# In the Heart of Another Country

## Erzählungen aus der Diaspora – Werke der Sharjah Art Foundation Collection

## The Diasporic Imagination in the Sharjah Art Foundation Collection

Halle für aktuelle Kunst /
Hall for Contemporary Art, Deichtorhallen Hamburg

Herausgegeben von / Edited by Omar Kholeif

Snoeck

DEICHTOR HALLEN
INTERNATIONALE KUNST UND FOTOGRAFIE
HAMBURG

SHARJAH ART FOUNDATION

# Künstler*innen / Artists

Bani Abidi

Sarah Abu Abdallah

Lawrence Abu Hamdan

Etel Adnan

Latif Al Ani

Khadim Ali

Halil Altindere

Minam Apang

Rasheed Araeen

Thuraya Al-Baqsami

Shiraz Bayjoo

Semiha Berksoy

Huma Bhabha

Huguette Caland

CAMP

Tony Chakar

Saloua Raouda Choucair

Tiffany Chung

Monir Shahroudy Farmanfarmaian

Simone Fattal

Marcos Grigorian

Abbas Habiballa

Joana Hadjithomas & Khalil Joreige

Rokni Haerizadeh

Taloi Havini

Susan Hefuna

Adam Henein

Lubaina Himid

Emily Jacir

Hayv Kahraman

Ali Kazim

Amal Kenawy

Aisha Khalid

Anuar Khalifi

David Koloane

Farideh Lashai

Tala Madani

Taus Makhacheva

Jumana Manna

Marwan

Ibrahim Massouda

Ahmed Mater

Ahmed Morsi

Fateh Moudarres

Khalil Rabah

Michael Rakowitz

Marwan Rechmaoui

Ibrahim El-Salahi

Mohan Samant

Hrair Sarkissian

Hassan Sharif

Wael Shawky

Anwar Jalal Shemza

Ahmed Shibrain

Shahzia Sikander

Rayyane Tabet

Richard Lokiden Wani

Nari Ward

Lionel Wendt

Kamal Youssef

Akram Zaatari

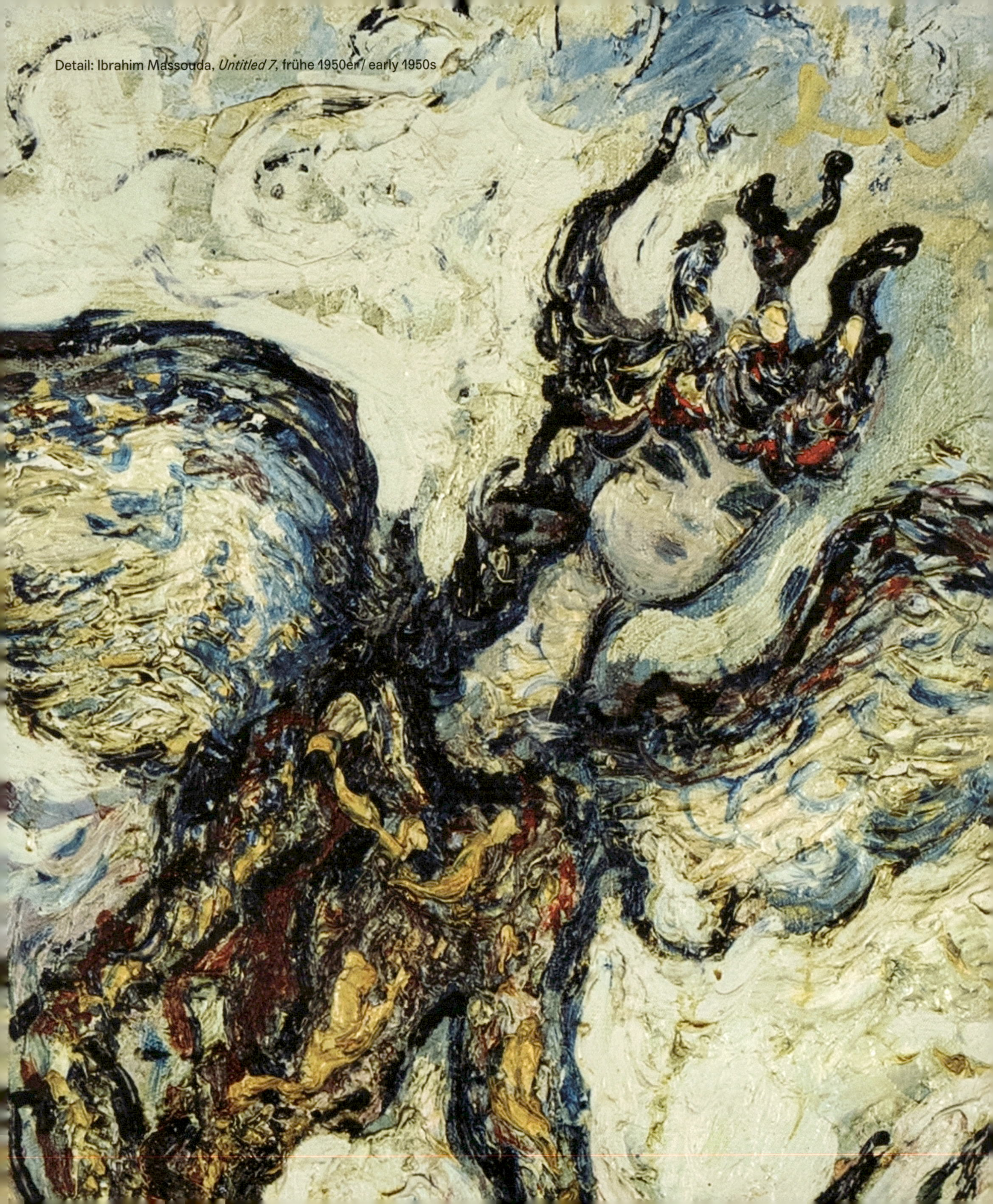

Detail: Ibrahim Massouda, *Untitled 7*, frühe 1950er / early 1950s

# Vorwort

# Dirk Luckow

*Intendant, Deichtorhallen Hamburg*

Die Sharjah Art Foundation (SAF), international bekannt für ihre Unterstützung von Künstler*innen durch Auftragsarbeiten und Ausstellungen zeitgenössischer Kunst, ist eine rechtlich unabhängige öffentliche Einrichtung unter der Schirmherrschaft der Regierung von Sharjah, einem der sieben Emirate der Vereinigten Arabischen Emirate. Sharjah, welches sich über eine Fläche von mehr als 2.500 Quadratkilometer erstreckt, ist das einzige Emirat, das an zwei Küsten liegt: am Golf von Oman und am Persischen Golf.

*In the Heart of Another Country* in den Deichtorhallen Hamburg ist die größte Einzelausstellung, die jemals aus der umfangreichen Sammlung der Stiftung gezeigt wurde. Für die Präsentation in Hamburg hat Omar Kholeif, Direktor*in der Sammlungen der Stiftung und Senior-Kurator*in, eine Auswahl mit fast 150 Werken von 61 Künstler*innen getroffen, die einen historischen Zeitraum von 1935 bis 2020 umspannt. Omar Kholeif erzählt in drei Kapiteln eine generationenübergreifende, in sich verwobene Geschichte, die uns zugleich die formale und stilistische Vielfalt der Werke in der Sammlung vor Augen führt. Kholeif hat sich insbesondere mit dem Begriff „Heimat" befasst – mit seinem Potenzial, Gefühle der Sehnsucht und Zugehörigkeit hervorzurufen. Was bedeutet es für einen Ort, ein Treffpunkt für Künstler*innen zu sein? Was bedeutet die „Diaspora" für Künstler*innen, und wie reflektieren ihre Werke die melancholischen Gefühle ihrer selbst und der Menschen aus verschiedenen Diasporagemeinden? Der Begriff Diaspora bezog sich ursprünglich auf das Exil des jüdischen Volkes und seine Zerstreuung über weite Teile der Welt. Darüber hinaus umfasst der Diasporabegriff das globale Phänomen von Exil, Zuflucht oder Migration religiöser, nationaler, kultureller oder ethnischer Gemeinschaften. Der künstlerische Umgang mit dem Diasporagedanken begründet den Untertitel der Ausstellung: *Erzählungen aus der Diaspora*.

Viele der hier gezeigten Künstler*innen lebten und leben weit von ihrem Geburtsort entfernt und haben somit mehrere kulturelle Bezugspunkte. Die Ausstellung verfolgt eine Route durch Süd- und Westasien, Afrika und die Karibik, die USA und Europa, auf der die Bedeutung des Konzepts „Diaspora" für Künstler*innen sowie Ausmaß und Möglichkeiten von Mobilität in verschiedenen historischen Epochen untersucht werden.

Die Kunst, die im Rahmen dieser Ausstellung in den Deichtorhallen präsentiert wird, ist von postkolonialen Erfahrungen, von Ankommen und Aufbruch, vielfältigen Bruchlinien und Globalisierungsformen charakterisiert. Die Künstler*innen versuchen, neue Formen von Schrift- und Bildsprachen zu erfinden und hybride Kunstwerke zu schaffen, die lange Zeit an den Rand der zeitgenössischen Kunstwelt verwiesen worden sind. Demgegenüber rückt das erste Kapitel

# Foreword

## Dirk Luckow

*General Director, Deichtorhallen Hamburg*

Recognised internationally for its history of supporting artists through commissions and exhibitions of contemporary art, Sharjah Art Foundation (SAF) is a legally independent public body under the auspices of the Government of Sharjah, one of the seven emirates of the United Arab Emirates. Spread across more than 1,000 square miles, Sharjah is the only emirate to inhabit two coasts: the Gulf of Oman and the Arabian Gulf.

The project, *In the Heart of Another Country*, at Deichtorhallen Hamburg is the single largest exhibition of work ever to be presented from the Foundation's expansive Collection. For this presentation, Omar Kholeif, the Foundation's Director of Collections and Senior Curator, has curated an exhibition featuring nearly 150 works by 61 artists, whose work spans a historical period from 1935 to 2020. Their concept seeks to narrate an intergenerational series of intertwined narratives across three chapters, which explore the formal and stylistic diversity of works held in the Collection. In particular, Omar Kholeif has homed in on the concept of 'home'—its possibilities of eliciting feelings of longing and belonging. What does it mean for a site to exist as a meeting point for artists? How can a place nurture the melancholic feelings of longing and belonging for individuals from different diasporas? The term diaspora originally referred to the exile of the Jewish people and their dispersion to many parts of the world. More broadly, it encompasses the global phenomena of exile, refuge, or migration of religious, national, cultural, or ethnic communities. The artistic exploration of the concept of the diaspora is what established the exhibition's subtitle, *The Diasporic Imagination in the Sharjah Art Foundation Collection*.

The artists herein occupy all four corners of the globe; many lived or live far from where they were born and thus embody multiple points of cultural reference. The exhibition traces a route across South and West Asia, Africa and the Caribbean, the United States, and Europe. Collectively, their work examines the significance of the concept of 'diaspora' for artists and explores the extent as well as possibilities of mobility over various periods throughout history.

The art presented on the walls of the Deichtorhallen is characterised by postcolonial experiences, arrival and departure, varied fault lines and forms of globalisation. These artists sought to invent new forms of languages, written and visual, presenting hybrid works of art that for long have existed at the margins of a contemporary art world. The exhibition at the Deichtorhallen instead presents you with what the exhibition's curator has deemed an 'Architecture by Other Means'—an exploration of how abstraction meets the contoured edges

der Ausstellung in den Mittelpunkt, was Omar Kholeif als eine „Architektur mit anderen Mitteln“ bezeichnet, und erkundet, wie Abstraktion auf die konturierten Ränder konkreter Städte trifft. Daran schließt sich das zweite Kapitel mit dem Titel *Zurückgewonnene Porträts: Unsichtbare Wiederherstellung* an, das die sich wandelnde Ontologie der Bildkultur von den 1930er Jahren bis heute zu entschlüsseln sucht. Schließlich folgt unter der Überschrift *Gen Süden: Reisen von Golf zu Golf, von Küste zu Küste* der „letzte Flug“, auf dem wir Künstler*innen begegnen, die historische Narrative re- und dekonstruieren, indem sie mit ihren Überlegungen zu Urbanismus und institutionellen Strukturen die vorherrschenden Erzählmuster der Moderne aufbrechen.

Die Sammlung der Sharjah Art Foundation umfasst moderne und zeitgenössische Kunst, die im perspektivischen Kontext globaler Ost-Ost- und Süd-Süd-Allianzen entstanden ist. Die Sammlung begann mit dem Erwerb von Werken, die speziell im Rahmen der 1993 gegründeten *Sharjah Biennale* in Auftrag gegeben wurden – einer Ausstellungsreihe, die noch während der Laufzeit der Hamburger Ausstellung im Jahr 2023 ihr 30-jähriges Bestehen mit der Realisierung der *Sharjah Biennale 15: Thinking Historically in the Present* feiern wird. Diese kommende Ausgabe ist eine wichtige Plattform, die von Hoor Al Qasimi, der Präsidentin und Direktorin der Stiftung, kuratiert und von einer internationalen Arbeitsgruppe und einem Beirat unterstützt wird.

Der bemerkenswerte Einfluss der *Sharjah Biennale* lässt sich an allen ausgestellten Werken ablesen, von denen viele auch speziell in ihrem Zusammenhang entstanden sind. Dazu gehören etwa die farbenfrohen Gemälde und Wandteppiche der verstorbenen Künstlerin und Schriftstellerin Etel Adnan, Aisha Khalids monumentale Installation *Kashmiri Shawl* (2011), Rayyane Tabets *Cyprus* (2013) und Lawrence Abu Hamdans *Saydnaya (The Missing 19db)* (2017). Schon diese wenigen Beispiele lassen den von der Sharjah Art Foundation ständig geführten Dialog mit internationalen Künstler*innen und Kurator*innen erkennen und spiegeln ihre Mission, insbesondere durch ihre ganzjährigen Programme eine globale Perspektive auf die Kunst zu richten. Die Ausstellung *In the Heart of Another Country* und damit auch diese Publikation zeugen aber nicht nur von der die Produktion von Kunst ermöglichenden Förderpraxis der Stiftung in der Golfregion, sondern vermitteln zugleich ein umfassendes Bild der bahnbrechenden Werke, die in dieser bedeutenden öffentlichen Sammlung aufbewahrt werden.

*In the Heart of Another Country* spiegelt zum anderen auch die globale Ausrichtung der Deichtorhallen Hamburg wider – eine Zielrichtung, die wir seit einigen Jahren mit Ausstellungen wie *Secret Signs. Kalligrafie in der zeitgenössischen chinesischen Kunst* (2014–2015), *Streamlines. Oceans, Global Trade and Migration* (2015–2016) oder in diesem Jahr *Currency. Photography Beyond Capture* (2022), die alle in Zusammenarbeit mit internationalen Partnern und Kurator*innen realisiert wurden, verfolgt haben und nun mit der aktuellen Schau, die uns transkulturelle Prozesse in der Kunst auf nuancierte Weise näherbringt, erneut aufgreifen.

Zuallererst möchte ich mich bei der Präsidentin der Sharjah Art Foundation, der hochgeschätzten Sheikha Hoor al Qasimi, für die großartige Zusammenarbeit und ihr außerordentliches Entgegenkommen bedanken. Die einzigartige Sammlung der Sharjah Art Foundation in Hamburg zeigen zu dürfen, ist eine überaus große Ehre. Vielen Dank dafür!

Die ersten Gespräche mit Omar Kholeif fanden im Mai 2016 in New York statt. Noch vor der eigenen Zeit bei der Sharjah Art Foundation schlug Omar Kholeif vor, sich auf die Sammlung der Sharjah Art Foundation zu konzentrieren, die diese*r im Rahmen der eigenen Rolle als Co-Kurator*in der *Sharjah Biennale 14: Leaving the Echo Chamber* erforschte. Das zentrale Thema der Ausstellung – die ständigen Bewegungen, denen Künstler*innen und Erzählungen unterliegen – stieß bei unseren beiden Institutionen auf großes Interesse. Die Präsentation in Hamburg,

of concrete cities. This is followed by their second chapter, 'Reclaimed Portraits: Invisible Acts of Repair', which seeks to decode the changing ontology of image culture from the 1930s to the present. Finally, they lead us to our 'Final Flight' down an exploratory path where artists can be seen reconstituting and intervening in historical narratives, rupturing dominant narratives of modernity with their reflections on urbanism and institutional structures.

The Sharjah Art Foundation Collection presents modern and contemporary art from an east-east and south-south perspective of alliances. The Collection began when the Foundation acquired works specially commissioned in the context of the Sharjah Biennial, which was initiated in 1993 and celebrates its 30th anniversary during the run of the Hamburgian exhibition in 2023 with the realisation of Sharjah Biennial 15: *Thinking Historically in the Present*. The forthcoming edition is a major platform curated by Hoor Al Qasimi, the Foundation's President and Director, supported by an international working group and advisory council.

The remarkable influence of the Sharjah Biennial is present throughout the displayed works, many of which were created specifically in the context of the Sharjah biennials. These include colourful paintings and tapestries by the late artist and writer Etel Adnan; Aisha Khalid's monumental installation *Kashmiri Shawl* (2011), Rayyane Tabet's *Cyprus* (2013) and Lawrence Abu Hamdan's *Saydnaya (The Missing 19db)* (2017). This cursory set of examples reflects the mission of the Sharjah Biennial to promote a global perspective on art and represents its constant dialogue with international artists and curators. The exhibition *In the Heart of Another Country* and, by proxy, this publication, not only stand as testament to a deeper understanding of the generative work of the Foundation in the Gulf region, but also reveal a comprehensive picture of the groundbreaking art being produced and held in one of its most significant public collections globally.

*In the Heart of Another Country* is a part of Deichtorhallen Hamburg's global strategy—one that we have been pursuing for several years now with exhibitions such as *Secret Signs: Calligraphy in Contemporary Chinese Art* (2014–2015), *Streamlines: Oceans, Global Trade and Migration* (2015–2016) or, this year, *Currency: Photography Beyond Captur*e (2022), which were all realised in cooperation with international partners. Similarly, *In the Heart of Another Country* reveals transcultural processes in art in a nuanced and fluent manner.

First and foremost, I would like to thank the President of Sharjah Art Foundation, Sheikha Hoor al Qasimi, for this great collaboration and her incomparable generosity. To be able to show the Foundation's unique Collection in Hamburg is an extremely great honour. Thank you very much for this opportunity.

The first discussions with Omar Kholeif took place in New York in May of 2016. Even before their arrival as a full-time staff member at Sharjah Art Foundation, Kholeif proposed to focus on the Sharjah Art Foundation Collection, which they were researching as part of their role as co-curator of Sharjah Biennial 14: *Leaving the Echo Chamber*. The exhibition's central theme, the constant movement of artists and narratives, was conceived by them and met with keen interest by both our institutions. The presentation in Hamburg offers a multifaceted cross-section of the SAF Collection, helping to shape, form and contour its stories and histories. Our greatest thanks go to them.

At the same time, discussions have been held since 2017 with Judith Greer, Director of International Programmes at Sharjah Art Foundation. Meetings took place in Hamburg on the occasion of the production, in glorious sunshine, of Wael Shawky's opera *The Song of Roland: The Arabic Version* and in Sharjah on the occasion of the 14th edition of the Sharjah Biennial in 2019. Greer supported the Hamburg project with great enthusiasm and circumspection,

die einen facettenreichen Querschnitt durch die SAF-Sammlung bietet, trägt entsprechend dazu bei, Geschichte und Geschichten zu gestalten, zu formen und zu konturieren. Dafür gebührt Omar Kholeif unser großer Dank.

Parallel dazu haben seit 2017 Gespräche mit Judith Greer, Director of International Programmes der Sharjah Art Foundation, stattgefunden. Die Treffen fanden 2017 in Hamburg anlässlich der Inszenierung von Wael Shawkys Oper *The Song of Roland: The Arabic Version* sowie 2019 in Sharjah anlässlich der 14. Ausgabe der *Sharjah Biennale* statt. Judith Greer hat das Hamburger Projekt mit großem Enthusiasmus und Umsicht unterstützt, wobei sie insbesondere bei der Vermittlung zwischen unseren Institutionen hilfreich war. Wir möchten auch Nawar Al Qassimi, der Vizepräsidentin der Sharjah Art Foundation, unseren Dank aussprechen. Ihr Besuch in den Deichtorhallen im Frühjahr 2022 brachte interessante Geschichten und Berichte über die Entwicklung, Bedeutung und Ausrichtung der Sharjah Art Foundation ans Licht – eine wichtige Ergänzung für den Katalog. Natürlich ist es für uns eine große Ehre, Gastgeber für die Künstler*innen zu sein, und wir möchten ihnen und ihren Nachlässen für das große Vertrauen danken, das sie uns bei der Vorbereitung der Ausstellung entgegengebracht haben.

Der Rundgang durch *In the Heart of Another Country*, der die einzigartigen räumlichen Möglichkeiten der Halle für zeitgenössische Kunst in den Deichtorhallen voll ausnutzt, wurde von Todd Reisz, Architekt, Wissenschaftler und Autor des Buches *Showpiece City: How Architecture Made Dubai*, entwickelt. Wir möchten ihm für sein überzeugendes architektonisches Ausstellungsdesign danken. Sein Layout, das in enger Zusammenarbeit mit Omar Kholeif und dem Team der Deichtorhallen entstanden ist, motiviert die Besucher*innen, sich mit den übergreifenden Themen zu beschäftigen, die für und durch die Ausstellung entwickelt wurden.

Omar Kholeif hat diesen Katalog verfasst, seinen Inhalt redigiert und die Fotografien der installierten Werke betreut. Als Teil dieses Prozesses haben Omar Kholeif und die Sharjah Art Foundation eine Reihe von Autor*innen eingeladen, um Texte zu den einzelnen Künstler*innen beizusteuern. Wir möchten uns bedanken bei: Skye Arundhati Thomas, Autorin und Mitherausgeberin von *The White Review*; Stephanie Bailey, Chefredakteurin des *Ocula Magazine*; Anne Barlow, Direktorin der Tate St. Ives; Chris McCormack, Mitherausgeber von *Art Monthly*; Sarah Perks, Professorin für Kuration und Leiterin der Abteilung an der MIMA School of Art and Design, Middlesbrough, England.

Neben diesen Beiträgen hat Sofia Victorino, Autorin und Wissenschaftlerin, die am UCL in London zu dekolonialen Konzepten forscht, einen Round Table mit den Künstler*innen Bani Abidi, Lubaina Himid und Hrair Sarkissian einberufen, der gemeinsam mit Omar Kholeif konzipiert wurde und hier mit einer Einführung der Moderatorin präsentiert wird. Wir danken ihr, den beteiligten Künstler*innen und Omar Kholeif sehr herzlich. Unser Dank gilt auch Nicholas Davies für seine Unterstützung beim Lektorat sowie dem ganzen fabelhaften Team der SAF, das mit Recherchen und Koordination auf allen Ebenen zu diesem Buch beigetragen hat. Auch gilt unser Dank dem Kernteam des SAF-Projekts einschließlich Zeina Al Kattan, kuratorische Assistentin, Souraya Kreideh, stellvertretende Registrarin, John Labib, Sammlungs- und Konservierungsmanager und Reem Sawan, Sammlungskoordinatorin der Sharjah Art Foundation, VAE. Außerdem sind Danko Stjepanovics präzises Auge und sein Blick in der Ausstellungsdokumentation deutlich zu spüren.

Vonseiten der Deichtorhallen bedanken wir uns auch bei Kathrin Hadeler, Martin Hager und Bram Opstelten für die jeweiligen Übersetzungen der englischen und deutschen Texte. Vielen Dank auch an das Londoner Grafikstudio Daly & Lyon für die äußerst gelungene Gestaltung des Katalogs. Außerdem freuen wir uns über die erneute Zusammenarbeit mit dem Verlag SNOECK. Das Hamburger Grafikbüro giraffentoast war verantwortlich für das Key Visual der Ausstellung

especially in drafting the cooperation agreement. We would also like to extend our gratitude to Sharjah Art Foundation Vice-President Nawar Al Qassimi. Her visit to the Deichtorhallen in spring 2022 revealed stories and histories, which were useful to our knowledge. Her accounts of the development, significance and focus of Sharjah Art Foundation were most insightful for our team and an important addition to the catalogue.

Of course, we are absolutely honoured to host the artists and would like to thank them and their estates for the great trust that they have placed in us while preparing the exhibition.

The route through *In the Heart of Another Country*, which takes full advantage of the unique spatial possibilities in the Hall for Contemporary Art at the Deichtorhallen, was brilliantly developed by Todd Reisz, a noted architect, academic and author of the book, *Showpiece City: How Architecture Made Dubai*. We would like to thank him for his compelling architectural exhibition design. His layout, conceived in close collaboration with Omar Kholeif and the Deichtorhallen team, motivates visitors to engage with the intersectional themes developed for and through the exhibition.

Omar Kholeif authored this catalogue, edited and fact-checked its content and supervised the photographs of the installed works. As part of this process, they and the Sharjah Art Foundation invited a series of authors to contribute texts to the book on individual artists. We would like to thank: Skye Arundhati Thomas, author and co-editor, *The White Review*; Stephanie Bailey, Editor-in-Chief, *Ocula Magazine*; Anne Barlow, Director, Tate St Ives; Chris McCormack, co-editor, *Art Monthly*; and Sarah Perks, Professor of Curating and Head of Department, MIMA School of Art and Design, UK.

Alongside these contributions, Sofia Victorino, author and academic, researching decolonial strategies at UCL, London, convened a roundtable with artists Bani Abidi, Lubaina Himid and Hrair Sarkissian, which was conceived with the exhibition curator and presented here with the moderator's introduction. We thank them fondly. Gratitude is also due to Nicholas Davies for stepping in to assist with copyediting and to the incredible team that contributed to this book with research and coordination at every level, as well as the core SAF project team, including, Zeina Al Kattan, Curatorial Assistant; Souraya Kreideh, Associate Registrar; John Labib, Collections and Conservation Manager; and Reem Sawan, Collections Coordinator, Sharjah Art Foundation, UAE. Danko Stjepanovic's precise eye and vision were warmly felt in the exhibition documentation.

At Deichtorhallen, we would also like to thank Kathrin Hadeler and Martin Hager for their translations of the English text. Many thanks also to the London-based graphic design studio Daly & Lyon for their attentive design of the catalogue. Moreover, we would like to extend our happiness to be collaborating again with publishing house, SNOECK. The Hamburg-based graphic design office giraffentoast was responsible for the key visual of the exhibition and assistance with the online microsite. We would also like to express our gratitude to the Hamburg-based journalist Melanie von Bismarck for her concept and realisation of the audio guide, in partnership with Omar Kholeif, who authored and narrated our first guide in the English language.

A great debt of gratitude is also due to the Ambassador of the United Arab Emirates in Berlin, H.E. Hafsa Al Ulama. We are equally grateful to Mohammed Khalifa, organizer of the Arabische Kulturwochen (Arab Culture Weeks) in Hamburg, for his support in bringing the exhibition to their audience and community in and beyond Hamburg.

The exhibition was made possible with the generous support of the Deichtorhallen Förderkreis chaired by Julia von Jenisch. We would like to thank her, the members of the board

und die Unterstützung bei der Online-Microsite. Unser Dank gilt auch der Hamburger Journalistin Melanie von Bismarck für die Konzeption und Umsetzung des Audioguides in Zusammenarbeit mit Omar Kholeif, welche*r unseren ersten englischsprachigen Guide verfasst und eingesprochen hat.

Ein großer Dank gebührt auch der Botschafterin der Vereinigten Arabischen Emirate in Berlin, I.E. Hafsa Al Ulama. Wir danken zudem Mohammed Khalifa, Organisator der Arabischen Kulturwochen in Hamburg, für seine Unterstützung bei der Vermittlung der Ausstellung an das eigene Publikum in und außerhalb Hamburgs.

Ermöglicht wurde die Ausstellung durch die großzügige Unterstützung des Deichtorhallen Förderkreises unter dem Vorsitz von Julia von Jenisch. Wir danken ihr, den Vorstandsmitgliedern und allen Förderer*innen der Deichtorhallen für die große finanzielle Unterstützung, die sie leisten. Wir danken der Behörde für Kultur und Medien der Freien und Hansestadt Hamburg, insbesondere Herrn Senator Carsten Brosda, für die großzügige Unterstützung aus dem Ausstellungsfonds der Stadt Hamburg. Ebenso dankbar sind wir unseren Partnern aus der Privatwirtschaft, namentlich unseren Stammpartnern Hapag Lloyd, Kölln Flocken und White Wall.

Ein großer Dank gebührt den großartigen Teams der Deichtorhallen Hamburg und der Sharjah Art Foundation. Bei den Deichtorhallen danken wir vor allem Bert Antonius Kaufmann, dem Kaufmännischen Direktor der Deichtorhallen, der mit seiner Planung und seinem Finanzmanagement entscheidend dazu beigetragen hat, dass die Ausstellung realisiert werden konnte. Cosima Grosser und Annette Sievert, die Projektleiterinnen, waren maßgeblich an der Umsetzung des komplexen Konzepts, der kuratorischen Realisierung der Ausstellung und der redaktionellen Betreuung des Katalogs beteiligt. Sie waren für die hervorragende Gesamtorganisation der Ausstellung verantwortlich. Unser besonderer Dank gilt auch Frances Fürst, welche*r sich unermüdlich und stets umsichtig in die komplexe internationale Korrespondenz und Realisierung der Ausstellung eingebracht hat. Unser Dank gilt zudem Lydia Jung, unserer Registrarin, für die Abwicklung des Leihverkehrs und die kompetente Leitung des Art Handling Teams. Ein herzliches Dankeschön auch an Sabine Seidel, Maren Willenbrock und Giovanna Engel, die uns bei der Terminplanung, den Videokonferenzen und der Korrespondenz tatkräftig unterstützt haben. Ausdrücklich bedanken möchten wir uns auch bei Angelika Leu-Barthel für ihre Öffentlichkeitsarbeit und bei Carolin Huzel, die sie dabei unterstützt hat, sowie bei Matthias Schönebäumer und Julia Schulze Darup für ihre umfangreichen Social-Media-Aktivitäten in Begleitung der Ausstellung. Unser Dank gilt auch Birgit Hübner und ihrer Abteilung Kulturelle Bildung für das umfangreiche Vermittlungsprogramm zur Ausstellung. Henning Best und Jutta Wasser von der Technischen Abteilung waren an der Planung und Installation der Architektur und der Montage der Ausstellung entscheidend beteiligt. Unser Dank gilt zudem Nils Handschuh und Karsten Chmielewski für die technische Umsetzung der Ausstellung; auch sie haben maßgeblich zum Gelingen des Projekts beigetragen. Gerhard Manthey und Torsten Stiller danken wir für die Betreuung der Ausstellungsarchitektur. Das Art-Handling-Team konnte sich einmal mehr bei der Montage und Installation der Werke bewähren. Sie werden hier stellvertretend für alle anderen Mitarbeiter*innen der Deichtorhallen genannt.

Alle biografischen und historischen Kontexte der Werke in *In the Heart of Another Country* sind vielschichtig, raffiniert, assoziativ – sie rufen eine Vielzahl von Orten und Momenten der Erinnerung auf. „Diese Ausstellung ist ein Akt des Weltenbaus, eine Schichtung von Geschichten“, sagt Omar Kholeif. In einem solchen Akt der Weltenbaus finden Solidarität, Bewegung und kollektives Handeln zu einer Einheit zusammen, die durch das poetische Zusammenspiel von Kunst und Architektur noch unterstrichen wird. Der Rest existiert in den Spuren unserer gemeinsamen Vorstellungskraft.

and all sponsors of Deichtorhallen for the major financial support that they provide. We would like to thank the Ministry of Culture and Media of the Free and Hanseatic City of Hamburg, especially Senator Carsten Brosda, for the generous support from the City of Hamburg's exhibition fund. We are equally grateful to our partners from the private economic sector; notable are our regular partners, Hapag Lloyd, Kölln Flocken and White Wall.

We owe an immense debt of gratitude to the great teams at Deichtorhallen Hamburg and Sharjah Art Foundation. At Deichtorhallen, we would like to thank first and foremost Bert Antonius Kaufmann, Commercial Director of Deichtorhallen, whose planning and financial management were decisive in making the exhibition a reality. Cosima Grosser and Annette Sievert, the project managers, were instrumental in implementing the complex concept, the curatorial realisation of the exhibition and the editorial support of the catalogue. They were responsible for the brilliant overall organisation of the exhibition. We are also particularly grateful to Frances Fürst, who tirelessly and always prudently contributed to the complex international correspondence and realisation of the exhibition. We would also like to thank Lydia Jung, our registrar, for her handling of the lending process and for her competent management of the art handling team. Many thanks also to Sabine Seidel, Maren Willenbrock and Giovanna Engel, who diligently assisted with all the scheduling, video conferences and correspondence. We would also like to expressly thank Angelika Leu-Barthel for her public relations work with the support of Carolin Huzel as well as Matthias Schönebäumer and Julia Schulze Darup for their extensive social media activities in support of the exhibition. We are also sincerely grateful to Birgit Hübner and her Cultural Education Department for the extensive educational programming accompanying the exhibition. Henning Best and Jutta Wasser from the Technical Department were part of planning and installing the architecture and mounting the exhibition. Our thanks are also due to Nils Handschuh and Karsten Chmielewski for their technical realisation of the exhibition. They, too, were instrumental in making the project a success. Gerhard Manthey and Torsten Stiller, we thank you for overseeing the architecture of the show. The art handling team was once again able to prove itself in the mounting and installation of the works. They are mentioned here vicariously for all other members of the Deichtorhallen's staff.

The biographies and context of the works in *In the Heart of Another Country* are nuanced and sophisticated; emotive and evocative—of many places and instances of memory. To quote the exhibition's curator, 'this exhibition is an act of world-building, a layering of histories'. In this act of world-building, we might find solidarity, movement and collective action elucidated through the poetic interplay of art and architecture. The rest exists in the vestiges of our common imagination.

# Vorwort

# Hoor Al Qasimi

*Präsidentin, Sharjah Art Foundation*

Die Ausstellung *In the Heart of Another Country* betrachtet die Arbeit von Künstler*innen der Sharjah Art Foundation Collection durch die Brille ihrer diasporischen Erfahrung und trägt ihre Kunst ins Herz eines anderen Landes. In Schardscha sind die meisten dieser Künstler*innen uns gut bekannt. Wir haben mit ihnen zusammengearbeitet, sie unterstützt und gefördert und von ihren oft tief bewegenden und bahnbrechenden künstlerischen Praktiken gelernt. Mit vielen von ihnen haben wir lange und dauerhafte Beziehungen aufgebaut, die Ausdruck der uns verbindenden Geschichten und Erfahrungen in Teilen der Welt mit komplexer Geschichte und umkämpfter Gegenwart sind.

Seit nunmehr 30 Jahren bietet die *Sharjah Biennial* Gelegenheit zur Zusammenkunft: für Künstler*innen, die anspruchsvolle neue Arbeiten präsentieren, für Kunstexpert*innen, die alte und neue Kolleg*innen treffen, und für alle zu reichlich Gedankenaustausch in der entspannten und geselligen Atmosphäre, die für unser Projekt grundlegend ist. Die *Sharjah Biennial* war und ist nach wie vor ein zentrales Element der Arbeit der Stiftung, ein Projekt, das es möglich gemacht hat, mit Formen künstlerischer Praxis, unterschiedlichen Herangehensweisen an die Produktion und Präsentation von Kunst und Formen der Auseinandersetzung mit dringenden Problemen in unserer heutigen gelebten Welt zu experimentieren.

Die Sharjah Art Foundation wurde 2009 gegründet, um diesen Motivationen eine tragfähige Struktur und eine Logik zu verleihen und so Künstler*innen kontinuierliche Unterstützung bieten und gleichzeitig ein lokales und regionales Publikum aufbauen zu können. Unlängst wies ein namhafter internationaler Kurator im Gespräch darauf hin, dass die Stiftung durch die große Zahl der von ihr in Auftrag gegebenen und produzierten Werke inzwischen obendrein ein breites internationales Publikum aufgebaut hat. Unser ganzjähriges Programm umfasst Ausstellungen, Initiativen mit den Schwerpunkten Film, Musik, Performance, Forschung und Publikationen sowie ein umfangreiches Kunstvermittlungsprogramm, die alle integraler Bestandteil unserer Arbeit auf lokaler wie internationaler Ebene sind.

Wie Sie in der Ausstellung und im vorliegenden Band sehen werden, spiegelt die Sammlung der Sharjah Art Foundation das Erbe der Biennale und der Stiftung wider. Sie dient nicht zur Dokumentation unserer Zusammenarbeit mit Künstler*innen, sondern zeigt auch unsere Bemühungen, Künstler*innen und Kunstbewegungen, die noch der genaueren Betrachtung und Anerkennung harren, Handlungsmöglichkeiten zu bieten. *In the Heart of Another Country*, die erste große internationale Präsentation unserer Sammlung, zeigt zahlreiche Arbeiten, die in und für Schardscha entstanden sind – einige davon werden jetzt erstmals international ausgestellt.

# Foreword

## Hoor Al Qasimi

*President, Sharjah Art Foundation*

*In the Heart of Another Country* considers the work of artists in the Sharjah Art Foundation Collection, through the lens of their diasporic experience, in a presentation that brings their art into the very heart of another country. Most of these artists are well known to us in Sharjah. We have worked with them, supporting and encouraging them, learning from their often deeply moving and groundbreaking practices. With many of them we have built long and enduring relationships, a reflection of our shared histories and experiences in parts of the world with complex histories and contested presents.

For the past 30 years, the Sharjah Biennial has offered a time and a place for us to gather: for artists to present challenging new works, for art professionals to meet old and new colleagues and for the generous exchange of ideas in the informal and convivial atmosphere so fundamental to our project. The Sharjah Biennial was, and remains, central to the work of the Foundation, a project that has allowed experimentation with modes of artistic practice, different approaches to producing and presenting art, and ways to consider urgent issues within our contemporary lived experience.

Sharjah Art Foundation was established in 2009 to provide these motivations both a sustainable structure and a logic that could offer continued support to artists whilst also building local and regional audiences. In a recent conversation, a prominent international curator pointed out that the extraordinary number of works commissioned and produced by the Foundation has now built a robust international audience as well. Our year-round programme includes exhibitions, initiatives focussed on film, music, performance, research and publications, and an extensive art education programme, all of which are integral to our work both locally and internationally.

As you will see in the exhibition and in this publication, the Sharjah Art Foundation Collection reflects the legacy of the Biennial and the Foundation. It not only serves as a record for our engagement with artists, but also reveals our efforts to offer agency to artists and art movements that have yet to be studied and acknowledged. *In the Heart of Another Country*, the first major international presentation of our Collection, features many works made in and for Sharjah—some of which are being shown internationally for the first time.

It has been a great privilege to have established this partnership with the Deichtorhallen Hamburg, one of the largest and most respected institutions presenting contemporary art and photography in Europe. I would like to thank Deichtorhallen Director Dirk Luckow for his tireless dedication to the realisation of this exhibition. While he has comprehensively thanked key staff from both of our institutions who have been deeply involved in the project, I would

Es ist uns eine große Ehre, dass wir diese Partnerschaft mit den Deichtorhallen Hamburg, einer der größten und angesehensten Institutionen für zeitgenössische Kunst und Fotografie in Europa, eingehen konnten. Mein besonderer Dank gilt Deichtorhallen-Direktor Dirk Luckow für seinen unermüdlichen Einsatz bei der Realisierung dieser Ausstellung. Obwohl er bereits allen wichtigsten am Projekt beteiligten Mitarbeiter*innen unserer beiden Institutionen seinen Dank ausgesprochen hat, möchte ich hier noch einmal den Teams der Deichtorhallen und der Sharjah Art Foundation für ihr außergewöhnliches Engagement danken, ohne das diese Ausstellung nicht hätte realisiert werden können.

Es scheint nur passend, dass noch während der Laufzeit dieser Ausstellung die *15. Sharjah Biennale* eröffnen wird: Mit *Thinking Historically in the Present* feiert die Biennale im Februar 2023 ihr dreißigjähriges Jubiläum. Obwohl diese 15. Biennale ursprünglich von dem in Hamburg und ganz Deutschland bekannten, leider aber verstorbenen Okwui Enwezor konzipiert wurde, habe ich die kuratorische Rolle für diese Ausgabe übernommen, die stark von Enwezors bahnbrechender *documenta 11* beeinflusst wurde. Jene Documenta im Jahr 2002 war der Auslöser für meine Rückkehr nach Schardscha, um dort die Biennale 2003 zu kuratieren, und markierte den Beginn meiner eigenen 20-jährigen Tätigkeit als Kuratorin. Enwezors Vermächtnis, wie es in der kommenden Biennale ebenso wie in der Sammlung der Stiftung zum Ausdruck kommt, reflektiert die vielfältige Art und Weise, wie Künstler*innen in der globalen Gegenwart sich mit der Gesellschaft auseinandersetzen – ein Ergebnis, das sich den Leser*innen dieser Publikation und den Besucher*innen der Ausstellung *In the Heart of Another Country*, wie wir hoffen, vermitteln wird.

like to thank, once again, the staff of the Deichtorhallen and Sharjah Art Foundation for their extraordinary efforts that have made this exhibition possible.

It seems fitting that this exhibition runs its course alongside the opening of Sharjah Biennial 15: *Thinking Historically in the Present*, which in February 2023 will mark the Biennial's 30th anniversary. Although this Biennial was originally conceived by the late Okwui Enwezor, who is well known in Hamburg and across Germany, I took over the curatorial role for this edition, which was deeply influenced by Enwezor's groundbreaking documenta 11. That 2002 documenta was the catalyst for my return to Sharjah to curate the Biennial in 2003 and marked the beginning of my own 20-year journey as a curator. Enwezor's legacy, as seen in both the upcoming Biennial and the Foundation's Collection, serves as testament to the myriad ways that artists engage with society in the global present—an outcome that we hope will be evident to readers of this publication and visitors to *In the Heart of Another Country*.

# In the Heart of Another Country

## Omar Kholeif

*Transcendent waves—*
*Accumulating*
*You are a conduit to the centre of this universe*
*The 'disordered individual' transpires.*
*...*
*It's 'okay to feel things deeply'*
*...*
*Keep filling the black hole, keep searching outwardly, more—*
— Auszug aus „Sonic Exile…" von Blake Karim Mitchell[1]

### Die Lebensbedingungen des Exils

Das Exil kann als Zustand, als Lebenskonzept oder vielleicht auch als endloses Lied beschrieben werden. Die Wege des Exils haben ganze Literaturkanons hervorgebracht, von den Schriften des deutschen Kulturkritikers Walter Benjamin bis hin zu den Romanen des in Tansania geborenen britischen Schriftstellers und Literaturnobelpreisträgers von 2021 Abdulrazak Gurnah. Exil bezeichnet im Allgemeinen die Vertreibung von Personen aus ihrem Geburtsland (oder Heimatland)[2] und wurde in der Vergangenheit als Gefühl der melancholischen Sehnsucht wahrgenommen, wie sie Dante in seinen Versen über das Exil verewigt hat. Mit den Worten „Wie jener, dem sich bei dem nahen Anfall / Des Wechselfiebers schon die Nägel bleichen, / Ganz zittert bei des Schattens bloßem Anblick" stellte er einen Bezug zwischen seiner Malaria-Erkrankung und seiner offiziellen Verbannung aus Florenz her.[3]

Seit dem 20. Jahrhundert sind Erzählungen über das Exil oft auch Berichte über eine Kultur des Konflikts. Das Individuum in Bewegung wird häufig als Flüchtling oder, in juristischen Kreisen, als Person auf der Flucht wahrgenommen, die von bestimmten Rechten wie dem Recht auf Arbeit oder Freizügigkeit ausgeschlossen ist.[4] In der kollektiven Vorstellung kursieren unzählige – klare wie auch verschwommene – Bilder von Vertreibung. Darunter Auswanderungswellen, die ausgelöst wurden durch den Völkermord an den Armenier*innen im Ersten Weltkrieg oder den Vietnamkrieg (1955–1975). Oder Emigration infolge der Zerstreuung der Menschen aus Afrika nach dem angeblichen Ende der Kolonialherrschaft, infolge der Machtübernahme von Diktatoren, des US-Irakkriegs und der Golfkriege (1990–1991 und 2003–2011), des Bürgerkriegs im Libanon (1975–1990) oder der seit dem Palästinakrieg 1948 andauernden Vertreibung der Palästinenser*innen, die im Arabischen als *Nakba* (Verlust oder Niederlage) bezeichnet wird.[5]

Die Vereinigten Staaten – im gängigen Sprachgebrauch trotz der geografischen Ungenauigkeit des Begriffs schlicht als Amerika bezeichnet – stützen sich als Ort, als Nation auf die

# In the Heart of Another Country

## Omar Kholeif

*Transcendent waves—*
*Accumulating*
*You are a conduit to the centre of this universe*
*The 'disordered individual' transpires.*
*...*
*It's 'okay to feel things deeply'*
*...*
*Keep filling the black hole, keep searching outwardly, more—*
— Extract from 'Sonic Exile...' by Blake Karim Mitchell[1]

### The Contours of Exile

Exile can be expressed as a condition, a concept, or, perhaps, as a ceaseless song. Routes of exile have formed the basis of entire canons of literature, from the writings of German cultural critic Walter Benjamin through to the 2021 Nobel Laureate for Literature, the Tanzanian-born British novelist Abdulrazak Gurnah. Exile, commonly defined as the expulsion of a person from their native country (or homeland),[2] was historically deemed a situation that produced melancholic longing, as memorialised in Dante's poems of exile, which noted, 'so ill his nails have lost all colour / trembles all over at the sight of shade', correlating the illness of malaria with Dante's official exile from Florence.[3]

The narration of exile since the twentieth century is often synonymous with a culture of conflict. The individual in movement, in motion, is often perceived as a refugee, or, in juridical spheres, as a fugitive, stripped of particular rights of work or onward mobility.[4] In the collective imagination, one can conjure innumerable images of displacement—some more recognisable than others. Examples include emigration induced through and after the Armenian genocide during World War I, or because of the Vietnam War (1955–1975), or as a result of the dispersion of African humanity after the perceived ends of colonial rule, or in the wake of the rise of dictatorships, or because of the US-Iraq and the Gulf Wars (1990–1991 and 2003–2011), or due to Lebanon's Civil War (1975–1990), or, the persistent displacement of Palestinians since 1948 during the Palestine War, referred to in Arabic by Palestinians as the Nakba (the loss or the defeat).[5]

The United States, referred to in common parlance, despite the geographic inaccuracy, as America, has been a site, a nation, built upon a contorted and conceivably analogous rhetoric as the global home to emigrés despite its violent history of settler-colonialism.[6] Franz Kafka's *Amerika*, Susan Sontag's *In America* and Jim Sheridan's feature film of the same name are but

verzerrte und dementsprechende Rhetorik, *die* weltweite Heimat von Auswander*innen zu sein, und das trotz ihrer brutalen Vergangenheit als Siedlerkolonie.[6] Franz Kafkas *Amerika*, Susan Sontags *In Amerika* und Jim Sheridans gleichnamiger Spielfilm sind nur einige wenige Beispiele für die Darstellung der einstigen Aussichten der „imaginierten Gemeinschaften", die von ihrem als Heimat wahrgenommenen Ort in „die freie Welt" versetzt wurden.

Beschäftigt man sich mit den Mustern der Indigenität, wird ein zentrales Konzept erkennbar, nämlich das einer fortdauernden Kreolisierung als jener mögliche Daseinsform in der Welt, die Ausgewanderten einen Anspruch auf ihre Identität verleiht.[7] Der haitianische Schriftsteller Edwidge Danticat, der heute in den USA lebt, hat in diesem Zusammenhang von der Möglichkeit der Haitianer*innen und anderer Schwarzer Menschen aus der Karibik gesprochen, „mobile Traditionen" bei sich zu tragen, die ihre Existenz sichern und ihnen gleichzeitig als Schutz gegen die mögliche Auslöschung ihrer kulturellen Identität oder des Erbes ihrer gelebten Erfahrungen dienen.[8] Als Vorreiter dieses Diskurses gilt der verstorbene Schriftsteller Sam Selvon aus Trinidad, der als Erster englische Umgangssprache in seiner Literatur verwendete, um die Verbindung zum historischen Kontext zu wahren. Abdulrazak Gurnah, der in seinen Romanen häufig die Verbindungen und Spannungen zwischen seinem Geburtsland Sansibar und Großbritannien thematisiert, geht noch weiter, indem er seine Romane auf Englisch, Arabisch und Swahili verfasst und sich weigert, nicht-englische Wörter in seinen Büchern kursiv darzustellen, weil sie in seinen Augen dadurch abgewertet würden.[9]

Das Aufkommen der postmodernen Theorie in den 1980er und frühen 1990er Jahren wurde von einer Popularisierung der postkolonialen Theorie begleitet, die in weltweiten Debatten innerhalb und außerhalb akademischer Kreise entwickelt und durch die 1978 erfolgte Veröffentlichung des Werks *Orientalismus* des 2003 verstorbenen Edward W. Said vorangetrieben wurde. In den 1980er und 1990er Jahren hielt Saids Literaturtheorie in die visuellen Künste Einzug, wie beispielsweise auf den Seiten der Zeitschrift *The Third Text*, die zum ersten Mal 1987 unter ihrem heutigen Titel erschien. *The Third Text* wurde in Großbritannien durch den minimalistischen Bildhauer, Maler und Schriftsteller Rasheed Araeen ins Leben gerufen, der später auch die Wanderausstellung *The Other Story: Afro-Asian Artists in Post-War Britain* kuratierte, deren erste Station 1989 die Londoner Hayward Gallery war und die für viel Gesprächsstoff sorgte.[10] Parallel dazu entwickelte sich in den 1980er Jahren eine große Solidarität unter Schwarzen Kunstschaffenden in den englischen Midlands. Beispielsweise formierten sich die BLK Group und der losere, aber umfassendere Zusammenschluss des British Black Art Movement, der als Reaktion auf die US-amerikanische Black Arts Movement der 1960er Jahre galt. Künstler*innen traten als Kurator*innen auf, z. B. Lubaina Himid, die ab 1983 Ausstellungen Schwarzer Künstlerinnen an Orten in London wie dem Africa Centre, dem Battersea Arts Centre und dem Institute of Contemporary Arts organisierte.[11]

Ein besonderes Merkmal dieser Phase des Kunstschaffens war der Glaube an ein „politisches Schwarzsein" (Political Blackness). Dieser Oberbegriff sollte nach außen die Einheit aller nichtweißen ethnischen Minderheiten gegen die Hegemonie des Weißseins und der Diskriminierung vermitteln.[12] Das Konzept griff auch jenseits des Atlantiks und beeinflusste den Identitätsbegriff Schwarzer US-amerikanischer Künstler*innen wie Lorraine O'Grady, die 2020 in der Einleitung zu ihren gesammelten Schriften *Writing in Space* anmerkte, sie habe den Begriff einmal verwendet, um intersektionale Gemeinschaften des Schwarzseins und der weiblichen Subjektivität zu erkunden. O'Grady plädiert für ein Bewusstsein, das viele Diasporagemeinschaften und -perspektiven miteinander verbindet. Aus ihrer Sicht bringt der Begriff des „politischen Schwarzseins" das Konzept der „Hybridität" klar zum Ausdruck.[13] Homi K. Bhabha hat diesen

a few examples of the erstwhile possibility engendered for the imagined communities that are transposed from their site of perceived origin to 'the free world'.

If one is to consider the schematics of indigeneity, there emerges a concept of significance here—of perpetual creolisation, a way of existing in the world that allows the expatriate to lay claim to their identity.[7] Edwidge Danticat, the Haitian author, now based in the United States, has spoken of the possibility for Haitians and other Black Caribbean peoples' potential to carry forth 'mobile traditions', which enable subsistence, and with that a preventative against the potential erasure of cultural identity, or the legacies of lived experience.[8] The late Trinidadian author Sam Selvon was a progenitor of this discourse with his literary use of nonstandard English as a means of maintaining connection to a historical context. Abdulrazak Gurnah's novels, which are often expressive of connections and tensions between Zanzibar, where he was born, and the United Kingdom, extends this, authoring novels in English, Arabic and Swahili, and declining to italicise non-English words in his books, which he intimates would denigrate them to a subaltern status.[9]

The rise of postmodern theory in the 1980s and early 1990s occurred in tandem with the popularisation of postcolonial theory, following global debates both within and outwith the formal academy, ushered in by the late Edward W. Said's publication of *Orientalism* in 1978. In the 1980s and 1990s, Said's literary theory expanded into the realm of the visual arts, such as in the pages of *The Third Text* journal, first published under its current banner, in 1987. *The Third Text* was founded in Britain by minimalist sculptor, painter and author Rasheed Araeen, who would go on to curate *The Other Story: Afro-Asian Artists in Post-War Britain*, a widely debated touring exhibition that began at the Hayward Gallery, London, in 1989.[10] In parallel, the 1980s bore witness to the proliferation of artist-led solidarity among Black artists in the English Midlands, with the formation of the BLK Group and the looser, but broader, framework of the British Black Art Movement—perceived as a rejoinder to the American Black Arts Movement of the 1960s. Artists acted as curators, among them Lubaina Himid, who organised exhibitions of Black women artists from 1983 onwards at venues including the Africa Centre, the Battersea Arts Centre and the Institute of Contemporary Arts, all in London.[11]

A distinctive feature of this cultural moment was a belief in 'political Blackness'—an umbrella term that outwardly proposed to unify all of Britain's non-white ethnic minorities against the hegemony of whiteness and discrimination.[12] The concept extended across the Atlantic, affecting the identarian positions of Black American artists such as Lorraine O'Grady, who in the introduction to her 2020 collected writings *Writing in Space* noted that she once used the term to explore intersectional communities of Blackness and female subjectivity. Arguing for a consciousness that embodies multiple diasporic communities and perspectives, O'Grady elucidates how this phrasing allows the concept of 'hybridity' to take shape.[13] Hybridity, a discourse that is deployed in theories of postcolonialism, anti-racism, globalisation and multiculturalism, to name but a few examples, was most profoundly articulated by Homi K Bhabha as an 'anxiety'-inducing field of study due to its ambiguous nature.[14] To simplify, Bhabha's suggestion has been that the 'liminal' nature of embodying hybridity leaves the individual subject to forms of mimicry—that the dispersed subject *when* hybrid may be perceived as prone to ambivalence regarding their difference, as opposed to forming a situated cultural knowledge about their own history as formerly colonised subjects.[15]

Writing these words from the vantage point of the third decade of the second millennium, where the mass medium of the internet has simultaneously connected and collected cultures, while at the same time it has perceivably flattened them, leaves the subject open to a different

Hybriditätsdiskurs, der in Theorien des Postkolonialismus, des Antirassismus, der Globalisierung und des Multikulturalismus geführt wird – um nur einige wenige Beispiele zu nennen –, besonders eindrücklich beschrieben. Für ihn ist es die inhaltliche Auseinandersetzung mit einer Materie, die durch ihre Mehrdeutigkeit „Ängste" verursacht.[14] Damit wollte Bhabha, vereinfacht ausgedrückt, sagen, dass das Individuum durch den Schwellenzustand seiner Verkörperung der Hybridität auf den Einsatz von Anpassung oder Nachahmung angewiesen ist. Vertriebene Personen im *Zustand* der Hybridität können in Bezug auf ihre Unterschiede als ambivalent wahrgenommen werden und nicht zwangsläufig über ein gemeinsames kulturgebundenes Wissen ihrer eigenen Geschichte als ehemals kolonisierte Subjekte verfügen.[15]

Aus dem Blickwinkel des dritten Jahrzehnts des zweiten Milleniums, in dem das Massenmedium Internet die Kulturen zusammengebracht und erfasst, aber gleichzeitig auch spürbar nivelliert hat, eröffnet sich dem Subjekt eine völlig neue ontologische Perspektive.[16] Unsere Form des „Seins" in der Welt hat sich grundlegend gewandelt. Durch sein unbeständiges Wesen erfährt das Sein eine fortwährende Aneignung und Wiederbelebung. Die Ausstellung *In the Heart of Another Country* widmet sich diesem Thema aus einer völlig neuen Perspektive, indem sie Kunstwerke und Künstler*innen aus drei Generationen und unterschiedlichen Diasporagruppen in einer imaginär konzipierten Inszenierung präsentiert. Ausgangspunkt für die Ausstellung war die Verbindung des Verfassers dieser Zeilen – und Kurators der Ausstellung – mit den unzähligen gelebten Erfahrungen der hier präsentierten Künstler*innen: Da sind zuallererst die Worte und Formen von Etel Adnan und Simone Fattal. Ihre gemeinsamen Leben und Biografien – ihre unterschiedlichen Herkünfte und ihre verschiedenen Akzente in vielen Sprachen. Beide waren durch Konflikte zu einem Leben an verschiedenen Orten gezwungen. Und beide waren queer. Ihre vielfältigen Erfahrungen sind ein Spiegel meiner eigenen Lebenswege. Mit der Zeit ist mir klar geworden, dass mich gerade diejenigen Aspekte bestimmter Lebensumstände, die „sich nicht in Worte fassen lassen", mit den Menschen verbinden, die in dieser Ausstellung vertreten sind. Für sie und mich allerdings mit dem *Unterschied*, dass sich keine unserer Verbindungen aus einem Gefühl der Unterwürfigkeit, sondern sich durch eine kollektive Affinität ergeben.

Der Titel der Ausstellung ist eine Hommage an Etel Adnans Pseudo-Memoiren *In the Heart of the Heart of Another Country*, die in ihrer aktuellen Fassung 2005 durch City Light Books in San Francisco ediert wurden. Vor dem Hintergrund persönlicher und politischer Turbulenzen, die Adnan vom Libanon, wo sie 1925 geboren wurde, nach Europa und in die USA brachten, ist das Buch auch ein stiller Rachefeldzug mit dem hartnäckigen Streben, einer Exilierten die kleinen Freuden des Alltags zu erlauben. Im Vorwort schreibt Adnan von einem „ununterbrochenen Strom kleiner Erfahrungen (…), Ekstasen"[17]. Und genau dieser Wunsch, eine völlig andere Lesart der Diaspora zu entwerfen, kommt in dieser Ausstellung zum Ausdruck. In einem Zeitalter der ständigen – als real oder virtuell empfundenen – Bewegung können vertriebene Körper bzw. Künstler*innen in der Diaspora eigenständig über ihre Form der Existenz und Außenwahrnehmung bestimmen. Diese These soll nicht allein über die Seiten dieses Katalogs, sondern auch über die unmittelbare körperliche Erfahrung während eines Besuchs der Ausstellung vermittelt werden, die einen kulturellen Wandel in sich und aus sich heraus bewirkt, und zwar nicht als untergeordnet oder in ständiger Opposition zu einer westlichen Hegemonie. Hier ist es Künstler*innen aus der Diaspora erlaubt, selbst über die Bedingungen der Rezeption ihrer Werke und ihrer Geschichten zu bestimmen.

ontological perspective.[16] Our way of 'being' in the world has shifted. It is unsettled by its very nature, subject to constant appropriation and re-animation. The exhibition *In the Heart of Another Country* proffers a reconsidered mode of looking through an imagined scenography of artworks and artists, who stretch across three generations and who hail from multiple diasporas. The starting point of the exhibition emerges through the alliance of the present author, the exhibition's curator, with the multiple lived experiences of the artists featured herein: first and foremost, with the words and forms of Etel Adnan and Simone Fattal. Adnan and Fattal's shared life and biographies—their being of multiple places; speaking in divergent accents, in various languages; their having been physically forced to live across multiple geographies due to the burdens of conflict, and their queerness—is a set of experiences that mirrors my own life. Over time, I have come to find the 'undefinable' aspects of this circumstance bear some connection to many of the individuals featured within this exhibition. Their, and my, *difference* here, however, is that no one is bound together by subaltern status, but rather, through a collective affinity.

The exhibition's title pays homage to Adnan's pseudo-memoir, *In the Heart of the Heart of Another Country*, first published in its current form in 2005 by the San Francisco-based publisher City Light Books. Set against a backdrop of personal and political turmoil, which sees Adnan moving between Lebanon, where she was born in 1925, Europe and the United States, the book, if anything, is quietly avenging in its persistent desire to allow the exiled subject to seek pleasure. As Adnan writes in the initial pages, through 'the flow of little experiences … small ecstasies …' emerge.[17] It is this very desire to give life to a different perceptual reading of a diaspora that this exhibition imagines. In an era of continuous movement, whether perceived as real or virtual, the dispersed body, the diasporic artist, can exist and be seen on their own terms. It is not merely the pages of this catalogue that will elucidate this argument but, rather, the visceral experience of the exhibition itself, which animates a form of cultural invention that exists in and of itself, not as subordinate, or in constant opposition, to a Western hegemony. The diasporic artist here has the right to set the terms by which their work is seen and their stories heard.

## The Radical Power of Personal Experience

*In trembling over the damp*
*petal-mound, palm-cupped,*
*I could but cry out,*
*stricken as the bird*
*who sees finally itself*
*reflected in the careful*
*accident of a bramble-knot*
— BLACKNESSS, WHICH WAS ALWAYS MOVING by Anaïs Duplan[18]

In *Body Work: The Radical Power of Personal Narrative*, through an interplay of memoir and analysis, Melissa Febos makes visible the complicit nature individuals play in forging shared narratives—intimacies familiar to many. In academia, it is intimated that the absence of the 'I' in scholarly writing, the avoidance of implicating the author within the text, suggests a vacuum,

*In trembling over the damp*
*petal-mound, palm-cupped,*
*I could but cry out,*
*stricken as the bird*
*who sees finally itself*
*reflected in the careful*
*accident of a bramble-knot*
— BLACKNESSS, WHICH WAS ALWAYS MOVING von Anaïs Duplan[18]

In *Body Work: The Radical Power of Personal Narrative* verdeutlicht Melissa Febos über ein Wechselspiel aus Erinnerung und Analyse, wie Menschen durch eine Art von Komplizenschaft – in einer weithin bekannten Form der Vertrautheit – gemeinsame Narrative entwickeln. In akademischen Kreisen heißt es, dass der Verzicht auf die Verwendung des Wortes „Ich" in wissenschaftlichen Texten, also die Vermeidung von Verweisen auf Verfasser*innen, den Eindruck eines Vakuums erzeugt. Es wird davon ausgegangen, dass bestimmte Geschichten keine spezifische Form der Subjektivität besitzen, sei es Klasse, ethnische Zugehörigkeit oder natürlich auch Erinnerung, Traumata oder Behinderung – weder in der Wahrnehmung noch tatsächlich.[19] In der Medizin bildet das Durchleben einer Krankheit eines der methodischen Hauptinstrumente für die Weiterentwicklung der Diagnosemöglichkeiten und der Forschung. In den Geisteswissenschaften hat die spürbare Spannung zwischen der dritten und der ersten Person deutlich abgenommen. Es hat sich gezeigt, dass vergessene Archive – die Geschichten der Unsichtbaren – einer Veranschaulichung durch persönliche Ausleuchtung und Konturengebung bedürfen. Das eindringlichste Beispiel für diesen methodologischen Ansatz bietet das wegweisende Konzept der „kritischen Fabulation", das Saidiya V Hartman, Professorin für Englisch und vergleichende Literaturwissenschaften an der Columbia University, zum ersten Mal 2007 in ihrem Essay „Venus in Two Acts" formulierte. Darin veranschaulicht sie mithilfe fiktionaler Narrative Aspekte der kritischen Theorie und Archivforschung, um sichtbar zu machen, was in offiziellen Aufzeichnungen und in der Geschichtsschreibung häufig nicht vorkommt.[20]

Der Künstler und Filmemacher Sky Hopinka erläutert dieses Konzept in seinem bedeutenden Essay "The Center of Somewhere" auf eindrucksvolle Weise. Darin liefert er eine vertiefte Analyse von Vorstellungen über Indigenität und Herkunft im Zusammenhang mit seinen eigenen künstlerischen Schaffensprozessen. Als amerikanischer Ureinwohner beschäftigt sich Hopinka eingehend mit den allgemeinen Definitionen von Kultur und ethnischer Zugehörigkeit und wirft insbesondere einen Blick auf „Identitäten und ihre Identifikatoren"[21]. Er geht auf das Spannungsfeld ein, das zwischen den spezifischen Absprachen über praktische Aspekte einer „empfundenen Ethnizität" und dem Akt der „Registrierung" in einer förmlichen Gemeinschaft besteht. So ist der Künstler zum Beispiel offizielles Mitglied der Ho-Chunk Nation in Wisconsin (wo er offiziell mit einer Nummer registriert ist), erhebt aber auch Anspruch auf seine Abstammung von der Pechanga Band der Luiseño Mission Indians (bei der er nicht registriert ist). Ein Widerspruch, der den Ureinwohnern das Leben erschwert, ein Lebensumstand, der von außen nicht erkennbar ist für all diejenigen, die mit den Prozessen der ethnischen

whereby, it is assumed, particular histories are devoid of specific forms of subjectivity—of class, race, gender, or, indeed, of memory, trauma, disability—perceived or otherwise.[19] In the medical sciences, the lived experience of illness is one of the primary methodological tools for diagnosis and research development. In the humanities, the notable tension of the third voice and the first person has increasingly disappeared. It has become evident that suppressed archives—that the stories of the unseen—require the contouring found in personal illumination. The clearest example in this methodological approach is evidenced in the significant concept of 'critical fabulation', articulated by Columbia University professor of English and comparative literature, Saidiya V Hartman, initially in 2007 in the essay, 'Venus in Two Acts'. Here, critical theory and archival research are illuminated through fictional narrative in order to give visuality to that which official record and history elides.[20]

A piercing example of this approach comes to life in artist and filmmaker Sky Hopinka's significant essay, 'The Centers of Somewhere', a reflective thesis of ideas that explores indigeneity and heritage in relation to the artist's own artmaking. Here, Hopinka, who is of Native American heritage, delves into broad concepts of culture and race, specifically, 'identities and their identifiers'.[21] The specificities of negotiating the practicalities of 'perceived ethnicity' versus the act of being 'enrolled' in a formal community, whether that be the artist's official membership in the Ho-Chunk Nation of Wisconsin (where he is officially enrolled with a number) or his claim to ancestry of the Pechanga Band of Luiseño Mission Indians (in which he is not enrolled), complicates the realities of Indigenous experience, a facet of being that is not outwardly evident to those who are not familiar with the processes of seeking to lay claim or who seek specific forms of 'belonging'. A survey of the visuality of Native Americans in popular culture deepens the disjuncture between these various ontological modes of living—revealing a hybrid form of consciousness that extends beyond the realm of W.E.B. Du Bois's notion of double consciousness to suggest what is arguably a kind of meta-consciousness.[22]

The life of the diasporic subject and, in turn, the diasporic artist, is an involved and entangled experience that extends beyond the mere notion that the 'diasporic' individual is 'displaced', 'exiled' or 'dispersed' from their homeland, or place of birth. Rather, to be diasporic, one has come to understand through intersectional forms of literature that artmaking is a form of embodiment that can be presented in myriad fashions. In the age of the internet, being or seeing through a creolised perspective that unsettles any concept of a master narrative of hegemony is increasingly assumed to be de rigueur due to the hyperlinked, remixed visual culture enabled by this field of vision.[23] Accordingly, to continue to see the world in binaries of East and West, within distinct formulations of hegemony and counter-hegemony, is to re-inscribe a culture of opposites and difference, as opposed to developing the specific shape of a present that is in constant flux. This feels ever more prevalent at a time when digital assimilation and fracture, digital forms of cultural cross-pollination, and newfound forms of consciousnesses have arisen.

The framework of stitching together the narrative of an exhibition, and with it, resuscitating the 'I' in the experience of both world-building and -framing, has been commensurate with a more fluent comprehension of what constitutes curatorial practice. Curating is still a field of study that remains largely confined to the examination of exhibition-histories. The physical acts involved in performing the curatorial—i.e., of primary archival research, fundraising, documenting, travelling, negotiating, presenting, acquiring, shipping, insuring, conserving, registering, cleaning, staging, fundraising again, licensing, authoring, presenting, contextualising and, finally, exhibiting—are, all too often, disciplinary details that are perceived to be at the margins of the curatorial narrative: on the cutting-room floor in a movie of flight and fancy.

Zuordnung oder der Suche nach spezifischen Formen der „Zugehörigkeit“ nicht vertraut sind. Eine nähere Beschäftigung mit der Sichtbarkeit US-amerikanischer Ureinwohner*innen in der Populärkultur zeigt, dass die Differenz zwischen den verschiedenen Lebensentwürfen noch größer ist als vermutet. Dabei wird eine hybride Form des Bewusstseins erkennbar, die weit über W.E.B. Dubois' Begriff des doppelten Bewusstseins hinausgeht und offenbar eine Art Metabewusstsein impliziert.[22]

Das Leben des Subjekts und des Kunstschaffenden in der Diaspora beruht auf einem komplexen Netz aus Erfahrungen, die die Grenzen dessen überschreiten, was gemeinhin als „Vertreibung“, „Exil“ oder „Zerstreuung“ von Menschen weg aus ihrer Heimat oder ihrem Geburtsort bezeichnet wird. Vielmehr lassen intersektionale Formen der Literatur und des Kunstschaffens den Schluss zu, dass der Zustand der Diaspora auf vielfältige Weise zum Ausdruck kommen kann. Im Zeitalter des Internets wird eine Existenz- oder Sichtweise aus einem kreolischen Blickwinkel, die jedem Konzept einer großen hegemonialen Erzählung zuwiderläuft, angesichts einer durch diese Perspektive begünstigten verlinkten und neu gemischten visuellen Kultur zunehmend als *de rigueur* erachtet.[23] Folglich würde eine Fortsetzung der binären Unterteilung der Welt in Ost und West mit einer klaren Unterscheidung zwischen hegemonialen und antihegemonialen Kräften dazu führen, eine Kultur der Gegensätze und Unterschiede fortzuschreiben, anstatt die spezifische Form einer Gegenwart im ständigen Fluss zu entwickeln – was sich in einer Zeit der digitalen Assimilationen und Umbrüche, der gegenseitigen kulturellen Befruchtung mit digitalen Mitteln und der neuartigen Bewusstseinsformen anscheinend immer mehr durchsetzt.

Das Zusammenweben eines Ausstellungsnarrativs und damit einhergehend die Wiederbelebung des „Ich“ in der Erfahrung des Aufbaus und der Gestaltung einer Welt beruht auch auf einer flexibleren Auffassung von den Inhalten der kuratorischen Praxis. In der Disziplin des Kuratierens geht es noch immer vor allem um die Auseinandersetzung mit den in einer Ausstellung präsentierten Geschichten. Die physischen Handlungen von Kurator*innen, z. B. erste Recherchen in Archiven, das Fundraising, Dokumentieren, Reisen, Verhandeln, Präsentieren, das Erwerben, Verschicken, Versichern, Einlagern, Registrieren, Reinigen, Aufstellen von Kunstwerken, das erneute Fundraising, Lizenzieren, Verfassen von Texten, Präsentieren, Kontextualisieren und schließlich das Ausstellen an sich werden viel zu häufig als reine Fleißarbeit wahrgenommen und finden keinen Platz im kuratorischen Narrativ – wie die herausgeschnittenen Szenen eines Films über kuratorische Höhenflüge.

Die Korrekturfunktion, die ich im Rahmen dieses aufwendigen Ausstellungsprojekts erkunden möchte, setzt voraus, dass das Kuratieren sowohl einen bekannten Kanon von Geschichten über Ausstellungen und Objekte als auch einen subjektiven Bereich der praktischen Recherche und Intervention im Rahmen einer präzisen Inszenierung beinhaltet. Dieser Text etwa entsteht in einer wenig romantischen Atmosphäre, in glühender Hitze zwischen angestaubten Zettelbergen mit flüchtig über einen Zeitraum von 17 Jahren hingekritzelten Notizen. Ordner in verschiedenen Zuständen und Formen verweisen auf meine wechselnden Arbeitsumstände und -materialien. Meine Referenzbilder der vergangenen sechs Jahre sind zwar ordentlich in Schutzhüllen verstaut, doch die billigen Blöcke mit den Notizen zu den Gesprächen mit vielen Künstler*innen dieser Ausstellung, von denen etliche nicht mehr am Leben sind, fristen ihr Dasein in auseinanderfallenden Kartons. Wird sich jemand ihrer annehmen? Haben sie ohne mich, der sie entschlüsseln kann, überhaupt irgendeinen Wert?

Auf digitalen Dateien sind, über mehrere Festplatten verteilt, unzählige Essays und Kritiken gespeichert. In einigen davon habe ich mich mit bestimmten künstlerischen Archiven beschäftigt.

The corrective function I seek to explore within the framework of this involved exhibition-project is that curating consists both of a known canonical field of exhibition and object histories, and of the subjective field of pragmatic research and intervention through precise scenography. There is little romance authoring these words in sweltering heat amidst dust-laden sheets of indexical information that have been scribbled opportunistically in meetings over the course of 17 years. Binders of different ilk and formation illustrate the changing possibilities of the resources at my disposal. My reference images of the past six years may be organised in protective sleeves, while conversations with many of the artists featured within this exhibition, many of whom are no longer alive, are scribbled on cheap notepads in decomposing boxes. Will someone come to their rescue? Do they hold any redeeming value beyond my ability to decode them?

Digital files spread across hard drives hold within them multiple essays and reviews, some of which I authored as a means of examining certain artistic archives, others are photographs of magazines; the ability to physically house them has become an impossibility, the consistently mobile nature of my type of profession does not guarantee that they can always be made visual, present or alive. I must often query whether I am examining the correct artwork, or if the magazine's picture editor has cropped one of the few pictures of an artwork by an artist they have deemed worthy of representing. This exhibition, in turn, was borne out of fluid historical experiences, which have required historical and visual anchoring. Traditionally, objects, ephemeral or otherwise, are waiting to be made animate by a keeper of some form, if not entirely re-authored in context—a practice that, in theatre and film (which tend to pull from the vestiges of literature), is commonly perceived as disciplinary rather than merely vernacular.

The act of the curatorial is often hollowed of the specific experience of narrating the journey as it were. Accordingly, the goal herein is not to contextualise less recognisable art forms within the frame of familiar genealogies or reference points, as this would be to ignore the historical involvement of archivists, librarians, publishers and exhibition designers, to name but a few examples. The articulation of the various processes and individuals involved in the staging of a curatorial experience intentionally and continuously proffers and allows for varied meanings to form around an artist or artwork. The hierarchy of how connotation is assumed is often the result of institutional forces—presumed seniority or even social standing being a determining factor. Thus, this essay, much like this exhibition, seeks, within the confines of the word limit, to take inventory of as much of the exhibition's curatorial processes as possible, in both a practical and theoretical sense, an exercise of accounting in real time, a porous assessment that will shift with the further exploration that occurs in the act of staging the project.[24]

Authoring an exhibition catalogue *before* the crucial act of staging, one of the economic thresholds that is difficult to parse within the field, ignores a certain 'distance of diplomacy'.[25] An exhibition as a proposition embodying a series of possibilities—of a scenography that seeks to embolden the latent meanings held within objects—is a curatorial practice that, at the time of writing a book such as this, is speculative. The realities of budgeting and the in situ experience of art is subject to constant change. This is not to say that the original curatorial intent cannot be realised, but that it is one of constant compromise. Accordingly, readers and audiences shall venture through a travelogue, through what for now is an imagined set of corridors that took six years to realise. Still, this exhibition project recognises relationships that have been developed in my work through primary research over more than 17 years. What is here is a site of accumulating acts that have been brought together to evoke what I hope shall be an affective act of witnessing—the result of which may demand continued investigation.

Dann gibt es Fotoaufnahmen aus Magazinen, von deren Originalen ich mich trennen musste, weil ich durch die mit meinem Beruf verbundene ständige Mobilität nicht sicherstellen kann, sie immer im richtigen Moment ansehen oder präsentieren zu können. Ich muss stets überprüfen, ob ich mich mit dem richtigen Werk befasse oder ob die Bildredaktion eines Magazins eines der wenigen Bilder aus dem Gesamtwerk einer*s von ihr als veröffentlichungswürdig betrachteten Künstlerin oder Künstlers beschnitten hat. Im Gegensatz dazu stützt sich diese Ausstellung auf zusammenhängende Erfahrungen der Vergangenheit, die eine historische und visuelle Verortung erforderten. Traditionell warten – vergängliche oder andere – Objekte darauf, von einer Art Hüter*in zum Leben erweckt oder sogar in einen völlig neuen Kontext gesetzt zu werden. Eine solche Praxis wird in der Welt des Theaters und des Films – die zum Teil auf literarische Fragmente zurückgreift – in der Regel eher als akademisch denn als volkstümlich betrachtet.

Die kuratorische Arbeit sieht in vielen Fällen nicht vor, die spezifische Erfahrung zu vermitteln, eine Geschichte so zu erzählen, wie sie sich zugetragen hat. Aus diesem Grund besteht das Ziel auch nicht darin, weniger eingängige Kunstformen mithilfe vertrauter Genealogien oder Bezugspunkte zu kontextualisieren, weil man auf diese Weise die bisherige Arbeit von Archivar*innen, Bibliothekar*innen, Verleger*innen und Ausstellungsdesigner*innen – um nur einige wenige Beteiligte zu nennen – ignorieren würde. Durch den Hinweis auf die verschiedenen Phasen und Mitwirkenden einer kuratorischen Erfahrung werden für Künstler*innen oder Kunstwerke ganz bewusst und fortwährend zahlreiche Interpretationsmöglichkeiten angeboten. Welche dieser Deutungen vorrangig berücksichtigt werden, wird häufig von den institutionellen Kräfteverhältnissen bestimmt. Dabei spielen Annahmen über Seniorität und sozialen Status eine entscheidende Rolle. Dieses Essay wie auch die Ausstellung unternehmen deshalb den Versuch, innerhalb der Grenzen des Ausdrückbaren eine möglichst umfassende praktische wie theoretische Bestandsaufnahme der kuratorischen Prozesse dieser Ausstellung zu erstellen – eine Echtzeitbilanz und zwangsläufig lückenhafte Bewertung, die sich im weiteren Verlauf des Projekts noch ändern wird.[24]

Das Verfassen eines Ausstellungskatalogs *vor* der eigentlichen Präsentation – eine der größten ökonomischen Hürden in diesem Zusammenhang – widersetzt sich einer gewissen „diplomatischen Distanz“[25]. Eine Ausstellung als Vorschlag, der eine Reihe von Möglichkeiten enthält – für eine Inszenierung, die verborgene Bedeutungen der ausgestellten Objekte ans Licht bringen will –, beruht auf einer kuratorischen Praxis, die sich in der Phase der Entstehung eines solchen Buches auf Spekulationen stützt. Die Realität der Finanzierung und das Erleben von Kunst an einem bestimmten Ort unterliegen ständigem Wandel. Dies soll nicht heißen, dass sich der eigentliche kuratorische Plan nicht umsetzen ließe, sondern vielmehr, dass dabei ständig Kompromisse erforderlich werden. Die Leserschaft und das Publikum mögen sich daher auf eine spannende Reise durch mehrere bislang noch imaginäre Korridore begeben, deren Vollendung ganze sechs Jahre in Anspruch genommen hat. In diesem Ausstellungsprojekt werden jedoch auch diejenigen Beziehungen gewürdigt, die ich im Verlauf meiner Primärforschung der vergangenen mehr als 17 Jahren aufbauen konnte. Folglich präsentiert sich hier eine Sammlung von Werken, die – so meine Hoffnung – ein emotionales Zeugnis ablegt und mit der die Auseinandersetzung womöglich noch nicht beendet ist.

*Burn me some music/send my roots rain/I'm swept*
*A struggle at the roots of the mind/Whoever said*
*it would go on and on like this*
*…*
*contraband calligraphy/against the war*
*poetry wages against itself*
— Extract from 'Waiting for Rain, for Music' by Adrienne Rich[26]

Longing—a set of associated feelings conjured by a specific place of perceived belonging—is notable for its potential to elicit endless bouts of melancholy.[27] The memorialisation of events and happenings serves as a persistent reminder for the diasporic subject: sites, memories, and places that are no longer in their immediate view or access. The distance in the dispersed image, whichever surface it may transpire upon, is evocative of a relentless despondency. Autobiographical prose, cinema and public events may all act as propulsive triggers.[28] For the present author, reading *Out of Egypt*, André Aciman's memoir of uncertainty from 2007, or Halima Bashir's *Tears of the Desert,* about the war in Darfur, summoned feelings of nostalgia, pain and interminable ambivalence. Although their experiences were distinct from mine—I could thread correlations—my queerness, disability, class and race, in that order, could be applied to specific details. The terror of attack, and the C-PTSD of a life lived in a trauma loop, made every detail all the more piercing.

These narratives, and many like them, form echoes that continue to hark back to a place—a site, even if one has sought (in this case, I) exile from it. In a different guise, Spike Lee's *Do the Right Thing* (1989)—the first motion picture screened during my tenure at film school—elicited anger, nostalgia and confusion, pushing me back into the recesses of memory and the years I spent as a child living in South Los Angeles. Although the setting in this instance was New York City, the encoded racial language and ensuing prejudice were all too familiar reminders of life in the City of Angels in the 1990s.

The dominion of art, and specifically of exhibition-making, plays a pivotal role in the activation of memory, especially in the nationalist contexts of exhibitions such as those of the art and architecture biennials of Venice, for example. I recall bearing witness to several 'firsts'—pavilions for Lebanon, Palestine and Sudan, which would transpire, only to disappear, and then resurface, before vanishing again as a result of economic or socio-political circumstance. In 2015, I curated the national representation of Cyprus—itself a contested and divided nation-state. Despite the curatorial team's aspiration to win the Golden Lion, I quietly estimated and hoped that my friend and collaborator Hrair Sarkissian, featured in the group show *Armenity*, would be given the prize. It was the centenary of the Armenian genocide, an event that elicits feelings of confusion when situated in a celebratory context such as a prize ceremony.

As *Armenity*'s curator, Adelina Cüberyan v. Fürstenberg held the prized gold statue, the late curator Okwui Enwezor—Artistic Director of the 56th Venice Biennale's international exhibition—stood behind her, gleaming.[29] In that moment, I felt both elation and sorrow. The award ostensibly served as a form of recognition, of a genocide that, to this day, is not publicly acknowledged by the perpetrators who incited the violence that led to mass displacement and

*Burn me some music/send my roots rain/I'm swept*
*A struggle at the roots of the mind/Whoever said*
*it would go on and on like this*
*...*
*contraband calligraphy/against the war*
*poetry wages against itself*
— Auszug aus „Waiting for Rain, for Music" von Adrienne Rich [26]

Sehnsucht – eine komplexe Gemütsverfassung, ausgelöst von einem Ort der tief empfundenen Zugehörigkeit – kann auf bemerkenswerte Weise endlose Wellen der Melancholie schlagen.[27] Der Rückblick auf Ereignisse der Vergangenheit verbindet Menschen in der Diaspora fortwährend mit Orten ihrer Erinnerung, die sie nicht mehr sehen oder besuchen können. In Darstellungen der Vertreibung – unabhängig von ihrer künstlerischen Form – erzeugt diese Distanz ein tiefes Gefühl der Verzweiflung. Autobiografische Schriften, Filme und öffentliche Veranstaltungen können diese Empfindung zusätzlich verstärken.[28] Für mich persönlich war die Lektüre von *Out of Egypt (Damals in Alexandria – Erinnerung an eine verschwundene Welt)*, André Acimans Memoiren aus einer Zeit der Unsicherheit aus dem Jahre 2007, oder von Halima Bashirs *Tears of the Desert (Tränen der Wüste)* über den Krieg in Darfur mit Gefühlen der Nostalgie, des Schmerzes und unendlicher Ambivalenz verbunden. Auch wenn sich die darin geschilderten Erfahrungen von meinen unterscheiden, konnte ich einige Schnittstellen ausmachen – mein Queersein, meine Behinderung, meine Klassen- und ethnische Zugehörigkeit waren, in dieser Reihenfolge, auf bestimmte Details übertragbar. Die Schrecken eines Angriffs und die Posttraumatische Belastungsstörung eines Lebens im Traumaloop ließen jede kleinste Einzelheit umso erschütternder erscheinen.

Diese und viele vergleichbare Narrative verweisen wie ein endloses Echo pausenlos auf einen bestimmten Ort – auch wenn ein Mensch (in diesem Fall ich) das Exil gewählt hat. Auf ganz andere Weise rief Spike Lees *Do the Right Thing* (1989) – der erste Spielfilm, der während meiner Zeit an der Filmhochschule gezeigt wurde – Wut, Nostalgie und Verwirrung in mir hervor und ließ mich erneut in die Abgründe der Erinnerung an meine Kindheit im Süden von Los Angeles abtauchen. Auch wenn der Film in New York City spielt, erinnerten mich die Codes der verschiedenen Sprachgemeinschaften und die damit verbundenen Vorurteile doch allzu sehr an mein Leben in der Stadt der Engel in den 1990er Jahren.

Das Kunstschaffen und insbesondere das Ausstellungsmachen tragen ganz wesentlich dazu bei, Erinnerungen zu wecken, insbesondere wenn Ausstellungen nach Nationen unterteilt sind, wie im Falle der Kunst- und Architekturbiennalen von Venedig. Ich erinnere mich an viele „erste Male" – im Zusammenhang mit den libanesischen, palästinensischen oder sudanesischen Pavillons, die errichtet wurden, sofort wieder verschwanden und dann wieder auftauchten, bevor sie erneut wirtschaftlichen oder soziopolitischen Umständen weichen mussten. Im Jahre 2015 kuratierte ich den Pavillon von Zypern – selbst eine umkämpfte und politisch geteilte Insel. Natürlich wollte unser Kurator*innenteam den Goldenen Löwen gewinnen. Doch insgeheim erwartete und hoffte ich, dass mein Freund und Kollege Hrair Sarkissian mit der Gruppenshow *Armenity* den Preis erhalten würde. Der Völkermord an den Armenier*innen lag damals 100

loss of life. I recall convening with Sarkissian in London afterwards—the two of us were about to prepare for his traveling survey exhibition, which I was curating. I queried his feelings, or, rather, sought to challenge my own assumptions. What emerged over the next five years was an open-ended conversation that spoke to the thorny nature of 'longing': is it a fictional construct of multiple imaginaries, as articulated by Joana Hadjithomas in the film *ISMYRNE* (2016), in which she and Etel Adnan sit together to piece together their relationship to a site of origin, a place they have chosen to relegate to the realm of the mind, perhaps? If displacement is a choice, can it still offer an emotional reverberation, entangling the diasporic individual in a frenzy? Or, rather, might it serve as a vessel, a means of unbuckling the practicalities of belonging to any particular place and, by proxy, identity?

Rather than fashion an exhibition of didactic inquisition, with prodding surveys and answers, I have adopted the methodological approach that was instilled in me by my closest of mentors. I was taught early on through the writings of Edward Said that one should use every opportunity—platforms and stages, small or large—'to speak truth to power'.[30] The shape and contour of that manifestation, however, shifted considerably in the historical juncture when I began working. Simply being 'seen' no longer served as a purposeful win for a community once vanquished or suppressed. Instead, I adopted Jean Fisher's position of play, as invoked through the figure of the 'trickster'.[31] Fisher's perceptual use of this characterful representative was concerned with unlocking the 'hermetic' field in favour of an interplay with 'hermeneutics'—i.e., a trailing, inquiring performance and composition of the senses. Invoking Michel Serres, my research under Fisher's supervision encouraged me to consider how the very act of encountering could be made manifest through trespassing, vectoring and capitalising on the opportunism offered to us. For the trickster, as Fisher argues, no form of 'hegemony' is 'ever absolute'.[32]

The formal aspects of note within *In the Heart of Another Country* are poetry and song, lyric and opera, as well as the relationship of architecture and the negotiation of tradition. I have used my years of research—amidst the archives and in public forums and beyond—to embody some form of Serres's 'troubadour of knowledge' and present an exhibition in three interleaving chapters.[33] The result is something layered: encrusted with sediments that have left imprints on or within each other.

I have long been preoccupied with ethnicity and its relationship to various forms of perceived cultural ideology, specifically in relation to geographic groupings of art from Africa and western Asia. But rather than speak of ethnicity, I have chosen to interlink the aesthetic, formal and conceptual connections amongst artists, listening to a distributed echo as it harkens, summoning a sense of return. Richard Bell, whose writing I was introduced to by the artist Michael Rakowitz, was influential in this unrelenting pursuit. His writing since the 1990s has argued that the context of 'Aboriginal art' is an anthropological categorical field constructed primarily for a white gaze.[34] Unlocking the triangles of discomfort formed by the agendas of Indigenous Australian communities, Bell compels his readers to return to the responsibility of art—whether it be political or purely the aesthetic form of art for art's sake. An artwork or artist's existence, visibly present or erased from history, it has been repeatedly argued in the reconstituted canon of twentieth and now twenty-first century art history, should not be deterministically linked with the ethnic identity of its maker.[35]

Deconstructing this topology, the exhibition's lyrics weave from a formal abundance of sculptures and maps—vessels and vestibules—through to a second chapter, where the portrait is sutured: a reparative context or simply a position to sing, scream and be heard. Here, a synthetic culture is deconstructed by Hassan Sharif, who is consciously positioned next to Rasheed Araeen, whose annotated portraits reflect a dissident energy that inadvertently links

Jahre zurück – ein Jahrestag, der sogar im feierlichen Kontext einer Preisverleihung Gefühle der Verwirrung auszulösen vermag.

Als die Kuratorin von *Armenity*, Adelina Cüberyan v. Fürstenberg, die begehrte Goldstatue entgegennahm, strahlte der inzwischen verstorbene Kurator und künstlerische Leiter der 56. Internationalen Kunstausstellung Biennale, Okwui Enwezor, hinter ihr vor Begeisterung.[29] In diesem Moment empfand ich Freude und Bedauern zugleich. Die Auszeichnung war eine Anerkennung – die Anerkennung eines Genozids, der von den Verursacher*innen dieser Gewaltexzesse trotz Massenvertreibungen und des Verlusts unzähliger Menschenleben bis heute nicht offiziell eingestanden wird. Ich erinnere mich an ein anschließendes Treffen mit Sarkissian in London. Wir wollten mit den gemeinsamen Vorbereitungen für eine von mir kuratierte Wanderausstellung beginnen. Ich fragte ihn nach seinen Gefühlen. Womöglich wollte ich auch meine eigenen Überzeugungen hinterfragen. Aus dieser Unterhaltung entwickelte sich in den nächsten fünf Jahren ein ununterbrochenes Gespräch über das heikle Thema „Sehnsucht" als fiktionales Konstrukt unzähliger Vorstellungswelten. Diesen Gedanken bringt auch Joana Hadjithomas in ihrem Film *ISMYRNA* (2016) zum Ausdruck, als sie im Gespräch mit Etel Adnan versucht, ihre gemeinsame Beziehung zu einem Herkunftsort, den sie in der Erinnerung möglicherweise in die Tiefen ihrer Seelen verbannt haben, zu einem gemeinsamen Bild zusammenzufügen. Wenn die Vertreibung selbst gewählt ist, kann sie dann noch einen emotionalen Widerhall erzeugen, der Menschen in der Diaspora in Aufruhr versetzt? Oder mag sie womöglich als Mittel dienen, um sich von den praktischen Aspekten der Zugehörigkeit zu einem bestimmten Ort und, stellvertretend, zu einer bestimmten Identität zu befreien?

Für die Ausstellung habe ich keinen didaktischen Ansatz gewählt, der Antworten aus Umfragen zitiert, sondern eine methodische Herangehensweise, den mir mein wichtigster Mentor, Edward Said, vermittelt hat. Durch die Lektüre der Schriften von Said habe ich mir schon früh angewöhnt, jede Möglichkeit zu nutzen – jede Plattform oder Bühne, sei sie auch noch so klein –, um „der Macht die Wahrheit zu sagen"[30]. Allerdings haben sich die Formen und Konturen einer solchen Meinungsäußerung mit den historischen Umwälzungen in meiner ersten Zeit als Kurator grundlegend verschoben. Der simple Akt des „Gesehenwerdens" wurde von einer einst besiegten oder unterdrückten Gemeinschaft nicht länger zwingend als Gewinn betrachtet. Stattdessen entschied ich mich für die spielerische Position von Jean Fishers Figur des „Tricksters"[31]. Fisher setzt diesen charaktervollen Stellvertreter bewusst ein, um das „hermetische" Feld zugunsten eines Zusammenspiels mit der „Hermeneutik" aufzubrechen – beispielsweise in Form einer drängenden, forschenden Performance und Komposition der Sinne. Durch die Auseinandersetzung mit Michel Serres' Thesen unter Fishers Ägide stellte ich mir schließlich die Frage, ob der eigentliche Akt der Begegnung nicht auch durch Grenzüberschreitung, Verschiebung und die Verwertung der uns zur Verfügung stehenden Möglichkeiten manifestiert werden könnte. Für den Trickster ist laut Fisher keine Form der „Hegemonie" jemals „absolut".[32]

Zu den formalen Besonderheiten von *In the Heart of Another Country* gehören Gedichte und Lieder, Lyrik- und Opernelemente sowie Bezüge zur Architektur und die Beschäftigung mit Traditionen. Im Anschluss an jahrelange Recherchen – unter anderem in Archiven und öffentlichen Foren – präsentiere ich als eine Art „Troubadour des Wissens" im Sinne von Serres eine Ausstellung mit drei miteinander verwobenen Kapiteln.[33] Das Ergebnis besteht aus mehreren Schichten – aus Verkrustungen mit Sedimenten, die Spuren auf- oder ineinander hinterlassen haben.

these individuals' practices. As one weaves their way through the echo chamber of a site that feels as limitless as it is confining, an inroad of possibility ensues. The final chapter, 'Going South', interrogates the language of the perceived 'Global South' through the lens of the artists and their active movement across multiple spaces and times. As the curtain descends on the final act, you—the visitor, the viewer, the spectator or, perhaps, the interloper—are invited to take your final flight: to extend beyond the realm of this reality and to enter into one anew.

## Chapter 1
## Architecture by Other Means: The Abstract Body Meets the Concrete City

1 *Noticing small details, patterns, smells, or sounds that others do not—*
*[they profess] this 'the core' affliction.*
2 *Finding it hard to understand what 'others' are thinking or feeling*
*Isn't this the most exquisite aspect of life's disease?*
3 *Anxiety everywhere…*
*Hasn't post-pandemonium entitled us to this aspect of 'the' disorder?*
4 *Avoiding eye contact—*
*Why should 'you' bear the privilege of entering into any 'other's' soul?*
*The practice of art is a dance of constant extraction.*
*The invitation doesn't come for free.*
5 *Getting upset if someone touches you?*
*The inner storm of touch and stimulation—the haptic, a choice, a right, or is*
*this the border of my body no longer contingent to the same rules as everyone else?*
*dawdle in shame.*
6 *Avoid your 'keen interests', i.e., hobbies*
*The curatorial disposition outputs in a swell of toxicity.*
*An abundance—an obsession with planning—*
*The danger of exhibition-making, worldbuilding, role-play?*
*The practice of enacting history presumes a perpetual death,*
*Murmurs expand and expound into an echo*
*The resonance of endless endlessness; a path to infinite ends, loop.*
— Extract from 'The Core Wound…' by Blake Karim Mitchell[36]

The disciplinary practice of producing exhibitions can materialise in myriad forms—as chronological displays, as formal groupings of artworks or as presentations that speak to grand societal themes. As a practitioner, I see exhibition-making as a distilled form of knowledge dissemination revealed through an interdisciplinary act of 'world-building'. The latter, a term commonly used in science-fiction literature, gaming and the realm of speculative futurism, considers that a world must be constructed as a universe unto itself.[37] World-building is akin to the contemporary reference of the 'metaverse'—a contained site with its own distinct feeling, its own language—real or invented, alongside inter-textual references, be they architectural or spatial, conditions that enable the viewer to feel emboldened to unpack latent meanings within the object-sphere, or to construct imagined contexts of their own.[38]

Ich habe mich lange Zeit mit Ethnizität und ihrem Verhältnis zu verschiedenen Formen einer vermeintlichen kulturellen Ideologie beschäftigt, insbesondere mit Blick auf Gruppen von Kunstschaffenden aus Afrika und Westasien. Dennoch möchte ich nicht von Ethnizität sprechen, sondern ästhetische, formale und konzeptuelle Verbindungen zwischen Künstler*innen herstellen und dabei dem Klang eines Echos der Vielfalt lauschen, das zu einer Art von Wiederkehr aufruft. Richard Bell, auf dessen Werk mich der Künstler Michael Rakowitz aufmerksam machte, war in meinem unablässigen Streben eine wichtige Inspirationsquelle. Seit 1990 vertritt er in seinen Schriften die These, der Begriff der „Aboriginal Art", also der Kunst der australischen Ureinwohner*innen, sei eine anthropologische Kategorie, die hauptsächlich dem weißen Blick diene.[34] Bell macht sich das vielgestaltige Unbehagen im Zusammenhang mit den Anliegen der australischen Ureinwohner*innen zunutze, um seine Leser*innen zu einer Rückbesinnung auf die Verantwortung der Kunst zu bewegen – ob nun aus politischer oder rein ästhetischer Sicht im Sinne einer L'art pour l'art. Im überarbeiteten Kanon der Kunstgeschichte des 20. und nun 21. Jahrhunderts wurde wiederholt darauf verwiesen, dass die sichtbare oder aus der Geschichte gelöschte Existenz von Kunstwerken oder Kunstschaffenden nicht zwingend mit ihrer ethnischen Identität verknüpft werden muss.[35]

Die Texte der Ausstellung lösen diese Topologie auf und winden sich durch ein Meer der Formen aus Skulpturen und Karten, die als Bindeglied und Übergang dienen, in ein zweites Kapitel voller zusammengestückelter Porträts – ein heilender Kontext oder einfach ein Ort, um zu singen, zu schreien und gehört zu werden. Hier dekonstruiert Hassan Sharif die synthetische Kultur. Seine Werke sind bewusst neben denen von Rasheed Araeen platziert. Dessen mit Kommentaren versehene Porträts strahlen eine rebellische Energie aus, die das Handeln der dargestellten Personen ganz zufällig miteinander verbindet. Auf den verschlungenen Pfaden der Echokammern dieser Ausstellung, die zugleich ein Gefühl der Grenzenlosigkeit und Enge vermitteln, öffnen sich schließlich überraschend neue Wege. Im letzten Kapitel, "Gen Süden" wird die Sprache des sogenannten Globalen Südens aus dem Blickwinkel der Künstler*innen auf ihrer Reise durch zahlreiche Räume und Zeiten hinterfragt. Wenn der Vorhang zum letzten Akt fällt, sind Sie – als Besucher*innen, Betrachter*innen oder vielleicht auch Eindringlinge – aufgefordert, sich auf Ihren letzten Flug zu begeben, bei dem Sie aus der aktuellen in eine völlig neue Realität eintreten.

## Kapitel 1
## Architektur mit anderen Mitteln: Der abstrakte Körper trifft auf die konkrete Stadt

1 *Noticing small details, patterns, smells, or sounds that others do not—*
*[they profess] this 'the core' affliction.*
2 *Finding it hard to understand what 'others' are thinking or feeling*
*Isn't this the most exquisite aspect of life's disease?*
3 *Anxiety everywhere…*
*Hasn't post-pandemonium entitled us to this aspect of 'the' disorder?*
4 *Avoiding eye contact—*
*Why should 'you' bear the privilege of entering into any 'other's' soul?*
*The practice of art is a dance of constant extraction.*
*The invitation doesn't come for free.*

The first time I stand in the Hall of Contemporary Art, I am alone, between exhibition installations. I do not recall bearing witness to dividing walls, simply an epic expanse—a site that simultaneously felt both too vast and yet, somehow, not eclectic enough for the specificity of the multiple artists whom I was eager to put into conversation. An exhibition as wide-ranging in periodisation and form as *In the Heart of Another Country* emerges as a result of an invitation to the curator, but that summoning quickly becomes a responsibility that demands a negotiation through contradictory politics, a cross-border engagement with language and a willingness to concede to the determinism that a venue weighs onto art itself.

The exhibition's architect, Todd Reisz,[39] begins his investigation into each particulate of my initial exhibition checklist before casting it aside. A situated world is fashioned by hand. I am presented with sheaths of paper, the sheets present interlocking forms, some overlaid, situated into tight-fitting corners. In these sketches, corridors emerge through which to summon different viewing experiences. Reisz created constellations of spaces, small and large, which I had begun to correlate with various artworks, moving through PDF documents, Excel sheets, sketch-up mock-ups and CAD drawings. The shaded areas of his drawings, contoured with his fine marker pen, began to resemble pools of water amidst an archipelago.

We meet several more times. On one occasion, he presents me with slide shows that criss-cross through a series of references, from the Bauhaus to Anni Albers's *On Weaving*. Another slide reveals these halls to have been markets, another shows similar venues in Germany used as processing sites for asylum seekers. These orientations swell, moving through to a contoured map in ebullient colour: Is this Pangea? Was the proposition of this exhibition to bring the world together, in stark opposition to the manner in which many group shows purporting to represent so-called 'regions' of the world have tended to function?[40]

I choose to peer through the map, imagining it as a site for the sensuous pleasures evoked by Huguette Caland and the rhythmic forms of Saloua Raouda Choucair, two pioneers of modern abstraction whose lyrical approach to material enraptures the spectator as it unsettles. Another illustration appears—an antiquated advertisement that reveals that the Deichtorhallen's hall was once the station for trains commuting to Berlin's Hamburger Bahnhof, another public visual arts institution that has held within its walls countless stories of travel and movement, enforced or imagined. The exhibition's theme had found its route in space and time.

With this scenography, the exhibition's curator could seek to reclaim the diasporic condition as a form of celebration through its hybrid artistic manifestations. The invocation, to produce *an architecture by other means*, is a proposition that speaks to the possibilities created by artists whose practices embrace vernacular architectures alongside references to academic tradition. Here, a topography unfurls through a series of alphabets that come to life, as both literal and lyrical, formal and immaterial. Collectively, they build an alterscape that is coated with personal histories of oppression, relief and reprieve. Ushering us into this arched convening of objects in the exhibition is Jumana Manna's *Theory of an Unfinished Building (landscape)* (2021), a piece of scaffold dust sheet six metres wide, transposed from the city of Beirut onto a wooden frame more than two-and-a-half metres high. As the narrator of this exhibit, I choose to see this not as a relic of a city in decay but as a transmutation of one form onto another, precarity inherent.[41] Here, it sits on the entry walls of the lobby at the Deichtorhallen, an acknowledgement that every story, every place, every history is perpetually under construction. Just like this experience of narration, there exists something of uncertainty ahead, a casting of doubt or foreshadowing—a demand or, rather, a request of the viewer to take inventory as they proceed into the heart of another country.[42]

5 *Getting upset if someone touches you?*
*The inner storm of touch and stimulation—the haptic, a choice, a right, or is*
*this the border of my body no longer contingent to the same rules as everyone else?*
*dawdle in shame.*
6 *Avoid your 'keen interests', i.e., hobbies*
*The curatorial disposition outputs in a swell of toxicity.*
*An abundance—an obsession with planning—*
*The danger of exhibition-making, worldbuilding, role-play?*
*The practice of enacting history presumes a perpetual death,*
*Murmurs expand and expound into an echo*
*The resonance of endless endlessness; a path to infinite ends, loop.*
— Auszug aus „The Core Wound…" von Blake Karim Mitchell[36]

Es gibt unzählige Formen der Ausstellungspraxis — chronologische Ausstellungen, Ausstellungen mit einer Auswahl von Kunstwerken nach äußeren Kriterien oder Ausstellungen zu großen gesellschaftlichen Themen. In der Praxis betrachte ich das Organisieren von Ausstellungen als destillierte Form der Wissensvermittlung in einem interdisziplinären Akt des „Weltenbaus". Dieser Begriff aus der Science-Fiction-Literatur, dem Gaming und dem spekulativen Futurismus setzt voraus, dass eine Welt als eigenes Universum erschaffen wird.[37] Dieser Weltenbau ist verwandt mit dem modernen Konzept des „Metaversums", einem geschlossenen Handlungsraum mit eigenen Gefühlswelten und eigenen Sprachen — real oder erfunden –, mit intertextuellen Bezügen zu architektonischen Räumen, um die Betrachtenden zu ermutigen, unterschwellige Bedeutungen auf der Objektebene zu entschlüsseln oder eigene imaginierte Kontexte zu schaffen.[38]

Bei meinem ersten Besuch in den Deichtorhallen stand ich allein inmitten von Exponaten. An Trennwände kann ich mich nicht erinnern – nur an unendliche Weiten. An einen Ort, der sich zu groß anfühlte und gleichzeitig nicht genug Abwechslung zu bieten schien für die besonderen Ausdrucksformen der vielen Künstler*innen, die ich hier in einen Austausch miteinander bringen wollte. Alles begann mit der Einladung, die Ausstellung *In the Heart of Another Country* zu kuratieren, die aufgrund ihrer formalen Vielfalt besondere organisatorische Anforderungen mit sich brachte. Schon bald stand ich vor der Aufgabe, alle Seiten trotz widersprüchlicher Ansichten über Länder- und Sprachgrenzen hinweg in die Vorbereitungen einzubinden und mich mit den Gegebenheiten dieses Ausstellungsorts für Kunst zu versöhnen.

Der Architekt der Ausstellung, Todd Reisz[39], schaute sich zunächst jedes kleinste Detail meiner ersten Checkliste genau an. Dann legte er die Liste zur Seite und schuf von Hand eine neue Ausstellungswelt. Er zeigte mir viele Blätter mit ineinandergreifenden Formen, einige überlappend und passgenau in Ecken platziert. Ich konnte Korridore mit unterschiedlichen Sichtachsen erkennen. Reisz entwarf eine Kombination aus kleinen und großen Räumen, in denen ich – nach einem Blick in PDF-Dokumente, Excel-Tabellen, Modellskizzen und CAD-Zeichnungen – bereits erste Kunstwerke unterbrachte. Die mit einem Finemarker schraffierten Flächen in seinen Entwürfen erinnerten mich an die Bassins in einem Archipel.

Dies war nur eines von vielen weiteren Treffen. Einmal zeigte er mir Dias, die wild von einem Thema zum nächsten sprangen, vom Bauhaus bis zu Anni Albers' *On Weaving*. Auf einem anderen Dia waren die Deichtorhallen als ehemalige Markthalle zu sehen, ein weiteres zeigte ähnliche Orte in Deutschland, die zu Auffangzentren für Asylbewerber umfunktioniert worden waren. Die immer vielfältigeren Assoziationen fügten sich schließlich zu einer scharf

*(I in body now alive)*
— From 'Fracture' by Adrienne Rich (2007)

Golden coil is swirling, spinning and looping. This work, by Khalil Rabah, greets the viewer from the corner of their field of vision. Take a turn and these glistening objects, arranged gracefully, almost politely, begin to suggest a fortress—a blockade, preventing view to another sightline. The cellular sculptures, *Area C Fields of Gold (Not everything that shines is Gold)* (1994), are not merely a metaphor for militarised lines drawn in the sand. Rather, the work is a performing situation, where 90 bantam objects can be seen accumulating through a formal act of repetition. For some, they may resemble luscious haystacks, inviting one to move to touch them—to consider the possibility of pressing one's body against the threshold of a fabricated wall—one that prickles as much as it entices. The floor beneath is saturated, the body sinks. Beneath you is Marwan Rechmaoui's *Beirut Caoutchouc* (2004–2008), a rubber map of his hometown of Beirut. Eyeballs examine the identifying streets, the gates to the city, but a perplexing set of questions arises. Here, the city-lines, the divisive marks delineating Christian and Muslim neighbourhoods—the fragmented scars of Lebanon's Civil Wars, which occurred from 1975 to 1990—do not appear. This is a speculative fiction of a reconciliation. A site that may have existed before the blood-soaked stains of sectarian violence seeped into the streets. I am walking with you across this expanse.

Before our gaze, leaning, floating, resting, is a tapestry by the late artist and poet Etel Adnan, the individual whose memoir inspired this exhibition's title. *Mount Tamalpaïs* (2015) convenes spectators around one of the artist's primary obsessions. Born in Lebanon in 1925, Adnan's life was dwelt in France, the United States and Lebanon—in circular loops of back and forth. These movements were dictated by the everyday experience of conflict, the wanton need for expression, comradery, and companionship. Mount Tam, as it is affectionately known, the artist's subject, is a site in Marin County, California. The peak often served as a visual respite for Adnan, becoming the subject of many of her small canvasses and tapestries. Its invocation could be interpreted as an act of longing, as much as it is a gratifying reconstitution of a feeling of ecstasy. The frenzy of such bliss is an intentional construction in this act of world-building, where the composition of these intertwined forms suggests a metaverse—a portmanteau that in Latin is suggestive of the act of 'transcending' into an altered state of being, of consciousness, beyond the present.[43]

Anchoring one's entry into the exhibition hall are two one-and-a-half-metre-high clay sculptures by Adnan's partner and frequent collaborator, the polymath, Simone Fattal. Fattal's arched reliefs form part of her *Warrior* series of works, here represented by *Zhat El Himma* and *Abdel Wahab* (both 2016). The genesis for these distorted bodies emerges from Fattal's literary interests and pursuits. Indeed, Fattal is the founder, publisher and designer of the Post-Apollo Press—undeniably one of the most significant international poetry presses of the twentieth century.[44] Inspired by prophetic biographies, one figure assumes the identity of a male character, while the other, *Zhat El Himma*, is suggestive of the early dynastic traditions of Palestinians, namely the life of Amina Dhat al Himma, also known as Princess Fatima, the only female subject of the 'epic novels' published in Arabic—in this case, *The Tale of Princess Fatima, Warrior Woman: The Arabic Epic of Dhat al Himma*.

umrissenen bunten Karte zusammen: Könnte es Pangäa sein? Und war es nicht die eigentliche Idee dieser Ausstellung, die Welt an einem Ort zusammenzubringen und sich damit von denjenigen Gruppenausstellungen abzuheben, die vorgeben, sogenannte Regionen der Welt abzubilden?[40]

Ich schaute mir die Karte genauer an und stellte sie mir als Projektionsfläche für die sinnlichen Freuden von Huguette Calands Werken und die rhythmischen Formen von Saloua Raouda Choucair vor – den beiden Pionierinnen der modernen Abstraktion, die ihre Betrachter*innen durch ihren lyrischen Umgang mit Materialien zugleich entzücken und verunsichern. Eine weitere Abbildung tauchte auf: eine alte Werbeanzeige für die Deichtorhallen als ehemaligen Ausgangspunkt für Züge zum Hamburger Bahnhof in Berlin – mittlerweile eine weitere öffentliche Institution für visuelle Künste, die in ihren Hallen unzählige Geschichten von Reisen und Bewegung beherbergt hat, durchgeführte wie erdachte. Das Thema der Ausstellung hatte seinen Weg durch Raum und Zeit gefunden.

Die hier beschriebene Szenografie bietet einen angemessenen Rahmen, um die Lebenswelten der Diaspora mithilfe ihrer vielfältigen künstlerischen Manifestationen zu feiern. Die Aufforderung, eine *Architektur mit anderen Mitteln* zu schaffen, ist als Vorschlag an Künstler*innen zu verstehen, die sowohl mit klassischen Architekturformen als auch mit Bezügen zur akademischen Tradition arbeiten. Dabei entfaltet sich eine Topografie aus unzähligen wörtlichen und lyrischen, formalen und immateriellen Assoziationen, die im Zusammenspiel eine *Alterscape* unter einer Schicht aus persönlichen Erfahrungen der Unterdrückung, Befreiung und Amnestie bilden. Den Weg in diese spannungsgeladene Ausstellungswelt weist Jumana Mannas *Theory of an Unfinished Building (landscape) / Theorie eines unfertigen Gebäudes (Landschaft)* (2021), eine sechs Meter breite Collage mit Abdeckfolien aus Beirut, die auf einen mehr als zweieinhalb Meter hohen Holzrahmen gespannt sind. Im Zusammenhang mit dem Narrativ dieser Ausstellung möchte ich das Werk nicht als Relikt einer Stadt im Untergang begreifen, sondern als Transmutation einer Form in eine andere unter prekären Bedingungen.[41] An der Wand im Eingangsbereich der Deichtorhallen erinnert es daran, dass keine Erzählung, kein Ort, keine Geschichte jemals abgeschlossen ist. Wie diese Erfahrung des Erzählens ist der Blick in die Zukunft immer mit Unsicherheit, leisen Zweifeln oder Vorahnungen behaftet – als Forderung oder vielmehr Wunsch an die Betrachtenden nach einer Bestandsaufnahme auf ihrem Weg in das Herz eines anderen Landes.[42]

## Unter den Bögen wandeln

*(I in body now alive)*
— Auszug aus „Fracture“ von Adrienne Rich (2007)

Goldene Spiralen drehen und winden sich durch Khalil Rabahs Werk, das die Besuchenden im Eingangsbereich der Ausstellung aus dem Augenwinkel wahrnehmen. Bei näherer Betrachtung erinnern die elegant, fast schon liebevoll angeordneten glänzenden Objekte an eine Befestigung, an eine Absperrung, die den Blick auf eine andere Sichtlinie versperren soll. Die netzartigen Skulpturen von *Area C Fields of Gold (Not everything that shines is Gold) / C-Zone Goldenes Feld (Es ist nicht alles Gold, was glänzt)* (1994) sind nicht nur eine Metapher für in den Sand gemalte Frontlinien. Vielmehr fügen sich hier performanceartig 90 kleine Objekte in einem repetitiven Akt

Along the passageways, filled with illustrious maps, dictionary pages and illuminated landscapes, Fattal resurfaces with her lava stone series, in the lyrical *In Our Land of the Drought the Rain is Forever Made of Bullets* (2006). Arabic-language inscriptions present a recurring, gestural act of naming—of the multiple massacres of Palestinian people during the 1948 war. Interwoven is a reference to Adnan's poem, 'Jebu', a critical text that invokes the piercing experiences of the everyday traumas associated with dictatorship, genocide and political unrest. Fattal's poignant musings emerge from conversations with the mythologies that encompass the Eastern Mediterranean, forming a vessel, a relief towards possible restitution.

## An Address without a Postcode

*Tonight I think*
*no poetry*
*will serve*
— Adrienne Rich [45]

I am standing outside 34 Marie Street in Sausalito, California. I am informed by Google Maps that this is the headquarters of the Post-Apollo Press, which is also where I assume Adnan and Fattal lived for many years. The house is barren, empty, hollowed of all life. It is December 2021 and the news of Adnan's passing is suddenly presenting itself as an impregnable weight. I have been asked to author an obituary of the poet and artist, whom I last saw during an evening of storytelling in the summer of 2018. She was present with Fattal, at the home of our mutual comrades, Joana Hadjithomas & Khalil Joreige, in Paris. Here I was, back in California, where I had spent a portion of my childhood in the dry and ashen landscapes of South, South, L.A. I had come to fulfil a promise of immigration with my paperwork, but instead, found myself wandering aimlessly, attempting to trace the sites that led to Adnan's modular forms and compositions.

Adnan started painting at the age of 34. She began writing poetry as a response to the Vietnam War. She studied at prestigious institutions, from Harvard to the University of California, Berkeley—of this, I was informed by her, out of thirst for knowledge and community, as opposed to a formal desire for validation, accreditation or certification. Her biography often reads like an act of mythmaking, but of all her expressions, it was the artist's rapturous desire to engage with life's questions that offered me subsistence in our few encounters.

On the final evening of my search for Adnan, I returned to my lodgings, where, in my backpack, I had kept a printed inventory of every possible work to be presented in a show that she had, in essence, inspired—her polyglot experience offering solace.[46] In the still of night, with but a single desk lamp, I cut out the hundreds of square and rectangular images, beginning to lay them out onto the floor. The decisions and associations were historically anchored by the interplay of abstract forms with the possibility of constructed architectural alphabets. The presentation also sought to create tense dualism—juxtapositions that could confound or reveal new meanings. The inspiration for this emerged as much from Adnan's illustrated leporellos, as it did from her innovative publication *The Arab Apocalypse* (1980). Here, writing by hand, the artist intuitively acted out her practice of drawing dissonant forms next to her lyric. Each picture only served to magnify the affective horror of the scenes of war re-imagined. Standing over the constellations before me, an indexical key revealed itself.

zu einem Gesamtbild zusammen. Manche mögen darin frische Heuhaufen sehen, die zur Berührung einladen – und möglicherweise dazu, den Körper gegen die Barriere einer aufgeschichteten Mauer zu pressen –, stoppelig und anziehend zugleich. Der Boden gibt nach, der Körper versinkt. Bis man auf Marwan Rechamouis *Beirut Caoutchouc / Beirut Kautschuk* (2004–2008) stößt, einen Stadtplan seiner Heimatstadt Beirut aus Kautschuk. Darauf sind die Hauptstraßen, die Tore in die Stadt zu sehen, doch kommen bei den verwirrten Betrachtenden dennoch Fragen auf. Die Sektorengrenzen, die als Narben des libanesischen Bürgerkriegs (1975–1990) die Stadt in christliche und muslimische Viertel unterteilen, sind nicht gekennzeichnet. Das Werk zeigt die Fiktion einer möglichen Versöhnung. Einen Ort, den es vielleicht einmal gab, bevor die religiös motivierte Gewalt ihre blutigen Spuren in den Straßen der Stadt hinterließ. Wir setzen unseren Besuch fort.

Der Blick wandert weiter und bleibt schließlich an einem Wandteppich der verstorbenen Künstlerin und Dichterin Etel Adnan hängen, deren Memoiren den Titel dieser Ausstellung inspiriert haben. Mit *Mount Tamalpaïs* (2015) präsentiert sie den Betrachtenden eines ihrer liebsten Motive. Adnan wurde 1925 in Beirut geboren und lebte abwechselnd in Frankreich, den USA und im Libanon. Das Hin und Her zwischen ihren verschiedenen Wohnorten war von täglichen Konflikterfahrungen und von dem dringenden Wunsch nach Ausdrucksmöglichkeiten, Kameradschaft und Gemeinschaft bestimmt. Auf diesem Werk ist der Mount Tam zu sehen – wie er im Volksmund genannt wird –, ein Berg in Marin County in Kalifornien. Adnan liebte den beruhigenden Blick auf seinen Gipfel, den sie auf vielen kleinen Gemälden und Wandteppichen verewigte. Mit der von diesem Berg ausgehenden Magie könnte die Künstlerin Sehnsucht, aber auch die dankbare Erinnerung an ein Gefühl der Verzückung verbunden haben. Die rauschhafte Begeisterung kommt ganz bewusst in diesem Akt der Weltenbildung zum Zuge. Die Anordnung der ineinander verschlungenden Formen deutet auf ein Metaversum hin – ein Kofferwort, das – ein altgriechisch-lateinisches Kompositum – für den Akt des „Übergangs“ in einen anderen Zustand des Daseins, des Bewusstseins außerhalb der Gegenwart steht.[43]

Der Eingang in die Ausstellungshalle wird von zwei eineinhalb Metern hohen Tonskulpturen von Adnans Lebenpartnerin und langjähriger Arbeitskollegin, der Universalgelehrten Simone Fattal, flankiert. Fattals verzerrte Reliefs *Zhat El Himma* und *Abdel Wahab* (beide 2016) sind Teil ihrer Werkreihe *Warrior / Krieger*in*. Die Entstehung dieser deformierten Körper liegt in Fattals literarischem Interesse und Schaffen begründet. Fattal ist Gründerin, Verlegerin und Grafikerin der *Post-Apollo Press* – zweifellos eine der wegweisenden internationalen Zeitschriften für Poesie im 20. Jahrhundert.[44] In Anlehnung an die Lebensgeschichten der Propheten stellt eine der Figuren einen Mann dar, während die andere, *Zhat El Himma*, eine Allegorie auf die frühen dynastischen Traditionen des palästinensischen Volkes sein soll. Es geht um das Leben von Amina Dhat al Himma, auch als Prinzessin Fatima bekannt, der einzigen weiblichen Figur in den in arabischer Sprache verfassten „epischen Romanen“ – hier *The Tale of Princess Fatima, Warrior Woman: The Arabic Epic of Dhat al Himma*.

Auf dem weiteren Weg durch die Ausstellung, vorbei an illustren Karten, Wörterbuchseiten und erleuchteten Landschaften, ist erneut Fattal zu sehen. In ihrer Lavastein-Reihe mit dem klangvollen Titel *In Our Land of the Drought the Rain is Forever Made of Bullets / In unseren Ländern der Dürre besteht der Regen für ewige Zeiten aus Kugeln* (2006) erinnert sie mit arabischen Inschriften wiederholt an die zahlreichen Massaker an der palästinensischen Bevölkerung während des Kriegs von 1948. Sie enthalten auch ein Zitat aus Adnans Gedicht „Jebu“, in dem die Künstlerin kritische Worte für die alltäglichen traumatischen Erfahrungen mit Diktaturen, Genoziden und politischen Unruhen findet. Fattal schöpft ihre ergreifenden Gedanken aus Mythologien, die das östliche Mittelmeer wie ein Gefäß umfassen – ein Hilfsmittel der möglichen Wiedergutmachung.

There is a key to the immortal alphabets of *In the Heart of Another Country*. It can be found in Huguette Caland's *Bribes de Corps* (1979)—an explosive painting in yellow, suggestive of an opulent embodied, non-binary form: two poles, soldered or, more appropriately, sutured together. Beside Caland, I have situated a painting from 1950 by Saloua Raouda Choucair, *Composition with Green Module*—a meticulously composed dreamscape that at once appears akin to a puzzle of overlaid forms, the fragments appearing ethereal, floating, suggestive of an act of transcendence. Palimpsest-like forms glide to the surface, scratching the edges of our gaze like the globules of a lava lamp, ascending, a surprise, a relief, a love affair. Finally, Etel Adnan's modestly sized composition *Untitled* (2012) is as much a calculated abstraction, as it is an evocation of the economy of spirit of the late artist Kazimir Malevich and his obsession with the mystical world, a milieu that has been articulated by Adnan as 'weightless', each square invoking a different action.[47]

The dissonant, spectral, floating forms found in these three works present a typological sketch of possibilities that bind the artists herein through their pursuit of a possible architecture—one that does not necessarily exist within the bounds of reality. From within this view and these vantage points, connotations begin to form across the work of artists, including Tiffany Chung, Hassan Sharif, Monir Shahroudy Farmanfarmaian and Adam Henein. What emerges in this assemblage is an articulation of how geometric forms locate the diasporic body—its encounter, its essence and material—into a situated place. The elegant, rounded forms in Choucair's painting spring into her gouaches, forging distinctive moons across altered horizons, such as the one found in the late David Koloane's *Untitled (the moon over Hillbrow Tower)* (1998–2010). The latter's architectonic vision of what was once the tallest high-rise in Africa returns the viewer to a long-standing question regarding the interrelationship between modernism's outmoded notion of progress and its resulting obsession with construction and, indeed, ultimately destruction.[48]

Sensorial dissonance emerges in a following instant in Anwar Jalal Shemza's *Advancing and Receding* (1963), a hallucinogenic, trance-like diptych that refracts the gaze through its overlaid tessellating composition of infinite circles and squares. Shemza was born and raised in Pakistan before emigrating to Britain after his undergraduate studies. Colloquial and official records note that the artist was exasperated by the epistemic prejudice against non-Western art within the academy in the United Kingdom. He was noted to have developed his distinctive style after attending a lecture by E.H. Gombrich, who chose to describe 'Islamic art' and its attendant forms, as 'purely functional'. It was believed that this moment fostered a significant shift in Shemza's practice, leading to what was called a 'double prism' or a dualistic vision, as is articulated in this representation.[49]

Continuous loops push and contort the body across the gallery, around corridors, moving from dimly lit spaces to the brightness of day. In these moments, floors become ceilings, and ceilings become floors. The precariousness of construction a returning motif, emblematised in expressions by Rasheed Araeen, such as in *Sculpture No. 2* (1965), Susan Hefuna's tri-part presentation of *Building* from 1991 and the horizon where one finds Saloua Raouda Choucair's *Interform* (1960–62).

Choucair, who was the subject of a retrospective at the Tate Modern in 2013, had aspirations of transforming her propositional structures into larger-than-life architectural forms, but such pursuits were uncommon in the 1940s for a woman with little financial means. Convention,

*Tonight I think*
*no poetry*
*will serve*
— Adrienne Rich[45]

34 Marie Street in Sausalito, Kalifornien. Laut Google Maps sollte sich hier der Hauptsitz der *Post-Apollo Press* befinden. Vermutlich haben auch Adnan und Fattal viele Jahre hier gelebt. Das leerstehende Haus bot einen trostlosen und verlassenen Anblick. Damals im Dezember 2021 legte sich die Nachricht von Adnans Tod wie ein tonnenschweres Gewicht auf meine Seele. Ich wurde gebeten, einen Nachruf auf die Dichterin und Künstlerin zu schreiben, die ich zuletzt im Sommer 2018 an einem vom Geschichtenerzählen erfüllten Abend gesehen hatte. Damals war sie gemeinsam mit Fattal im Pariser Haus unserer gemeinsamen Freunde, Joana Hadjithomas & Khalil Joreige, zu Besuch. Und nun war ich zurück in Kalifornien, wo ich in den trockenen und staubigen Landschaften des Südens, im tiefsten Süden Los Angeles', einen Teil meiner Kindheit verbracht hatte. Eigentlich wollte ich mich endlich um die Papiere für meine Einwanderung kümmern. Doch stattdessen wanderte ich ziellos umher, auf der Suche nach den Orten, die Adnans modulare Formen und Bildkompositionen geprägt hatten.

Adnan begann mit der Malerei im Alter von 34 Jahren. Erste Gedichte schrieb sie als Reaktion auf den Vietnamkrieg. Ihr Studium führte sie an namhafte Institutionen, von Harvard bis an die University of California in Berkeley. Wie sie mir erzählte, stand dabei vor allem ihr Streben nach Wissen und Gemeinschaft und weniger der Wunsch nach einem formalen Ausbildungsbeleg im Vordergrund. Ihre Biografie liest sich an vielen Stellen wie ein Akt der Mythenbildung. Und doch war es in all ihrer expressiven Vielfalt vor allem dieser ungestüme Wunsch, die großen Fragen des Lebens zu ergründen, der mich bei unseren wenigen Begegnungen am nachhaltigsten beeindruckte.

Als ich am letzten Abend meiner Spurensuche zu meiner Unterkunft zurückkehrte, kramte ich in meinem Rucksack nach einer ausgedruckten Liste aller Werke für eine Ausstellung, zu der mich Etel Adnan maßgeblich inspiriert hatte. Ihre polyglotte Lebensweise hatte ich schon immer als tröstend empfunden.[46] In der Stille der Nacht, im schummerigen Licht einer Schreibtischlampe, schnitt ich Hunderte von quadratischen und rechteckigen Abbildungen aus und verteilte sie auf dem Boden. Bei meinen Entscheidungen für bestimmte Konstellationen orientierte ich mich am traditionellen Zusammenspiel abstrakter Formen und den vielfältigen Möglichkeiten der Architektur. Diese Form der Präsentation sollte auch eine dualistische Spannung erzeugen, und zwar durch eine Gegenüberstellung von Werken, die Verwirrung erzeugt, aber auch neue Bedeutungen entstehen lässt. Als Inspiration dienten Adnans illustrierte Leporellos und ihr innovatives Buch *The Arab Apocalypse* (1980). Hier hatte die Künstlerin intuitiv handschriftliche Einträge und schnell angefertigte Zeichnungen neben ihren Gedichten eingefügt. Mit jedem einzelnen Bild wollten sie den emotionalen Schrecken der von ihr erinnerten Kriegsszenen hervorheben. Die Arrangements vor mir am Boden fügten sich fast wie von selbst in eine Ordnung.

then, would become a practice the artist would persistently eschew. Choucair studied biology and took art lessons, avoiding what was then deemed 'formal' training in favour of pursuits developed from her travels in Paris and Cairo.[50] It was after an extended period in Egypt in the mid-1940s that Choucair returned to Beirut to work at the American University library and began her exploration of a 'non-objective form' of artmaking, as she described it, alongside her continued pursuit and study of sculpture.[51] In the intervening years, the artist lived in relative obscurity, as she innovated with her stacked poem walls in accumulating verses, her dual sculptures and her infinite propositional reliefs, fusing what some have deemed to be Islamic motifs with a Sufi-like form of pure transcendental abstraction.[52]

Choucair's art sought to inhabit what could also be correlated as the One Dimension, a movement and principle articulated by Iraqi modernist Shakir Hassan Al-Said, a distilled and pure experience—a total art.[53] To connote the spiritual within the frame of the abstract does not deny the work's politic or polemic. The artist, who, by the age of 100, began to be recognised formally as one of the global pioneers of abstract modernism, committed herself to practising despite the perpetual conflict that ensnared her living conditions. Little financial success as an artist throughout much of her working life meant that much of her art was kept in unregulated storage, some of her beloved pieces lost to the shroud, or still wounded in disrepair. Nonetheless, Choucair was relentless, arguing that the pursuit of 'making art' was tantamount to the expression of 'thought itself'. Thus, she forged a path that persists in its evocative potential—an artist insistent against odds unbalanced.[54]

## The First Finissage

*No unclaimed, cremated mothers this year*
*Nor collateral white skin*
...
*The prison foot races the museum*
*My instrument ends*
*I mean, what is a calendar to the slave?*
...
— Extract from 'I Make Promises Before I Dream' by Tongo Eisen-Martin[55]

The multitude of stories that a corner of an exhibition can hold are intended to surprise and to nourish expressions, emotions and animations in the perceptual field. But the story does not end here. In the composed gallery that interleaves the first chapter with the second in the exhibition, palimpsests by Ahmed Shibrain appear—stained with the wounds of memory, mapping inner musings created after he criss-crossed from Britain back to Sudan. Here, Shibrain co-developed the Khartoum School, living and working as an educator for most of his life. Cross-border conversations emerge from paintings on these walls around the delicate material of paper, in particular, papyrus, an ancient form produced from the pithy stem of a water plant. Here, it is saturated in zigzagged colour by the late draughtsman Adam Henein.

Hassan Sharif, the late pioneer of contemporary art in the United Arab Emirates, has created a playful and performative language for the expression of art amidst the pages of his

Es gibt Schlüssel zu den unendlichen Ausdrucksformen von *In the Heart of Another Country.* Sie finden sich zum Beispiel in Huguette Calands *Bribes de Corps* (1979) – einem bildgewaltigen Gemälde in gelber Farbe mit einen ausladenden nicht-binären Körper aus zwei Teilen, die zusammengeschweißt oder besser zusammengenäht zu sein scheinen. Daneben habe ich ein Gemälde von Saloua Raouda Choucair aus dem Jahr 1950 platziert, *Composition with Green Module / Komposition mit grünem Modul* – eine sorgfältig arrangierte Traumlandschaft, die zugleich wie ein Puzzle aus übereinanderliegenden Figuren anmutet, dessen Teile ätherisch, fließend, im Akt der Transzendenz verhaftet scheinen. Palimpsestartige Formen gleiten an die Oberfläche, kratzen auf ihrem Weg an unseren Blickwinkeln wie die Bläschen in einer Lavalampe und vermitteln ein Gefühl der Überraschung, Erleichterung, Verliebtheit. Die kleinformatige Bildkomposition *Untitled / Ohne Titel* (2012), in der Etel Adnan bewusst das Mittel der Abstraktion einsetzte, erinnert schließlich auch an die gegenstandslose Malerei des verstorbenen Künstlers Kasimir Malewitsch und seinen Hang zur Mystik. In Adnans Werk kommt dieser Aspekt über eine gewisse „Schwerelosigkeit" zum Ausdruck – jede Form scheint in eine andere Richtung zu streben.[47]

Die unstimmigen, geisterhaft fließenden Formen in diesen drei Werken verbinden die beteiligten Künstlerinnen miteinander als typologische Muster der Möglichkeiten für ihr gemeinsames Streben nach neuen Ausdrucksformen, die sich auch jenseits der Realität bewegen können. Aus diesem Blickwinkel entstehen Assoziationen mit den Werken von Künstler*innen wie Tiffany Chung, Hassan Sharif, Monir Shahroudy Farmanfarmaian und Adam Henein. Die Anordnung der Werke macht deutlich, wie geometrische Formen den Körper in der Diaspora – sein Ausgesetztsein, sein Wesen, seine Materialität – an einem bestimmten Punkt verorten können. Die eleganten, abgerundeten Formen aus Gouache, die sich auf Choucairs Gemälden entfalten, bilden deutlich erkennbare Monde vor einem diffusen Horizont – wie auch auf *Untitled (the moon over Hillbrow Tower) / Ohne Titel (Der Mond über dem Hillbrow Tower)* (1998–2010) des verstorbenen Künstlers David Koloane. Dessen architektonische Vision eines Gebäudes – einst das höchste Hochhaus in Afrika – fordert die Betrachtenden auf, sich erneut die alte Frage zu stellen: Was ist das Verhältnis zwischen dem überholten Fortschrittsbegriff der Moderne und dem daraus resultierenden Bauwahn, der letzten Endes auch eine Zerstörungswut in sich trug?[48]

Anwar Jalal Shemzas sinnlich dissonantes Diptychon *Advancing and Receding* (1963) versetzt die Betrachtenden mit seinen übereinanderliegenden Mosaiken aus einer unendlich anmutenden Abfolge von Kreisen und Quadraten in einen halluzinations-, ja tranceartigen Zustand. Shemza wuchs in Pakistan auf und emigrierte im Anschluss an erste Studienjahre nach Großbritannien. Aus informellen und öffentlichen Quellen ist bekannt, dass der Künstler von den erkenntnistheoretischen Vorurteilen gegenüber nicht-westlicher Kunst in akademischen Kreisen seiner neuen Heimat frustriert war. Seinen charakteristischen Stil soll er im Anschluss an eine Vorlesung bei E. H. Gombrich entwickelt haben, der die „Islamische Kunst" und ihre Elemente als „rein funktional" bezeichnete. Diese Erfahrung hatte offenbar einen maßgeblichen Einfluss auf Shemzas künstlerische Neuausrichtung, bei der er sich fortan auf das sogenannte Doppelprisma oder eine dualistische Vision konzentrierte – wie im ausgestellten Werk zu sehen.[49]

Auf gewundenen Pfaden irren wir weiter durch die Ausstellung und passieren schwach beleuchtete Räume, bis wir schließlich wieder ans Tageslicht gelangen. Die Begriffe oben und unten verlieren in diesen Momenten an Bedeutung. Die Vergänglichkeit des Gebauten als wiederkehrendes Motiv versinnbildlichen Rasheed Araeens *Sculpture No. 2 / Skulptur Nr. 2*

notebooks. Only as we bear witness to them, we notice that they have been stitched shut. Concealed, a summoning of and for revelation, awaits. A constant double take is required of the spectator. Earthly forms appear as squares, as cubes, free-flowing and stacked in the art of Marcos Grigorian. Next to his relief of nine squares, a small table is occupied by Kamel Youssef, a surrealist of a fashion. This arrangement reveals limp bodies that have become seized, appearing comatose, but the spectre of life lingers in the distance. The passageway through these alphabetic routes leads to a waiting room, past *Before the Departure (Black Paintings)* (1963–64) by Rasheed Araeen. His black-and-white matrices, expressive of his signature form of postcolonial restitution, lead to our destination: a wall with a picture by Ali Kazim. With but one gleaming eye visible to viewer, a gentleman presents himself, staring. His face, concealed by a giant white bird—a suggestion of potential movement, of chance, of flight; phantastic and dream-like, much as the artists herein, artists, who have lived, wept, and leapt—springs forward onto the pages.

## Chapter 2
## Reclaimed Portraits: Invisible Acts of Repair

*remember we were brought here from the clear waters of our dreams*
*that we might be named, numbered and forgotten*
*that we were made visible that we might be looked on with contempt*
*that they gave us their first and last names…*
…
*close our smoky mouths around their dreams*
*swallow them as they gaze upon us*
*never to be full —*
*snap, crackle*
*amen.*
— Excerpt from 'Arrival' by Jay Bernard[56]

*[the story actually, perhaps, maybe, begins in the middle—somewhere]*[57]

What is the impetus in reclaiming a portrait of oneself? To stitch and solder the seams of a canvas—a fabric, a given material—to fill in the interstices of what history has obfuscated, or, perhaps, to serve a corrective function within the realm of one's own imagination? For many, this author included the first memories of the places that we have been routed from, may have been experienced through the lens of Orientalist painting, a tradition that grew in popularity in Africa and western Asia in the 19th century. These paintings, created by Western European flâneurs, presented what Nasser Rabbat distilled as some of the key 'Orientalist stereotypes'.[58] Paintings across an expansive arch of history, by artists from Eugène Delacroix, David Roberts and Frédéric de Buzon, to Hermann David Salomon Corrodi and Charles Théodore Frère, to cite a few, presented large 'history-style' paintings of oil on canvas, where 'tribal chieftains, guards or mystics' were the central subjects. But as a cursory glance of these examples reveals, the site of the harem, which proffered the potential of Said's 'exoticised East', is perhaps one of the most popular of rendered scenes.[59]

(1965), Susan Hefunas dreiteiliges Werk *Building / Gebäude* (1991) und Saloua Raouda Choucairs *Interform / Zwischenform* (1960–1962).

Choucair, der 2013 eine Retrospektive in der Tate Modern gewidmet war, wollte ihre ausdrucksstarken Skulpturen ursprünglich in überlebensgroße architektonische Formen übertragen. Doch solche Pläne waren in den 1940er Jahren für eine Frau mit geringen finanziellen Mitteln nicht zu verwirklichen. Gerade darum konzentrierte sie sich in ihrer Kunst fortan auf andere unkonventionelle Ausdrucksformen. Sie studierte Biologie, nahm Kunstunterricht und vermied alles, was zu dieser Zeit als „formale" Ausbildung galt. Stattdessen entwickelte sie künstlerische Ansätze aus ihrer Zeit in Paris und Kairo weiter.[50] Nach einem längeren Aufenthalt in Ägypten kehrte Choucair Mitte der 1940er Jahre nach Beirut zurück, um in der Bibliothek der Amerikanischen Universität zu arbeiten. Damals begann sie ihre Arbeit mit – wie sie es nannte – „ungegenständlichen Formen" des Kunstschaffens und widmete sich weiterhin dem Studium der Bildhauerei.[51] In dieser Zeit lebte die Künstlerin relativ zurückgezogen und experimentierte mit Poesiewänden aus sich kumulierenden, gestapelten Versen, mit modularen Skulpturen und mit aussagestarken Reliefs, in denen sie nach Meinung einiger Betrachter*innen islamische Motive mit einer Sufi-inspirierten Form reiner metaphysischer Abstraktion verband.[52]

Mit ihrer Kunst wollte sich Choucair der Form der One Dimension nähern, einer Bewegung, die in ihrem Grundsatz durch den irakischen Modernisten Shakir Hassan Al-Said als destillierte und reine Erfahrung – als absolute Kunst – geprägt worden war.[53] Sie geht davon aus, dass politische oder polemische Elemente eines Werks nicht beeinträchtigt werden, wenn auch spirituelle Elemente auf der abstrakten Ebene mitschwingen. Die Künstlerin, die im Alter von hundert Jahren schließlich auch offiziell weltweit als eine der Vorreiter*innen des abstrakten Modernismus anerkannt wurde, gab ihre Arbeit trotz der ständigen Konflikte, die ihr Leben bestimmten, niemals auf. Da ihr zu Lebzeiten kein großer finanzieller Erfolg vergönnt war, konnte sie viele ihrer Kunstwerke nicht sicher lagern, sodass einige der von ihr besonders geliebten Stücke nicht überlebten oder bis heute Narben davontragen. Nichtsdestotrotz hielt Choucair an ihrer Überzeugung fest, dass jedes „Kunstschaffen" mit einer „Meinungsäußerung" gleichzusetzen sei. Ihr Lebensweg steht damit stellvertretend für das Schicksal von Menschen, die allen Widrigkeiten zum Trotz an ihrer Kunst festhalten.[54]

## Die erste Finissage

*No unclaimed, cremated mothers this year*
*Nor collateral white skin*
…
*The prison foot races the museum*
*My instrument ends*
*I mean, what is a calendar to the slave?*
…
— Auszug aus „I Make Promises Before I Dream" von Tongo Eisen-Martin[55]

Die vielen Geschichten, die in jedem Winkel dieser Ausstellung Platz finden, sollen überraschen und die Wahrnehmung für neue Ausdrucksformen, Emotionen und Animationen öffnen. Doch

With the enveloping interest in the genre during the 1980s, a generation that was brought up in the 1980s was schooled to believe that these paintings served as one of the few representative examples where one's perceived culture could be seen. The Royal Academy of Arts in London in 1984 staged an exhibition, *The Orientalists: Delacroix to Matisse*, which travelled to the National Gallery of Art in Washington, D.C., an exhibit that, as Rabbat infers, seemed to avoid the global implications generated by the debates that ensued following the 1978 publication of Edward Said's treatise on 'Orientalism', even while 'quoting it' in their interpretative material.[60]

The narrative is complicated by the matter of education. The earliest art schools in megapolises such as Cairo, where the Cairo College of Fine Arts (formerly the fine art school) was founded in 1908 by Prince Yusuf Kamal, welcomed trans-border, international groups of students.[61] The curriculum was notable for its engagement with Western art and artists.[62] The school's first director, the French artist Guillaume Laplagne, if not a customary Orientalist per se, is recognised for sculptural forms of acquiescent female figures as well as festooned metal reliefs of Black and Brown bodies, producing a perceived tribal representation from up and down his travels of the African countries along the Nile. Returning to the matter of the affective—and the potential—of the diasporic subject's desire to feel a connection towards felt and perceived notions of 'home', the question of ambivalence surfaces. If the visual references of one's perceived self, generated from within the walls of the nation-the continent-the culture's very own walls was deemed mimetic, a poor, or reductive facsimile of western modernism, and the alternative presented are the workings of the orientalist narrative, how then does the diasporic subject lay claim to their artistic pursuits, without being conceivably reduced to one's ethnic or geographic point of origin?[63]

The intimation in the realm of modern art, or more appropriately from the current vantage point of the contemporary, has traditionally necessitated that the diasporic artist adopts an identity that is not one's own. This claim of becoming and living is often dubbed impostor syndrome.[64] In 1980, the literary critic, author and poet Michelle Cliff, who was born in Jamaica, held US citizenship and was educated in the United Kingdom, presented her penetratingly precise treatise on race and the act of 'passing' in her collection, *Claiming an Identity They Taught Me to Despise*. In 'passing', she unfolds the tense dualism of embodying a form of identity that is expected of the racialised or othered subject, noting that 'this camouflage terrorises me / This pattern of skin which makes a being invisible against its habitat'.[65] The contour of assimilating comes into fuller view when Cliff professes that 'passing' demands a desire to become invisible. '[To live a] ghost life'. The melancholy espoused in these sentences is suggestive of a figure who can no longer look themselves in a mirror, or lay claim to themselves; they are situated within 'an ignorance of contradictions'.[66]

The tone of Cliff's text opens with a probing interior self-inquiry, but develops into action, serving to salvage the ruin. It was this instrumental book, whose first edition sits before me in weathered form, that inspired the ongoing ontological journey of the exhibition *In the Heart of Another Country*. When Cliff professes, 'We are not exotic / or aromatic / or poignant... / we are ordinary / All this has happened before', we are, indeed, born with the realities of inevitable violence experienced by the racially encoded, prejudiced imagination. It is thus assumed that a mindset, developed by ulterior forces, has sought to situate art in hierarchical categorical fields and folds that are not our own. The inference drawn from this narrative is that if one is not willing to 'accept' the realities of variances in ontology and perception as inherent, that they are themselves complicit in the acts of mythmaking around specific subjects and histories. This creates ongoing dissociating—distancing subjects from history's field of vision.[67]

The exhibition's second chapter endeavours to cluster and unbuckle through association and formal interrogation the concept of what it means to reclaim one's images, and by proxy, one's

wir haben das Ende der Geschichte noch nicht erreicht. Die Bildergalerie, die das erste mit dem zweiten Kapitel der Ausstellung verbindet, zeigt Palimpseste von Ahmed Shibrain, in denen die Wunden der Erinnerung und der emotionale Aufruhr seiner verschlungenen Rückkehr von Großbritannien in den Sudan deutlich zutage treten. Im Sudan war Shibrain maßgeblich am Aufbau der Khartoum School beteiligt und fast sein gesamtes Leben lang als Lehrmeister tätig. Andere Gemälde an diesen Wänden vermitteln grenz- und grenzenüberschreitende Dialoge. Der verstorbene Zeichner Adam Henein hat hier großzügig Aquarellfarben in abstrakten Mustern auf feine Bögen aus Papyrus aufgetragen – einer antiken Form von Papier aus dem Mark einer Wasserpflanze.

Hassan Sharif, der verstorbene Pionier der zeitgenössischen Kunst in den Vereinigten Arabischen Emiraten, schuf eine spielerische und performative Sprache, um aus den Seiten seiner Notizbücher kleine Kunstwerke zu machen. Bei genauerer Betrachtung stellen wir jedoch fest, dass sie zugenäht wurden und uns in diesem Zustand förmlich dazu einladen, die Geheimnisse ihres Inneren aufzudecken. Genaues Hinsehen ist erforderlich. In den Werken von Marcos Grigorian tauchen irdische Formen als freischwebende und übereinandergeschichtete Rechtecke und Würfel auf. Neben seinem Relief aus neun Quadraten ist auf einem Tisch ein Werk von Kamel Youssef zu sehen, einem ganz eigentümlichen Surrealisten. Das Arrangement zeigt schlaffe Körper in scheinbar bewusstloser Erstarrung, über die das Gespenst des Lebens in der Ferne wacht. Entlang dieser Vielfalt an Ausdrucksformen passieren wir auf dem Weg in einen Warteraum das Werk *Before the Departure (Black Paintings) / Vor der Abreise (Schwarze Bilder)* (1963–1964) von Rasheed Araeen. Vorbei an den schwarz-weißen gitterartigen Strukturen, die charakteristisch für seinen künstlerischen Umgang mit der postkolonialen Restitution sind, haben wir unser Ziel erreicht und blicken an der Wand auf ein Bild von Ali Kazim: darauf ein Mann, der uns mit nur einem sichtbaren Auge anschaut. Sein Gesicht wird von einem großen weißen Vogel verdeckt, der für Bewegung, Gelegenheit, Flucht stehen könnte. Ali Kazim bietet ein fantastisches und träumerisches Bild, wie die meisten der hier präsentierten Künstler*innen, die gelebt, geweint und mit ihrer Kunst den Sprung nach vorn gewagt haben.

## Kapitel 2
## Zurückgewonnene Porträts: Unsichtbare Wiederherstellung

*remember we were brought here from the clear waters of our dreams*
*that we might be named, numbered and forgotten*
*that we were made visible that we might be looked on with contempt*
*that they gave us their first and last names…*
*…*
*close our smoky mouths around their dreams*
*swallow them as they gaze upon us*
*never to be full –*
*snap, crackle*
*amen.*
— Auszug aus „Arrival" von Jay Bernar[56]

*[the story actually, perhaps, maybe, begins in the middle—somewhere]*[57]

heritage. It seeks to articulate in diaphanous, often contradictory, form without the taxing microscope of being held as subaltern in a view fashioned through or by the minds of a Western interloper, moving freely due to the privileges afforded them through and by the legacies of colonial rule.

This clustering comes to full life in a scenography I have entitled, 'The Painted Crowds'. I had to resist the desire to insert the word 'shroud' within this constellation of formal and aesthetic imaginings. Here, Anuar Khalifi summons the spectator to enter the world through a gaze entirely his own—a portrait of Jesus on water this is not. Rather, *MAWQIF* (2020) serves as a recouped reading of history's most politicised of religious events. In the centre of this magisterial site is work by Ibrahim El-Salahi, who presents miniature forms anchored around a ghost that has been summoned to life in a swooping concave cell that evokes the prison in which he was once held in Sudan. Mohan Samant's grouping of buoyant figures, peering at us in saturated watercolours, bursts with ebullience, as they, his subjects—the onlookers—continue peering at the audience from within.

Ahmed Morsi's funerary scene presents gaunt, sketch-like figures of humanity, raising a tense evocation of the earliest humans on Earth. Semiha Berksoy's painting on board represents a singular longing for the maternal—an homage, as much as it as a gesture of self-care. Meanwhile, Huguette Caland's rounded forms give breath to a kind of opacity of difference in form and colour. In these canvases, the rendered body of flesh—whether it is natively female or not, whether it is non-gendered or non-binary, is a porous suggestion left for the onlooker to decipher. This, like everything presented here, is a place where, once again, the philosophical concept of hermeneutics resurfaces; it is for your senses to complete and convene with the details of the story.

## Chapter 3
## Going South: Travels from Gulf to Gulf, from Coast to Coast

*desire intensifies on the*
*silver edge of the sea. my friends,*
*don't wait for me any longer, my heart*
*is in the abundance of the same*
*spring as yours*
— An Excerpt from 'Time' by Etel Adnan[68]

The concept of the 'Global South' became more pronounced in the 1990s when global leaders felt that that a field of reference was required to refer to the differing socioeconomic and political context of sites inclusive of South America, Africa and parts of Asia; the south was also a visual—a perceptual—reality.[69] For numerous reasons, many of the decolonising movements and efforts in both the academy and the field of aesthetics have deployed this term as an interlinking reference even within discussions of solidarity. Still, academic Walter D Mignolo was quick to point out the polemical reverence for the phrase, which he argued had in some respects merely replaced the use of the now-derogatory expression, Third World.[70] Indeed, much of the reason that the 'Global South' is still referred to as such is because of ongoing debates around what in the West might seem unfathomable: 'the digital divide'.

Was könnte einen Menschen dazu bewegen, eine Darstellung von sich selbst zurückzufordern? Oder eine Leinwand – einen Stoff oder ein anderes Material – zusammenzunähen oder -zuzurren, um die Zwischenräume der vergessenen Geschichten zu füllen oder vielleicht auch korrigierend in die eigenen Vorstellungswelten einzugreifen? Viele mögen die von mir ausgesuchten ersten Erinnerungen an die Orte unserer Herkunft durch die Linse der orientalischen Malerei wahrgenommen haben, einer Tradition, die im 19. Jahrhundert in Afrika und Westasien an Popularität gewann. Die davon beeinflussten Gemälde westeuropäischer Flaneure bildeten ab, was Nasser Rabbat als zentrale „orientalistische Stereotype" herausgearbeitet hat.[58] Künstler verschiedener historischer Epochen, von Eugène Delacroix, David Roberts und Frederic de Buzon bis hin zu Hermann David Salomon Corrodi und Charles Théodore Frère – um nur einige wenige zu nennen – schufen großformatige Ölgemälde auf Leinwand im Stil der „Historienmalerei", auf denen Stammesfürsten, Wachen oder Mystiker die Hauptfiguren waren. Ein flüchtiger Blick auf diese Beispiele zeigt jedoch, dass der Harem als Ort der von Said postulierten „Exotisierung des Orients" vermutlich am häufigsten als Motiv verwendet wurde.[59]

Im Zuge eines umfassenden Interesses für das Genre in den 1980er Jahren wurde eine ganze Generation angehender Künstler*innen in dem Glauben gelassen, diese Gemälde gehörten zu den wenigen repräsentativen Darstellungen dessen, was sie als eigene Kultur wahrnahmen. Die Royal Academy of Arts in London veranstaltete 1984 eine Ausstellung mit dem Titel *The Orientalists: Delacroix to Matisse / Die Orientalisten: Von Delacroix bis Matisse*, die anschließend auch in der National Gallery of Art in Washington DC zu sehen war – eine Ausstellung, die laut Rabbat ganz offensichtlich die Augen vor den weltweiten Entwicklungen verschloss, die durch die Debatten im Anschluss an die Veröffentlichung von Edward Saids Studie zum „Orientalismus" im Jahr 1978 ausgelöst worden waren.[60]

Das Narrativ wird durch die Frage der Bildung noch verkompliziert. Die ersten Kunsthochschulen in Metropolen wie Kairo, wo Prinz Yusuf Kamal im Jahr 1908 das Cairo College of Fine Arts (ehemals Schule der Schönen Künste) gegründet hatte, empfingen über die Landesgrenzen hinweg auch Studierende aus aller Welt.[61] Der Lehrplan sah in besonderem Maße die Auseinandersetzung mit Kunst und Kunstschaffenden aus der westlichen Welt vor.[62] Erster Direktor der Schule war der französische Künstler Guillaume Laplagne. Obwohl kein Orientalist der alten Schule, war er für seine skulpturalen Darstellungen fügsamer Frauenfiguren und seine mit schwarzen und braunen Körpern geschmückten Metallreliefs bekannt. Mit diesen Kunstwerken wollte er Stämme darstellen, die er auf seinen Reisen durch afrikanische Länder entlang des Nils getroffen hatte. Ausgehend von der Gefühlsebene und dem – möglichen – Wunsch des Individuums in der Diaspora nach einer Verbindung zu einem gefühlten und wahrgenommenen „Heimat"-Begriff, springt an diesem Punkt die Frage der Ambivalenz auf. Wenn die visuellen Bezüge der eigenen Selbstwahrnehmung, die sich ausschließlich innerhalb der Grenzen einer Nation, eines Kontinents, einer Kultur [sic] bilden, als mimetisch, unzureichend oder als schlechte Kopie des westlichen Modernismus wahrgenommen werden und Werke auf Grundlage des orientalistischen Narrativs die einzige Alternative bieten, wie sollen Kunstschaffende in der Diaspora dann ihre eigene Stimme finden, ohne Gefahr zu laufen, auf ihre ethnische oder geografische Herkunft reduziert zu werden?[63]

Mit dem Eintritt in das Reich der modernen oder, aus heutiger Perspektive besser gesagt, zeitgenössischen Kunst ist für Kunstschaffende in der Diaspora seit jeher das Erfordernis verbunden, eine andere als die eigene Identität anzunehmen. Der damit verbundene Anspruch an das eigene Werden und Leben wird häufig als Moment eines Hochstaplersyndroms gewertet.[64] Im Jahr 1980 präsentierte die in Jamaika geborene und in Großbritannien ausgebildete

Here, the 'Global South' is denoted as alternative not because the internet does not exist in these sites, but even more so because there is a gross inequity amongst the local populaces. The cost of and access to high-speed broadband being prime impediments.[71]

The invocation of 'Going South' in this case—the exhibition's finale is intended with irony—refers both to how political terminology often frames the politics of artmaking and, equally, to the presumptive cultural notion in vernacular English that 'going south' is equivalent to a nosedive towards failure. Conversely, in these repurposed rooms, Taus Makhacheva resuscitates a displaced museum by literally placing it on a tightrope walker's journey in *Gamsutl* (2009) and CAMP studio presents the interiority of lives lived on multiple ships, fashioning a route that merges auto-ethnography with fiction in *From Gulf to Gulf to Gulf* (2009–13). Meanwhile, Ahmed Mater reconstitutes an archive of the holiest of cities in Islam, Mecca, presenting nostalgic images of the Kaaba (The Cube) taken with various view finders, alongside elements gleaned from an archive of more than 100 found objects gathered during his lifetime. The veracity of these performing entities may be brought into question by some, but they are intended to be expressive of the codification and commoditisation of a culture that many believe should be held sacred—unsullied by any form of economic intervention.

In a gallery alcove, the late Egyptian artist Amal Kenawy's face, flat and stretched out on a mixed-media canvas, glints at the viewer. She is suspended between the world of the living and an imaginary afterlife. This painting, *You Will Be Killed 2* (2006), which is also the subject of a film by the same name, reflects Kenawy's examination of life in an Egyptian state governed psychiatric hospital. Is it ever possible to heal when the very sight of a person's image, such as in this painting or their attendant biography, presumes them dead? Are there means to disrupt the industrial complex, medical or otherwise, in order to fashion spaces where an individual is able to heal?

At the very end of this breadth of space sit the skulls of seven birds—an extinct specimen, the northern bald ibis. They would travel, according to the artist Hrair Sarkissian, from Palmyra in Syria, across Saudi Arabia to Ethiopia and back. The female bird, Zenobia, is a sacred entity, recognisable from antiquity, found in hieroglyphics. Sarkissian's birds, whose extinction was declared to have been reversed temporarily with the discovery of a group of seven birds, despite humanity's efforts, were lost again to history. The bald ibis could not be rescued from the inevitable violence that had come to subsume the life of its flight path. Here, 3D-printed skulls gleam above meticulously formed museum stands, which anchor them into the ground; they become embodied, almost human in form. On one wall, a glinting silver plate traces the birds' historic route; on another, a photograph shows the last time they were believed to have been seen in the sky. Ahead of them is a looping path—a sweeping satellite film of the world as they may have seen it. If this installation, *Final Flight* (2017–19) leaves us with one thing, it is that the world of the northern bald ibis is still out there for us; it exists, it lives, it breathes, and it is for all of us who remain on this Earth to take a hold, a sense of accountability for it.

US-Amerikanerin und Literaturkritikerin, Schriftstellerin und Dichterin Michelle Cliff in ihrer Schriftensammlung *Claiming an Identity They Taught Me to Despise* eine messerscharfe Studie zur ethnischen Herkunft und Identitätsfindung (Passing). Im Beitrag „Passing" analysiert sie die dualistischen Spannungen, die mit der von einer rassifizierten oder „zum Anderen gemachten" Person erwarteten Verkörperung einer bestimmten Identität einhergehen. Sie stellt fest: „Diese Tarnung macht mir Angst / Diese Hautfarbe, die ein Lebewesen in seinem Lebensraum unsichtbar macht."[65] Das Ausmaß dieser Anpassung tritt klarer zutage, wenn Cliff bekennt, ein solches Passing setze den Wunsch voraus, unsichtbar zu werden, das Leben eines Phantoms zu führen. Derart düstere Gedanken sind charakteristisch für Menschen, die nicht mehr in den Spiegel schauen oder Anspruch auf eine eigene Identität erheben können. Sie sind in einem „fehlenden Bewusstsein für die Widersprüche"[66] gefangen.

Am Anfang ihres Textes richtet Cliff den Blick zunächst nach innen, entwickelt dann jedoch aktive Strategien, um zu retten, was noch zu retten ist. Ihr Buch, dessen zerknitterte Erstausgabe ich in Händen halte, hat den Entstehungsprozess der Ausstellung *In the Heart of Another Country* ganz wesentlich beeinflusst. Cliff stellt treffend fest: „Wir sind weder exotisch / noch aromatisch / oder rührend … / wir sind ganz normal / Das ist alles schon einmal passiert." Tatsächlich werden wir nach unserer Geburt mit einer Realität der unausweichlichen Gewalt durch rassistisch kodierte, vorurteilsbehaftete Vorstellungen konfrontiert. Äußere Einflüsse haben die Unterteilung der Kunst in hierarchische Kategorien bestimmt, die uns nicht entsprechen. Folglich machen sich alle, die starren Unterscheidungen von Daseins- und Wahrnehmungsformen nicht als gegeben „akzeptieren" wollen, mitschuldig an der Mythenbildung um bestimmte Menschen und Geschichten. Dies hat zur Folge, dass diese Menschen aus dem Blickwinkel der Geschichte verschwinden.[67]

Im zweiten Kapitel der Ausstellung soll das Konzept der Restitution des eigenen Bildes und stellvertretend des eigenen Erbes über Assoziationen und formale Fragestellungen zusammengefasst und analysiert werden. Dabei steht eine transparente und oft auch widersprüchliche Form der Darstellung im Mittelpunkt. Die belastende Herabwürdigung zu Untertanen nach den Vorstellungen westlicher Eindringlinge, die dank ihrer Privilegien während der Kolonialzeit alle Freiheiten genossen, findet hier keinen Platz.

Zur besseren Verdeutlichung habe ich eine Inszenierung mit dem Titel *The Painted Crowds / Die bemalten Menschenmassen* zusammengestellt. Dabei musste ich dem Drang widerstehen, das Wort „shroud" (Leichentuch, Totenhemd) in diese Konstellation aus formalen und ästhetischen Gedankenwelten einzufügen. Anuar Khalifi fordert uns hier auf aus seinem ganz persönlichen Blickwinkel die Welt zu betrachten – und er sieht darin keinesfalls ein Bildnis von Jesus, der über das Wasser geht. Vielmehr bietet *MAWQIF* (2020) eine weitere Lesart für eines der am stärksten politisierten religiösen Ereignisse der Geschichte. Im Mittelpunkt des formvollendeten Arrangements findet sich ein Werk von Ibrahim El-Salahi. In diesem Werk hat er Miniaturfiguren um einen Geist herum angeordnet, der in einer gewölbeartigen Zelle zum Leben erweckt wurde, die seiner eigenen Gefängniszelle im Sudan nachempfunden ist. Mohan Samants Gruppe von Figuren in kräftigen Aquarellfragen hingegen hat ihren Blick voller überschäumender Lebensfreude von innerhalb des Bildes auf die Betrachtenden gerichtet.

In Ahmad Morsis Begräbnisszene beschwören hagere, skizzenhafte Gestalten in einer spannungsgeladenen Darstellung die ersten Menschen auf Erden. Semiha Berksoys Ölgemälde auf Hartfaserplatte zeigt die ungezügelte Sehnsucht nach dem Mütterlichen zugleich als Huldigung und Geste der Selbstfürsorge. Huguette Caland lässt mit ihren abgerundeten, fast atmenden Körpern alle Unterschiede zwischen Formen und Farben verschwimmen. Beim Blick

auf ihre Gemälde müssen sich die Betrachtenden selbst die Frage beantworten, ob die dargestellten Körper von Geburt aus weiblich, geschlechtslos oder nicht-binär sind. Auch dieser Teil der Ausstellung erschließt sich erneut auf dem Wege der philosophischen Hermeneutik – alle weiteren und abschließenden Details der Geschichte liegen in der Auslegung der Betrachtenden.

## Kapitel 3
## Gen Süden: Reisen von Golf zu Golf, von Küste zu Küste

*desire intensifies on the*
*silver edge of the sea. my friends,*
*don't wait for me any longer, my heart*
*is in the abundance of the same*
*spring is yours*
— Auszug aus „Zeit" von Etel Adnan[68]

Das Konzept des „Globalen Südens" gewann in den 1990er Jahren an Bedeutung, als die internationalen Staats- und Regierungschefs nach einem gemeinsamen Bezugsrahmen für die unterschiedlichen sozioökonomischen und politischen Kontexte in den Ländern Südamerikas, Afrikas und Teilen Asiens suchten. Der Süden war auch eine visuelle – eine wahrgenommene – Realität.[69] In mehreren akademischen und ästhetischen Dekolonisierungsbewegungen wurde das Konzept als verbindendes Element sogar in Solidaritätsdebatten aufgegriffen. Allerdings bezeichnete der Wissenschaftler Walter D. Mignolo den Begriff schon bald als streitbar, da er seiner Meinung nach nur als Ersatz für die Verwendung der inzwischen als abwertend geltenden Bezeichnung Dritte Welt diente.[70] Tatsächlich liegen zahlreiche Ursachen, dass der „Globale Süden" immer noch als solcher bezeichnet wird, in der Tatsache begründet, dass viele laufende Debatten um die aus westlicher Sicht möglicherweise nicht nachvollziehbare Problematik der „digitalen Kluft" kreisen. Hier wird der „Globale Süden" nicht nur deshalb als Alternative verwendet, weil es an diesen Orten kein Internet gibt, sondern vor allem, weil die Ungleichheit zwischen den Bevölkerungsgruppen hier besonders groß ist. Die Kosten für und der Zugang zum Hochgeschwindigkeitsbreitbandnetz stellen für die Menschen ein zentrales Hindernis dar.[71]

In diesem Fall ist die Aufforderung „Gen Süden" – am Abschluss der Ausstellung kommt bewusst das Element der Ironie zum Einsatz – sowohl als Anspielung darauf zu verstehen, dass die politische Wortwahl häufig einen Einfluss auf Strategien in der Kunst hat, als auch darauf, dass mit dem Begriff „going south" in der englischen Umgangssprache offenbar ein völliger Misserfolg bezeichnet wird. Im Umkehrschluss erweckt Taus Makhacheva in umfunktionierten Galerieräumlichkeiten ein verlassenes Museum zum Leben, indem er das Gebäude in *Gamsutl* (2009) wie ein Seiltänzer durchschreitet. CAMP-Studio präsentiert Einzelheiten aus dem Leben von Menschen auf verschiedenen Schiffen und zeichnet in *From Gulf to Gulf / Von Golf zu Golf* (2009–2013) eine Fahrtroute nach, die Autoethnografie mit Fiktion verbindet. Ahmed Mater rekonstruiert ein Archiv der heiligsten Stadt des Islam, Mekka, mit nostalgischen Bildern der Kaaba – des „Würfels" –, die mit zahlreichen Bildsuchern aufgenommen wurden, und kombiniert sie mit Objekten aus einem Archiv mit mehr als 100 gefundenen Objekten, die er in seinem Leben bisher zusammengetragen hat. Die Aussagekraft dieses Arrangements erschließt sich möglicherweise nicht allen Betrachtenden. Dennoch steht es

sinnbildlich für die Kodifizierung und Kommodifizierung einer Kultur, die aus Sicht vieler Menschen als heilig gelten und keinen ökonomischen Gesetzmäßigkeiten unterliegen sollte.

Aus einer Nische schaut uns das Gesicht der verstorbenen ägyptischen Künstlerin Amal Kenawy von einer Mixed-Media-Leinwand an. Offenbar flach am Boden liegend, scheint sie zwischen der Welt der Lebenden und einem imaginären Jenseits zu schweben. Das Gemälde *You Will Be Killed 2 / Du wirst getötet werden 2* (2006) ist auch das Thema eines gleichnamigen Films, in dem sich Kenawy mit dem Leben in einer staatlichen psychiatrischen Klinik in Ägypten auseinandersetzt. Besteht jemals die Möglichkeit auf Heilung, wenn allein der Anblick einer Person – wie in diesem Gemälde – und ihre Biografie auf ihren baldigen Tod hindeuten? Können wir von den vorgesehenen – medizinischen oder anderen – Abläufen abweichen, um für das Individuum Räume der Heilung zu schaffen?

Ganz am Ende der großen Halle sind sieben Vogelschädel des ausgestorbenen Waldrapps aufgereiht. Nach Angaben des Künstlers führt die Zugroute dieser Vögel alljährlich vom syrischen Palmyra über Saudi-Arabien nach Äthiopien und zurück. In Hieroglyphen finden sich Darstellungen des Vogelweibchens Zenobia, einer Heiligen aus der Antike. Sarkissians Vögel, deren offizielles Aussterben mit der Entdeckung einer Kolonie von sieben Vögeln noch einmal revidiert wurde, gelten heute allen menschlichen Bemühungen zum Trotz als verschollen. Der Waldrapp konnte der allgegenwärtigen Gewalt, die das Leben auf seiner Flugroute erschütterte, nicht entkommen. Für die Ausstellung wurden die Knochenabgüsse eines 3D-Schädelmodells des Vogels auf eleganten Sockeln aufgereiht, um sie mit dem Boden zu verankern. Sie erhalten dadurch etwas Körperliches, fast schon Menschliches. An einer Wand ist eine silberglänzende Karte mit der Zugroute der Vögel zu sehen, an einer anderen zeigt eine Fotografie den Moment, als die Vögel vermutlich zum letzten Mal am Himmel gesichtet wurden. Darüber läuft in einer Endlosschleife ein aus der Perspektive der Vögel aufgenommener Satellitenfilm von ihrer Zugroute. Wenn uns diese Installation *Final Flight / Letzter Flug* (2017–2019) eines sagen will, dann dies: Die Welt des Waldrapp wartet dort draußen noch immer auf uns. Sie existiert, sie lebt, sie atmet. Und wir, die wir noch auf dieser Erde weilen, haben die Aufgabe und die Verantwortung, uns ihrer anzunehmen.

## Endnoten

1 Blake Karim Mitchell, „Sonic Exile…" (2022), in: O. Kholeif, *The Bad Self/I AM HIGHLY SENSITIVE PEOPLE*, erscheint voraussichtlich 2023 in London.

2 Edward W. Said, *Out of Place: A Memoir*, London 2000.

3 Guy P. Raffa, „Dante's Exile", in: *Lapham's Quarterly*, 2020. Verfügbar unter: https://www.laphamsquarterly.org/roundtable/dantes-exile, Zugriff am 31. Juli 2022.

4 E. S. Kim, *The Fugitive: Murder and Exile in the Age of Heroes* (Dissertation), 2017.

5 Siehe Donald Bloxham, *The Great Game of Genocide: Imperialism, Nationalism, and the Destruction of the Ottoman Armenians*. Oxford 2005; Walid Khalidi, *Before Their Diaspora: A Photographic History of the Palestinians 1876–1948*. Washington, D.C., 1984; sowie Stephen Sheehi, „The Nahda After-Image, or All Photography Expresses Social Relations", in: *Third Text*, Vol. 26, No. 4 (Juli 2012), S. 401–414; Adel Manna, „Nakba and Survival: The Story of Palestinians Who Remained in Haifa and the Galilee, 1948–1956", Oakland 2022.

6 Siehe George M. Fredrickson, *Not Just Black and White: Historical and Contemporary Perspectives on Immigration, Race, and Ethnicity in the United States*, New York 2005; Desmond King, *Making Americans*, Cambridge, MA, 2000; Sarah M.A. Gualtieri, *Between Arab and White: Race and Ethnicity in the Early Syrian American Diaspora*, Berkeley, CA, 2009.

7 Für einen Überblick über die Konzepte der Kreolisierung, insbesondere im Zusammenhang mit dem Schriftsteller und Philosophen Édouard Glissant aus Martinique, siehe: Sanyu Ruth Mulira, „Édouard Glissant and the African Roots of Creolization", in: *Ufahamu: A Journal of African Studies*, 38(2); verfügbar unter: https://escholarship.org/content/qt083om6m8/qt083om6m8.pdf?t=nlj870 (Zugriff am 1. August 2022).

8 Dany Laferrière und Martin Munro, *Edwidge Danticat: A Reader's Guide*, Charlottesville, VA, 2010.

9 Alexander Alter und Alex Marshall, „Abdulrazak Gurnah Awarded Nobel Prize in Literature", in: *New York Times*, 2021; verfügbar unter: https://www.nytimes.com/2021/10/07/books/nobel-prize-literature-abdulrazak-gurnah.html (Zugriff im Juli 2022).

10 Rasheed Araeen, *The Other Story: Afro-Asian Artists in post-war Britain*. London 1989; also see: Jean Fisher, „The Other Story and Past Imperfect", in: *Tate Papers*, 2009; verfügbar unter: https://www.tate.org.uk/research/tate-papers/12/the-other-story-and-the-past-imperfect (Zugriff am 15. Januar 2022).

11 Ausführliche Informationen bietet das Archiv *Making Histories Visible* der University of Central Lancashire, an der Himid, die das Archiv gründete und verwaltete, Professor Emerituş ist. Hinweise zu *The Thin Black Line* und dem Folgeprojekt *The Thin Black Lines* finden sich unter: https://makinghistoriesvisible.com/curations/thin-black-lines/ (Zugriff am 7. August 2022).

12 Ein Überblick über diese Debatten findet sich bei Aamna Mohdin, „‚Political Blackness': A Very British Concept with a complex history", in: *Quartz*, 2018; verfügbar unter: https://qz.com/1219398/political-blackness-a-very-british-concept-with-a-complex-history/ (Zugriff am 7. August 2022).

13 Lorraine O'Grady, *Lorraine O' Grady: Writing in Space 1973–2019*, hg. v. Aruna D'Souza, Durham, NC, 2020), S. 1–6. Vgl. „Lorraine O'Grady with Jarrett Earnest", in: *Brooklyn Rail*, 2016; verfügbar unter: https://brooklynrail.org/2016/02/art/lorraine-ogrady-with-jarrett-earnest (Zugriff am 31. Juli 2022).

14 Siehe Homi K. Bhabha, *The Location of Culture*. London 1994; Paul Gilroy, *The Black Atlantic: Modernity and Double Consciousness*, Cambridge, MA, 1993; und Stuart Halls Essay von 1990, „ Cultural Identity and Diaspora", in: J. Rutherford (Hg.), *Identity: Community, Culture, Difference*, London 1990.

15 Marjorie Perloff, „Cultural Liminality/ Aesthetic Closure?: The Interstitial Perspective of Homo Bhabha", 1998; verfügbar unter: https://writing.upenn.edu/epc/authors/perloff/bhabha.html (Zugriff am 7. August 2022).

16 Zu diesem Thema gibt es zahlreiche Bücher, unter anderem James Bridle, *New Dark Age: Technology and the End of the Future*, London und Brooklyn, NY, 2018; Shoshana Zuboff, *The Age of Surveillance Capitalism: The Fight for a Human Future at the New Frontier of Power*, New York 2019; Legacy Russell, *Glitch Feminism*. London and Brooklyn, New York 2020. An acht Büchern war ich als Autor oder Co-Autor beteiligt. Zu den wichtigsten Referenzen gehören *You Are Here: Art After the Internet* (Cornerhouse and SPACE, 2013/14); *Re-thinking Trust in the Age of the Internet* (Sternberg Press, 2015), *Moving Image* (MIT Press/Whitechapel, 2015), *Art in the Age of Anxiety* (MIT Press, 2021) und *Internet_Art: From the Birth of the Web to the Rise of NFTs* (Phaidon 2023).

17 Etel Adnan, *In the Heart of the Heart of Another Country*, San Francisco 2005, S. 1–4; dt.: *Im Herzen des Herzens eines anderen Landes*, Frankfurt a. M. 2018. S. 142.

18 Anaïs Duplan, „BLACKNESS, WHICH WAS ALWAYS MOVING'", in: id., *Take This Stallion*, New York 2016, S. 5

19 Melissa Febos, *Body Work: The Radical Power of Personal Narrative*, Manchester 2022, S. 4, 65, 82, 105–153.

20 Saidiya V. Hartman, „Venus in Two Acts", in: *Small Axe 12*, Nr. 2 (Juni 2008), S. 1–14.

21 Sky Hopinka, „The Centers of Somewhere"; in: K. Nguyen und J Gerrity (Hg.), *Why are they So Afraid of the Lotus?*, London und San Francisco 2021, S. 24.

22 Folgendes Zitat steht sinnbildlich für Dubois' Begriff des doppelten Bewusstseins: „Es ist sonderbar, dieses doppelte Bewusstsein, dieses Gefühl, sich selbst immer nur durch die Augen anderer wahrzunehmen, der eigenen Seele den Maßstab einer Welt anzulegen, die nur Spott und Mitleid für einen übrig hat." Dieser Text ist ein Auszug aus W.E.B. Dubois, *The Souls of Black Folk* (1903), Reprint: Oxford (Oxford World Classics), dt.: *Die Seelen der Schwarzen*, Freiburg 2003.

23 Hier beziehe ich mich auf kulturelle Bewegungen, die wie Black Lives Matter über soziale Medien zu Protesten mit Veranstaltungen wie dem „Blackout Tuesday" aufrufen. Diese anspruchsvolle Form des Bürger*innen-journalismus wurde als Möglichkeit, den Staat zur Rechenschaft zu ziehen, wohl erstmals mit dem Aufkommen von Blogs während der US-Invasion im Irak 2003 genutzt. Sie rückte erneut in den Fokus der Öffentlichkeit mit dem „Arabischen Frühling", der 2010 in Tunesien seinen Anfang nahm und schließlich auch auf Ägypten übergriff. Der mediale Output, insbesondere von Kollektiven wie Mosireen, die ihre Beiträge auf YouTube veröffentlichten, war ein beeindruckendes Beispiel für die Möglichkeiten medialer Kommunikationskampagnen im Internet-Zeitalter.

24 Kritiker*innen werden meinen Rückschluss auf Rosalind Krauss' gesammelte Schriften *Perpetual Inventory* und auf ein Konzept erkannt haben, dem ich mich immer wieder in mehreren von mir initiierten Ausstellungen gewidmet habe. Dafür veranstalte ich dieselbe Ausstellung am selben Ort einige Jahr später, um den spezifischen Kontext des historischen Zeitpunkts in unserem Leben zu verdeutlichen. Krauss reflektiert in ihrer hochgeschätzten Textsammlung über den modernistischen Impuls der Kunst als „Medium" und seiner Spezifizität und plädiert gemeinsam mit Lyotard für die postmodernistische Auflösung des modernistischen Konzepts der „großen Erzählung". Siehe R. E. Krauss, *Perpetual Inventory*, Cambridge, MA, 2010.

25 Vgl. Richard Dyers Beitrag im Katalog zur Ausstellung *Near*. Sharjah Art Museum: Sharjah, UAE, 1998, S. 20.

26 Adrienne Rich, „ Waiting for Rain, for Music" (2007), in: id., *Tonight No Poetry Will Serve*, New York 2011, S. 13–14.

27 Gavin Doyle, „Diaspora blues: Eileen Myles, Melancholia, and the Loss of Irish-American identity", in: *Irish Studies Review*, Vol: 26, No:1, 2018, S. 80–97.

28 Sara Clarke Kaplan, „Souls at the Crossroads, Africans on the Water: The Politics of Diasporic Melancholia", in: *Callaloo* 30, no. 2, 2007, S. 511–26.

29 Siehe die officielle Website von Armenity, der nationalen Repräsentanz von Armenien auf der 56. Biennale von Venedig; verfügbar unter: https://www.armenity.net/ (Zugriff am 16. August 2022).

30 Edward W, Said, „Speaking truth to power", in: id., *Representations of the Intellectual*, London 1994, S. 65.

31 Jean Fisher, „ Coyote Comes Laughing" (1986), in: id., *Vampire in the Text: Narratives of Contemporary Art*, London 2003, S. 214-218.

32 Jean Fisher, „Tricksters, Troubadours, and Bartleby" (2009), Norma U Lifton Lecture, School of the Art Institute of Chicago 2013.

33 Michel Serres, *The Troubadour of Knowledge*, Ann Arbor, MI, 1997; dt.: *Troubadour des Wissens – Versuch über das Lernen*, Zürich 2015.

34 Richard Bell, „Bell's Theorem: Aboriginal Art – It's a White Thing!", 2002; verfügbar unter: http://www.kooriweb.org/foley/resources/art/bellessay.html (Zugriff am 15. August 2022).

35 „Equality and Diversity in the Cultural Sector in England (Report)", Arts Council England, 2011; verfügbar unter: https://www.artscouncil.org.uk/sites/default/files/download-file/Equality_and_diversity_within_the_arts_and_cultural_sector_in_England.pdf (Zugriff am 16. August 2022).

## Notes

1 Blake Karim Mitchell (2022) 'Sonic Exile…'. In O. Kholeif (ed. Forthcoming 2023) *The Bad Self/I AM HIGHLY SENSITIVE PEOPLE*. London: Sylvia and Cathy. Pg: TBD.

2 Edward W. Said (2000) *Out of Place: A Memoir*. London: Granta Books.

3 Guy P. Raffa (2020) 'Dante's Exile' in *Lapham's Quarterly*. Available at: https://www.laphamsquarterly.org/roundtable/dantes-exile, accessed 31 July 2022.

4 E. S. Kim (2017). *The Fugitive: Murder and Exile in the Age of Heroes* (Doctoral dissertation).

5 See: Donald Bloxham (2005) *The Great Game of Genocide: Imperialism, Nationalism, and the Destruction of the Ottoman Armenians*. Oxford: Oxford University Press and Walid Khalidi (1984) *Before Their Diaspora: A Photographic History of the Palestinians 1876–1948*. Washington D.C.: Institute for Palestine Studies, 1984, as well as Stephen Sheehi (2012). 'The Nahda After-Image, or All Photography Expresses Social Relations.' *Third Text*. Volume: 26. No. 4 (July 2012). Pgs.: 401–414.

6 See: George M. Fredrickson (2005) *Not Just Black and White: Historical and Contemporary Perspectives on Immigration, Race, and Ethnicity in the United States*. New York: Russell Sage Foundation and Desmond King (2000) *Making Americans*. Cambridge, MA: Harvard University Press and Sarah M.A. Gualtieri (2009) *Between Arab and White: Race and Ethnicity in the Early Syrian American Diaspora*. Berkeley, CA: UC Press.

7 For an overview of concepts of creolisation, most precisely associated with the Martinican writer and philosopher, Édouard Glissant, see: Sanyu Ruth Mulira (2005) 'Edouard Glissant and the African Roots of Creolization'. Ufahamu: A Journal of African Studies, 38(2) Available at: https://escholarship.org/content/qt083om6m8/qt083om6m8.pdf?t=nlj870, accessed 1 August 2022.

8 Dany Laferrière and Martin Munro (2010) *Edwidge Danticat: A Reader's Guide*. Charlottesville, VA: University of Virginia Press.

9 Alexander Alter and Alex Marshall (2021) 'Abdulrazak Gurnah Awarded Nobel Prize in Literature'. *New York Times*, available at: https://www.nytimes.com/2021/10/07/books/nobel-prize-literature-abdulrazak-gurnah.html, accessed July 2022.

10 Rasheed Araeen (1989) *The Other Story: Afro-Asian Artists in post-war Britain*. London: Hayward Gallery. Also see: Jean Fisher (2009) 'The Other Story and Past Imperfect'. *Tate Papers*. Available at: https://www.tate.org.uk/research/tate-papers/12/the-other-story-and-the-past-imperfect, accessed 15 January 2022.

11 Detailed information can be accessed through the 'Making Histories Visible' archive at the University of Central Lancashire, where Himid is Professor Emeritus, and founded and oversaw this archive. Reference to *The Thin Black Line* and its successor, *The Thin Black Lines* is available here: https://makinghistoriesvisible.com/curations/thin-black-lines/, accessed 7 August 2022.

12 For an overview of these debates, view: Aamna Mohdin (2018) '"Political Blackness": A Very British Concept with a complex history.' *Quartz*. Available at: https://qz.com/1219398/political-blackness-a-very-british-concept-with-a-complex-history/, accessed 7 August 2022.

13 Lorraine O'Grady (2020) *Lorraine O' Grady: Writing in Space 1973–2019*, ed. Aruna D'Souza (Durham, NC: Duke University Press, 2020), 1–6. Also see: 'Lorraine O'Grady with Jarrett Earnest' (2016) in *Brooklyn Rail*. Available at: https://brooklynrail.org/2016/02/art/lorraine-ogrady-with-jarrett-earnest, accessed 31 July 2022.

14 See: Homi K. Bhabha (1994) *The Location of Culture*. London: Routledge and Paul Gilroy (1993) *The Black Atlantic: Modernity and Double Consciousness*. Cambridge, MA: Harvard University Press and Stuart Hall's essay from 1990, 'Cultural Identity and Diaspora'. In J. Rutherford (ed.) *Identity: Community, Culture, Difference*. London: Lawrence Wishart.

15 Marjorie Perloff (1998) 'Cultural Liminality/ Aesthetic Closure?: The Interstitial Perspective of Homo Bhabha.' Available at: https://writing.upenn.edu/epc/authors/perloff/bhabha.html, accessed 7 August 2022.

16 A constellation of books exists on the subject including, but not limited to, James Bridle (2018) *New Dark Age: Technology and the End of the Future*. London and Brooklyn, NY: Verso; Shoshana Zuboff (2019) *The Age of Surveillance Capitalism: The Fight for a Human Future at the New Frontier of Power*. Also: Legacy Russell (2020) *Glitch Feminism*. London and Brooklyn, NY: Verso. I have also authored or co-authored 8 books. Key references here include, *You Are Here: Art After the Internet* (Cornerhouse and SPACE, 2013/14); *Re-thinking Trust in the Age of the Internet* (Sternberg Press, 2015), *Moving Image* (MIT Press/Whitechapel, 2015), *Art in the Age of Anxiety* (MIT Press, 2021) and *Internet_Art: From the Birth of the Web to the Rise of NFTs* (Phaidon 2023).

17 Etel Adnan (2005) *In the Heart of the Heart of Another Country*. San Francisco: City Light Books. Pgs.: 1–4.

18 Anaïs Duplan (2016) 'BLACKNESS, WHICH WAS ALWAYS MOVING'. *Take This Stallion*. New York: Brooklyn Arts Press. Pg. 35.

19 Melissa Febos (2022) *Body Work: The Radical Power of Personal Narrative*. Manchester: Manchester University Press. Pgs.: 4, 65, 82, 105–153.

20 Saidiya V. Hartman, 'Venus in Two Acts', Small Axe 12, no. 2 (June 2008). Pgs.: 1–14.

21 Sky Hopinka (2021) 'The Centers of Somewhere'. In K. Nguyen and J Gerrity (eds.) *Why are they So Afraid of the Lotus?* London, UK and San Francisco, USA: Sternberg Press and The Wattis Institute. Pg. 24.

22 Dubois's concept of double consciousness is emblematized in the following excerpt: 'It is a peculiar sensation, this double consciousness, this sense of always looking at oneself through the eyes of others, of measuring one';s soul by the tape of a world that looks on in amused contempt and pity.' This text is excerpted from W.E.B. Dubois (1903) *The Souls of Black Folk* (Reprint). Oxford: Oxford University Press (Oxford World Classics).

23 Here, I am invoking cultural movements such as the Black Lives Matters movement's mobilisation of social media in protest movements with events such as 'Blackout Tuesday', a sophisticated form of citizen journalism—a mechanism of holding the state accountable, which arguably began with the rise of blogging during the U.S. invasion of Iraq in 2003, with a forceful return to public attention during the 'Arab Uprisings' that began in 2010 in Tunisia, with clustered activity in Egypt. The media output, in particular, of collectives such as Mosireen, who outputted their content through YouTube, was a phenomenal example of the ways in which media communication campaigns can function in a networked era.

24 Critics will recognise my inference of Rosalind Krauss's collected writings, *Perpetual Inventory*—a framework, which I have paid regular attention to via a series of exhibitions that I have initiated, whereby I re-stage the same exhibition, in the same site, a number of years later, bringing into view the context-specificity of the historical moment in which we live. Krauss's widely revered collection reflects on the modernist impulse of art's 'medium' and its specificity, deploying Lyotard as a means to argue for post-modernism's dilution of modernism's concept of the 'master narrative'. See R. E Krauss (2010) *Perpetual Inventory*. Cambridge, MA: The MIT Press (October Books).

25 Richard Dyer (1998) contribution in the exhibition catalogue for *Near*. Sharjah Art Museum: Sharjah, UAE. Pg. 20.

26 Adrienne Rich (2007/2011) 'Waiting for Rain, for Music'. *Tonight No Poetry Will Serve*. New York: W.W. Norton & Co. Pgs.: 13–14.

27 Gavin Doyle (2018) 'Diaspora blues: Eileen Myles, Melancholia, and the Loss of Irish-American identity.' *Irish Studies Review*. Vol: 26. No:1. Pgs.: 80–97.

28 Sara Clarke Kaplan (2007) 'Souls at the Crossroads, Africans on the Water: The Politics of Diasporic Melancholia.' *Callaloo* 30, no. 2. Pgs.: 511–26.

29 See: Official Website of 'Armenity', the national representation of Armenia at the 56 th Venice Biennale. Available at: https://www.armenity.net/, accessed 16 August 2022.

30 Edward W Said (1994) 'Speaking truth to power'. *Representations of the Intellectual*. London: Vintage. Pg. 65.

31 Jean Fisher (1986/2003) 'Coyote Comes Laughing' *Vampire in the Text: Narratives of Contemporary Art*. London: Iniva. Pgs:214–218.

32 Jean Fisher (2009/2013) 'Tricksters, Troubadours, and Bartleby'. Norma U Lifton Lecture, School of the Art Institute of Chicago.

33 Michel Serres (1997) *The Troubadour of Knowledge*. (Trans: Sheila Glaser and William Paulson). Ann Arbor, MI: University of Michigan Press.

34 Richard Bell (2002) 'Bell's Theorem: Aboriginal Art – It's a White Thing!' Available at: http://www.kooriweb.org/foley/resources/art/bellessay.html, accessed 15 August 2022.

35 Equality and Diversity in the Cultural Sector in England (Report) (Arts Council England, 2011). Available at: https://www.artscouncil.org.uk/sites/default/files/

36 Blake Karim Mitchell, „The Core Wound…" (2022), in: O. Kholeif, *The Bad Self/I AM HIGHLY SENSITIVE PEOPLE*, erscheint voraussichtlich 2023 in London.

37 Trent Hergenrader, *Collaborative Worldbuilding for Writers and Gamers*, London 2019.

38 Eddie Paterson, Timothy Simpson-Williams, Will Cordner, *Once Upon a Pixel: Storytelling and Worldbuilding in Video Games*, Boca Raton, FL, 2020.

39 Reisz erhielt das Angebot für eine Zusammenarbeit, nachdem er 2020 erfolgreich an der Konzeption der lichtbrechenden zellenartigen Räume der Ausstellung *Art in the Age of Anxiety* (2020) in der Sharjah Art Foundation mitgewirkt hatte. Die Wahl fiel nicht allein deshalb auf ihn, weil er unser Anliegen einer Wieder verwertung von Materialien im Sinne des Klimaschutzes teilt, sondern auch, weil er als Künstler in der Sammlung der Sharjah Art Foundation vertreten ist.

40 Morad Montazami, „Réviser le canon, revivre les mondes arabes", in: *CRITIQUE D'ART* (46), 2016.

41 Joseph Choonara, „The Precarious Concept of Precarity", in: *Review of Radical Political Economics*, Vol. 52(3), 2020, S. 427–446.

42 Ansgar F. Nünning, „Reconceptualizing the Theory and Generic Scope of Unreliable Narration", in: „Recent Trends in Narratological Research", in: John Pier (Hg.), *Recent Trends in Narratological Research*, 1999; verfügbar unter: http://books.openedition.org/pufr/3950 (Zugriff am 13. August 2022).

43 „The Origin of Metaverse", in: „What is the metaverse?", in: *Merriam Webster Dictionary*; verfügbar unter: https://www.merriam-webster.com/words-at-play/meaning-of-metaverse (Zugriff am 13. August 2022).

44 Siehe https://litmuspress.org/about/the-post-apollo-press/#:~:text=The%20Post%2DApollo%20Press%20%E2%80%93%20Litmus%20Press&text=Founded%20in%201982%20by%20Simone,translation%20for%20over%20thirty%20years ( Zugriff am 14. August 2022); Karl Roesler, „An Interview with Simone Fattal of the Post-Apollo Press", in: *Rain Taxi*, 2020; verfügbar unter: https://www.raintaxi.com/counting-the-new-age-an-interview-with-simone-fattal-of-the-post-apollo-press/ (Zugriff am 14. August 2022); Mirene Arsanios, „Post Apollonian", in: *Ibraaz*, 2013; verfügbar unter: https://www.ibraaz.org/interviews/74 (Zugriff am 14. August 2022).

45 Adrienne Rich, *Tonight No Poetry Will Serve*, New York 2007/2011, S. 25.

46 In meinem kurzen Tribut an Etel Adnan im Poetry Magazine bringe ich, wenn auch womöglich nur andeutungsweise, den Trost zum Ausdruck, der mit dem für Menschen in der Diaspora erforderlichen Sprachenwechsel verbunden ist. Siehe O. Kholeif, „To Speak with Many Tongues at Once", in: *Poetry*, Issue: April 2016; verfügbar unter: https://www.poetryfoundation.org/poetrymagazine/articles/88728/to-speak-with-many-tongues-at-once (Zugriff am 14. August 2022).

47 Sébastien Delot, „Etel Adnan", Bern und Luxembourg: Zentrum Paul Klee and MUDAM, 2018, S. 55 und S. 314.

48 Errol Haarhoff, „Appropriating modernism: Apartheid and the South African Township", in: *ITU A/Z*, Vol. 8, S. 184–195.

49 Aphra Shemza, „My grandfather, Anwar Jalal Shemza", in: *Tate Papers*, 2015; verfügbar unter: https://www.tate.org.uk/tate-etc/issue-35-autumn-2015/my-grandfather-anwar-jalal-shemza (Zugriff am 14. August 2022).

50 Jessica Morgan, *Saloua Raouda Choucair*, London 2013.

51 Salwa Mikdadi, *Forces of Change: Artists of the Arab World*, Washington, D.C.: International Council for Women in the Arts, 1994.

52 Helen Khal, *The Woman Artist in Lebanon*, Beirut 1988, Beirut University College: Institute for Women's Studies in the Arab World.

53 Charbel Dagher, *Shakir Hassan Al Said: The One and Art*, Paris 2021.

54 Kaelen Wilson-Goldie, „Saloua Raouda Choucair: Beirut Exhibition Center", in: *Artforum*. Vol. 50, No.5, 2012.

55 Tongo Eisen-Martin, „I Make Promises Before I Dream", in: *Blood on the Fog*. San Francisco 2021, S. 67–68.

56 Jay Bernard, „Arrival", in: *Surge*, London 2019, S. 1.

57 Anmerkung des Verfassers.

58 Nasser Rabat, „Occidental Tourists", in: *Artforum*, Juli/August 2020; auch verfügbar unter: https://www.artforum.com/print/202006/nasser-rabbat-on-inspired-by-the-east-83284 (Zugriff am 16. August 2022).

59 Ebd.

60 Ebd.

61 Elina Sairanen, „Cairo's School of Fine Arts", 2020; verfügbar unter: http://mathqaf.com/2020/12/16/cairos-school-of-fine-arts/ (Zugriff am 16. August 2022).

62 Dina Ramadan, „Modernity and Artistic Subjectivity", Vortrag auf der Konferenz *Tracing an Imperfect Chronology*, 22. Oktober 2016, Whitechapel Gallery, London; Programm verfügbar unter: https://www.whitechapelgallery.org/events/barjeel-art-foundation-conference/ (Zugriff am 16. August 2022).

63 Hier beziehe ich mich auf mehrere Werke, insbesondere jedoch auf E. H. Gombrich, *The Preference for the Primitive: Episodes in the History of Western Taste and Art*, London und New York 2006 (Neuauflage). Für eine erste Lektüre finden sich weitere Anregungen und Auseinandersetzungen bei Mohamed El Metmari, „Re-reading the Exotic Other in Western Paintings"; Khalid Chaouch, „American Painters' Pre-Colonial Morroco"; Adrienne L. Childs, „The Black Exotic: Tradition and Ethnography in Nineteenth Century Orientalist Art"; und in Salwa Mikdadis bereits erwähntem „ Forces of Change".

64 Ein kurzer Überblick über die mit dem Hochstaplersyndrom verbundenen Verhaltensweisen findet sich bei Jaruan Sakulku, „The Impostor Phenomenon", in: *The Journal of Behavioural Science*, Vol. 6, Issue 1, 2011, S. 75–97.

65 Michelle Cliff, „Passing", in: id., *Claiming an Identity They Taught Me to Despise*, Watertown, MA, 1980, S. 3.

66 Ebd. S. 5.

67 Ebd. S. 7.

68 Etel Adnan, *Time* (übers. v. Sarah Riggs), New York 2003/2019, S. 37; dt.: *Zeit* (übers. v. Klaudia Ruschkowski), Hamburg 2021.

69 Amitav Acharya, „Studying the Bandung conference from a Global IR perspective", in: *Australian Journal of International Affairs*, Vol. 70, No. 4, 2016, S. 342–357.

70 Walter D. Mignolo, „THE GLOBAL SOUTH and WORLD DIS/ORDER"; in: *Journal of Anthropological Research*, Vol. 67, No. 2, 2011. S. 165–188.

71 Dhwani Goel, „the global digital divide is reminiscent of colonialism", 2021; verfügbar unter: https://blogs.lse.ac.uk/brexit/2021/05/06/the-global-digital-divide-is-reminiscent-of-colonialism/ (Zugriff am 15. August 2022).

download-file/Equality_and_diversity_within_the_arts_and_cultural_sector_in_England.pdf, accessed 16 August 2022.

36 Blake Karim Mitchell (2022) 'The Core Wound…'. In O. Kholeif (ed. Forthcoming 2023) *The Bad Self/I AM HIGHLY SENSITIVE PEOPLE*. London: Sylvia and Cathy. Pg: TBD.

37 Trent Hergenrader (2019) *Collaborative Worldbuilding for Writers and Gamers*. London, UK: Bloomsbury Academic.

38 Eddie Paterson, Timothy Simpson-Williams, Will Cordner (2020) *Once Upon a Pixel: Storytelling and Worldbuilding in Video Games*. Boca Raton, FL: CRC Press, an imprint of the Taylor & Francis Group.

39 Reisz was invited to collaborate with me, after successfully co-conceiving the refractive, cellular spaces of the exhibition, *Art in the Age of Anxiety* at Sharjah Art Foundation in 2020. Reisz was selected not only for his sensitivity to one of our primary concerns of material re-use in the age of climate emergency, but equally, because he himself, is an artist featured in the Sharjah Art Foundation Collection.

40 Morad Montazami (2016) 'Réviser le canon, revivre les mondes arabes'. In *CRITIQUE D'ART* (46).

41 Joseph Choonara (2020) 'The Precarious Concept of Precarity'. *Review of Radical Political Economics*. Voume: 52(3). Pgs.: 427–446.

42 Ansgar F. Nünning (1999) 'Reconceptualizing the Theory and Generic Scope of Unreliable Narration In: Recent Trends in Narratological Research'. In John Pier (ed.) Recent Trends in Narratological Research. Available at: http://books.openedition.org/pufr/3950, accessed 13 August 2022.

43 'The Origin of Metaverse'. In 'What is the metaverse?' *Merriam Webster Dictionary*. Available at: https://www.merriam-webster.com/words-at-play/meaning-of-metaverse, accessed 13 August 2022.

44 See the following: https://litmuspress.org/about/the-post-apollo-press/#:~:text=The%20Post%2DApollo%20Press%20%E2%80%93%20Litmus%20Press&text=Founded%20in%201982%20by%20Simone,translation%20for%20over%20thirty%20years., accessed 14 August 2022. Also: Karl Roesler (2000) 'An Interview with Simone Fattal of the Post-Apollo Press'. *Rain Taxi*. Available at: https://www.raintaxi.com/counting-the-new-age-an-interview-with-simone-fattal-of-the-post-apollo-press/, accessed 14 August 2022. Also see: Mirene Arsanios (2013) 'Post Apollonian'. *Ibraaz*. Available at: https://www.ibraaz.org/interviews/74, accessed 14 August 2022.

45 Adrienne Rich (2007/2011) *Tonight No Poetry Will Serve*. New York: W.W. Norton & Co. Pg. 25.

46 My short tribute to Etel Adnan in Poetry Magazine, while not perfect, articulates the comfort through andfrom the acts of code-switching demanded of the diasporic individual. See: O. Kholeif (2016) 'To Speak with Many Tongues at Once'. Poetry. Issue: April 2016. Available at: https://www.poetryfoundation.org/poetrymagazine/articles/88728/to-speak-with-many-tongues-at-once, accessed 14 August 2022.

47 Sébastien Delot (2018) Etel Adnan. Bern and Luxembourg: Zentrum Paul Klee and MUDAM. Pg. 55 and Pg. 314.

48 Errol Haarhoff (2011) 'Appropriating modernism: Apartheid and the South African Township.' *ITU A/Z*. Volume 8. Pgs.: 184–195.

49 Aphra Shemza (2015) 'My grandfather, Anwar Jalal Shemza'. In *Tate Papers*. Available at: https://www.tate.org.uk/tate-etc/issue-35-autumn-2015/my-grandfather-anwar-jalal-shemza, accessed 14 August 2022.

50 Jessica Morgan (2013) *Saloua Raouda Choucair*. London: Tate Publishing.

51 Salwa Mikdadi (1994). *Forces of Change: Artists of the Arab World*. Washington, D.C.: International Council for Women in the Arts.

52 Helen Khal (1988). The Woman Artist in Lebanon. Beirut, Lebanon: Beirut University College: Institute for Women's Studies in the Arab World.

53 Charbel Dagher (2021) *Shakir Hassan Al Said: The One and Art*. Paris: Editions Skira Paris.

54 Kaelen Wilson-Goldie (2012) 'Saloua Raouda Choucair: Beirut Exhibition Center'. *Artforum*. Volume 50. No.5.

55 Tongo Eisen-Martin (2021) 'I Make Promises Before I Dream'. *Blood on the Fog*. San Francisco: City Light Books. Pgs.: 67–8.

56 Jay Bernard (2019) 'Arrival'. *Surge*. London: Chatto & Windus. Pg. 1.

57 Intervention by the author.

58 Nasser Rabat (2020) 'Occidental Tourists'. *Artforum*. July/August. Also available at: https://www.artforum.com/print/202006/nasser-rabbat-on-inspired-by-the-east-83284, accessed 16 August 2022.

59 Ibid.

60 Ibid.

61 Elina Sairanen (2020) 'Cairo' School of Fine Arts'. Available at: http://mathqaf.com/2020/12/16/cairos-school-of-fine-arts/, accessed 16 August 2022.

62 Dina Ramadan (2016) 'Modernity and Artistic Subjectivity'. Presented at the conference, *Tracing an Imperfect Chronology*, Saturday 22 October 2016, Whitechapel Gallery, London. Programme available here: https://www.whitechapelgallery.org/events/barjeel-art-foundation-conference/, accessed 16 August 2022.

63 In these citations I am invoking a range of references, but in particular, E.H. Gombrich (re-print 2006) *The Preference for the Primitive: Episodes in the History of Western Taste and Art*. London and New York: Phaidon. For other references and debates, consider, Mohamed El Metmari's 'Re-reading the Exotic Other in Western Paintings'; Khalid Chaouch's 'American Painters' Pre-Colonial Morroco'; Adrienne L. Childs's 'The Black Exotic: Tradition and Ethnography in Nineteenth Century Orientalist Art' and Salwa Mikdadi's aforementioned, 'Forces of Change', as a starting point.

64 For a cursory definition or examination of the tendencies of Imposter Syndrome, see: Jaruan Sakulku (2011) 'The Impostor Phenomenon'. *The Journal of Behavioural Science*. Volume: 6. Issue:1. Pgs.: 75–97.

65 Michelle Cliff (1980) 'Passing'. *Claiming an Identity They Taught Me to Despise*. Watertown, MA.: PersephonePress. Pg.3.

66 Ibid. Pg. 5.

67 Ibid. Pg. 7.

68 Etel Adnan (2003/2019) *Time* (translated by Sarah Riggs). New York: Nightboat Books. Pg. 37.

69 Amitav Acharya (2016) 'Studying the Bandung conference from a Global IR perspective'. *Australian Journal of International Affairs*. Volume: 70, No:4. Pgs.: 342–357.

70 Walter D. Mignolo (2011) 'THE GLOBAL SOUTH and WORLD DIS/ORDER." *Journal of Anthropological Research*. Vol: 67. No. 2 (2011). Pgs.: 165–88.

71 Dhwani Goel (2021) 'the global digital divide is reminiscent of colonialism'. Available at: https://blogs.lse.ac.uk/brexit/2021/05/06/the-global-digital-divide-is-reminiscent-of-colonialism/, accessed 15 August 2022.

# Architektur mit anderen Mitteln: Der abstrakte Körper trifft auf die konkrete Stadt

# 1

# Architecture by Other Means: The Abstract Body Meets the Concrete City

# Etel Adnan

„Ich bin in einem Teil der Welt geboren, der seit Beginn des 20. Jahrhunderts von Krieg gezeichnet ist“, schrieb Etel Adnan in einem Essay über ihre Kindheit und Jugend im Libanon. „Meine Erinnerung und mein Alltag sind mit Krieg verwoben. Oft habe ich mich gefragt, wie ein so verletzlicher Organismus wie der des Menschen solche schier endlosen Umwälzungen aushalten kann, wie sie der Nahe Osten erfahren hat und bis heute erfährt.“* Das komplexe Spannungsfeld zwischen physischer Fragilität und Erfahrungen im Exil zeigt sich in Adnans jahrzehntelanger Praxis, in der sie Malerei, Schreib- und Dichtkunst sowie Film miteinander verknüpft. In ihren Arbeiten sucht sie eine Welt festzuhalten, die durch Konflikte, Traumata und erzwungene Migration im Verschwinden begriffen ist. Zudem entwickelt sie ein tiefes Gefühl für ein Konzept von Heimat, das nicht nur die eigene Identität betrifft, sondern auch die Entwicklung zu einem breiten Beziehungsgeflecht mit einschließt.

Etel Adnan wurde 1925 in Beirut als Tochter eines hochrangigen muslimisch-osmanischen Offiziers aus Damaskus und einer griechisch-christlichen Mutter aus Izmir geboren. Ihre Kindheit erinnert Adnan als von Sonnenlicht durchflutet. Sie beschreibt das intensive Licht der Stadt als „lebendiges Wesen“, das oftmals versucht habe, in ihren Schatten zu treten wie ein naher Begleiter. Die Stadt eröffnete ihr zudem eine Vielzahl von Sprachen und Perspektiven: Zu Hause sprach sie Griechisch und Arabisch, im Alltag aber auch Türkisch und vor allem Französisch, in einer späteren Lebensphase dann hauptsächlich Englisch. Nach einem Studium an der Sorbonne ging Adnan in die USA und studierte erst in Harvard, dann an der University of California in Berkeley. Sie zog nach Sausalito in der Bay Area und unterrichtete Kunst und Philosophie am Dominican College in San Rafael. Dort schuf sie am Ende der 1950er Jahre im Alter von 34 Jahren auch ihr erstes Gemälde. Ihr bevorzugtes Werkzeug wurde der Spachtel, mit dem sie Farbe direkt von der Tube auf die Leinwand übertrug. Leitmotiv ihrer Arbeit waren unberechenbare Momente, die sich aus Beobachtungen im Verlauf der Zeit ergeben – ein sehnsüchtiger Blick, ein Nachglimmen, eine eingehende Betrachtung.

Mit dem Beginn des Vietnamkriegs Ende der 1960er Jahre ging Adnan zurück nach Beirut. Sie beschäftigte sich noch tiefgehender mit dem Konzept von Ort und Erinnerung und erfuhr dabei eine zunehmende Entfremdung in einer im ständigen Wandel begriffenen und konfliktreichen Gegenwart. Sie gab unumwunden zu: „Im eigenen Heimatland und von der eigenen Kultur exiliert zu sein, ist vielleicht die schlimmste Form des Exils. Es ist die Hölle auf Erden.“* Zu dieser Zeit lernte Adnan auch ihre Lebensgefährtin kennen, die Künstlerin Simone Fattal, die zu einer ihrer wichtigsten Gesprächspartnerinnen wurde. Der Ausbruch des Libanesischen Bürgerkriegs ließ die beiden nach Sausalito zurückkehren, wo Adnan sich in der Nähe des Mount Tamalpais – eines ihrer wichtigsten Motive – wusste.

Möglicherweise bietet der Fokus auf die starre, unnachgiebige Formation eines Berges eine solide Basis, auf der Erinnerung ihr richtiges Maß findet: eines, das so flüchtig wie fragil ist.

'I originated in a part of the world that war has been made and unmade since the beginning of this century', Etel Adnan reflected in an essay about her life growing up in Lebanon. 'My memory as well as my daily life are woven with war. I often wondered how a system as fragile as the human body could bear upheavals become chronic as the ones that the Arab East has known and is still experiencing'. These delicate tensions between the fragility of a body and the experiences of exile are woven throughout Adnan's decades-long practice, which combined painting, writing, poetry and film. Her body of work attempts to capture a world disappearing through conflict, trauma and forced migration, as well as a profound sense of how one's homeland is not only related to one's identity, but consolidates a broader network of relationships across time.

Born in Beirut in 1925 to a notable Muslim Ottoman officer from Damascus and a Greek Christian mother from Ismyrna (Izmir), Adnan's early life in Lebanon was one filled with sunlight. Adnan describing the intensity of light in the city as a being of life in itself, often trying to step into her own shadow as if it were a companion. The city also exposed her to a polyphony of languages and perspectives; conversing in Greek and Arabic at home, she also spoke Turkish, but adopted French as her principal mode of expression. English would take precedence later in life. After studying at the Sorbonne, Adnan ventured to the United States to study first at Harvard and then the University of California, Berkeley, settling in Sausalito in the Bay Area. Her day job was teaching art and philosophy at Dominican College, San Rafael. Her first painting emerged in the late 1950s at the age of 34. Adnan's paintings were produced almost solely with a palette knife, transferring paint directly from tube to canvas. Her work evokes the incalculable relationships offered and conferred in the physical encounter of seeing in time—be it a longing glance, searing after-image or studied observation.

Returning to Beirut in the late 1960s with the advent of the Vietnam War, Adnan thickened her relationship towards place and memory, encountering her formative experiences as increasingly alienated from the ever-changing and conflicted present, starkly affirming that 'to be exiled on one's own homeland and from one's culture is maybe the most desperate of all forms of exile. It is living hell'. It was during this time that Adnan met her life partner, the artist Simone Fattal, who would become one of Adnan's primary interlocutors. The onset of the Lebanese Civil War led the pair to return to Sausalito, where Adnan could be in proximity with one of her chief subjects, Mount Tamalpais.

It is perhaps the focus upon the stationary, unyielding formation of a mountain that one's memory finds its righting scale: one fleeting and fragile.

Chris McCormack

*Dt. Übersetzung aus dem Englischen von Moritz Müller-Schwefe aus: Etel Adnan „Reise, Krieg und Exil“, 2020

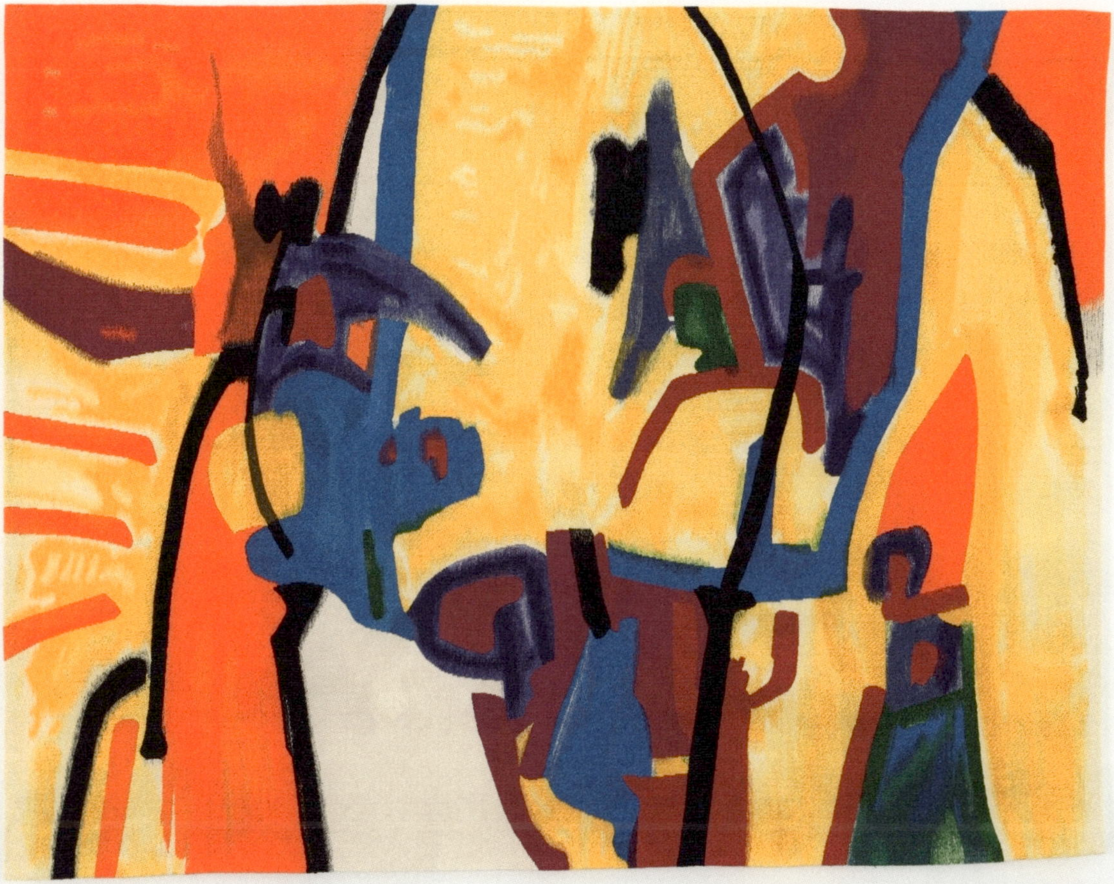

*Arbres [Trees] / Bäume [Trees]*, 2015. Wandteppich (Wolle) / Wool tapestry. 220 × 165 cm. Im Auftrag der Sharjah Art Foundation / Commissioned by Sharjah Art Foundation

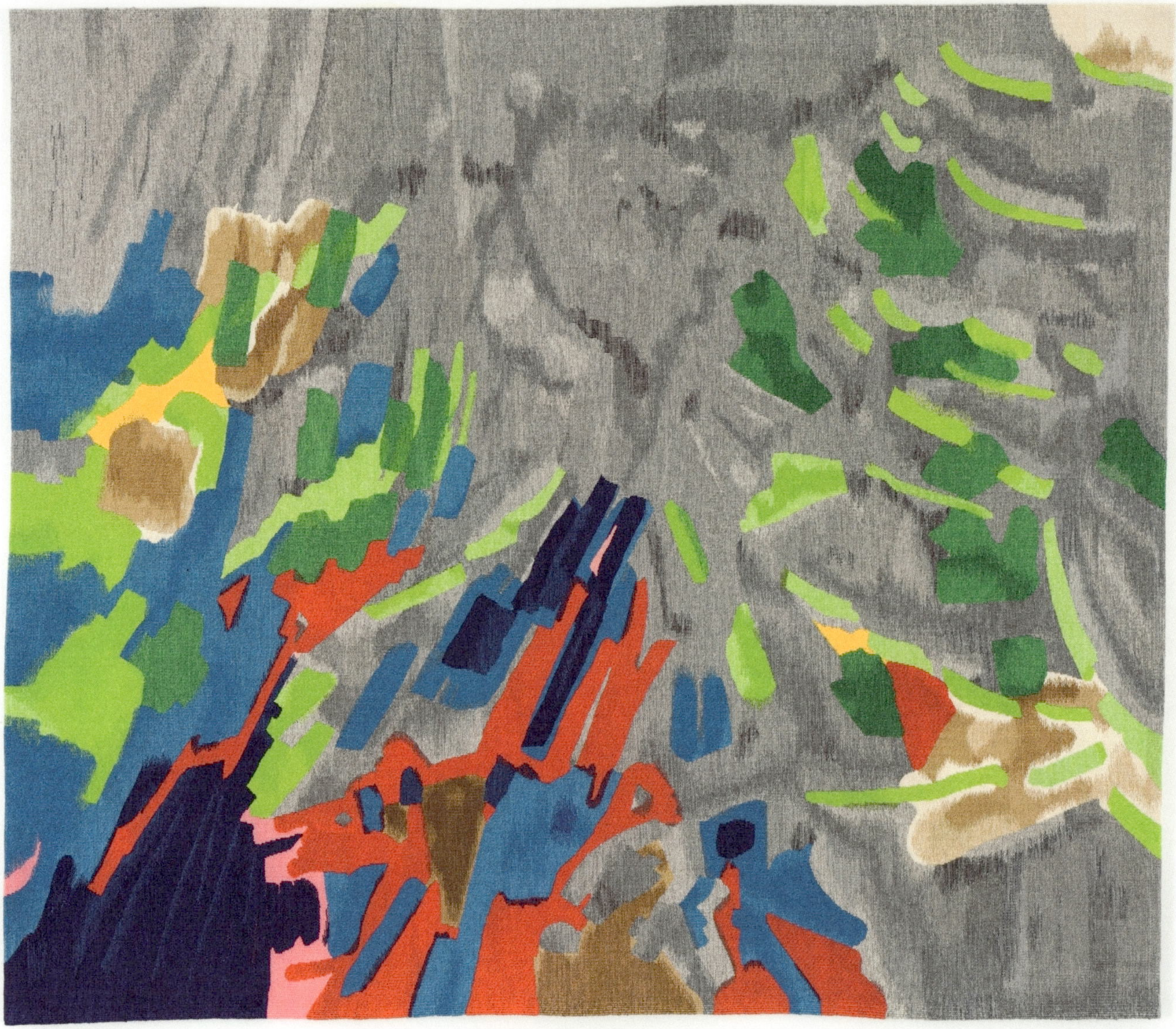

*Mount Tamalpaïs*, 2015. Wandteppich (Wolle) / Wool tapestry. 212 × 170 cm. Im Auftrag der Sharjah Art Foundation / Commissioned by Sharjah Art Foundation

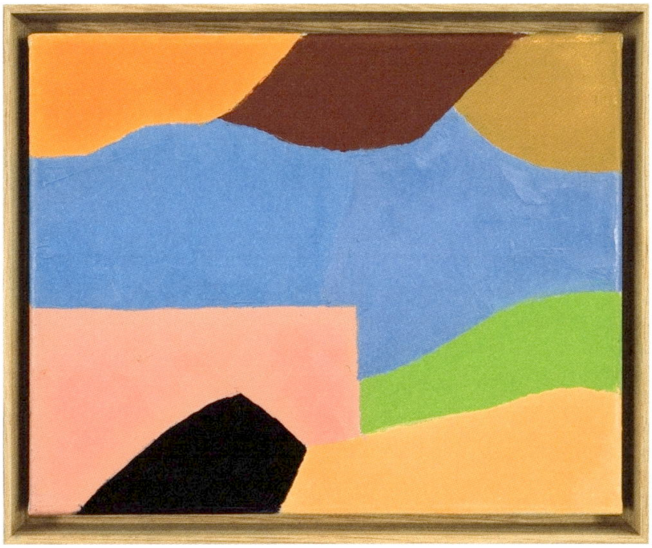

*Untitled* / *Ohne Titel*, 2012. Öl auf Leinwand / Oil on canvas. 30 × 24 cm. Im Auftrag der Sharjah Art Foundation / Commissioned by Sharjah Art Foundation

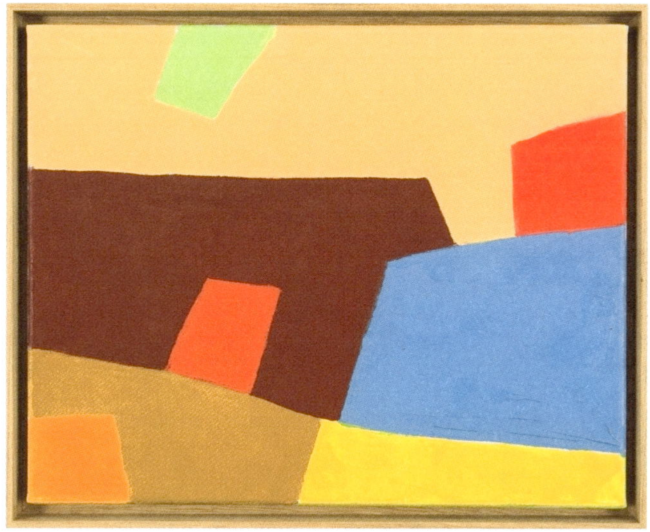

*Untitled* / *Ohne Titel*, 2012. Öl auf Leinwand / Oil on canvas. 41 × 32 cm. Im Auftrag der Sharjah Art Foundation / Commissioned by Sharjah Art Foundation

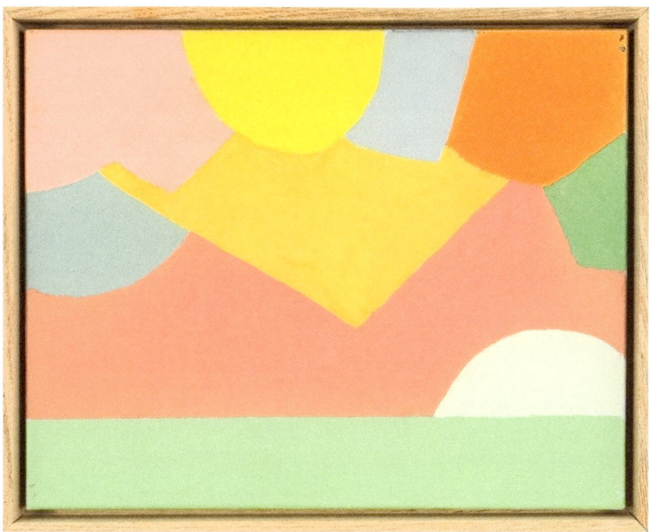

*Untitled* / *Ohne Titel*, 2013. Öl auf Leinwand / Oil on canvas. 45 × 35 cm. Im Auftrag der Sharjah Art Foundation / Commissioned by Sharjah Art Foundation

# Rasheed Araeen

Rasheed Araeen arbeitet seit über sechs Jahrzehnten als Bildhauer, Publizist, Maler, Kurator und Performer. Er wurde nicht nur in Großbritannien, sondern weltweit zu einer der Schlüsselfiguren der Entwicklung des postkolonialen Denkens. Jedoch wurde seinem Werk bis vor Kurzem so gut wie keine institutionelle Anerkennung zuteil. Rasheed Araeens künstlerischer Leitgedanke ist die Öffnung des vorherrschenden restriktiven eurozentrischen Erbes der Moderne sowie des damit einhergehenden Anspruchs auf Universalität, um die Errichtung neuer praktikabler Ziele für eine gerechtere Gesellschaft zu fördern. Für ihn liegt das entsprechende Potenzial in der „einzigartigen Geschichte […] jener Männer und Frauen, die ihrem ‚Anderssein' trotzten und den modernen bis dato verbotenen Raum betreten haben – nicht nur, um ihren historischen Anspruch darauf zu erheben, sondern auch, um den Rahmen infrage zu stellen, der diese Grenzen definierte und schützte".

Araeen leitete aus seiner Zeit als Bauingenieur in Karachi eine eigene Handschrift ab und entwickelte die geometrische Formsprache seiner britischen Kolleg*innen Anthony Caro, Kenneth und Mary Martin und Anthony Hill weiter. Sein Werk umfasst unterschiedlichste Formen und Materialien, von industriellen Werkstoffen wie Stahlträgern in *Sculpture No. 2* („Skulptur Nr. 2", 1965) bis zu bunt bemalten filigranen Holzmatrizen einer Projektarbeit für die *documenta14* mit dem Titel *Shamiyaana – Food for Thought: Thought for Change* („Shamiyaana – Denkanstöße: Gedanken über Veränderungen", 2017); und aus Fundstücken fertigte er zart gebogene Drahtrahmen für *My First Sculpture (Variation 1)* („Meine erste Skulptur [Variation 1]", 1959).

Araeens Arbeiten folgen einem Leitgedanken: dem Zentralmotiv des Minimalismus und der entsprechenden Positionierung eines Gitters, um einen Raum mit aktivistischem Potenzial zu bilden, in dem neben seinen gleichseitigen Formen die suggestive Kraft der Diagonalen als Handlungsaufforderung wirkt. Dieser Ansatz wird deutlich in seinen frühen, in den Deichtorhallen ausgestellten Gemälden *Before the Departure (black paintings)* („Vor der Abreise [schwarze Bilder]", 1963–1964). Die gitterartigen Formen fügen sich zu dichten architektonischen Gebilden zusammen, ganz so, als ob die Sinnhaftigkeit eines Raumes nur durch ständiges Übermalen gefunden werden könnte.

In den späten 1970er Jahren veränderte sich Araeens Praxis deutlich. Parallel zu den politischen Unruhen im Vereinigten Königreich und in Europa nahm das Werk des Künstlers offenere und konfrontativere Züge an. Fortan schien er seine ursprünglichen modernistischen Formen vollständig verworfen zu haben. Frustriert über die fehlende Wertschätzung seiner Arbeit auf institutioneller Ebene – wo seiner Meinung nach versucht wurde, sein Werk ausschließlich im Hinblick auf seine Identität zu kategorisieren – schuf Araeen eine Reihe von Porträts, in denen er seine eigenen Bilder mit Hakenkreuzen und schmerzhaften Sätzen wie „Paki Go Home" brandmarkte. Diese Reihe steht symbolisch für die Kulturkriege, die zu jener Zeit in der westlichen Welt tobten, und spiegelt das rassistische Trauma wider, das dem eigenen Empowerment dem Subjekt gegenüber vorausgeht, von dem die Unterwerfung droht. Diese berührenden Arbeiten sind Ausdruck einer komplizierten Praxis, die die systemische Dauerfortsetzung der orthodoxen institutionellen Denkweise unterbricht, vergrößert darstellt und kritisch bekämpft.

Spanning over six decades, Rasheed Araeen's practice comprises sculpture, publishing, painting, curating and performance. He has served as a pivotal figure in the call towards postcolonial thinking in Britain and globally. His work has largely deflected institutional recognition until recently. A key aspect of Araeen's complete project is the opening up of the restrictive and Eurocentric legacies of modernism, as well as their attendant claims of universality, in order to foster new, workable aims for a more equitable society. He recognises this potential as 'the unique story … of those men and women who defied their "otherness" and entered the modern space that was forbidden to them, not only to declare their historic claim on it, but also to challenge the framework which defined and protected its boundaries'.

Araeen rerouted his formative work as a structural engineer in Karachi into a personal language of his own, extending the geometrical forms of his British counterparts such as Anthony Caro, Kenneth and Mary Martin and Anthony Hill. His work encompasses numerous forms and materials, such as industrial materials like the steel girders in *Sculpture No.2* (1965), the colourfully painted delicate wooden matrices that underpin the societal project work for documenta 14, *Shamiyaana – Food for Thought: Thought for Change* (2017) or the found materials that comprise the delicate bent wire frame of *My First Sculpture (Variation 1)* (1959). A guiding principle is Araeen's use of the central motif of Minimalism, the positioning of the grid, to form a space of activist potential, implicating the equilateral forms of space, alongside the suggestive power of the diagonal, as a conceptual strike mark into action. These formulations are evident in his early paintings *Before the Departure (black paintings)* (1963–64), presented at the Deichtorhallen, which assemble grid-like forms into dense architectural vistas, as if the intelligibility of a space might only be found by continually drawing over it.

The late 1970s witnessed a significant shift in Araeen's practice. Coinciding with broader political unrest in the United Kingdom and Europe at the time, the artist's work took a more overtly confrontational approach, appearing to completely reject the modernist forms he had initially developed. Frustrated at the wilful rejection of his work at an institutional level, which, he argued, sought to categorise his work solely within the confines of his identity, Araeen created a series of portraits in which he seemed to vandalise his own image with swastikas and painful phrases such as 'Paki Go Home'. This body of work displays the culture wars that were in play in the Western world at the time, reflecting the racist trauma in advance of its claim to power over the subject it seeks to subjugate. These affecting works further complicate a practice that disrupts, magnifies and critically rejects systems of institutional orthodoxy.

Chris McCormack

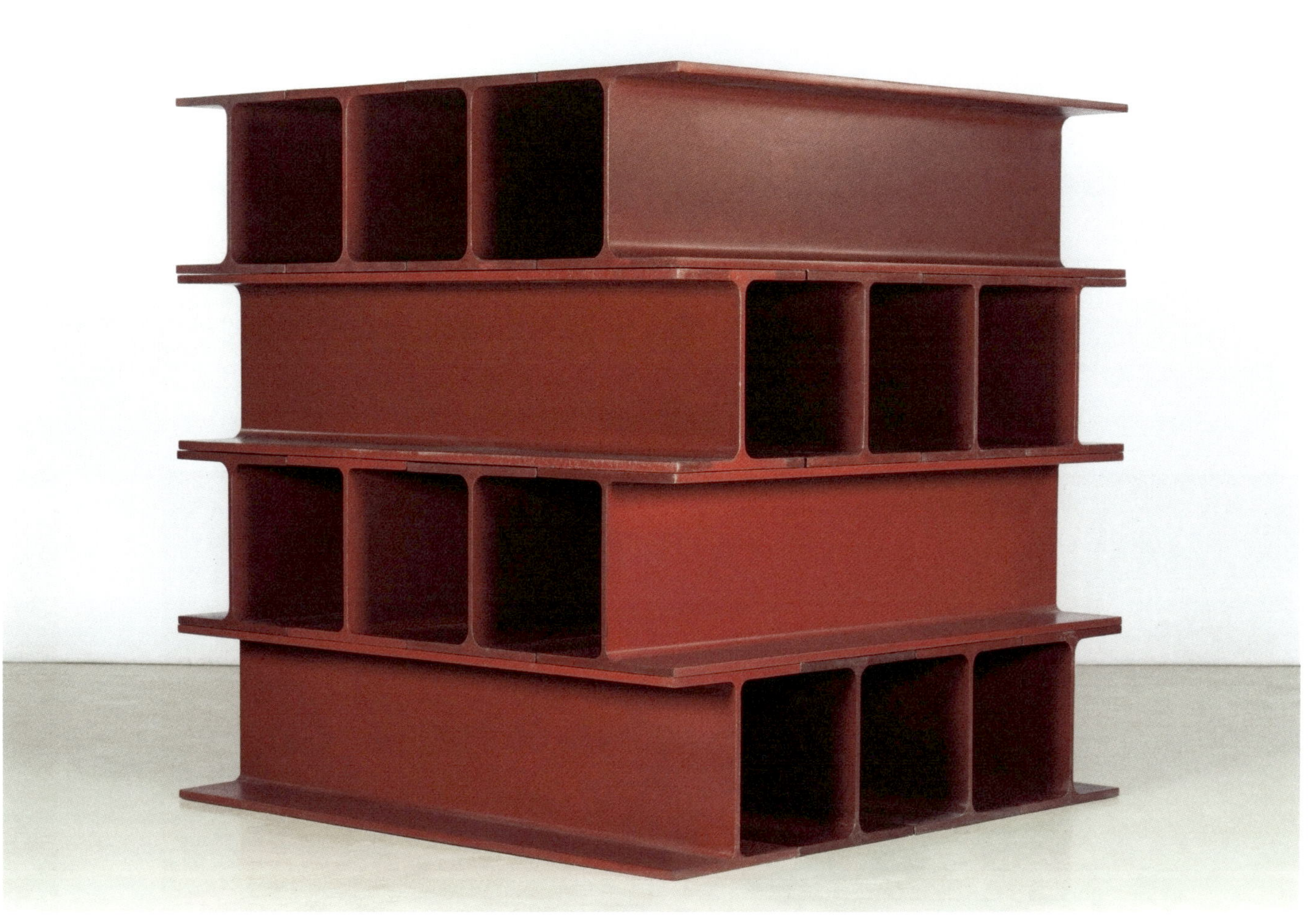

*Sculpture No.2* / *Skulptur Nr. 2*, 1965. 16 Stahlträger, eisenoxidrote Sprühfarbe / 16 steel girders, iron-oxide red sprayed paint. 122 × 122 × 122 cm.
Reproduziert von der Sharjah Art Foundation (2014) / Reproduced by Sharjah Art Foundation (2014)

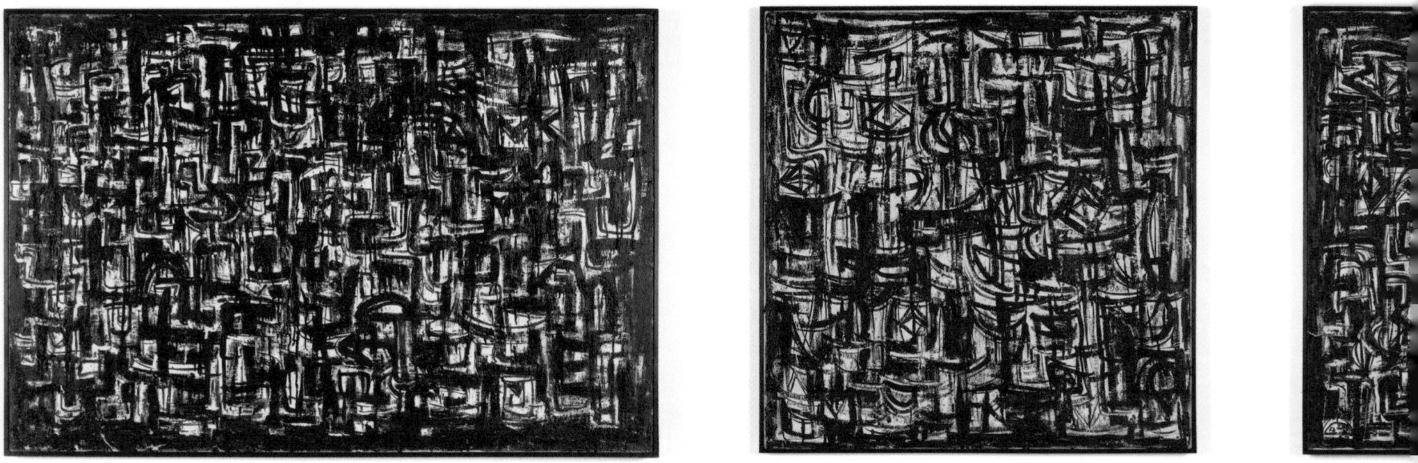

*Before the Departure (Black Paintings) | Vor der Abreise (Schwarze Gemälde)*, 1963–1964. 5 Gemälde, Öl auf Leinwand / 5 paintings, oil on canvas. Maße variabel / Dimensions variable

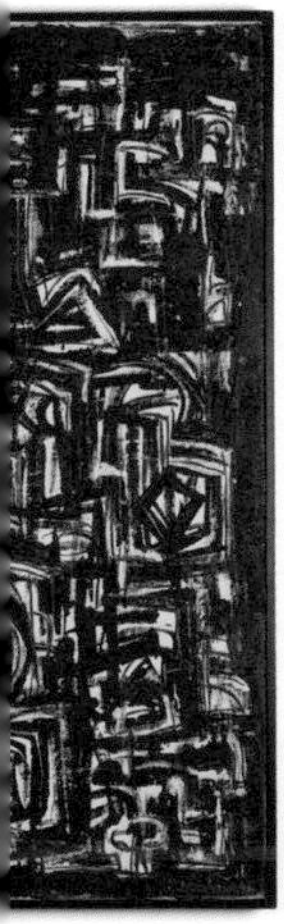
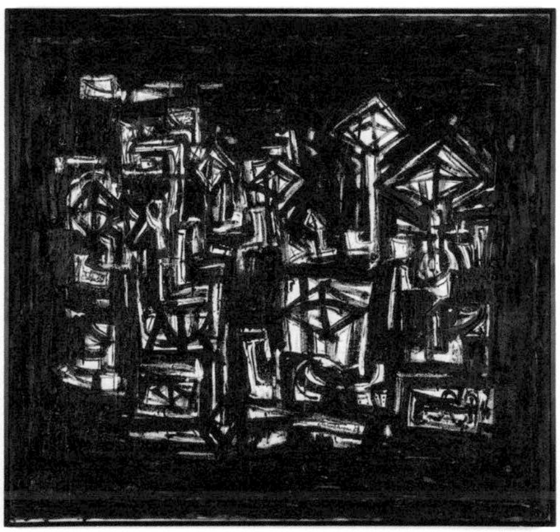
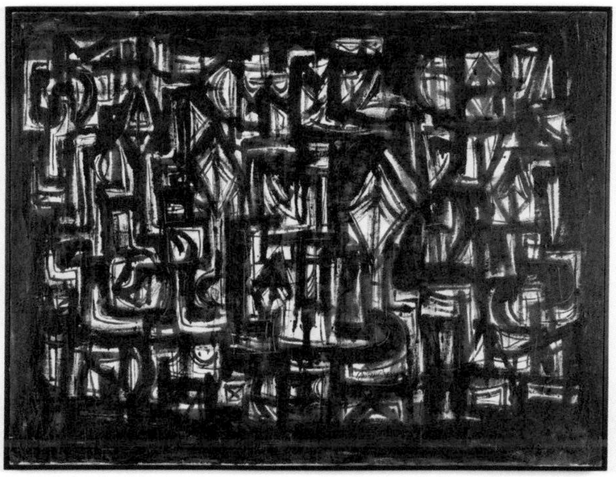

# Huguette Caland

Das Gemälde *Maameltein* (1970) gehört zu den frühesten Arbeiten von Huguette Caland. Es verweist auf ein Viertel der Stadt Jounieh, nördlich von Beirut, wo ihr Vater, der erste Präsident des unabhängigen Libanon, zum Ende seines Lebens wohnte. Die üppigen Farben in Edelsteinschattierungen sind typisch für diese Phase in Calands Schaffen. Die von schwarzen Linien umgebenen Farbflächen verbinden sich zu einer abstrakten Komposition, die an die geschwungene Küstenlinie des Stadtteils erinnert. 1970 war für Caland ein entscheidendes Jahr, denn es brachte eine Reihe internationaler Ausstellungen, ihre erste Einzelausstellung in Beirut und den Abschied vom Familienleben. Huguette Caland verließ den Libanon, um sich in Paris ihrer künstlerischen Karriere zu widmen. Bis zu ihrer Rückkehr nach Beirut im Jahr 2013 lebte sie in der Diaspora – zunächst in Paris, später in Los Angeles.

In den 1970er Jahren beschäftigte sich die Künstlerin ausgiebig mit dem menschlichen Körper. Bei *Red II* („Rot II", 1974) beherrscht ein geschwungener Torso mitsamt Oberschenkeln die Leinwand, während in *Flash* („Aufblitzen", 1978) eine suggestive Wölbung aus etwas herausragt, das wie rosafarbene Fleischmasse anmutet. Caland schuf zudem eine neue Werkreihe mit dem Titel *Bribes de Corps* („Körperfragmente") – erotisch aufgeladene Gemälde zwischen Figuration und Abstraktion, die gängige Darstellungen weiblicher Schönheit und weiblichen Begehrens hinterfragen.

Calands spätere Arbeiten sind komplexer aufgebaute „Landschaften", die häufig die Oberfläche von Stoffen suggerieren. *Rossinante Diptychon* („Rossinante-Diptychon", 2011), eines ihrer jüngsten Werke, in Acryl und mit Stiften ausgeführt, erinnert in Form und Linienführung an ihre frühen Zeichnungen aus den 1960er und 1970er Jahren, während die fast „gestochen" anmutenden Punktmuster den palästinensischen Stickereien ähneln, denen Caland ebenfalls in den späten 1960er Jahren begegnete.

One of Huguette Caland's earliest works, *Maameltein* (1970) refers to a district in Jounieh, north of Beirut, where her father, Lebanon's first post-independence president, lived towards the end of his life. The painting's rich, gem-like hues are characteristic of this period in Caland's work, seeing her deploy resilient colour forms surrounded by black lines, which develop an abstract composition that, in this instance, also brings to mind the curved bays of the neighbourhood. A momentous year for Caland, 1970 marked a number of international exhibitions, her first solo show in Beirut and her departure from family life in Lebanon to pursue her artistic career in Paris. Until returning to Beirut in 2013, Caland had lived an entirely diasporic life, first in Paris and subsequently in Los Angeles, California.

The 1970s saw an exuberant focus on the body in the artist's work. In *Red II* (1974), a curvaceous torso and thighs dominate the canvas, while in *Flash* (1978), a suggestive protuberance emerges from what appear to be mounds of pink flesh. Caland also created a new series of works titled *Bribes de Corps* (*Body Bits* or *Body Parts*)—erotically charged paintings that shifted between figuration and abstraction—challenging conventions around the presentation of female beauty and desire.

Caland's later works are more intricately constructed 'landscapes' that often resemble the surface of textiles. *Rossinante Diptych* (2011), one of the artist's latest works, produced in acrylic and pen, is evocative of the interior lines and forms of some of her early drawings from the late 1960s and '70s, while the dots, fashion 'stitch-like' marks, evoke terrains akin to the Palestinian embroideries Caland first encountered in the late 1960s.

Anne Barlow

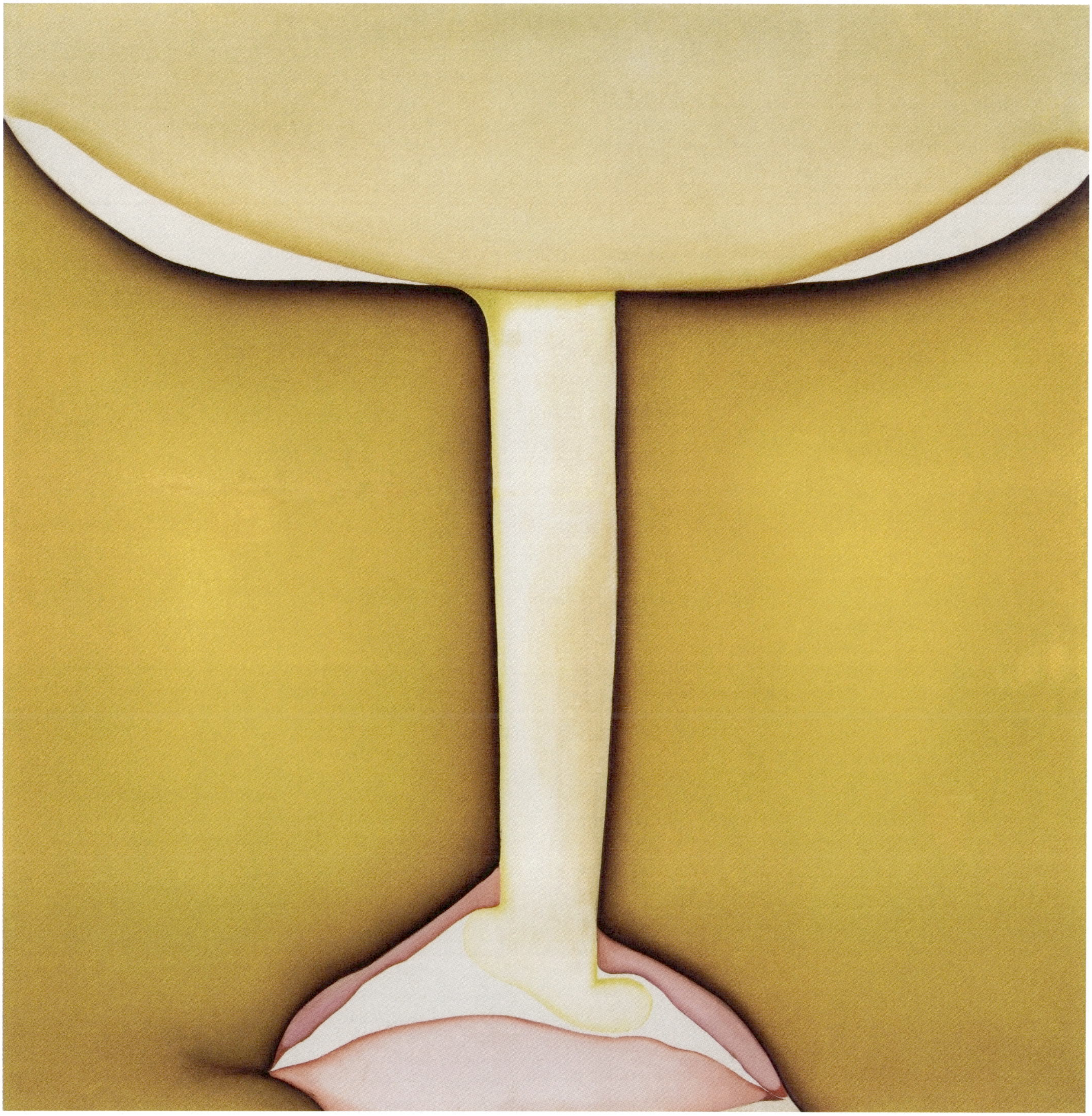

*Bribes de Corps / Körperfragmente*, 1979. Öl auf Leinen / Oil on linen. 99,7 × 99,7 cm

# Saloua Raouda Choucair

Saloua Raouda Choucair lebte zwischen 1948 und 1951 in Frankreich. Dort studierte sie an der École des Beaux-Arts, schloss sich dem Atelier d'art abstrait in der Nähe des Studios von Fernand Léger an und besichtigte die Cité Radieuse von Le Corbusier. Diese Erfahrungen haben Choucairs Abstraktionstechnik beeinflusst, die sich durch eine modulare organische Geometrie auszeichnet. Ihr Streben nach dem Ungegenständlichen – einer reinen Form des Kunstschaffens – ist jedoch vor allem in der islamischen Kunst der arabischsprachigen Städte und ihrer Architekturen verankert. Für die Kunsthistorikerin Ann Coxon haben Choucairs „Studien der modernen Meister lediglich ihre Überzeugung bestätigt, dass bestimmte arabische und islamische Verfahren bereits Jahrhunderte zuvor den Weg zur ‚reinsten Form' oder ‚Essenz' der Kunst geebnet hatten", wie sie 2013 im Katalog zur Einzelausstellung der Künstlerin in der Tate Modern schrieb.

Choucairs Zeit in Frankreich trug also nur einen weiteren Baustein zu ihrem künstlerischen Verfahren bei, bei dem sie bereits zuvor die Möglichkeiten der Abstraktion für einen transzendenten Lyrismus genutzt hatte. Die Farbgebung nahm dabei einen wichtigen Stellenwert ein. In der Gouache auf Papier *Gradual Rhythmical Composition* („Graduelle rhythmische Komposition"), die sie 1953 im Anschluss an ihre Rückkehr nach Beirut malte, scheinen blaugrüne, ocker-, orange- und fuchsiafarbene sowie schwarze Formen auf einer horizontalen Ebene zu vibrieren. Die Künstlerin nannte solche Kompositionen „Module". Als Choucair in den 1960er Jahren die Malerei aufgab, waren diese Module reif für ihre dreidimensionale Umsetzung. *Interform* („Zwischenform") aus Holz, das zwischen 1960 und 1962 entstand, ist ein frühes Beispiel dieser Weiterentwicklung. Ein mit geschwungenen Aussparungen versehener Holzblock, der an das Skelett eines Hochhauses erinnert, zeugt von Choucairs anhaltendem Interesse für die Architektur. Ihre folgenden Serien nannte Choucair „skulpturale Gedichte" und verwies damit auf den strukturellen Einfluss der arabischen Poesie. „Ich wollte, dass der Rhythmus so wie das lyrische Versmaß unabhängiger und gleichzeitig stärker in sich verschränkt ist", bemerkte sie einmal.

Between 1948 and 1951, Saloua Raouda Choucair lived in France. While there, she studied at the École des Beaux-Arts, joined the Atelier d'art abstrait, working adjacent to Fernand Léger's studio, and visited Le Corbusier's Cité Radieuse. But while these experiences influenced Choucair's abstraction, which is defined by a modular, organic geometry, it was the vernaculars of Islamic art found in Arabic-speaking cities and their architectures that anchored Choucair's reach for non-objectivity—a pure form of artmaking. As art historian Ann Coxon wrote in the catalogue for the artist's solo show at Tate Modern in 2013, Choucair's 'studies of the modern masters simply confirmed her belief that certain Arab and Islamic practices had already prepared the ground in reaching "the purest form" or "essence" of art centuries earlier'.

Choucair's time in France, then, was but a moment that expanded a practice already engaged with abstraction's capacity for transcendent lyricism. Colour played an essential role. Teal, ochre, orange, fuchsia and black shapes seemingly vibrate on a horizontal plane in the gouache on paper *Gradual Rhythmical Composition*, painted in 1953 after Choucair's return to Beirut. The artist referred to such compositions as 'modules', and, by the time she stopped painting in the 1960s, they were ripe for three-dimensional translation. The wooden *Interform*, created between 1960 and 1962, is an early example of this evolution. Speaking to Choucair's enduring interest in architecture, a wood block carved with curved voids recalls the skeleton of a high-rise building. Choucair would title subsequent series 'sculptural poems', pointing to Arabic poetry's structural influence. 'I wanted rhythm like the poetic meter, to be at once more independent and interlinked', she once noted.

Stephanie Bailey

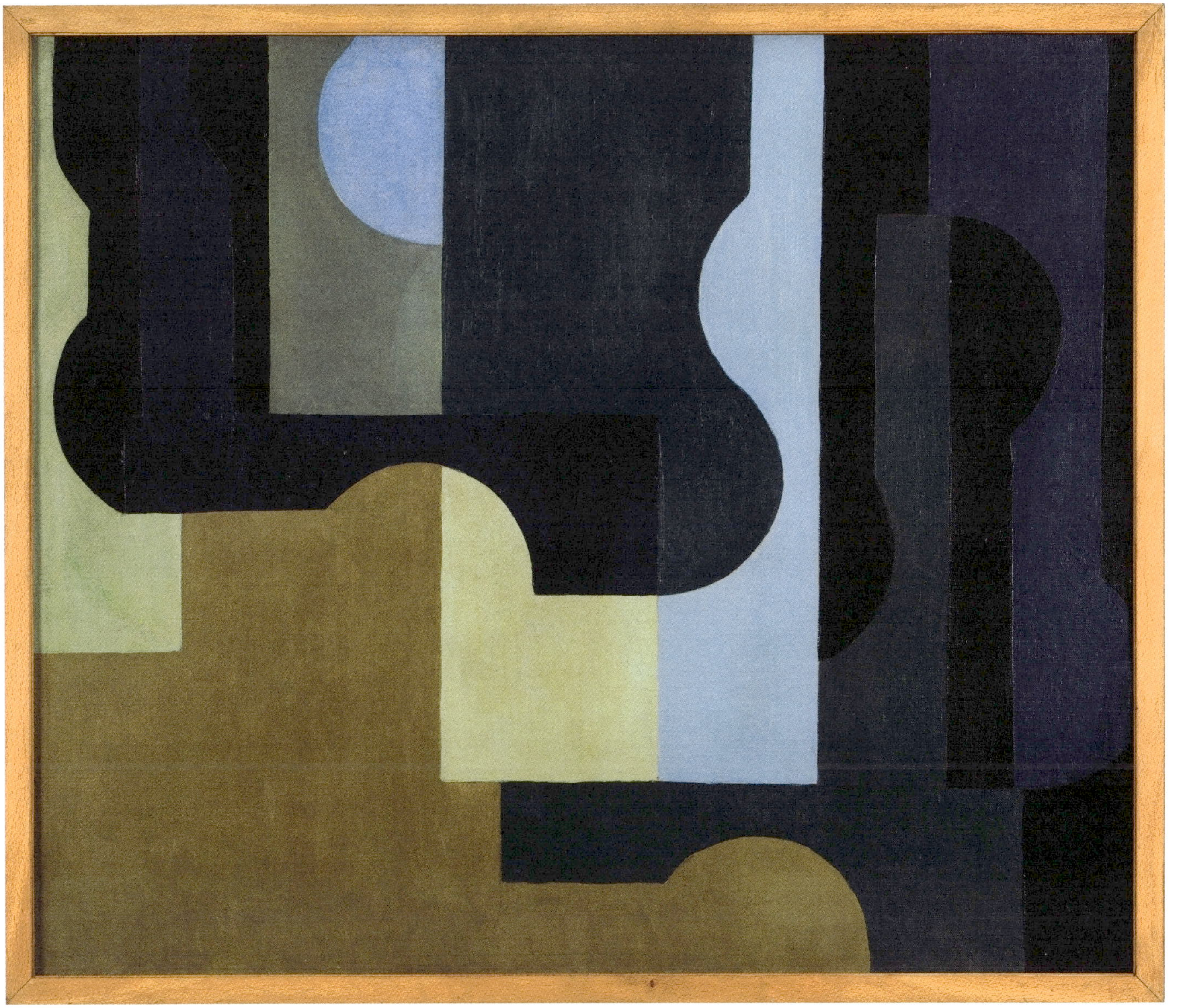

*Composition with Green Module* | *Komposition mit grünem Modul*, 1950. Öl auf Leinwand / Oil on canvas. 67 × 58 cm

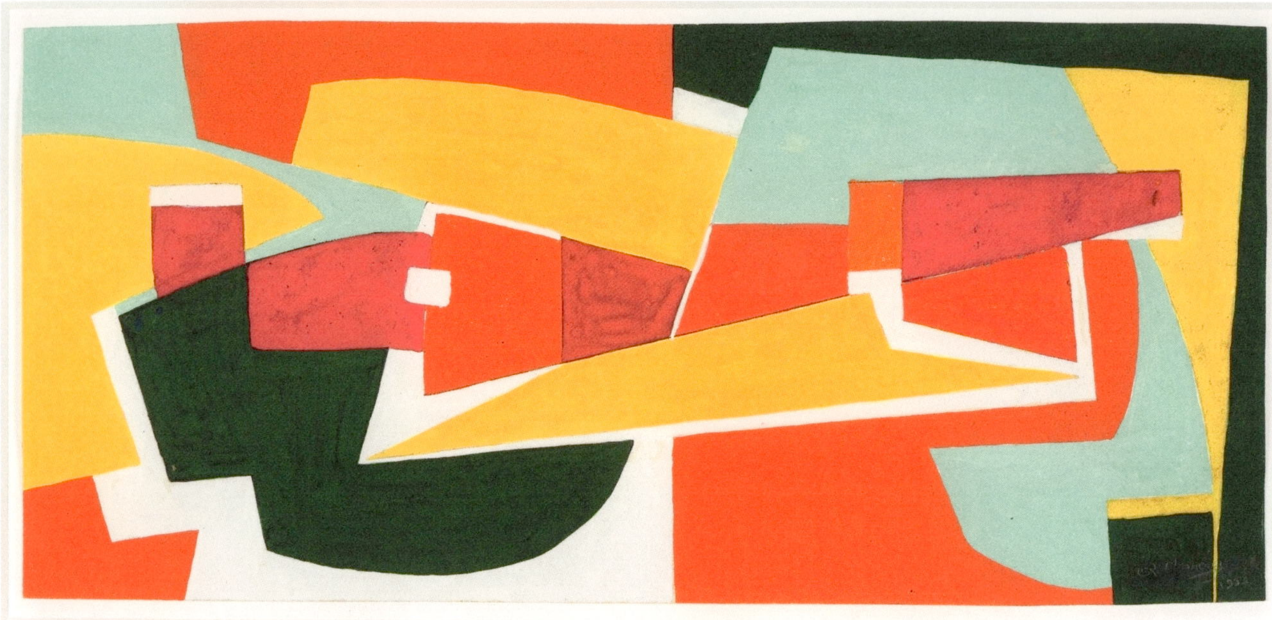

*Gradual Rhythmical Composition | Graduelle rhythmische Komposition*, 1953. Gouache auf Papier / Gouache on paper. 50 × 22 cm

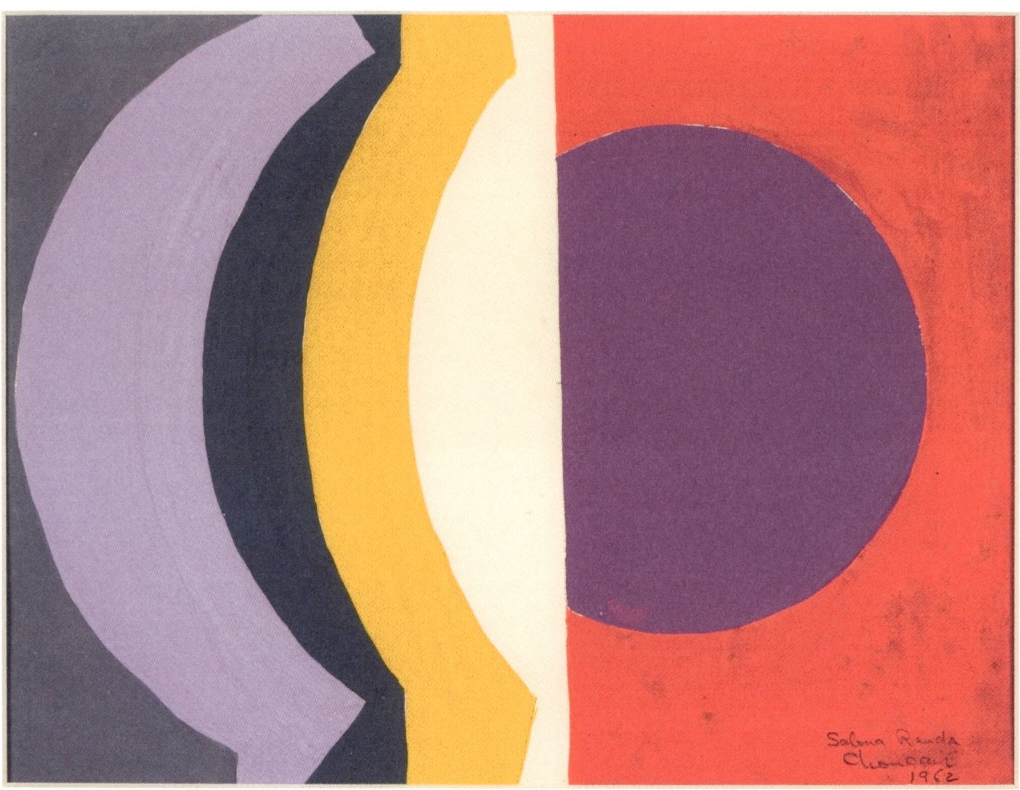

*Composition with a Circle | Komposition mit Kreis*, 1952. Gouache auf Papier / Gouache on paper. 32 × 25 cm

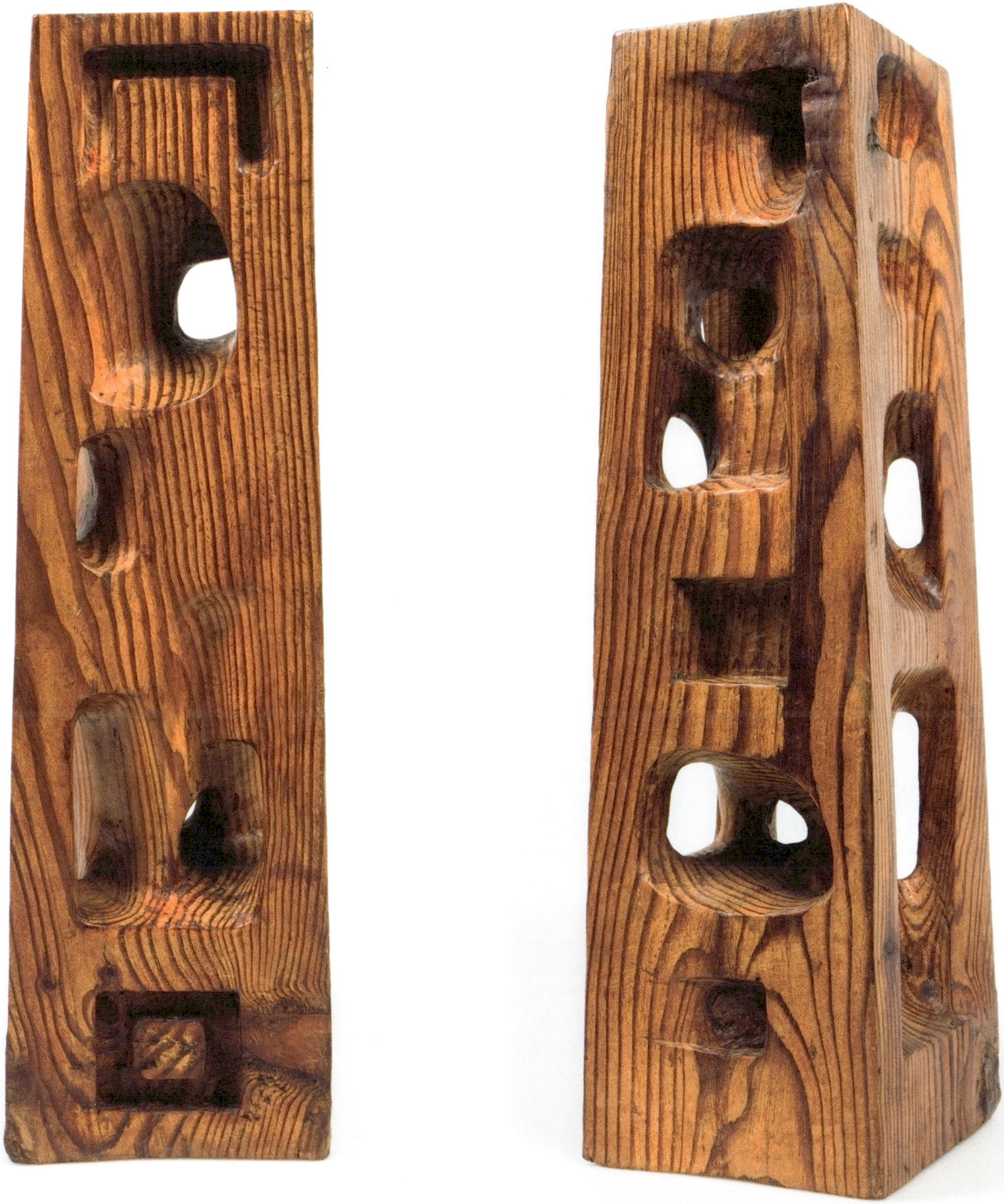

*Interform* / *Zwischenform*, 1960–1962. Holz / Wood. 12 × 49 × 12 cm

# Tiffany Chung

Tiffany Chung ist für ihre komplexen und farbenfrohen kartografischen Arbeiten bekannt. Für das *The Heart of Sharjah Project 2025* hat sie im Anschluss an umfangreiche Recherchearbeiten Kartenmaterial und historische Narrative miteinander verknüpft. Auf mehreren übereinanderliegenden Schichten Transparentpapier zeichnete Chung freihändig nach alter kartografischer Tradition eine Karte der Altstadt von Sharjah. Für das Kartennetz mit seinen Linien und Punkten verwendete sie verschiedene Ölfarben und Tinten. In der auf einen Rahmen gezogenen Zeichnung im Format 75 × 91,5 cm gehen reale und imaginierte Räume ineinander über. Die Künstlerin vermischt auf der Karte ganz bewusst tatsächliche und fiktionale Angaben.

Der Souk in der historischen Altstadt soll als „Herz von Sharjah" bis 2025 rekonstruiert und restauriert werden. Darauf spielt Chung in ihrem Werktitel an. Im Verlauf dieses Stadtsanierungsprojekts, das als das größte seiner Art in den Emiraten und der Golfregion gilt, ist bereits ein neues Kultur-, Hotel- und Restaurantviertel entstanden. Chung will mit ihren nicht näher definierten Linien und Punkten die Komplexität einer solchen Aufgabe verdeutlichen. Außerdem will sie vermitteln, dass durch Architekturentwürfe und Städtebauprojekte allein die Erinnerungen nicht wiederaufleben, die solche Kulturer-Kulturerbe-stätten bestätten in den Menschen wachrufen. Chungs Markierungen verweisen wie verschlüsselte Codes auf verborgene Objekte, die sich die Betrachtenden ohne weitere Erläuterungen vorstellen müssen. Wie Mikroorganismen ballen sich die Punkte an den Durchgangsstraßen der Altstadt, ganz so, als breiteten sich die Menschen und ihre Unternehmungen dort wie ansteckende Krankheiten aus.

Chung verwendet in ihren Werken historische Karten unterschiedlicher Epochen, um die Sedimente der Geschichte freizulegen. Sie will damit zeigen, wie sehr das Anfertigen und Lesen von Karten durch subjektive Vorstellungen geprägt sind. In ihrer künstlerischen Praxis verarbeitet Chung ihre eigenen Kindheitserfahrungen aus der Zeit der Flucht vor dem Vietnamkrieg und die Erfahrungen ihres Vaters in der Kriegsgefangenschaft. Sie stellt die Frage, wie Migration, Bewegung und Konflikte das eigene Orts- und Zugehörigkeitsgefühl prägen.

Known for her intricate and colourful cartographic works, Tiffany Chung applies her in-depth research process combining geographical documents and historical narratives to *The Heart of Sharjah Project 2025*. Layers of translucent paper build a map of the old town of Sharjah that Chung has drawn using the precise tradition of a cartographer's grids overlaid with lines and dots drawn freehand with different types of ink and oil. A mounted illustration measuring roughly two-thirds of a square metre, the image is a synthesis of real and imagined space, presenting a map that is as intentionally accurate as it is fictional.

The old town souq district now referred to as the Heart of Sharjah is a historical preservation and restoration area due to be completed by the year 2025, as is referenced in the title of Chung's piece. At one point, the urban development project—perceived to be the largest project of its kind in the Emirates and the Arabian Gulf—already transformed and rebuilt a new cultural and hospitality district. Chung's unexplained lines and dots evoke the complexity of such a task, intimating that architectural design and urban construction alone cannot re-create the memories these heritage sites evoke. Chung's markings are unknown codes that insinuate hidden objects the viewer must imagine without a literal key. Clustered like microbes, the dots are congested along the old town's thoroughfares, as if people and activity were spreading through them contagiously.

In her practice, Chung uses historical maps from multiple time periods in order to reveal the sediments of history, highlighting the subjective practice of both making and reading cartography. Influenced by her childhood departure from her home during the Vietnam War and her father's experience as a prisoner of war, Chung's artistic practice considers how migration, movement and conflict affect one's concept of place and belonging.

Sarah Perks

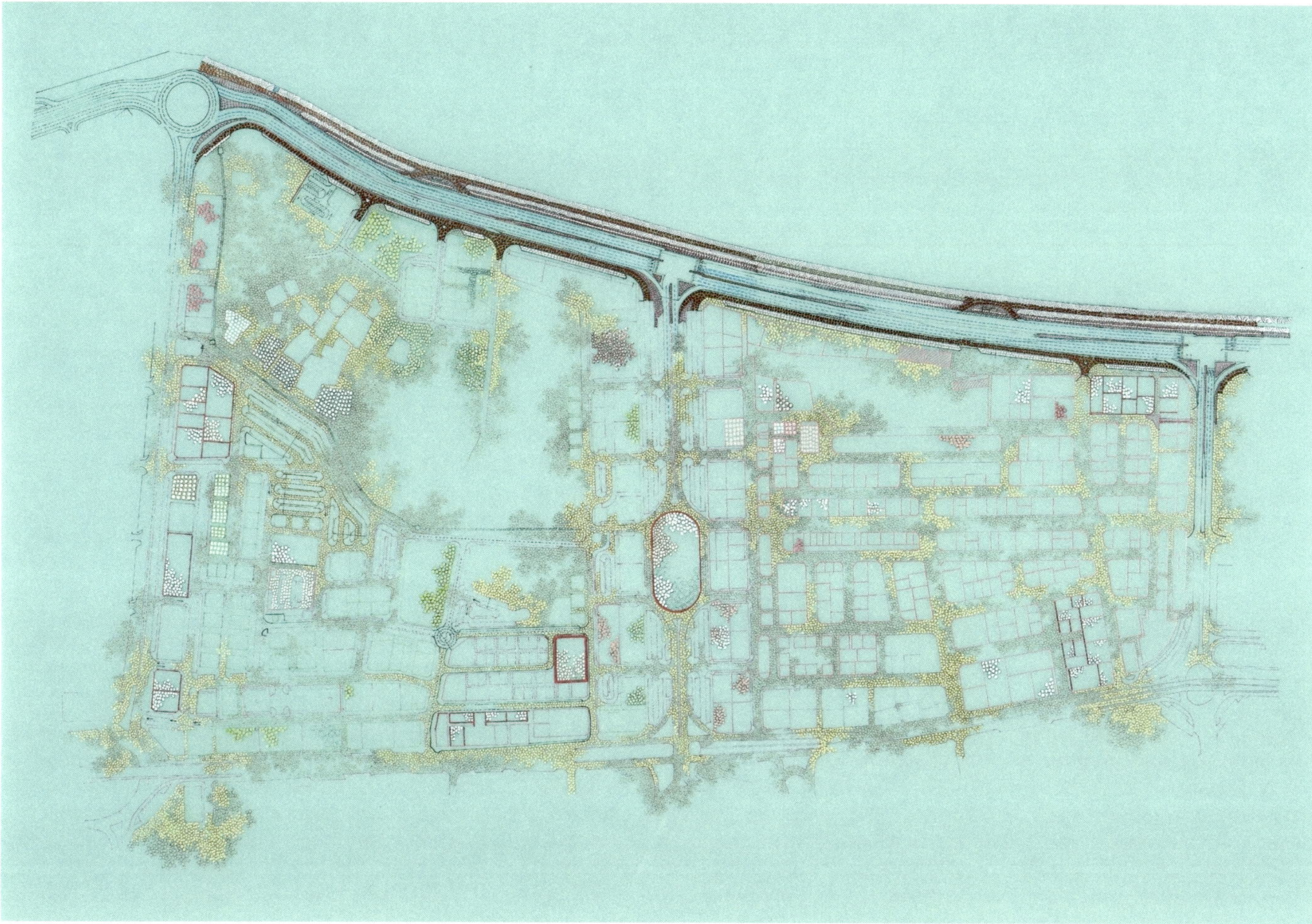

*The Heart of Sharjah Project 2025 | Das Heart of Sharjah-Projekt 2025*, 2012. Mikropigment-Tinte, Geltinte, Ölmarker auf Pergament und Papier / Micropigment ink, gel ink, oil marker on vellum and paper. 91,5 × 75 cm. Im Auftrag der Sharjah Art Foundation / Commissioned by Sharjah Art Foundation

# Monir Shahroudy Farmanfarmaian

Monir Shahroudy Farmanfarmaian ist insbesondere für ihre spektakulären Spiegelmosaike bekannt, die von der iranischen Hinterglasmalerei und den dortigen Spiegelmosaiken beeinflusst sind – traditionelle Kunstformen, die vor allem die Wände persischer Paläste, Schreine und Moscheen schmücken. Die kaleidoskopartige Linienführung von Farmanfarmaians glitzernden geometrischen Skulpturen findet sich auch in ihren zweidimensionalen Zeichnungen wieder. Zum Beispiel in den unbetitelten Tafelbildern von 2008, bei denen feine farbige Linien aus Filzstiften und Spiegeln auf einem Gipsuntergrund zarte schematische Landkarten entstehen lassen, die wie geometrische Sternkarten wirken.

Farmanfarmaian hat sich bei der Gestaltung ihrer edlen, klar umrissenen Skulpturen nicht nur von der Architektur der Städte Isfahan, Shiraz und Tabriz inspirieren lassen, sondern auch von den iranischen Souks, die für sie „voller Farben, Muster und Collagen“ steckten, wie sie dem Kurator Hans Ulrich Obrist einmal erklärte. Anklänge an diese Orte finden sich in den freieren, expressiveren Linien, die für Farmanfarmaians Teppicharbeiten typisch sind: etwa *Untitled (C3)* („Ohne Titel [C3], 1993) aus natürlich gefärbter Seide und handgewebter Wolle aus Tabriz. Ebenso sind sie in ihren Mixed-Media-Collagen aus organischen Formen zu entdecken, die sich mit übereinanderliegenden, oftmals netzartigen Oberflächen verweben.

Farmanfarmaians Collagen wie *CG8* (1982), in der eine Reihe von Schmetterlingen inmitten ineinandergreifender Formen aus Rosatönen und dunklem Blau schweben, sind ein weniger bekannter Teil ihrer Arbeit. Ihre erste Collage entstand in New York, wo sie nach dem Beginn der Iranischen Revolution Ende der 1970er Jahre im Exil lebte. Den Anstoß gaben, so erzählte sie Obrist, Reparaturarbeiten auf der Terrasse ihrer Wohnung an der Fifth Avenue. Dabei beobachtete sie, wie Arbeiter*innen ein Netzgewebe über den Asphalt spannten. Fasziniert von der Schönheit dieses Werkstoffes, bat sie um ein Stück davon, fing an, mit Zeitungs- und Zeitschriftenfetzen auf Pappe herumzubasteln und bedeckte die Komposition mit ihrem neu entdeckten Material.

Monir Shahroudy Farmanfarmaian is best known for her spectacular mirror mosaics, which draw from traditional Iranian reverse-glass painting and mirror mosaics that adorn the walls of Persian palaces, shrines and mosques. The kaleidoscopic lines of Farmanfarmaian's glittering geometric sculptures are mapped out in the artist's two-dimensional drawings, like her untitled panels created with felt markers and mirrors on plaster made in 2008, where fine colourful lines create delicate, diagrammatic maps that take on the appearance of geometric star maps.

But, while Farmanfarmaian certainly drew on the architectures of Isfahan, Shiraz and Tabriz to create her exquisite, clean-cut sculptures, she also found inspiration in Iran's souqs, which she once described to curator Hans Ulrich Obrist as being 'full of colour and patterns and collages'. Echoes of these spaces can be found in the more freewheeling, expressive lines that pattern Farmanfarmaian's carpet works, such as *Untitled (C3)* (1993), with naturally dyed silk and wool hand-woven in Tabriz, alongside her mixed-media collages, defined by organic shapes that move in and out of layered, often netted surfaces.

Farmanfarmaian's collages, such as *CG8* (1982), in which a series of butterflies float amid a depth of interlocking shapes in rose scales and dusky blues, are a lesser known part of her practice. She made her first collage in New York, where she lived in exile following the outbreak of the Iranian Revolution at the end of the 1970s. The triggers, as she informed Obrist, were repairs to the terrace of her Fifth Avenue apartment. Farmanfarmaian remembers watching workers putting netting over the asphalt. Struck by the fabric's beauty, she asked for a piece and began tinkering with bits of newspaper and magazine on cardboard, covering the composition with her newfound material.

Stephanie Bailey

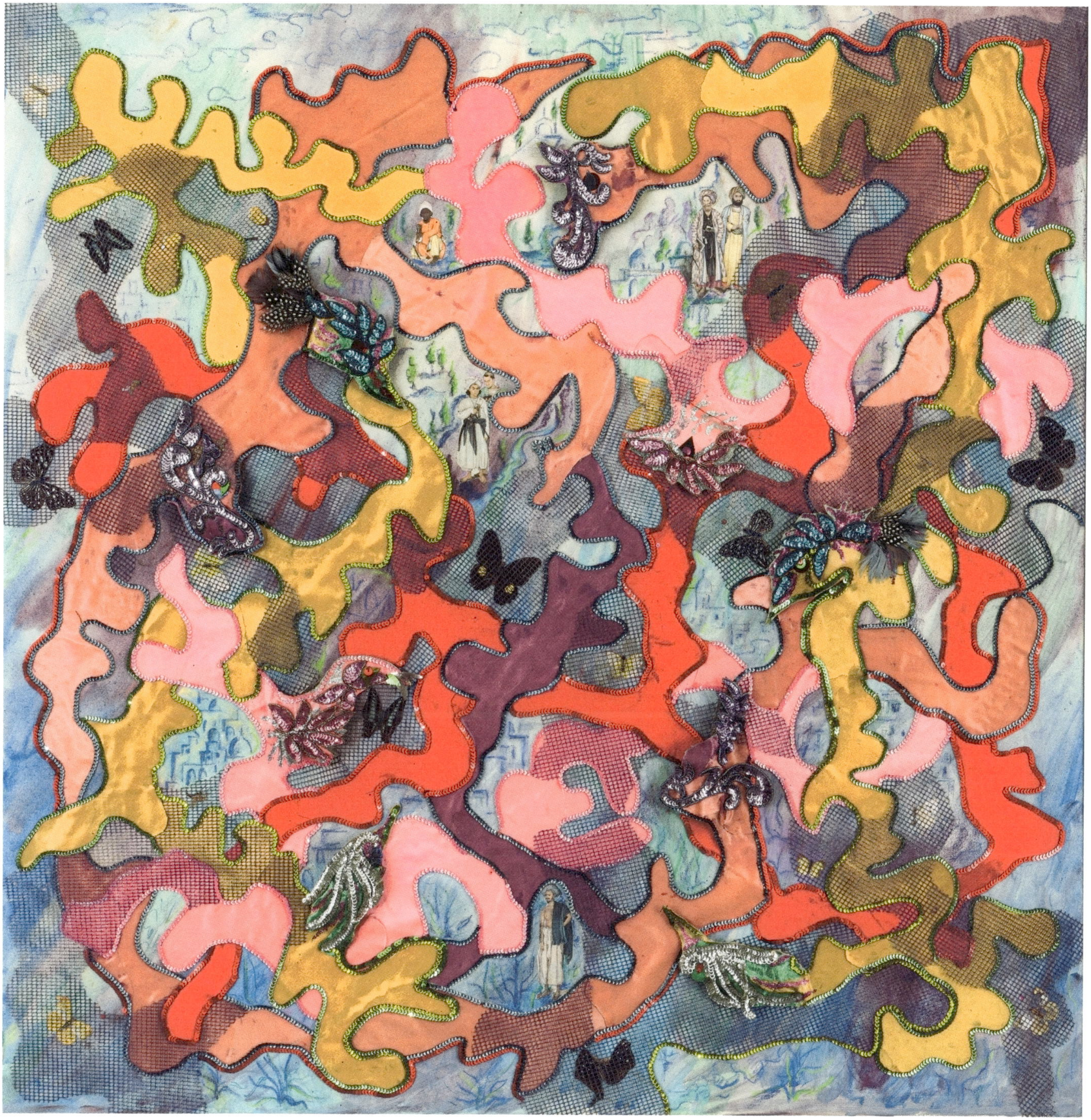

*CG8*, 1982. Mixed-Media-Collage / Mixed media collage. 128 × 128 cm

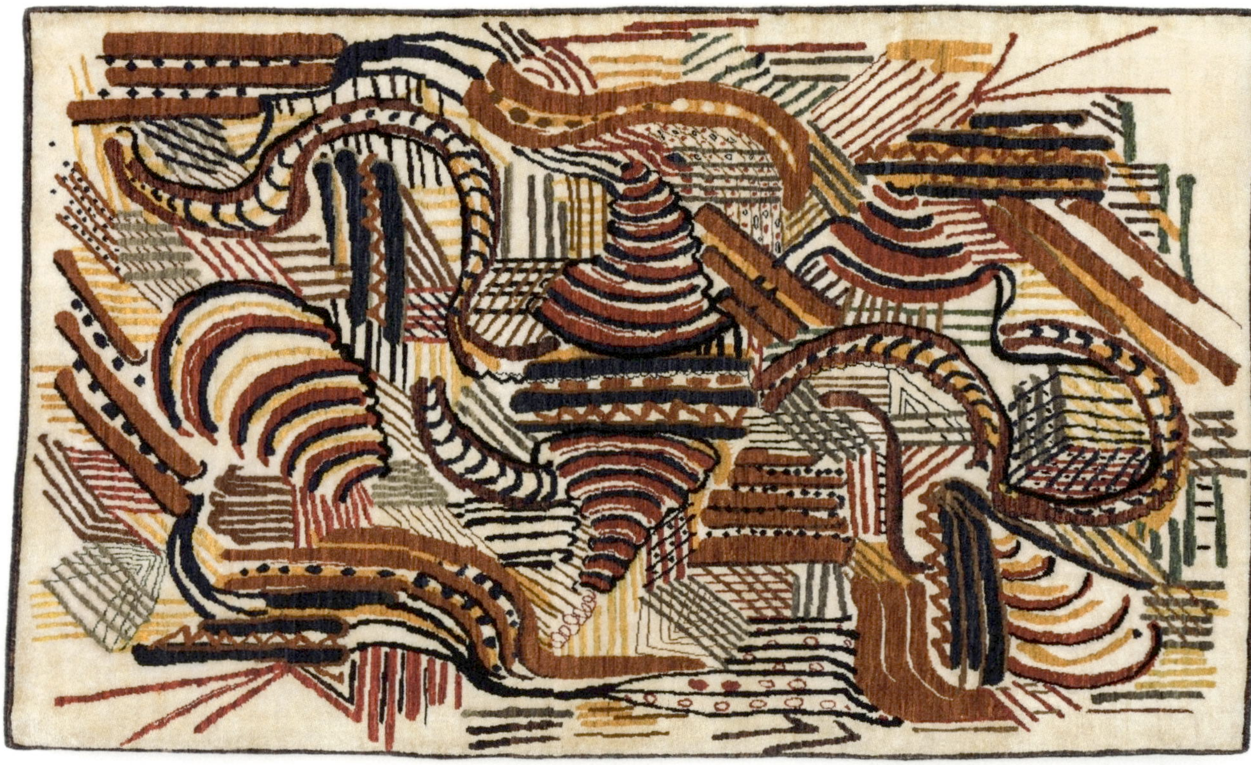

*Untitled (C3) | Ohne Titel (C3)*, 1993. Natürlich gefärbte Seide und handgewebte Wolle aus Tabriz / Naturally dyed silk, wool handwoven in Tabriz.
177 × 103 cm

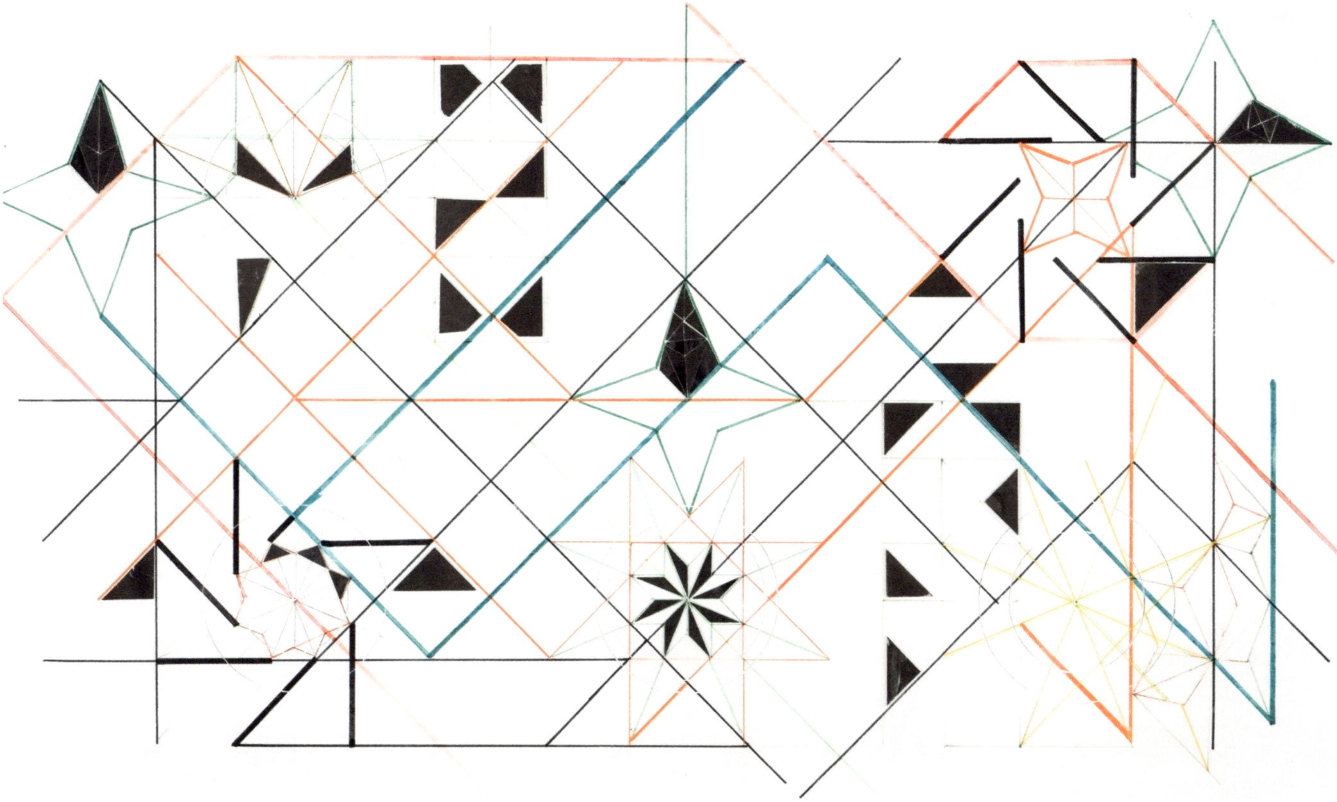

*Untitled* / *Ohne Titel*, 2008. Bunte Filzstifte, Spiegel auf Gips / Colour felt tip pens, mirror on plaster. 132 × 97 × 5 cm

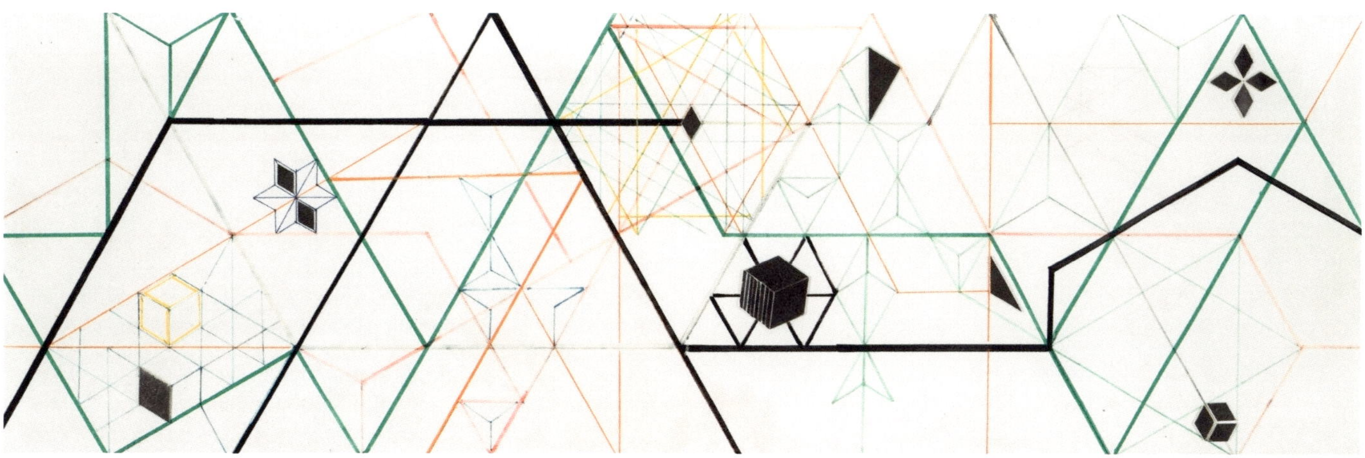

*Untitled* / *Ohne Titel*, 2008. Bunte Filzstifte, Spiegel auf Gips / Colour felt tip pens, mirror on plaster. 96 × 39 × 5 cm

# Simone Fattal

Als Simone Fattal sieben Jahre alt war, verfasste sie eine Novelle und versteckte sie unter ihrer Matratze. Einige Monate später bekam sie von einer Freundin ihre ersten Farbtuben geschenkt. „Und seitdem", so Fattal in einem Interview mit *apartamento*, „habe ich nie mehr aufgehört." Der literarische Impuls wirkt in ihren Kunstwerken fort und hat sich durch die Zusammenarbeit mit ihrer verstorbenen Partnerin Etel Adnan noch weiterentwickelt. Ein Beispiel dafür ist ihre gemeinsame Interpretation des Gedichts „Jebu" von 1973. In ihrer Arbeit aus dem Jahr 2006 greift Fattal eine Zeile aus diesem Gedicht auf – „In unseren Ländern der Dürre besteht der Regen für ewige Zeiten aus Patronen" – und malt sie in breiten schwarzen arabischen Schriftzügen auf Lavasteinfliesen. Fattal ist eine große Meisterin der Abstraktion; ihren Einsatz weißer Farbe in einer Reihe monochromer Gemälde beschreibt sie als die Verwendung von „Weiß bis zu dem Punkt, an dem ich keine Fragen mehr hatte ".Auf ähnliche Weise beschäftigt sie sich mit Form und Sprache: Oftmals versucht sie in ihren Werken, ein einziges Register zu ziehen, eine einzige emotionale Aussage zu treffen, die klar ist und nachwirkt. Den entscheidenden Antrieb für ihre Arbeit erfährt Fattal, wenn sie als Künstlerin „plötzlich von der Eindringlichkeit einer Beobachtung überwältigt wird (...) hat sie etwas verstanden und sieht es als ihre Pflicht an, diese Erkenntnis weiterzutragen". Wenn sie mit Ton arbeitet, fertigt Fattal repräsentative Totems von Gestalten aus der Poesie, Geschichte und Erzählkunst. Ton „ist geschwätzig", bemerkt sie fast beiläufig: „Er ist ein starkes Material, er lässt mich nicht machen, was ich will." Solche Anforderungen stellt auch das historische Erzählen: eine Geschmeidigkeit und Standhaftigkeit, die man einkalkulieren und gestalten muss. Zwei Skulpturen aus dem Jahr 2006, *Zhat El Himma* und *Abdel Wahab*, wurden im selben Ofen gebrannt und sind nach Motiven desselben Epos *Sira* geformt, das vornehmlich in der mündlichen Überlieferung existiert. Für die Künstlerin ist Geschichte fortlaufend und dynamisch und wird durch die Überzeugungskraft des Materiellen vorangetrieben.

When Simone Fattal was seven years old, she wrote a novella and hid it under her mattress. A few months later, a friend handed Fattal her first tubes of paint, after which, she says in an interview with *apartamento*, 'I never stopped'. The literary impulse carries on in her artworks and is further developed through collaborative works with her late partner, Etel Adnan. One such example is their interpretation of the poem 'Jebu' from 1973. Fattal's work from 2006 takes a line from the poem—'In our land of drought the rain forever is made of bullets'—and paints it in Arabic over a composite of lava stone. Fattal is a profound abstractionist; she describes her use of white in a series of monochrome paintings as taking 'white to the point where I had no more questions'. She has a similar preoccupation with form and language: often her works seek to stroke a single register, one single emotive remark—clarified and resounding. Fattal finds impetus to make work when she, as an artist, 'suddenly finds herself possessed by the urgency of her observation ... she has understood something, and it is her duty to translate her understanding'. When Fattal works in clay, she makes representative totems of figures from poetry, history and legend. Clay 'talks a lot', Fattal notes, it is almost flippant: 'it's a strong thing, it doesn't let you do whatever you want'. Such are also the demands of historical telling: an elasticity and endurance that must be reckoned with and shaped. Two sculptures from 2006, *Zhat El Himma* and *Abdel Wahab*, were fired in the same kiln and are built from the residue of the same epic, *Sira*, which exists primarily as an oral history. For the artist, history is continuous and dynamic, rendered further itinerant by her material persuasions.

Skye Arundhati Thomas

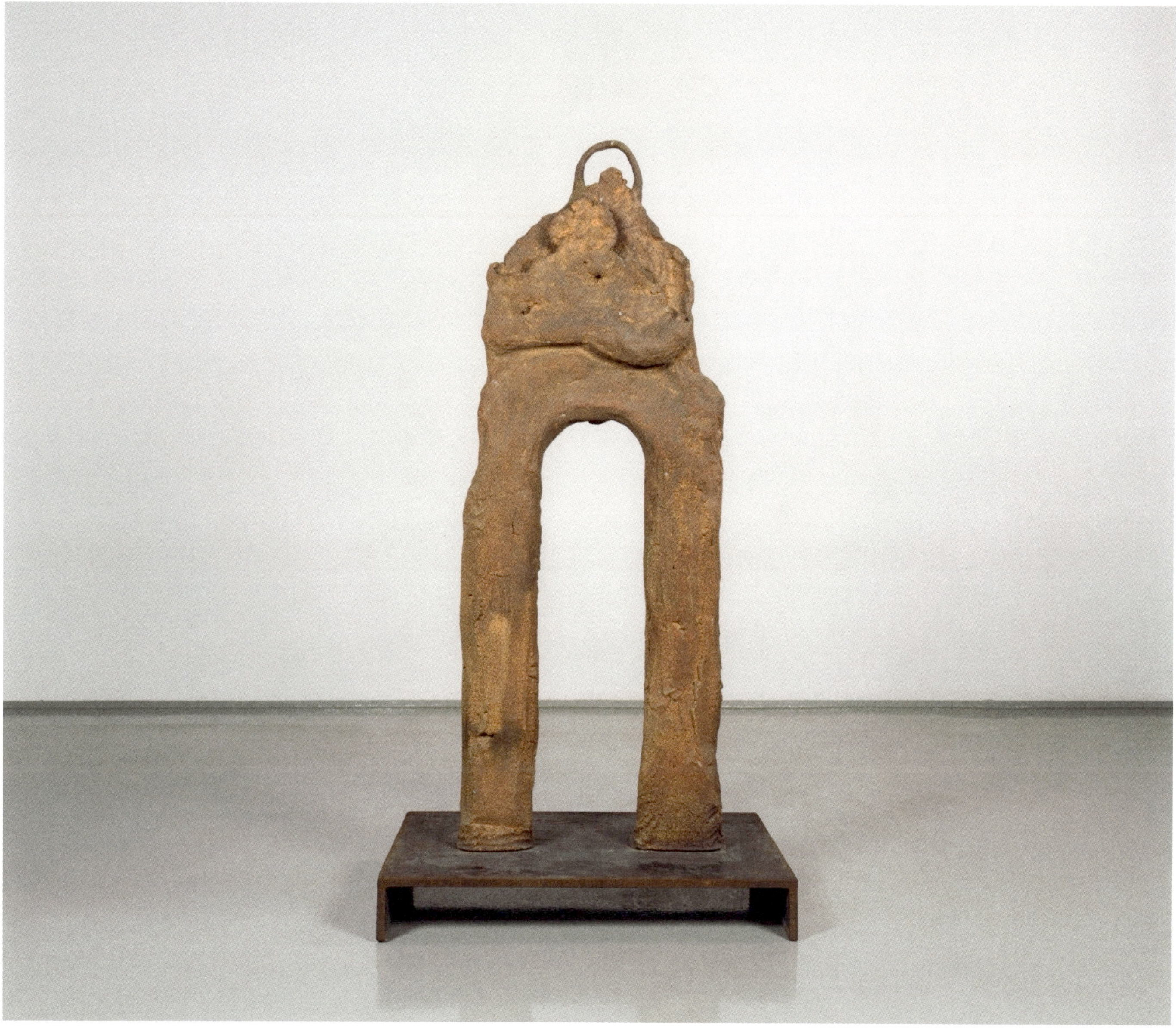

*Abdel Wahab*, 2006. Ton / Clay. 80 × 154,5 × 60 cm

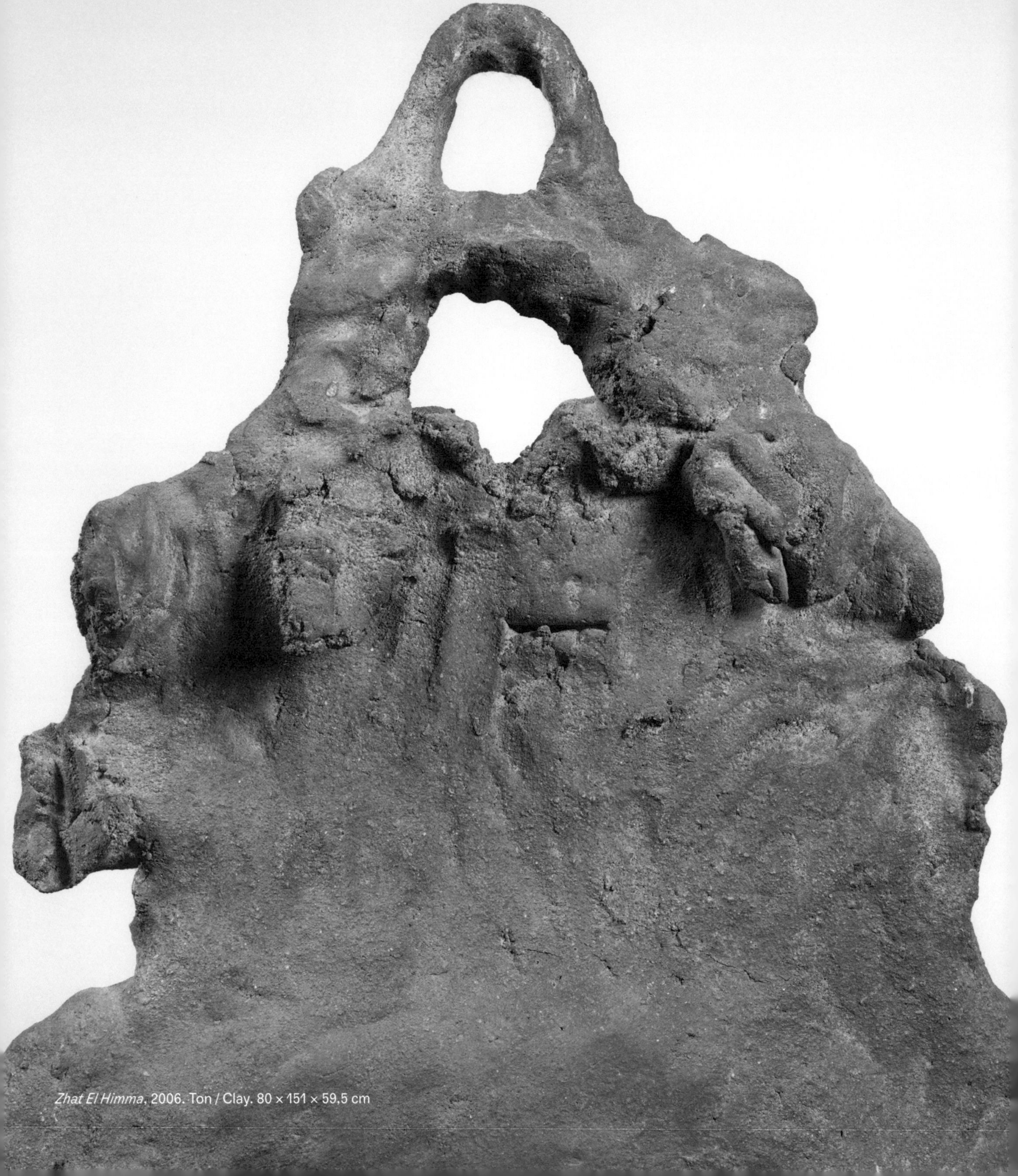

*Zhat El Himma*, 2006. Ton / Clay. 80 × 151 × 59,5 cm

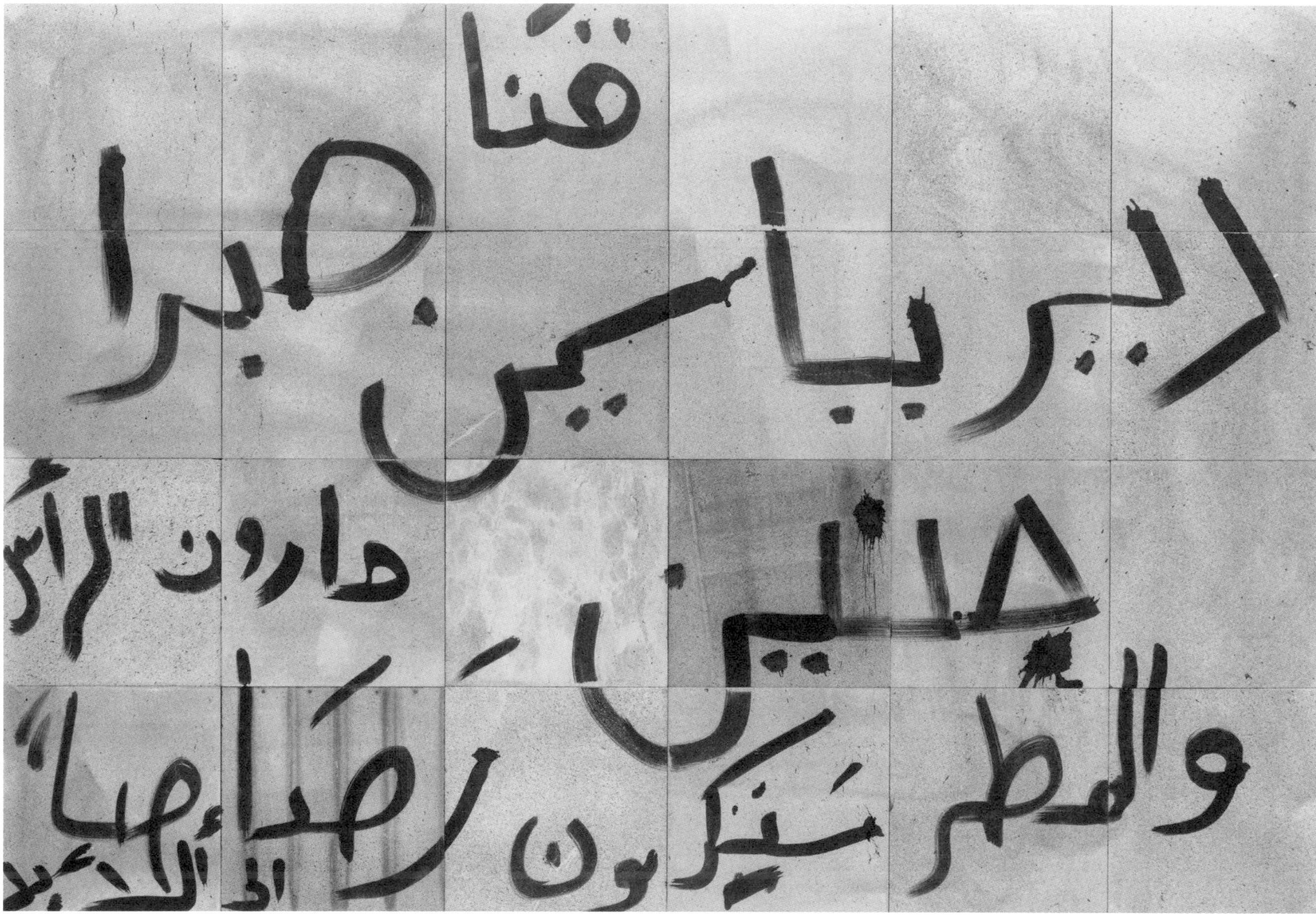

*In Our Lands of Drought the Rain Forever is made of Bullets / In unseren Ländern der Dürre besteht der Regen für ewige Zeiten aus Patronen*, 2006.
Lavastein / Lava stone. 300 × 200 cm

# Marcos Grigorian

*Eight of nine* („Acht von neun", 1964) ist aus acht Holzquadraten zusammengesetzt, die auf mit Sackleinen bedeckter Erde angeordnet sind. Bei diesem Musterbeispiel für Grigorians Beschäftigung mit der Kunstform Land Art sind die bemalten Oberflächen in erdigen Braun- und Burgundertönen ausgeführt, die an die hybriden bemalten skulpturalen Formen von Grigorians Freund und zeitweiligem Mitarbeiter Alberto Burri erinnern. Es scheint, als könnten sich die einzelnen Platten trotz ihrer präzisen Positionierung durch Raum und Zeit bewegen – die leere Stelle der imaginären neunten Platte ermöglicht die Aktivierung und Bewegung der anderen acht. *Eight of nine* gehört zu der berühmten Serie von Arbeiten mit Erde, die der Künstler zwischen den frühen 1960er und den 1980er Jahren geschaffen hat. Innerhalb dieser Serie gestaltete Grigorian verschiedene Reliefs aus natürlichen Materialien wie Erde, Sand, Schlamm und unkonservierten Lebensmitteln, wie sie für das Landleben im Iran charakteristisch sind. Zusammen bilden sie dreidimensionale Skulpturen, die man als lebendige Gebilde bezeichnen könnte.

Der armenisch-iranische Künstler Grigorian war allgemein für seine interdisziplinäre Arbeitsweise bekannt. Zu Lebzeiten gab er sich auch den Namen Marc Gregory. In seinen verschiedenen Rollen als Schauspieler, Filmemacher, Pädagoge, Kunsthändler und Künstler bewegte er sich zwischen den entsprechenden Welten – weil er es spannend fand, aber auch um sein Leben zu retten. Grigorian, der die meiste Zeit seines Lebens in der Diaspora verbrachte, schuf ein vielfältiges Werk mit figurativen und expressionistischen Gemälden, die er in kürzester Zeit aus preiswerten, oft alltäglichen Materialien fertigte. Sein Werk gilt posthum als ein wesentlicher Beitrag zur Land Art und zur politischen Abstraktion.

*Eight of nine* (1964) consists of eight wooden squares arranged atop burlap-covered earth. A prime example of Marcos Grigorian's interest in land art, the painted surfaces are earthy in tones of brown and burgundy, evocative of the hybrid painted sculptural forms of Grigorian's friend and sometime collaborator, Alberto Burri. Here, it appears as though there is room for the tiles to move, to traverse across space and time, against their precise designations—the empty expanse of the imagined ninth tile leaving a site of possible activation and movement. *Eight of nine* forms part of the artist's renowned series of earthworks, which were produced between the early 1960s and the 1980s. In these frames, Grigorian fashions assorted reliefs of natural ingredients, such as soil, sand, mud and unpreserved foodstuffs, which are representative of everyday life in rural Iran. Collectively, they construct structured three-dimensional sculptures that arguably could be considered living forms.

An Armenian Iranian artist, Grigorian was widely known as a polymath and also went by the name Marc Gregory during his lifetime. Embodying different identities—actor, filmmaker, educator and art dealer, in addition to artist—Grigorian traversed these worlds out of excitement as well as the necessity for survival. A diasporic citizen for most of his life, Grigorian produced a varied œuvre that features figurative and expressionistic paintings made hurriedly from inexpensive, often everyday, materials. Since his death, the artist's work has been interpreted as a vital contribution to the field of land art as well as political abstraction.

Omar Kholeif with Reem Sawan

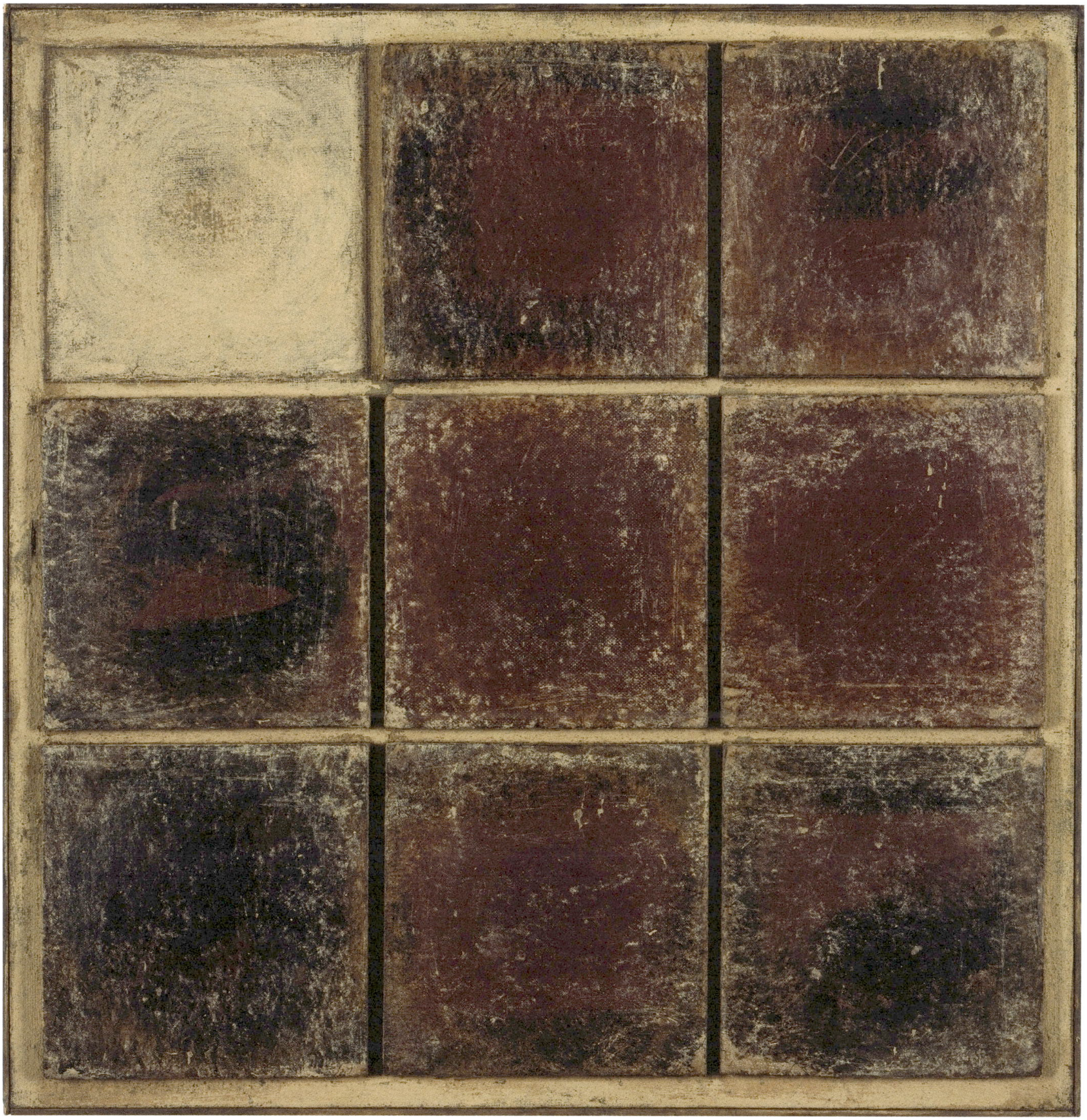

*Eight of nine / Acht von neun*, 1964. Acryl und Dichtungsmasse auf 8 Holzquadraten auf mit Sackleinen bedeckter Erde / Acrylic and sealant on 8 wooden tiles on earth compound on burlap. 99,4 × 99,2 cm

# Susan Hefuna

Die Werkserie von Susan Hefuna mit dem Titel *Building* („Gebäude“, 1991) besteht aus vollständig mit schwarzer Tinte eingefärbten Holzskulpturen. Über die Struktur verteilte weiße Punkte erzeugen einen Bruch. Die Skulpturen werden üblicherweise in Gebäudenischen – an einer Wand, einer Decke – installiert und erzeugen so eine impressionistische Landschaft von Auswüchsen – Stalaktiten der Fantasie – eine Fülle von Gittern, die aus dem Nichts zu kommen scheint. Zu ihrem Werk inspiriert haben Hefuna Erkundungen des gitterartigen Straßennetzes von New York City, das auf einem anschaulichen und einfachen, aber dicht gedrängten und überwältigenden Stadtkonzept beruht.

Die Gitterstruktur wird hier zusätzlich verstärkt und durch klassische Formen des islamischen Maschrabiyya durchbrochen, einem zur Abtrennung dienenden Gitterfenster. Die geschnitzten Holzfenster bieten Stadtbewohner*innen in ihren traditionellen „arabischen“ Häusern eine Möglichkeit der Belüftung und gleichzeitig ein gewisses Maß an Privatsphäre. Man könnte daraus schließen, dass sich die Künstlerin in ihrer gesamten abwechslungsreichen Karriere – sie schuf Zeichnungen, Gemälde, Performances und Installationen – diesen horizontalen und vertikalen Linien widmete, die für die Städte der Moderne in ihren Traumlandschaften so typisch sind. Häufig nimmt sie Bezug auf konkrete Orte, wie in London mit dem Projekt *On the Edgware Road* für die Serpentine Gallery, aber auch in Kairo oder in Deutschland, wo sie geboren wurde und noch heute lebt und arbeitet.

Die drei hier ausgestellten Objekte aus der Serie *Buildings* widmen sich der ästhetischen Erkundung durch Austausch und Beobachtung. Bei einer Installation im symbolträchtigen denkmalgeschützten Haus Bait Al Serkal in Sharjah platzierte die Künstlerin ihre Arbeiten in Nischen, als seien sie fest installierte Reliefs – ähnlich den gitterförmigen Strukturen, die traditionell in dieser Form der islamischen Architektur zu finden sind.

Sculptures of wood, doused in black ink, each painted precisely. White dots, scattered across these forms, generate a rupture. This series of works, titled *Building* (1991), is traditionally installed in the crevices of buildings (on a wall, within a ceiling) creating an impressionistic landscape of growths—stalactites of the imagination—a cornucopia of grids that seemingly appear from nowhere. Susan Hefuna's inspiration for these works, it has been noted, was an exploration of the grid system of New York City, an iconic, simple, but deeply congested and overwhelming urban plan.

The grid here becomes aggravated; it is ruptured by the invocation of the forms of the Islamic *mashrabiya*, a mesh window that acts as a sealant. It offers the city-dweller the possibility of ventilation whilst maintaining a modicum of privacy in traditional 'Arab' homes. We might infer that the horizonal and vertical lines that characterise the modernist cities of Hefuna's dreamscapes have been explored throughout the artist's career, an expansive one realised through drawing, painting, performance and installation. She often responds to specific sites, as in London for the Serpentine Gallery's Edgware Road Project, or in Cairo, or indeed, in Germany, where she was born and continues to live and work.

The three renderings of *Buildings* presented here offer an aesthetic exploration developed through both exchange and observation. At one point, when they were installed and situated in Sharjah's iconic heritage house, Bait Al Serkal, the artist placed these pieces in crevices, such that they resembled permanent reliefs—not unlike the latticed shapes that cohere to the tradition of this form of Islamic architecture.

Omar Kholeif with Reem Sawan

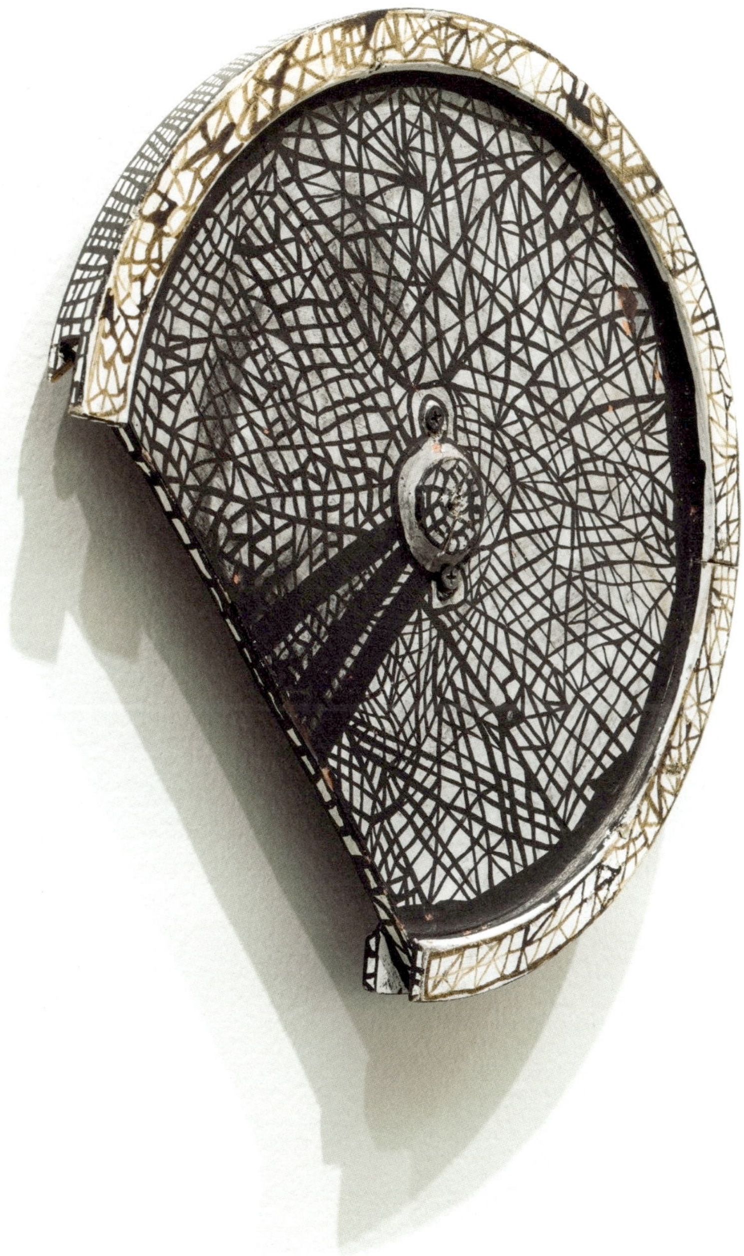

*Building | Gebäude*, 1991. Skulptur, Holz, Tinte / Sculpture, wood, ink. 26 × 31 × 5 cm

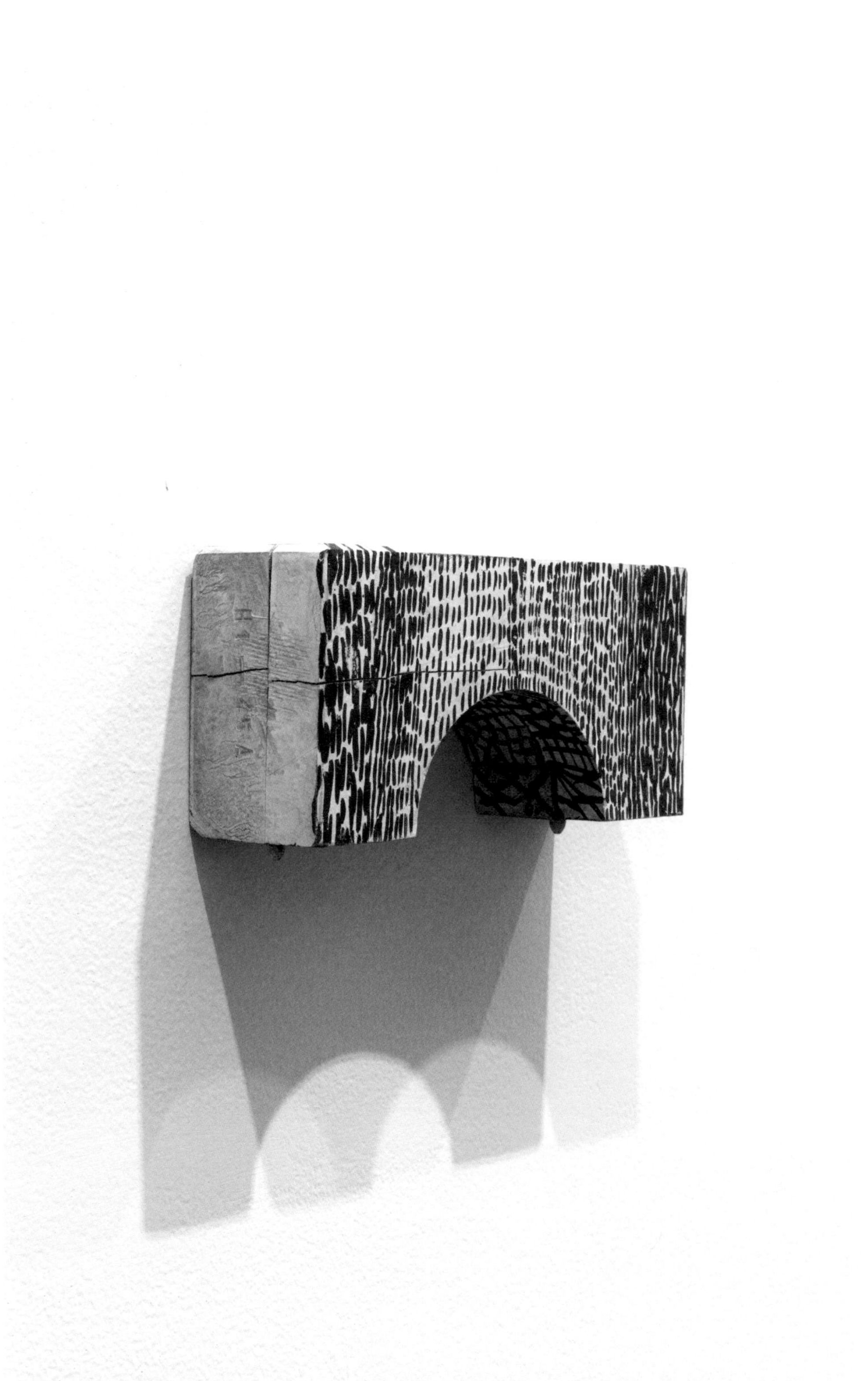

*Building / Gebäude*, 1991. Skulptur, Holz, Tinte / Sculpture, wood, ink. 27,5 × 18,5 × 14 cm

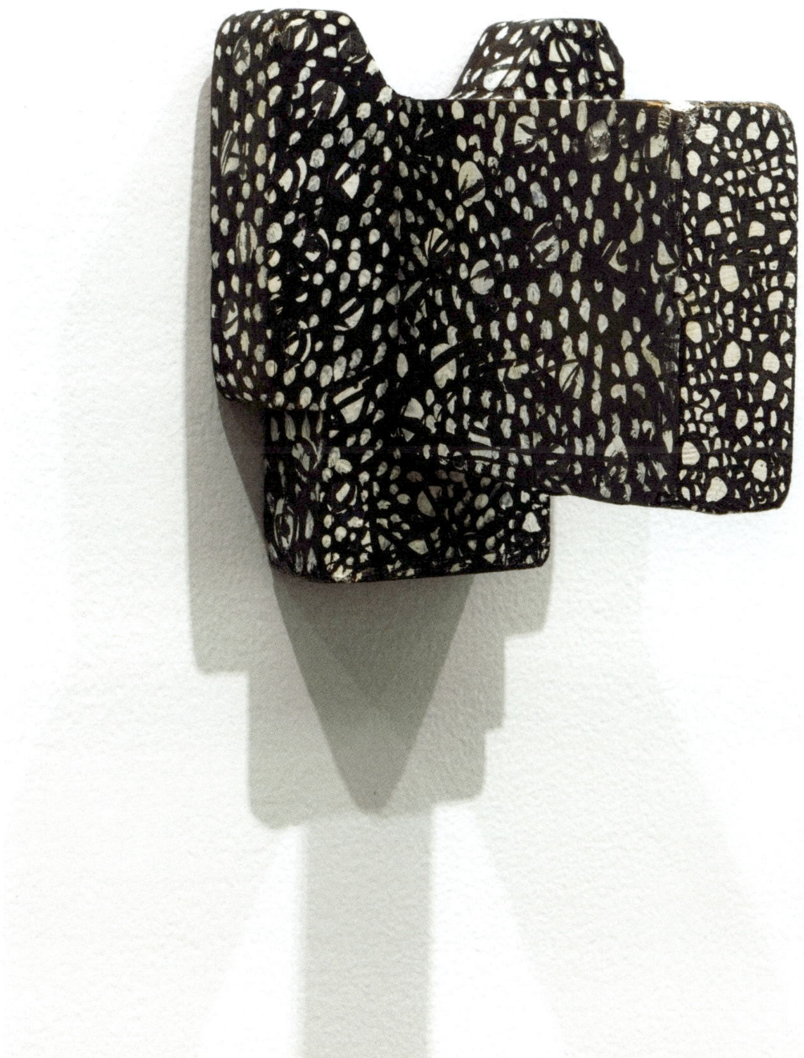

*Building | Gebäude*, 1991. Skulptur, Holz, Tinte / Sculpture, wood, ink. 17,5 × 23 × 26 cm

# Adam Henein

Der renommierte Zeichner Adam Henein wurde in Kairo als Sohn einer ursprünglich aus Assiut stammenden Metallarbeiterfamilie geboren. Er zählt zu den herausragendsten Künstlerpersönlichkeiten Ägyptens. Zu Lebzeiten war er vor allem für seine Mitwirkung an der Restaurierung der Großen Sphinx von Gizeh bekannt – der mythischen Kalksteinstatue eines liegenden Löwen mit Menschenkopf, die zu Ehren des Pharaos Khafre errichtet worden war.

Nach seinem Abschluss in Bildhauerei 1953 wollte er vor allem die formalen Grenzen der Skulptur ausloten und erweitern. Er schuf lebensgroße Figuren aus vielen unterschiedlichen Materialien. Aus grobem Granit, Stein und Marmor gestaltete er – inspiriert von Legenden und Hieroglyphen – mystisch anmutende Tiere. Überdimensionale Eulen als Symbole der Weisheit wurden zu einem immer wiederkehrenden Motiv, ebenso seine fast schon lebhaften menschlichen Körper, die sich lang gen Himmel strecken und den Eindruck von Erhabenheit vermitteln.

Im Jahre 1971 ging Adam Henein nach Paris. Dort widmete er sich der Malerei eleganter Formen auf Papyrus, einem altägyptischen Papier aus dem Mark einer Wasserpflanze. Diese im gesamten Mittelmeerraum verbreiteten Faserbögen sind porös und hauchdünn – so zart, dass Tinte und Aquarellfarbe auf die Rückseite durchfließen. Ihre Materialität steht für die mythologische Tradition, in der Papyrus mit Hieroglyphen und anderen in Ägypten beheimateten kulturellen Darstellungsformen assoziiert wird. In Heineins Werken saugt das Papier die von ihm aufgetragenen Aquarellfarben, die Tempera, auf. Dabei bilden sich amorphe Abstraktionen, die aus heutiger Sicht wie ein Akt des Widerstands gegen die Kunst der Moderne im damaligen Ägypten anmuten. Der Künstler arbeitete jenseits des Mainstreams und entzog sich den figürlichen Strömungen, die in der damaligen Kunstszene seiner Heimat vorherrschten.

Nach 25 Jahren in Paris kehrte Henein in den 1990er Jahren nach Ägypten zurück. Im Jahr 2014 wurde ihm zu Ehren ein Museum in Kairo eröffnet. Kurz vor seinem Tod 2020 veranstaltete die Sharjah Art Foundation eine Retrospektive seines Werks: Die Ausstellung *Lasting Impressions* („Bleibende Eindrücke"), die sich über beide Flügel des Sharjah Art Museums erstreckte, präsentierte das Leben und Werk eines Künstlers, der von einem unbändigen Forscherdrang und schier unersättlichem Wissensdurst erfüllt war.

Widely recognised as a draughtsman, Adam Henein, one of Egypt's emblematic artistic figures, was popularly known in his lifetime for assisting with a partial restoration of the Great Sphinx of Giza, the mythical limestone statue of a stationary human with the body of a lion, honouring the pharaoh Khafre. Born Samuel Henein to a family of metalworkers in Cairo who originally hailed from Assiut, the artist's formative training was completed in 1953 when he received a degree in sculpture.

Henein's concerns shifted to contouring and expanding the formal limits of sculpture, producing life-size figures using an assortment of materials. Coarse granite, stone, and marble were deployed to form mystical-looking animals, conjured from legend and hieroglyphs. Oversized owls, bearers of wisdom, became a recurring motif, as did his seemingly buoyant human bodies: elongated, stretching to the sky, a feeling of transcendence arrives. In 1971, the artist moved to Paris, where he began his devoted act of painting shapely forms on papyrus, an ancient Egyptian paper gleaned from the pithy stem of a water plant. These sheets of fibre, used throughout the Mediterranean, are porous and delicate—so fragile that ink and watercolour seep through their very form. Their materiality is representative of the mythological tradition linked with papyrus's associations to hieroglyphics, among other cultural forms native to Egypt. Here, the paper imbibes the watercolours, the tempera, applied by the artist. The resulting artworks present amorphous abstractions, which when looked at through the lens of the present, seem akin to an act of resistance within the modernist art from his nation at the time. Henein was working against the grain, avoiding the figurative tendencies that were dominant at the time in his home country.

After 25 years in Paris, Henein returned to Egypt in the 1990s. In 2014, a museum opened in his honour in Cairo. Shortly before his death in 2020, Sharjah Art Foundation staged a retrospective of his work at the Sharjah Art Museum. Taking over both wings of the institution, *Lasting Impressions* surveyed the life and work of an artist whose inquisitive nature was boundless—constantly consumed by his curiousity.

Omar Kholeif

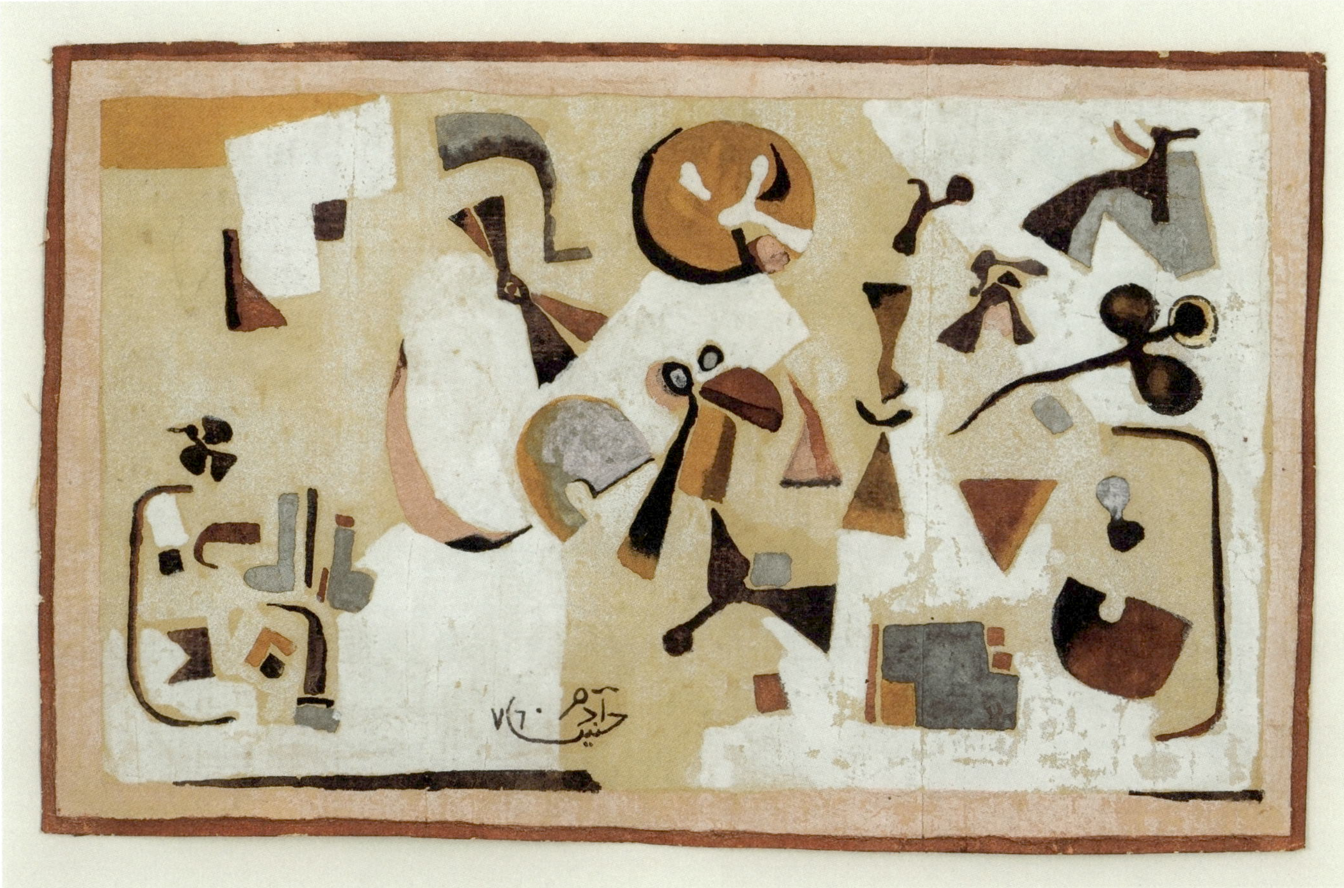


*Falling Flowers* | *Fallende Blumen*, 1976. Papyrus. 35,7 × 22 cm

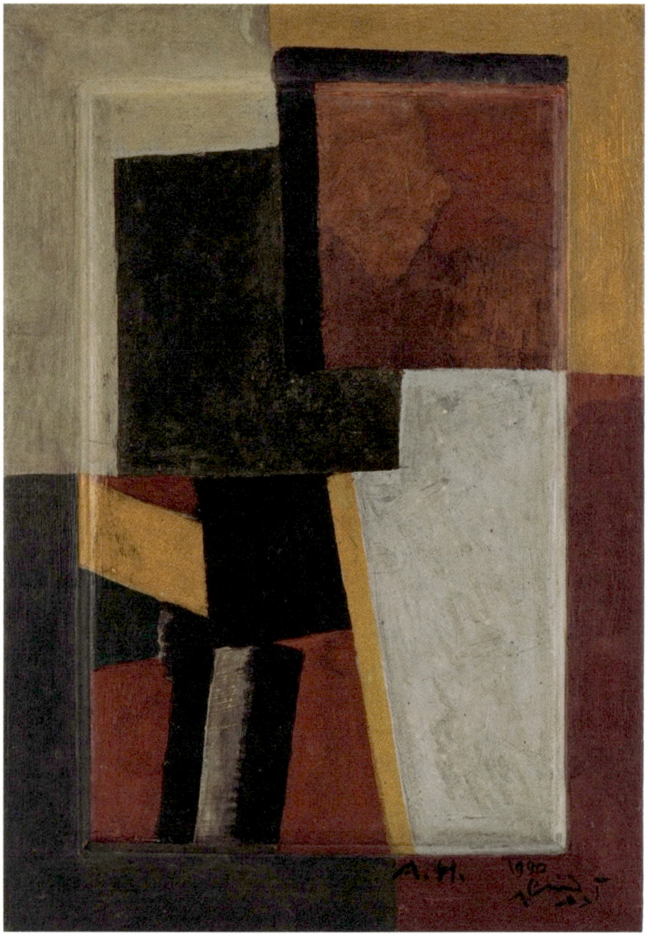


*Untitled | Ohne Titel*, 1990. Tempera auf Papyrus / Tempera on papyrus. 26 × 36,6 cm

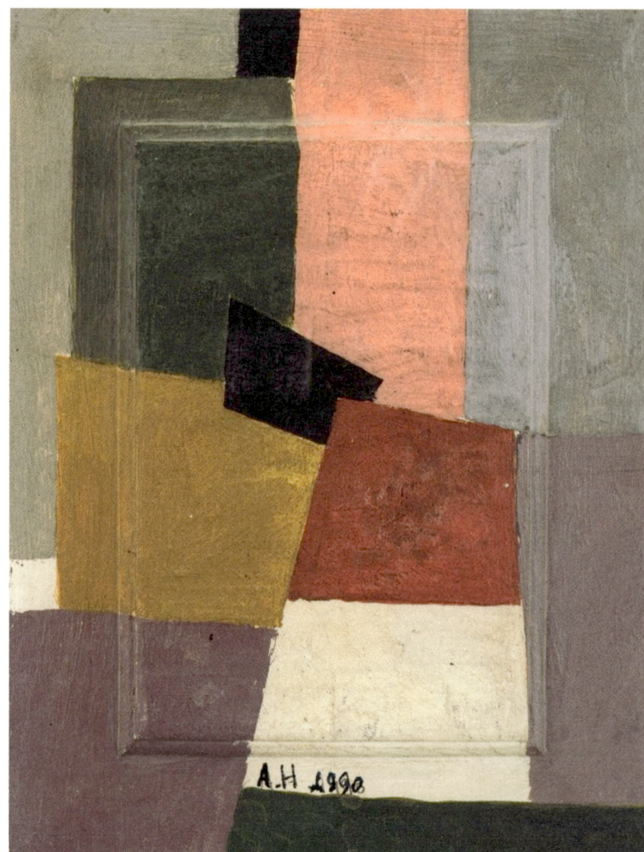


*Untitled | Ohne Titel*, 1990. Tempera auf Papyrus / Tempera on papyrus. 18,2 × 23,5 cm

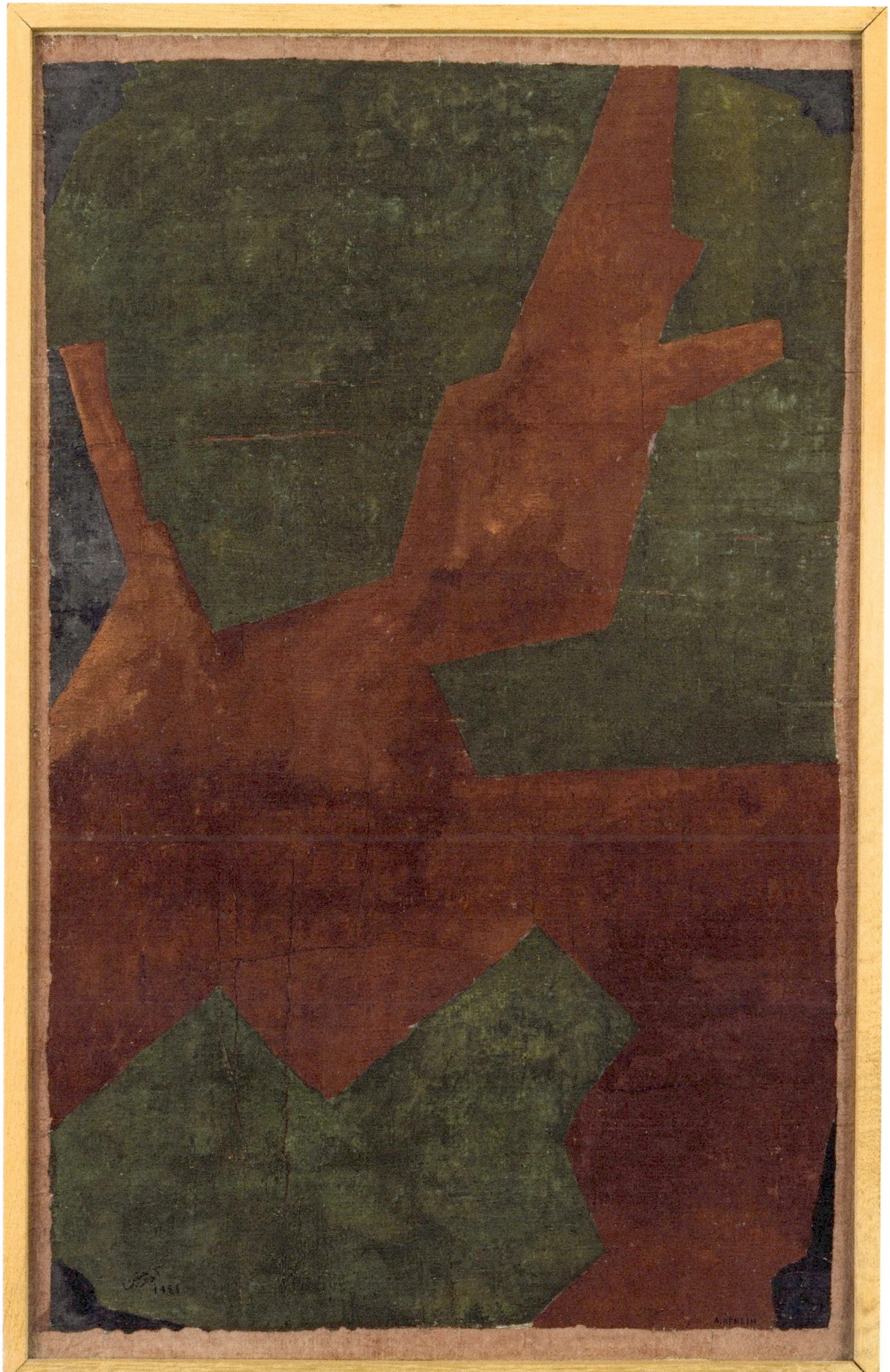

*Obligatory Silence* / *Vorgeschriebene Ruhe*, 1986. Natürliche Pigmente, Gummiarabikum auf Papyrus / Natural pigments, acacia gum on papyrus. 91 × 134,1 cm

# Lubaina Himid

Mit der Überführung individueller Erinnerungen in ein „kollektives“ Gedenken versuchen Staaten, ihre Macht oder ihren Einfluss über ihre eigene Sphäre hinaus zu manifestieren. Dem liegt die Absicht der Administration zugrunde, die von ihr vertretenen positiven Werte zu vernetzen und zu reproduzieren.

Indem Lubaina Himid in die vermeintlich hermetische kulturelle Erinnerung des weißen Westens eindringt, verschränkt sie das Schwarze Trauma und die transatlantische Sklaverei mit Aspekten, die sonst nicht in das (Geschichts-)Bewusstsein Einlass gefunden hätten.

Himids Arbeit zieht ans Licht, was sonst aus dem öffentlichen Leben getilgt worden wäre. Sie betont wichtige Details aus dem Leben von Schwarzen Menschen, denen nach wie vor kein Platz im öffentlichen Bewusstsein eingeräumt wird. Die Künstlerin hingegen taucht sie in einen Farbenreichtum, der die lebendige und strahlende Bedeutung dessen bekräftigt, was verloren gegangen ist. „Wenn das Mahnmal ein Mahnmal für den Beitrag ist, den Schwarze Menschen zu jedem einzelnen Aspekt der westlichen Kultur leisten, dann braucht es ein solches Mahnmal. Ich habe es satt, in einer Kultur zu leben, in der dieser Beitrag unsichtbar gemacht wird“, erklärt Himid.

Die multimediale Arbeit *Bone in the China: Success to the Africa Trade* („Knochen im Porzellan: Erfolg dem afrikanischen Sklavenhandel“, 1985) verbindet die zentralen Themen der Künstlerin. Eine kreisrunde, heraldisch anmutende Scheibe ist zart mit den propagandistischen Zeilen „Success to the Africa Trade“ beschrieben. Die Scheibe thront auf der neoklassizistischen Form einer aus dem Gleichgewicht geratenen kannelierten Säule, deren Sockel mit dem titelgebenden Knochen abgerundet wird – eine Andeutung darauf, wie viele Leben ihre Errichtung gekostet hat. Die Säule ist von vielen kleinen schwarzen Scheiben umgeben, die sie vermeintlich beschweren. Deren Inschrift lautet „Unsere Erinnerungen, unsere Heldinnen, unsere Beiträge, unsere Kreativität“. Das Werk entstand als Reaktion auf eine Punsch-Schale, die der Künstlerin in einem Museum im englischen Stoke-on-Trent auffiel und die den afrikanischen Sklavenhandel feiert.

Lubaina Himid erstellt Gegennarrative zu den verzerrten Darstellungen der Kolonialkriege und der gewaltsamen Unterdrückung von indigenem Leben. Zudem bieten ihre Werke auch eine potenzielle Neupositionierung des heutigen Lebens jenseits der festgefahrenen Grenzen und des Erbes weißer Vorherrschaft.

The passage of memory into what might be termed a 'collective' memorial is predicated on a state's aim to extend the grip of its power or influence beyond the span of a lifetime. It also demonstrates an attempt to cohere and reproduce a state's revered values around it. Stepping into this otherwise seemingly sealed space of white Western cultural recollection, Lubaina Himid's work entangles Black trauma and transatlantic slavery into subjects that have otherwise remained beyond the place of history and consciousness. By returning to what has otherwise been expunged from public life, Himid's work actively makes manifest the meaningful details of Black lives that continue to be erased, emblazoning them with a material richness of colour that reaffirms the vivid, shimmering sense of what has been lost. As Himid asserts: 'If the memorial is a memorial to the contribution that Black people make to every single aspect of Western culture, then it's a memorial worth making. I'm sick and tired of living in a culture where that contribution is invisibilised'.

The mixed-media work *Bone in the China: Success to the Africa Trade* (1985) brings together core themes of Himid's work. A herald-like circular disc is delicately painted with the propagandistic line 'Success to the Africa Trade' and sits atop the neo-classical form of an off-balance fluted column, its base pointedly rendered as the titular bone, hinting at the lives taken to support the resulting edifice. Numerous small black discs surround the column, as if weighting down the structure, and are inscribed with 'our memories, our heroines, our contributions, our creativity'. The work was produced in response to a punch bowl the artist witnessed in a museum in Stoke-on-Trent, England, which celebrated the African slave trade.

Into the absence of usable paths, which have hereto obscured the consequences of colonial wars and violent suppression of indigenous lives, Himid conjures not only the depiction of counter-narratives but also the speculative repositioning of lives beyond the reaches of entrenched forms of white supremacy and its legacies today.

Chris McCormack

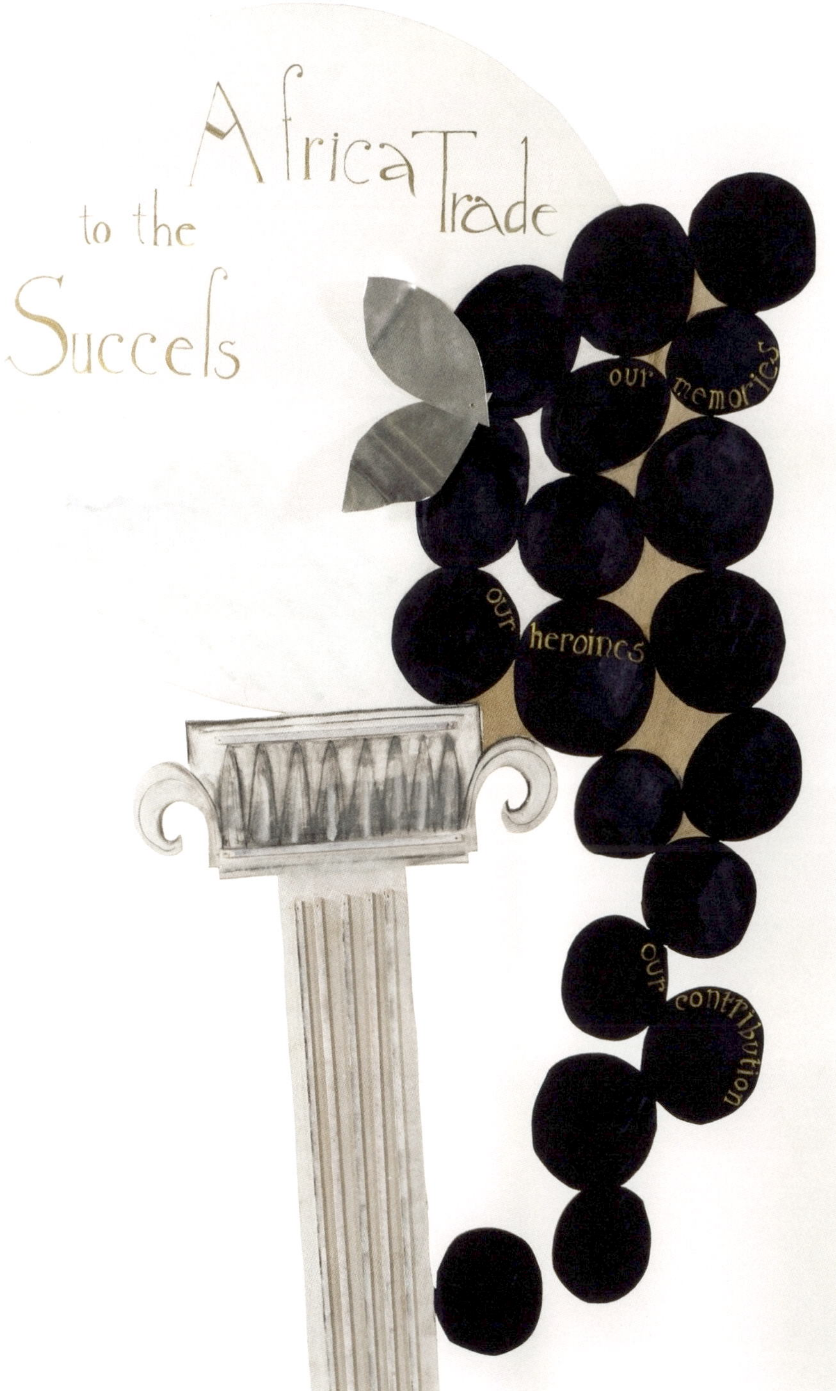


*Bone in the China: Success to the Africa Trade* | *Knochen im Porzellan: Erfolg für den afrikanischen Sklavenhandel*, 1985. Holzkonstruktion, Acryl auf Sperrholz mit Aluminium, Acryl auf Leinwand / Wooden construction, acrylic on plywood with aluminium, acrylic on canvas. 122 × 244 × 270 cm

# Ali Kazim

Die Maler des indischen Subkontinents übten sich im 18. und 19. Jahrhundert in den Techniken des ausgehenden Mogulreichs. Sie fertigten detaillierte Porträts vor sorgfältig komponierten Hintergründen aus ineinander verschlungenen einheimischen Blumen, Vögeln, Tieren und Blätterdächern. Dieser Stil entwickelte sich in der Kolonialzeit, denn viele der Künstler gehörten der Company School an, die aus dem *East India Company College* hervorgegangen war, und erhielten Aufträge nach den Vorlieben des Empires. Der pakistanische Maler Ali Kazim stellt dieses Genre geschickt auf den Kopf: Das mit Aquarellpigmenten auf Papier gemalte Bild *Untitled (The Bird Hunter Series II)* („Ohne Titel, Vogelfängerserie II") ist ein Porträt vor flächigem, einfarbigem Hintergrund. Der Oberkörper des Dargestellten mit glatten Schlüsselbeinen und gewölbten Muskeln ist nackt, sein einziger Schmuck ein Vogel, der wie eine Maske auf seinem zerzausten braunen Haar thront. Eines seiner Augen blickt zwischen luftig gemalten Federn hervor und fängt den Blick der Betrachtenden sofort ein. Kazim durchbricht die vierte Wand. Er stellt die Motive des Werks frei. Hier ist eine rätselhafte Geschichte im Spiel, die nur entschlüsseln kann, wer Fragen stellt. Die Pinselstriche sind zart, filigran und zugleich entschlossen. Mit den dunklen Federn um den dottergelben Schnabel könnte der Vogel ein weißer Silberreiher sein, ein Zugvogel, der von Sibirien aus auf den Subkontinent fliegt. Kazim ist ein raffinierter Klassizist, der seine Technik jedoch auf die Gegenwart anwendet. So strahlt sein Bild auch eine Verletzlichkeit aus, die den hauchdünnen Schichten von Aquarellfarbe und Tusche auf dem Papier geschuldet ist, das der Künstler abschließend noch einmal wässert. Kazim bedient sich zudem der Technik der Mogul-Miniatur: Nach dem Malen taucht er seinen dünnsten Pinsel in schwarze Tinte und fährt damit über das Bild – ein Verfahren, das Siya Qalam heißt (der letzte Schritt, wörtlich: schwarze Schreibfeder). Die Linienführung des Künstlers ist weich und überzeugt auf sanfte Weise, jedes Werk zeigt einen zarten und intensiven Augenblick.

The 18th- and 19th-century painters of the Indian subcontinent trained in late Mughal techniques, making immaculate portraits of people in highly composed scenes of intertwined native flowers, birds, animals and leafy canopy. There was a colonial impulse to this; many were a part of the 'Company School', which emerged after the East India Company College, and were commissioned to suit the eyes of empire. Pakistani painter Ali Kazim elegantly turns this genre on its head: the watercolour pigment on paper *Untitled (The Bird Hunter Series II)* (2020) is a portrait set against a flat, single-colour backdrop. Its protagonist's torso is bare—all smooth collarbones, curved muscle—and all that adorns him is a bird, placed atop his ruffled brown hair, like a mask. One's eye peers from between the lightly painted feathers, and it locks immediately with the viewer of the painting. Kazim breaks the fourth wall and abstracts the subjects of the work. There is narrative at play here: in part mysterious, and in part to be decoded only if you ask more questions. The brushstrokes are fine, delicate and purposeful. The bird could be a white egret, characterised by the darkened feathers that encase its yolk-yellow beak; it's a migratory bird that flies into the subcontinent down from Siberia. Kazim is a refined classicist, but one that thrusts technique right into a contemporary moment. There is also vulnerability, encased in the filmy nature of how paint ink and paint dry onto paper—intensely set through the eventual soaking of thin layers of watercolour wash, as is Kazim's process. He also borrows from the Mughal miniaturists, and after painting, he will dip the thinnest brush in black ink and go over the image, the *siya qalam* (the last step, meaning literally 'black pen'). The artist's use of line is soft and gently persuasive, each work a moment of tender saturation.

Skye Arundhati Thomas

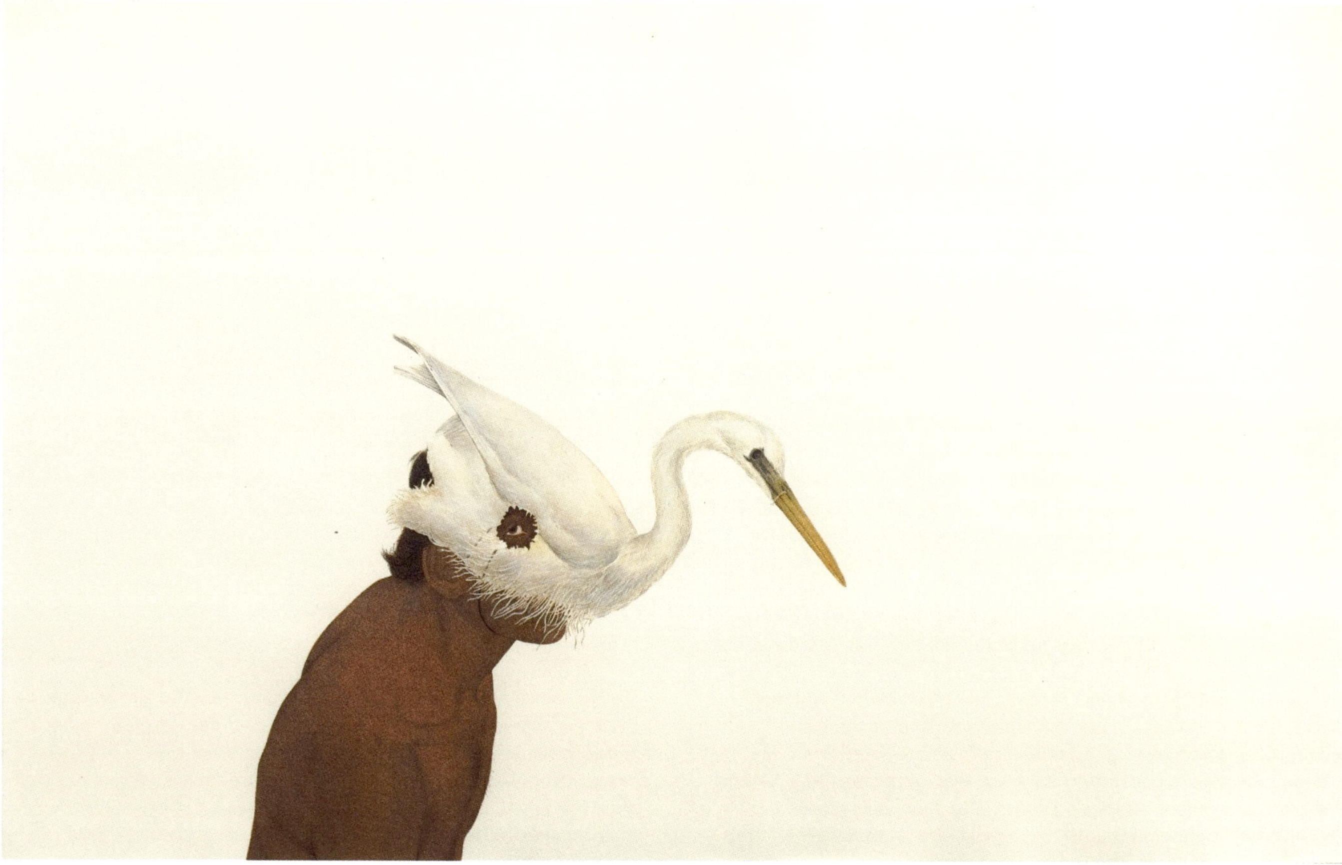

*Untitled (The Bird Hunter Series II) | Ohne Titel (Vogelfängerserie II)*, 2020. Aquarellpigmente auf Papier / Watercolour pigments on paper. 114 × 70 cm

# Aisha Khalid

Auf den ersten Blick erscheint *Kashmiri Shawl* (2011) – ein großflächiger, schwerer Pashmina im Hochformat – wie ein exquisites dekoratives Kunstwerk in Schwarz-Gold. Die traditionelle Webarbeit aus Ziegenwolle zeigt klassische Muster aus Kaschmir, der umkämpften nördlichsten Region des sogenannten Subkontinents.

Naturmotive auf der Vorderseite des Werkes stehen für die rauschenden Feste der lokalen adligen Oberschicht. In Abwandlungen tauchen diese Muster auf Tüchern in aller Welt wieder auf, beispielsweise auf den im Westen beliebten Paisley-Schals. Auf der Rückseite des Kunstwerks bietet sich ein widersprüchliches Bild von Gewalt und Verfall: Aus einem roten Stoffuntergrund ragen 360.000 vergoldete Stahlstifte hervor, die auch auf den heiklen Prozess der Gestaltung des Goldmusters auf der Vorderseite verweisen.

In einem arbeitsintensiven Verfahren wird jede einzelne Nadel von Hand durch vier Gewebeschichten geführt. Normalerweise widmet sich die Künstlerin dieser spirituellen und meditativen Aufgabe allein. Für die gigantische Arbeit an ihrem *Kashmiri Shawl* heuerte sie jedoch Unterstützung an. So konnte sie auch den sozialen Aspekt in ihren Produktionsprozess einbeziehen, den sie selbst als kollektive *Chikankari*-Stickarbeit bezeichnet. Ein ganzes Team war nur für die Vergoldung der einzelnen Nadeln zuständig. Diese mühselige und monotone Tätigkeit findet ihren Ausdruck im dichotomischen Charakter des Werks: Auf der Vorderseite präsentiert sich ein vorzügliches Kunstwerk, auf der Rückseite eine Referenz an in Blut getränkte schmerzvolle und traumatische Erfahrungen. Beide Seiten erzählen unmittelbar von der bewegten Geschichte Kaschmirs. Sowohl die aufwendige Handarbeit als auch der traumatische Alltag in der Region, wo die Pashminas hergestellt werden, erhalten in unserer Konsumwelt viel zu selten die gebührende Aufmerksamkeit.

In ihren Gemälden, Textilarbeiten und Videos begreift Aisha Khalid Tradition als wandelbares und veränderliches Konzept. Sie entwirft ausgefeilte Muster von nahezu erhabener Schönheit, jedoch mit sichtbaren Lücken, um ein Gefühl von Verlust oder Abwesenheit zu vermitteln. Das Tuch wechselt im wörtlichen wie im übertragenen Sinne den Kontext und dient so der Kritik an der Ignoranz gegenüber seinem Ursprungsort. Zudem leistet das Werk einen Beitrag zum anhaltenden Dialog über den Neuen Materialismus (oder den „Material Turn“, die Wende zum Material) in der zeitgenössischen Kunst: Es geht um die Interpretation von Kunstwerken auch aus soziopolitischer oder ökologischer Sicht und um den Übergang von der Konzeption zur Rezeption, wie es Arjun Appadurai in seiner Theorie nahelegt: „Wir müssen den Dingen selbst folgen.“

At first, *Kashmiri Shawl* (2011), a large-scale, vertical, heavy pashmina, appears as a luxurious black-and-gold decorative artwork. The traditional pattern outlined on goat wool references the Kashmir region—the contested, northernmost geographical region of what is often referred to as the 'subcontinent'.

Motifs from nature on one side of the work represent the luxurious celebrations held by local nobility, variations of which have been appropriated into patterns in shawls across the globe, such as fashionable paisley shawls in the West. The other side of the shawl reveals a contradiction: here, 360,000 gold-plated steel pins protrude from red fabric, evoking an image of violence and disrepair, which also exposes the hazardous process of the creation of the gold pattern on the reverse.

Aisha Khalid's labour-intensive process involved inserting each pin by hand through four layers of fabric, a spiritual and meditative experience that is usually completed by the artist alone. For the gargantuan task of composing *Kashmiri Shawl*, the artist hired a team of collaborators, embracing the social aspect of production, for what she has referred to as a generative process of collective *chikan kari*-style embroidery. A separate team plated each individual pin with gold. The arduous and repetitive actions of making serve to highlight a dichotomy, the exquisiteness of the one side juxtaposed against the intimation of the blood-soaked pain or trauma on the other, both of which directly reference the experience of Kashmir's fraught history. Both the extensive work and the traumatic realities of life in the region of Kashmir, where the pashminas are produced, are expressions the average global consumer rarely considers.

Khalid's practice across painting, textile and video sees tradition as adaptive and responsive; embracing the space of the sublime, she concocts rich patterns, which leave visible space for voids that intimate loss or absence. As the shawl literally and metaphorically changes context to critique the ignorance around its place of origin, it also functions to elucidate contemporary art's ongoing dialogue with new materialism (or the 'material turn'). This focuses on expanded interpretations of artworks across the social-political and environmental, and from conception to reception, as Arjun Appadurai's theory proposes, 'we have to follow the things themselves'.

Sarah Perks

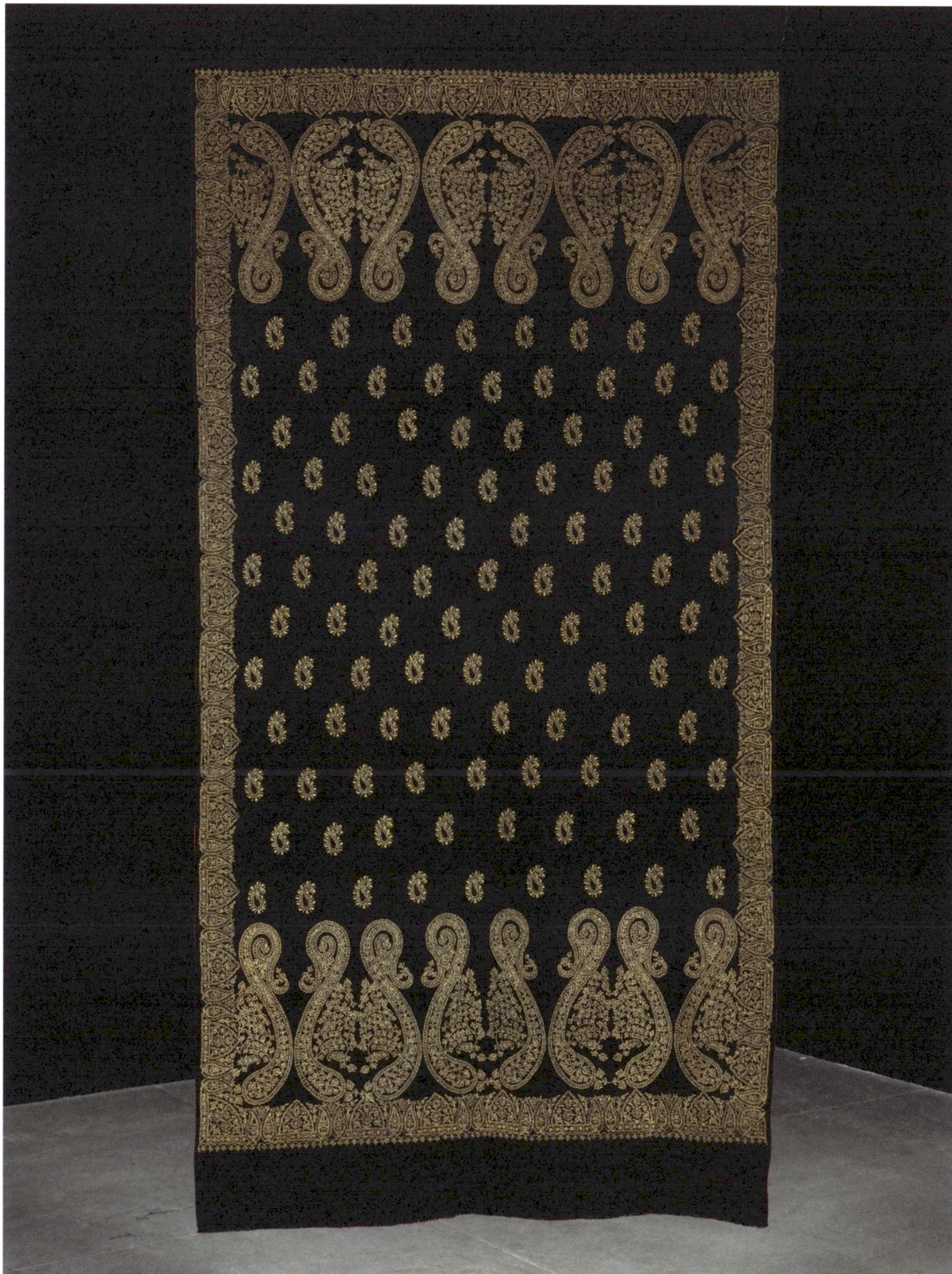

*Kashmiri Shawl* / *Kaschmir-Schal*, 2011. Pashmina-Schals, vergoldete Stahlstifte / Pashmina shawls, gold-plated steel pins. 129,54 × 256,54 cm. Im Auftrag der Sharjah Art Foundation / Commissioned by Sharjah Art Foundation

# David Koloane

„Die durch das Apartheidregime geschaffenen gesellschaftspolitischen Bedingungen“, so der südafrikanische Künstler David Koloane in einem Interview mit *artnews*, „haben die *Conditio humana* zum unverrückbaren Dreh- und Angelpunkt meiner Arbeit gemacht.“ *Untitled (The Moon Over Hillbrow Tower)* („Ohne Titel – Der Mond über dem Hillbrow Tower“, 1998–2010) ist eine Arbeit in Öl und Mischtechnik auf Leinwand, in der Koloane mit dem für ihn typischen schroffen Pinselstrich die Silhouetten der Hochhäuser im Johannesburger Stadtteil Hillbrow nachzeichnet. Im Mittelpunkt der Szenerie steht der gleichnamige 90-stöckige Turm – einst das höchste Gebäude in ganz Afrika und weit über die Grenzen der Stadt hinaus zu sehen. Hillbrow gilt als einer der lebhaftesten Bezirke Johannesburgs. Zunächst war der Turm nach Premierminister J. G. Strijdom benannt, einem erklärten Verfechter der weißen Vorherrschaft, der die Apartheidpolitik in den frühen 1950er Jahren aktiv vorantrieb. Beim Treason Trial, einem fünfjährigen Gerichtsprozess gegen eine Gruppe verhafteter Aktivisten – darunter Nelson Mandela –, die des Landesverrats beschuldigt wurden, war Strijdom seit 1956 federführend gewesen. Koloane wählte das Motiv seines Gemäldes also ganz bewusst: Über Hillbrow leuchtet ein strahlend weißer Mond.

In seinen Werken verarbeitet der Künstler seine persönlichen Erfahrungen mit zwei Gesetzen, die für besonders willkürliche Formen der Rassentrennung in Südafrika standen: der Group Areas Act („Gruppengebietsgesetz“) und der Separate Amenities Act („Gesetz über getrennte Einrichtungen“). Erst mit Mitte dreißig betrat er zum ersten Mal ein Kunstmuseum. Viele seiner Werke sind düster und schemenhaft, in einer Art expressionistischem Stil gemalt, der dynamisch und kraftvoll die diffuse, finstere Brutalität der eigenen Segregationserfahrung einfängt. Koloane verwendet vornehmlich satte Rot- und Brauntöne sowie stahlgraue Schattierungen, die an die Metallzäune der Stadt und den Rost in ihren Straßen erinnern. Man könnte fast sagen, dass er sich dabei stets einer aktiven Verarbeitung des Raumkonflikts widmet: In einem Interview mit Kritiker Ivor Powell im Jahr 1995 bemerkte er: „Die Apartheid war vor allem anderen eine Politik des Raums.“ Auf den oft dicht bemalten Leinwänden des Künstlers ist die Bewegung gehemmt, es herrscht eine bedrückende und klaustrophobische Atmosphäre. Obwohl seine Werke von Einschränkungen erzählen, sind sie von hoher Dringlichkeit – rastlos, energiegeladen, an der Schwelle zur Revolution.

‘The socio-political conditions created by the apartheid system of government’, said South African artist David Koloane in an interview with *ARTnews*, ‘transfixed the human condition as the axis around which my work evolves’. *Untitled (The Moon Over Hillbrow Tower)* (1998–2010) is an oil and mixed-media work on canvas in which Koloane’s characteristic scraggly lines silhouette the high-rises of Johannesburg’s Hillbrow neighbourhood. At the centre of this scene is the 90-storey eponymous tower, once the tallest structure in all of Africa, that can still be spotted far beyond the city’s limits. Hillbrow is known as one of the city’s most turbulent districts; the tower was first named after Prime Minister JG Strijdom, an open white supremacist who actively strengthened apartheid policies in the early 1950s. When the 1956 Treason Trial took place—during which a group of activists, including Nelson Mandela, were arrested and tried over five years—Strijdom oversaw them. Koloane thus chose the subject of this painting carefully; over Hillbrow, a slinky white moon gleams.

Koloane’s practice negotiates his own lived experiences routing through the Group Areas Act and the Separate Amenities Act—two crucial pieces of legislature that kept the most arbitrary distinctions of apartheid in place. The artist, himself, only entered an art museum for the first time in his mid-30s. Many of the artist’s works are shaded and misty, a kind of Expressionist style of painting that captures—with dynamism and vigour—the uncertain, shadowed brutalities of the lived experience of segregation. His palette is dominated by richly steeped reds and browns, as well as steely greys that evoke the armature of the city’s metallic fences and the rust found in its streets. One might say that there is always an active mediation of spatial quandary: in a 1995 interview with critic Ivor Powell, Koloane remarked: ‘Apartheid was a politics of space more than anything’. The artist’s canvases are often tightly packed, movement is inhibited, atmospheres overcast and claustrophobic. Despite their mirroring of constraint, a quickened pace runs through the works—restless, electric, grasping at the edges of revolution.

Skye Arundhati Thomas

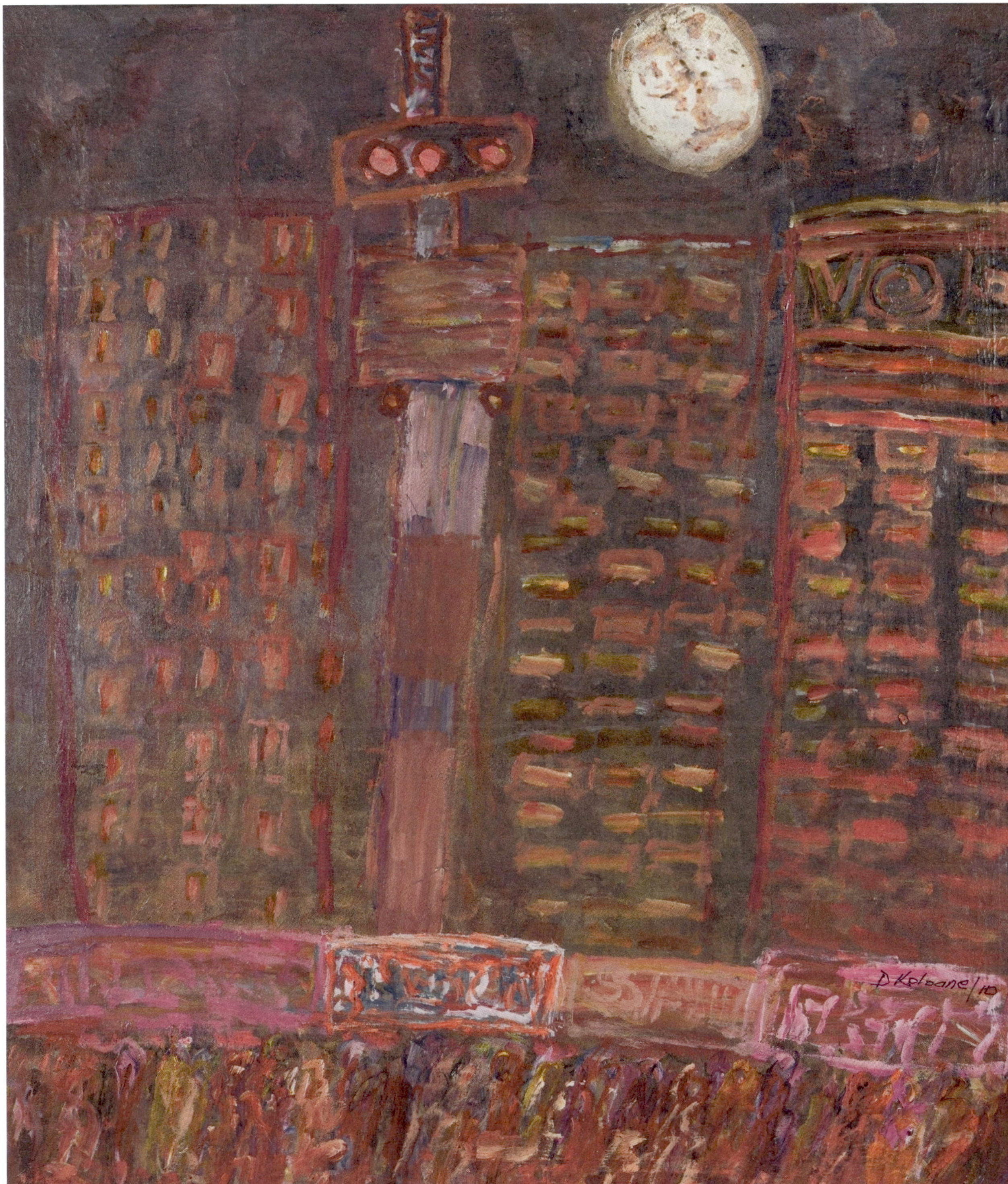


*Untitled (The Moon Over Hillbrow Tower) / Ohne Titel (Der Mond über dem Hillbrow Tower)*, 1998–2010. Öl und Mixed Media auf Leinwand / Oil and mixed media on canvas. 110 × 124 cm

# Jumana Manna

*Kopf* aus der Installation *The Contractor's Heel* („Die Ferse des Bauunternehmers", 2016) ist eine Skulptur der Künstlerin Jumana Manna, welche Teil einer Skulpturengruppe für die 6. *Marrakesch Biennale* im Jahre 2016 war. Jene Skulpturen wurden auf der Ausstellung in den Ruinen des El-Badi-Palastes aus dem 16. Jahrhundert präsentiert. Sie belegen, wie stark die Künstlerin fasziniert ist von der Archäologie und der Art und Weise, wie Kulturdenkmäler Geschichte und Kunstwerke erhalten, archivieren und interpretieren; und dabei durchaus eigene „moderne Mythen" schaffen können. Gleichzeitig verweist Manna in ihren Skulpturen, Filmen und Texten auch auf die den Dingen innewohnende Spannung, die durch den menschlichen Wunsch erzeugt wird, sie bewahren zu wollen – trotz ihres unaufhaltsamen Verfalls in der Zeit.

Die Formen und Texturen in *The Contractor's Heel* leiten sich aus Konturen und Abdrücken in den Palastmauern ab. Ihre Namen erinnern an Körperteile (Kopf), Verzierungen (Amulett) oder urbane Elemente (Rinnstein). Sie stehen in Beziehung zueinander wie Charaktere auf einer Bühne. Manche von ihnen werden zudem von gerüstähnlichen Gebilden und Brettern gehalten. Für die Künstlerin symbolisiert diese Aufstellung einerseits die Fremdheit von archäologischen Artefakten und anderseits die Isolation der Gips-, Faser- und Lackkörper von ihrer Umgebung.

Elemente von Baustellen oder Renovierungsarbeiten erscheinen auch in *Theory of An Unfinished Building (landscape)* („Theorie eines unfertigen Gebäudes [Landschaft], 2021), das ursprünglich Teil der Ausstellung *Thirty Plumbers in the Belly* des Museums für Zeitgenössische Kunst Antwerpen war. Die an der Wand hängende Collage aus weißen, blauen und grünen Abdeckfolien vor einer bemalten Holzstruktur erinnert an die provisorische Abdeckung eines Baugerüsts. Sie wirkt wie von der Witterung gezeichnet. Kleine Risse und Löcher in der Oberfläche suggerieren Brüchigkeit. Für Jumana Manna symbolisiert das Werk die „Landschaften" von Baustellen, in denen einige Teile abgedeckt sind und andere offen liegen – sowohl im wörtlichen als auch im übertragenen Sinne: „Theaterbühnen mit Körpern und Materialien, die im sich verändernden Architekturraum ihre Wirkung entfalten", um die Künstlerin zu zitieren.

*Head*, from *The Contractor's Heel* (2016) was among a group of sculptures commissioned for the 6th Marrakech Biennale in 2016. Presented in the remains of the 16th-century El Badi Palace, these sculptures reflect Jumana Manna's ongoing interest in archaeology and the ways in which heritage sites preserve, archive and interpret specific histories and artefacts, thereby creating their own forms of 'modern myth'. Across her sculpture, filmmaking and writing, Manna observes the inherent tension that arises from the human drive to conserve things in the face of inevitable deterioration over time.

The forms and textures of *The Contractor's Heel* are derived from contours and indentations in the clay surface of the palace walls, with names that evoke body parts, adornments and urban features (such as *Head*, *Amulet*, *Gutter*). Set in relation to one another as though characters on a stage, several are supported by scaffold-like structures and wooden planks; on one hand, they have the appearance of strange artefacts excavated from the site, while, on the other, they feel alien to their surroundings due to their plaster, fibre and lacquer bodies.

Elements from sites of construction or renovation are also apparent in *Theory of An Unfinished Building (landscape)* (2021), which was originally presented as part of the exhibition, *Thirty Plumbers in the Belly* at the Museum of Contemporary Art in Antwerp. Hung against a wall and resembling the temporary 'skin' that often covers scaffolding, this work is a collage of dust sheets in white, blue and green attached to a painted wooden armature. Its appearance is weathered as if it has been exposed to the elements; the small tears and gaps that punctuate its surface emote a certain fragility. The work evokes the 'landscapes' of building sites, where some elements are revealed while others are covered, both literally and metaphorically: 'theatres of bodies and materials labouring in the shifting spaces of architecture', to quote the artist.

Anne Barlow

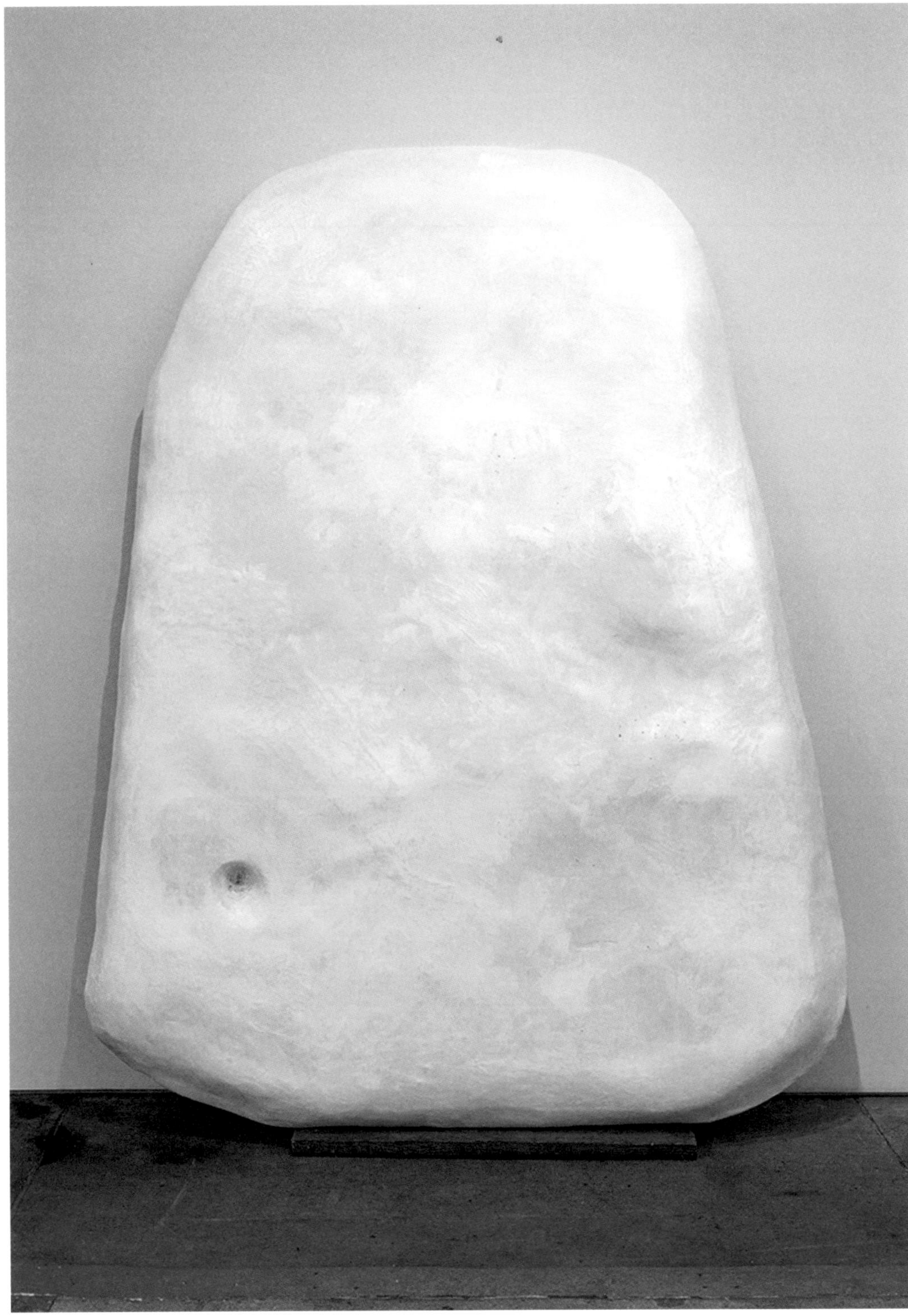

*Head,* from *The Contractor's Heel* / *Kopf,* aus *Die Ferse des Bauunternehmers*, 2016. Gips, Faser, Lack, Metallgerüst / Plaster, fibre, lacquer, metal scaffold. 150 × 190 × 10 cm

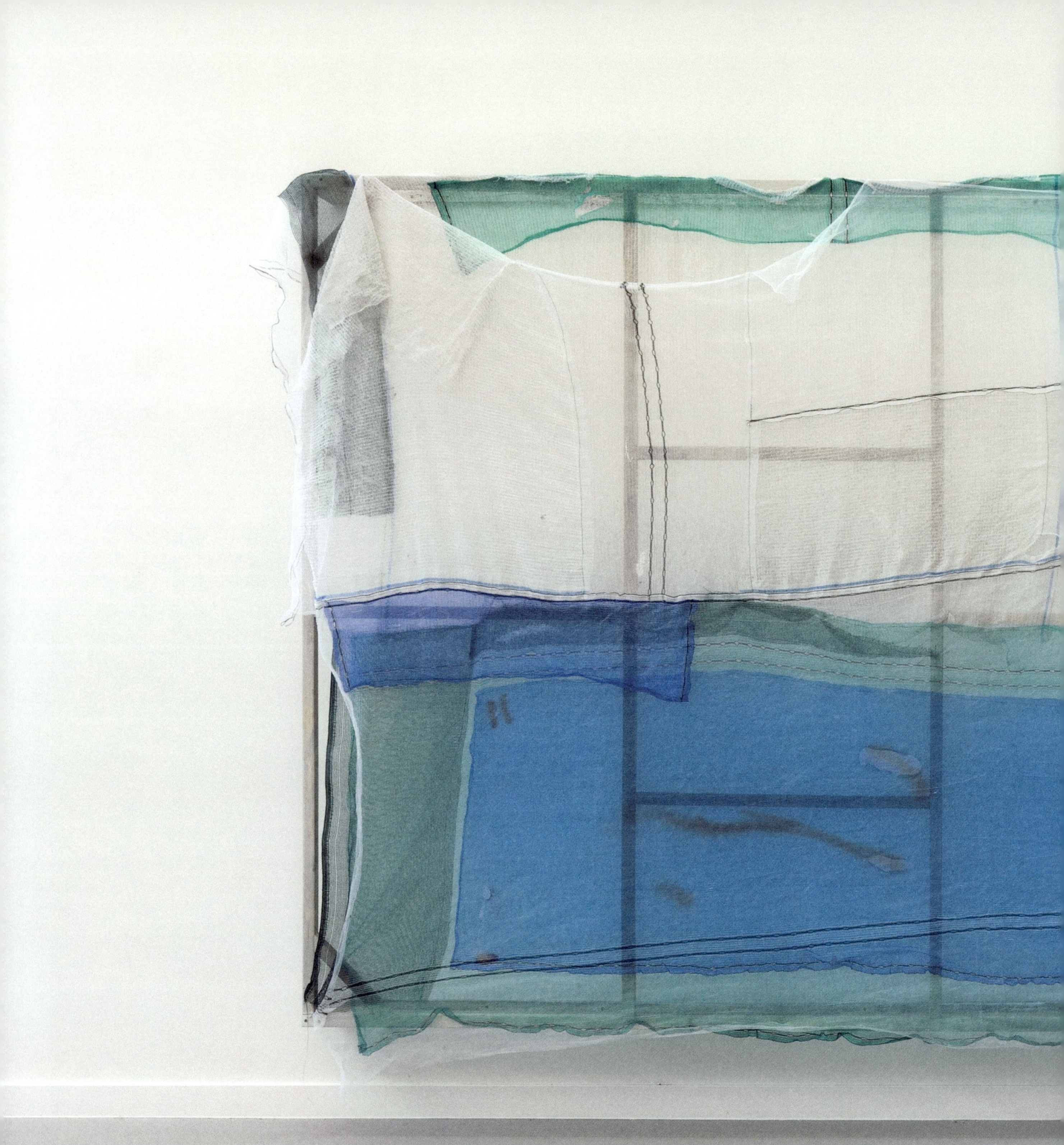

*Theory of An Unfinished Building (landscape) | Theorie eines unfertigen Gebäudes (Landschaft)*, 2021.
Abdeckfolie für Baugerüste, Holzrahmen / Scaffold dust sheet, wooden frame. 600 × 250 × 40 cm

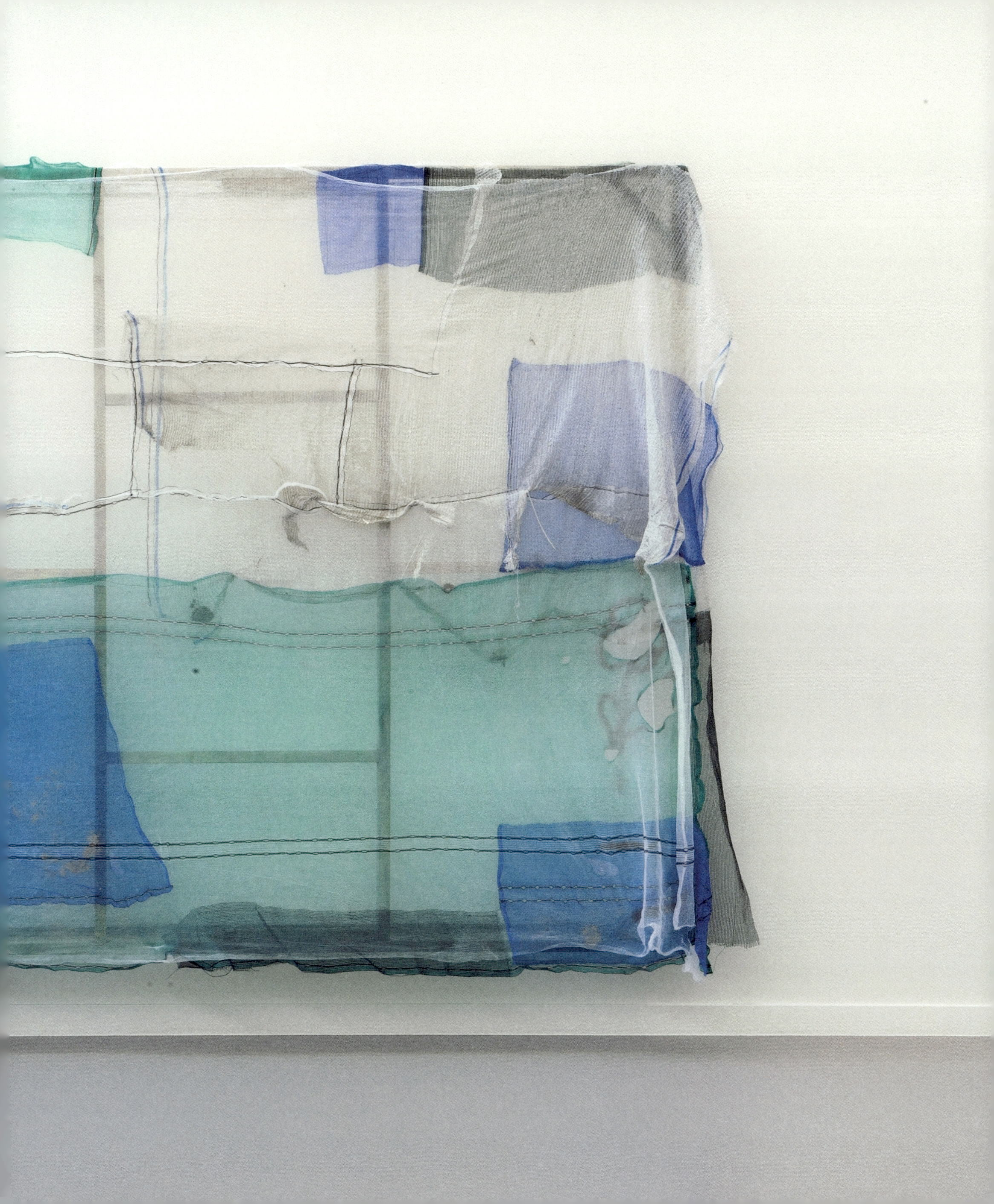

# Ibrahim Massouda

Das Leben des ägyptischen Künstlers Ibrahim Massouda liest sich für viele wie ein unerfülltes Mysterium. Der vermutlich 1925 als Sohn jüdischer Eltern geborene Künstler erlangte in der ägyptischen Kunstszene Anerkennung als Vertreter zweier ineinandergreifender Kunstbewegungen – der ägyptischen Surrealisten und der Gruppe für Zeitgenössische Kunst in Kairo. Wie die Kunsthistorikerin und Kuratorin Salwa Mikdadi 2004 in einem Essay für das Metropolitan Museum of Art erklärte, wuchs Massoudas Generation zu einer Zeit auf, als Künstler in Ägypten „populäre figurative Traditionen kritisch hinterfragten und mit Surrealismus, Kubismus, Dadaismus und Abstraktion experimentierten".

Die Bewegung der später so genannten ägyptischen Surrealisten formierte sich 1939 unter dem offiziellen Namen Gruppe Kunst und Freiheit. Dieser bis 1948 aktiven Gruppe gehörten Künstler an, die sich, so Mikdadi, „mit dem europäischen antifaschistischen Widerstand identifizierten und sich für Meinungsfreiheit einsetzten". Ein neu erwachtes Interesse an diesem historischen Moment führte in den 2000er Jahren zu Ausstellungen, die von Kurator*innen wie Hoor Al Qasimi, Salah M Hassan, Sam Bardouil und Till Fellrath zusammengestellt wurden. Sie beleuchteten die verschiedenen Phasen der Bewegung, wobei Ibrahim Massouda in späteren Ausstellungen der Gruppierung auftaucht, neben Figuren wie Kamal Youssef, der auch in *In the Heart of Another Country* vertreten ist.

Mitte der 1940er Jahre wurde die Gruppe für Moderne Kunst, besser bekannt als Gruppe für Zeitgenössische Kunst, in Kairo gegründet. Massouda wurde neben namhaften ägyptischen Künstler*innen wie Abdel Hadi Al-Gazzar, Hamed Nada und Gazbia Sirry als Mitglied aufgeführt. Wie Mikdadi feststellt, ging es dieser Konstellation von Künstler*innen, analog zu der in den frühen 1950er Jahren entstandenen Bagdader Gruppe für Moderne Kunst, in ihrer Kunst darum, nach der „Seele" Ägyptens zu suchen und durch die Appropriation und Umgestaltung nationalistischer oder ikonografischer Referenzen zur Geschichte ihres Landes ein „kollektives Unbewusstes" sichtbar zu machen. In dem hier gezeigten unbetitelten Ölgemälde, das Massouda in den frühen 1950er Jahren schuf, umreißen expressionistische Pinselstriche eine scheinbar geschlechtslose, amorphe Figur. Sie schwebt über einen goldbraunen Ort, der dem Blick entzogen bleibt. Man könnte hier eine metaphorische Lesart des Körpers bemühen, der sich nach dem Exodus von Juden aus vielen Teilen Nordafrikas in den frühen 1950er Jahren neu zu verorten sucht. Ebenso aber suggeriert die ruhige Leichtigkeit des Ausdrucks und der Bewegung dieser goldenen Figur innerhalb des Bildrahmens potenziellen Optimismus und mögliche Versöhnung – die Möglichkeit des Fliegens: eine Reise in ein Reich möglicher Fülle.

The life of Egyptian artist Ibrahim Massouda reads like an unfilled, or rather, as an unfulfilled mystery to many. Assumed to have been born in 1925 to Jewish parents, the artist came to recognition in the sphere of the Egyptian art scene as part of two interleaving art movements, the Egyptian Surrealists and as a member of Cairo's Contemporary Art Group. As curator and historian Salwa Mikdadi articulated in an essay for the Metropolitan Museum of Art in 2004, Massouda's generation came of age at a time when artists in Egypt were 'challenging popular figurative traditions, experimenting with Surrealism, Cubism, Dadaism and abstraction'.

It was in and around 1938/9–48 that various accounts reveal the formation of those who would later become referred to as the Egyptian Surrealists, formally identified as the Art and Freedom Group (also known as the Art and Liberty Group). These were artists who 'identified with the European antifascist resistance and rallied for freedom of expression', noted Mikdadi. A newfound interest in this historical moment in the 2000s has led to exhibitions curated by the likes of Hoor Al Qasimi, Salah M Hassan, Sam Bardaouil and Till Fellrath, which have revealed the iterative stages of this movement, with Ibrahim Massouda's name appearing in later exhibitions of community, alongside the likes of Kamal Youssef, who is also featured within *In the Heart of Another Country*.

In the mid-1940s, the Group of Modern Art, more commonly referred to as the Contemporary Art Group, was founded in Cairo circa 1945. Massouda was listed as a member, alongside notable Egyptian artists Abdel Hadi Al-Gazzar, Hamed Nada and Gazbia Sirry. As Mikdadi notes, much like movements such as the Baghdad Modern Art Group, which emerged in the early 1950s, this constellation of artists was keen to search for the 'soul' of Egypt in their artistic approach, revealing a 'collective unconscious' by appropriating and recasting nationalistic or iconographic referents to local history. In the *Untitled* oil on canvas piece by Massouda featured here, produced in the early 1950s, expressionistic brushstrokes reveal a seemingly genderless, amorphous figure. Here, they float above a burnished site, which is withheld from view. One could invoke a metaphorical reading of the body negotiating its place after the exodus of Jews from many parts of Northern Africa in the early 1950s. Yet equally, this gilded figure's tranquil ease of expression and movement within the frame suggest a potential optimism and reconciliation—a possibility of flight, a journey to a realm of possible abundance.

Omar Kholeif

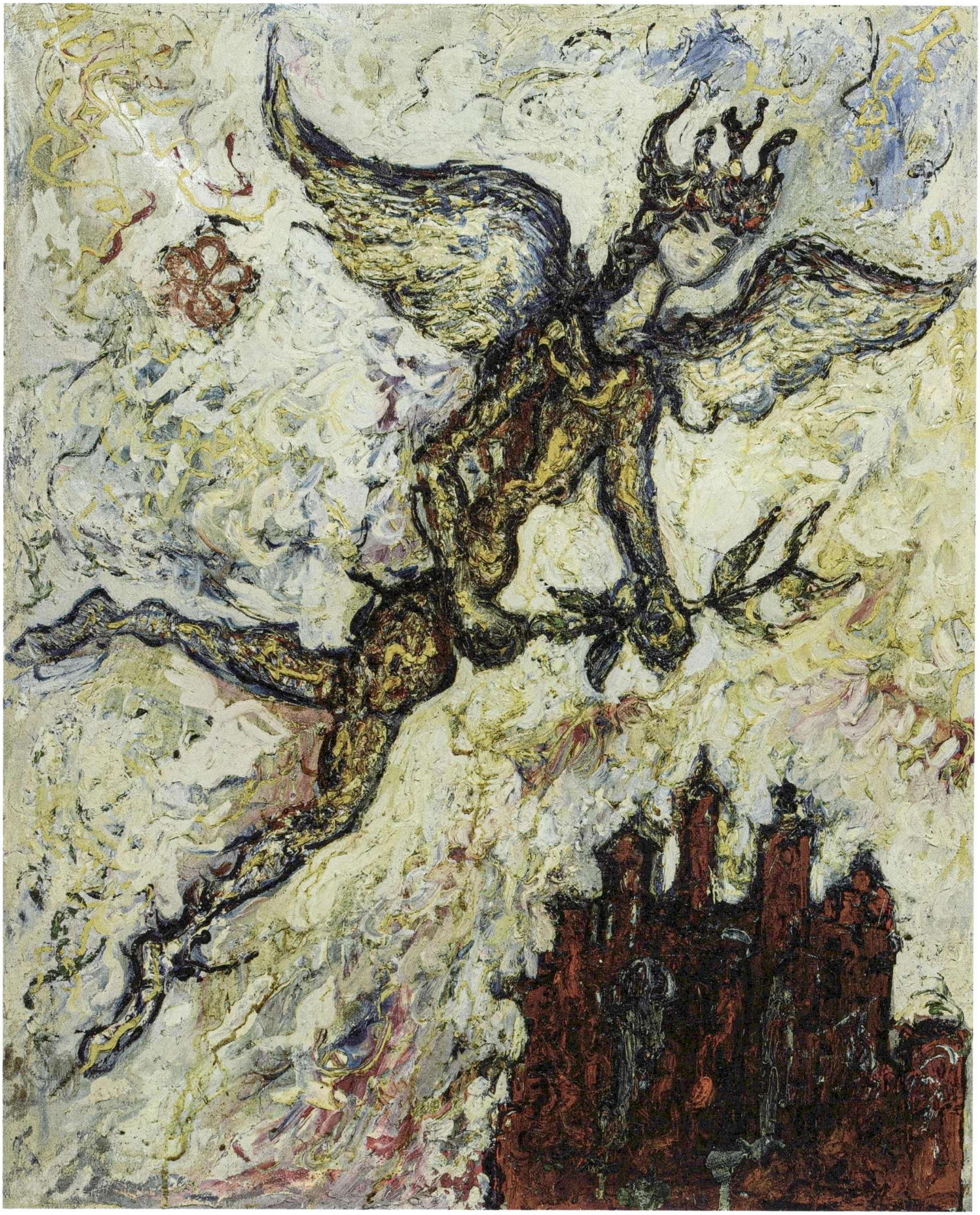

*Untitled 7*, frühe 1950er / early 1950s. Öl auf Leinwand / Oil on canvas. 72 × 82.5 cm

# Marwan Rechmaoui

Marwan Rechmaoui stellt in seinem Architekturmodell ein Gebäude so originalgetreu wie möglich dar, um die Ausführbarkeit und die Finesse des Entwurfs – oder auch sein Potenzial als lukratives Renditeobjekt – zu beurteilen. In seiner Arbeit setzt er spekulative Investitionen des Modellbaus kritisch mit allen politischen Realitäten in Verbindung, die während der Lebensdauer eines Gebäudes eine Rolle spielen könnten.

Rechmaoui, der 1964 in Beirut geboren wurde und in der Golfregion und den USA aufwuchs, kehrte erst als Erwachsener in den Libanon zurück. Seither erforscht er seine Heimatstadt Beirut wie ein Archäologe und rekonstruiert in seinen Kunstwerken das Stadtbild höchst detailverliebt. Auf diese Weise will er den historischen Wertewandel und die Brüche nachvollziehen, die in die architektonische Gestaltung der Stadt eingebettet sind. Seine Figuren aus industriellen Werkstoffen wie Beton, Gummi und Stahl sowie gefundenen Gebäudefragmenten ähneln glyphenartigen minimalistischen Totems, die den scheinbar endlosen Wiederaufbau einer von Krieg, Erdbeben und Explosionen erschütterten Stadt, die dazu gegenläufige Gentrifizierung und den Kampf um urbane Kontrolle symbolisch miteinander verschmelzen.

Diese Themen tauchen in *Monument for the Living* („Denkmal für die Lebenden", 2001–2008) wieder auf. Die Betonreplik bildet den im Zentrum von Beirut emporragenden Burj al Murr (bekannt als Murr) nach. Der Bau des 34-stöckigen Büroturms im Stadtkern von Beirut wurde 1974 von der Familie El-Murr in Auftrag gegeben, einem Clan, der bis heute für seinen Einfluss auf die Finanzwelt und die Politik des Landes bekannt ist. Während des libanesischen Bürgerkriegs (1975–1990) stoppten jedoch die Bauarbeiten, und das Gebäude blieb Bauruine. Die oberen Stockwerke wurden zu einem berüchtigten Versteck für Scharfschützen zahlreicher politischer Gruppierungen, während das Untergeschoss für Verhöre und als Munitionslager genutzt wurde. Das dem Verfall geweihte Gebäude ist zu hoch, um es abzureißen, und steht zu nah an anderen Bauten, um es sicher implodieren zu lassen. Sein Schatten über der Stadt bleibt ein gespenstisches Vermächtnis des Krieges oder vielmehr einer Reihe von Kriegen, deren Folgen bis in die heutige Zeit hineinwirken.

If an architectural model typically renders a building as faithfully as possible in order to assess the design's workability and finesse—or, indeed, its potential as an object of lucrative financial return—then Marwan Rechmaoui's work critically returns the speculative investment of modelmaking to the political realities that take hold throughout a building's life. Born in Beirut in 1964 and growing up in the Gulf and the United States before returning to Lebanon as an adult, Rechmaoui surveys his home of Beirut as an archaeologist might, intimately reconstructing the cityscape in his artworks as a way to comprehend the shifting historical currencies and ruptures that are embedded in its architectural planning. Using industrial materials, such as concrete, rubber and steel, as well as found fragments of buildings, Rechmaoui's sculptures resemble glyph-like, minimalist totems that thread together the seemingly endless reconstruction of a city beset by war, earthquakes and explosions, its countermovement of gentrification and the fight for its urban control.

These themes are redolent in *Monument for the Living* (2001–08), which re-creates a concrete replica of the towering Burj al Murr (known as the Murr) in central Beirut. Construction of the 34-storey office tower in downtown Beirut was begun in 1974 by the El-Murr family, a fraternity who remain well-known for their influence in the country's financial and political seats. However, the Lebanese Civil War (1975–90) halted the building's construction, leaving it abandoned. The top floors became an infamous lookout used by snipers by numerous political factions, while its basement became a site for interrogation and ammunition storage. The building remains derelict; too tall to demolish and too dense to safely implode, its shadow across the city remains a haunting legacy of a war, or rather, a series of wars that continue to ricochet into present-day reality.

Chris McCormack

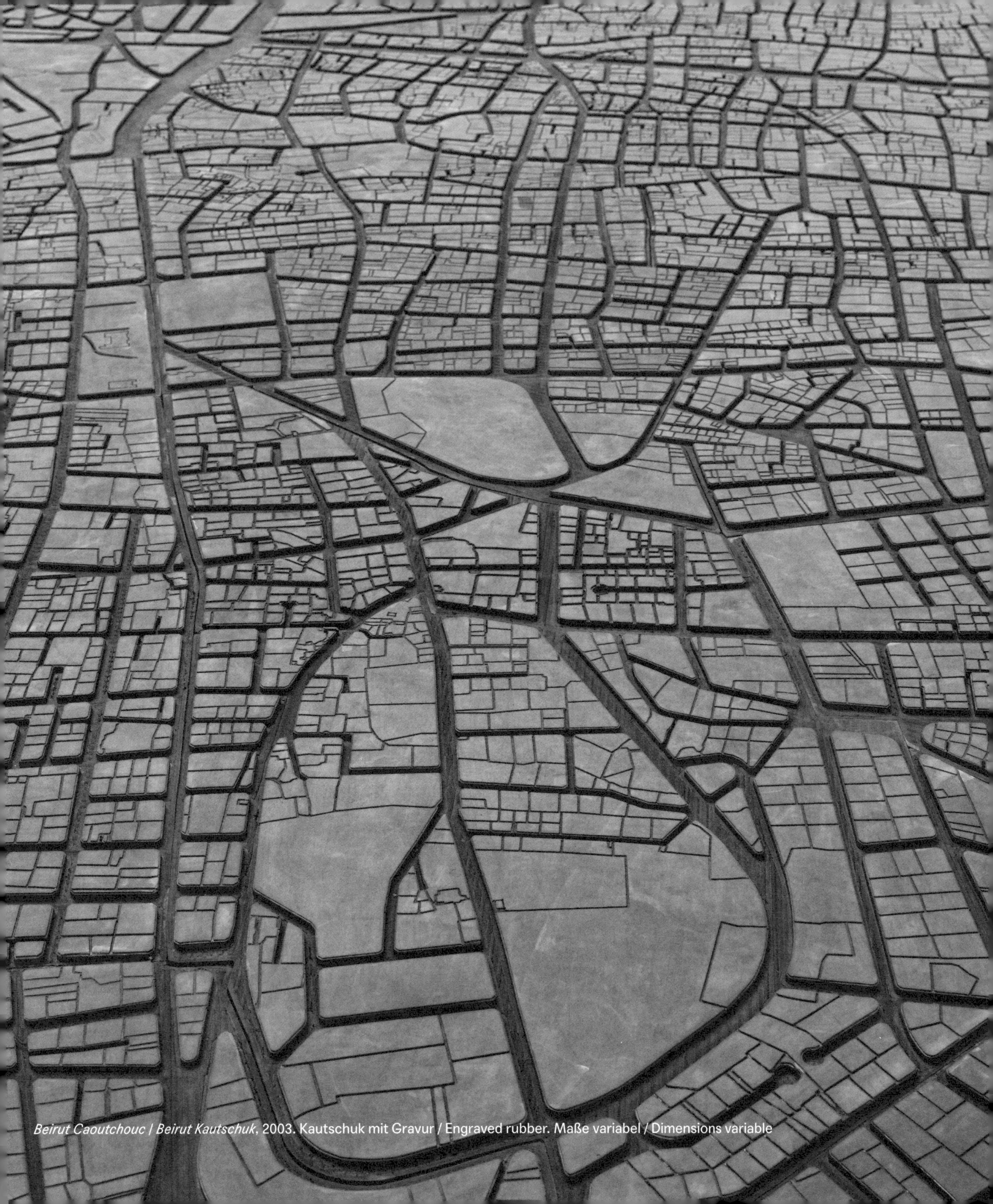

*Beirut Caoutchouc | Beirut Kautschuk*, 2003. Kautschuk mit Gravur / Engraved rubber. Maße variabel / Dimensions variable

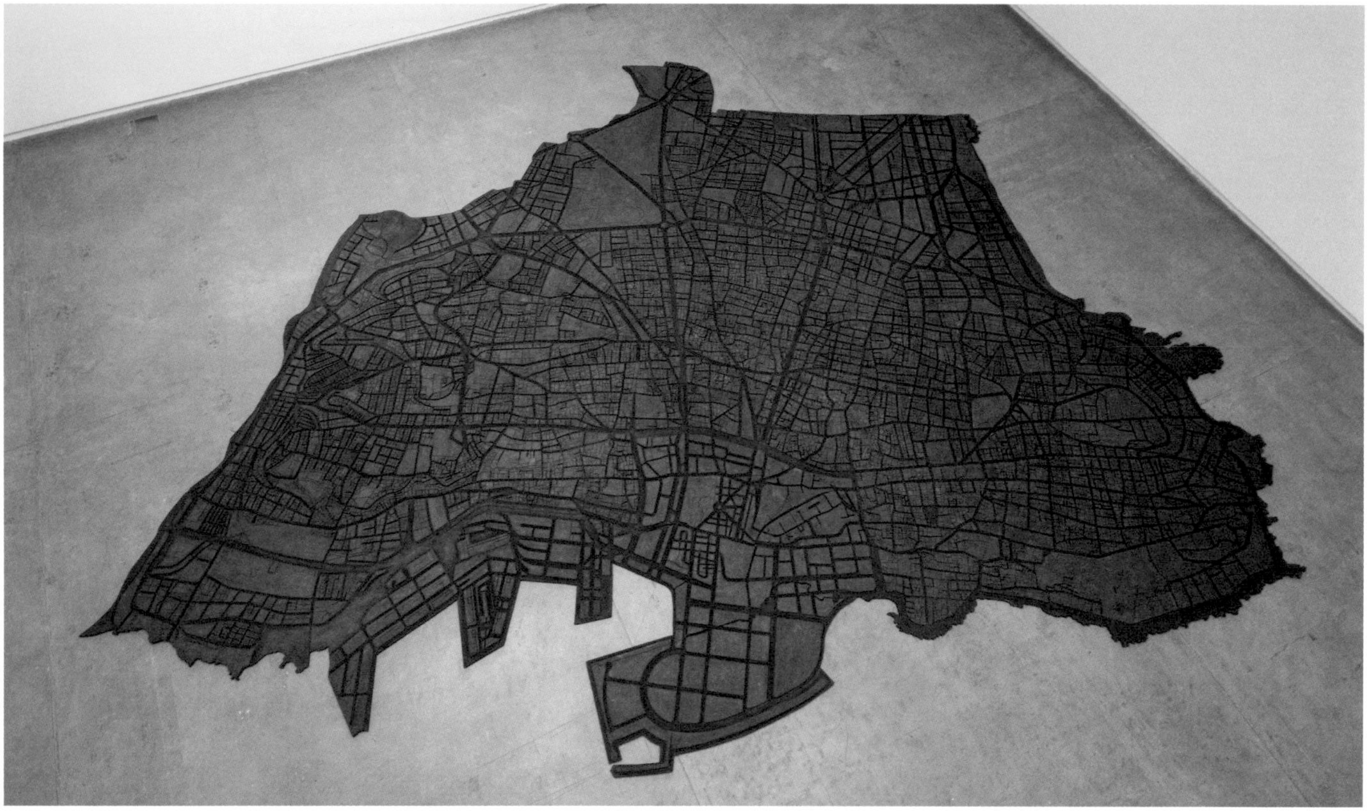

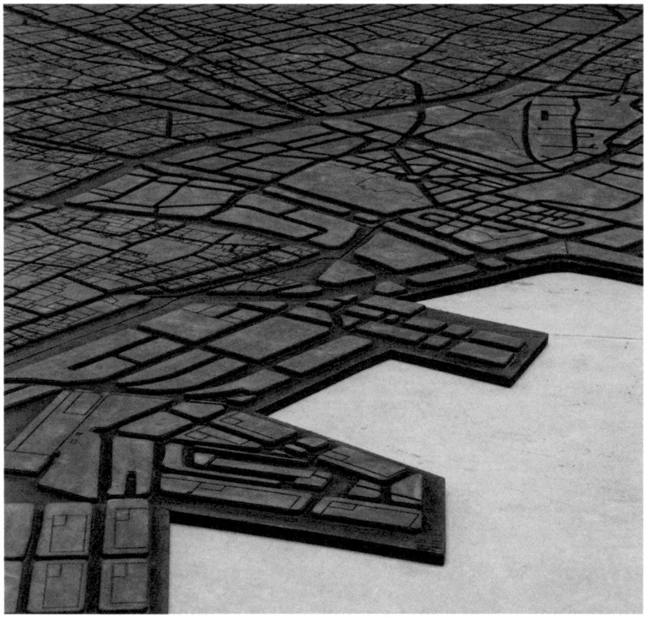

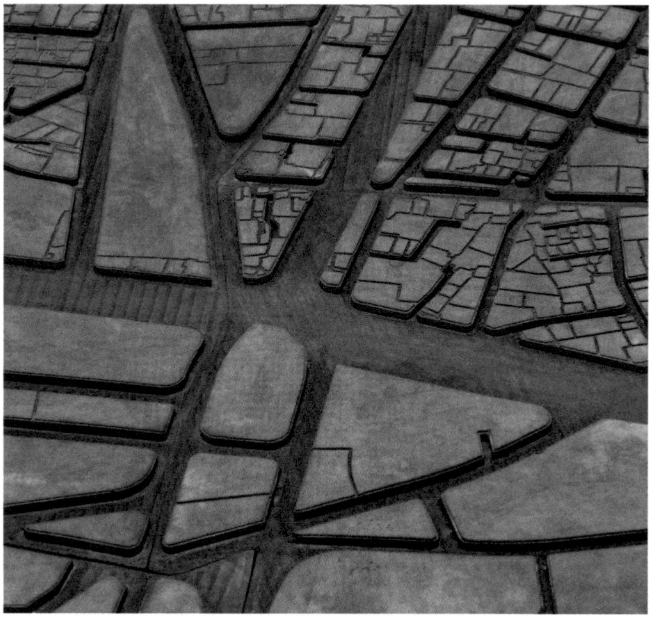

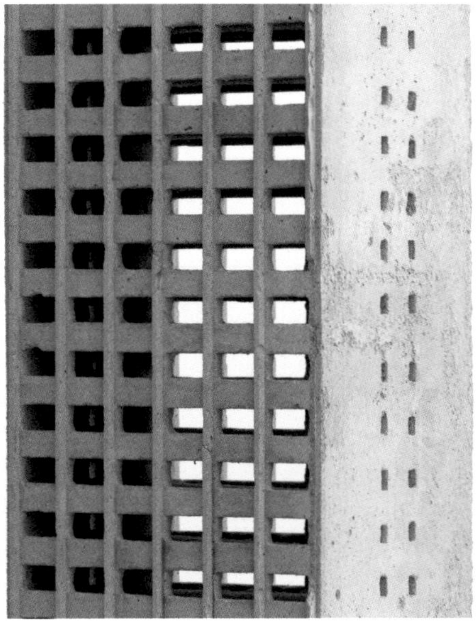

*Monument for the Living / Denkmal für die Lebenden*, 2000.
Gussbeton / Casting cement. 60 × 230 × 40 cm

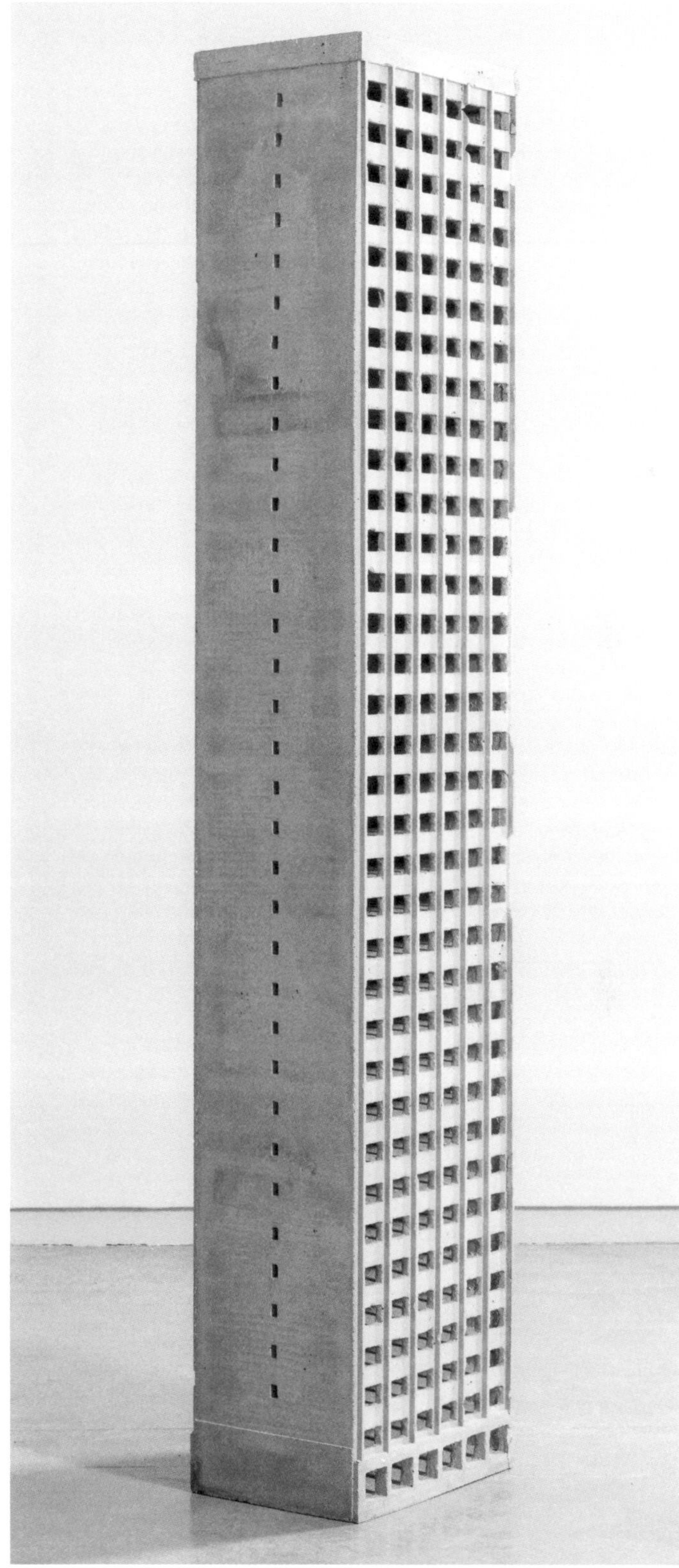

# Hassan Sharif

Hassan Sharif produzierte seine ersten „Bücher“ in London, wo er sich mit den Gedanken des Konstruktivisten Kenneth Martin zum Thema „Zufall und System“ auseinandersetzte. Martin entwarf Zeichnungen und Gemälde, indem er nach dem Zufallsprinzip Zahlen auswählte, die den Kanten eines quadratischen Rasters entsprachen.

Dagegen fotografierte Sharif für die Serie *Dictionary* („Wörterbuch“) von 1981 einzelne Seiten aus seinem arabisch-englischen Wörterbuch auf Londoner Bürgersteigen, wobei der Abstand zwischen Seite und Kamera von der Seitenzahl abhing (zum Beispiel entsprach 301 dem Wert 3 + 0 +1, war also vier Schritte entfernt). Im Jahr 2015 trug Sharif sieben illustrierte arabisch-englische Wörterbücher zusammen, darunter das von ihm in London verwendete, und klebte ihre Seiten an Baumwollschnüre, um daraus eine monumentale, kaskadenartige Wandskulptur entstehen zu lassen. Dieser maximalistische Umgang mit alltäglichen Materialien ist für einen Großteil von Sharifs Arbeiten charakteristisch. In *Slippers and Wire* („Hausschuhe und Draht“, 2009) verwandelte er das Durcheinander eines bunten Haufens von Plastikpantoffeln in eine formale Einheit.

In London hatte man Sharif erklärt, er könne sich ohne Englischkenntnisse nicht das notwendige Wissen für konzeptionelles Arbeiten aneignen. „Dafür habe ich mich gerächt“, sagte er einmal. *Dictionary*, das Übersetzung als konzeptionellen Prozess verstand, war Teil dieser Rache. Ebenso seine „Buch“-Skulpturen, darunter *Book of Numbers* („Buch der Zahlen“, 1982/2006), ein Stapel Papier in einem einfachen Pappordner, auf dessen oberstem Blatt eine Spalte mit maschinengeschriebenen Zahlen zu sehen ist, und *Book of Different Pens* („Buch der verschiedenartigen Stifte“, 1983), ein rotes Ringbuch, das auf einer aufgeschlagenen Seite den verwendeten Berol-Magnum-Marker nennt. Auch *Sewing Notebook No. 1* („Nähbuch Nr. 1“) und *Sewing Notebook No. 2* („Nähbuch Nr. 2“), die beide aus dem Jahr 1983 stammen und 2006 bzw. 2007 rekonstruiert wurden, sind mit Juteseilen zugenähte Notizbücher, deren Seiten so gefaltet sind, dass diese in deren Innerem ein voluminöses Papierbündel bilden, während in *Colourful File No. 2* („Bunte Mappe Nr. 2“) Papier- und Stoffstücke aus den vernähten Kanten einer Plastikmappe herausquellen.

Nach seiner Rückkehr in die Vereinigten Arabischen Emirate im Jahr 1984 wurde Sharif zum Pionier der konzeptuellen performativen Kunst in seinem Heimatland. Ein prägendes Ereignis im Jahr 1985 war eine eintägige Ausstellung auf dem Zentralmarkt von Schardscha zusammen mit dem Künstler Abdul Rahim Salem – ein Ereignis, das in den auf Karton aufgezogenen Fotografien von *Central Market, Sharjah* („Zentralmarkt, Schardscha“) dokumentiert ist. Die Ausstellung zeigte u. a. geometrische Gemälde, die waagerecht auf oder unter stehende Wasserflaschen gelegt worden waren. Heute setzt sich der performative Impuls des Künstlers in den Arbeiten einer ganzen Generation jüngerer Künstler*innen aus den Vereinigten Arabischen Emiraten fort, die im Land oder in der Diaspora leben.

Hassan Sharif made his first ‘books’ in London. There, he engaged with Constructionist Kenneth Martin’s notion of ‘chance and order’, with Martin creating drawings and paintings by randomly selecting numbers corresponding to the edges of a squared grid.

In turn, Sharif photographed pages from his Arabic-English dictionary on London sidewalks for the 1981 series *Dictionary*, with the distance between page and camera dictated by page number (for example, 301 equalled 3 + 0 + 1, thus four steps away). In 2015, Sharif gathered around seven illustrated Arabic-English dictionaries, including the one he used in London, and glued their pages to cotton ropes, creating a monumental cascading wall sculpture. This maximalist approach to everyday materials defines much of Sharif’s practice. In *Slippers and Wire* (2009), he turned a multicoloured pile of plastic slippers from disarray into an expression of formal unity.

In London, Sharif was told that if he didn’t learn to speak English, he would not gain the knowledge required to work conceptually—this is ‘something I retaliated against’, he once said, and *Dictionary*, which interpreted translation as a conceptual process, was part of that retaliation. As were his *Book* sculptures, including *Book of Numbers* (1982/2006), a stack of paper, the top page of which features a column of typed numbers, contained within a rough cardboard file, and *Book of Different Pens* (1983), a red ring binder open to a page where writing announces the Berol Magnum marker that was used. Likewise, *Sewing Notebook No. 1* and *Sewing Notebook No. 2*, both from 1983 and reconstituted in 2006 and 2007 respectively, present notebooks sewn shut with jute rope, their pages folded to create a flowering volume within; while in *Colourful File No. 2* (2006), pieces of paper and cloth seep out from a plastic file’s sewn edges.

Returning to the UAE in 1984, Sharif pioneered conceptual performative art in his home country. One defining happening in 1985, documented in the card-mounted photographs of *Central Market, Sharjah*, was a one-day exhibition staged at Sharjah’s central market with artist Abdul Rahim Salem. The show included, among other things, geometric paintings laid horizontally under and over water bottles. Today, Sharif’s performative impulse continues through the work of an entire generation of younger artists from the UAE, living both within the country and its diaspora.

Stephanie Bailey

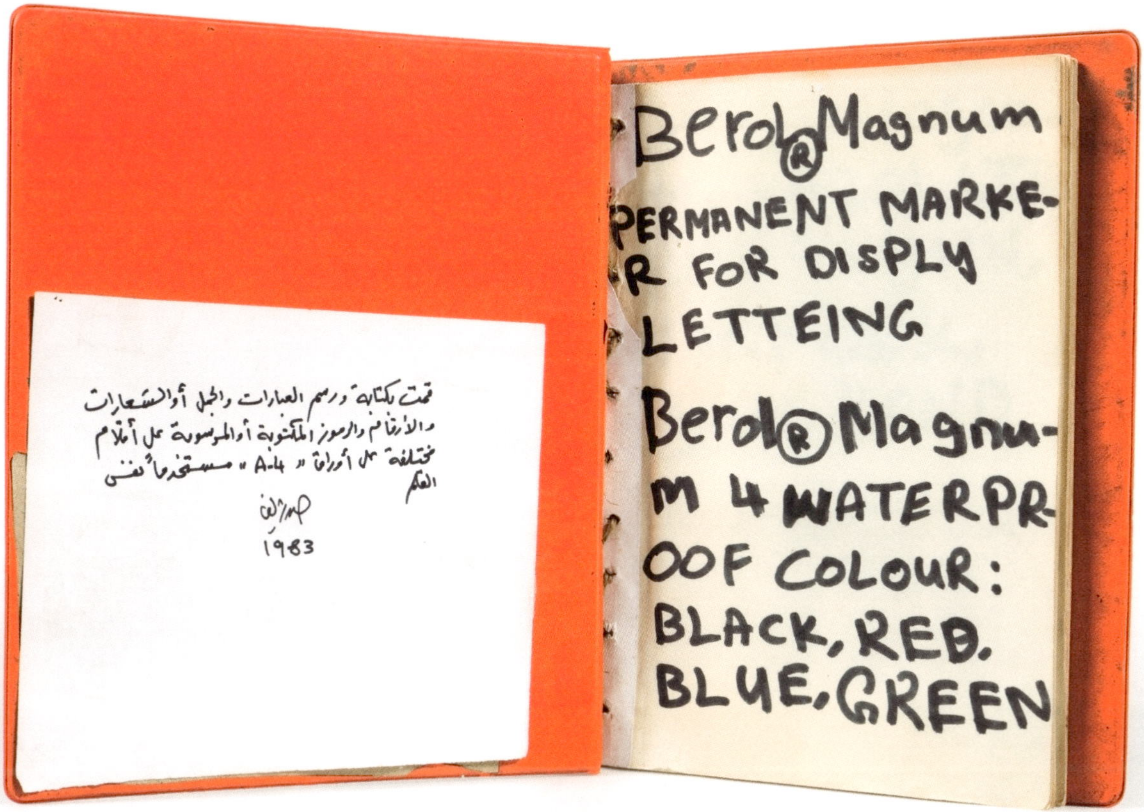


*Book of Different Pens / Buch der verschiedenartigen Stifte*, 1983. Ringbuch aus Kunststoff, Tinte auf Papier / Plastic ring binder, ink on paper. 28,8 × 30,3 × 2,5 cm (geschlossen / closed). 46,9 × 30,3 × 2,4 cm (geöffnet / open)

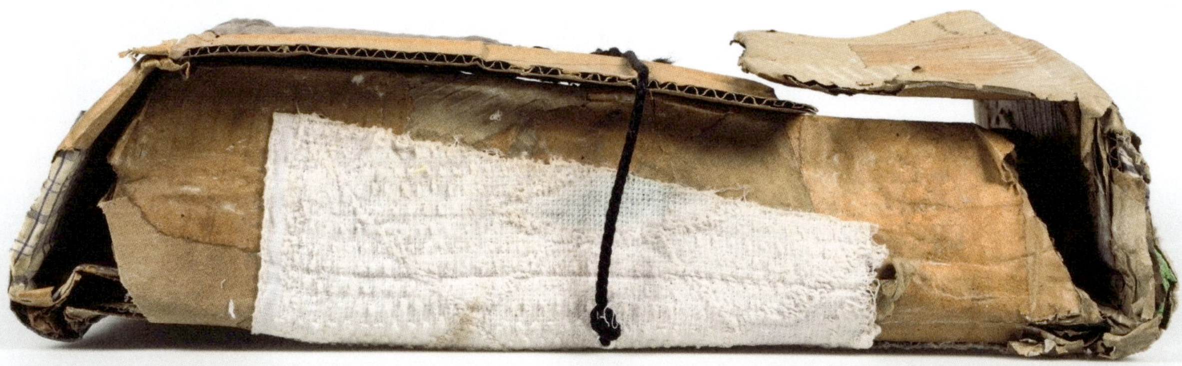

*Book of Numbers / Buch der Zahlen*. Innenseiten 1982, Papparbeit 2006 / Inside pages 1982, cardboard work 2006. Pappe, Stoff, Juteband, Schnur, Marker, Tinte auf Papier / Cardboard, cloth, jute rope, cord, marker, ink on paper. 30,5 × 34,5 × 10,2 cm (geschlossen / closed), 47 × 93 × 10,5 cm (geöffnet / open)

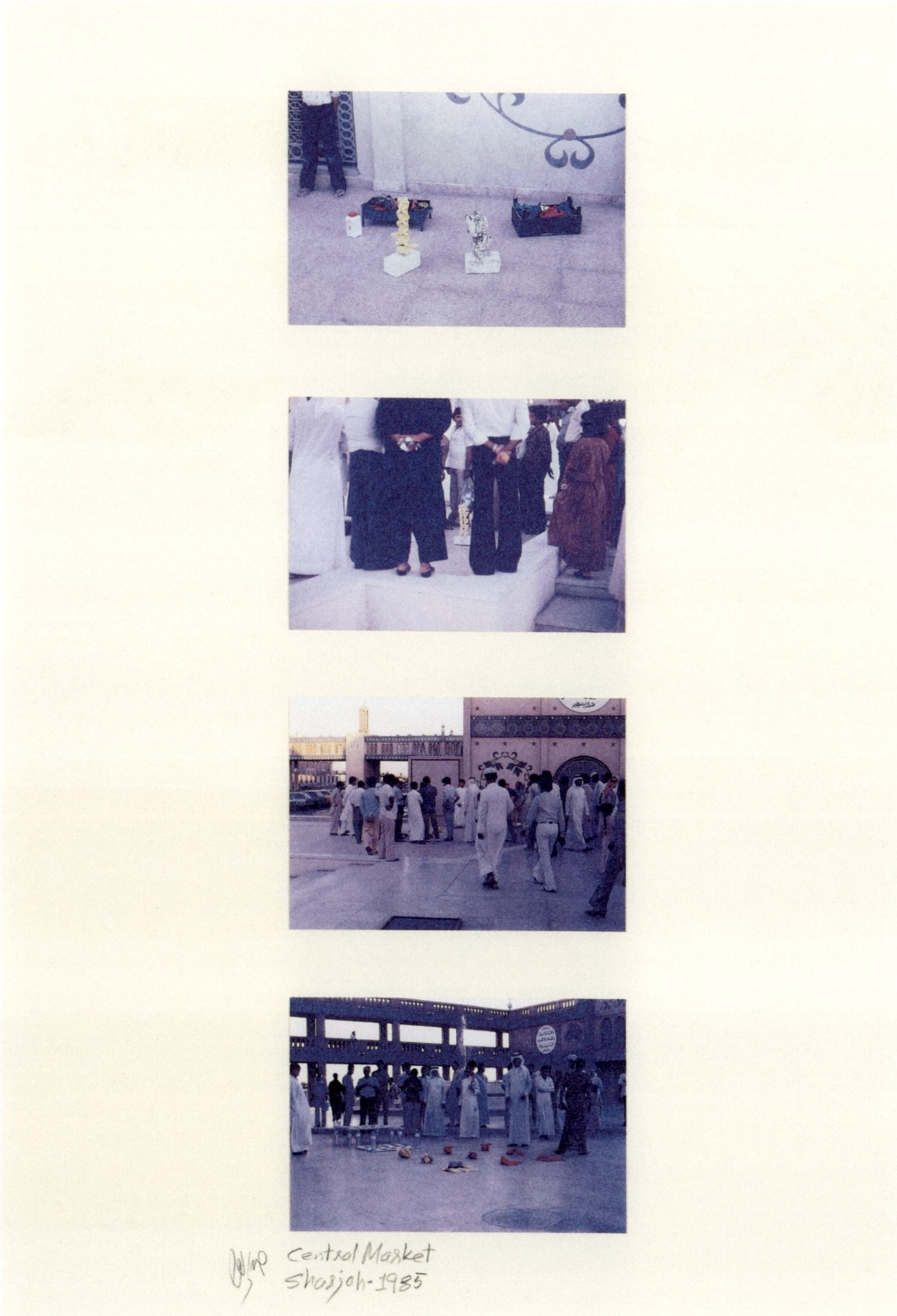


*Central Market, Sharjah* / *Zentralmarkt, Sharjah*, 1985. Auf Karton aufgezogene Fotografien, Bleistift / Photographs mounted on cardboard, pencil. Reihe mit 3 Werken, jeweils 42 × 59,5 cm / Group of 3 works, 42 × 59,5 cm each

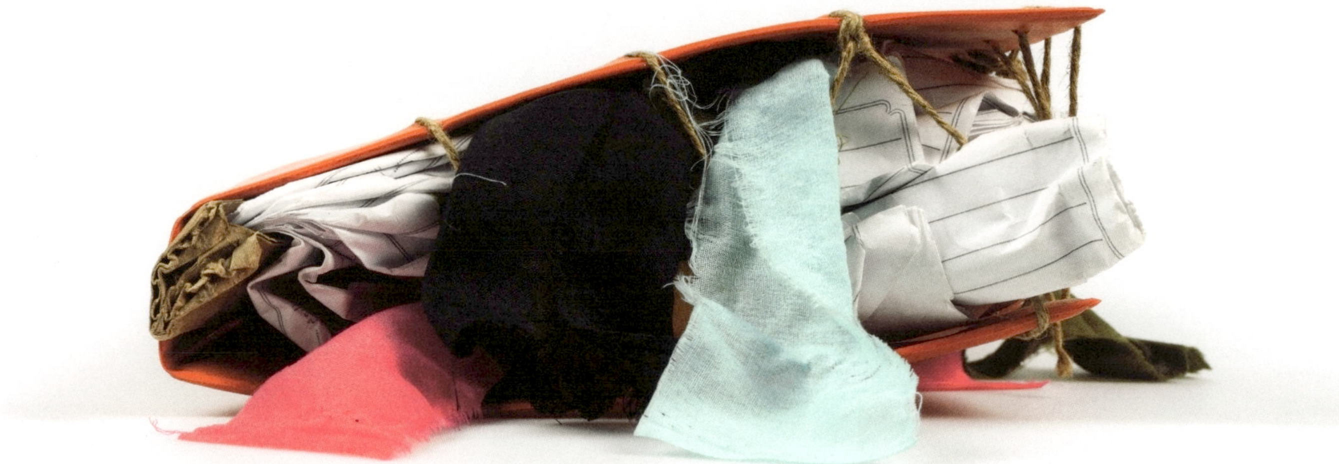

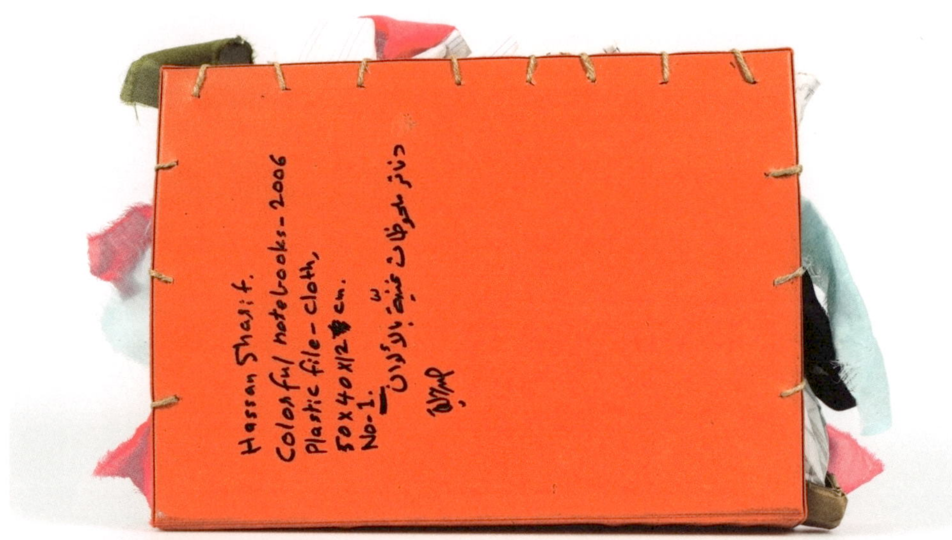


*Colourful File No. 2 | Bunte Mappe Nr. 2*, 2006. Plastikmappe, Jute, Papier, Stoff / Plastic cover, jute, paper, cloth. 24 × 35,5 × 10,5 cm

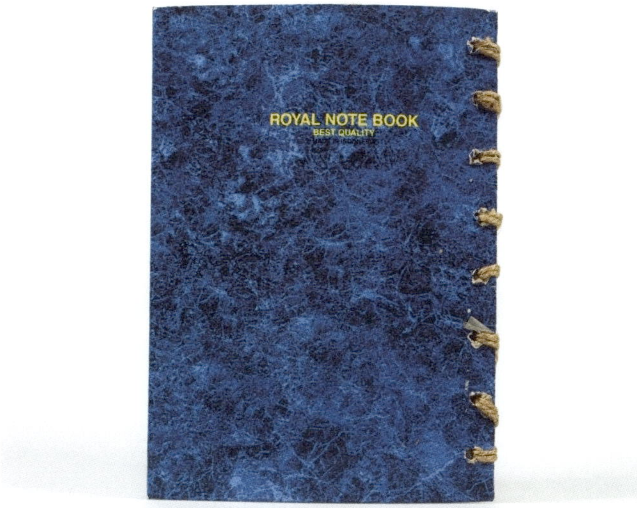


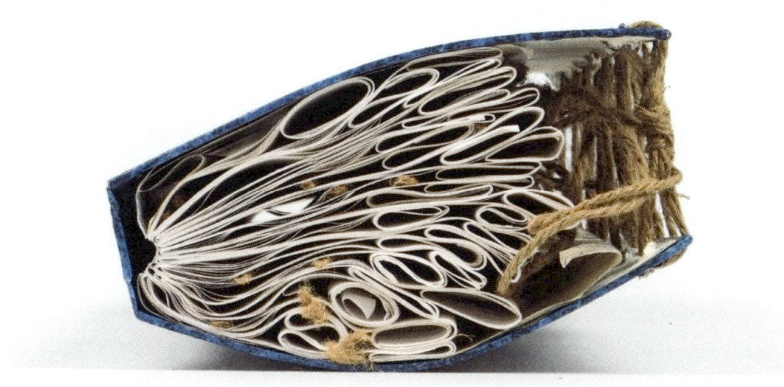

*Sewing Notebook No. 1 | Nähbuch Nr. 1.* 1983, rekonstruiert 2006 / 1983, reconstituted in 2006. Notizbuch, Juteseil / Notebook, jute rope. 16 × 22 × 9,8 cm

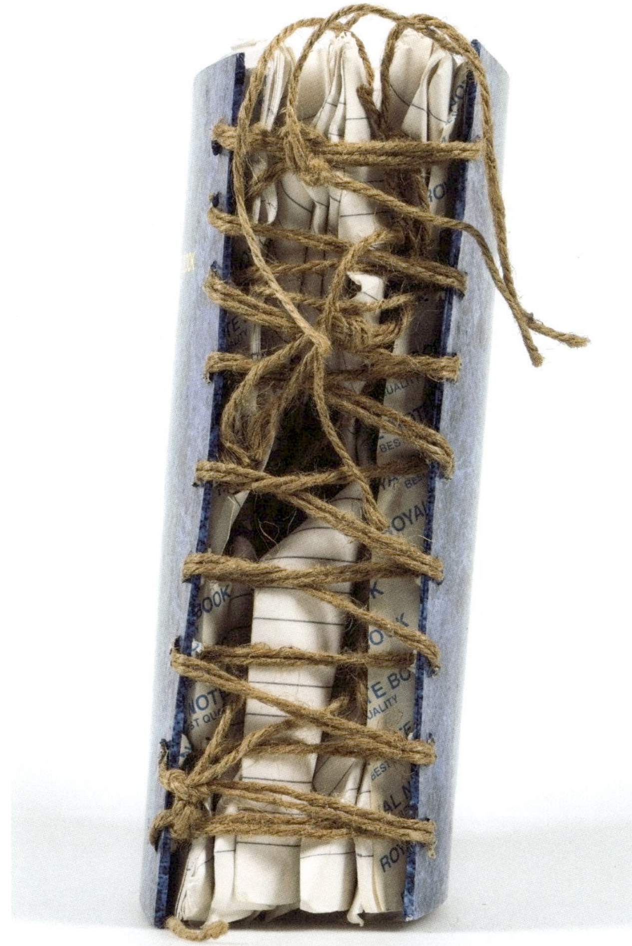

*Sewing Notebook No. 2 | Nähbuch Nr. 2. 1983*, rekonstruiert 2006 / 1983, reconstituted in 2006. Notizbuch, Juteseil / Notebook, jute rope. 15,5 × 22 × 10 cm

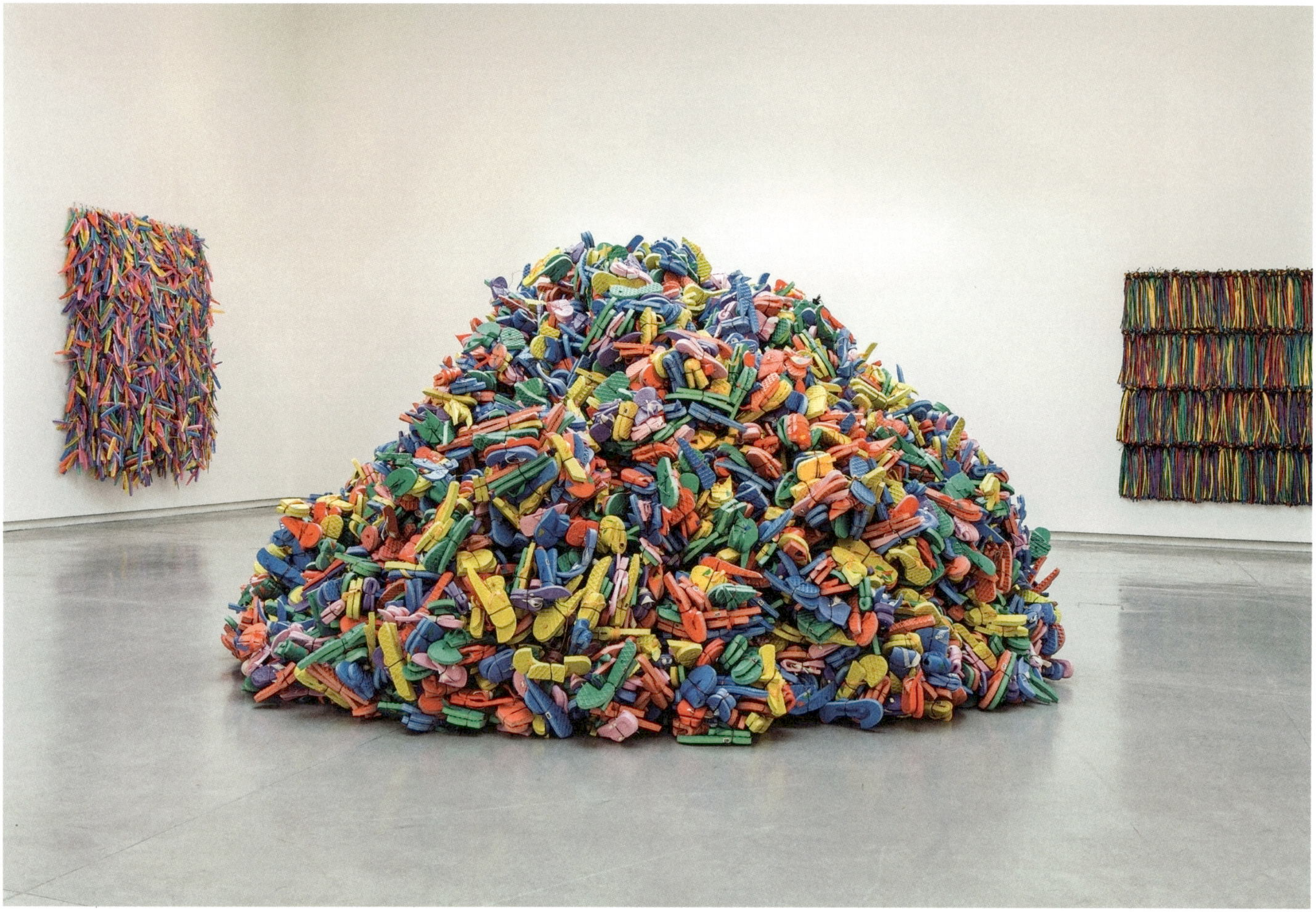

*Slippers and Wire* / *Hausschuhe und Draht*, 2009. Hausschuhe, Kupferdraht / Slippers, copper wire, Maße variabel / Dimensions variable. Installationsansicht / Installation view, Hassan Sharif: *I Am The Single Work Artist*, Sharjah Art Foundation, 2017.

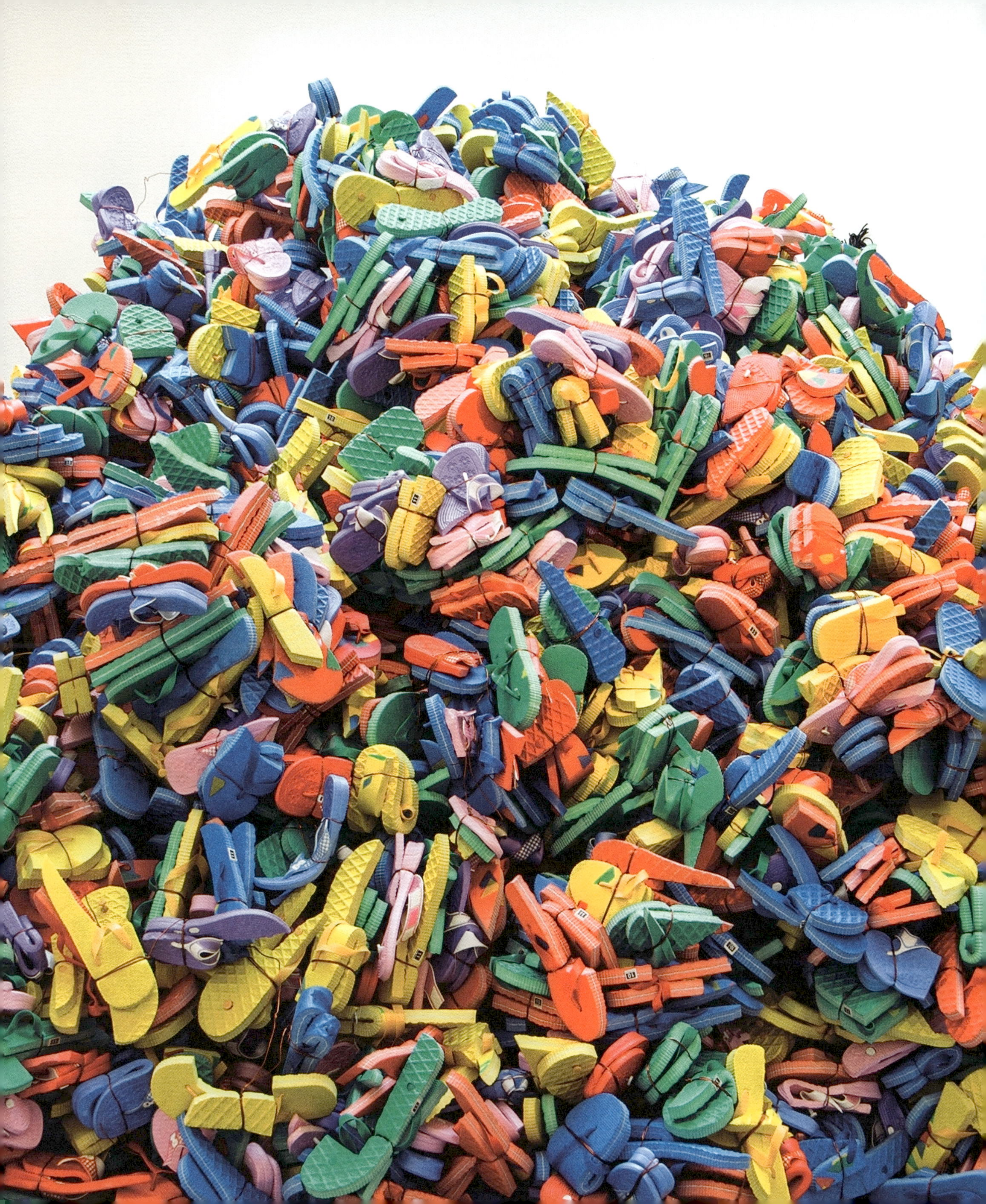

# Anwar Jalal Shemza

*Love Letter* („Liebesbrief", 1962) von Anwar Jalal Shemza ist ein Ölgemälde auf handgefärbtem Stoff, das wie ein filigranes Gitterwerk arrangiert ist: Dicht an dicht ziehen sich zarte schwarze Linien in engen Windungen und Netzen über das Gewebe. Shemza wurde Ende der 1920er Jahre in Shimla geboren. Er stammt aus einer Familie von Kunsthandwerkern aus Kaschmir, die handgefertigte Teppiche und feine Stickereien herstellten. Die Schlaufen und zusammengedrängten Rechtecke in seinen Gemälden wirken so zart und geheimnisvoll wie die geschnitzten Holz- oder Marmor-Jalis der Mogulpaläste, die Balkone zierten, als Paravents frei im Raum standen oder den Frauen des Hofes als diskreter Sichtschutz für ihre Audienzen dienten. Shemza wuchs in Lahore auf, wo sich noch immer zahlreiche Spuren des Mogulreichs finden; die Ästhetik dieser Epoche floss in seine Arbeiten ein. Sich selbst betrachtete der Künstler als Vertreter der Moderne, was sich in seinen Werken auch durch die Kombination kleinteiliger, zarter Motive widerspiegelt, darunter ineinandergreifende oder schlicht nebeneinander angeordnete Kreise, Vierecke oder Rauten. Für *Sun and the Sea* („Sonne und das Meer", 1966) klebte er eine Reihe runder Holzstücke zu einem einfachen Muster auf ein Stück Hartfaserplatte. Durch die unterschiedliche Größe, Dicke und Maserung der Holzstücke entstanden so wellenartige Arrangements, die das Bild lebendig wirken lassen. Shemzas Arbeiten sind oft sehr konstruktiv gestaltet: Sie bilden strukturierte Flächen, erzeugen Tiefe, beeinflussen das Licht und verändern den Raum. In *Advancing & receding* („Voranschreiten & Zurückweichen", 1963) überlagern sich Kreise und Quadrate so, dass fast schon hypnotisch anmutende, schwalbenschwanzförmige farbige Muster und Strukturen entstehen. Das Werk ist eine Art Palimpsest: In der Ölzeichnung auf Hartfaserplatte werden zwei entgegengesetzte geometrische Figuren zum Leben erweckt.

Shemza ließ hier die Formen des arabischen Abjad und des lateinischen Alphabets lebendig werden. In seiner künstlerischen Praxis bediente er sich zunächst antiker Techniken, um dann allmählich die überlieferten Codes zu abstrahieren. Wie R. Garfield 2015 in einem Essay schrieb, bringt Shemza „alles an die Oberfläche, indem er eine Gegenbewegung erzeugt, die im Widerspruch zu der Tiefenwirkung seiner Bildkomposition steht".

*Love Letter* (1962) by Anwar Jalal Shemza is an oil painting on hand-dyed cloth that resembles delicate lattice work: lissome black lines shift in small undulations and grids in a tightly packed movement across the fabric. Shemza was born in Shimla in the late 1920s, and his family, who are Kashmiri, were artisans who worked on handmade carpets and fine embroidery. The loops and tight rectangles of his paintings appear as slim and mysterious as the carved wooden or marble *jalis* of Mughal palaces that adorned balconies, stood freely in rooms as dividers or, more discreetly, functioned as privacy screens behind which the women of the court would hold audience. Shemza grew up in Lahore, a city full of traces of the Mughal Empire, and the aesthetics of that time are pressed into his work. The artist considered himself a modernist, and his configurations and use of slight, subtle motifs reflect this: interlocking or simply juxtaposed circles, squares, diamonds. In *Sun and the Sea* (1966), we see an assembly of round pieces of wood, glued together on a piece of hardboard in a slender pattern. The wood undulates as it is of different sizes, heights and grain, animating the view. Shemza's work is often architectural: building structural planes, creating depth, shifting light and altering space. *Advancing & receding* (1963) is a vivid, almost hypnotic, overlay of circles and squares in dovetailed paint and texture. The work is a kind of palimpsest: two sets of geometry on oil on hardboard, one the inverse of the other, come to life. Shemza enlivened the shapes of the Arabic *abjad* and Latin alphabets through his work. His is a practice that takes root in the ancient before slowly abstracting history's codes. As R. Garfield writes in a 2015 essay, Shemza brings 'everything to the surface, setting up a push/pull that contradicts the deep space of composition'.

Skye Arundhati Thomas

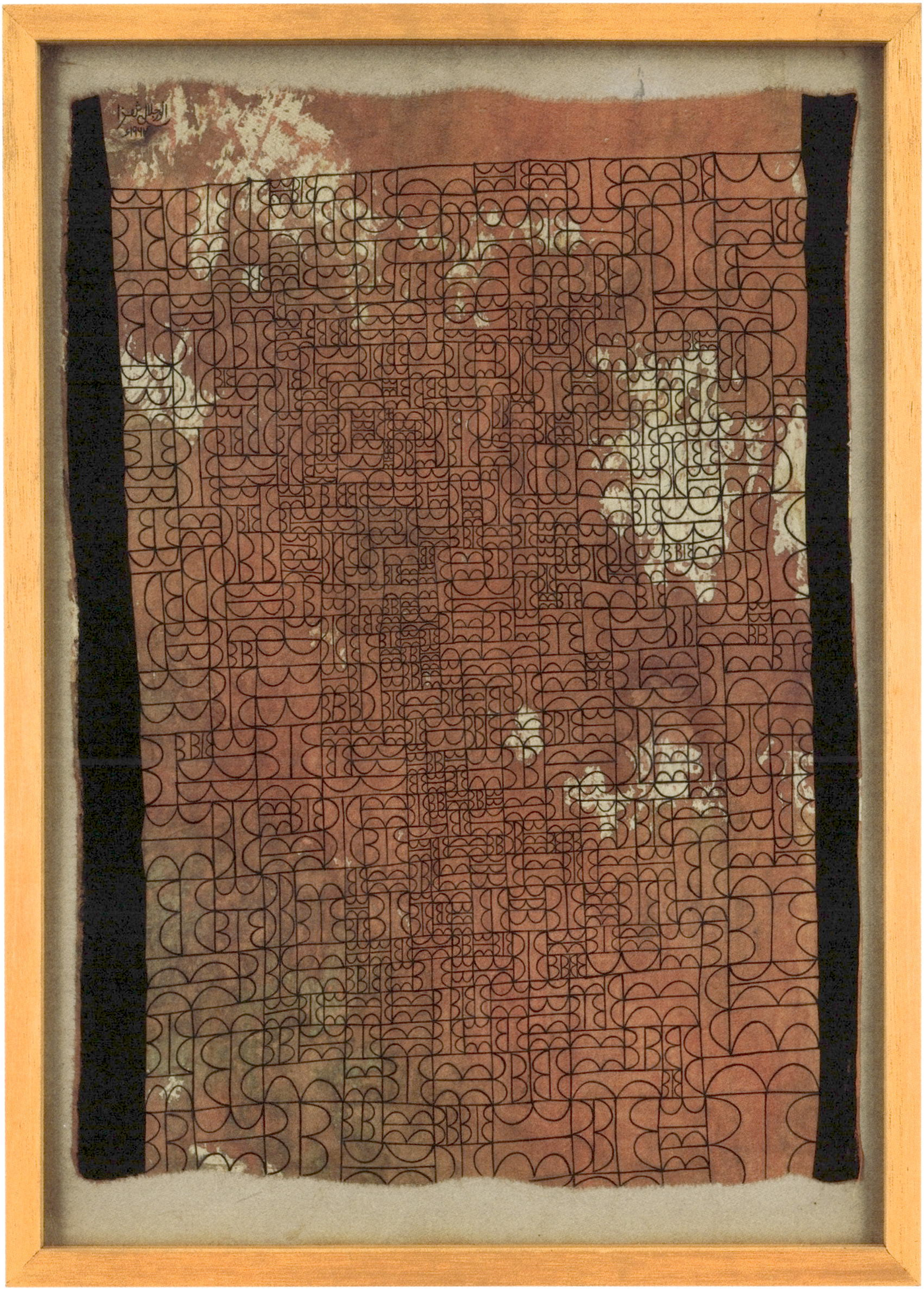

*Love Letter* / *Liebesbrief*, 1962. Öl auf handgefärbtem Stoff / Oil on hand-dyed cloth. 56 × 76 cm

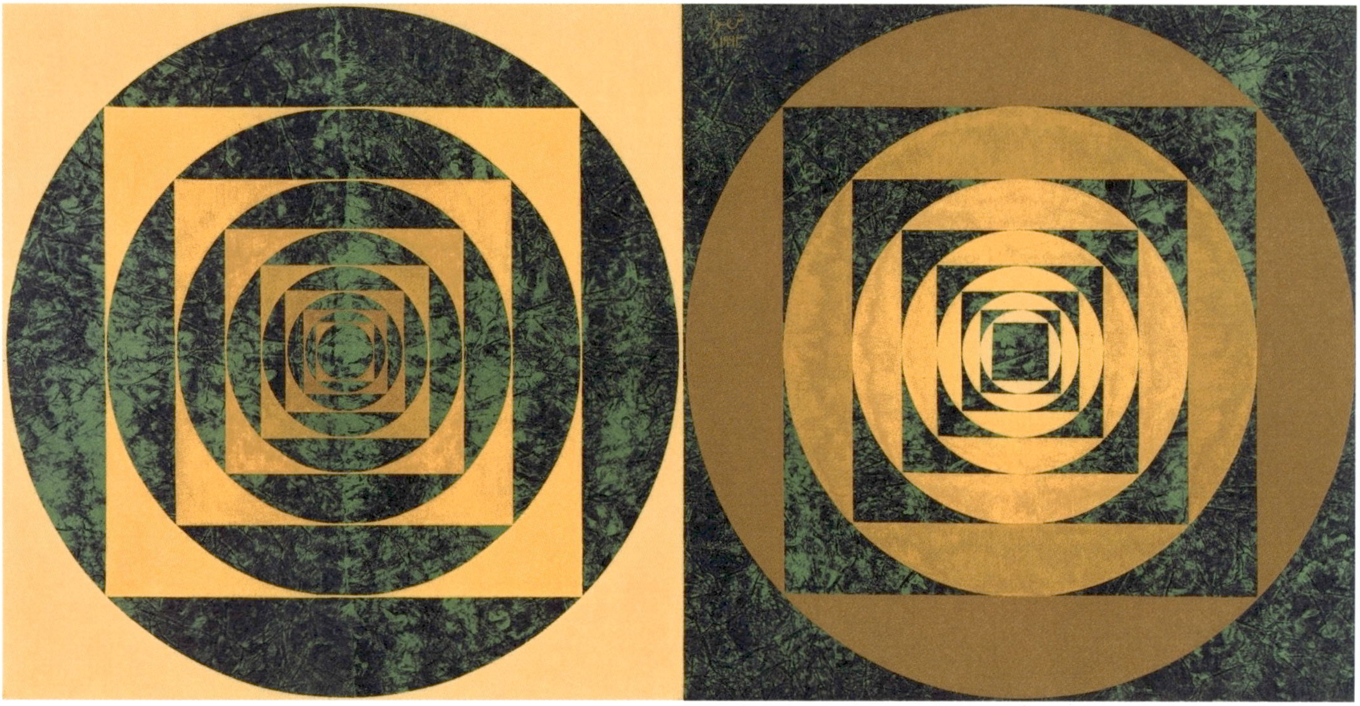

*Advancing & receding: yellow ochre on olive green* | *Voranschreiten & Zurückweichen: Ockergelb auf Olivgrün*, 1963. Öl auf Hartfaserplatte / Oil on hardboard. 123 × 61 cm

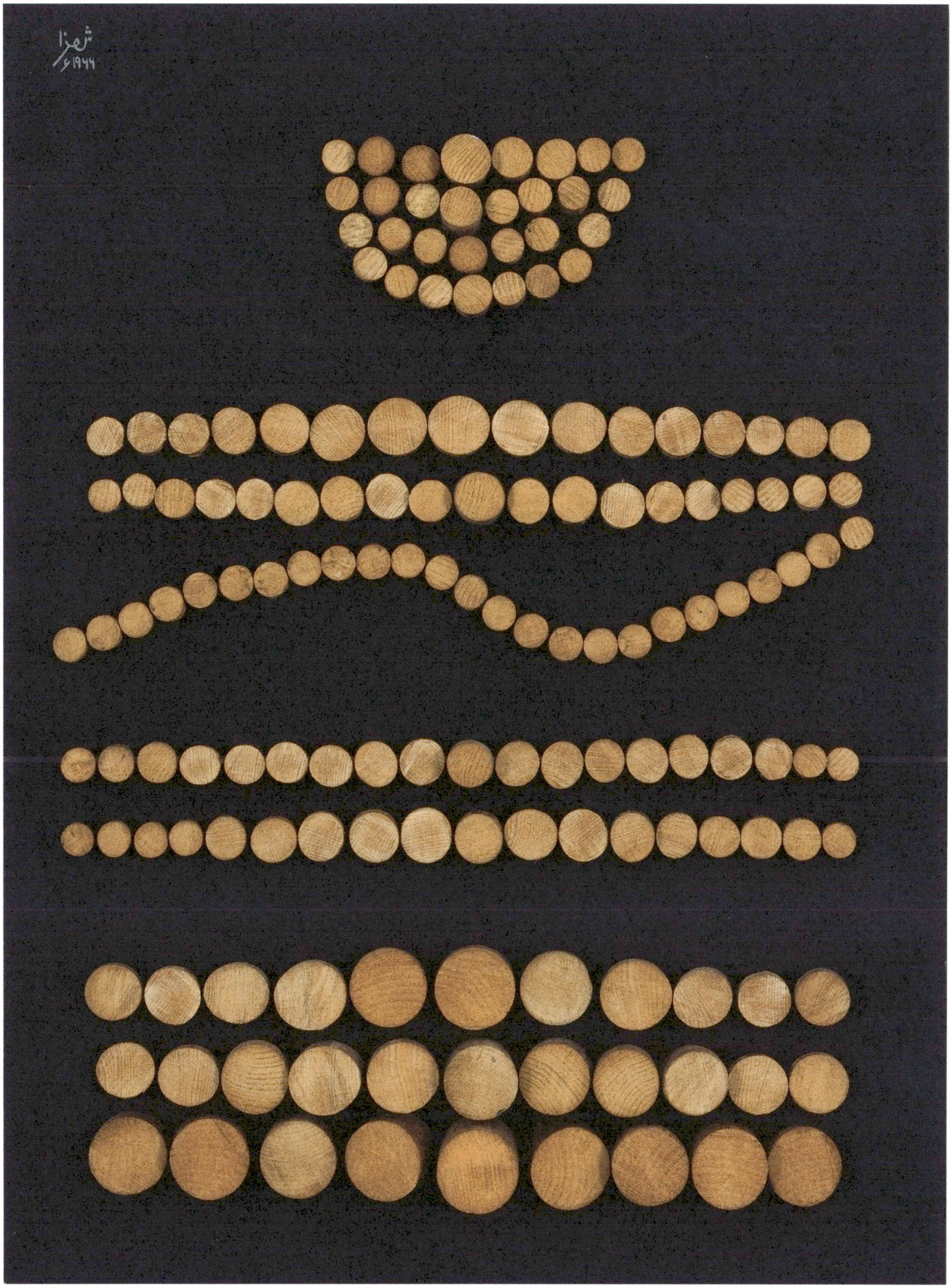

*Sun and the Sea / Sonne und das Meer*, 1966. Holz auf Hartfaserplatte / Wood on hardboard. 45 × 61 cm

# Ahmed Shibrain

Unter Ahmed Shibrains Werk aus den 1960er Jahren findet sich auch das Ölgemälde *Sonnet XVII* („Sonett XVII", 1960), von dem der Künstler einmal sagte, er habe damit das „kulturelle Wesen" seiner sudanesischen Heimat einfangen wollen. Shibrains Werk ist von einer intensiven Auseinandersetzung mit den figurativen Aspekten der arabischen Kalligrafie geprägt, die sich häufig in seinen Arbeiten auf Leinwand und Papier wiederfinden. Seine künstlerische Methode entstand als Teil der *Hurufiyya*-Bewegung: Die unverwechselbare Kombination aus Schrift und Bild knüpft an die Geschichte der Ästhetik afrikanischer und arabischer Sprachen an. Seine Gemälde greifen klar erkennbar Farben aus sudanesischen Landschaften auf: Die Blau- und Blaugrüntöne des Oberen Nils, die Rot-, Gelb- und Brauntöne der traditionellen Architektur in sudanesischen Städten und Dörfern sowie die Aschtöne des Bodens. Häufig dekonstruiert Shibrain islamische Ornamente wie die Mondsichel und deutet Arabesken und/oder Rosetten an. Ebenfalls zu sehen ist *Untitled* („Ohne Titel", 1960), das die kulturelle Vielfalt in Shibrains Lebensumfeld widerspiegelt. Der Künstler kombiniert dafür sprachliche Elemente mit Referenzen auf das kulturelle Erbe und kleinen Ausflügen in die zeitgenössische abstrakte Malerei.

Neben seiner Arbeit als Künstler war Shibrain auch ein angesehener Lehrmeister und beeinflusste eine ganze Generation von Kunstschaffenden im Sudan. Gemeinsam mit seinen Zeitgenoss*innen Ibrahim El-Salahi (geb. 1930) und Kamala Ibrahim Ishag (geb. 1939) gründete er die Khartoum-Schule, eine der wichtigsten Wegbereiterinnen der sudanesischen Moderne. Sie trugen maßgeblich zur Entwicklung einzigartiger Stilrichtungen bei, indem sie afrikanische und islamische Einflüsse miteinander verbanden, um so das Wesen der Republik Sudan nach der Unabhängigkeit von der britischen Kolonialherrschaft einzufangen.

Ahmed Shibrain's works from the 1960s include *Sonnet XVII* (1960), an oil painting the late artist once articulated seeks to capture the 'cultural essence' of his homeland of Sudan. Shibrain's influences emerge from extensive examination of the figurative aspects of Arabic calligraphy, which are often reflected in his works on canvas and paper. He utilises a method that emerged as part of the Hurufiyya movement, a distinctive hybrid of the literary and the visual that is tethered to the histories of African- and Arabic-language aesthetics. His paintings recognisably incorporate colours from Sudanese landscapes, including the blues and blue-greens of the Upper Nile, and the red, yellow and brown tones that represent the traditional architecture of Sudanese cities and villages, as well as the ashen ground. Shibrain frequently deconstructs Islamic decorative motifs such as the crescent moon, alongside suggestions of the arabesque and/or the rosette. Also on view is *Untitled* (1960), which seeks to reflect the cultural diversity of Shibrain's immediate locale by combining elements of language and references to cultural heritage, while giving a nod to contemporary abstract movements.

Aside from his work as an artist, Shibrain was a prominent educator and influenced a generation of creative individuals in Sudan. He co-established the Khartoum School, the best-recognised of Sudan's modern art movements, alongside his contemporaries Ibrahim El-Salahi (b. 1930) and Kamala Ibrahim Ishag (b. 1939). Together, they developed and encouraged distinctive styles that combined African and Islamic influences, reflecting the quintessence of the newly founded nation of Sudan after the end of British colonial rule.

Reem Sawan

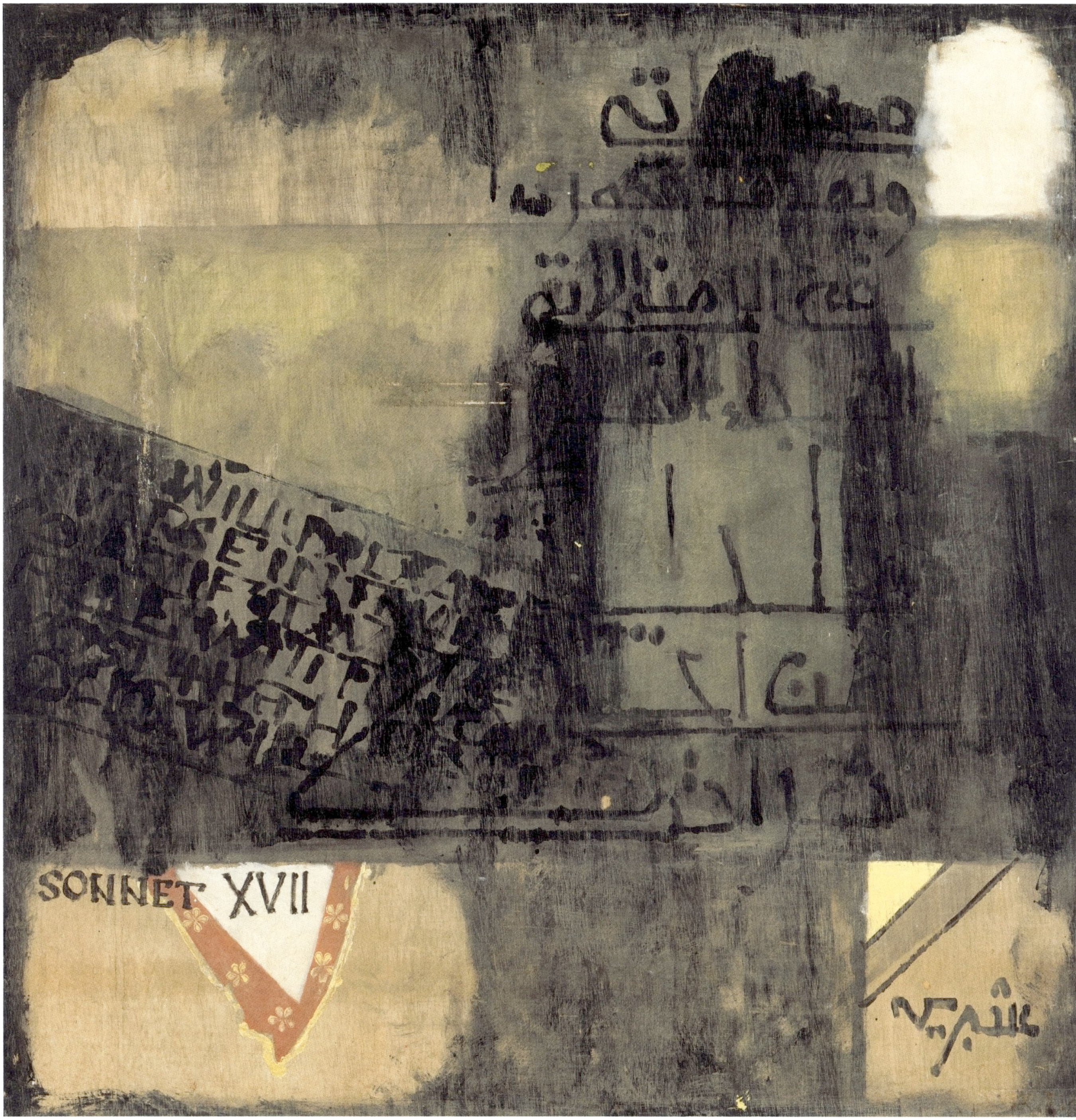


*Sonnet XVII* / *Sonett XVII*, 1960. Öl auf Leinwand / Oil on canvas. 80 × 80 cm

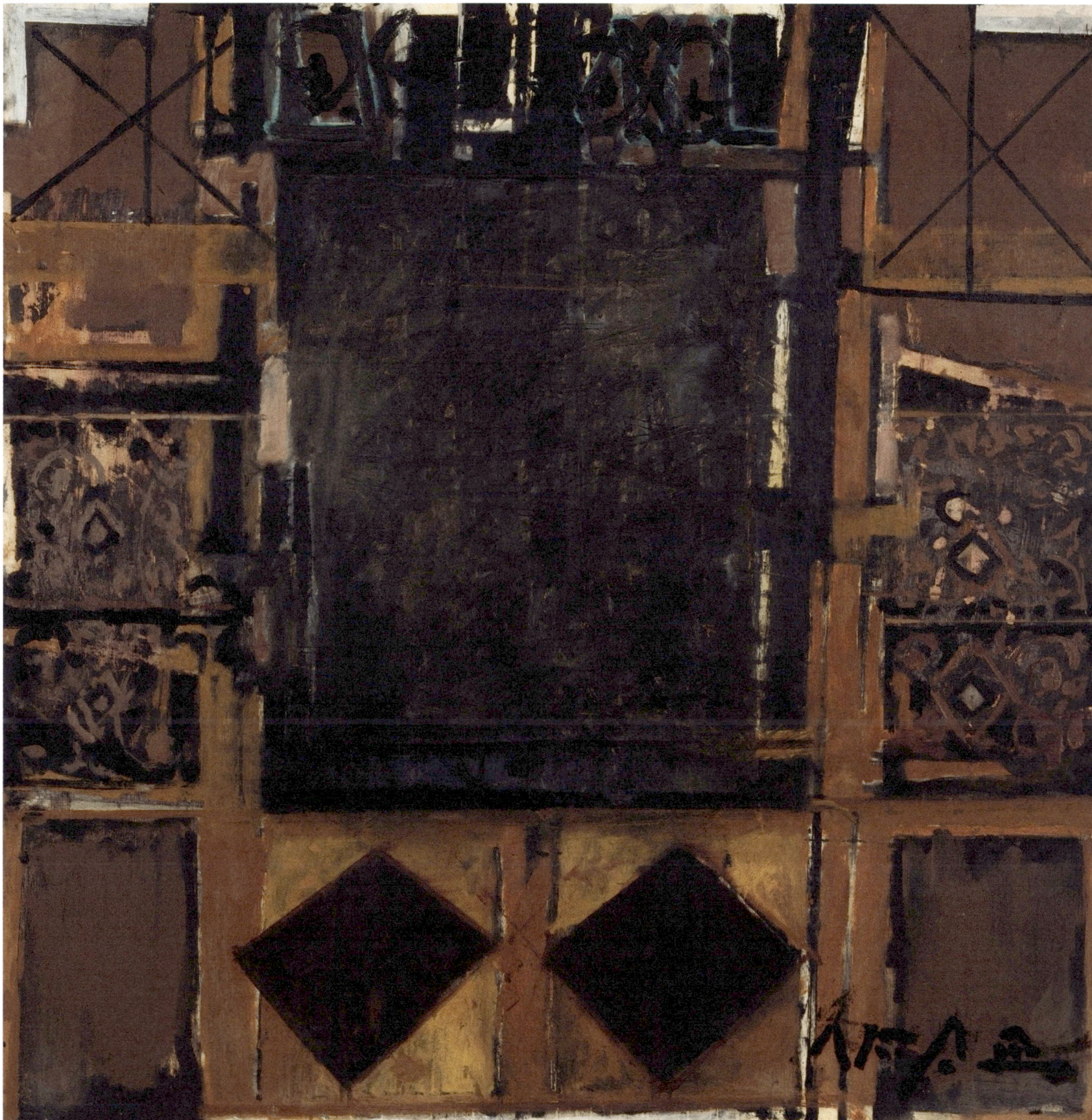

*Untitled* / *Ohne Titel*, 1960. Tinte auf Papier / Ink on paper. 82 × 81 × 3,5 cm

# Nari Ward

Nari Wards Wandskulptur trägt den Titel *We the People (Arabic version)* („Wir, das Volk“ [Arabische Fassung], 2018). Mit Hilfe von Schnürsenkeln schreibt er die arabische Transkription genau dieser Worte ‘الشعب نحن’, „We the People“. Es sind die ersten Worte der Präambel der Verfassung der Vereinigten Staaten von Amerika aus dem Jahre 1787. Der Künstler hat sein Werk ursprünglich in Philadelphia produziert, wo die Verfassung einst erarbeitet und niedergeschrieben wurde. Mit der Zeit erfolgten sprachliche Anpassungen, um der Bedeutung der Worte in unterschiedlichen sozialen und politischen Zusammenhängen Rechnung zu tragen.

In englischer oder arabischer Sprache benötigen die Betrachter*innen ein wenig Zeit, um Wards Schriftzug zu entziffern. Vor der wörtlichen Bedeutung vermittelt sich zunächst die Form der Wörter. Die miteinander verknoteten Schnürsenkel überlagern sich und erinnern ästhetisch an eine nicht vollendete Stickarbeit, die als kunstvolle Wandgestaltung in einem staatlichen oder öffentlichen Kunstmuseum hängen könnte. Die Schnürsenkel wurden von Menschen getragen und entsorgt oder Nari Ward gespendet, der sie als leicht wiedererkennbare Alltagsgegenstände für sein Werk wählte. Aus Sicht des Künstlers repräsentieren sie die Energie der Gehwege – für ihn selbst ein unwägbarer Zwischenraum und Treffpunkt unterschiedlichster Menschen. Die Zweckentfremdung von Fundstücken und Alltagsgegenständen steht im Mittelpunkt von Wards künstlerischer Praxis, die von seinem mehr als 25-jährigen Wirken in Harlem, New York City, inspiriert ist. Hier stellt er die „Zufälligkeit der Straße der systematischen Ordnung einer Ausstellung gegenüber“, wie er selbst sagt.

*We the People (Arabic version)* dient als Anregung und öffentliche Ankündigung. Losgelöst von ihrem ursprünglichen US-amerikanischen Kontext werfen die Worte dennoch dieselbe grundlegende Frage auf: Wer sind die „wir“ dieses „Volkes“? Ist das Statement als Aufruf zur Einheit oder als Mahnung an all diejenigen zu verstehen, die in der Regel nicht mit der Bezeichnung „Volk“ gemeint sind? Ward ist weniger an den tatsächlichen Antworten interessiert, die sehr unterschiedlich ausfallen können, als vielmehr daran, über die kontextuelle Entwicklung seiner Materialien Fragen nach den sozialen, politischen und ökonomischen Beziehungen zwischen den Menschen aufzuwerfen.

Nari Ward’s wall-mounted sculpture *We the People (Arabic version)* (2018) uses shoelaces to spell out ‘الشعب نحن’, an Arabic calligraphic translation of ‘We the People’, the opening words in English of the preamble of the United States Constitution from 1787. The artist originally produced the work in Philadelphia, where the Constitution was written and created, transposing language across eras in order to consider the significance of words when applied in different social and political contexts.

In English or Arabic, Ward’s words demand time of the viewer to interpret and construct. Their form is apparent before their literal meaning. The shoelaces, placed in an overlaid and interlocking fashion, present an aesthetic statement reminiscent of unfinished embroidery, perhaps for a hanging to be treasured material in a national or public art gallery. The shoelaces were collected from individuals who discarded them, or were donated to Ward, who chose them as an easily recognisable quotidian object. For him, they represent the energy of the pavement, which the artist has described as an unpredictable and liminal space that connects different types of people. Repurposing found and everyday objects is at the centre of Ward’s practice, inspired by his more than 25 years working in Harlem, New York City, where he juxtaposes what he refers to as the ‘randomness of the street with the order of the exhibition’.

*We the People (Arabic version)* serves as a proposition and a public announcement. Now detached from its original US context, it still evokes the same fundamental question: Who is the ‘we’ of this ‘people’? Is this statement a call to unison or a reminder of those who are usually excluded when ‘the people’ are called upon? Ward is less interested in the actual answers, which might be multiple, as he is in using the contextual journey of his objects to posit questions about the social, political and economic relationships between human beings.

Sarah Perks

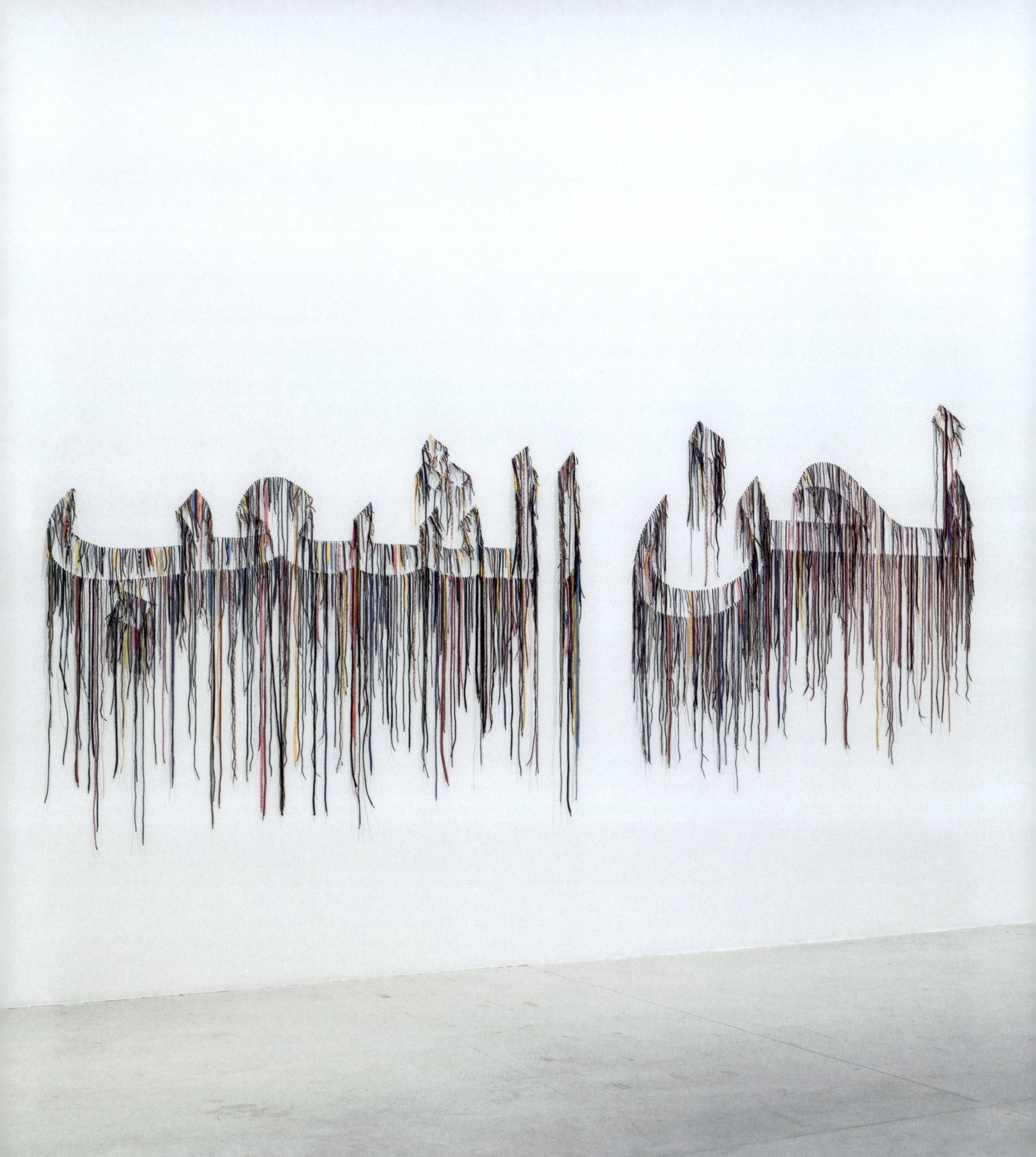

*We the People (Arabic version) | Wir, das Volk (Arabische Fassung)*, 2018. Schnürsenkel / Shoelaces. 569 × 152,4 cm. Installationsansicht / Installation view, *When I Count, There Are Only You…*, Sharjah Art Foundation, 2021.

# Kamal Youssef

Von den vier unverwechselbaren Skulpturen Kamal Youssefs, die in der Ausstellung gezeigt werden, stammen drei aus den späten 1960er, eine aus den frühen 1990er Jahren. Youssef ist seit mehr als 70 Jahren als aktiver Vertreter der ägyptischen Kunstszene und ihrer Diaspora bekannt. Eines seiner Markenzeichen ist die Einbindung kultureller Idiome aus dem reichen Fundus der Kunstgeschichte in seine Werke. Seine Figuren sind oftmals von einer großen Melancholie erfüllt: Sie schauen die Betrachter*innen aus einem tatsächlichen oder symbolischen Gefängnis heraus an. Zudem haftet seinen figurativen Formen und Skulpturen etwas Sinnliches und bisweilen fast schon etwas Komisches an.

Zu Beginn seiner Karriere entwickelte Youssef gemeinsam mit einer Gruppe aufstrebender Kunstschaffender eine eigene künstlerische Ausdrucksform, die an das ägyptische kulturelle Erbe und die Traditionen aus der Zeit vor der britischen Kolonialherrschaft anknüpfte. Das Kollektiv mit dem Namen Groupe de L'Art Contemporain machte national wie international auf sich aufmerksam. Als in den 1950er Jahren das Interesse an einer neuen, als ägyptischer Surrealismus bekannt werdenden Bewegung zunahm, arbeitete auch Youssef in seinen malerischen Kompositionen mit fantastischen, bizarren und absurden Elementen. Seinen Lebensunterhalt verdiente der Künstler fast sein gesamtes Leben lang als Bauingenieur. In seiner Freizeit widmete er sich ununterbrochen der Malerei und Bildhauerei.

Featured in this exhibition are four of Kamal Youssef's idiosyncratic sculptures, of which three were produced in the late 1960s and one in the early 1990s. Youssef has been an active proponent of art in Egypt and its diaspora for more than 70 years, and is recognised for his interpolation of cultural idioms from across the expanse of art's history. The characters in the artist's work are often steeped in melancholy—peering out at the viewer from a prison, whether literal or metaphorical. Too, there is a sensuality to his figurative forms and sculptures, which occasionally veer towards humour.

Early in his career, Youssef, along with a group of emerging artists, sought to create a situated formal artistic practice, invoking heritage and tradition that stemmed from a period prior to the British colonial rule of Egypt. The collective went by the name Groupe de L'Art Contemporain and were recognised nationally and throughout the world. From the 1950s onwards, with the rise and consciousness of a movement recognised as Egyptian Surrealism, Youssef adopted notions of the fantastical, the bizarre and the incongruous into his painterly compositions. To earn his living, the artist pursued a career as a civil engineer for much of life, painting and sculpting consistently throughout it all.

Omar Kholeif with Reem Sawan

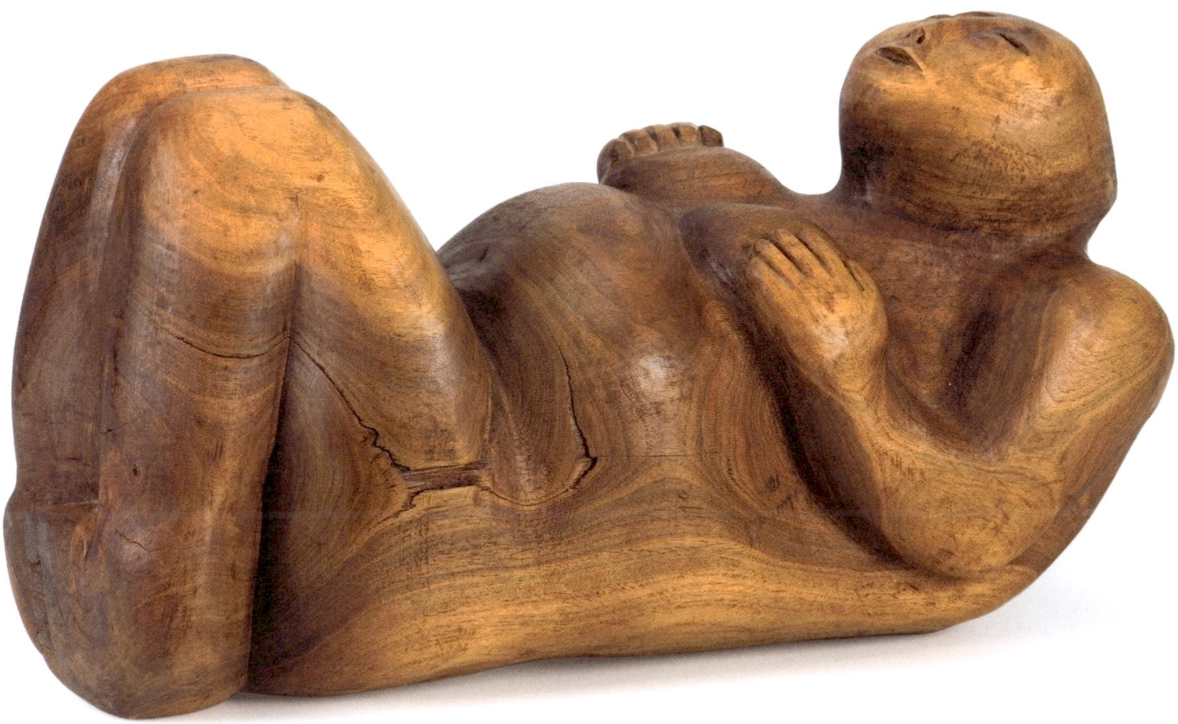

*Pregnant Daughter | Schwangere Tochter*, 1991. Holz / Wood. 48,26 × 25,4 × 20,32 cm

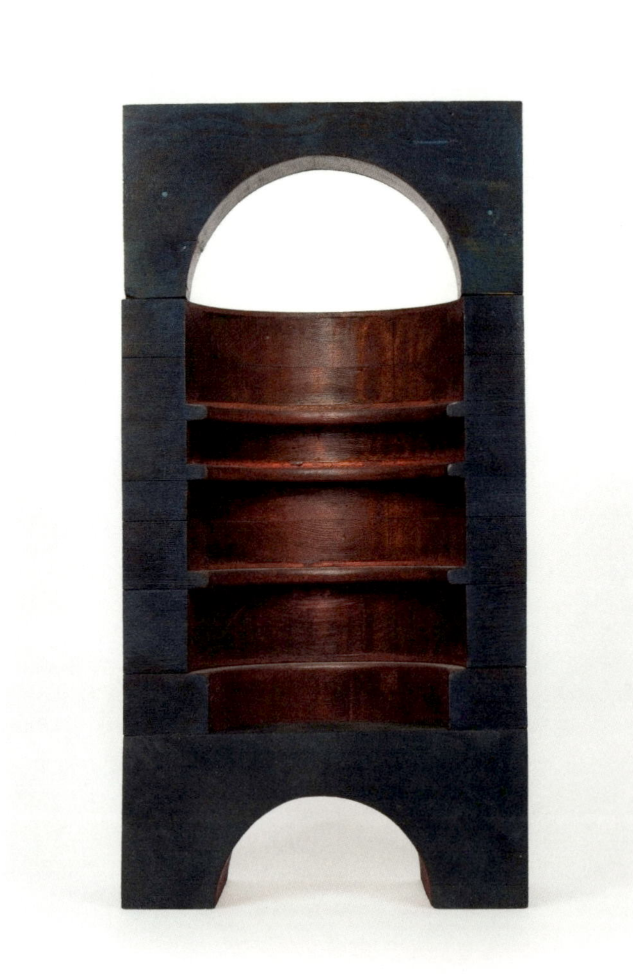

*Pattern 1* / *Muster 1*, 1968–1969. Holz, Farbe / Wood, dye.
24 × 40,64 × 11,5 cm

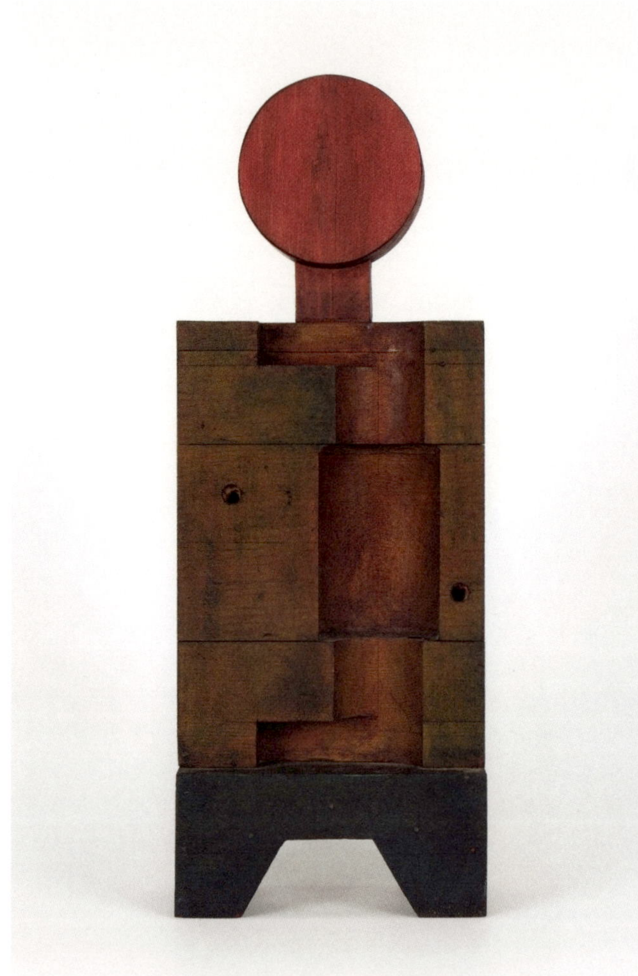

*Pattern 3* / *Muster 3*, 1968–1969. Holz, Farbe / Wood, dye.
23 × 55,88 × 13 cm

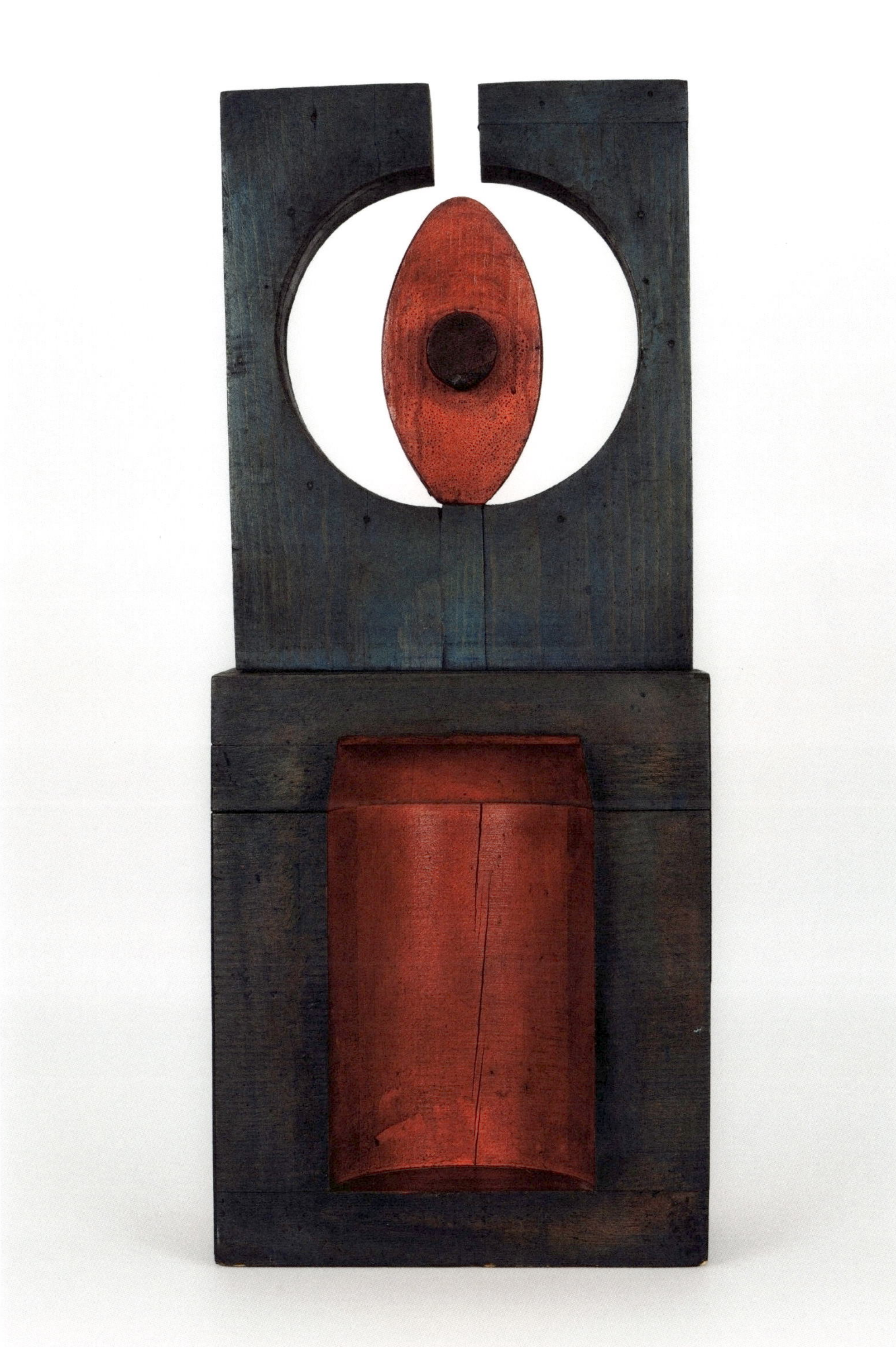

*Pattern 5* / *Muster 5*, 1968–1969. Holz, Farbe / Wood, dye. 20,32 × 53,34 × 10,16 cm

# Zurückgewonnene Porträts: Unsichtbare Wiederherstellung

# 2

# Reclaimed Portraits: Invisible Acts of Repair

# Sarah Abu Abdallah

Ein Video zeigt die Künstlerin beim Bemalen eines Autowracks mit blassrosa Farbe. Dasselbe Auto steht als Teil der Installation neben dem Bildschirm. In einer zehnminütigen Videoschleife ist zu sehen, wie Abdallah das Auto in einer performativen Geste mit Farbe bespritzt und immer wieder zurücktritt, um den Fortschritt ihrer Arbeit zu überprüfen. Am Ende legt sie den Pinsel zur Seite und klettert – unübersehbar erschöpft von der Gluthitze unter ihrer schweren Abaya (einem dunklen Überkleid) – demonstrativ auf den Beifahrersitz. Das Werk entstand zu einer Zeit, als Frauen in Saudi-Arabien, dem Heimatland der Künstlerin, das Autofahren noch nicht erlaubt war.

Abdallah hatte den Wagen zwei Jahre zuvor entdeckt. Jemand hatte ihn vor ihrem College in Sharnah zurückgelassen. Sie beschloss, das Auto an sich zu nehmen. Über den heruntergekommenen Blechhaufen bemerkte die Künstlerin: „Ich wollte ihm Leben einhauchen und einen Wert geben." Mit dem Kunstwerk wolle sie zum Ausdruck bringen, welche Ängste sie im Zusammenhang mit ihrer eingeschränkten Mobilität in Saudi-Arabien empfindet. Das Ergebnis ist für sie ein Versuch, den Möglichkeitsspielraum in einer ansonsten offenbar hoffnungslosen Situation aufzuzeigen. Die stereotype Verwendung der Farbe Rosa für den Wagen einer Frau ist beabsichtigt.

Die Installation ist Teil von Abdallahs Frühwerk. Seitdem hat sich die Künstlerin in ihrer Praxis mit der Frage beschäftigt, wie poetische und absurde Gesten die latenten Mechanismen des häuslichen Lebens in Saudi-Arabien und der Staaten des Golf-Kooperationsrats ingesamt aufzudecken vermögen. Das Verhältnis zwischen Bildschirm und Objekt in der Installation *Saudi Automobile* (2011) zeugt auch von dem anhaltenden Interesse der Künstlerin am Internet als Möglichkeit des – ortsunabhängigen – Zugangs zu neuen Orten und gemeinsam geteilten Realitäten. Bei diesen und anderen Multimedia-Arbeiten geht es Abdallah nicht so sehr darum, die Öffentlichkeit herauszufordern. Vielmehr zeigen sie die Folgen möglicher Reaktionen auf verschiedene Formen der Unterdrückung im privaten Bereich auf.

A video shows the artist painting a wrecked car with a pale pink paint, the same car that forms the installation across from it. A 10-minute loop, the video follows the artist's performative gesture of splashily painting the automobile, occasionally stepping back to view her progress. At the end, clearly exhausted from the sweltering heat under the weight of her *abaya* (a dark overgarment), she puts down the brush and pointedly enters the passenger seat. The work was produced at a time when women were not yet permitted to drive in Saudi Arabia, the artist's home country.

Sarah Abu Abdallah had located the car a couple of years before, abandoned outside her college in Sharjah, before she decided to claim it. Referring to the worn heap of metal, in her own words, the artist has noted, 'I decided to give it life and give it value'. The work articulated her fears about her lack of mobility in Saudi Arabia, and the resulting work is perceived as an attempt to instil the prospect of the possible in an otherwise seemingly hopeless situation. The stereotypical use of pink for a female-owned car is intentional.

The piece is one of Abdallah's earliest completed works; her practice has since evolved to consider how poetic and absurd gestures can reveal the inner workings of domestic life in Saudi Arabia and the broader GCC context. The relationship between screen and object of the *Saudi Automobile* (2011) installation also manifests the artist's ongoing interest with the internet as a point of access—one based not on geographical proximity, but providing an opportunity to connect to new locations and shared realities. This, and other multimedia works by Abdallah, do not so much mount a grand challenge on a public level; instead revealing potential responses to, and effects of, different forms of oppression within the realm of the personal.

Sarah Perks

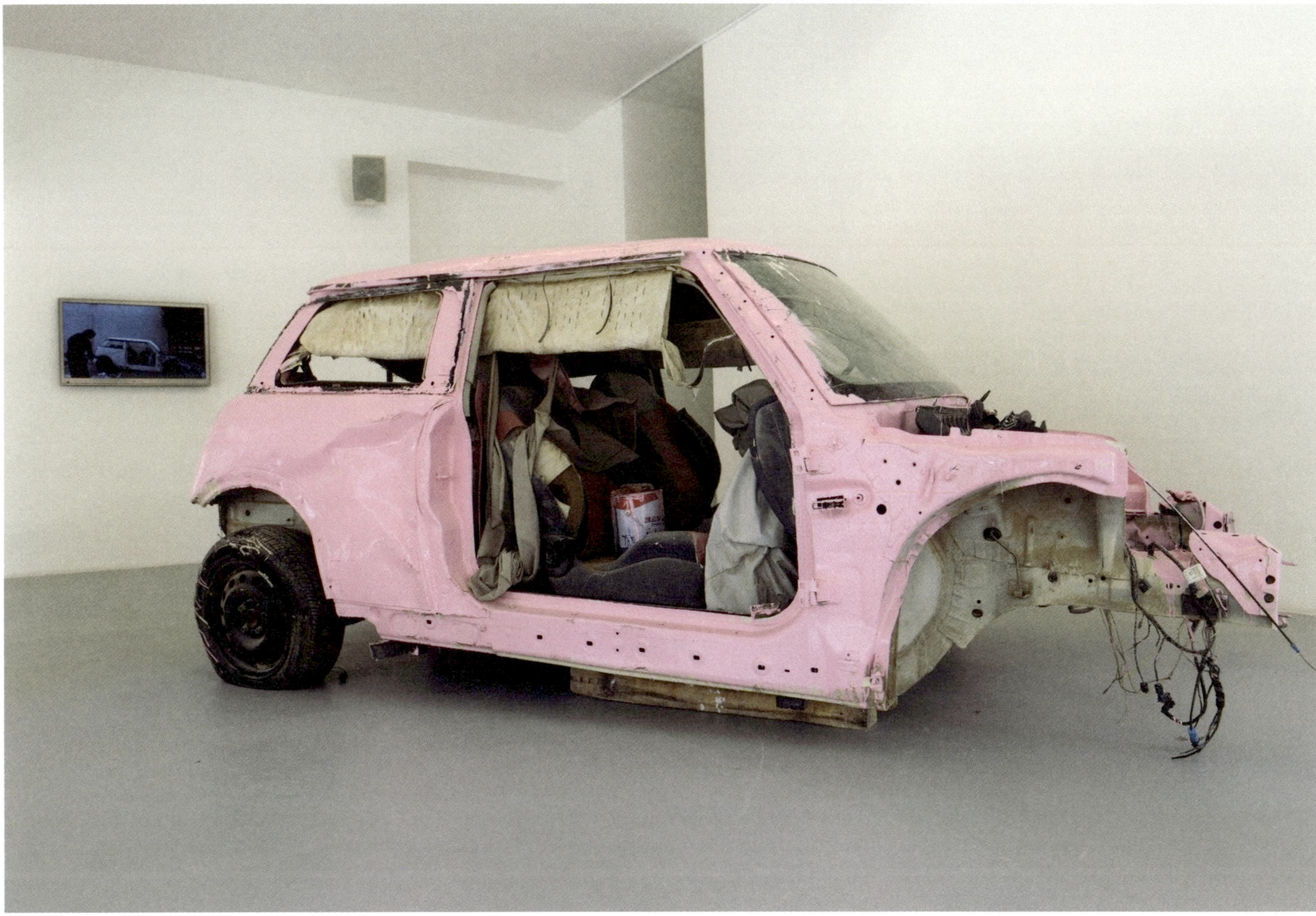

*Saudi Automobile*, 2011. Einkanal-HD-Farbvideo, Sound; Auto, rosa Farbe / Single-channel HD colour video, sound; car, pink paint. 10 Minuten (Videoschleife) / 10 minutes (looped). 162 × 316 × 186 cm. Reproduziert von der Sharjah Art Foundation / Reproduced by Sharjah Art Foundation. Installationsansicht / Installation view, *Sharjah Biennial 11*, Sharjah Art Foundation, 2015.

# Latif Al Ani

Latif Al Anis fotografisches Werk, zwischen den 1950er und dem Ende der 1970er Jahre entstanden, ist die Chronik einer komplexen und wechselhaften Zeit im Irak. Der Ölhandel entwickelte sich, der Tourismus blühte auf, und das Land wurde zunehmend kosmopolitisch. Al Ani war einer der wenigen Fotografen, die zu dieser Zeit im Irak arbeiteten, wodurch sein umfangreiches Archiv zu einem unvergleichlichen Porträt einer Nation wurde. Al Ani bezeichnet diese Ära als „goldenes Zeitalter", da seine Bilder die Neugierde des Landes auf die moderne Welt und dessen nach der Revolution und dem raschen Abzug der Briten im Jahr 1958 aufkeimende Unabhängigkeit festhielten.

Die Vielfalt der erhaltenen Bilder seines Archivs zeugt auch von Al Anis Reisefreudigkeit, mit der er das Land im Rahmen seiner Arbeit für die Magazine der irakischen Ölindustrie *Ahl Al Naft* [„Menschen des Öls"] und *Iraq Petroleum* durchstreifte. Die dabei entstandenen Werke zeigen die zunehmende industrielle Modernisierung des Landes und der Arbeit und gleich daneben antike Ruinen und ländliche Szenen von Schafhirten, die von Touristen fotografiert werden, oder von Frauen, die einkaufen gehen oder unverschleiert Sport treiben.

*US Couple at Taq Kasra (Ruins of Ctesiphon), Al Mada'in, Salman Pak, Bagdad* („US-amerikanisches Paar in Taq Kasra [Ruinen von Ktesiphon], Al Mada'in, Salman Pak, Bagdad", 1965) zeigt einen Rabāb-Spieler mit einem amerikanischen Paar aus Colorado bei den Ruinen von Ktesiphon nahe Bagdad. Es ist eine symbolische Szene für das frühe kulturelle und finanzielle Interesse der USA am Irak, das allerdings in den 1990er und 2000er Jahren während der Golf- und Irakkriege eine verheerende Wendung nahm. „Damals ging es Amerika um die Freiheit (…) es war unser Traum, Amerika zu sehen. Jetzt steht Amerika für die Kontrolle und Herrschaft über die Welt", erklärte Al Ani. *Fashion show at the Nineveh ruins in Mosul, Iraq* („Modenschau bei den Nineveh-Ruinen in Mossul, Irak", 1965) bezeugt den modernen Impuls für die Emanzipation der irakischen Frauen. Das unbeschwerte Ereignis fand an einem Ort statt, der heute zu den am meisten gefährdeten historischen Stätten der Welt gehört und in großen Teilen unwiederbringlich zerstört ist.

Seine zweite Anstellung fand Al Ani im irakischen Informationsministerium, wo er mit dem Aufbau eines Fotoarchivs betraut war. Mit der Machtübernahme Saddam Husseins im Jahr 1979 und dem Beginn des Iran-Irak-Kriegs im Jahr 1980 klang jedoch seine Faszination für die Fotografie ab. Das von ihm aufgebaute Archiv wurde im dritten Golfkrieg ab 2003 weitgehend zerstört. Die noch erhaltenen Fotos wurden von der Arab Image Foundation und dank der Arbeit der Kuratorin Tamara Chalabi verwahrt. Al Anis Weitsicht bei der Darstellung einer Welt, die inzwischen verschwunden ist, verleiht seinem Werk eine zusätzliche Bedeutung. Sie bietet aber auch eine Vision für eine mögliche neue Ära nach der jüngsten blutigen Geschichte des Irak: „Angst war eines meiner Hauptmotive, alles so zu dokumentieren, wie es war. Ich habe alles getan, was ich konnte, um diese Zeit zu dokumentieren und zu bewahren."

Produced from the 1950s to the end of the 1970s, Latif Al Ani's photographic work chronicles a complex and fragile period in Iraq, one that ushered a developing oil trade, burgeoning tourism and cosmopolitan possibility in the country. Al Ani was one of the few photographers working in Iraq at that time, while his remaining archive provides an unrivalled portrait of a nation. The era is referred to as a 'golden age' by Al Ani, his pictures capturing the country's moment of curiousity with the modern world and its prospering independence after the quick departure of the British in 1958 after the Revolution.

The richness of the surviving archive is a testament to Al Ani's access to travel, criss-crossing the country as part of his work for Iraq's oil industry magazines *Ahl Al Naft* (*People of Oil*) and *Iraq Petroleum*. The resulting works portray an influx of industrial modernisation and labour alongside ancient ruins and rural scenes of shepherds herding sheep with tourists taking photographs, or women shopping, playing sports unveiled.

*US Couple at Taq Kasra (Ruins of Ctesiphon), Al Mada'in, Salman Pak, Baghdad* (1965) depicts a *rabāb* player with an American couple from Colorado at the ruins of Ctesiphon, near Baghdad. It is indicative of the United States' early cultural and financial interest in Iraq, which ultimately took a devasting turn through the 1990s and 2000s during the Gulf and Iraq wars. Al Ani has stated: 'At that time America cared about freedom … It was our dream to see America. Now what America means is to control and rule the world'. *Fashion show at the Nineveh ruins in Mosul, Iraq* (1965) exemplifies the modern moment of female independence and pleasure standing in what now remains as one of the most imperilled historical sites in the world, with numerous of its sections vandalised beyond repair.

Al Ani found his second job at the Iraqi Ministry of Information, where he was tasked with establishing a photography archive. However, he ended his fascination with photography during the ascendency of Saddam Hussein in 1979 and the beginning of the Iran-Iraq War in 1980. The archive he built was largely destroyed in the war that began in 2003, the remaining images being preserved by the Arab Image Foundation and through the work of the curator Tamara Chalabi. Al Ani's prescience to record a world now vanished adds further poignancy to his body of work. It also offers a vision of a possible new era from Iraq's recent bloody history: 'Fear was a major motive to document everything as it was. I did all that I could to document, to safeguard that time'.

Chris McCormack

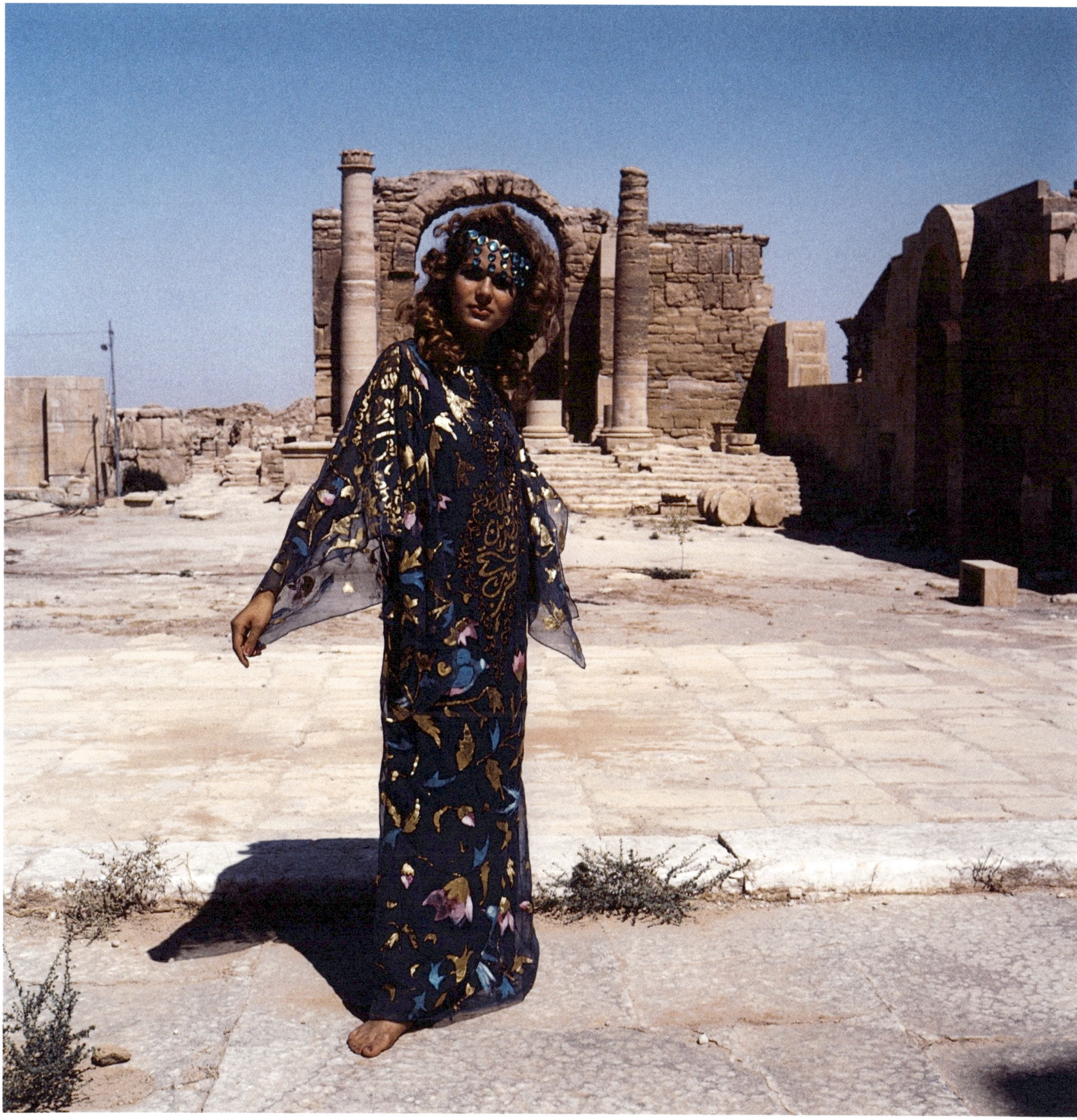

*Fashion show at the Nineveh ruins in Mosul, Iraq / Modenschau bei den Niniveh-Ruinen in Mossul, Irak*, 1965 (Abzug / printed 2019). Digitale Reproduktion eines im chromogenen Verfahren entwickelten Negativs / Digital reproduction of chromogenic process film negative. 60 × 60 cm

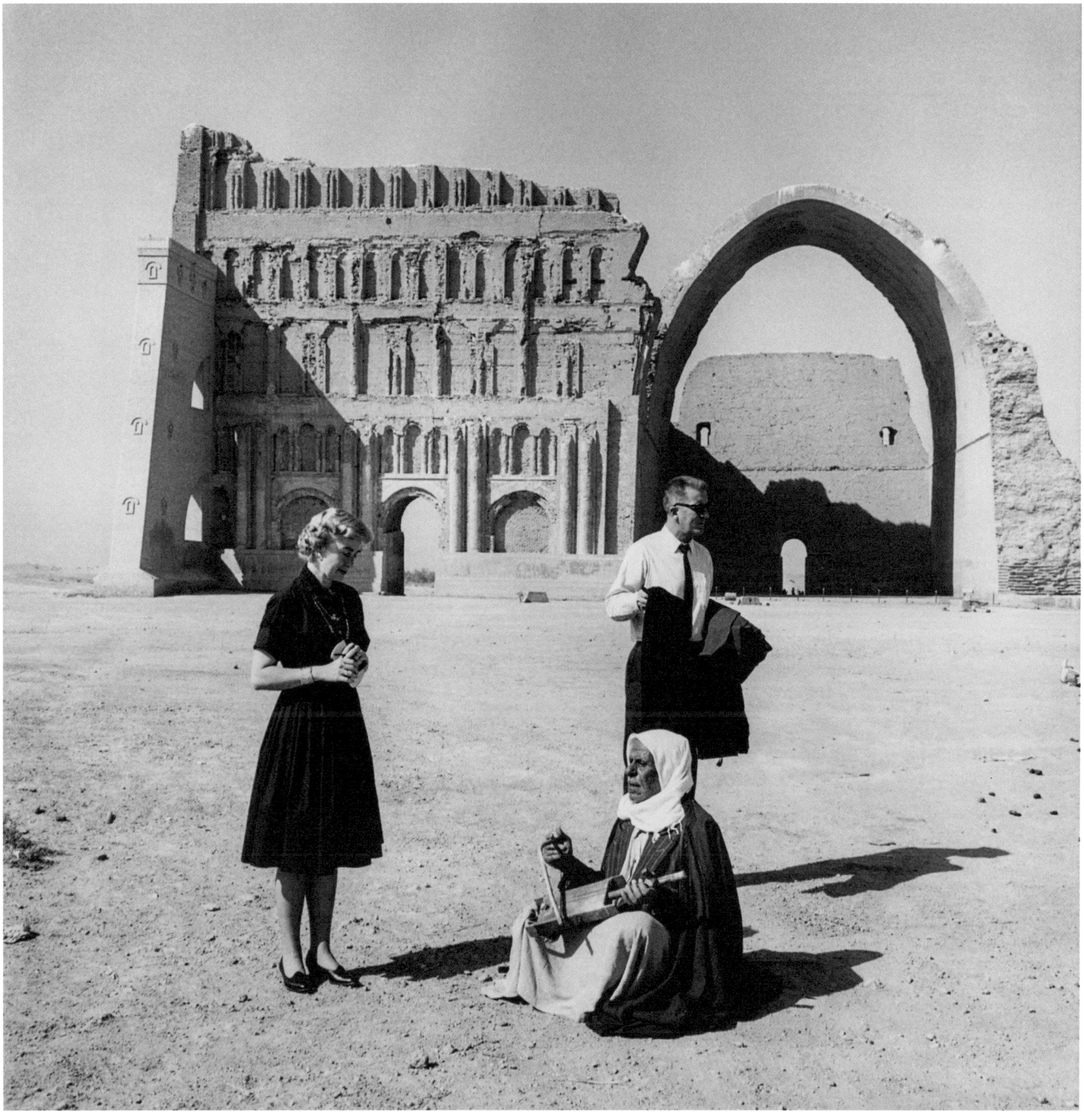

*Family from the American Friends of the Middle East organization on a visit to Iraq Ctesiphon Arch, Iraq* / *Familie aus der American-Friends-of-the-Middle-East-Organisation bei einem Besuch am Taq Kasra (Bogen von Kthesiphon), Irak*, ca. 1964. Digitale Reproduktion eines Silbergelatineabzugs auf Film / Digital reproduction of gelatin silver negative on film. 60 × 60 cm

Text siehe S. 66
see p. 66

# Rasheed Araeen

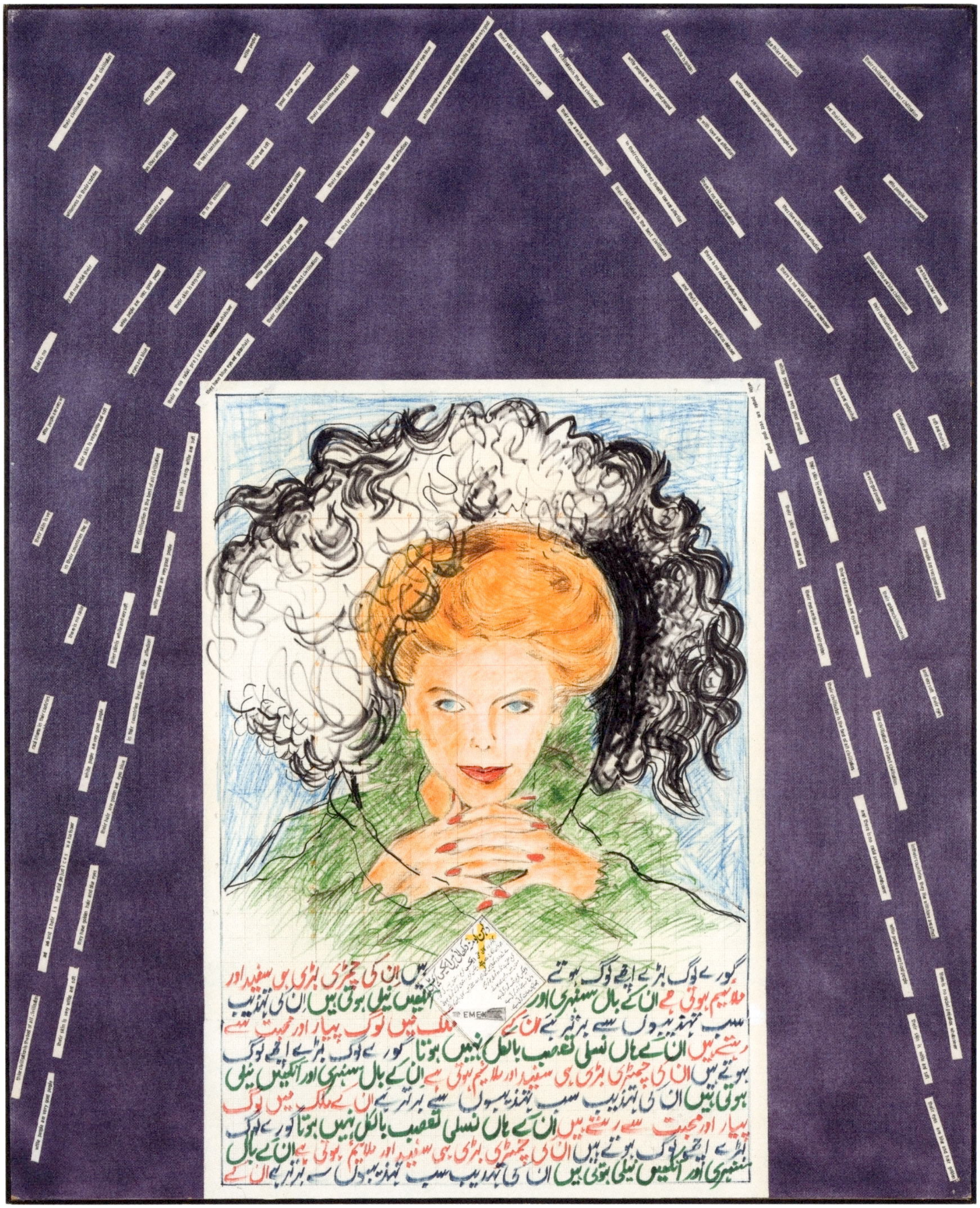

*Black Sheep* / *Schwarzes Schaf*, 1983–1984. Acryl, Papier, Farbstift, Filzstift auf Platte / Acrylic, paper, coloured pencil, felt pen on board. 91,5 × 122 cm

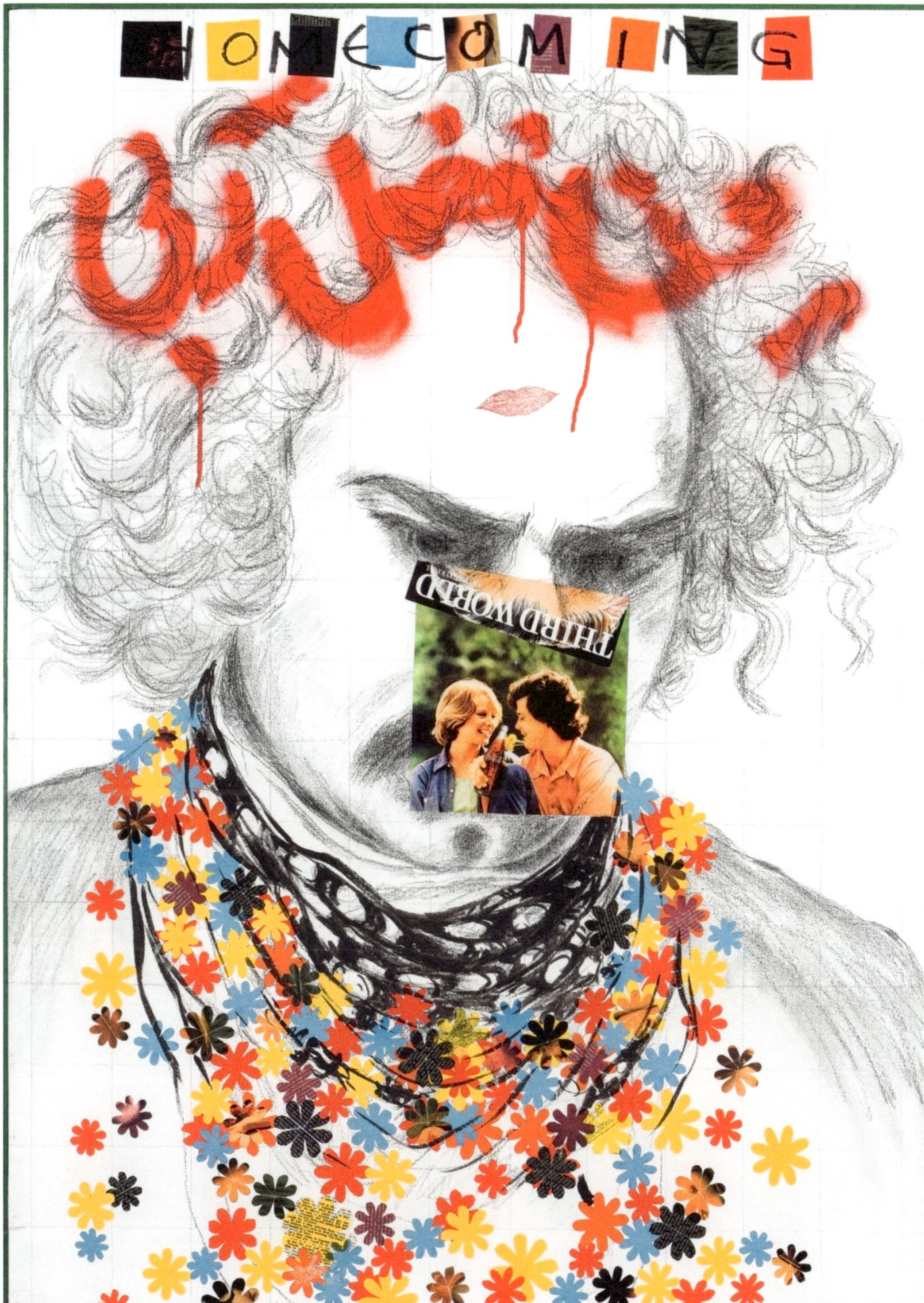


*Homecoming | Heimkehr*, 1982. Bleistift, Acryl, Collage auf Platte / Pencil, acrylic, spray paint, collage on board. 76,25 × 122 cm

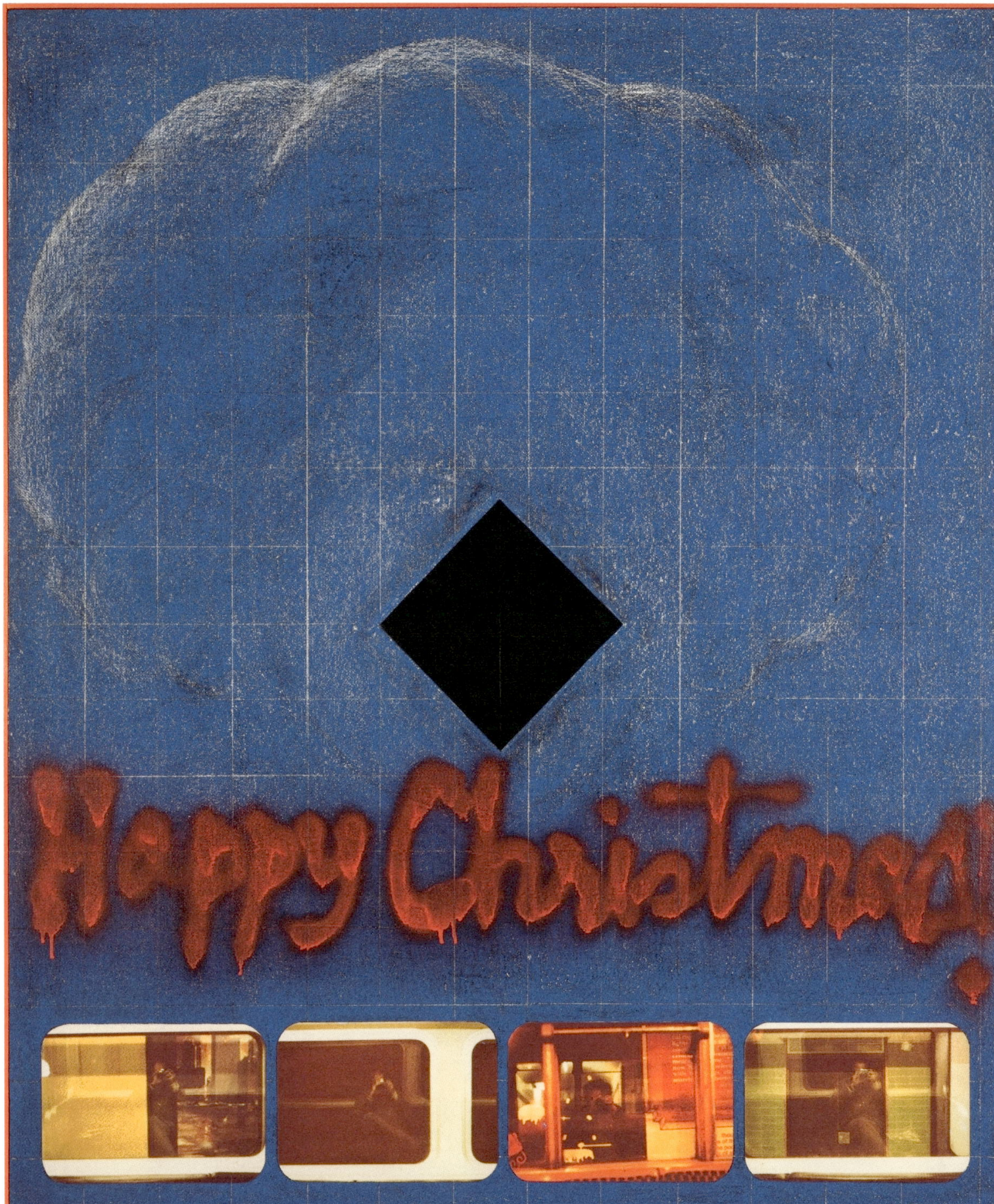


*Happy Christmas / Frohe Weihnachten*, 1979–1983. Acryl, Sprühfarbe, Farbfotografien, Spiegel / Acrylic, spray paint, colour photographs, mirror. 91,5 × 122 cm

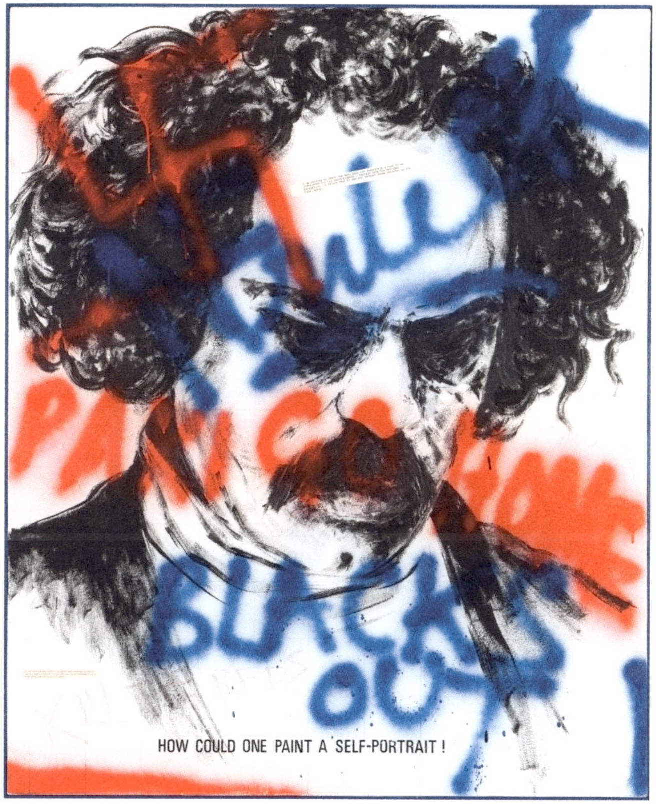


*How Could One Paint a Self-Portrait / Wie könnte man ein Selbstporträt malen*, 1978–1979. Acryl, Sprühfarbe, Papier auf Platte / Acrylic, spray paint, paper on board. 91,5 × 122 cm

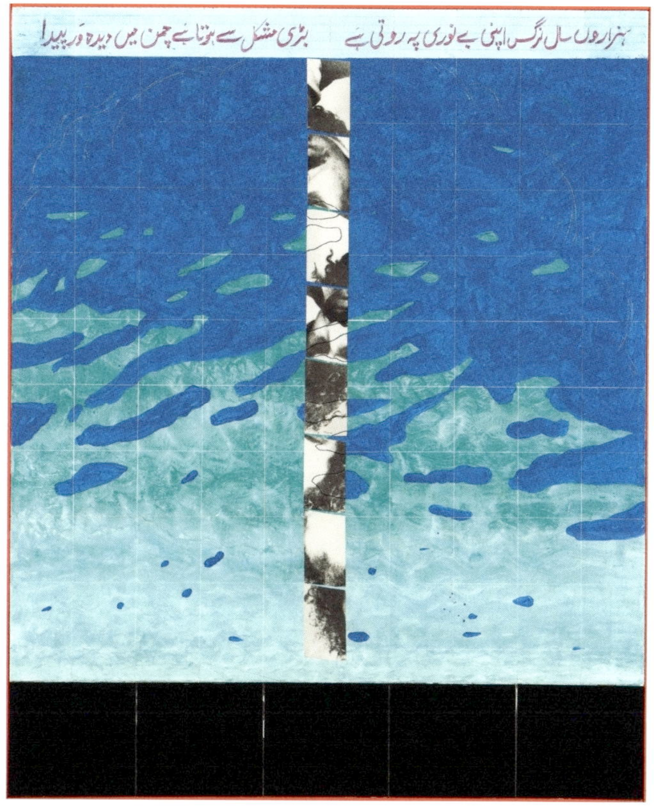


*Narcissus / Narziss*, 1979–1983. Acryl, Papier, Urdu-Schriftzug, Spiegel / Acrylic, paper, Urdu script, mirror. 91,5 × 122 cm

# Thuraya Al-Baqsami

2017 zeigte das CCS Bard in Zusammenarbeit mit der Barjeel Art Foundation in New York eine Ausstellung mit Werken aus den Jahren 1990 und 2016, die den gemeinsamen geopolitischen Raum der arabischen Welt reflektieren. Die erste Hälfte des Titels der von Fawz Kabra kuratierten Ausstellung *No to the Invasion* („Nein zur Invasion") stammt von einem Linolschnittplakat, das Thuraya Al-Baqsami im August 1990 kurz nach dem irakischen Einmarsch in Kuwait entwarf und unter Widerstandsgruppen verteilte. Vor einem dunkelblauen Hintergrund sind in weißer Farbe nebeneinander die Gesichter eines Mannes und einer Frau dargestellt. Darunter steht auf Arabisch der Satz „Nein zur Invasion".

Der Golfkrieg (1990–1991) führte zu einer spürbaren Neuausrichtung der Kunst von Al-Baqsami, die zunächst in Kairo und Moskau studierte. Anschließend lebte sie mit ihrem Mann, dem kuwaitischen Diplomaten Mohammed Al-Qadiri, der später in Kriegsgefangenschaft geriet, eine Zeit lang in Afrika. Die Leinwände, Drucke und Arbeiten auf Papier, die Al-Baqsami während dieser Zeit schuf, enthalten eine unmittelbare, intuitive Symbolik, die eine Reaktion auf das kollektive Trauma der Menschen in Kuwait war. Es war eine Zeit, in der Al-Baqsami sich selbst darüber wunderte, dass sie im Begriff war, „tote Menschen zu malen", wie sie es einmal formulierte.

Die in dieser Ausstellung gezeigte Arbeit *The Last Shot* („Der letzte Schuss") von 1991 ist charakteristisch für diese Phase. Auf der mit Pastell- und Acrylfarben bemalten Leinwand sind zwei kahlköpfige Gestalten von den Schultern an aufwärts zu sehen – eine wiederkehrende Form im Werk der Künstlerin. Die Figuren sind aschfahl und stehen Rücken an Rücken, als stützten sie sich gegenseitig, wobei die eine ihren Kopf zurückgeworfen hat, um im Nacken der anderen Trost zu finden. Rote Kreise markieren die Schläfe der einen und das Herz der anderen Figur, bei Letzterer ist seitlich am Kopf auch eine Zielmarkierung zu sehen, die an Schusswunden erinnert. Die Augen der Figuren sind schwarz, mit Ausnahme der rot geränderten weißen Iris und der schwarzen Pupillen. Dadurch wird der das Bild beherrschende Schrecken noch verstärkt, zu dem auch ein aus dem schwarzen Himmel auf die beiden Figuren zuschießender roter Pfeil beiträgt.

In 2017, CCS Bard, in collaboration with the Barjeel Art Foundation, staged an exhibition in New York bringing together works made between 1990 and 2016 that reflected the Arab World's shared geopolitical space. Curated by Fawz Kabra, the first half of the exhibition's title, *No to the Invasion*, was taken from a linocut-printed poster created by Thuraya Al-Baqsami in August 1990, just after Iraq invaded Kuwait, and distributed among resistance groups. Against a dark blue background, the face of a man and woman rendered in white are shown side by side. The phrase 'No to the Invasion' is written below them in Arabic.

The Gulf War (1990–91) instigated a marked shift in the art of Al-Baqsami, who studied in Cairo and Moscow before spending time living in Africa alongside her husband, Mohammed Al-Qadiri, a Kuwaiti diplomat who would become a prisoner of war. The canvases, prints and works on paper that Al-Baqsami made during that period express a visceral symbolism that responded to the trauma being experienced collectively in Kuwait. It was a time when, as Al-Baqsami once put it, she found herself 'painting dead people'.

*The Last Shot*, featured in this exhibition, is characteristic of this moment. Created in 1991 with pastels and acrylics on canvas, two bald figures—recurring forms in the artist's work—are seen from the shoulders up. Rendered ashen white, they stand back-to-back as if they are leaning on each other for support, with one head thrown back to find comfort in the nook of the other's neck. Red circles mark one figure's temple and the other's heart, the latter also bearing the mark of a target on the side of their head, suggesting bullet wounds. Their eyes are black, save for red-lined white irises and black pupils, amplifying a state of terror that infuses the image, as a red arrow shoots down towards them from a black sky.

Stephanie Bailey

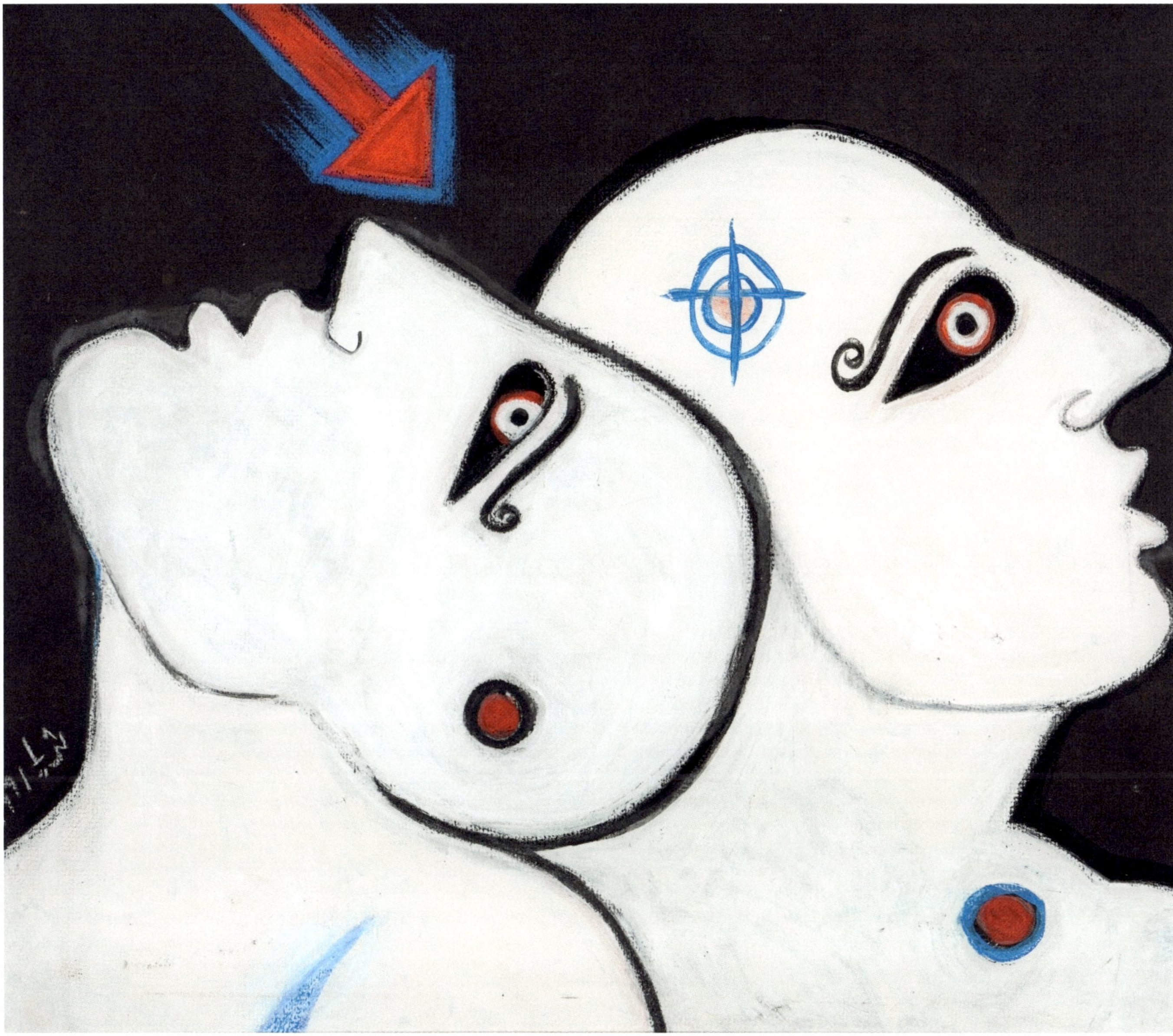

*The Last Shot* | *Der letzte Schuss*, 1991. Pastellfarben, Acryl auf Leinwand / Pastels, acrylic on canvas. 60 × 50 cm

# Semiha Berksoy

Semiha Berksoy war ein Multitalent: Sie wirkte als Opernsängerin, Schauspielerin, Dichterin und Malerin und gilt gemeinhin als Ikone des türkischen Kulturbetriebs im Istanbul des späten 20. Jahrhunderts. Berksoy hatte ein ausgeprägtes Talent zur Selbstmythologisierung. Sie war eine Mystikerin mit überschäumender und gleichzeitig kristallklarer Fantasie und hatte die Begabung, mit jeder von ihr gewählten Ausdrucksform zu begeistern. Im Selbstporträt *Chain Breaker* („Kettenbrecherin“, 1968), in Öl auf Hartfaserplatte gemalt, taucht sie als schwarz umhüllte Gestalt aus einer dreiecksförmigen dunklen Leere auf. Die ungleichmäßigen Pinselstriche im Hintergrund wirken wie Wasser. Als reflexives Totem verweist das Bild auf Berksoys turbulentes Privatleben und gibt einen Eindruck von ihrem unbeständigen Selbstbild. „Alle Energie geht nur von mir aus“, erklärte Berksoy, „und Sie, mit anderen Worten, meine Rezipientinnen und Rezipienten, sollten verstehen, dass sie mir allein gehört.“ Die Künstlerin setzte ihre Fähigkeiten souverän und klug ein – sie war unermüdlich und gleichzeitig oft am Ende ihrer Kräfte. Auf dem Selbstporträt nähern sich Ketten aus Ringen unheilvoll und bedrohlich Berksoys Füßen, ohne jedoch ihre Sohlen zu berühren. *My Mother and I* („Meine Mutter und ich“, 1974) ist ein Ölgemälde mit verwirbeltem aquamarinfarbenem Hintergrund, vor dem Berksoys Mutter – in puderrosa Bluse und engem Rock – in dem unmöglichen Versuch über ihren Kopf greift, um die Hand ihrer Tochter zu ergreifen. Berksoy malt sich selbst als winzigen Säugling mit flatternden Ärmeln und einem Stirnband, das sie wie einen Heiligenschein über ihrem kurz geschnittenen Haar platziert. Auch wenn sie in unterschiedlichsten künstlerischen Bereichen tätig war, malte Berksoy bis zu ihren letzten Lebensjahren weiter – und jedes ihrer Werke zeugt von einem intensiven und scharfsinnigen Selbstgespräch. Im Alter von 90 Jahren präsentierte sie im New Yorker Lincoln Centre eine ergreifende Interpretation der Liebestodarie aus Wagners *Tristan und Isolde*, die Isolde im letzten Akt der großen Tragödie singt, wenn sie über Tristans Leichnam wacht. In der Oper finden die beiden Liebenden erst dort Ruhe, wo sich ihre inneren Welten miteinander vereinen – so erging es auch Berksoy, nur eben in ihrer ganz eigenen Welt.

Semiha Berksoy was a polymath: an opera singer, actor, poet and painter; she was a revered icon of the late-20th-century Turkish cultural milieu of Istanbul. She was also a vivid self-mythologiser and mystic, with a sparkling, crystal imagination that had the capacity to enchant through each of her chosen expressive mediums. In the oil on hardboard self-portrait *Chain Breaker* (1968), she is a hooded black figure emerging from a triangular dark void set against aquatic, uneven brushstrokes. It is the record of a stormy private realm, a reflective totem and an insight into Berksoy's flighty imagination of the self. 'All energies flow only out of me', Berksoy famously declared, 'and you, in other words, the consumers, should understand, that they are mine'. The artist wielded her powers with a knowing self-autonomy—she was inexhaustible and yet tortured. In the self-portrait, looped chains slink toward Berksoy's feet, ominous and threatening, yet they do not touch her soles. *My Mother and I* (1974) is an oil painting with a swirling, aquamarine backcloth, and Berksoy's mother, dressed in a powder rose blouse and tight skirt, reaches over her head in an impossible manoeuvre to clasp her daughter's hand. Berksoy paints herself as a tiny infant, dressed in flowing sleeves and a headband that sits like a halo over her close-cut hair. The artist continued to paint right into the final years of her life, with each work offering a trace of an intense and penetrating monologue. At age 90, she performed a moving rendition of the 'Liebestod' aria from Wagner's *Tristan and Isolde* at Lincoln Centre in New York, where Isolde stands over Tristan's body in the final act of the great tragedy. In the opera, the two lovers only find requiem where their inner worlds entwine; Berksoy did too, but simply, and wholly, in her very own.

Skye Arundhati Thomas

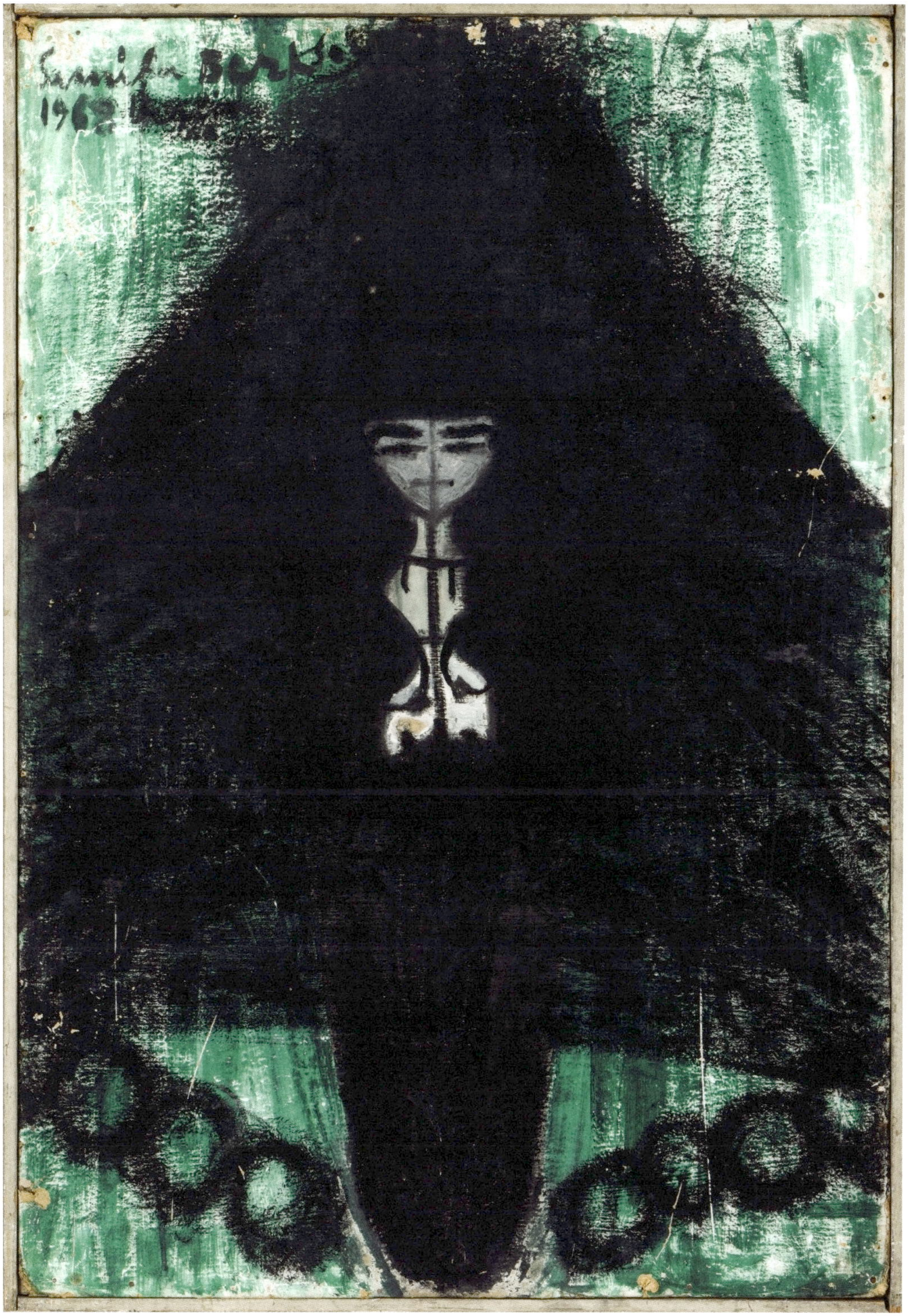

*Chain Breaker (Self-Portrait) | Kettenbrecherin (Selbstporträt)*, 1968. Öl auf Hartfaserplatte / Oil on hardboard. 70 × 100 cm

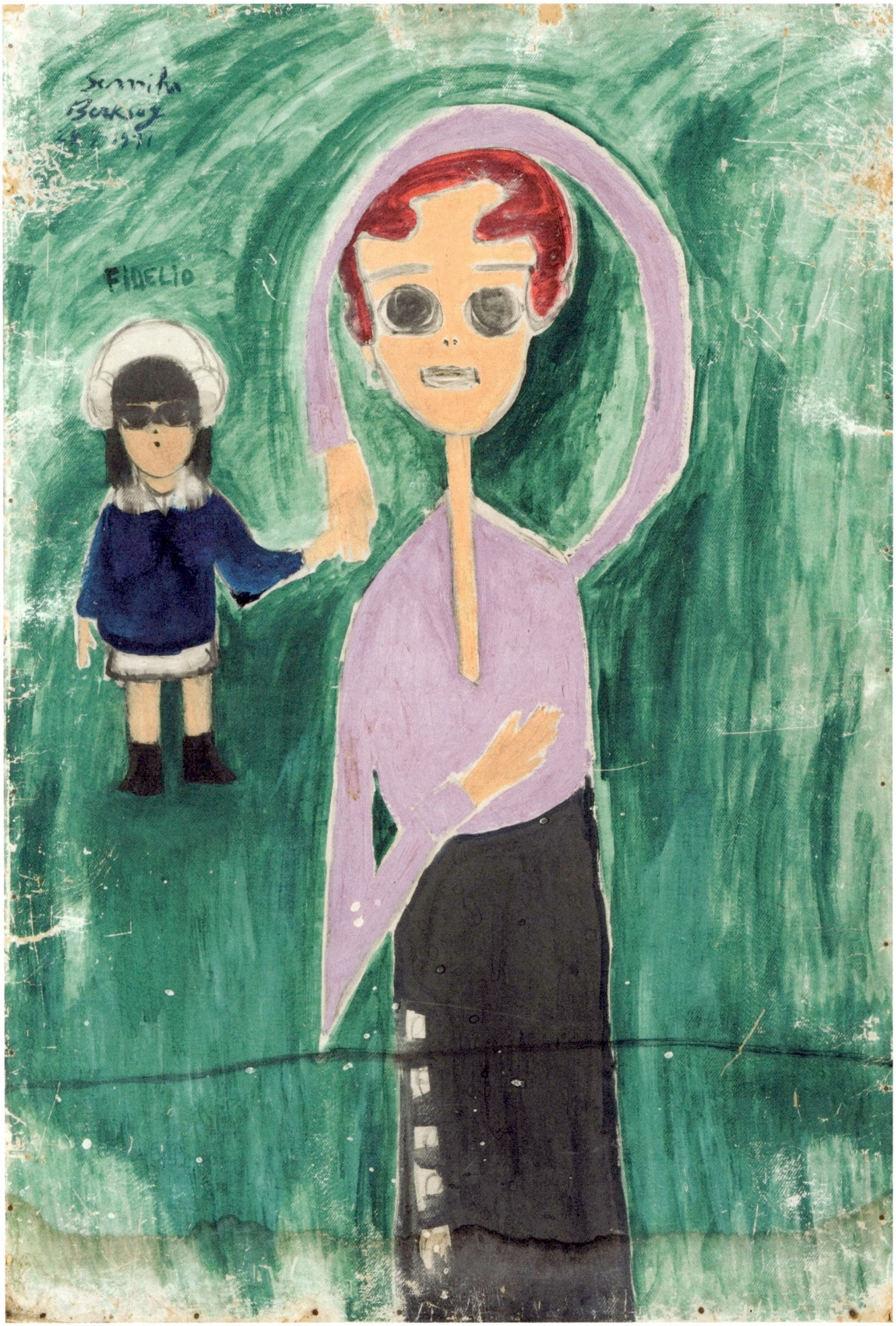


*My Mother and I* | *Meine Mutter und ich*, 1974, Öl auf Hartfaserplatte / Oil on hardboard. 70 × 100 cm

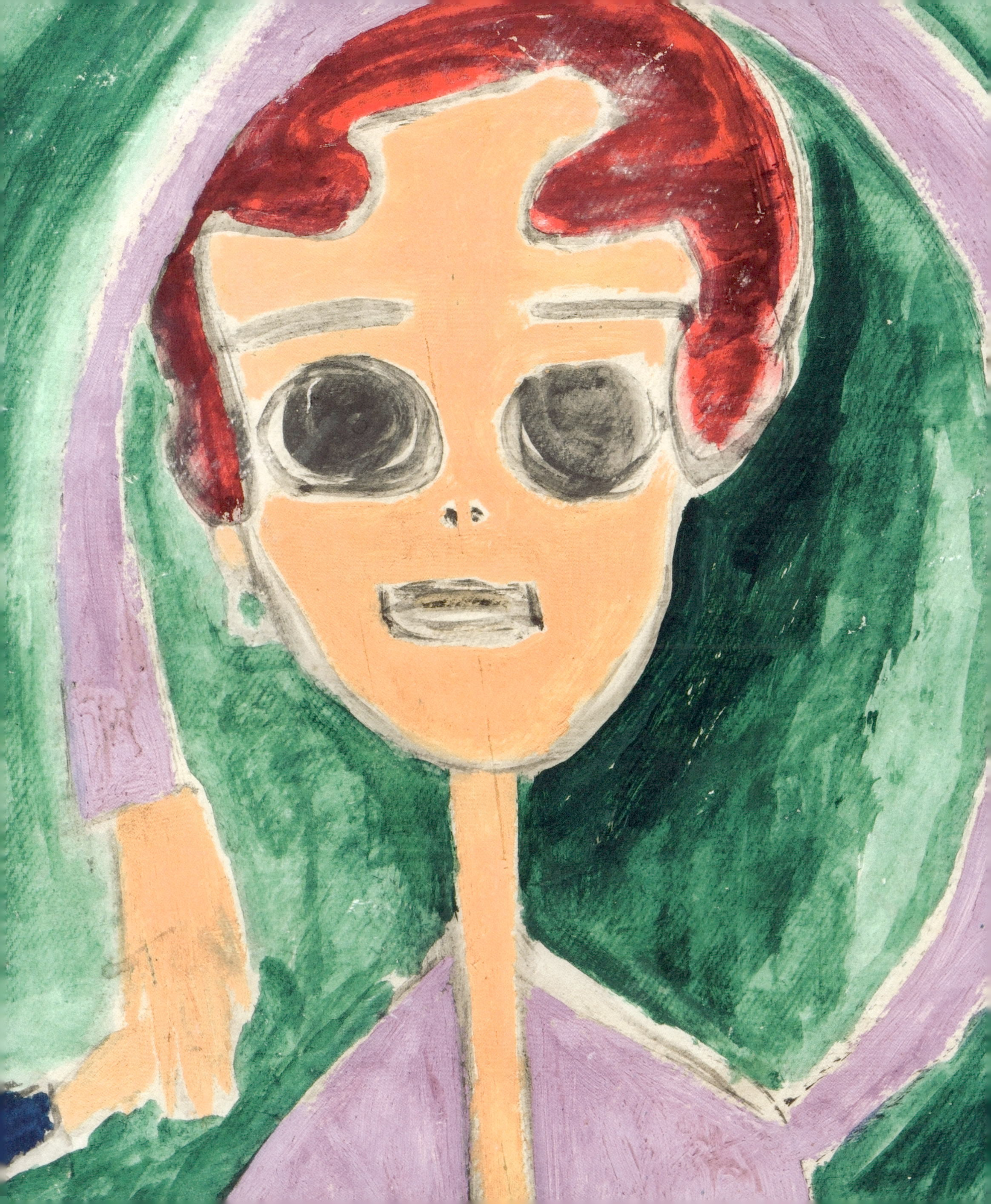

# Huma Bhabha

*Bumps in the Road* („Holprige Straße", 2008) ist eine Installation, die aus einem übergroßen Kopf, Augen aus Metallteilen und einem Gesicht aus Hühnerdraht besteht, an dem teilweise „Fleischstücke" hängen. Der Hinterkopf fehlt und lässt Zuschauer*innen in das Innere blicken, das einer Hausruine ähnelt – verfallen oder vielleicht im Kampf zerstört. Vom Kopf separiert, stehen zwei Beine mit „Füßen" aus Metall, durch einen Balken verbunden, auf dem jeweils die Worte „vorne" und „hinten" zu lesen sind. Beide Skulpturen scheinen in der Vorwärtsbewegung innezuhalten – eine postapokalyptische Szene in einer vernarbten und scheinbar verkohlten Landschaft.

Huma Bhabha hat bei diesem Werk hauptsächlich mit Ton und Styropor gearbeitet. Wie bei ihren früheren Arbeiten in den 2000er Jahren platziert sie ihre Installationen auf Sockel, die dadurch zur Bühne werden. Bhabhas Faszination für antike griechische Statuen, die sie als „wandelnde Monumente" bezeichnet, zeigen sich auch in *Bumps in the Road*. Die Figuren sind in der Bewegung erstarrt, den linken Fuß angehoben. Gleichzeitig erinnern sie an die filigranen Werke des Bildhauers Alberto Giacometti und unterstreichen den Reichtum an Inspirationsquellen, aus dem Bhabha schöpft: von antiken und modernen Skulpturen bis zu den Filmgenres Science-Fiction und Horror. Sie selbst verglich die Figuren aus *Bumps in the Road* einmal mit Don Quijote und Sancho Panza und stellte sie sich als die Reisenden in Cormac McCarthys Roman *Die Straße* (2006) vor.

Den Titel ihres Werks griff die Künstlerin nach eigener Aussage aus dem Radio auf. „Bumps in the Road" beziehe sich auf die Worte eines US-Soldaten, der im Irak über Leichen fuhr. Für Bhabhas Arbeiten aus dieser Zeit, die sie als „Landschaften aus menschlichen Trümmern" beschreibt, ist dieser bis in die Eingeweide dringende Ausdruck von Krieg und Gewalt besonders treffend. Bhabha begreift Narrative über Heimat, Vertreibung, Kolonialisierung und Konflikte als die ewigen Themen etlicher Regionen und Kulturen. Unabhängig von ihren Quellen, die historisch, futuristisch oder fiktiv sein können, ist der rote Faden ihrer Arbeiten immer die menschliche Sichtweise auf die Welt.

In *Bumps in the Road* (2008), a figure with a disproportionately large head with metal parts for eyes leans forward, the partial 'flesh' of its face clinging to an armature of chicken wire. The back of its head is missing, exposing what resembles the internal structure of a building ruined over time, or perhaps damaged in conflict. Separate from this character are two legs with metal 'feet' held together by a beam with the words 'front' and 'back' on either side. Both characters appear to be paused in forward motion—a post-apocalyptic scene in a scarred and seemingly charred landscape.

Clay and Styrofoam are core materials and, as with several works from the mid-2000s, Huma Bhabha has used the device of stacking as armature and plinths as a 'stage' on which to place her sculptures. Reflecting her fascination with ancient sculpture such as Greek *kouroi*, which she refers to as 'walking monuments', the figures in *Bumps in the Road* are similarly mid-stride, with left foot forward. At the same time, they recall the fragile figures of the sculptor Alberto Giacometti, underscoring the extraordinary range of sources Bhabha draws upon, from ancient to modern sculpture, to the genres of science fiction and horror movies. Years later, Bhabha would liken the figures in *Bumps in the Road* to Don Quixote and Sancho Panza, imagining them as the travellers in Cormac McCarthy's 2006 novel *The Road*.

According to the artist, the title *Bumps in the Road* refers to a US soldier's term (that she heard used on the radio) for driving over dead bodies in Iraq. Bhabha referred to much of her work in that period as 'landscapes of human debris', a description that feels particularly apt for this visceral expression of war and violence. For Bhabha, narratives around home, displacement, colonialisation and conflict are, however, eternal themes that span multiple geographies and cultures. While her sources might be historic, futuristic or even fictional, her work affectively relates to the ways in which humans experience and see the world today.

Anne Barlow

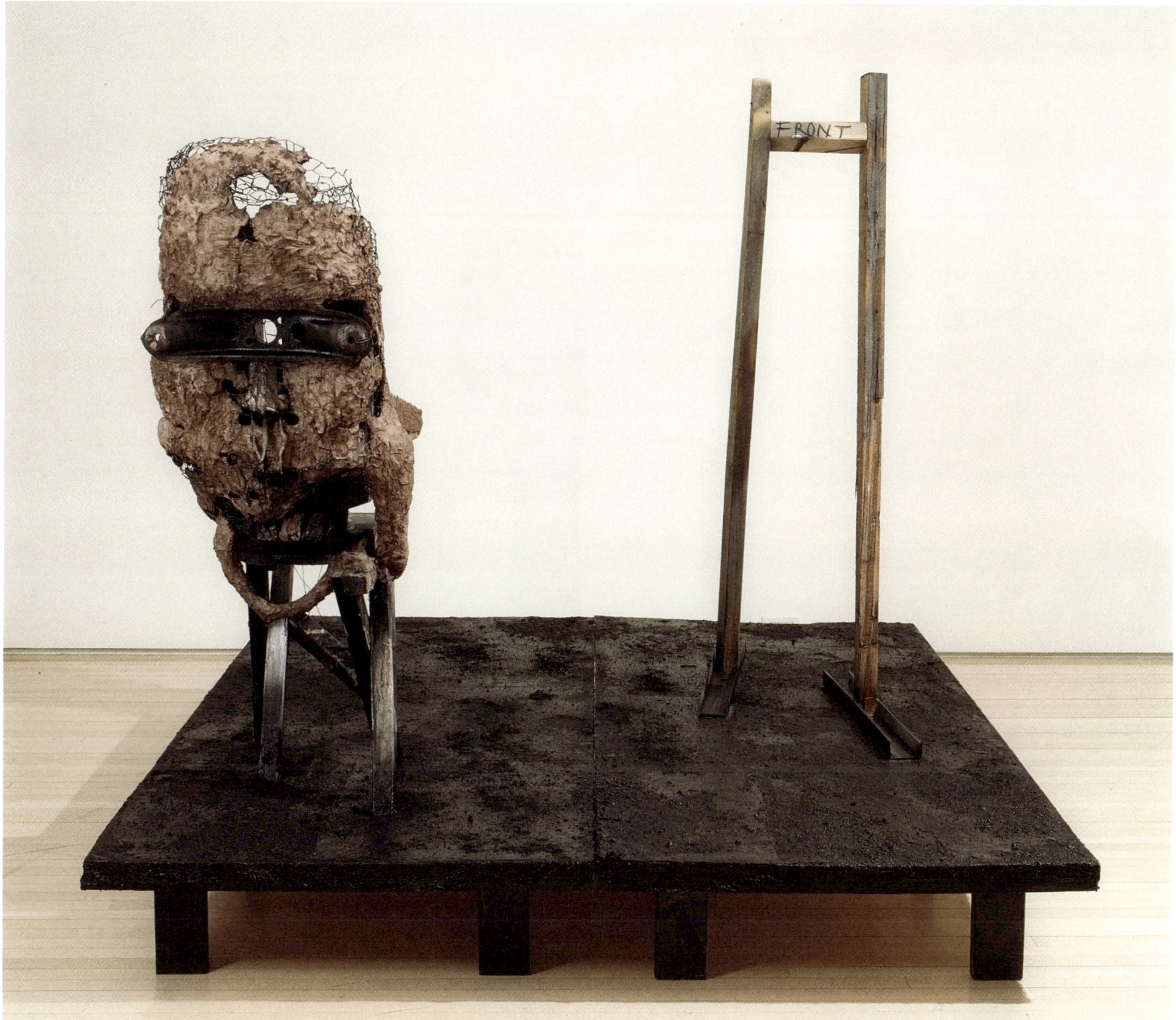


*Bumps in the Road / Holprige Straße*, 2008. Ton, Holz, Draht, Styropor, Metallstifte, Acryl, Farbe, Gusseisen, Sackleinen, Zeitungspapier, Sand, Asche / Clay, wood, wire, Styrofoam, metal studs, acrylic, paint, cast iron, burlap, newsprint, sand, ash. 168,3 × 153,7 × 203,8 cm

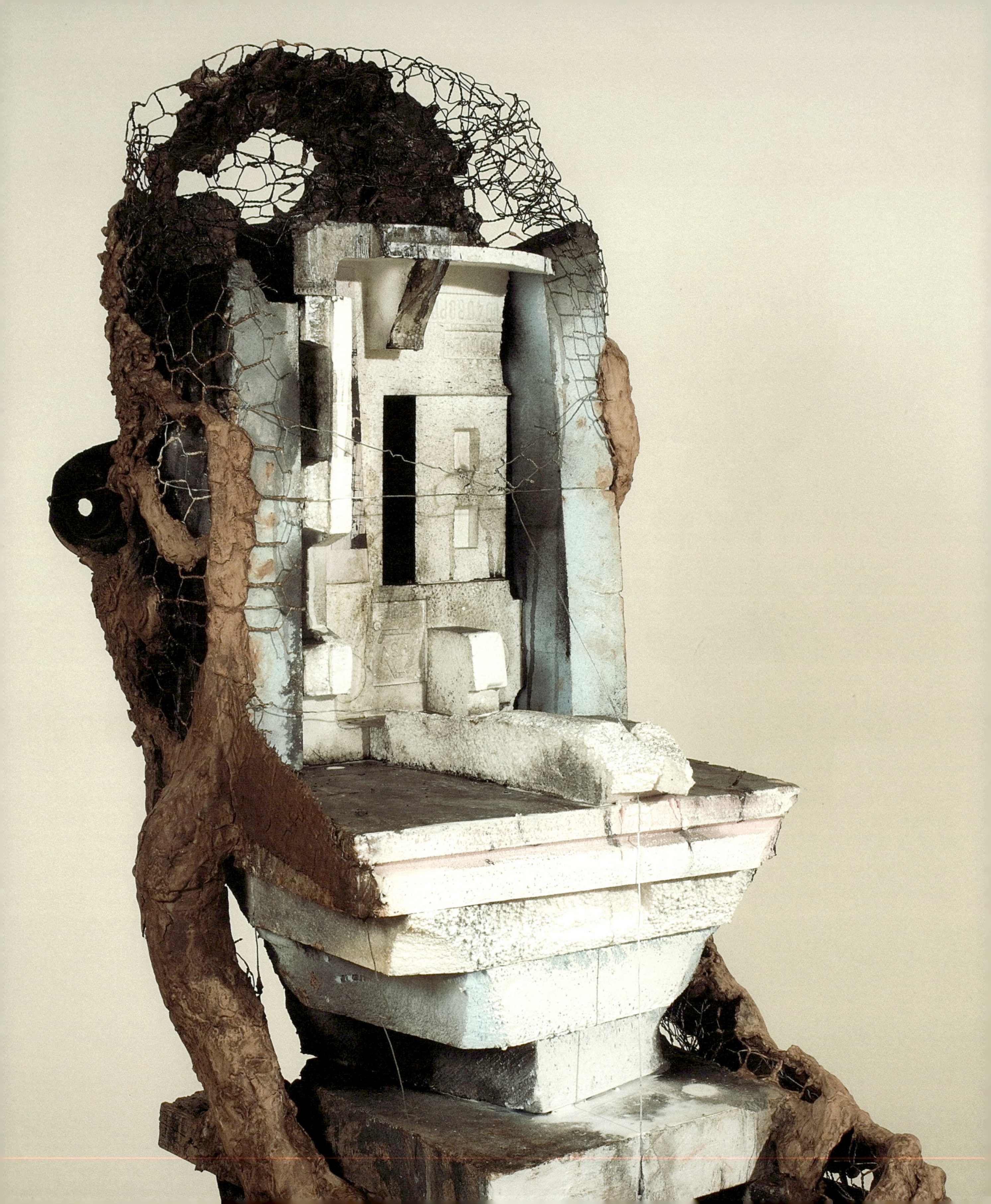

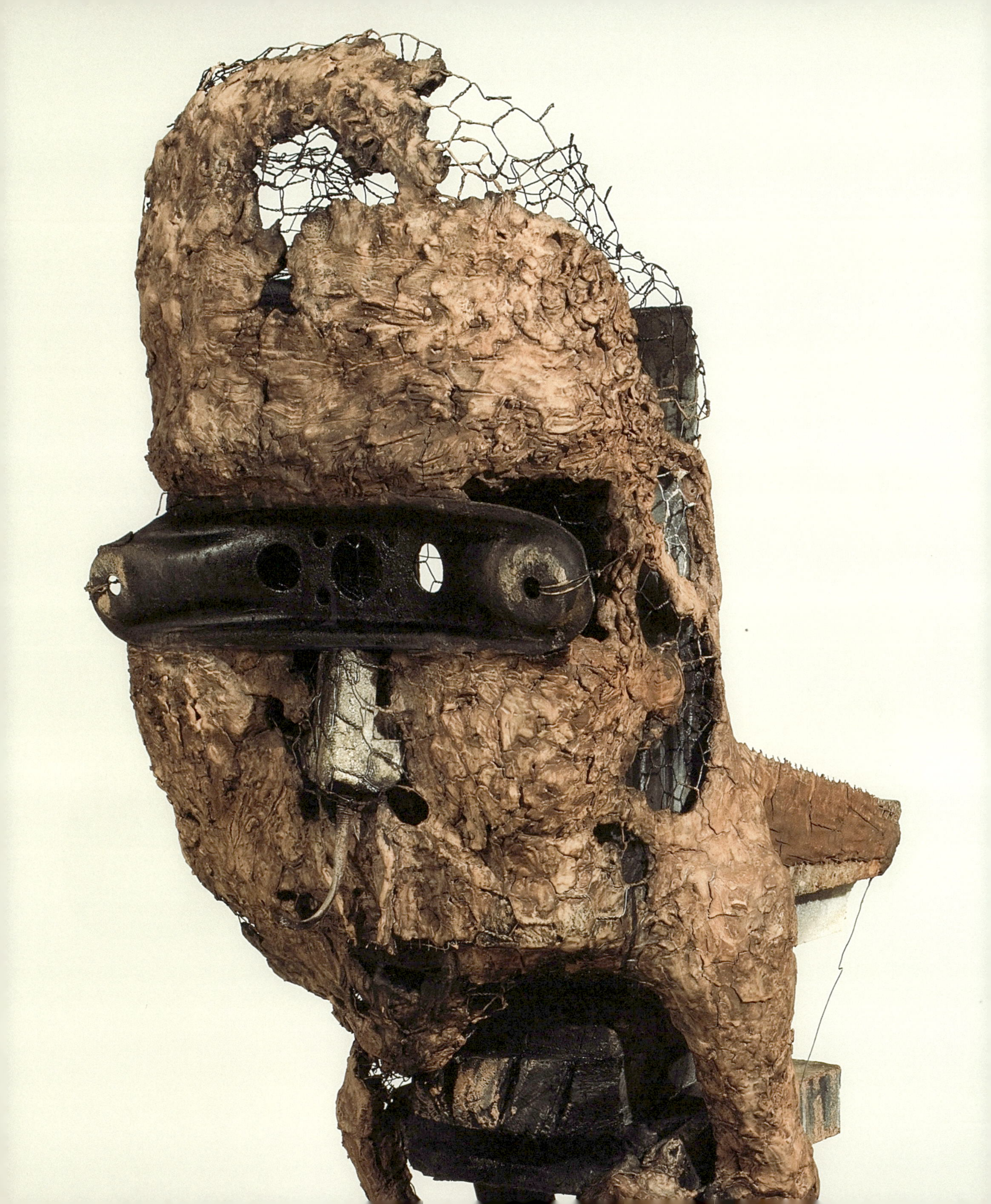

Text siehe S. 70
see p. 70

# Huguette Caland

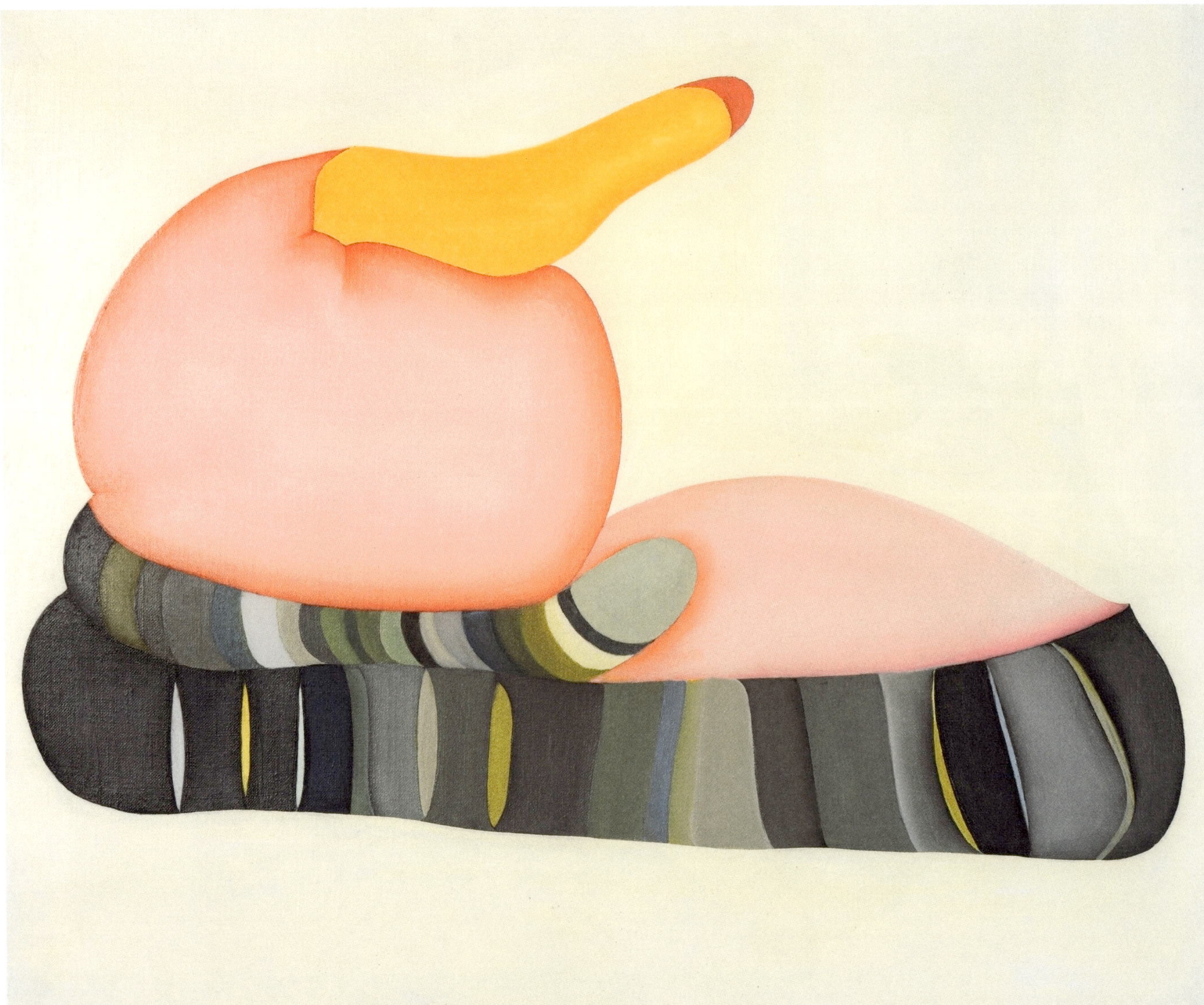

*Flash* | *Aufblitzen*, 1978. Öl auf Leinen / Oil on linen. 45,7 × 38,1 cm

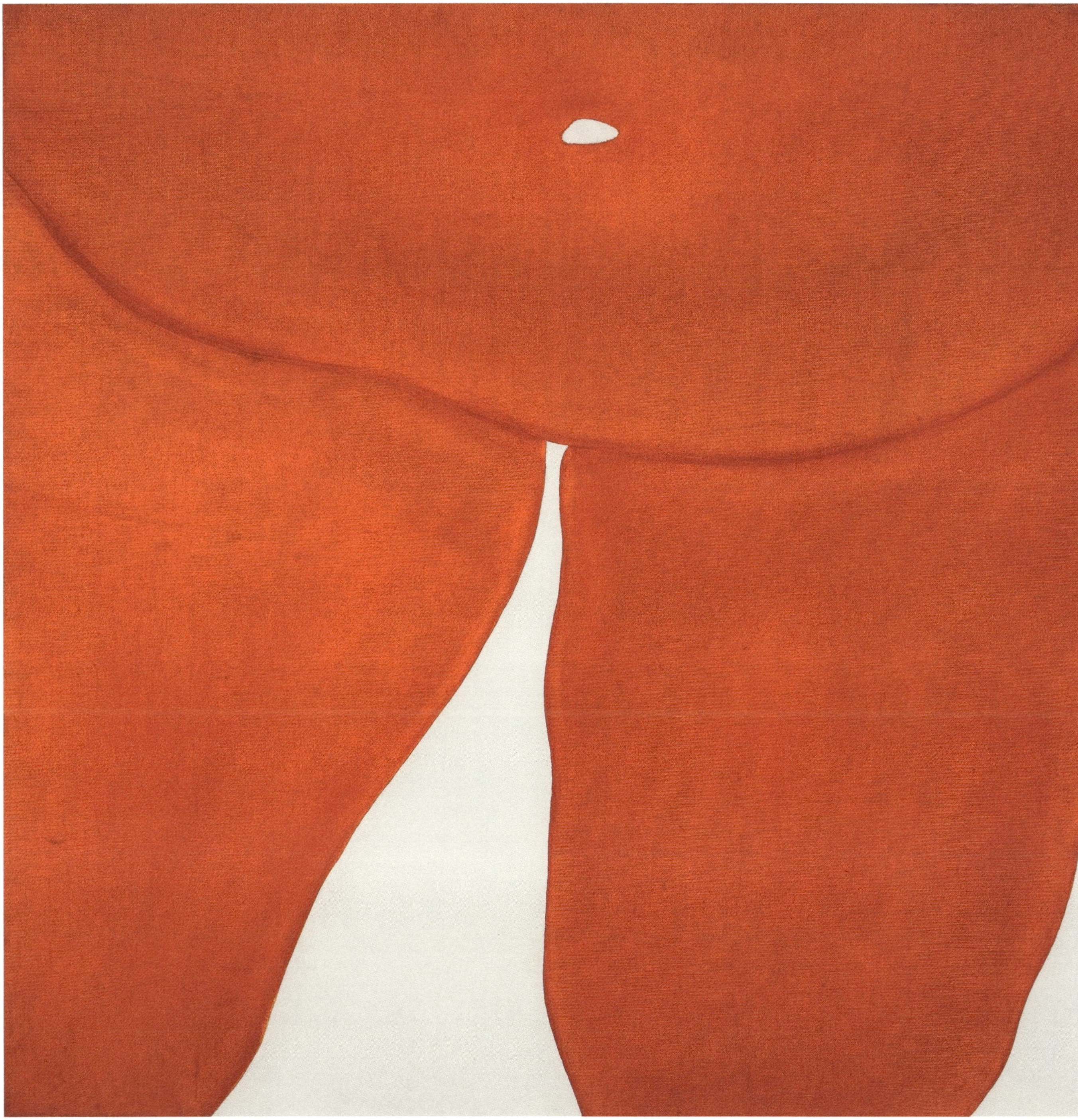

*Red II* / *Rot II*, 1974. Öl auf Leinen / Oil on linen. 79,7 × 79,7 cm

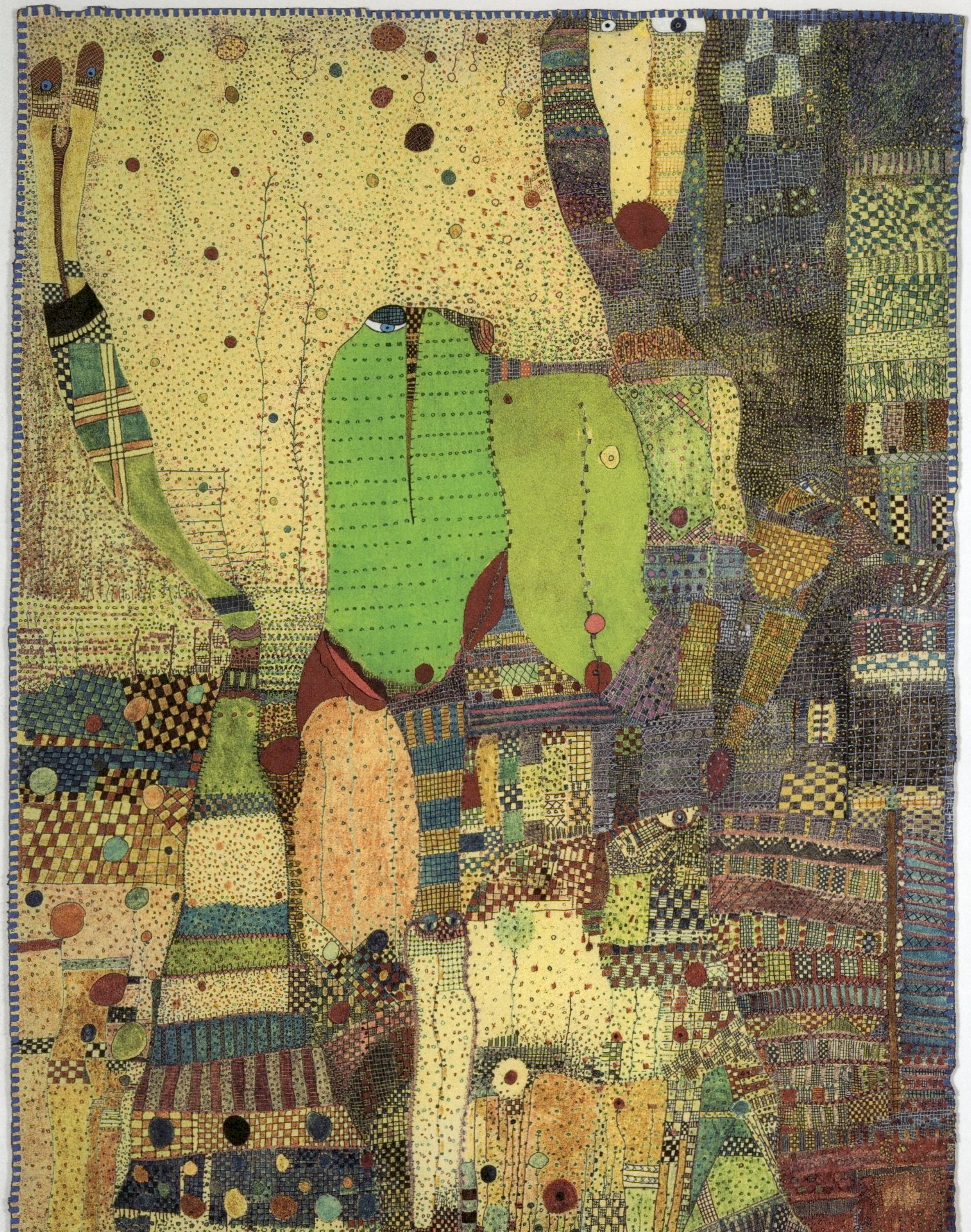

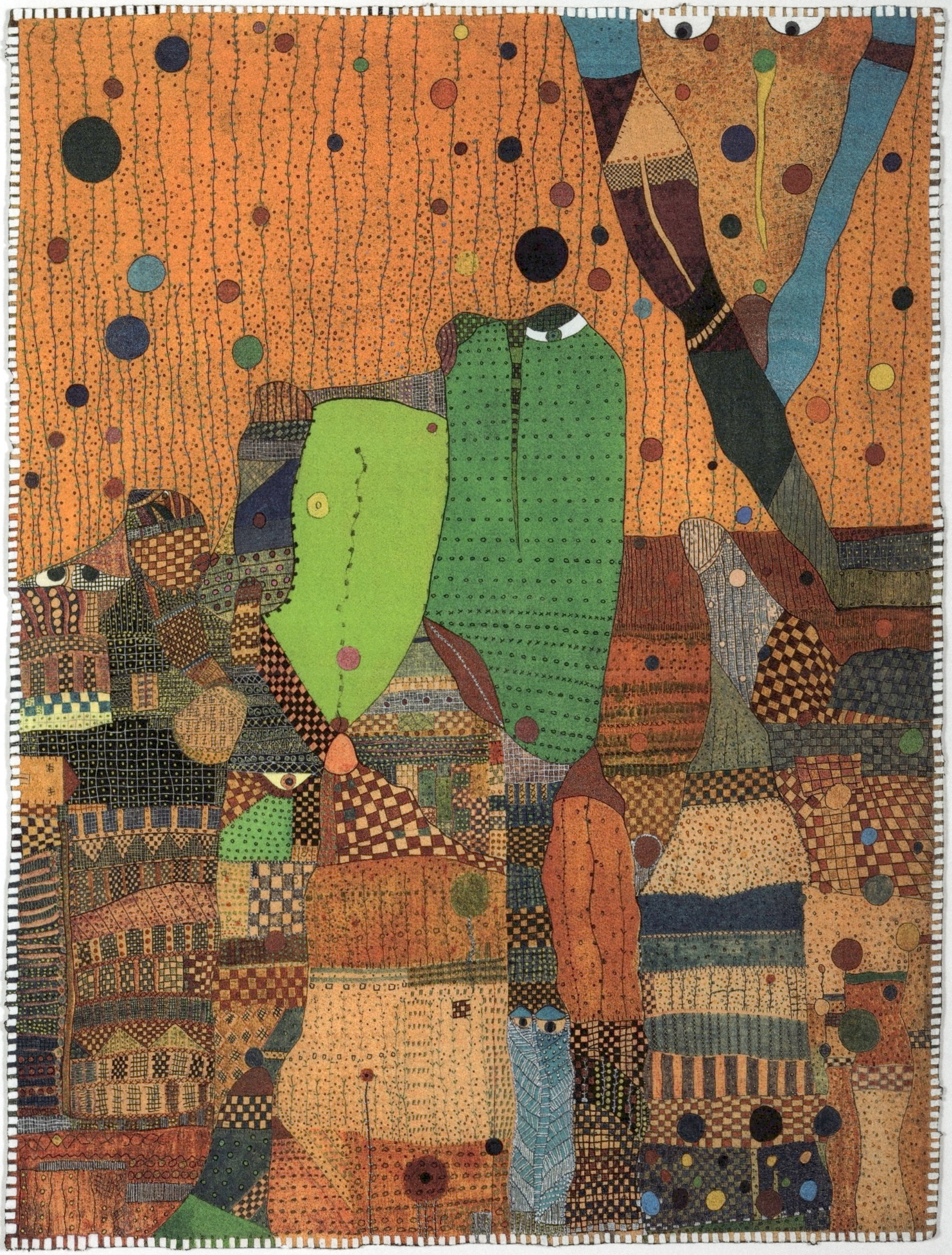

*Rossinante Diptych* / *Rossinante-Diptychon*, 2011. 2 Gemälde, Acryl, Stift auf Leinwand / 2 paintings, acrylic, pen on canvas. Jeweils / Each 130 × 100 cm

# Abbas Habiballa

*Tea Time, A Friday Outside El Obeid* („Tea Time, Ein Freitag außerhalb von El Obeid"), *Gerari dance for Official visit / El Obeid* („Gerari tanzen bei Staatsbesuch / El Obeid") und *Abbas Photography Teacher At the Minister of Culture / Khartoum* („Abbas Fotografielehrer im Kulturministerium / Khartum") sind Fotografien von Abbas Habiballa aus den 1970er Jahren, die 2017 in einer Neuauflage gedruckt wurden. Zu Beginn seiner Laufbahn arbeitete Habiballa als Fotograf für die sudanesische Regierung. Anschließend hielt er das Alltagsleben seiner Verwandten und Nachbar*innen im Sudan mit der Kamera fest. Mit seinem fotografischen Ansatz erzeugte er einen reizvollen Kontrast zwischen den offiziellen und inoffiziellen Dokumenten der Landesgeschichte. Fast schon zärtlich fing er ungeschönte Szenen aus dem Alltag ein, sei es bei Familienfeiern oder in seinem täglichen Umfeld, und entwickelte auf diese Weise eine eigene Form der Dokumentarfotografie. Bei seiner Arbeit verwendete er bei Tag und bei Nacht häufig eine Rolleiflex-Kamera mit Blitz. Die Rolleiflex war für ihre besondere Bauart und ihre unerschöpflichen optischen Möglichkeiten bekannt. Die vom Künstler selbst entwickelten Silbergelatineabzüge zeichnen sich im Druckbild durch ihre warme Tongebung aus. Diesen Effekt erzielte er durch die Kombination von faserhaltigem Fotopapier mit der brillanten Bildqualität seiner Langzeitbelichtung.

Abbas Habiballa war nicht nur Künstler und Fotograf – er wurde auch vielfach mit der sudanesischen Kunstbewegung der Moderne in der Mitte des 20. Jahrhunderts und mit der Khartoum School in Verbindung gebracht. Wie seine Weggefährten Mohamed Yahia Issa, Fouad Hamza Tibin, Osman Hamid Khalifa, Omar Addow, Richard Lokiden Wani und viele andere nutzte Habiballa die Fotografie als Versuchsfeld und präsentierte gleichzeitig einen experimentellen Einblick in die sudanesische Kultur, der sich deutlich von der Darstellung in den Mainstream-Medien abhob. Die tiefe Emotionalität seiner Werke, die er mit dieser Arbeitsweise erzeugte, nahm im Verlauf seiner Karriere immer weiter zu.

*Tea Time, A friday Outside El Obeid, Gerari dance for Official visit / El Obeid* and *Abbas Photography Teacher At the Minister of Culture / Khartoum* are photographs taken by Abbas Habiballa in the 1970s and re-printed in 2017. At the start of his career, Habiballa worked for the Sudanese government as a photographer, then he went on to capture the daily lives of his relatives and neighbours in Sudan. His approach to photography presents a beguiling contrast between official and unofficial records of history in Sudan. Habiballa captures raw, commonplace environments—sites of family gatherings and daily surroundings out of affection—creating a vernacular form of photography. He frequently used a Rolleiflex camera, with flash, both during the day and at night. The Rolleiflex was renowned for its exceptional construction and boundless optical potential. The silver gelatin prints produced by the artist emerge in warm tones when printed. Habiballa utilised a fiber base of paper combined with the brilliance of his long exposures.

Aside from being an artist and photographer, Habiballa was often associated with the modernist art movement in Sudan during the mid-20th century, including the Khartoum School. Alongside fellow companions Mohamed Yahia Issa, Fouad Hamza Tibin, Osman Hamid Khalifa, Omar Addow, Richard Lokiden Wani and many others, Habiballa utilised photography as a method of experimentation, but also presented a window of experimentation into Sudan's culture that diverged from mainstream media representation. The inner realm of emotions this approach provokes continued to swell in affect throughout his career.

Reem Sawan

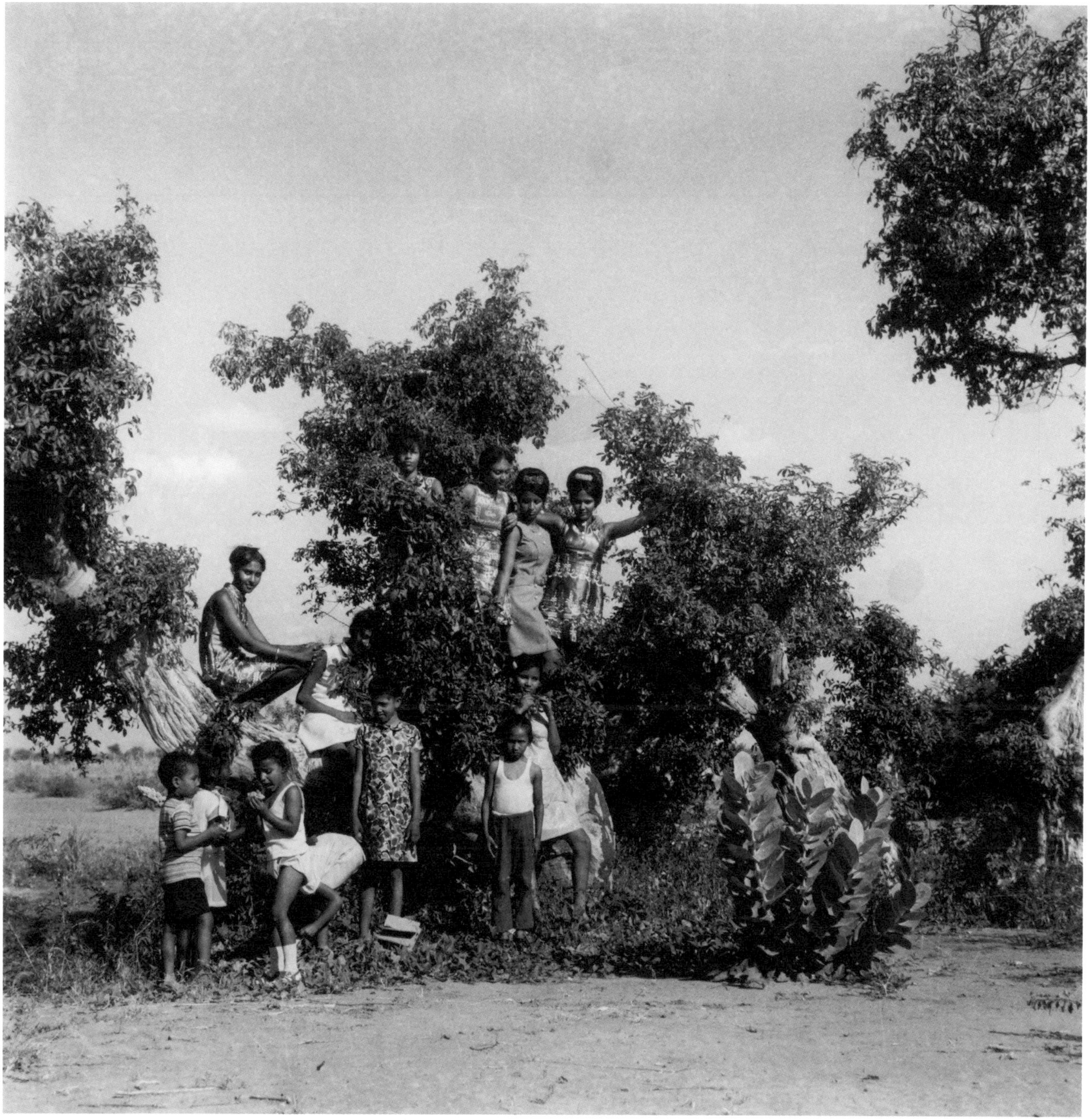

*A Friday Outside El Obeid* / *Ein Freitag außerhalb von El Obeid*, ca. 1975 (Abzug / printed 2017). Silbergelatineabzug (warme Färbung), faserhaltiges Fotopapier / Gelatin silver print (warm tone), fibre-based paper. 40 × 30 cm

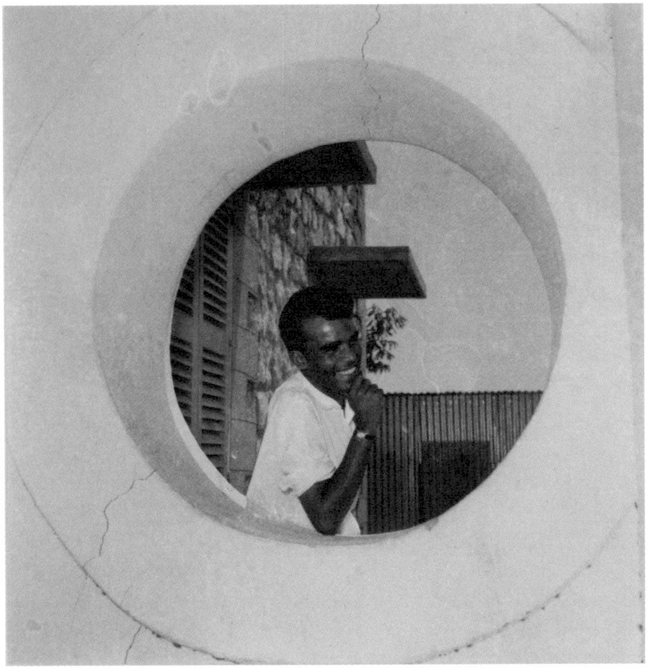

*Abbas Photography Teacher at the Minister of Culture / Khartoum / Abbas' Fotografielehrer im Kulturministerium / Khartum*, ca. 1975 (Abzug / printed 2017). Silbergelatineabzug (warme Färbung), faserhaltiges Fotopapier / Gelatin silver print (warm tone), fibre-based paper. 40 × 30 cm

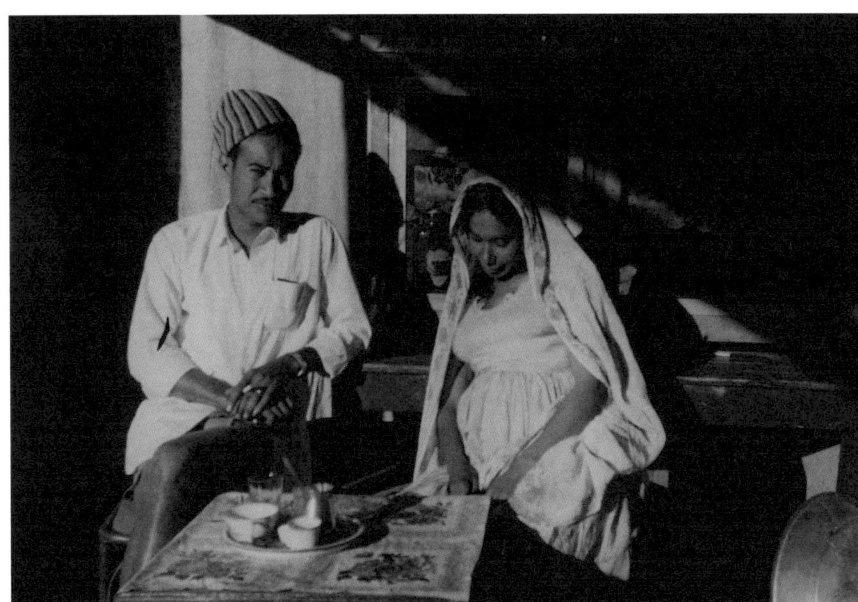

*Tea Time*, ca. 1970 (Nachdruck / reprinted 2017). Silbergelatineabzug (warme Färbung), faserhaltiges Fotopapier / Gelatin silver print (warm tone), fibre-based paper. 30 × 24 cm

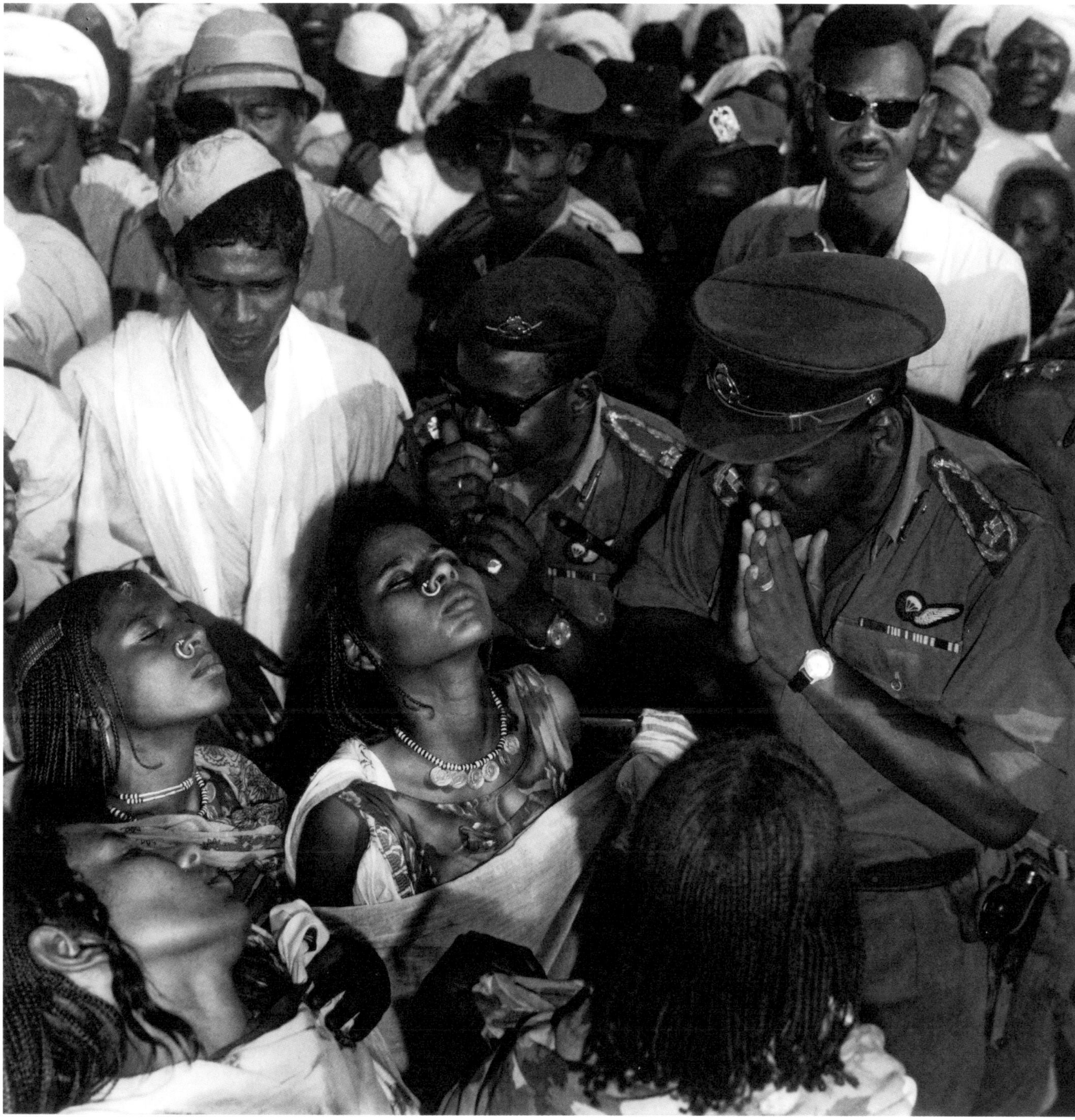

*Gerari dance for Official visit / El Obeid / Gerari tanzen bei Staatsbesuch / El Obeid*, ca. 1975 (Abzug / printed 2017). Silbergelatineabzug (warme Färbung), faserhaltiges Fotopapier / Gelatin silver print (warm tone), fibre-based paper. 40 × 30 cm

# Joana Hadjithomas & Khalil Joreige

Der Dokumentarfilm *ISMYRNE* („Ismyrna", 2016) ist den Geschichten und Erfahrungen der Filmemacherin Joana Hadjithomas und der Künstlerin Etel Adnan gewidmet. Die beiden Frauen verbindet ihre familiäre Herkunft aus einer Stadt, die sie selbst nie besucht haben und aus der ihre Familien einst ins Exil getrieben wurden. Hadjithomas' griechische Familie väterlicherseits wurde von der türkischen Armee zum Verlassen des damaligen Smyrna gezwungen, während Adnans griechische Mutter ihren Vater, einen syrischen Offizier der Osmanischen Armee, heiratete und nach dem Zusammenbruch des Osmanischen Reichs mit ihm nach Beirut ging. In persönlichen Gesprächen erkunden die beiden Frauen, deren Familien sich jeweils an verschiedenen Fronten historischer Konfliktlinien befanden, die tiefgreifenden geopolitischen Veränderungen und Konflikte in der Region im Verlauf des Jahrhunderts, seit ihre Familien Smyrna (heute das türkische Izmir) verlassen mussten. Unter Zuhilfenahme von Poesie, Humor und herzlichen Umarmungen stellt das generationenübergreifende Zweiergespann dabei fest, dass Smyrna ein Ort ist, der besser in und mit ihrer Fantasie weiterlebt.

*The President's Album* („Das Album des Präsidenten", 2011) ist eine Fotoinstallation aus 32 identischen Fotografien, die jeweils unterschiedlich gefaltet und zusammengesetzt das lebensgroße Bild einer Rakete ergeben. Jede der Fotografien besteht aus zwei Bildern: Das eine war dem ehemaligen libanesischen Präsidenten Fouad Chehab aus einem Fotoalbum überreicht worden, in dem das Wirken der inspirierten Träumer der Lebanese Rocket Society (Libanesische Raketengesellschaft) dokumentiert wurde. Das zweite ist eine weitere Aufnahme, allerdings von einer Nachbildung der Cedar IV Rocket. Sie wurde in den Originalfarben der libanesischen Flagge bemalt und im Hof der Haigazian University in Beirut – dem Gründungsort der Gesellschaft – aufgestellt. Die Lebanese Rocket Society war der Zusammenschluss einer Gruppe von Studierenden der Universität, die mit geringem Budget – und mäßigem Erfolg – eine Weltraumrakete ins All schießen wollten. Mit ihren Aktionen erregten sie auch die Aufmerksamkeit des Präsidenten. Als das wissenschaftliche Versuchsprojekt schließlich von der Politik für den Einsatz als militärische Waffe vereinnahmt wurde, verließ der Vorsitzende die Gesellschaft und das Projekt wurde aus den Geschichtsbüchern und dem nationalen Bewusstsein gelöscht. Auch wenn die Bilder zusammen ein Ganzes bilden, zeigt jedes für sich doch nur ein Fragment und verbirgt fast den gesamten Rest der Fotografie, um zu zeigen, dass eine verlorene Geschichte nicht durch Bilder allein wieder vollständig zum Leben erweckt werden kann.

The projected film *ISMYRNE* (2016) is an investigation in stories and experiences between filmmaker Joana Hadjithomas and artist Etel Adnan, connected by ancestors through a city both of their families had been exiled from, a place neither had ever been to. Hadjithomas's paternal Greek family was forced to leave the city of Smyrna by the Turkish Army, whilst Adnan's Greek mother was to marry her father, a Syrian Ottoman Army officer who left for Beirut after the fall of the Ottoman Empire. Their personal exchanges—existing at opposite ends of historical battle lines—foreground the epic geopolitical changes and conflicts in the region over the century since their families left Smyrna (now Izmir, Turkey). Together, through poetry, laughter and warm embrace, the trans-generational duo concede that Smyrna is a site best left to and of the imagination.

*The President's Album* (2011) is a photographic installation comprised of 32 identical photographs, each folded differently, that reveal a life-size composite image of a rocket. The photograph is itself a configuration of two images, the first an image offered to former Lebanese President Lebanon Fouad Chehab from a photo album that documented the inspiring dreamers who formed the Lebanese Rocket Society. The second is another image of the Cedar IV Rocket, albeit a reproduction—painted its original Lebanese flag colours, installed at Haigazian University in Beirut, where the society was founded. The Lebanese Rocket Society refers to a group of students at the university who had achieved limited success in launching a space rocket on a miniscule budget and attracted the attention of the president. When the propositional science project was politically commandeered as a military weapon, the leader of the society left the group and the project was written out of history and the national consciousness. Whilst collectively the images create a whole, each only displays a fragment of the full photograph, hiding the majority of its existence in this exploration of how a lost history cannot be fully resurrected through image alone.

Sarah Perks

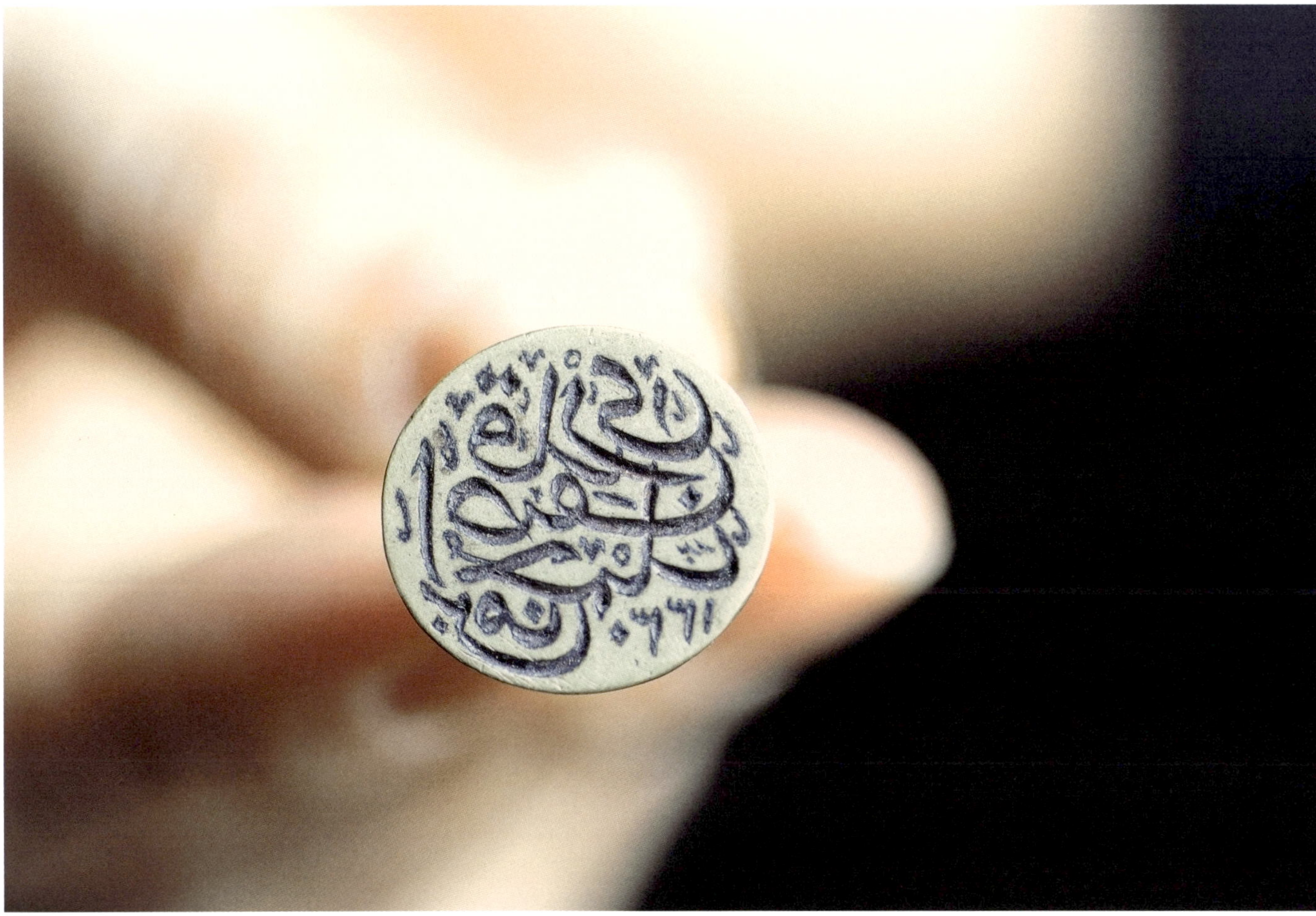

*ISMYRNE / ISMYRNA*, 2016. Einkanal-HD-Video / Single-channel HD video. 50 Minuten / 50 minutes. Im Auftrag der Sharjah Art Foundation und des Jeu de Paume, Paris / Co-Commissioned by Sharjah Art Foundation and Jeu De Paume, Paris

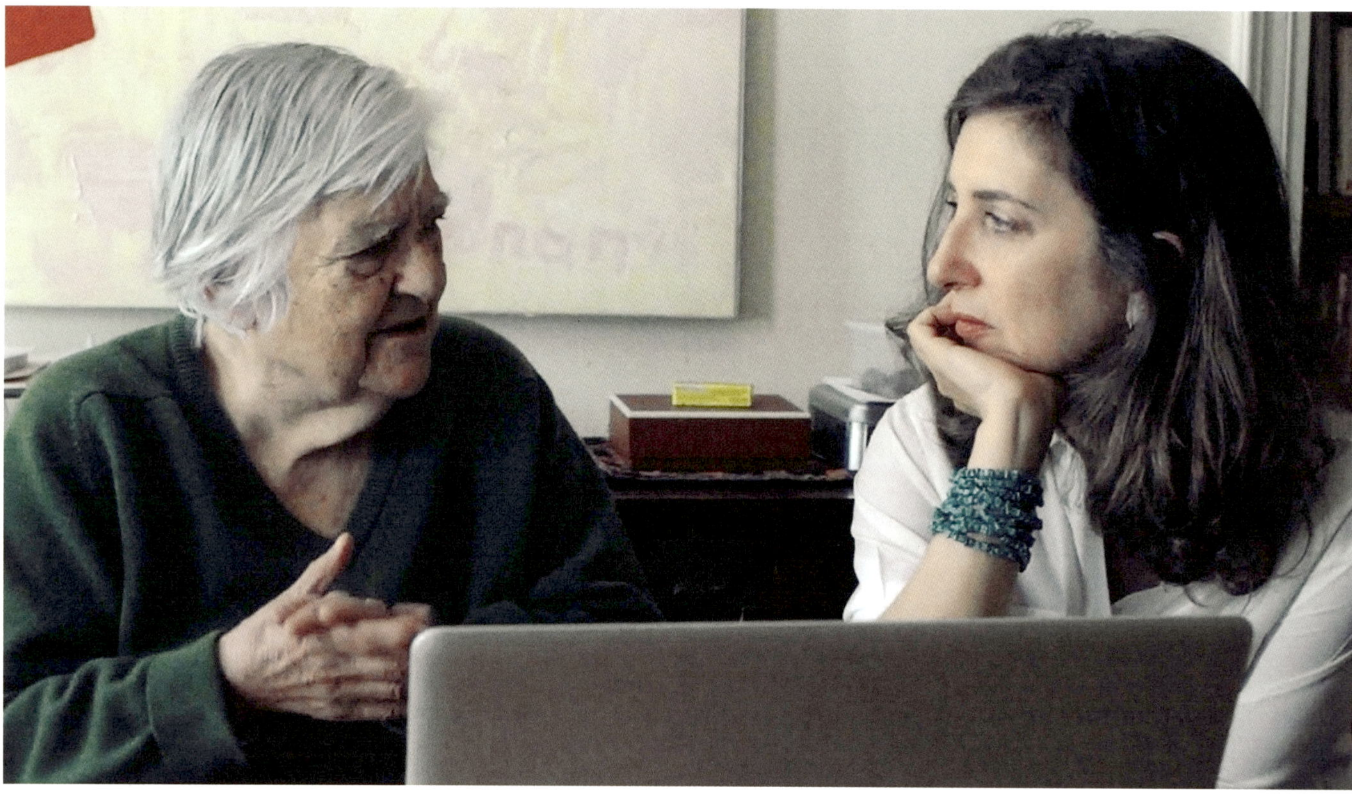

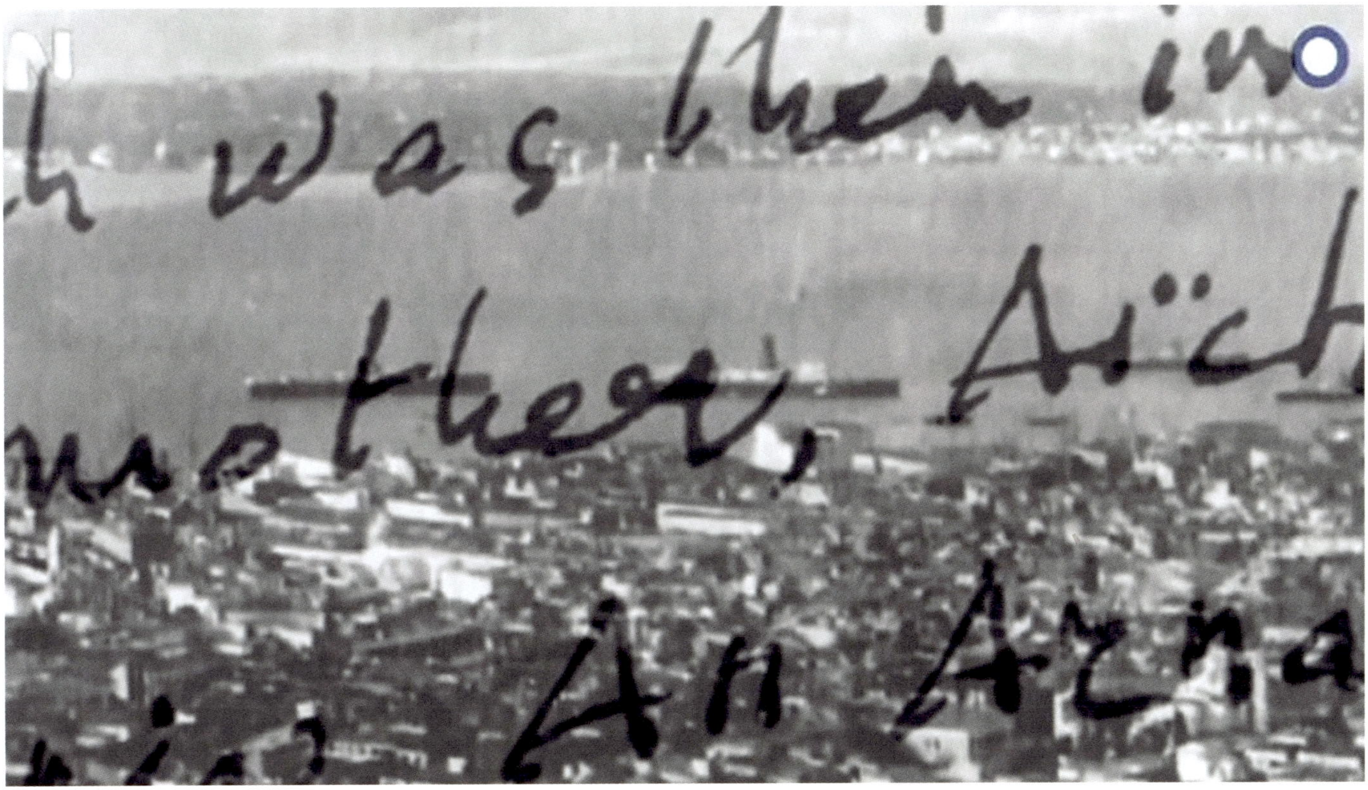
was then
mother,

# Hayv Kahraman

Hayv Kahramans Bilder bieten eine Zuflucht für Heimatlose. Ihre als kraftlos dargestellten Figuren verkörpern eine Art Gegenpol zu den häufig gewalttätigen Bedingungen, die Menschen vertreiben – aus einem Zuhause, einem Land und oft dem Leben selbst. Im Alter von elf Jahren floh Hayv Kahraman mit ihrer Mutter vor dem Golfkrieg (1990–1991) aus dem Irak nach Schweden. Auf der Suche nach Asyl am Stockholmer Flughafen angekommen, zerrissen die beiden ihre Pässe und spülten die Überreste die Toilette hinunter, erinnert sie sich. Ab 2006 lebte die Künstlerin in Los Angeles, wo sie eine Gemäldeserie begann, in der sie stets dieselben Figuren darstellt: Knochenbleiche, halbierte Körper werden als durchscheinende, gespenstische Hautmembranen auf einen grau-braunen Untergrund gepresst. Dabei stehen die apfelförmigen Brüste und glänzend rote Lippen für „westliche Freuden", die Kahraman letztlich aufspießen will. Indem die Künstlerin persische Miniaturmalerei, japanische Tuschmalerei und Kompositionen aus der neoklassischen europäischen Malerei verfremdet, verweist sie auf das traumatische Erbe, das in westlichen Sammlungen und Museen marginalisiert wird oder lediglich einen schmerzhaften, nicht rekonstruierten Schatten hinterlassen hat.

Kahramans Werke stehen nicht nur für Widerstand und Sensibilität, sondern orchestrieren auch die komplexe Phänomenologie der Architektur, der Erinnerung und des Geschlechts. Besonders deutlich wird dies durch die Einschnitte, die Kahraman in die Oberfläche ihrer Leinwände macht, wie etwa in *Identification (Facial Hair)* („Identifikation [Gesichtsbehaarung]", 2016). Sechs identische Gesichter sind von Kahraman mit forensischer Detailtreue kopiert worden, wobei jedes Gesicht unterschiedliche Frisuren und Gesichtsbehaarungen vorweist – eine tastende Systematik des Lebens auf der Suche nach Verkleidung, die gleichzeitig staatliche Untersuchung auf den Plan ruft. Quer über die Kehlen der porträtierten Gesichter verlaufen eingebrannt zwei Linien zu einem „X". Indem die Fähigkeit zu atmen annulliert wird, verwandelt Kahraman die Bedingung der Möglichkeit, Gehör zu finden, in ein Schnappen nach Luft.

Hayv Kahraman's paintings offer shelter to the exiled body, her languid figures a seeming counter-pressure to the often violent conditions that ushered lives out of a home, a country and, often, existence itself. The artist fled to Sweden as an 11-year-old refugee from Iraq during the Gulf War (1990–91). Kahraman recounts seeking asylum in Stockholm's airport with her mother, both tearing their Iraqi passports apart and flushing the pieces down a toilet. The artist settled in Los Angeles in 2006, where she began a series of paintings in which the same figure continually resurfaces into view. Pale, bone-white bodies are bisected and flattened into transparent and ghostly membranes of skin over greyed and brown grounds, their apple-shaped breasts and glossy red lips suggestive of the 'occidental pleasures' Kahraman ultimately seeks to skewer. By contorting references that include Persian miniature-style painting, Japanese ink painting and certain neoclassical European painting compositions, Kahraman's work touches on the traumatic legacies that have been constricted or remain a painful unreconstructed shadow over national collections in museums and paintings in the West.

If Kahraman's body of work is one of resistance and receptivity, it is also one in which the intricate phenomenology of architecture, memory and gender are in concert. This is most strikingly rendered in the incisions Kahraman makes in the surface of the canvas, such as in *Identification (Facial Hair)* (2016). The six portraits represented here are repeated by Kahraman forensically, each identical face proffering differing styles of hair and facial hair—appearing as wary taxonomies of lives in search of disguise and necessitating state scrutiny. Into the surface of the canvas appear a series of 'x's brandished across the throats of each portrait. By perforating the capacity for breathing, Kahraman renders the physical possibilities of being listened to into a gasp for air.

Chris McCormack

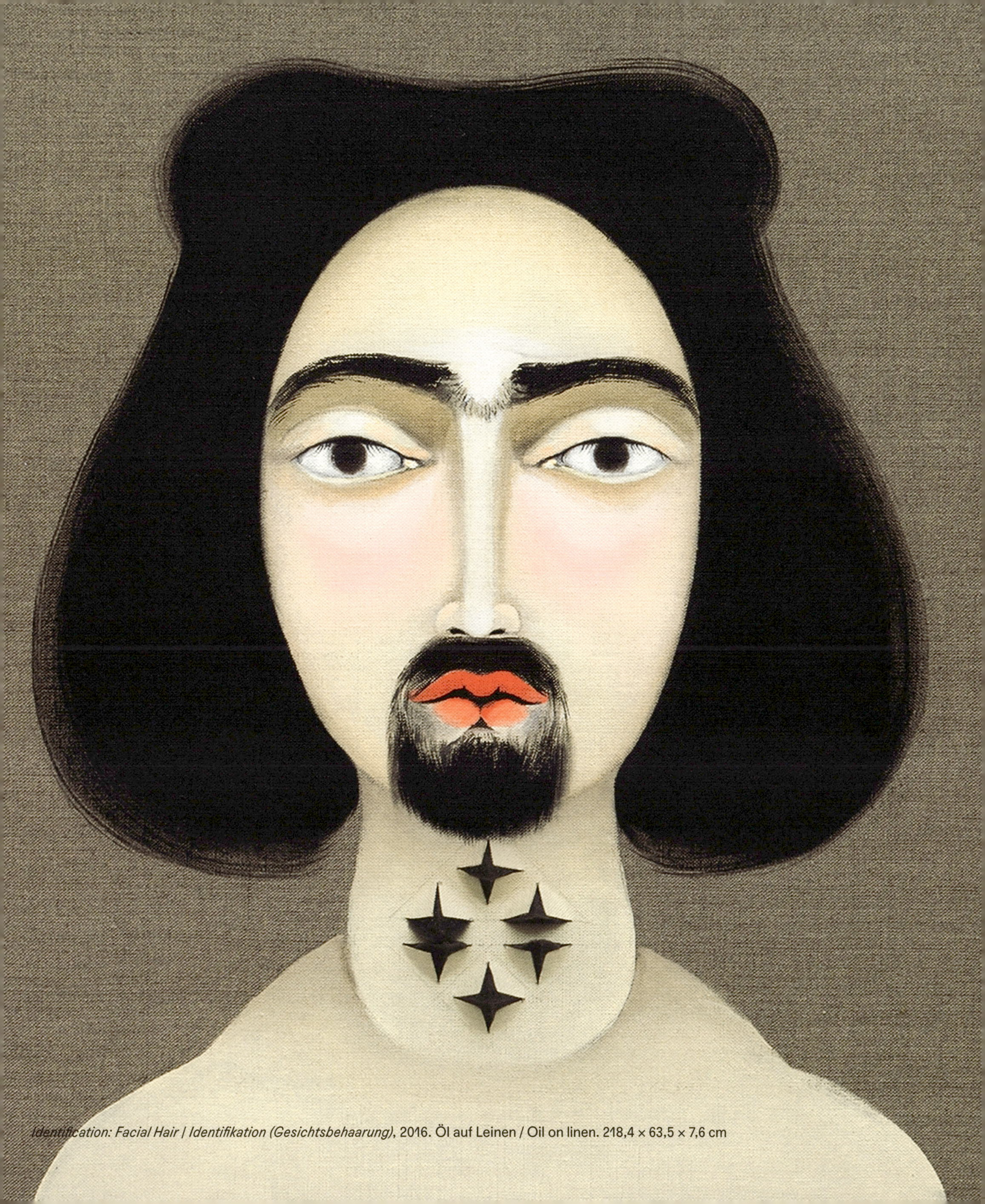

*Identification: Facial Hair | Identifikation (Gesichtsbehaarung)*, 2016. Öl auf Leinen / Oil on linen. 218,4 × 63,5 × 7,6 cm

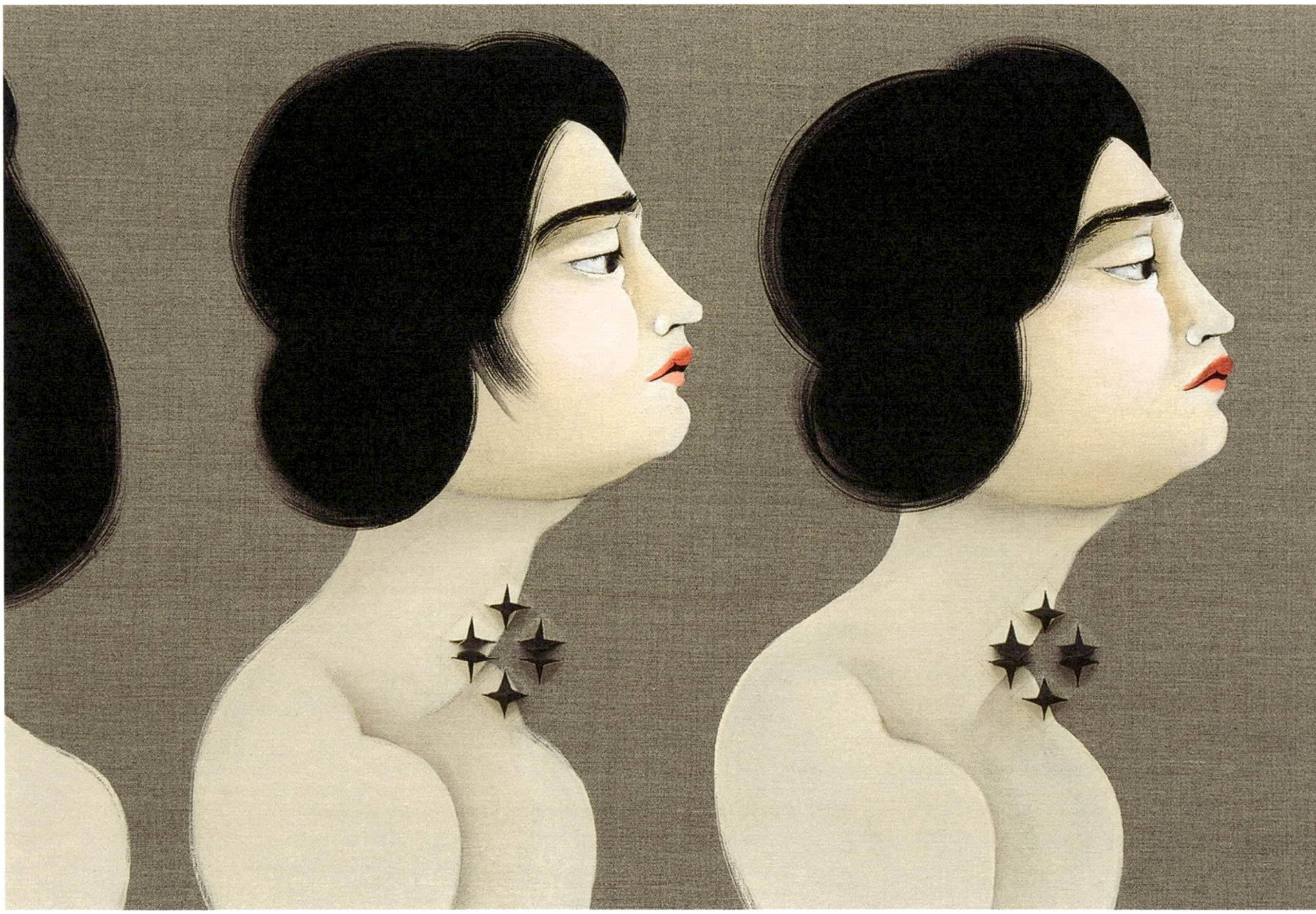

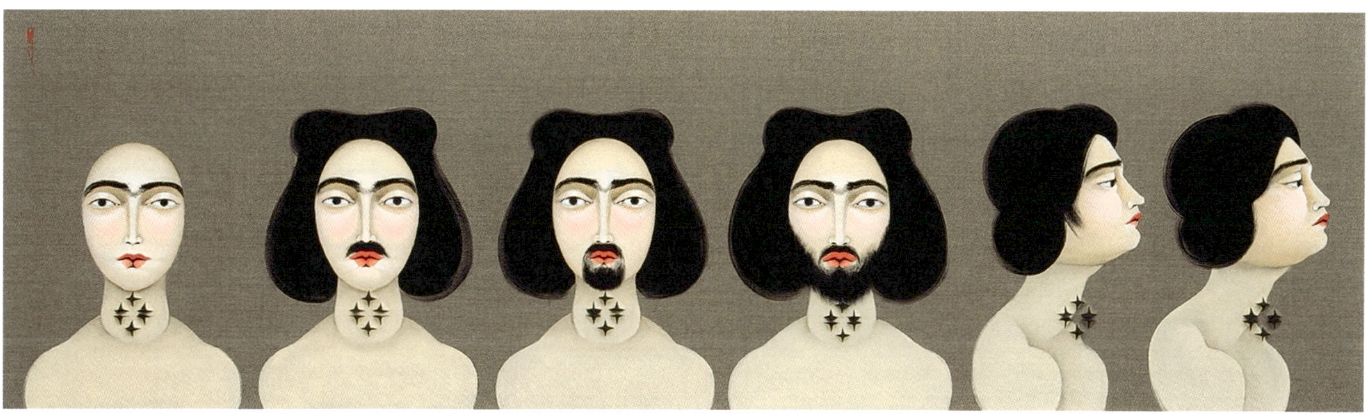

# Anuar Khalifi

Anuar Khalifi verbindet mit seinen Gemälden einen Appell – und manchmal auch eine Abrechnung. Er will in den geschlossenen Bereich der westlichen „Historienmalerei" vordringen, indem er Braune und Schwarze Körper darstellt, die in den prunkvollen Szenen berühmter Maler des Neoimpressionismus wie Georges Seurat und Henri-Edmond Cross üblicherweise nicht erscheinen.

Khalifi lebt und arbeitet in Tanger und Barcelona. Mit raschen Pinselstrichen entwirft er fantasievolle Szenen und Figuren, die Elemente aus der Sufi-Dichtung mit historischen Bezügen zu Matisse und Seurat verbinden und thematische Orientierungspunkte wie Fußball, Rap und andere Bezugsgrößen miteinander kombinieren. Eines seiner anspruchsvollsten Gemälde ist das epische Werk *Mud Bricks* („Schlammziegel", 2022), das einen Braunen und einen Schwarzen Mann mit verdeckten Gesichtern zeigt. Einer von beiden lehnt sich zum anderen hinüber. Der Welt entrückt, beugen sie sich einer höheren Gewalt. Die wechselnden europäischen und afrikanischen Bezugsrahmen des Gemäldes veranschaulichen auf eindrucksvolle Weise die Zerrissenheit, die sich aus der Zugehörigkeit zu verschiedenen Kulturen der Diaspora ergibt: in diesem Fall Europa und Afrika, Marokko und Spanien, die durch den *schmalsten* aller Pfade, die Straße von Gibraltar, voneinander getrennt sind.

Eines von Khalifis bedeutsamsten Gemälden, *The Wounded Raver* („Der verwundete Raver", 2021), wirkt wie ein Mahnmal des Antagonismus und der Erneuerung. Ein blondierter Mensch im Teenageralter – möglicherweise der Künstler selbst – wird von zwei barmherzigen Derwischen getragen. Das rote Arsenal-Trikot der zentralen Figur erinnert an den penetranten Geruch des Erbrochenen in den Straßen rund um ein Fußballstadium nach einem Spieltag. Die Träger ähneln eher maskierten Helden als götzenartigen Gestalten. Ihre Gewänder spielen auf den Tanz der drehenden Derwische aus dem 12. Jahrhundert an. Für den Künstler, der zwischen seinen entgegengesetzten Identitäten pendelt, ist das Malen sowohl ein Akt des Protests als auch der Wiedergutmachung. Es geht um die Erneuerung eines Narrativs und die Kreolisierung der Protagonist*innen der Kunstgeschichte. Tatsächlich ist dieses Gemälde wie viele andere seiner Werke eine Nachbildung – in diesem Fall eine Neuinterpretation von Francisco Goyas romantischem Werk *Der verwundete Maurer* bzw. *Der verletzte Maurer* (1786–1787). In Khalifis Gemälde ist der Originalhintergrund vollständig durch ein grünes Leichentuch ersetzt – eine Farbe, die traditionell für die islamische Kunst steht.

In seinem ätherischen Werk *Musk* („Moschus", 2021) durchbricht ein leuchtend gelbes Rechteck im abstrakten Stil eines Kasimir Malewitsch die sich überlagernden Schichten aus smaragdgrüner Acrylfarbe. Durch die sorgfältige Platzierung des Rechtecks verschiebt sich die Perspektive vom Gesicht des Jugendlichen in der Bildmitte auf die leuchtend gelbe Fläche. Einen Zugang zu vielen Gemälden des Künstlers erhält man über das Symbol des *Fana*. Dabei handelt es sich um einen in Marokko nicht heimischen Baum, der wegen seiner Exotik häufig Ortswappen ziert. Im Arabischen hingegen steht *Fana* für die mögliche Auflösung oder vielmehr für das Zügeln des eigenen Ichs – ein wiederkehrendes Motiv in Khalifis ausdrucksstarker künstlerischer Praxis.

Die beiden Gemälde von Khalifi, die in der Ausstellung *In the Heart of Another Country* zu sehen sind, enthalten viele dieser Symbole. *MAWQIF* (2020), arabisch für „Der Stehende", spielt auf die ikonische

Anuar Khalifi's paintings serve as a summoning—at times, a reckoning. They seek to pierce the hermetic field of western 'history painting'—reifying Brown and Black bodies, traditionally excluded from the scenes of splendour composed by noted neo-impressionist painters, among them Georges Seurat and Henri-Edmond Cross.

Living and working between Tangier and Barcelona, Khalifi uses rapid brushstrokes to construct scenes and characters from the imagination that merge lyrical Sufi forms, alongside historical references from Matisse and Seurat, while intermingling orientations, such as football, rap music, and other points of fixation. One of Khalifi's most ambitious canvases is an epic piece entitled *Mud Bricks* (2022), which presents two figures, a Brown and a Black man, their faces concealed, one leaning into the other, submitting to a state of otherworldliness—acquiescing to a higher power. The painting's deviating frames, both European and African, are an evocative vessel for comprehending the dysphoria of belonging of and to different cultures of the diaspora. In this case, Europe, and Africa—Morocco and Spain, separated by the *narrowest* of trails, the Strait of Gibraltar.

One of Khalifi's most significant paintings, *The Wounded Raver* (2021), serves as an antagonistic and restorative memorial. Here, a bleached-blonde human—a teenage boy, potentially a stand-in representation for the artist, is supported by two altruistic dervishes. The central figure's red Arsenal football top harkens to the vomit-filled streets of post-match-day stadiums—their pungent smell lingering. The characters anchoring him resemble masked heroes as opposed to objects to be fetishised. Their garments allude to the 12th-century whirling dervish dance. For the artist, who oscillates between his diagonal identities, the act of painting is one of both reclamation and restitution—of modernising a narrative and creolising the protagonists of art's history. Indeed, this image, like many he has created, is a reconstruction—in this case, a re-imagining of Francisco Goya's Romantic-era work, referred to as either *The Wounded Mason or The Injured Mason* (1786–87). In Khalifi's art, the aggrieved bricklayer's backdrop is replaced with an all-encompassing shroud of green—a colour emblematic of Islamic artistic tradition.

In the ethereal *Musk* (2021), thickets of overlaid emerald acyclic paint are interrupted by a shimmering yellow square, seemingly transposed from Kazimir Malevich's era of abstraction. A perspectival shift occurs from the central youthful prospect's face to the lustrous glow of yellow invoked by the meticulously placed square. A key to many of the artist's paintings is a decoding of the emblem that is the *fana*—a tree that is non-indigenous to Morocco and that has often been deployed as a crest of place due to its exoticism. To the contrary, in Arabic *fana* represents the potential obliteration or, indeed, the reigning-in, of one's ego—a recurring motif in Khalifi's expressive practice.

The two paintings by Khalifi on view in *In the Heart of Another Country* contain many of the symbols articulated above. *MAWQIF* (2020), whose Arabic title translates as 'the stand', is suggestive of the iconic scenes of Jesus walking on water, here reconceived with an African body. He stands, centre-frame, in a detailed jellabiya, invoking a different form of cultural specificity—a possibility expressed beyond the formal limits of western ideology. Contrarily, the brown figure shrouded in white atop a horse amidst a green landscape in *THE LIGHT BLOSSOM* (2020) invokes the narrativisation

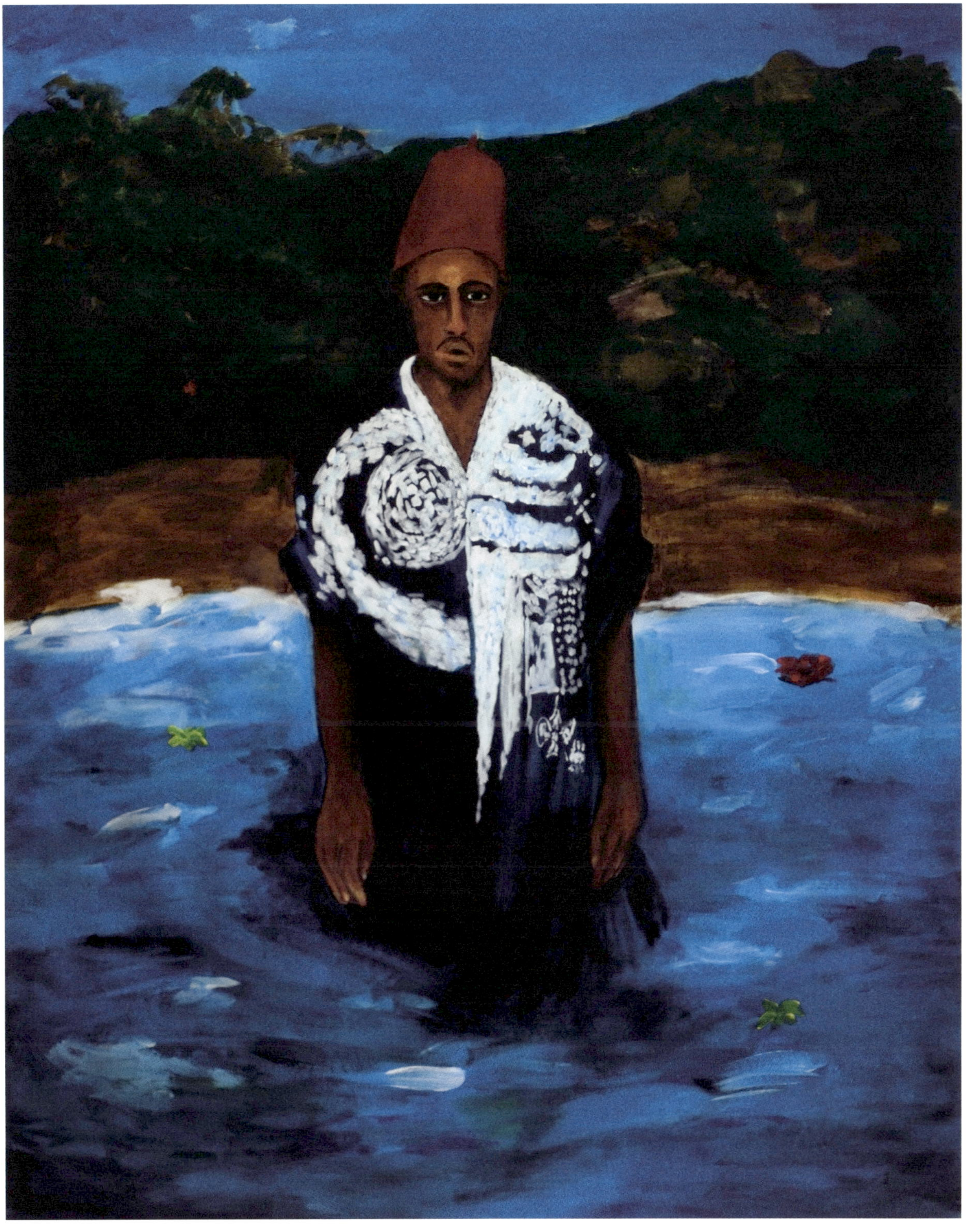

*MAWQIF / DER STEHENDE*, 2020. Acryl auf Leinwand / Acrylic on canvas. 114 × 145 cm

Szene an, in der Jesus über das Wasser geht. Hier wird er im Körper eines Afrikaners dargestellt. Er steht in einer reich gemusterten Dschellaba in der Bildmitte und präsentiert damit eine andere Form der kulturellen Besonderheit – eine Möglichkeit jenseits der formalen Grenzen der westlichen Ideologien. Dagegen verweist die Braune Person im weißem Gewand auf einem Pferd inmitten einer grünen Landschaft in *THE LIGHT BLOSSOM* („Die helle Blüte", 2020) auf die narrative Verwendung der Farbe Weiß in der Ikonografie und auf die Metapher des Pferdes in der Geschichte der Malerei – von der höfischen Malerei des Mogulreichs bis hin zur narrativen Malerei des Islam. Die magische „Blüte", die der Figur im Bild mit ihren strahlend weißen Blütenblättern und ihrem glänzenden Blütenstaub aus der Hand fällt, erinnert an eine Opfergabe – an die Möglichkeit eines Lebens nach dem Tod.

of the colour white in visual iconography, and of the metaphor of horses in the history of painting—from the Mughal Court era through to Islamic narrative painting. The invocation of the 'blossom'—shimmering, flailing from the palm of the protagonist's hand as he clenches the petal—the pollen blossom—sparkling, luminous and looming, is suggestive of an offering—the possibility of afterlife.

Omar Kholeif

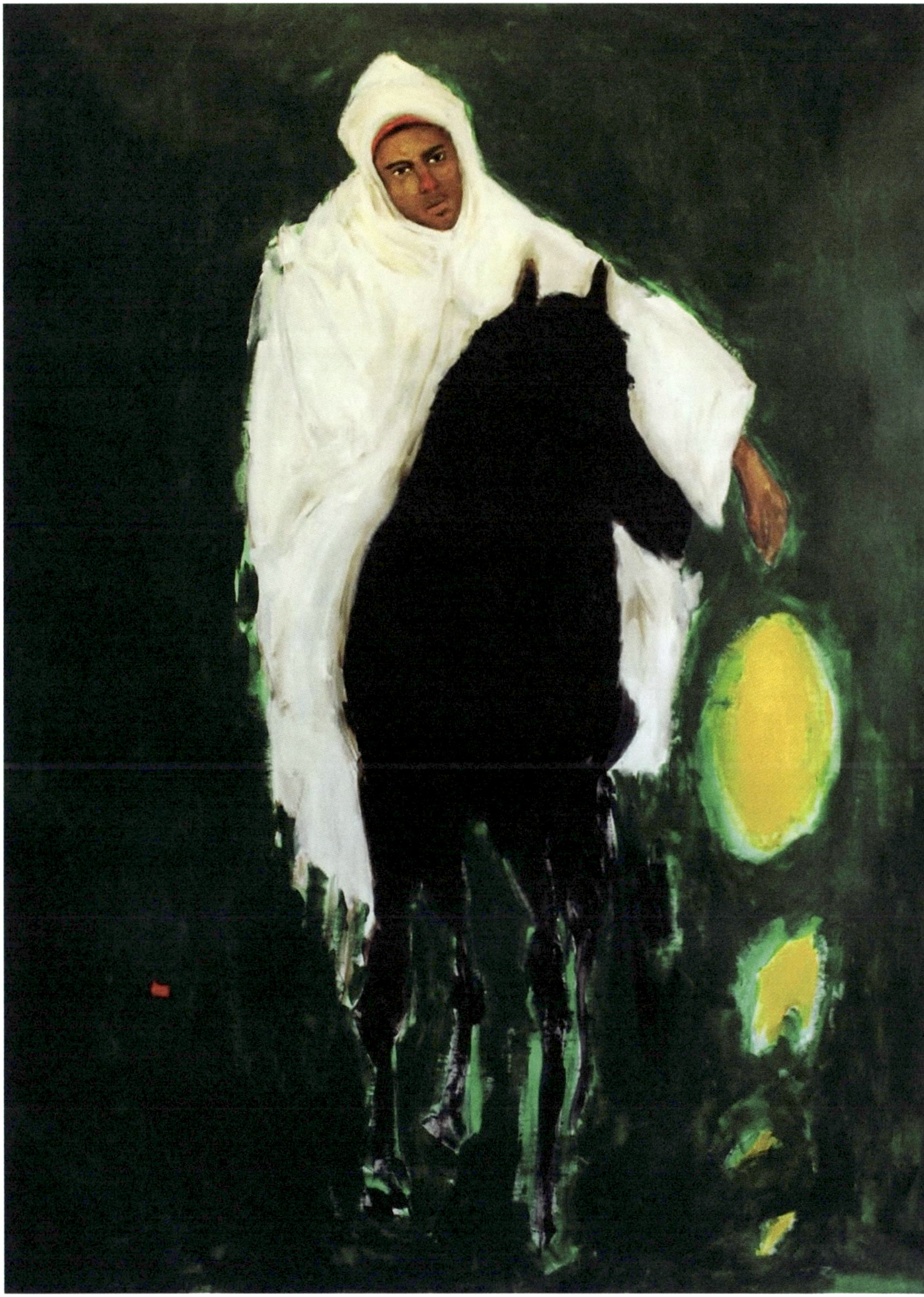

*THE LIGHT BLOSSOM / DIE HELLE BLÜTE*, 2020. Acryl auf Leinwand / Acrylic on canvas. 139 × 190 cm

# Farideh Lashai

Farideh Lashais Multimedia-Installation, die im Rahmen von *In the Heart of Another Country* gezeigt wird, ist eine Neuinterpretation von Francisco Goyas *Die Schrecken des Krieges* (1810–1820). Für die Installation hat Lashai die Hintergründe von 80 der 82 Blätter aus Goyas Originalzyklus in einem Rechteckgitter angeordnet. Im Rhythmus einer der *Nocturnes* von Frédéric Chopin werden die Blätter abwechselnd von einem Punktstrahler angeleuchtet. Sobald der Lichtkegel auf eine der leeren Landschaften fällt, werden die Figuren aus Goyas Originalen als animierte Figuren auf das Bild projiziert und füllen so für einen kurzen Moment die Leere. Mit dieser künstlerischen Dramaturgie aus „leeren" Blättern und bewegten Figuren arrangiert Lashai eine Konfliktkonstellation, die über den eigentlichen Kontext von Goyas Werk hinausgeht und die Brutalität des Krieges als globale und ortsunabhängige Erfahrung offenbart.

Die Dichterin und Landschaftsmalerin Lashai hat in dieser Installation – einem der letzten vor ihrem Tod im Jahr 2013 vollendeten Werke – mehrere ihrer wichtigsten Einflussquellen miteinander verquickt. Der erste Teil des Werktitels „When I count, there are only you… But when I look" („Wenn ich zähle, sind nur du (…) Aber wenn ich vorschaue") stammt aus T. S. Eliots eindringlichem Gedicht *The Waste Land* (1922) über die gesellschaftliche und kulturelle Lage in Europa nach dem Ersten Weltkrieg. Der zweite Teil, „There is Only a Shadow", verweist auf den wichtigen Einfluss des Dramatikers Bertolt Brecht auf ihr Schaffen. Die menschenleeren und öden Landschaften sind Resultate eines Brecht'schen Strebens, die innere Logik von Raum und Zeit zu ergründen. Auf diese Weise entsteht eine dramatische Kluft – die Vierte Wand wird durchbrochen und die kritische Distanz der Zuschauer*innen auf diese Weise noch verstärkt. Womöglich ist es die bewusste Wahrnehmung des Entweichens, das hier ein Gefühl des Schreckens erzeugt.

Lashai arbeitete in ihren Werken häufig mit abstrakten Landschaften und Naturdarstellungen, die sie vielfach mit ihren Lebenserfahrungen aus der konfliktreichen soziopolitischen Geschichte ihrer Heimat Iran verknüpfte. Im Verlauf ihrer mehr als fünf Jahrzehnte währenden Karriere schuf Lashai eine breite Palette künstlerischer Formate. Sie gilt weithin als eine der wichtigsten iranischen Künstlerinnen des 20. Jahrhunderts.

Reinventing and reimagining Francisco Goya's *The Disasters of War* (1810–20) as a multimedia installation, Farideh Lashai's installation featured within *In the Heart of Another Country* presents 80 of the 82 backgrounds from Goya's original series in a rectangular grid format, each illuminated in turn by a synchronised spotlight moving to one of composer Frédéric Chopin's *Nocturnes*. As the spotlight crosses one of the empty landscape images, the original Goya characters momentarily return as projected animated figures that fill the void. Lashai's dramatic composition of the 'empty' prints with lively characters configures a representation of conflict that transcends the original context of Goya's work to expose the brutality of war as a global experience, wherever it takes place.

Lashai, who was both a poet and a landscape painter, united several of her primary influences in this installation, one of the last completed works before her death in 2013. The first part of the work's title, *When I count, there are only you… But when I look*, is taken from T. S. Eliot's influential poem of post-war landscapes, *The Waste Land* (1922). The second part, *There is only a shadow*, reflects the major inspiration of the playwright Bertolt Brecht on her work. The landscapes, devoid of people and activity, follow the Brechtian desire to reveal the inner workings of space and time. In doing so, they create a theatrical disconnect—a breaking of the fourth wall, fostering a critical distance for the spectator. Indeed, it may be the awareness of disappearance that incites one's feeling of horror here.

Much of Lashai's work presented or amalgamated a recurrent use of abstract landscapes, as well as depictions of nature. These were often presented in the context of her experiences of Iran's conflicted sociopolitical history during her lifetime. With a career spanning over five decades, which saw the artist working with a vast array of artistic formats, Lashai is widely considered one of the most significant Iranian artists of the 20th century.

Sarah Perks

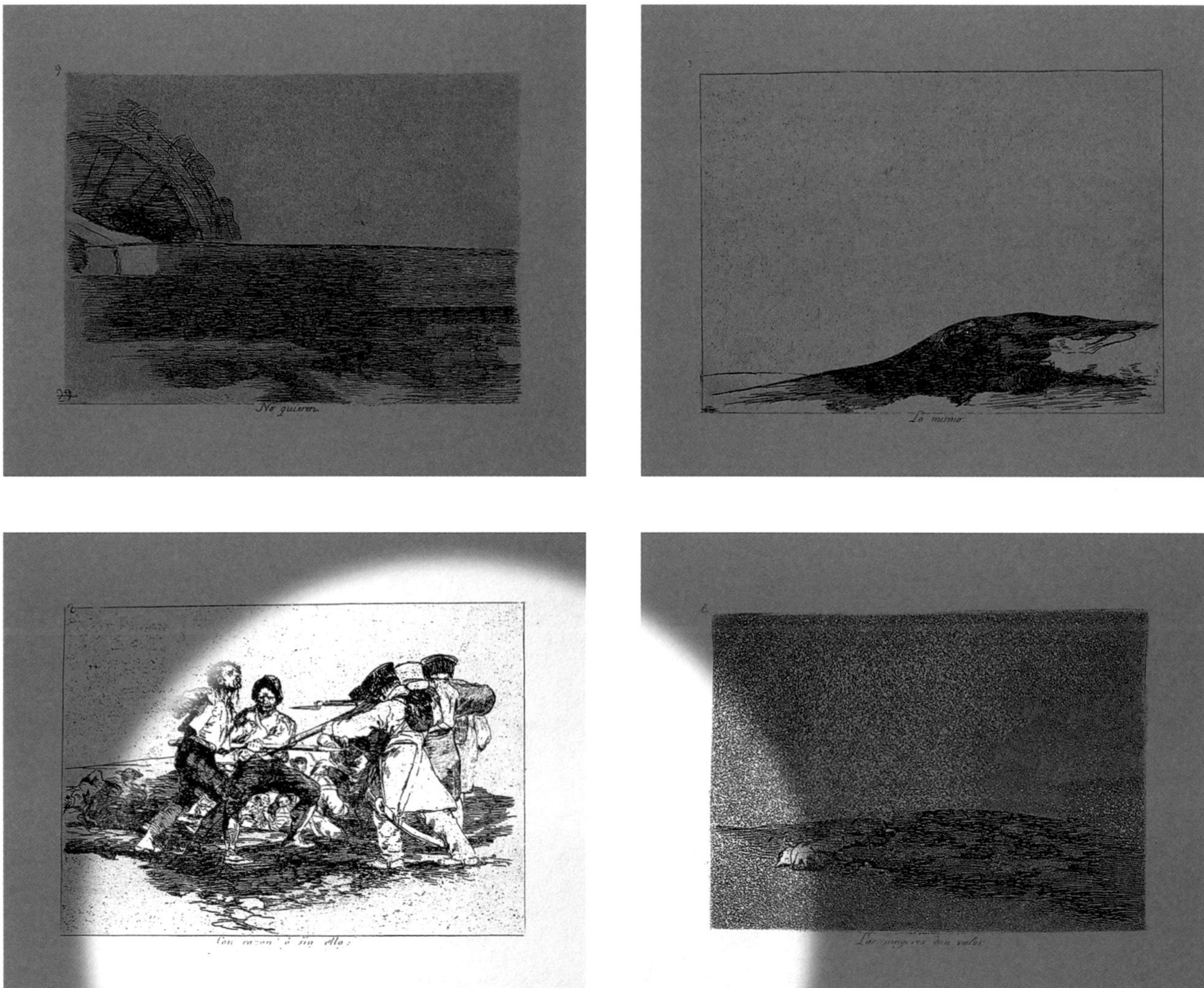

*When I count, there are only you… But when I look, there is only a shadow / Wenn ich zähle, sind nur du … Aber wenn ich vorschaue, ist da nur ein Schatten*, 2012–2013. Projektion animierter Bilder auf eine Abfolge von 80 im Tiefdruckverfahren entwickelten Fotoabzügen / Projection of animated images on a suite of 80 original photo-intaglio prints. 310 × 192 cm. Installationsansicht / Installation view, *When I Count, There Are Only You…*, Sharjah Art Foundation, 2021.

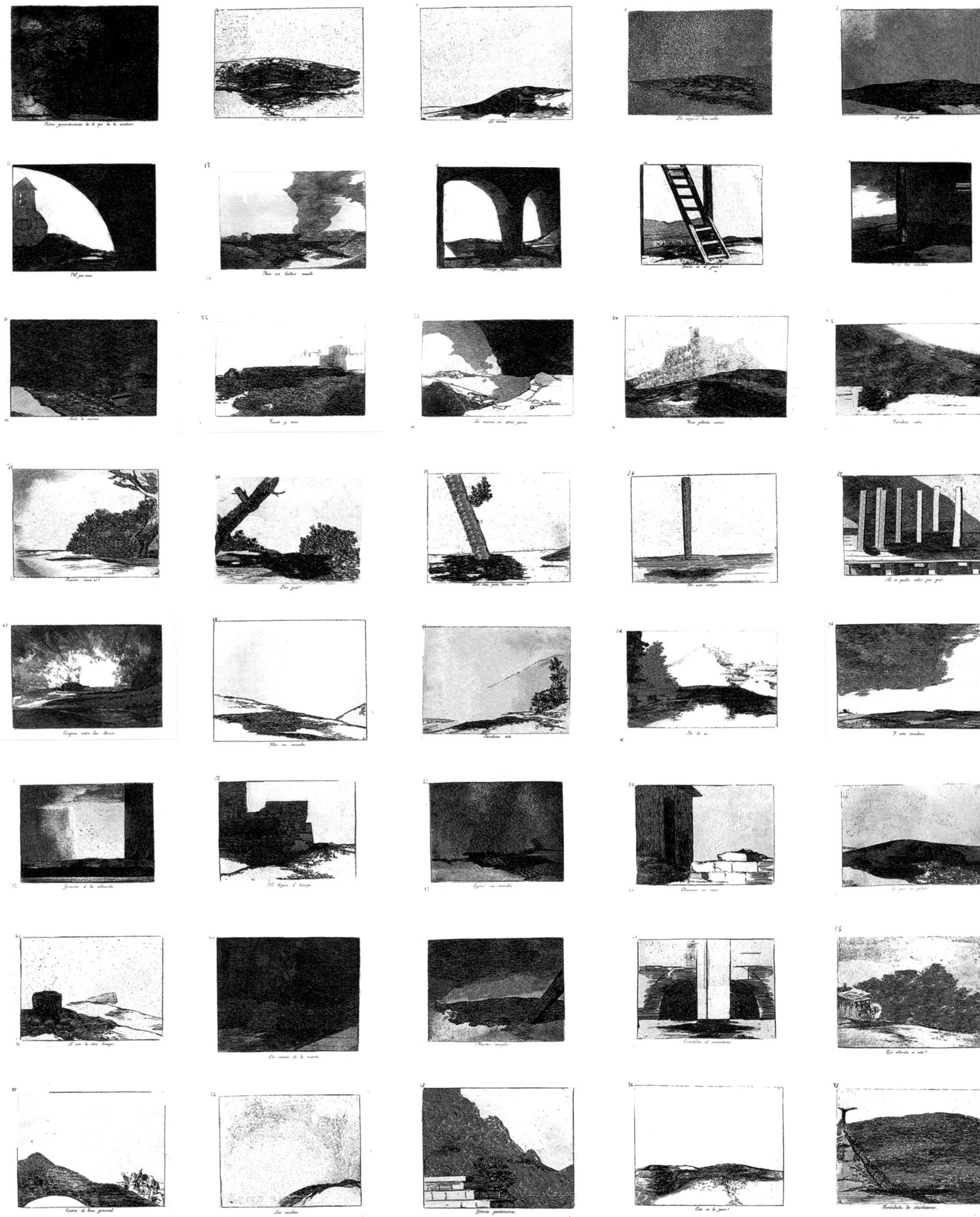

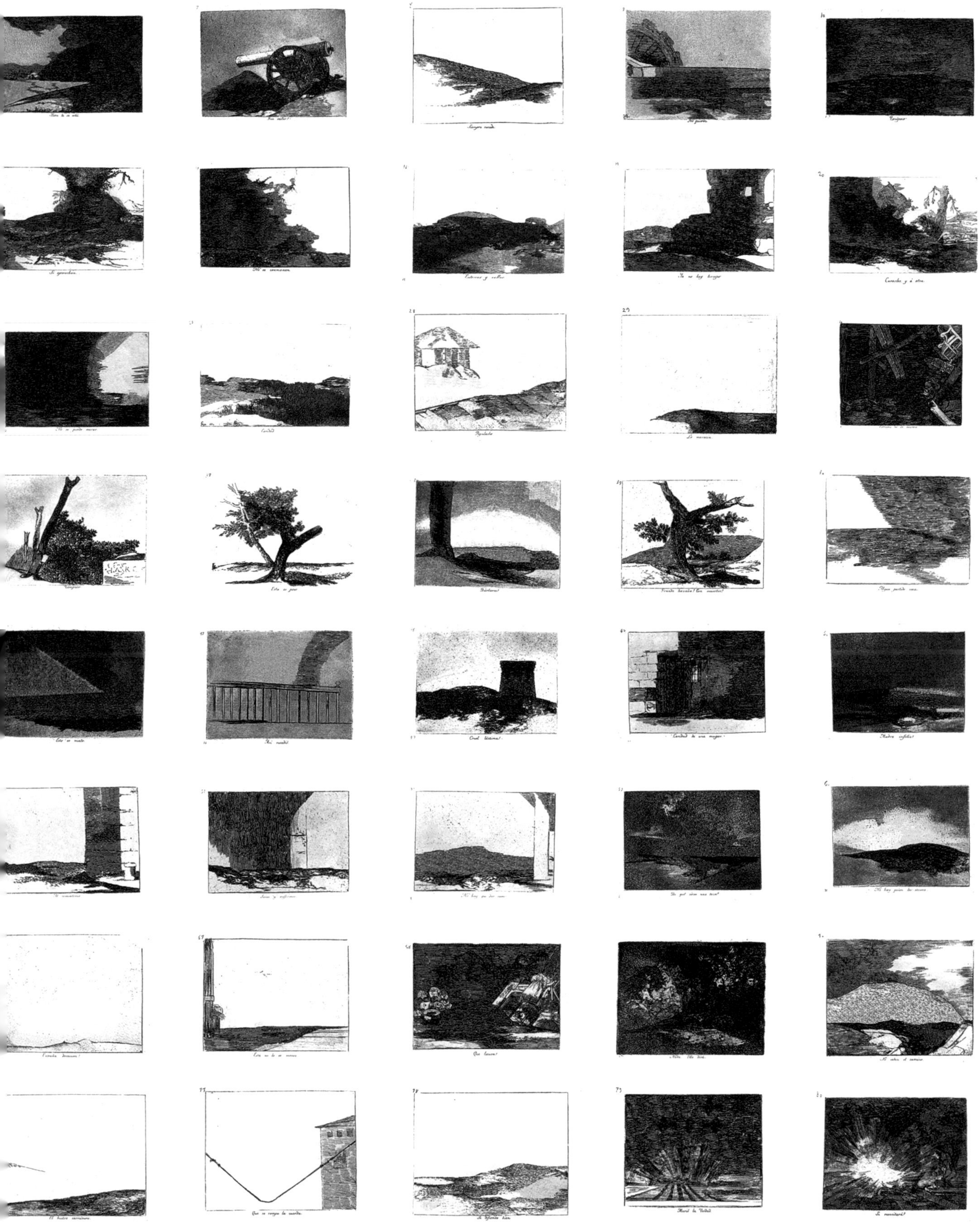

# Marwan

Marwan malte in Syrien zunächst Landschaftsbilder und Porträts, bevor er die beiden Genres dann in Berlin verband, wo er sich 1957 an der Hochschule für Bildende Künste einschrieb und in Kontakt mit der Neuen Figuration und dem Neoexpressionismus kam. Dieses Ölgemälde ohne Titel aus dem Jahr 1969 ist ein Beispiel für die Arbeiten Marwans aus seinen frühen Berliner Jahren: zwei gewundene, aus feinen fließenden Linien bestehende Figuren vor einem Hintergrund, dessen gedeckte Farbgebung zu ihren Hauttönen und ihrer Kleidung passt.

Wie die Galeristin Andrée Sfeir-Semler 2016 berichtete, reiste Marwan im Anschluss an seinen Umzug nach Deutschland regelmäßig nach Damaskus, um Porträts von Politiker*innen anzufertigen. „Ich würde sagen, er war politisch genug, um in den 1960er Jahren mehrere Ermahnungen von syrischen Behörden zu erhalten. Danach hat er aufgehört, solche Werke zu malen“, sagte sie der in den Vereinigten Arabischen Emiraten erscheinenden Zeitung *The National*. Zu den Porträtierten gehörte auch der Politiker Munif al-Razzaz, ein panarabischer Sozialist, der vor dem Staatsstreich von 1966 Generalsekretär der syrischen Baath-Partei war und 1977 in den Irak zog, um sich der irakischen Baath-Partei anzuschließen, wo er 1984 im Hausarrest starb.

Im Jahr 1965 fertigte Marwan zwei Porträts von al-Razzaz an, die aufeinander verweisen. Auf dem Gemälde in der Sammlung der Sharjah Art Foundation befindet er sich in der Mitte einer Leinwand, deren Hintergrund durch zwei erdige, pastellige Mauvetöne unterteilt ist. Er steigt bis auf Brusthöhe vom unteren Bildrand auf; sein Kinn ruht auf einem Holzklotz, der sein müdes, besorgtes Gesicht noch deutlicher hervortreten lässt. Das zweite Gemälde, das sich in der Sammlung der Barjeel Art Foundation befindet, stellt al-Razzaz in derselben Pose dar, diesmal vor einer dunkelolivfarbenen Fläche und einer Holzsäule, die hinter seinem Kopf aufragt. Im Jahr 2021 erwähnte der Kulturkritiker Sultan Sooud Al-Qassemi dieses Bild in einem Tweet und suchte die Verbindung zu al-Razzaz' Sohn Omar Razzaz, einem ehemaligen jordanischen Ministerpräsidenten. „Er muss meinen Vater gut gekannt haben“, antwortete Razzaz, „denn das Bild enthält eine Reihe von Anspielungen.“

Marwan began painting landscapes and portraits in Syria before melding the two genres in Berlin, where he moved in 1957, enrolling at Hochschule für Bildende Künste and becoming associated with New Figuration and Neo-Expressionism. This untitled 1969 oil on canvas is exemplary of those created during Marwan's early years there: two sinuous figures painted with fine, fluidly gradated lines appear over a smooth plane whose muted shading matches their skin tones and clothing.

As gallerist Andrée Sfeir-Semler noted in 2016, Marwan regularly visited Damascus after arriving in Germany, creating portraits of political figures: 'I would say he was political enough for him to receive some warnings in the 1960s from Syrian officials. Afterwards, he stopped painting such works', she informed *The National*, UAE. Among his subjects was politician Munif al-Razzaz, a pan-Arab socialist and secretary-general of the Syrian Ba'ath Party before the 1966 coup d'état, who moved to Iraq in 1977, joined the Iraqi Ba'ath Party and died in 1984 under house arrest.

In 1965, Marwan created two portraits of al-Razzaz that echo one another. The painting in the Sharjah Art Foundation's Collection positions him at the centre of a canvas whose background is divided by two shades of earthen, pastel mauve. He rises, torso up, from the bottom; his chin rests on a wooden block, amplifying a face expressing weary concern. Another painting, found in the Barjeel Art Foundation's collection, repeats al-Razzaz's pose, this time against a dark olive plane with a wooden pillar extending upwards from behind his head. In 2021, the cultural critic Sultan Sooud Al-Qassemi tweeted about the latter painting, seeking a connection to al-Razzaz's son, Omar Razzaz, a former prime minister of Jordan. 'He must have known my father well', Razzaz responded, 'because there are several clues in it'.

Stephanie Bailey

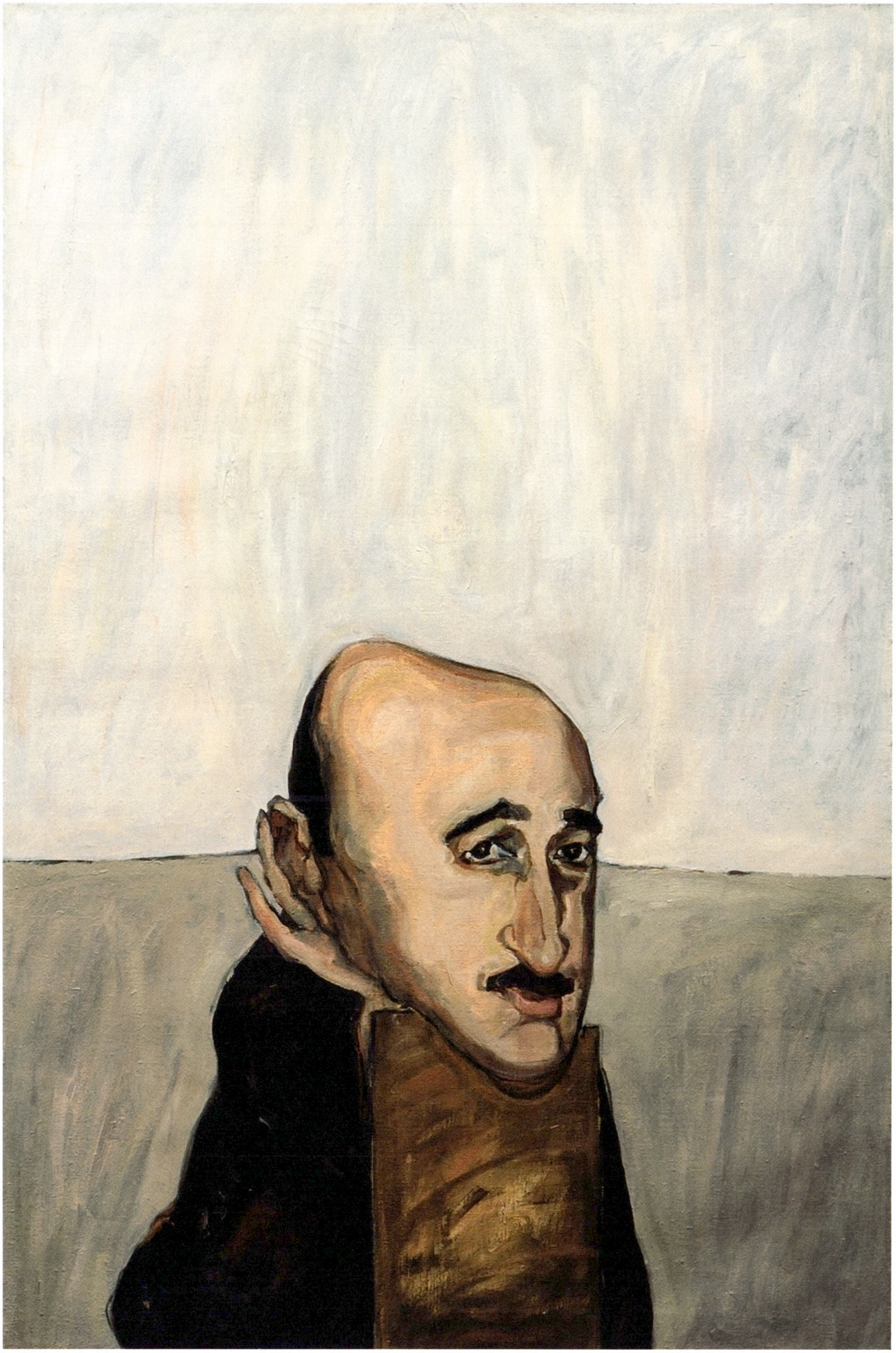

*Munif al Razzaz*, 1965. Öl auf Leinwand / Oil on canvas. 89 × 130 cm

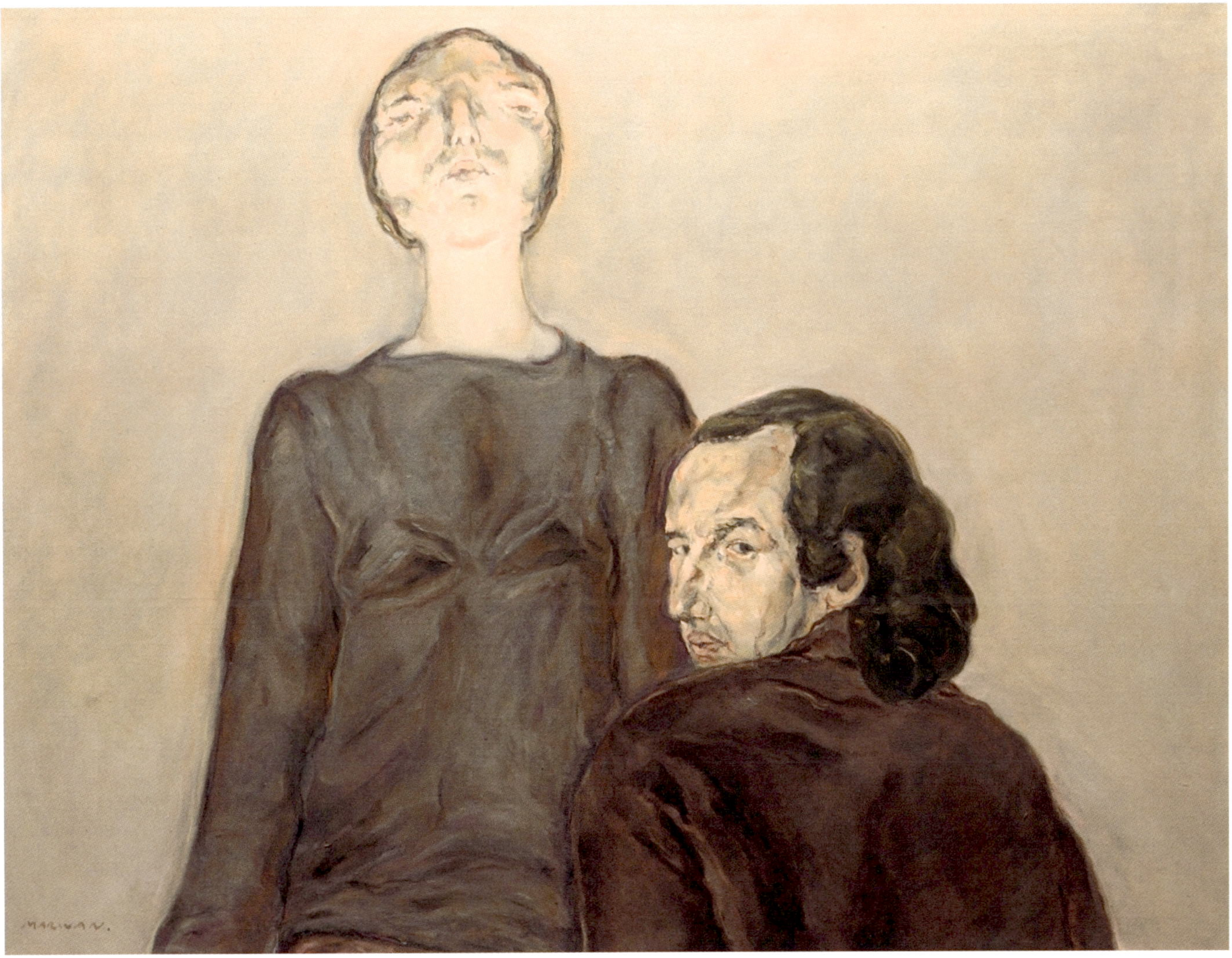

*Untitled* / *Ohne Titel*, 1969. Öl auf Leinwand / Oil on canvas. 130 × 89 cm

# Ahmed Morsi

Die komplexen Erzählungen in Ahmed Morsis Gemälden schaffen eine Welt, die seine vielschichtigen Lebenserfahrungen der letzten 50 Jahre widerspiegelt. Ahmed Morsi hat sich im Laufe seines Lebens neben der Malerei auch der Poesie, dem Schreiben, dem Verlegen und dem Journalismus gewidmet. Geboren 1930 in Alexandria, stammt er aus einem literarisch geprägten Elternhaus. Beide Eltern waren Übersetzer, und auch seine eigene erste Veröffentlichung war die Übersetzung eines Gedichts ins Griechische. Als Erwachsener entwickelte sich Morsi zu einem Meister des Netzwerkens in der Kunstszene. Er wurde zum Aushängeschild der sogenannten Alexandria School, der auch der prominente surrealistische Schriftsteller Edwar Al Kharrat und die Künstler Seif Wanly und Mahmoud Moussa angehörten. Eine lebenslange Freundschaft pflegte er mit dem ägyptischen Modernisten Abdel Hadi Al Gazzar, der heute Kultstatus besitzt. Gemeinsam mit ihm organisierte er mehrere Gruppenausstellungen, in denen auch die Vorreiter der ägyptischen Modernisten- und Surrealisten-Bewegung eine Rolle spielten. Auf dieser fruchtbaren Periode des Experimentierens beruht der bemerkenswerte stilistische Reichtum in Morsis Werk. *Man and Son* („Mann und Sohn“, 1954) zeigt beispielsweise eine Person in andachtsvoller Pose, die von einem Kind in den Armen gehalten wird. Bemerkenswert sind dabei die Details: der Abdruck einer geschwärzten Hand oder Handfläche auf der Stirn des Kindes; eine Anordnung von Punkten, die ein Dreieck auf dem Handrücken des Vaters bilden. Jedes Element steht für ein geheimnisvolles Beziehungsgeflecht, in dem familiäre Abhängigkeit als spannungsreicher Balanceakt zwischen Gesagtem und Ungesagtem abgebildet wird.

Morsi lebte zwischen 1955 und 1957 für kurze Zeit in Bagdad und unterrichtete Englisch an einer höheren Schule. Die Stadt erlebte zu dieser Zeit eine künstlerische und kulturelle Renaissance. Morsi versuchte sich hier auch als Kritiker und schrieb u. a. eine kontrovers diskutierte Kritik über die Bagdad-Gruppe, die Teile der internationalen Kunstwelt erschütterte.

Als er 1957 aus dem Irak nach Ägypten zurückkehrte, ließ er sich in Kairo nieder, wo er als Maler, Schriftsteller und Übersetzer arbeitete und erste Schritte als Bühnenbildner machte. In einer nächsten experimentellen Phase war er ab 1968 Mitgründer, Herausgeber und Layouter der Avantgarde-Literaturzeitschrift *Gallery 68*. Der Start der von Kritikern gefeierten Publikation fiel mit Morsis Entscheidung zusammen, keine Lyrik mehr zu verfassen, nachdem Ägypten und eine Koalition arabischer Staaten im Sechstagekrieg (Naksah) von 1967 durch Israel besiegt worden waren – obgleich Morsi zuvor in der Zeitschrift eine alternative Perspektive auf diese schwierige Periode der ägyptischen Geschichte eingenommen hatte.

In dieser Lebensphase verfeinerte Morsi zudem seinen unverwechselbaren Malstil, eine Entwicklung, die nicht zuletzt auch durch ein einschneidendes biografisches Ereignis ausgelöst wurde: Im Jahr 1974 zog er mit seiner Familie nach New York. Werke wie *Woman's Head* („Frauenkopf“, 1972) oder *Adam and Eve* („Adam und Eva“, 1994) zeugen von Morsis surrealistischer Bildsprache – regungslose Figuren vor kargen Landschaften, gespenstische Erscheinungen zwischen diesem Leben und dem nächsten. Seine totemartigen Bilder gehen über europäische Vorstellungswelten vom Tod hinaus und ziehen neue Grenzen des Unbewussten.

The complex fabulations Ahmed Morsi produces in his paintings present a world that finds its echo in the artist's expansive approach to life over the past 50 years. His is one that has encompassed the practices of poetry, writing, editing and journalism alongside his painting. Born in Alexandria in 1930, Morsi's formative life was one filled with literature (both his parents were translators and his first published work was, fittingly, a poem translated into Greek). As an adult, Morsi developed a community of lifelong friendships, becoming a figurehead for the Alexandria School, which comprised figures such as the Surrealist writer Edwar Al Kharrat and the artists Seif Wanly and Mahmoud Moussa. Morsi developed a lifelong friendship with the now-iconic Egyptian Modernist Abdel Hadi Al Gazzar, producing multiple group exhibitions that included pioneers in the Modernist and Surrealist Egyptian movements. This fortuitous period of significant experimentation fomented notable richness in Morsi's style of work. For example, *Man and Son* (1954) depicts a solemnly seated figure gripped in the arms of a child. Curious details emerge: the mark of a blackened hand or palm print on the boy's forehead; an arrangements of dots in a triadic form on the back of the father's hand. Each element forges a mystical set of relations, one in which familial dependency is rendered as a taut balancing act of what is said and unsaid.

Morsi briefly lived in Baghdad between 1955 and 1957, teaching English at a senior school. The period was one of artistic and cultural renaissance in the city. Baghdad was also the place where he tried his hand at criticism, including a controversial review of works by the Baghdad Group, which upset certain orders of art world power.

Morsi chose Cairo as his base after his return to Egypt from Iraq in 1957, continuing his diverse career as a painter, writer and translator in addition to venturing into theatre set design. Morsi experimented again in 1968, becoming the co-founder, editor and layout designer of the Cairo-based avant-garde literary journal *Gallery 68*. The launch of the critically lauded publication also coincided with Morsi's retreat from writing poetry when Egypt and a coalition of Arab states were overpowered by Israel in the Six-Day War (Naksah) of 1967, the publication itself ushering a different perspective to a difficult period in Egypt's history.

It was also during this period that Morsi honed his distinctive style, not least in part to the momentous shift in 1974 when he left Egypt with his family for New York. Works such as *Woman's Head* (1972) and *Adam and Eve* (1994) form part of Morsi's surrealist idiolect of statuesque figures set against barren landscapes, haunting apparitions between this life and the next. The totemic images Morsi produces reroute the lines of where the unconscious realm is found, one which exceeds the European imaginary.

Chris McCormack

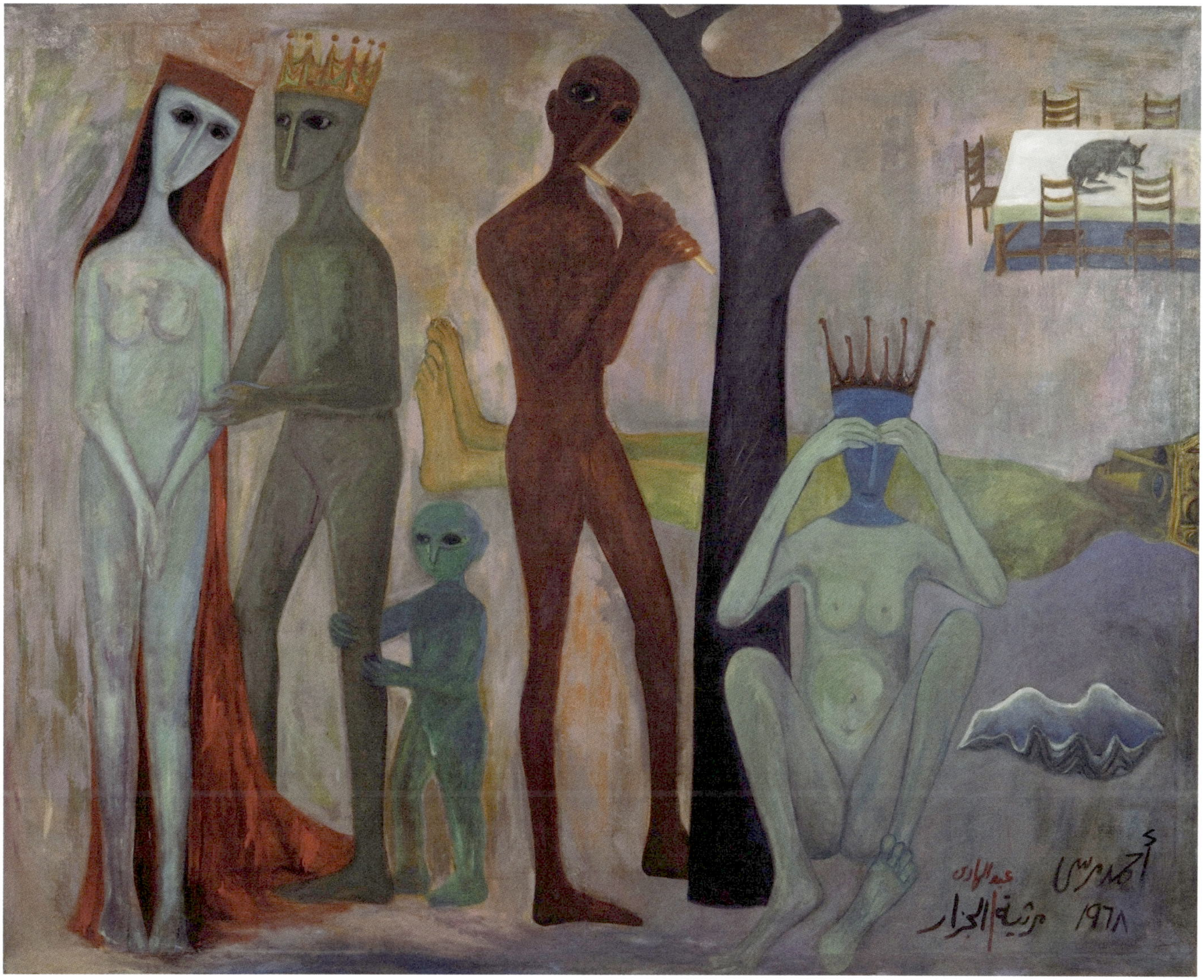


*Elegy of Al Gazzar* | *Klagelied von Al Gazaar*, 1968. Öl auf Leinwand / Oil on canvas. 184 × 235 cm

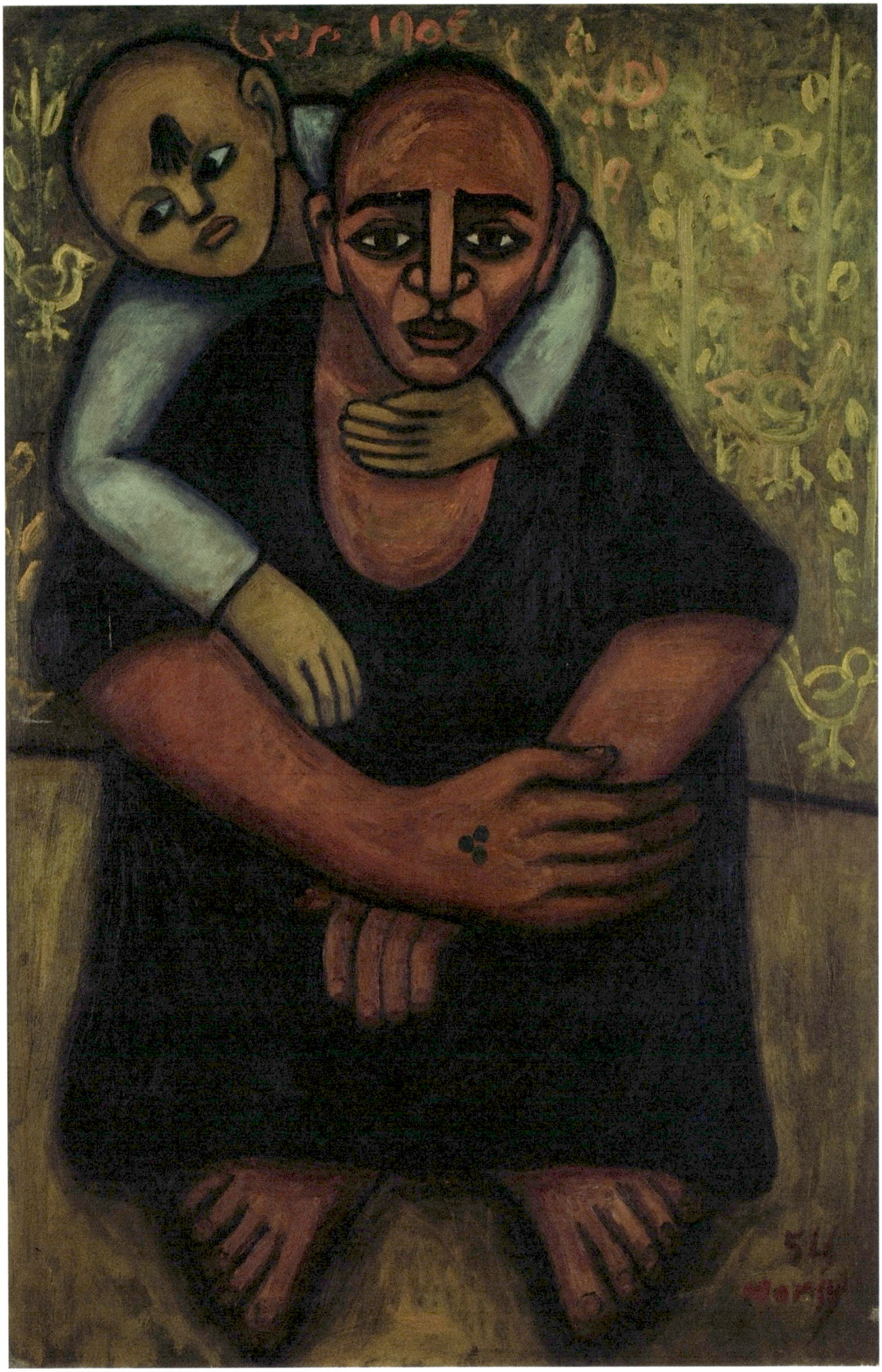

*Man and Son* / *Mann und Sohn*, 1954. Öl auf Holz / Oil on wood. 79 × 111 cm

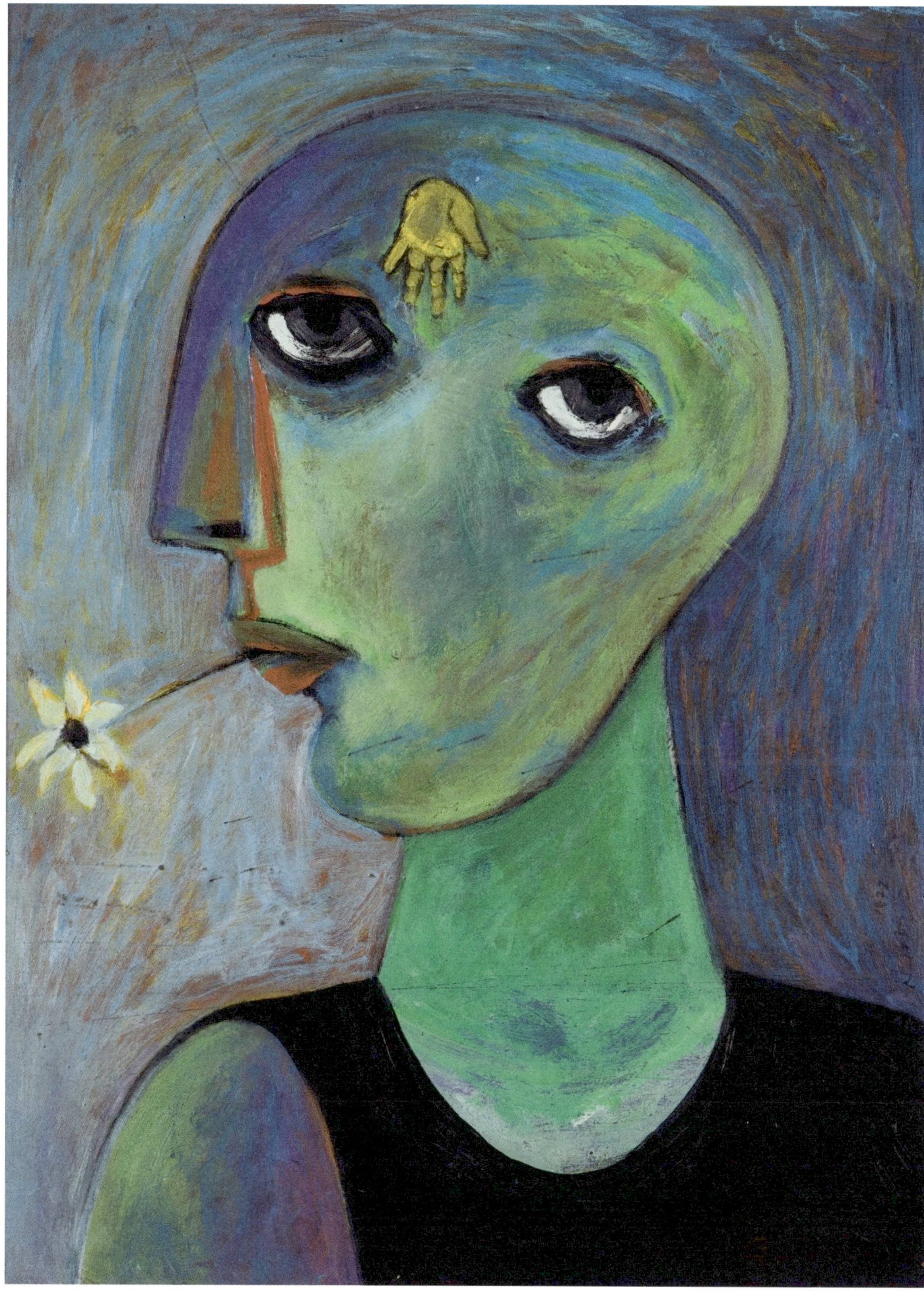

*Woman's Head* / *Frauenkopf*, 1972. Öl auf Leinwand / Oil on canvas. 46 × 52 cm

# Fateh Moudarres

Der Künstler Fateh Moudarres malte *Two Children Astride a Goat* („Zwei Kinder reiten auf einer Ziege“, 1960) kurz nach Abschluss seines Studiums an der Accademia di Belle Arti in Rom, wo er über seine zunehmende Begeisterung für den Surrealismus auch seinen unverkennbaren Stil entwickelte. Zu dieser Zeit gab Moudarres auch seine intensive künstlerische Beschäftigung mit religiösen Figuren auf und konzentrierte sich stattdessen auf Darstellungen des syrischen Alltagslebens und seines persönlichen Umfelds.

Auf seinem Gemälde stellte er mit dicken Schichten von Ölfarbe in einfachen Grün-, Rot- und Gelbtönen zwei junge Menschen dar, die auf einer Ziege durch eine ländliche Umgebung reiten – aus der Gegenwart in ein Reich der Fantasie. Für die Körper der Kinder wählte er kräftige Farben, die einen harten Kontrast zu den tristen Grautönen im Vordergrund der Leinwand bilden.

Moudarres zählt zu den bekanntesten Maler*innen Syriens und gilt weltweit als Wegbereiter der Moderne in seiner Heimat. Sein einzigartiger Stil wurde von den lokalen Sitten und Gebräuchen beeinflusst. Er stellte den harten Alltag der syrischen Landbevölkerung ebenso dar wie die konfliktgeladenen Unruhen, die sein tägliches Leben bestimmten. Der Künstler war zunächst Autodidakt und verbrachte seine Zeit hauptsächlich mit Beobachtungen. Zudem engagierte er sich in seiner lokalen Gemeinschaft und war als Revolutionär und ausdauernder Demonstrant bekannt. Er porträtierte das Leid und die Nöte der Menschen anhand von Szenen aus der Krise der syrischen Landwirtschaft und dem Bürgerkrieg im Libanon. Auf diese Weise setzte er sich mit dem gesellschaftlichen und politischen Wandel in den Ländern der Levante im Verlauf der Kriegsjahre des 20. Jahrhunderts auseinander.

*Two Children Astride a Goat* (1960) was painted just after the completion of Syrian artist Fateh Moudarres's studies at the Accademia di Belle Arti in Rome, where his fascination with Surrealism surfaced to inflect his distinctive style. It was during this time that Moudarres ceased his continuous and repetitive exploration of religious figures, choosing instead to focus on portrayals of Syrian daily life and his community. Thick layers of oil paint in unpretentious greens, reds and yellows are used to depict two young people riding a goat across a rural environment—out of the present into a realm of the imaginary. The children's flesh is presented in textured tones, in stark contrast to the desolate greys in the canvas's foreground.

One of Syria's most well-known painters, Moudarres is recognised worldwide as the country's progenitor of modernism, having developed an individual style influenced by local cultural norms and mores. The artist represented the hardships felt in the daily lives of Syria's rural citizens, as well as the conflicted uprisings that ensnared his everyday existence. Initially self-taught, Moudarres spent much of his time in observation mode, becoming active in his local community, and also operating as a revolutionary and relentless protestor. His portrayals of human suffering and difficulty are explored through depictions of the Syrian agriculture crisis and the Lebanese Civil War, reflecting the shifting social and political landscapes of 20th-century wartime in the Levant.

Reem Sawan

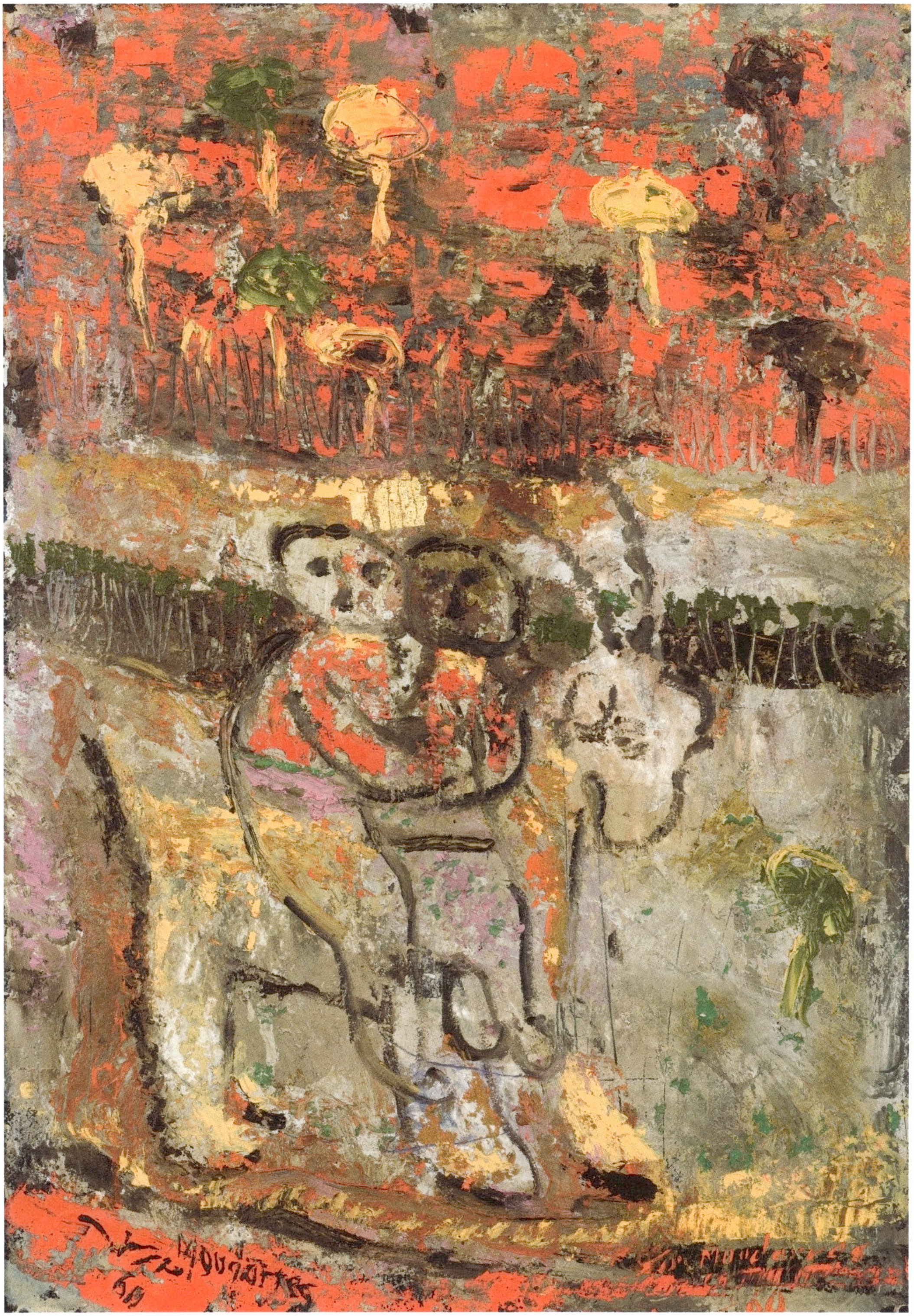

*Two Children Astride a Goat* | *Zwei Kinder reiten auf einer Ziege*, 1960. Öl auf Leinwand / Oil on canvas. 50 × 70 cm

# Michael Rakowitz

*The invisible enemy should not exist...* („Der unsichtbare Feind sollte nicht existieren ...") ist ein fortlaufendes Projekt, das der irakisch-amerikanische Künstler Michael Rakowitz 2007 begonnen hat. Es stellt eine Reaktion auf die Plünderung von Artefakten aus dem irakischen Nationalmuseum in Bagdad, die auf die US-amerikanische Invasion folgte. Aus Lebensmittelverpackungen, die er in „orientalischen" Lebensmittelgeschäften gesammelt hat, und oftmals unter Verwendung arabischer Zeitungen fertigt Rakowitz anhand von Informationen der Interpol-Website und der Datenbank des Orientalischen Instituts der Universität Chicago maßstabsgetreue Pappmaschee-Nachbildungen von im Irak geraubten und zerstörten Artefakten.

Das Orientalische Institut ist auch Schauplatz von Rakowitz' Stop-Motion-Film *The Ballad of Special Ops Cody* („Die Ballade von Special Ops Cody", 2017). Vor diesem Setting stellt der Künstler das spannungsreiche Verhältnis zwischen der Rolle der Vereinigten Staaten im „Nahen Osten" – ein militärischer Begriff, der zu Beginn des 20. Jahrhunderts von einem US-Marineoffizier geprägt worden sein soll – und dem Verlust von Kulturstätten und dazugehörigen Objekten aus der Region dar. Den Ausgangspunkt des Films bildet die wahre Geschichte von Special Ops Cody, eine US-Infanterie-Actionfigur, die auf US-Militärbasen in Kuwait und im Irak verkauft wurde. Eine irakische Rebellengruppe nutzte diese Figur 2005, um der US-amerikanischen Regierung (erfolglos) weiszumachen, sie halte einen amerikanischen Soldaten als Geisel gefangen.

*The Ballad of Special Ops Cody* erweckt diesen Spielzeugsoldaten zum Leben. Er dringt in eine Vitrine des Orientalischen Instituts ein, in der mesopotamische Votivstatuen verwahrt werden – offensichtlich um sie zu befreien. Doch die Statuen bleiben stumm an ihrem Platz, als wären sie mit den Folgen der Rückkehr in eine Heimat überfordert, die sie nicht mehr kennen und die womöglich sogar verloren gegangen ist. Solch komplizierte Restitutionsfragen knüpfen an *The invisible enemy should not exist...* an, das sich in den letzten Jahren anderen Fällen von kultureller Zerstörung und Diebstahl gewidmet hat. Das 2018 initiierte Projekt *The invisible enemy should not exist (Northwest Palace of Nimrud)* („Der unsichtbare Feind sollte nicht existieren [Nordwest-Palast von Nimrud]") konzentriert sich auf die Reliefskulpturen des assyrischen Palastes von Nimrud im irakischen Mossul, deren Zerstörung durch den Islamischen Staat (IS) im Jahr 2015 die Entfernung von Hunderten von Palastreliefs vorausging, die an internationale Sammlungen gegeben wurden.

*The invisible enemy should not exist...* is an ongoing project commenced in 2007 by Iraqi American artist Michael Rakowitz; it is a response to the looting of artifacts from the National Museum of Iraq in Baghdad, following the US invasion of Iraq in 2003. With food packaging gathered from 'Middle Eastern' food shops, and often using Arabic newspapers, Rakowitz created scaled papier-mâché replicas of looted and destroyed artefacts in Iraq based on information posted on Interpol's website and the database of the University of Chicago's Oriental Institute.

The Oriental Institute is the stage on which the fraught connection between the role of the United States in 'the Middle East'—a military term believed to have been coined by a US naval officer at the turn of the 20th century—and the loss of cultural sites and their attendant objects from the region, plays out in Rakowitz's 2017 stop-motion film *The Ballad of Special Ops Cody*. The film departs from the true story of Special Ops Cody, a US infantry action figure sold on US military bases in Kuwait and Iraq, which was used by an Iraqi insurgent group in 2005 to (unsuccessfully) fool the US government into believing they were holding an American solider hostage.

*The Ballad of Special Ops Cody* brings this toy soldier to life. He enters a vitrine at the Oriental Institute containing Mesopotamian votive statues, seemingly to free them. But the statues remain silent and in place, as if unable to contend with the implications of returning to a home they no longer know, and indeed, which may well have been lost. Such complicated questions surrounding restitution connect back to *The invisible enemy should not exist...*, which has turned its gaze in recent years to other moments of cultural destruction and theft. Initiated in 2018, *The invisible enemy should not exist (Northwest Palace of Nimrud)*, focuses on the relief sculptures of the Assyrian Palace of Nimrud in Mosul, Iraq, whose destruction by ISIS in 2015 was preceded by the removal of hundreds of gypsum reliefs that were sent to international collections.

Stephanie Bailey

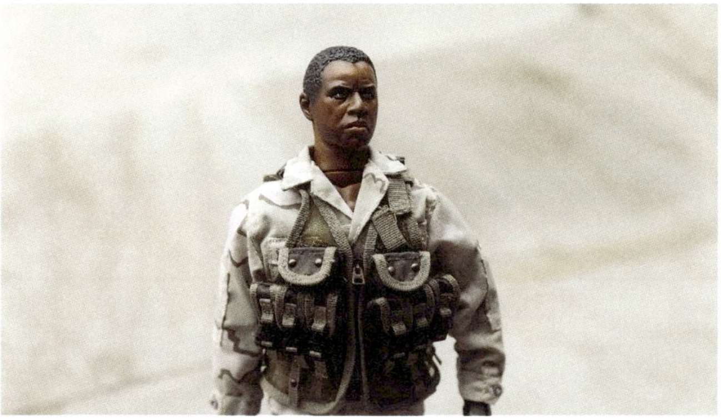

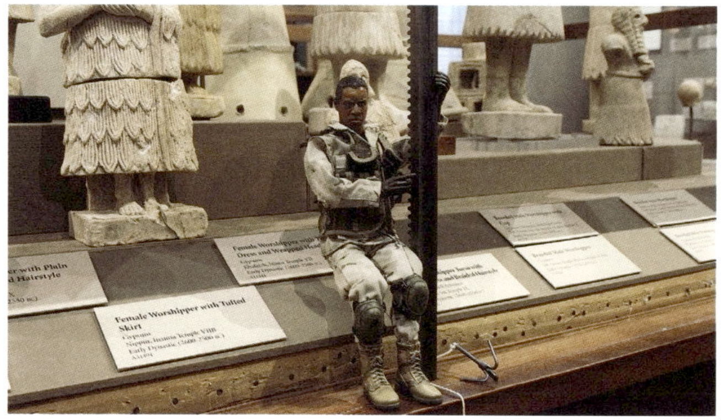


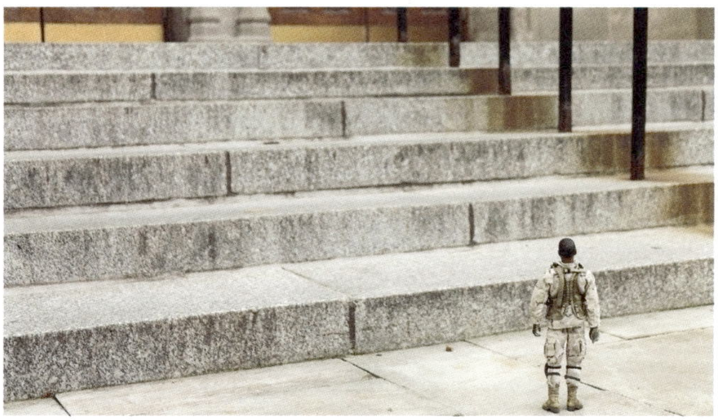

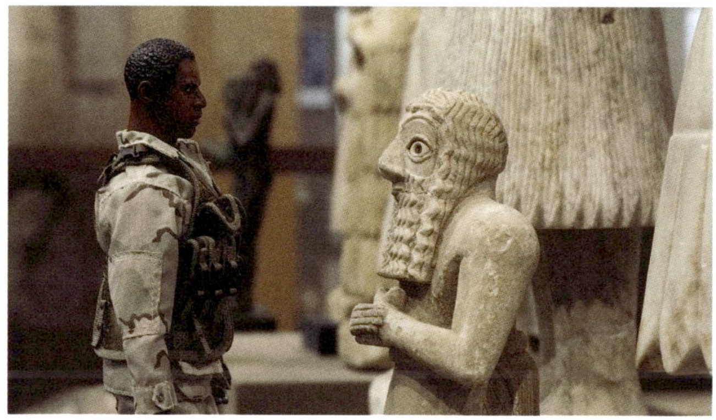

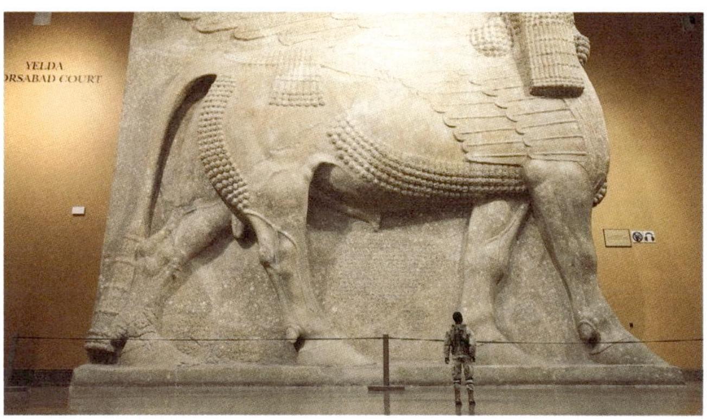


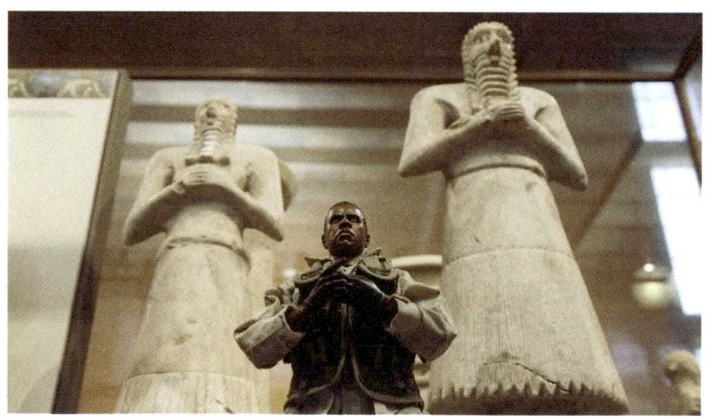

*The Ballad of Special Ops Cody | Die Ballade von Special Ops Cody*, 2017. Stop-Motion-Video / Stop-motion video. 14 Minuten, 42 Sekunden / 14 minutes 42 seconds. Im Auftrag des Museum of Contemporary Art Chicago / Commissioned by Museum of Contemporary Art Chicago

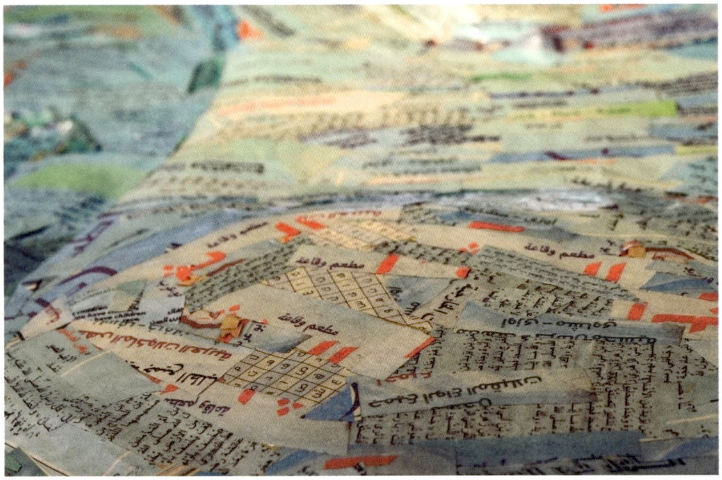

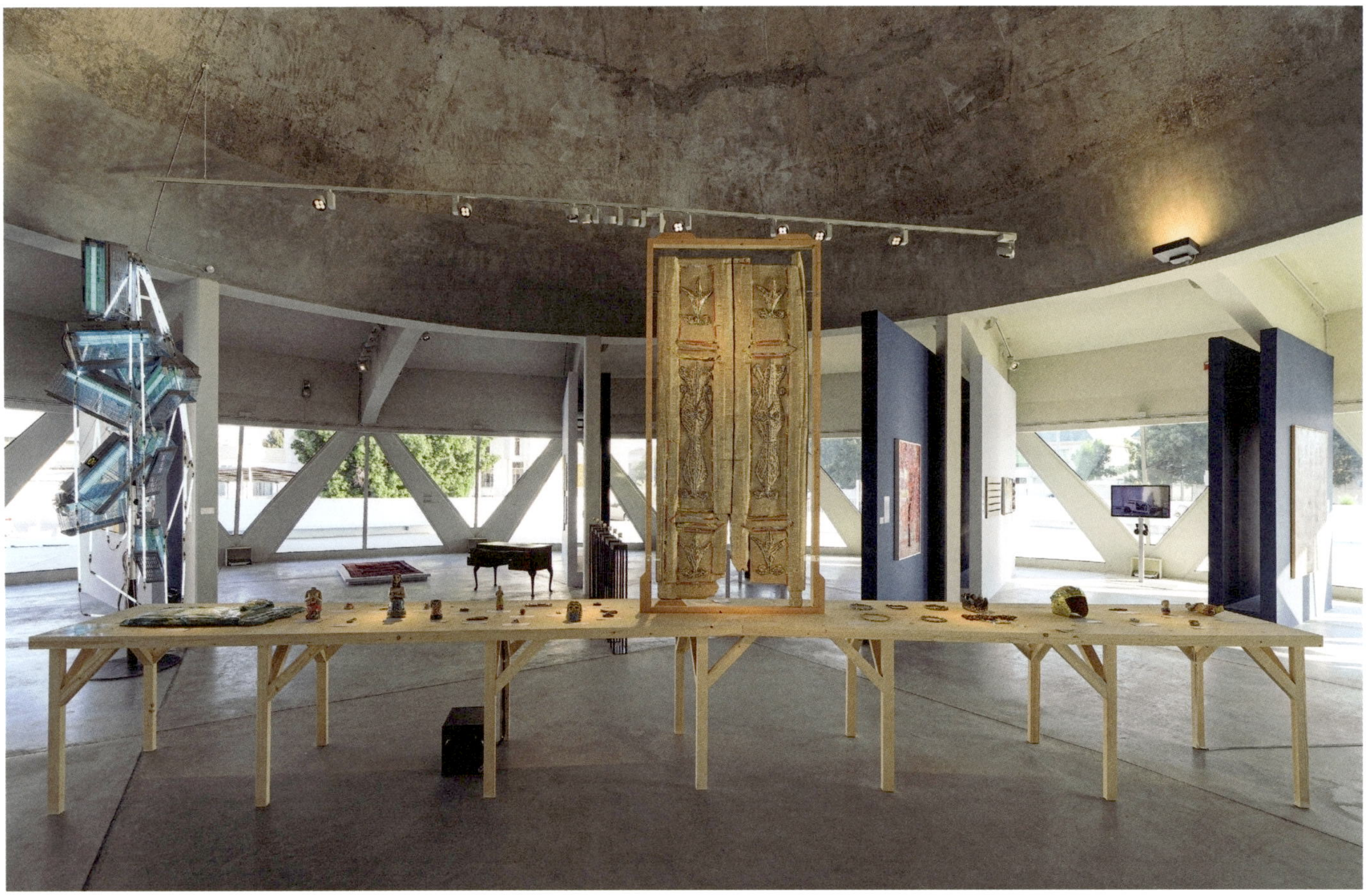

*The invisible enemy should not exist... / Der unsichtbare Feind sollte nicht existieren...*, 2007 bis heute / 2007–ongoing. Artefakte, Verpackung und Zeitungspapier, Klebstoff, 4 Zeichnungen, Schautafel, Sound / Artefacts, packaging and newspapers, glue, 4 drawings, display table, sound. Maße variabel / Dimensions variable. Installationsansicht / Installation view, *Unsettled Objects*, Sharjah Art Foundation, 2021.

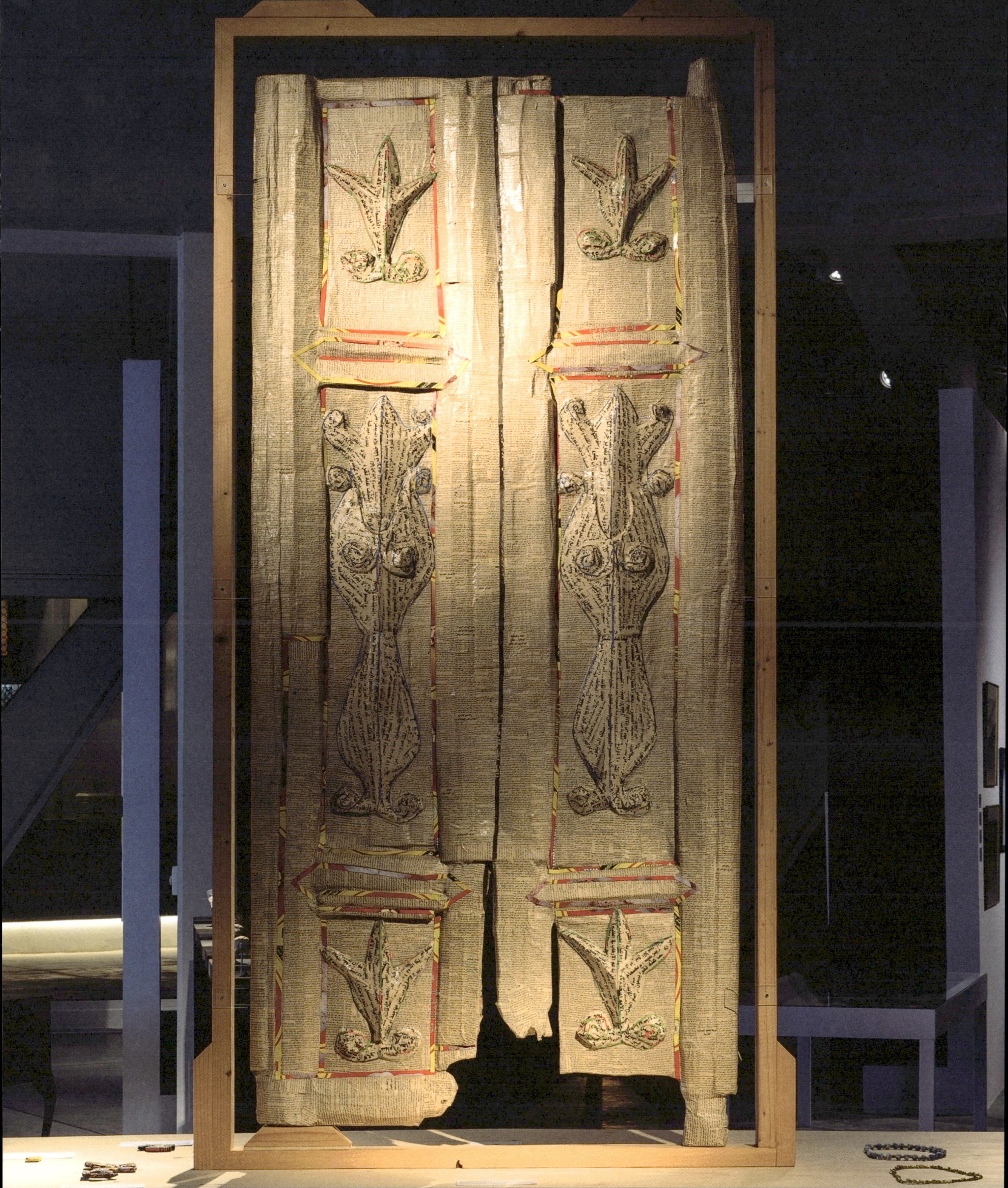

# Ibrahim El-Salahi

Die fließenden, figurativen Formen im Werk von Ibrahim El-Salahi verweisen auf die langjährige Beziehung des Künstlers zur Kalligrafie – von seiner Kindheit in Omdurman im Sudan, wo er in der Koranschule seines Vaters die Schrifttafeln verzierte, bis zu seiner Zeit als erwachsener Künstler, der seine künstlerischen Erfahrungen in Afrika, Europa und Lateinamerika zusammenzuführen versucht.

Als in der Londoner Tate Modern 2013 seine Retrospektive gezeigt wurde, beschrieb El-Salahi dem *Guardian*, wie sein künstlerisches Schaffen eine Wende genommen hatte, als er 1957 nach seinem Studium an der Slade School of Art in den Sudan zurückkehrte und dort mit Werken von Cézanne, Giotto und Mondrian in Berührung kam. El-Salahi stieß mit seinen Stillleben, Porträts und Aktbildern, die er in Khartum ausstellte, auf kein Interesse. Er begann, mit Kalligrafie zu experimentieren, um eine Verbindung zu seinem Publikum herzustellen. Als er „anfing, die Buchstaben zu zerlegen, um herauszufinden, was ihnen Sinn verleiht, öffnete sich eine Büchse der Pandora", berichtete der Künstler. „Aus diesen ursprünglich abstrakten Zeichen entwickelten sich Tier-, Menschen- und Pflanzenformen."

Solche Figuren werden in dem Ölgemälde *Untitled* („Ohne Titel") von 1962 lebendig, auf dem sich ein Körper, der einen Bogen führt, hinter einer langgestreckten zentralen Figur in die Höhe reckt. Die Farbpalette des Gemäldes verweist auf einen weiteren wichtigen Zusammenhang, den El-Salahi in seinen Gemälden herstellt: Er verbindet die Farben mit dem Staub der Savanne und der Wüste des Sudan. Kontextbezogene Texturen finden sich auch in dem Ölgemälde *Fatima* (1968), einer reliefartigen abstrakten Komposition aus organischen Formen in Sandfarben. Jahrzehnte später inspirierten El-Salahi die Farben und Formen Andalusiens zu seinem sechsteiligen Ölgemälde auf Leinwand *Flamenco Dancers* („Flamencotänzer", 2011–2012). Ein von der islamischen Architektur und den maurischen Spuren der Alhambra beeinflusster Hintergrund in Wüstenfarben umgibt hier eine unruhige Gruppe von Figuren. Der Kontrast zwischen ihren schwarzen Silhouetten und dem zentralen weißen Torbogen, in dem sie sich befinden, lässt die Figuren in scharfen Konturen hervortreten.

Ibrahim El-Salahi's fluid, figurative forms invoke the artist's long-standing relationship with calligraphy—from the time he grew up in Omdurman in Sudan, where he decorated the writing boards at his father's Qur'anic school, to his adult years as an artist seeking to synthesise his artistic encounters across Africa, Europe and Latin America.

As El-Salahi informed Mark Hudson of *The Guardian* in 2013, the same year his retrospective was staged at the Tate Modern in London, a turning point in his practice came after his return to Sudan in 1957 after studying at the Slade School of Fine Art, where he encountered works by Cézanne, Giotto and Mondrian. El-Salahi found no interest in the still-lifes, portraits and nudes he showed in Khartoum, prompting him to experiment with calligraphy in a bid to connect with his audiences. When he 'began to break down the letters to find what gave them meaning', he noted, 'a Pandora's box opened. Animal forms, human forms and plant forms began to emerge from these once-abstract symbols'.

Such figures come alive in the 1962 oil on canvas work *Untitled*, in which a body wielding a bow stretches up from behind an elongated central figure. The painting's palette echoes another important point of contextual connection El-Salahi developed in his paintings, with colours he connected to the dust, savanna and desert of Sudan. Contextual textures also appear in the oil on canvas *Fatima* (1968), a sand-scale abstract composition defined by organic shapes rendered in textured relief. Decades later, El-Salahi found resonance in the colours and shapes of Andalusia, which inspired the six-panel oil on canvas *Flamenco Dancers* (2011–12). A desert-hued background, informed by the place's Islamic architecture and the Moorish relics of Alhambra, frames a flurry of central figures sharply defined by the contrast of their black silhouettes and the white central arch in which they are contained.

Stephanie Bailey

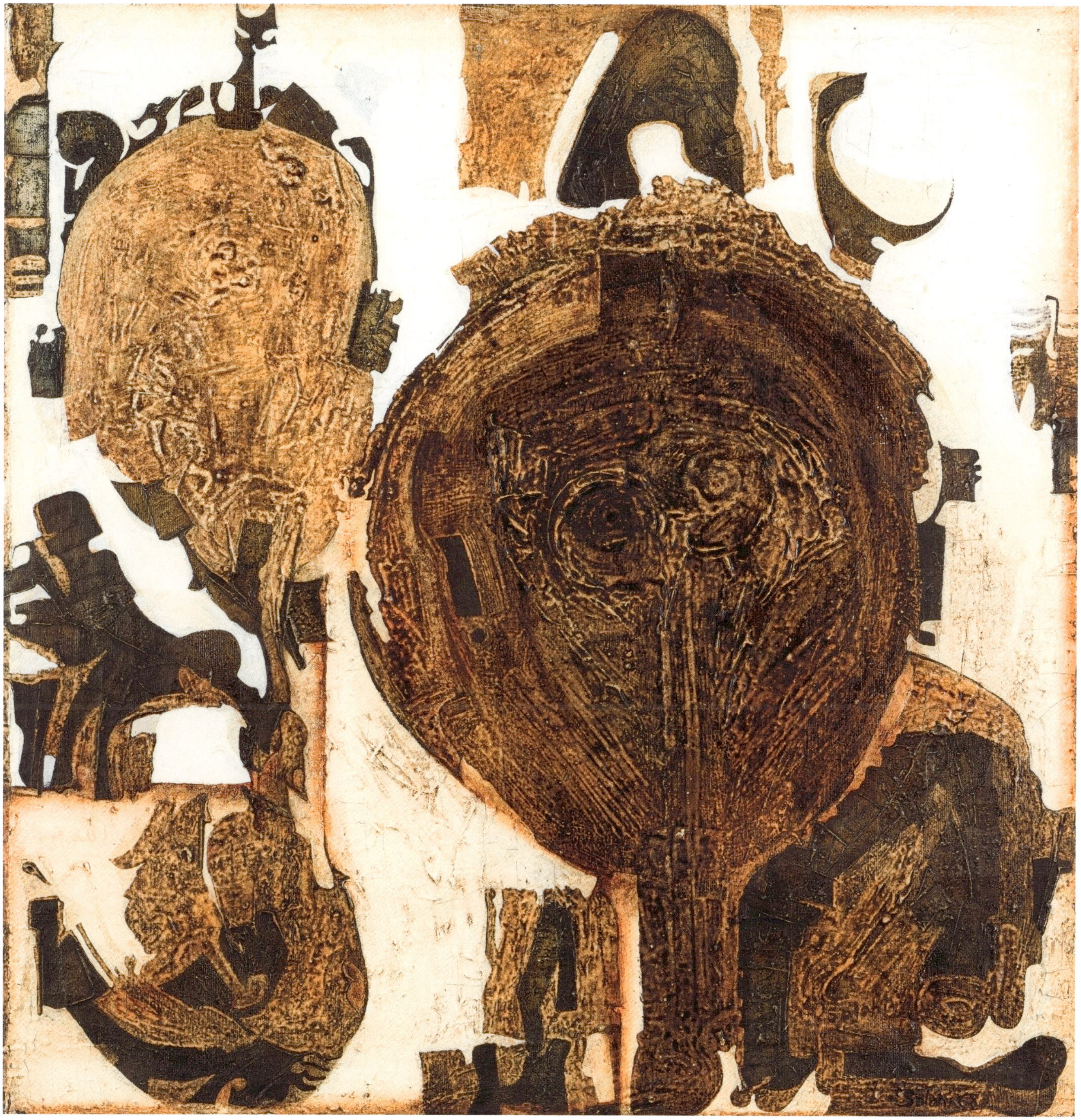

*Fatima*, 1968. Öl auf Leinwand / Oil on canvas. 82,5 × 72 cm

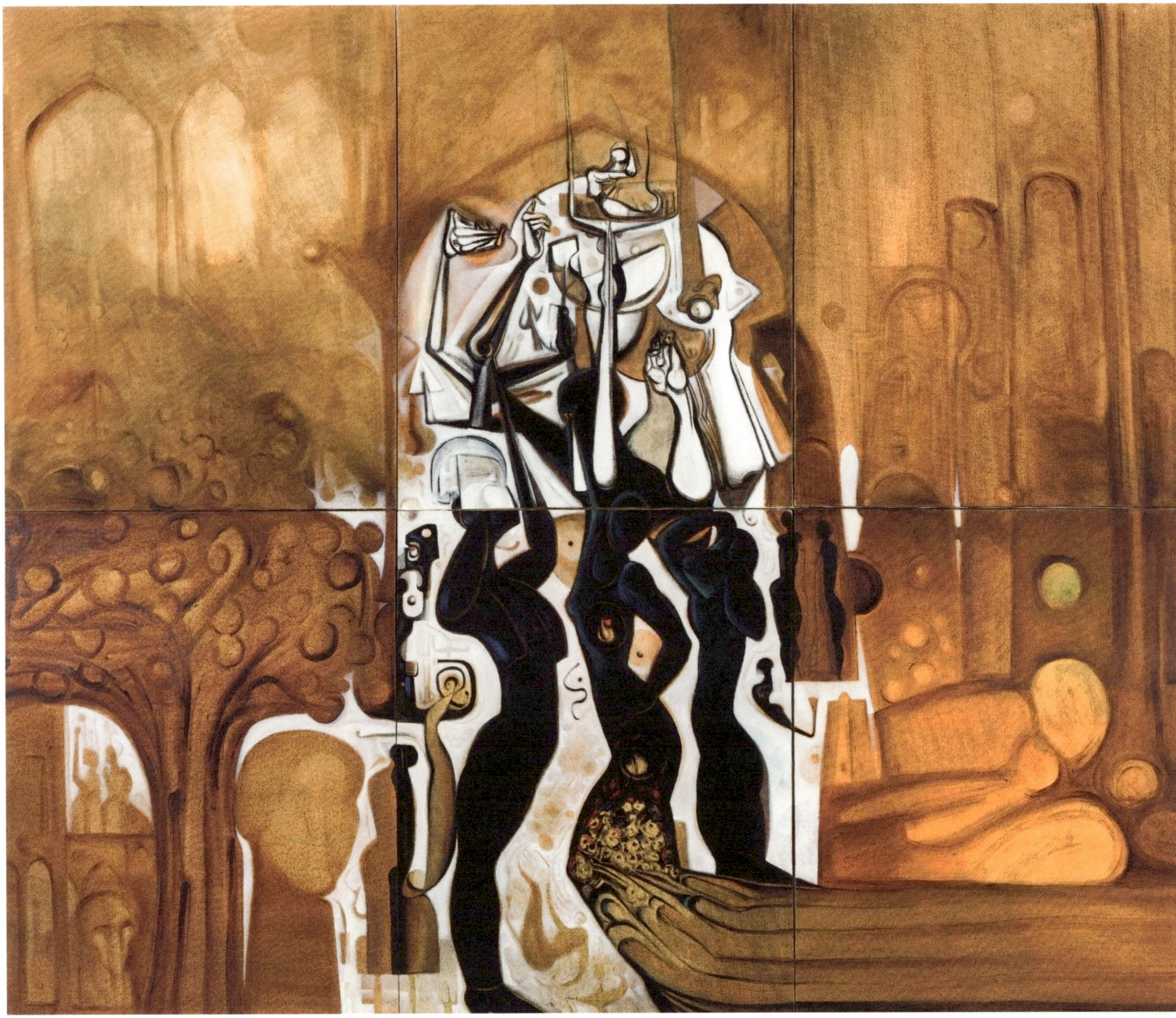

*Flamenco Dancers / Flamencotänzer*, 2011–2012. Öl auf Leinwand / Oil on canvas. 243 × 203,6 cm

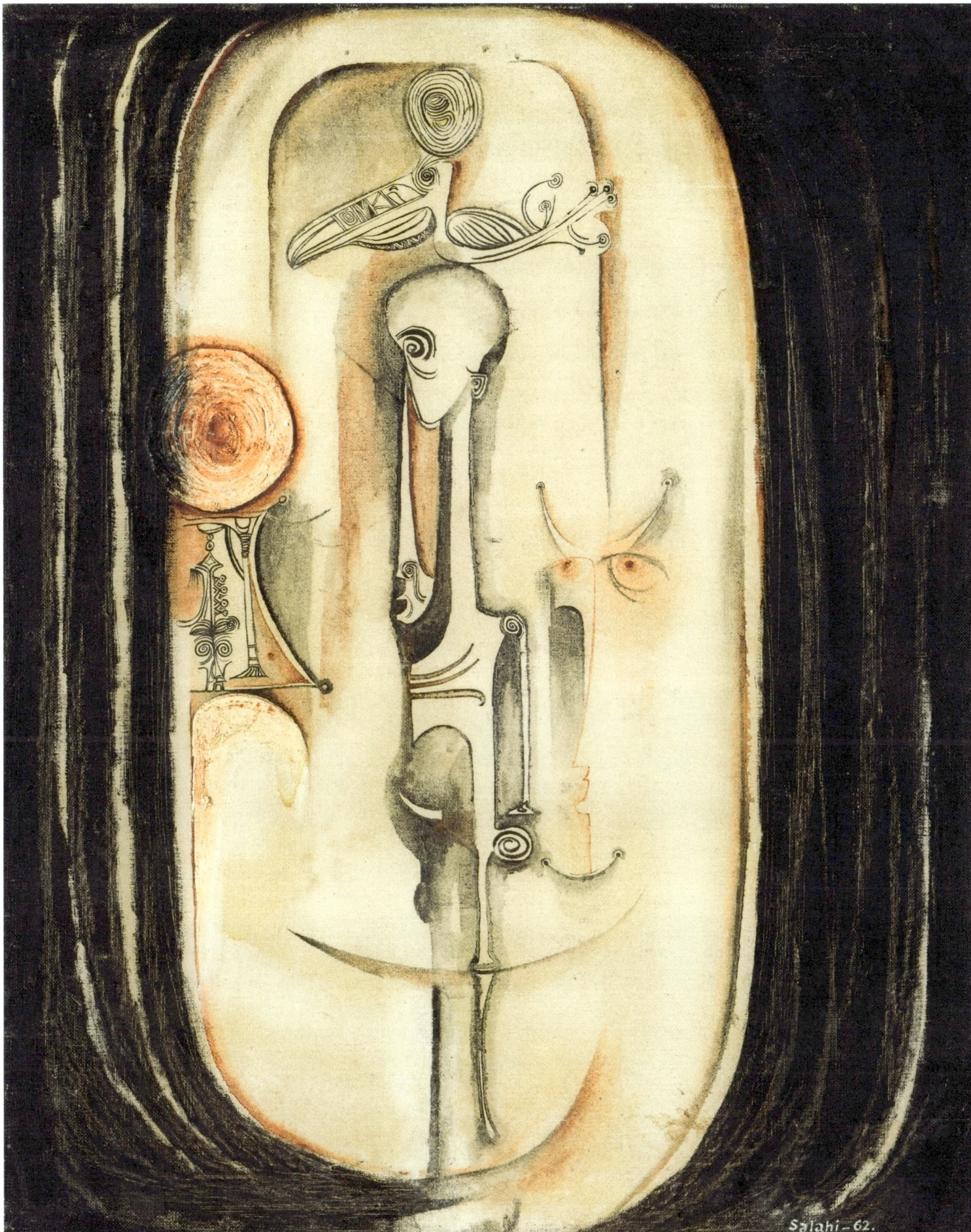


*Untitled* / *Ohne Titel*, 1962. Öl auf Leinwand / Oil on canvas. 53,5 × 66,2 cm

# Mohan Samant

Die Ausstellung präsentiert sechs Werke von Mohan Samant auf Papier und eine seiner großartigen Mixed-Media-Arbeiten auf Leinwand. All diese Werke, die über einen Zeitraum von 20 Jahren entstanden sind, erstrahlen in einer üppigen Farbenpracht.

Seine Bilder unterscheiden sich in ihrem charakteristischen Aufbau deutlich von dem, was viele seiner indischen Zeitgenoss*innen in den 1950er Jahren und danach hervorbrachten. Obwohl er allgemein als früher Vertreter der indischen Moderne gilt, könnte man Samant – er verbrachte einen Großteil seiner Schaffensphase bis zu seinem Tod 2004 in New York City – ebenso gut als wegweisenden amerikanischen Künstler bezeichnen.

Seine bildhaften Darstellungen sind von hypothetischen und suggestiven gesellschaftlichen Szenarien durchdrungen, die sich als Halluzinationen erweisen – sie zeigen mumifizierte Gestalten, die zugleich einen körperlichen wie ätherischen Eindruck vermitteln. Die vorliegende Werkreihe widmet sich Erkundungen, die von Samants Reisen und seinem Leben in New York inspiriert wurden. Dort verbrachte er die Sonntage mit seiner Ehefrau im Museum of Modern Art und in der ägyptischen Abteilung des Metropolitan Museum of Art. Das antike Ägypten wurde zu einem wichtigen Bezugspunkt, ebenso die Möglichkeiten der ökonomischen Abstraktion, die sich in Paul Klees kubistischen Formen finden. Dank seines ausgeprägten Interesses für den Surrealismus beschäftigte sich Samant in einer späteren Schaffensphase ausführlich mit Materialität. Er fertigte Arbeiten auf zerknittertem Papier an und ließ Bilder mit unterschiedlich intensiven Tusche- und Farbschichten entstehen, die ihre Betrachtenden zum genaueren Hinschauen zwingen.

Samant war Mitglied der Progressive Artists' Group, eines wegweisenden Künstler*innenkollektivs mit Schwerpunkt in Bombay. Seine Mitglieder richteten den Blick in künstlerischen Untersuchungen, Ausstellungen und Kooperationen sowohl nach innen als auch nach außen, um die Besonderheiten der indischen Kunstgeschichte, des Kubismus, des Postimpressionismus und des Expressionismus zu erforschen. Samant schöpfte seine Inspiration aus einer „totalen Kultur", die er in seinen Werken würdigte. In vielen seiner Darstellungen kommen Musikinstrumente vor – vermutlich eine Hommage an die Sarangi, ein indisches Streichinstrument, für das er eine lebenslange Leidenschaft empfand.

Six of Mohan Samant's works on paper and one of his magnificent mixed-media pieces on canvas, representing a 20-year time span, are presented here, each bursting with colourful luminosity.

Samant's painterly constructions encompass an idiom that diverges from what many of his contemporaries in India were producing in the 1950s and onwards. Although widely considered an early Indian modernist, it would be just as apt to argue that Samant was equally a pioneering American artist, having spent much of his working life in New York City until his death in 2004.

The artist's pictorial representations are suffused with depictions of hypothetical and suggestive social scenes, which unfold as hallucinations—as mummified figures, invoking the corporeal and the ethereal. This collection of works represents explorations inspired by Samant's travels and life in New York. He spent his Sundays with his wife at the Museum of Modern Art and in the Egyptian galleries of the Metropolitan Museum of Art. Egyptian antiquity became a point of fixation, as did the potentialities of economic abstraction found in the cubist forms of Paul Klee. Buoyed by an interest in Surrealism, Samant later became consumed with materiality, producing pieces on wrinkled paper, embodying various intensities of ink wash and dye, creating images that demand that the spectator look twice.

Samant was a member of the Progressive Artists' Group, a significant collective of artists mostly based in Bombay whose investigations, exhibitions and collaborations looked both inwards and outwards, examining the specificities of Indian art history, Cubism, Post-Impressionism and Expressionism. Samant drew influence from and paid homage to a 'total culture'—musical instruments are invoked in many of his representations, perhaps an homage to his lifelong passion for the *sarangi*, an Indian bowed instrument.

Omar Kholeif with Reem Sawan

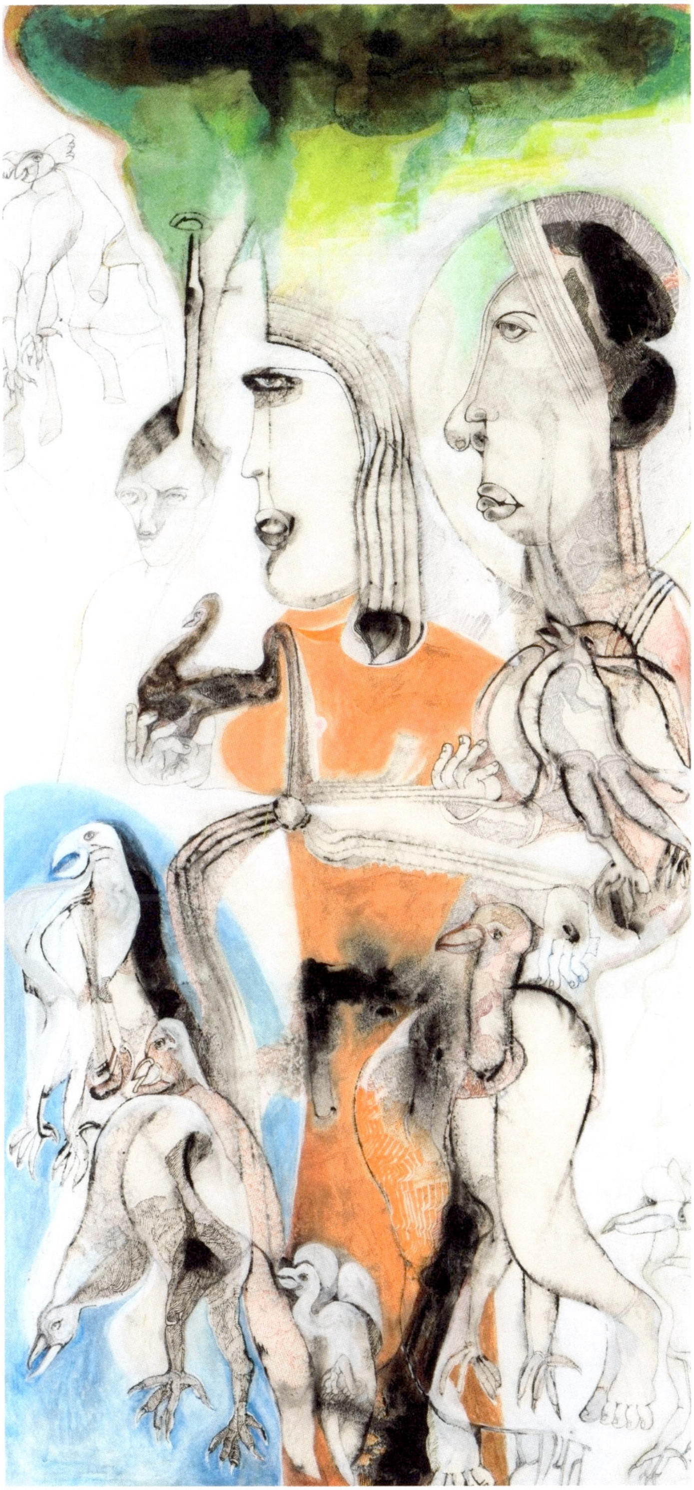

*Bird Sanctuary* | *Vogelschutzgebiet*, 1997. Aquarellfarbe auf Papier / Watercolour on paper. 90,2 × 185,4 cm

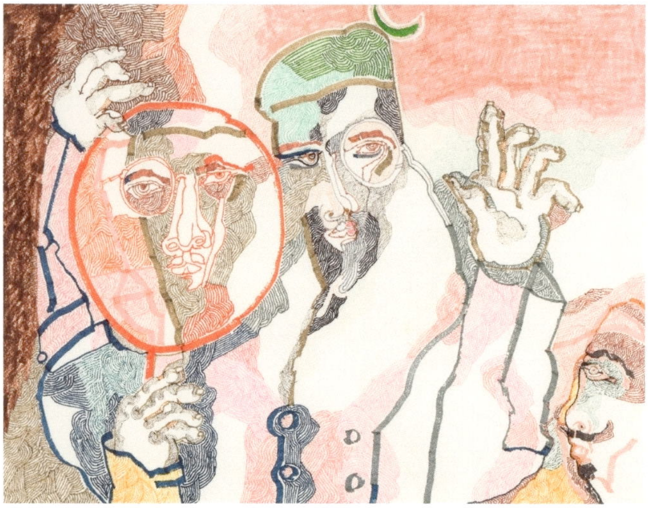

*Bride / Braut*, ca. 1991. Aquarellfarbe auf Papier / Watercolour on paper. 60 × 46 cm

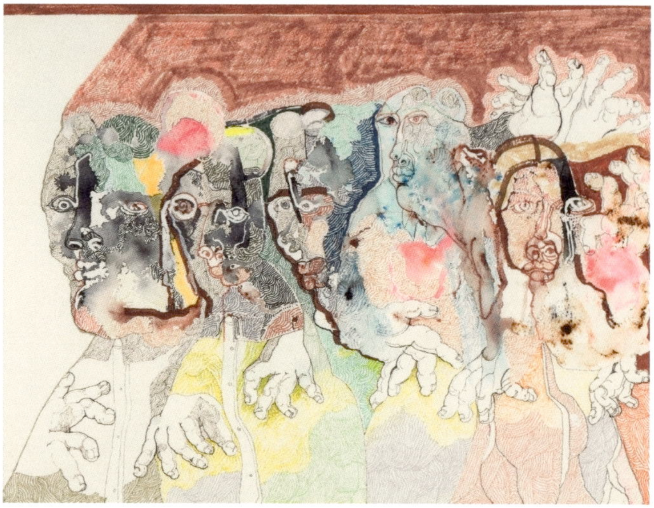

*Pointing Fingers / Zeigende Finger*, 1991. Stift und Tinte, Aquarellfarbe auf Papier / Pen and ink, watercolour on paper. 59,1 × 44,5 cm

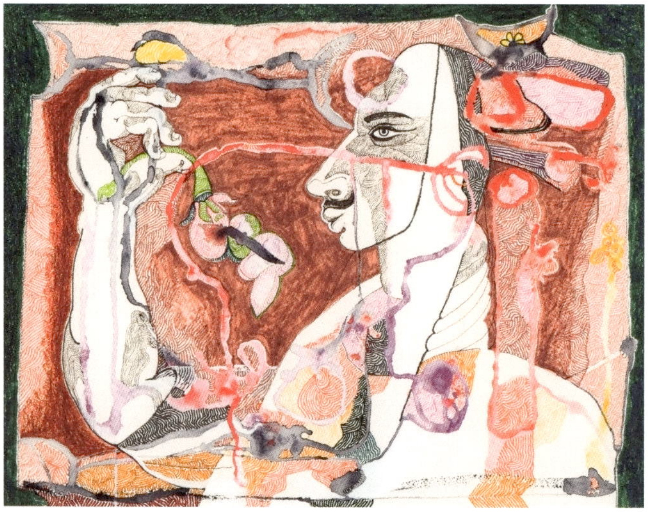

*Untitled / Ohne Titel*, ca. 1980–1999. Stift und Tinte, Aquarellfarbe auf Papier / Pen and ink, watercolour on paper. 60,6 × 46 cm

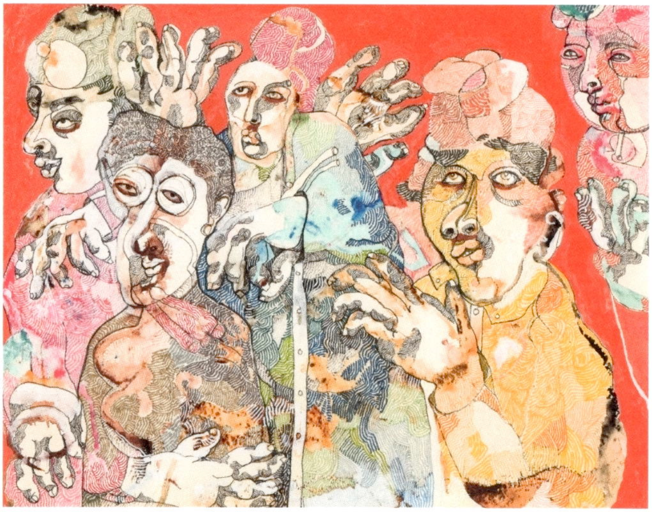

*Untitled / Ohne Titel*, ca. 1980–1999. Stift und Tinte, Aquarellfarbe auf Papier / Pen and ink, watercolour on paper. 60,6 × 46 cm

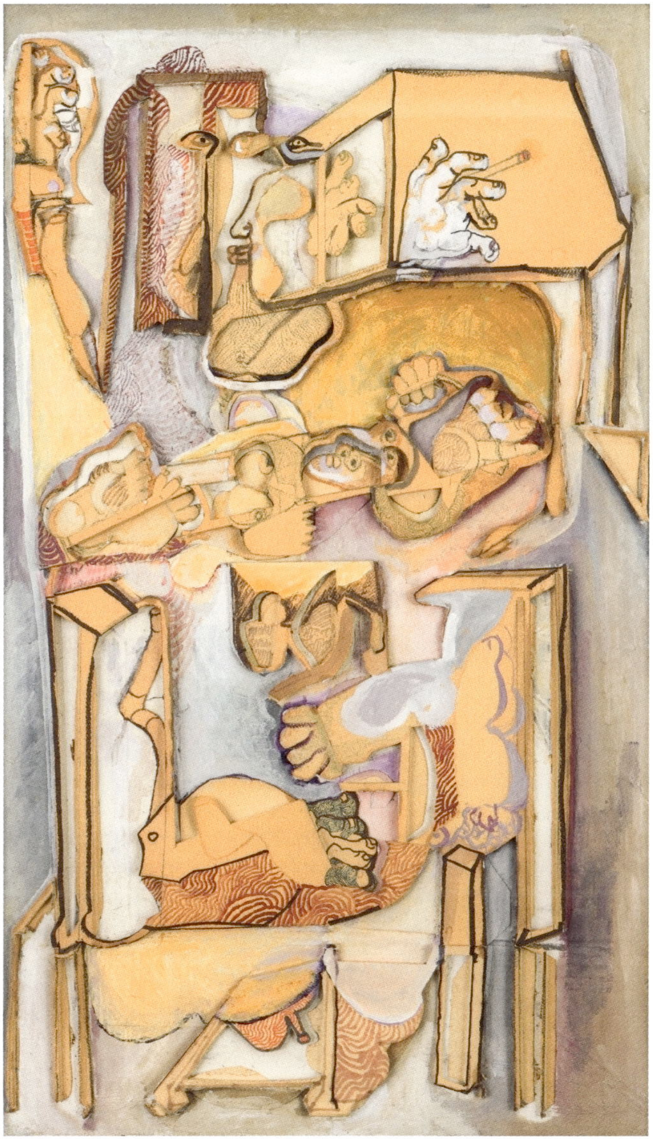

*Man with a Child in a Chair / Mann mit Kind auf Stuhl*, 1982. Mixed Media, gefaltetes Papier auf gegipster Leinwand / Mixed media, folded paper on plastered canvas. 66 × 111,8 cm

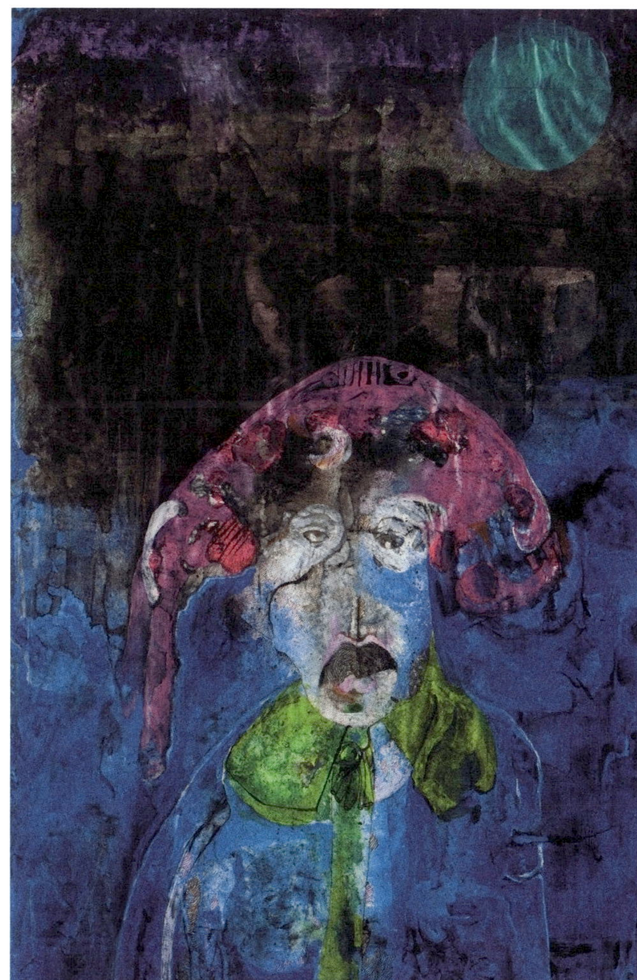

*Sad Man Wandering / Trauriger Mann wandert umher*, 1998. Aquarellfarbe auf Papier / Watercolour on paper. 80 × 120,7 cm

# Wael Shawky

Der multidisziplinäre Künstler Wael Shawky enthüllt in seinen Videos, Skulpturen, Installationen, Zeichnungen und Malereien verborgene Erzählungen, mythische Rituale und religiöse Machtstrukturen, um die verschlungenen Wege mündlicher Geschichtsüberlieferung an jüngere Generationen zu erkunden. Für das vielschichtige Porträt seiner Heimat Ägypten schöpft Shawky aus der über tausendjährigen Geschichte des Landes, um metaphysische Beziehungsgeflechte aufzudecken, die in religiösen Schriften, geheimen Ritualen oder im Alltagsleben selbst verborgen sind – sei es, dass es um die Freilegung unterirdischer Gänge geht, in denen angeblich geheime Schätze lagern, sei es die kritische Auseinandersetzung mit gefährlichen Formen eines „blinden Glaubens", die sich mit dem Kolonialismus im Nahen Osten verbreitet haben.

Das multidisziplinäre Werk *Al Araba Al Madfuna* (2012 bis heute) verdeutlicht die Bandbreite von Shawkys künstlerischer Praxis. Nach zehnjähriger Forschung, Entwicklung und Produktion verbindet das Werk eine Filmtrilogie mit zahlreichen Gemälden und Zeichnungen. Sein Titel geht auf ein Dorf in Ägypten zurück, das Shawky vor über 15 Jahren besuchte. Dort beobachtete er, wie Dorfbewohner mit den Leichen von Pharaonen sprachen, um verborgene Schätze zu finden, wobei sie sich, wie Shawky es beschreibt, „magischer" Künste bedienten und gleichzeitig Verse aus dem Koran und manchmal auch aus der Bibel zitierten. „Es ist unmöglich, ein Grab zu finden", verrät Shawky, „es sei denn, man überwindet den Fluch des Pharao, der die Tür der Grabkammer schützt." Aus dieser Dualität der Welten, der Vergangenheit und Gegenwart, des Mythischen und des Realen, schmiedet Shawky ein in sich kohärentes und gleichzeitig eindrucksvoll esoterisches Porträt einer von gemeinsamen Riten und Ritualen beeinflussten Kultur.

Shawky bezieht sich in seinen Werken auch auf die Kurzgeschichten des ägyptischen Schriftstellers Mohamed Mustagab (1938–2006), etwa *Horsemen Adore Perfumes* oder *The Offering*. Erst kürzlich hat Shawky Mustagabs Schriften zusammen mit von ihm selbst stammenden träumerischen und fließend geschwungenen Tuschezeichnungen neu aufgelegt. Diese zart gezeichneten Werke verdeutlichen den roten Faden in Shawkys Werk: Eine Tuschelinie scheint diese Welt von einer anderen zu trennen, während der Pinselstrich wie von Pharaonenhänden über das Blatt geführt wird.

Wael Shawky's art, comprising video, sculpture, installation, drawing and painting, uncovers hidden narratives, mythical rituals and routes of religious power that explore the contingent manner in which stories have passed through oral traditions from one generation to the next. Shawky's mercurial portrait of his homeland of Egypt draws on over a millennium of the country's history as a way to parse metaphysical relations accrued in religious scripture, esoteric ritual or the land itself—be it the excavation of underground passageways filled with the promise of riches or critical portrayals of the way in which perilous forms of 'blind faith' have spread along colonial tributaries in the Middle East.

The multi-form project *Al Araba Al Madfuna* (2012–ongoing) is indicative of Shawky's depth of practice. Spanning over a decade of research, development and production, the work brings together a trilogy of films alongside numerous paintings and drawings. The work takes its name from a village in Egypt that Shawky visited over 15 years ago. There, he witnessed villagers communing with the corpses of pharaohs, attempting to find buried treasures using, as Shawky describes them, systems of 'magic' while quoting verses from the Qur'an and, at other times, the Bible. 'It is impossible to discover a tomb', Shawky reveals, 'unless you break the spells of the pharaohs that act as protection on the door of the chamber'. This duality of worlds, of past and present, mythical and real, is forged by Shawky as an internally coherent yet compellingly esoteric portrait of a culture influenced by shared rites and rituals.

Shawky also uses the writings of Egyptian novelist Mohamed Mustagab (1938–2006) as a reference, layering his short stories, such as *Horsemen Adore Perfumes* and *The Offering*, into his work. Shawky recently reprinted Mustagrab's writings alongside his own dream-like and fluidly sinuous ink drawings. These delicately rendered works further calibrate the images found throughout Shawky's practice, one in which the inked line seems to separate this world from another, the marks as if guided by the hands of the pharaohs across the page.

Chris McCormack

*Al Araba Al Madfuna Drawings* / *Al Araba Al Madfuna Zeichnungen*, 2013–2014. 12 Zeichnungen, Tinte, Grafit, Öl auf Papier / 12 drawings, ink, graphite, oil on paper. Maße variabel / Dimensions variable

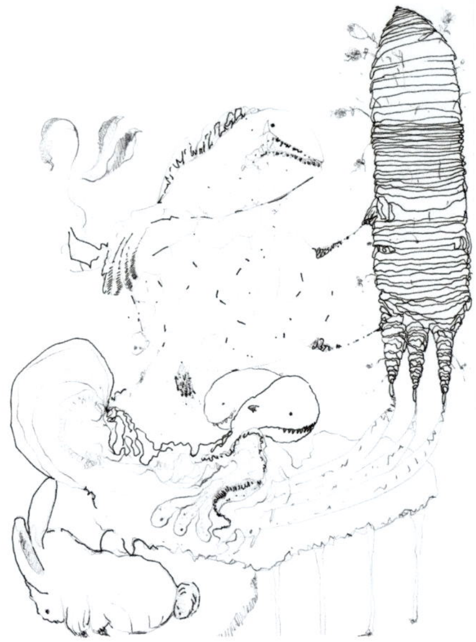

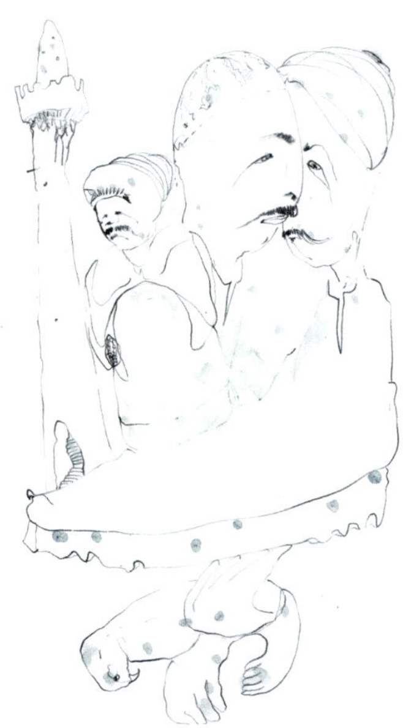
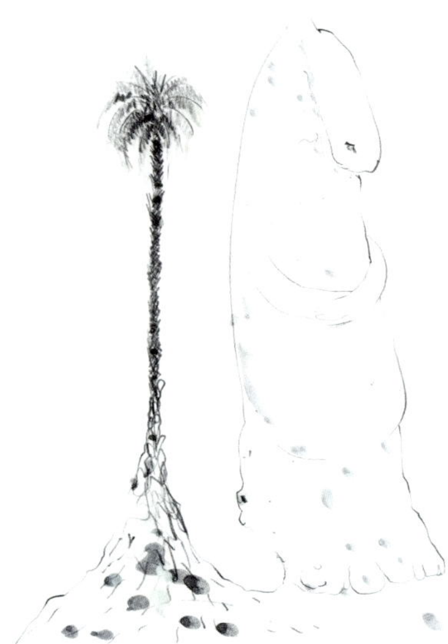
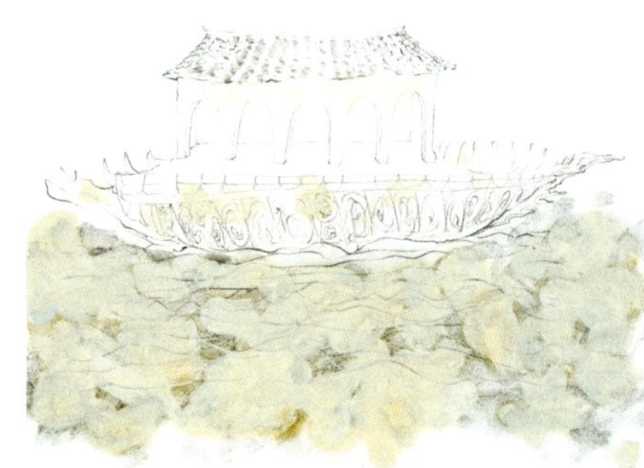

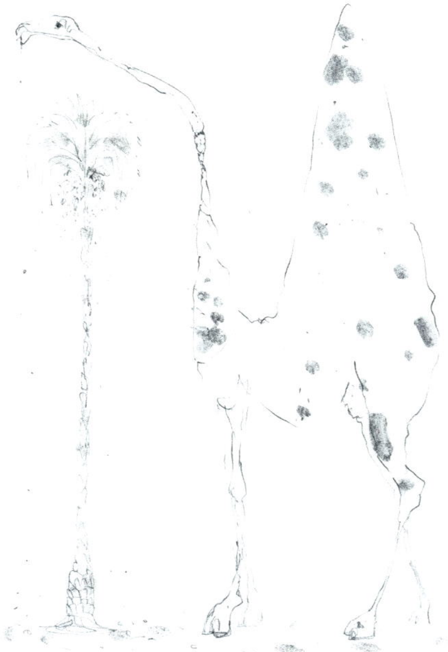
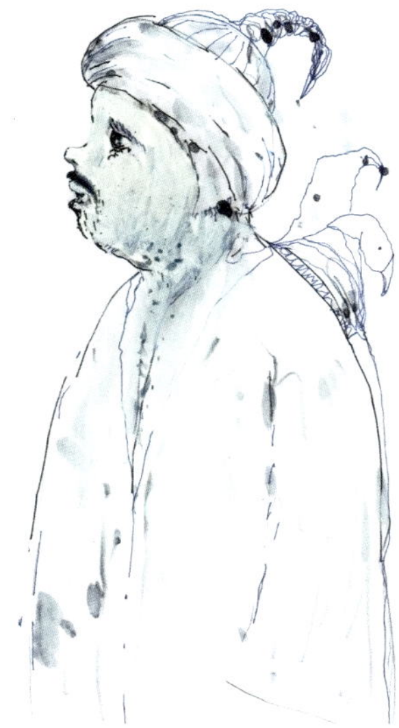
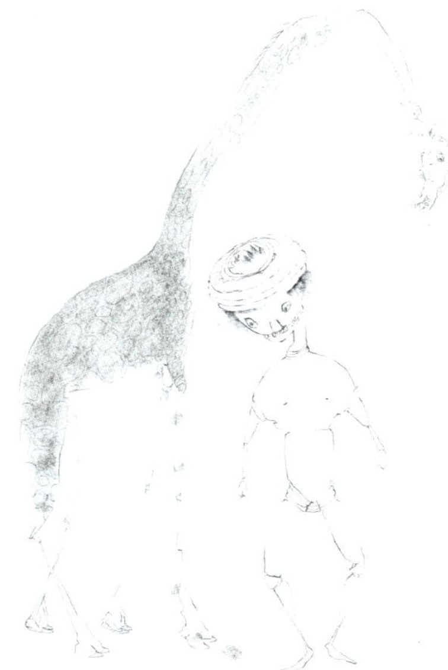
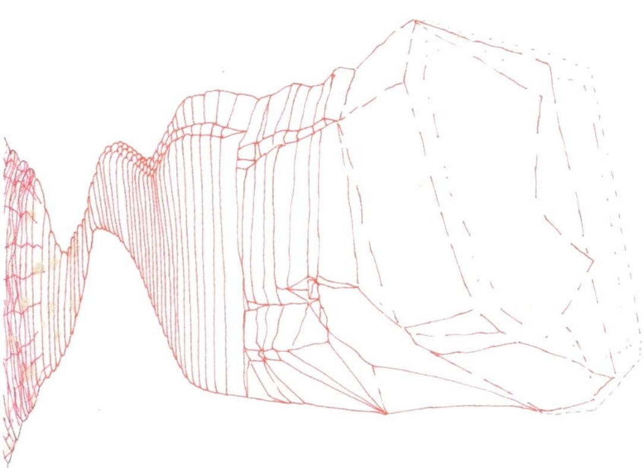
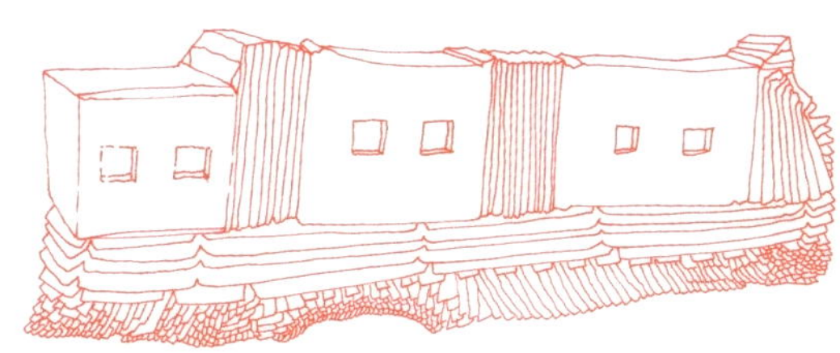

# Shahzia Sikander

Die beiden Fotografien von Shahzia Sikdander, die in dieser Ausstellung präsentiert werden, zeigen jeweils die Innen- und Außenansicht eines alten Kino in der Stadt Khorfakkan in Sharjah. Die Künstlerin projiziert ihr Werk auf die große Leinwand des heute verfallenden und leerstehenden Kinos, um diesen Ort, der einst für sein abwechslungsreiches Filmprogramm und seine farbenfrohen Architekturmotive geliebt wurde, erneut mit Leben zu erfüllen. Das Gebäude erinnert in seiner Formsprache an die Lichtspielhäuser der 1960er und 1970er Jahre in Karachi, gelegen in Pakistan, dem Geburtsland Sikanders.

Bei der Inszenierung und Aufnahme der Fotografien fiel Sikander auf, dass der Direktor des Kinos noch immer im Gebäude lebte. Er gehörte dem pakistanischen Team an, das 1976 für den Bau des Kinos in die Stadt gekommen war. Seitdem ist er geblieben und hat sein Leben dem Kino gewidmet. Treu wahrt er das Andenken dieses Hauses, obwohl dessen Niedergang allgegenwärtig ist.

Der Titel des Werks, *The cypress, despite its freedom, remains captive to the garden* („Die Zypresse, wenngleich frei, bleibt eine Gefangene des Gartens", 2012) ist eine übersetzte Zeile aus einem Ghazal (einer lyrischen Gedichtsform, die ursprünglich aus der persischen Literatur stammt) von Ghalib – einem bekannten Dichter des Mogulreichs, der im 19. Jahrhundert auf Urdu und Persisch schrieb. Der Künstlerin ist das Verhältnis zwischen Werktiteln und Bildern ganz besonders wichtig, denn es öffnet den Raum für die Frage, inwiefern Geschichte durch die Linse der Gegenwart immer wieder neu betrachtet wird. Im vorliegenden Werk spiegelt sich der Titel unmittelbar im Motiv des Fotos wider, während die Rahmenhandlung eine persönliche Migrationsgeschichte losgelöst von den Aspekten wirtschaftlicher Zwänge erzählt.

Shahzia Sikander hat zusammen mit Kunstschaffenden wie Imran Qureshi und Aisha Khalid den Weg für ein erfolgreiches Revival der zeitgenössischen Miniaturmalerei geebnet, das in den 1990er Jahren vom pakistanischen National College of Arts in Lahore ausging. Gemeinsam entwickelten sie diese Kunstform grundlegend weiter. Sikanders Interesse an der arbeitsintensiven Miniaturmalerei steht hier im Zusammenhang mit der Verlagerung von Arbeitsplätzen und der Funktion des Kinos. Die Künstlerin selbst sagt dazu: „Mein Ziel war es, die Form der Miniaturmalerei von innen heraus zu erweitern, indem ich mich mit dem Handwerk, der Technik, der Präzision, der Detailgenauigkeit und dem kleinen Format sowie mit den historischen Zusammenhängen auseinandersetzte."

The two photographs presented by Shahzia Sikander in this exhibition show the interior and exterior of an old cinema in the town of Khorfakkan in Sharjah. The artist projects her work onto the screen of the now-derelict, unused cinema in an attempt to bring back to life a site that was once feted for its diverse cinematic programming and its colourful architectural motifs. The cinema's design evokes the cinemas of 1960s and '70s Karachi, Pakistan, the nation where Sikander was born.

Whilst staging and photographing these pictures, Sikander found the cinema's manager still living in the building. He was a member of the team from Pakistan that had arrived to build the cinema in 1976. He has since dedicated his life to the cinema and remains faithful to its memory, despite its discernible decline.

The title of the work, *The cypress, despite its freedom, remains captive to the garden* (2012), is a translated line from a *ghazal* (a lyrical poem format, originally associated with Persian literature) by Ghalib, a well-known Mughal figure writing in Urdu and Persian during the 19th century. The relationships evoked between her titles and images is of particular importance to Sikander, offering, as it does, a space to interrogate how history is continually re-authored through the lens of the present. In this case, the photographs' subject suggests a literal representation of the title, whilst the backstory holds a personal testimony to migration beyond economic imperative.

Sikander is recognised as a successful pioneer of the contemporary miniature revival that emerged from Pakistan's National College of Art in Lahore during the 1990s, alongside figures such as Imran Qureshi and Aisha Khalid. These artists expanded this practice significantly. Here, Sikander's interest in the intense labour of the miniature can be traced to a labourer's dislocation from a geographical context and the functional role of the cinema. As the artist explains, 'my interest in miniature painting was to expand the medium from within, embracing its craft, technique, rigour, detail and small scale, as well as its historical contexts'.

Sarah Perks

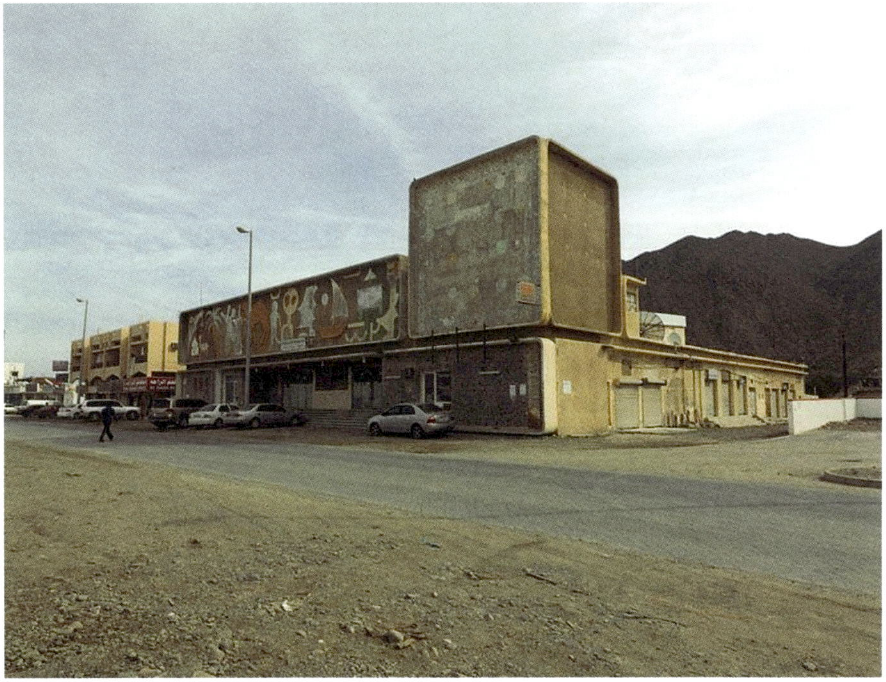

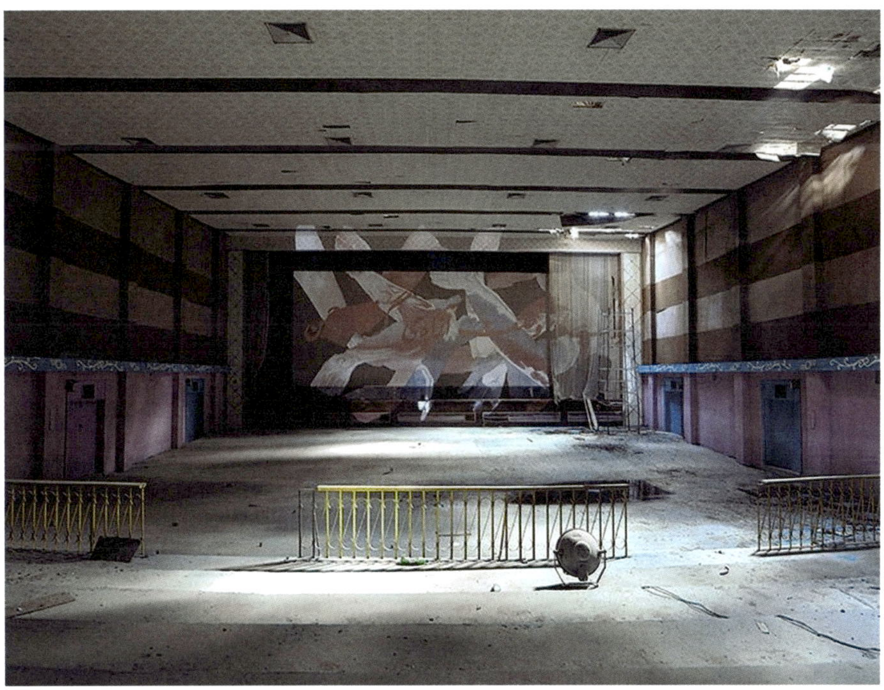

*The cypress, despite its freedom, remains captive to the garden / Die Zypresse, wenngleich frei, bleibt eine Gefangene des Gartens*, 2012. 2 C-Prints auf Hartschaumplatte / 2 C-prints mounted on sintra board. 124,46 × 99,06 × 5,08 cm. Im Auftrag und produziert von der Sharjah Art Foundation / Commissioned and produced by Sharjah Art Foundation

# Richard Lokiden Wani

Richard Lokiden Wani macht Porträtaufnahmen von Menschen, die aus seinem Lebens- und Arbeitsumfeld in Juba stammen, der heutigen Hauptstadt des Südsudan. Für seine um die Jahrtausendwende entstandenen Aufnahmen *Couple at night* („Paar bei Nacht") und *Family Portrait* („Familienporträt") fotografierte er Leute in ihrem Alltag – in der für seine Arbeit charakteristischen Inszenierung blicken die sitzenden oder stehenden Personen frontal in die Kamera. Wani fotografiert auch bei Tageslicht mit Blitz. Auf diese Weise werden alle Porträtierten in ein reflexives, spirituelles Licht gehüllt. Die Fotografien sind zwar gestellt, aber nicht professionell arrangiert. Bei den Personen auf den Aufnahmen handelt es sich um Bekannte, die in vielen Fällen die Fotoporträts kaufen und damit das Eigentum an ihrem Bild erwerben.

Wani entwickelte seine zwanglose Bildkompositionstechnik im Rahmen von Ausbildungsprogrammen bei amerikanischen und norwegischen Nichtregierungsorganisationen und bei Missionaren, die während der jahrzehntelangen Konflikte in Evangelikalen-Gemeinden im ganzen Südsudan tätig waren. Mittels Wanis Blick durch die Linse erhalten die Betrachtenden Gelegenheit, die Porträtierten in einer selbstbewussten Haltung als ebenbürtig zu erleben. Ein solches Bild entspricht nicht dem stereotypen Bild des Südsudan, der von der internationalen Gemeinschaft als Hort der ungezügelten Gewalt wahrgenommen wird. Das glückliche Paar und die Kernfamilie auf den Bildern sind sich ihrer lässigen Pose und Kleidung, die sofort ins Auge fallen, sehr wohl bewusst. Auf dem Familienporträt dominiert das Kleid der jungen Frau mit dem Eiffelturmmotiv die Aufnahme und lenkt die Aufmerksamkeit auf die Distanz zur französischen Hauptstadt und zu den ehemaligen Kolonialmächten des Globalen Nordens.

Von den Bildern wurden etwa 17 Jahre nach ihrer Entstehung C-Prints (analoge Farbabzüge) angefertigt. Die Aufnahmen stehen für den andauernden Dekolonialisierungsprozess in der Fotografie, den der britische Wissenschaftler Mark Sealy als „das Selbst (…) im Moment des Auftauchens" bezeichnet. Wanis Werk stützt insbesondere mit Blick auf seine afrikanische Heimatregion Sealys Postulat, dass ganz entgegen der dokumentarischen Tradition der westlichen Kolonialmächte ein Besitzanspruch auf das eigene Bild erhoben werden kann.

Richard Lokiden Wani takes portraits of the community where he lives and works in Juda, now the capital of South Sudan. Taken around the turn of the millennium, *Couple at night* and *Family Portrait* follow his distinctive on-location style, in which subjects sit or stand up to face the camera, and for which Wani uses a flash, whether it is night or day. This effect generates a reflective, spiritual light on each and every one of the people in his photographs. The subjects are posed, but not expertly framed; they are complicit subjects who often then purchase these portraits, so they effectively own their own image.

Wani's informal composition was developed through training programmes provided by both American and Norwegian non-government organisations and missionaries who often operated in evangelist communities throughout Sudan during its many decades of conflict. Through Wani's lens, the viewer is privy to an equitable encounter, a stance of self-representation that defies the international community's stereotypical perception of South Sudan as a site of unbridled violence. Instead, the happy couple on view and the nuclear family presented here are aware of their casual poses and clothing, which feature prominently. In the family portrait, the Eiffel Tower-print dress worn by the young woman in the frame dominates the image, drawing attention to their distance from the French capital and former colonial powers of the Global North.

These images have been reproduced as C-Prints (colour analogue processing) some 17 years after the photographs were taken. They represent an ongoing decolonising movement within photography, one that British academic Mark Sealy describes as 'the self … caught emerging'. With particular respect to this region of Africa, Wani's work epitomises Sealy's theory—staking a claim and taking ownership, contrary to the colonial Western documentary tradition.

Sarah Perks

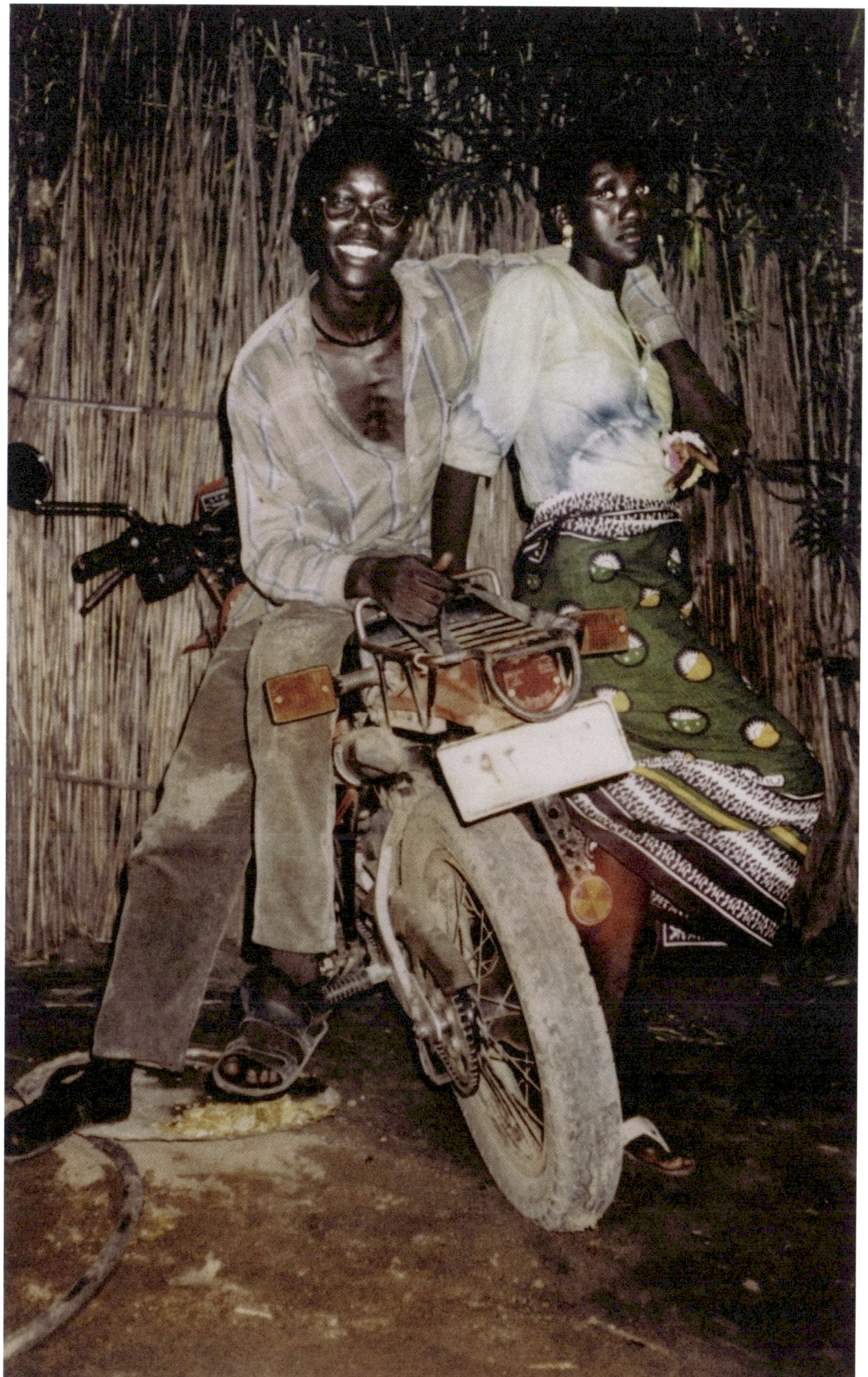

*Couple at night / Juba / Paar bei Nacht / Juba*, 2000 (Abzug / printed 2017). Lambda-Silberabzug auf hochglänzendem RC-Fotopapier / Lambda silver print on RC glossy paper. 28 × 22 cm

# Lionel Wendt

Der sri-lankische surrealistische Fotograf Lionel Wendt hielt seine Kamera immer nah an die Gesichter und Körper seiner anmutigen Modelle – ob Menschen, figürliche Skulpturen oder Objekte mit ebenmäßiger Struktur. Die geschwungenen Körper auf den Studioaufnahmen des frühen 20. Jahrhunderts fangen das Licht ein, während ihre tiefen Schatten durch den von Wendt gewählten Silbergelatineabzug noch verstärkt werden. In *Untitled (Man with palm made fan)* („Ohne Titel, Mann mit Fächer aus Palmwedeln", ca. 1935) steht der Protagonist des Bildes auf einem hölzernen Podest, die Haltung aufrecht, die Ellbogen angewinkelt, die Hand am Griff eines langen, geflochtenen Strohfächers – eines Punkahs, der breiter und höher ist als sein Träger selbst. Dessen Haut wirkt im flachen, direkten Licht weich, der Sarong um seine Hüften locker und seidig. In *Untitled (Portrait from Memory, Bromid)* („Ohne Titel, Porträt aus dem Gedächtnis, Bromid", ca. 1936) lehnt eine Frau mit spitzem Kinn an einer Säule. Über ihr schimmert ein breites Blätterdach. Sie hält einen fedrigen Blumenstrauß in den Händen, ihr Kleid scheint aus fließendem Mitternachtssamt zu bestehen. Der Blick der Frau ist gesenkt, ihre Handflächen sind im Schoß gefaltet. Das Bild hat die kompositorische Klarheit eines gemalten Porträts. Es strahlt Melancholie, Bewegtheit und eine düstere Poesie aus. Wendt hat das Bild solarisiert. Die lange Belichtung kehrte die Farbtöne des Drucks um, das Dunkle erscheint hell. In Wendts Arbeiten finden sich immer wieder Dunkelkammerexperimente: Papiernegative, Bromradierungen, Reliefdrucke, Dias und Fotomontagen. *Sailing Boats* („Segelnde Boote", um 1942) zeigt den Hang des Künstlers zur Collage: Boote mit flossenartigen Segeln durchschneiden das Wasser. Eines wird eingefasst von einem schwebenden Bilderrahmen mit geriffeltem Profil. Darüber liegt ein weiteres verschwommenes Bild und im unteren Teil der Szenerie weiß anmutendes Gras. Wendt betrachtet seine Motive sehr genau. All seine Bilder sind sorgfältig ausgearbeitete Ergebnisse dieser intensiven Analyse. Dabei ist jedes Arrangement von Körper und Gegenstand von einem verführerischen Schimmer überzogen.

Lionel Wendt, Surrealist Sri Lankan photographer of the early 20th century, held his camera close to the faces and torsos of his graceful, long-limbed subjects—whether people, figurative sculptures or steadily composed objects. In his studio photography, bodies curve, catching the light in deep shadows that are further thrown into relief by Wendt's choice of gelatin silver printing. In *Untitled (Man with palm made fan)* (c. 1935), the image's protagonist stands lean and tall upon a wooden platform, elbows angled and fingers slipped into the handle of a long, woven straw fan, a *punkah* wider and taller than its carrier. His skin turns creamy in the flat, direct light that hits him; the sarong at his hips loose and silky. In *Untitled (Portrait from Memory, Bromide)* (c. 1936), a sharp-jawed woman leans against a fluted column, with a wide canopy of leaves shimmering above her. She holds a feathered bouquet in her hands, her dress appears made of a slippery midnight velvet. Here, Wendt has solarized the image, and owing to a long exposure, the tones of the print are reversed, where dark appears light. The gaze of Wendt's sitter is downcast, her palms folded on her lap. There is melancholy, movement and a sombre poetic here, with the compositional alertness of portraitist painting. Wendt's images are full of experiments in the darkroom: paper negatives, brom etchings, relief prints, transparencies and photomontages. In *Sailing Boats* (c. 1942), we see Wendt's collagist tendencies: the fin-like sails of the boats cut through waters framed by a floating ridged picture frame, over which another image blurs, with whitened grass shifting at the bottom of the scene. Wendt studies figure, and each image becomes the watchful upshot of his intense analysis; each arrangement of body and object draped in an alluring sheen.

Skye Arundhati Thomas

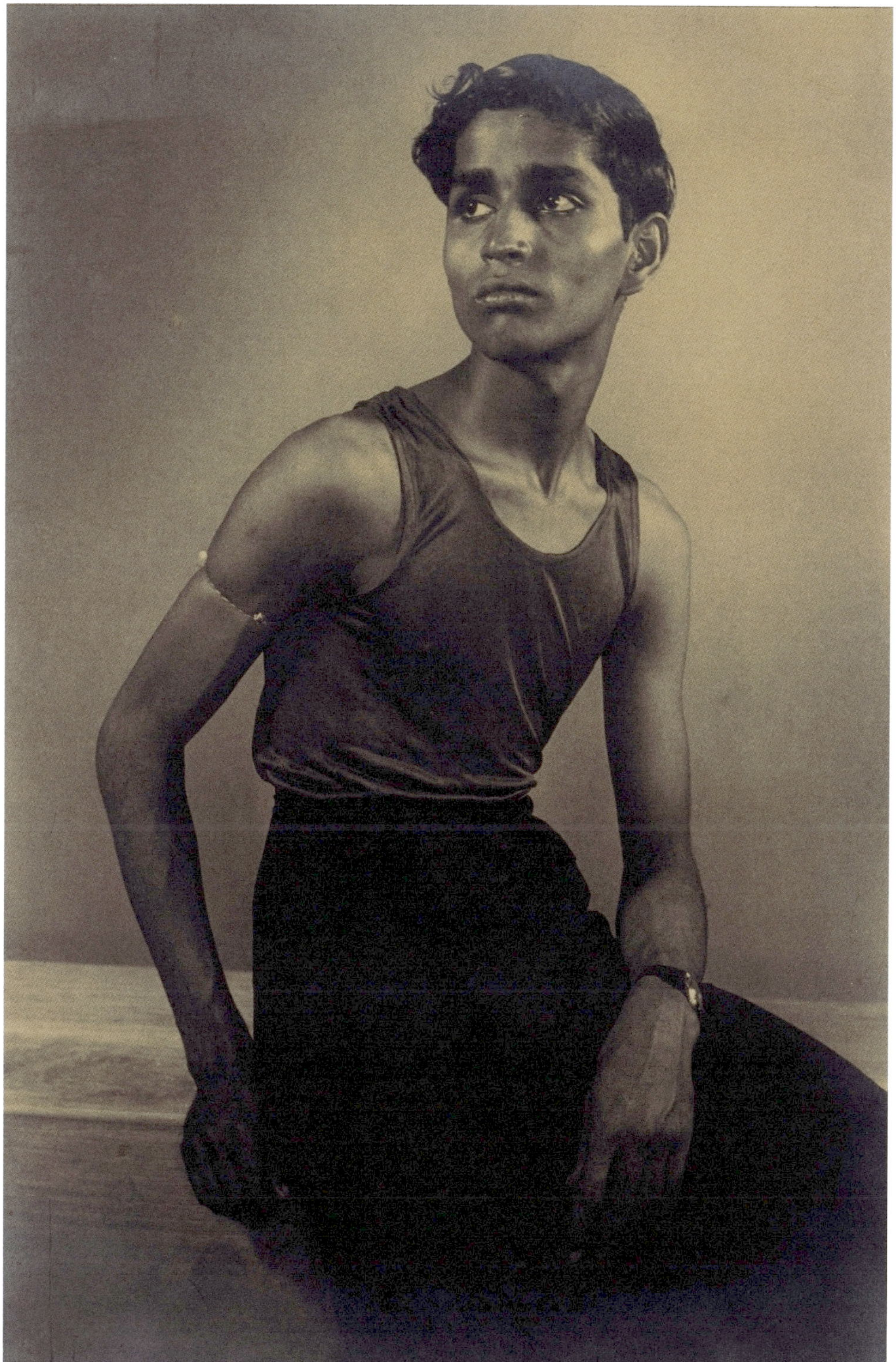

*Man with watch and amulet* / *Mann mit Uhr und Oberarmspange*, ca. 1935. Silbergelatineabzug / Gelatin silver print. 24,3 × 36,4 cm

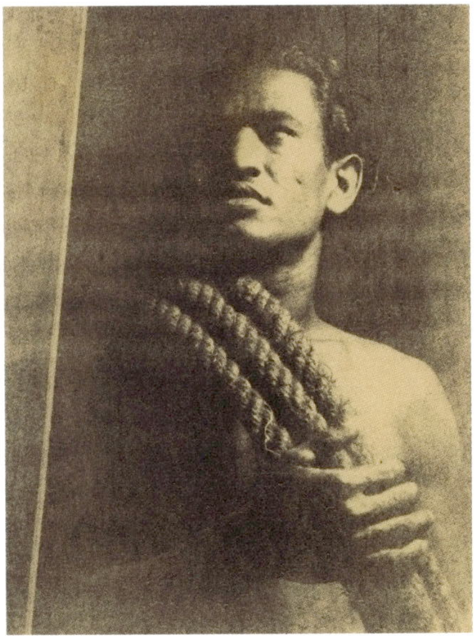

*Untitled (Man with Rope) | Ohne Titel (Mann mit Seil)*, ca. 1935. Silbergelatineabzug (kupferfarben) / Gelatin silver print (copper-toned). 21 × 27,7 cm

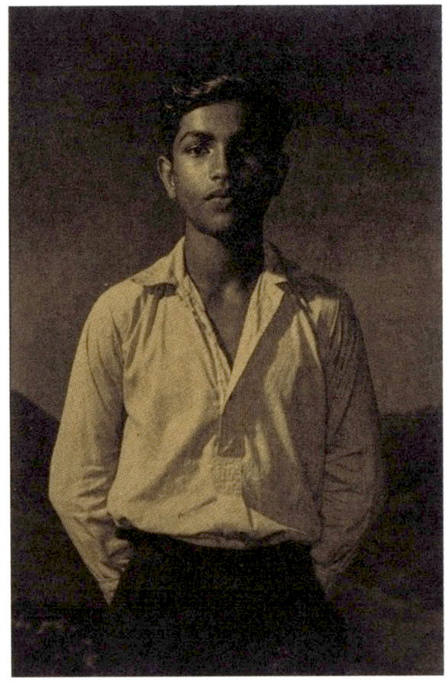

*Untitled (Boy in White Shirt and Trouser) | Ohne Titel (Junge in weißem Hemd und Hose)*, ca. 1935. Silbergelatineabzug / Gelatin silver print. 15,9 × 23,7 cm

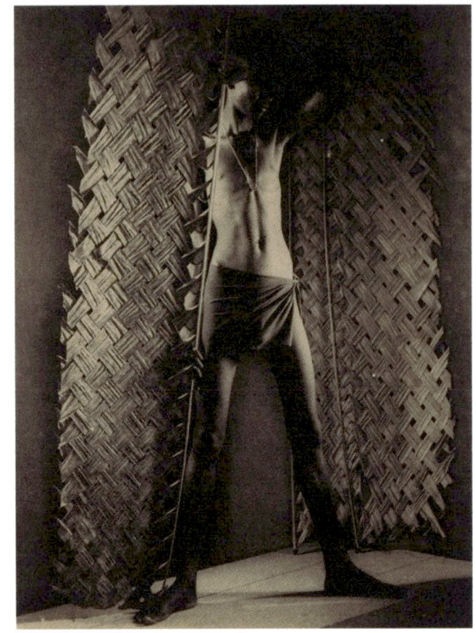

*Untitled (Man with palm made fan) | Ohne Titel (Mann mit Fächer aus Palmwedeln)*, ca. 1935. Silbergelatineabzug / Gelatin silver print. 26,4 × 36,2 cm

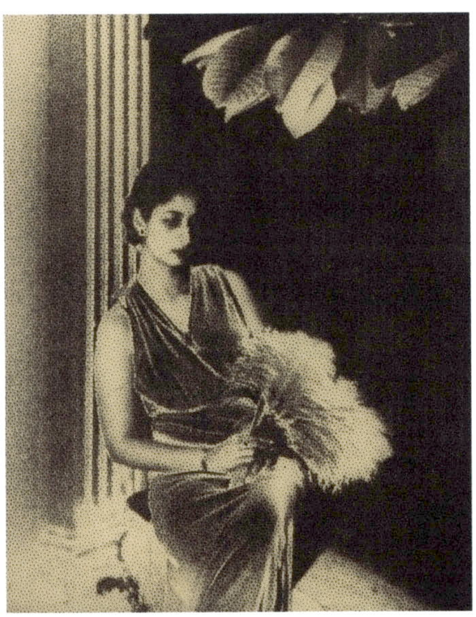

*Untitled (Portrait from Memory, Bromide) | Ohne Titel, Porträt aus dem Gedächtnis, Bromid*, ca. 1936. Silbergelatineabzug, Solarisation / Gelatin silver print, solarisation. 29,5 × 36,8 cm

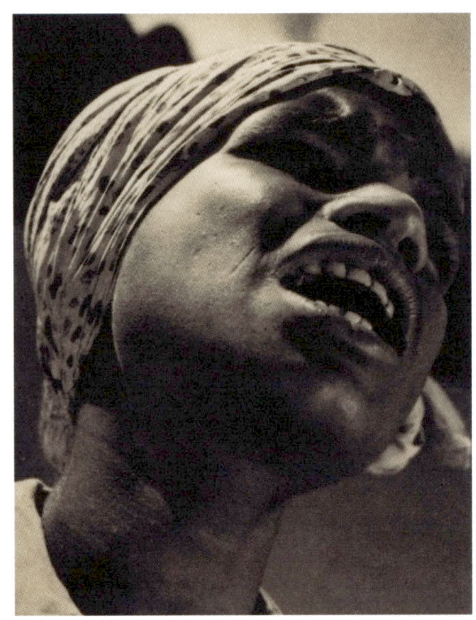

*Untitled (Singer in Sunshine) | Ohne Titel (Sängerin im Sonnenschein)*, ca. 1938–1939. Silbergelatineabzug / Gelatin silver print. 26,9 × 35 cm

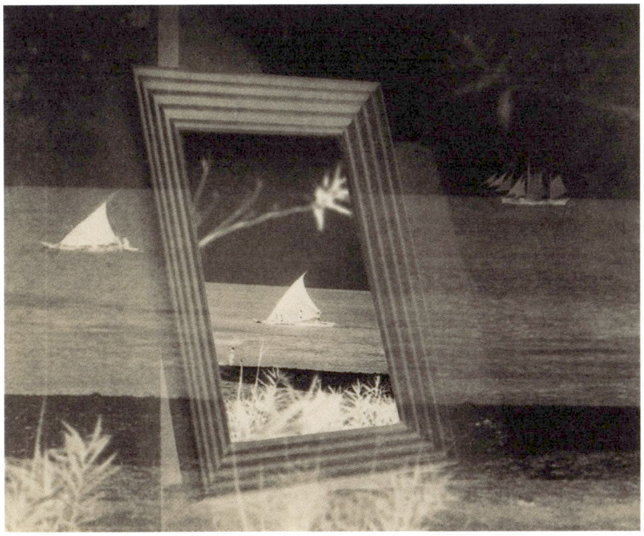

*Sailing Boats / Segelboote*, ca. 1942. Fotomontage, Silbergelatineabzug, Solarisation / Photo montage, gelatin silver print, solarisation. 38 × 30,5 cm

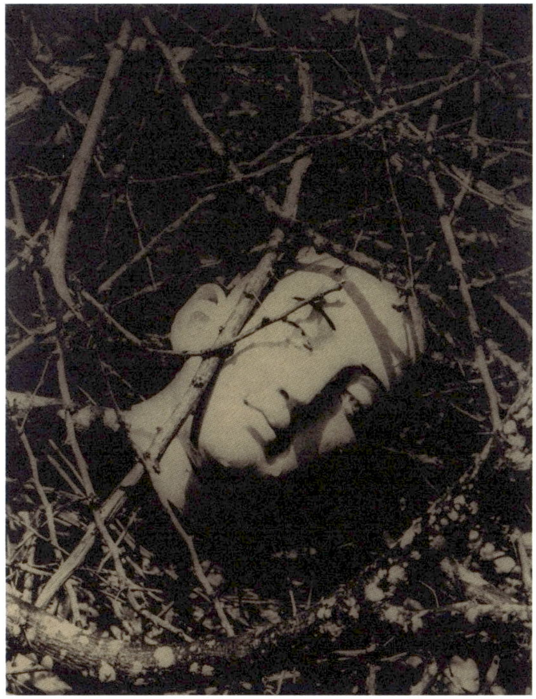

*Untitled (Head Among Twigs 2) / Ohne Titel (Kopf zwischen Zweigen 2)*, ca. 1942. Silbergelatineabzug / Gelatin silver print. 37,8 × 30,1 cm

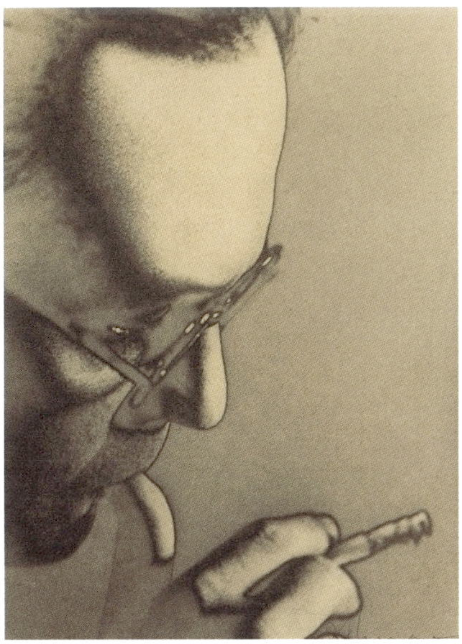

*Untitled (Profile of Lionel Wendt Smoking) / Ohne Titel (Profil von Lionel Wendt, rauchend)*, ca. 1937. Silbergelatineabzug, Solarisation / Gelatin silver print, solarisation. 25,3 × 30,3 cm

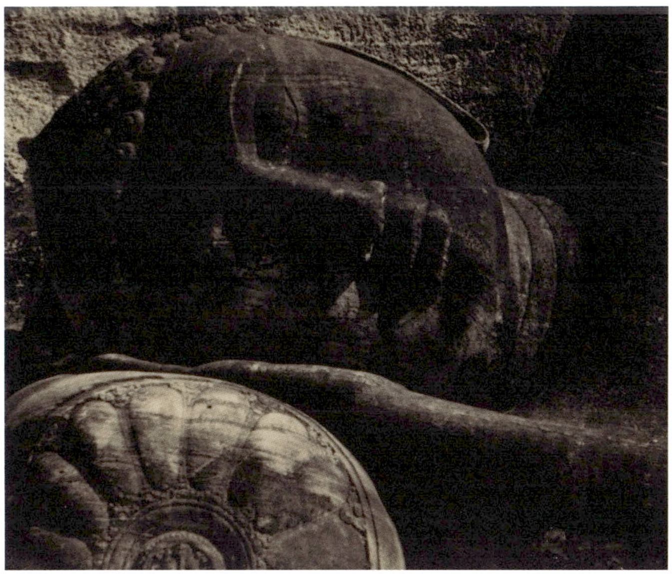

*Reclining Buddha / Liegender Buddha*, ca. 1935. Silbergelatineabzug / Gelatin silver print. 29 × 23,9 cm

# Gen Süden: Reisen von Golf zu Golf, von Küste zu Küste

# 3

# Going South: Travels from Gulf to Gulf, from Coast to Coast

# Bani Abidi

„In einem Raum seines Ateliers liegt das Modell seiner Traumstatue", schreibt die Künstlerin Bani Abidi über Ram Sutar, den Protagonisten ihrer Arbeit *Proposal for a man in the sea* („Entwurf für einen Mann im Meer", 2012). Als Abidi den 87-jährigen Sutar in seinem Atelier besuchte, war er seit sechs Jahrzehnten mit der Anfertigung öffentlicher Denkmäler in Gestalt von – meist männlichen – indischen Staatsoberhäuptern befasst. Der Pomp der politischen Führung, der üblicherweise für die Zurschaustellung im öffentlichen Raum entworfen und gebaut wird, hatte sich bis in Sutars Haus und Atelier ausgebreitet. Abidi stößt überall auf verstreute Erinnerungsstücke, Statuen, Büsten, Fotografien und Zeichnungen von nicht vollendeten, nur angedachten Werken. Mahatma Gandhi ist eine der wichtigsten Figuren in diesem Fundus, den die Künstlerin als dissonantes Sammelsurium bezeichnet – ein winziger ideologischer Mikrokosmos, gefiltert vom Leben und Wirken eines Mannes, der es als seine Aufgabe sah, die kraftvolle Rhetorik einer Generation schwieriger und ambivalenter Führungspersönlichkeiten greifbar zu machen. Es ist ein Traum, „den niemand mehr in Auftrag geben will", bemerkte die Künstlerin. Abidi ist eine Meisterin darin, genau diesen besonderen Nerv der Menschen auf dem indischen Subkontinent zu treffen, die mit den Praktiken und Mechanismen falscher und enttäuschter politischer Versprechen vertraut und von ihnen gekränkt sind. Das reflexive Verfahren der Künstlerin besticht durch seine Präzision. Es zeigt, auf welche Weise kleine, persönliche Gesten ideologische Abstraktionen am stärksten hervortreten lassen. Abidi traf Sutar während ihrer Recherche für den Zweikanalfilm *Death at a 30 Degree Angle* („Tod aus einem 30-Grad-Winkel", 2012, ebenfalls Teil der SAF-Sammlung). Darin gibt die Figur eines unbedeutenden indischen Politikers eine Statue von sich selbst in Auftrag. Gemeinsam mit seinen Gefolgsleuten betritt der Politiker das Atelier eines Bildhauers. Wir sehen den Besucher*innen dabei zu, wie sie ihr Spiel der Repräsentation und Mythenbildung betreiben. Und während die Hybris des Politikers auf dem Bildschirm deutlich hervortritt, mahnt sie gleichzeitig an die zerbrochenen Gliedmaßen zerschlagener Standbilder, die die Parks und Plätze der politischen Zentren der Welt verunstalten.

'In one room of his studio lies the model of his dream statue', writes artist Bani Abidi about Ram Sutar, the protagonist of her work *Proposal for a man in the sea* (2012). At the time Abidi visits Sutar's studio, he is 87 years old and has been in the profession of making public monuments in the shape of—mostly male—Indian state leaders for six decades. The pageantry of political leadership, usually designed and built for display in public space, enters Sutar's home and studio. Abidi finds scattered memorabilia, statues, busts, photographs and drawings of unrealised, purely aspirational pieces. Mahatma Gandhi is a primary character among these findings, which the artist intimates to be a dissonant and peculiar context—a tiny microcosm of ideology filtered through the life and practice of a man who dedicated his life to making physical the mighty rhetoric of a generation of difficult and ambivalent leaders. It is a dream 'that no one is interested in commissioning anymore', Abidi writes. The artist is a master at finding that special nerve carried by people of the Indian subcontinent—the one attuned to, and wounded by, the rehearsals and mechanisms of corrupt and disappointing political promise. Her reflective practice strikes with precision, often revealing how the abstractions of ideology filter most intensely through small, personal gestures. Abidi met Sutar while undertaking research for the two-channel film *Death at a 30 Degree Angle* (2012)—also part of the SAF Collection). Here, the character of a small-time Indian politician commissions a statue of himself. With his cronies, he enters the studio of a sculptor and soon we watch as they play with representation and myth-building. We see his hubris move across the screen, only to remember that the broken limbs of collapsed public statues litter the parks and public squares of political centres across the world.

Skye Arundhati Thomas

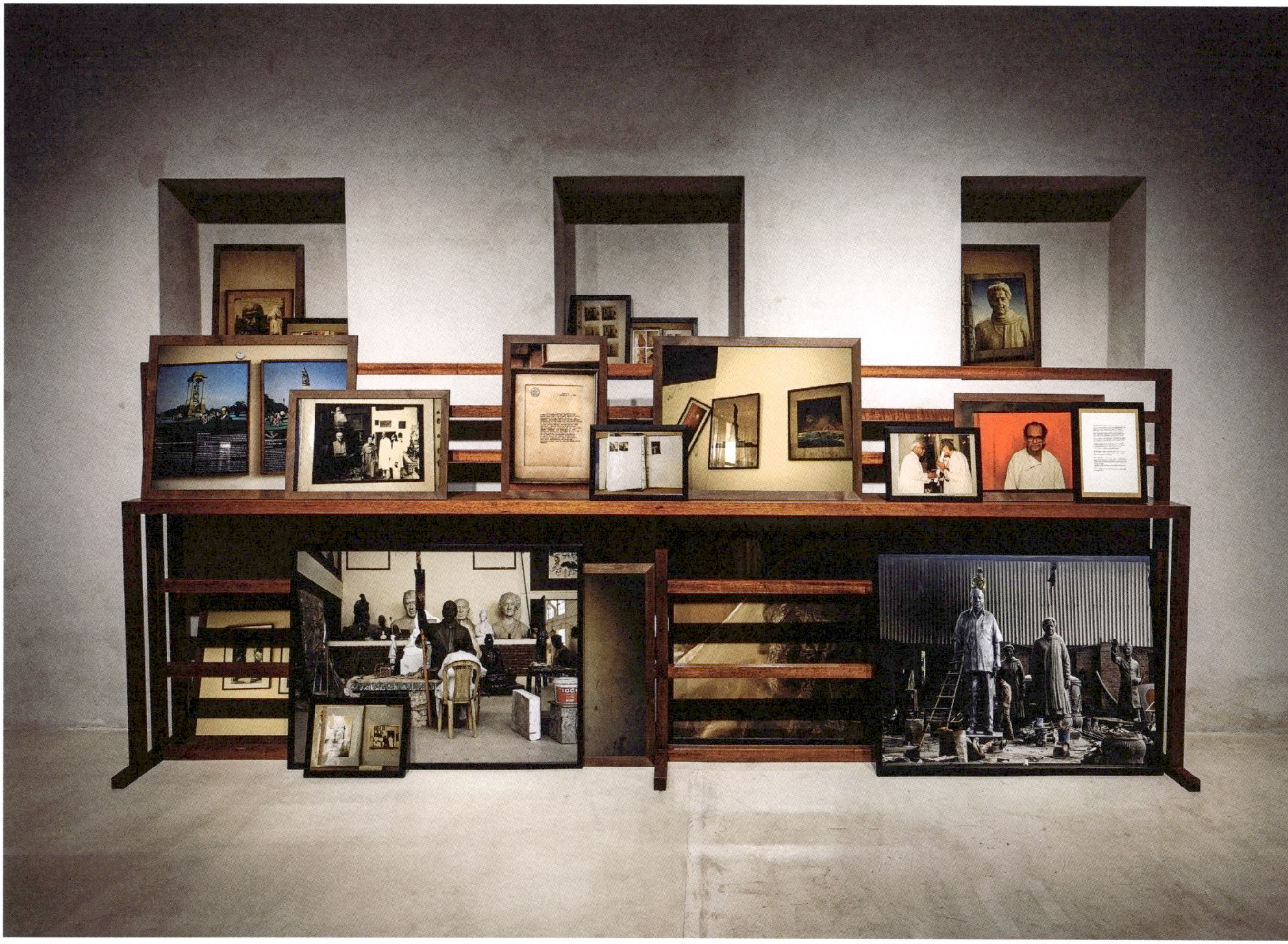

*Proposal for a man in the sea / Angebot für einen Mann im Meer*, 2012. Serie von 26 Abzügen auf Archivpapier, verschiedene Rahmen / Suite of 26 prints on archival paper, assorted frames. Maße variabel / Dimensions variable. Installationsansicht / Installation view, *Bani Abidi: Funland*, Sharjah Art Foundation, 2019.

# Lawrence Abu Hamdan

Lawrence Abu Hamdan, der sich selbst als „private ear“ (privater Klangdetektiv) bezeichnet, hinterfragt die politischen Ursachen, die die Menschen zum Schweigen verurteilen. Er widmet sich Berichten von Ohrenzeug*innen, die aus der offiziellen Geschichtsschreibung getilgt wurden. Abu Hamdans Videos, Performances und Installationen analysieren die politischen Bedingungen, die entscheiden, warum manche Leben hörbar sind, während andere durch staatliche Interessen, koloniale Unterdrückung, Invasion oder Krieg zum Schweigen gebracht – oder, wie Abu Hamdan es ausdrücken würde, noch nicht verstanden – werden.

Die Schwellen der Hörbarkeit, die auch politischer Natur sind, werden in *Saydnaya (The Missing 19db)* („Saydnaya [Die vermissten 19db]“, 2017) zum Ausgangspunkt der Rekonstruktion. Die Installation aus „akustischen Erinnerungen“ legt in herzzerreißenden Berichten von Überlebenden Zeugnis davon ab, wie im syrischen Saydnaya-Gefängnis Gefangenen die Augen verbunden und sie durch Folter zum Schweigen gebracht wurden. In Jahren 2011 bis 2015 fanden in diesem Gefängnis zwischen 5.000 und 13.000 Hinrichtungen statt, die menschenrechtlich bislang noch nicht aufgearbeitet worden sind. Viele der Hingerichteten waren politische Gefangene unter dem Regime des syrischen Präsidenten Bashar al-Assad. Bei ihrer Ankunft im Gefängnis wurden ihnen die Augen verbunden, und sie wurden gezwungen, sich die Augen zuzuhalten, sobald Wachen im Raum waren. So wurden die vier Zellenwände zu den einzig sichtbaren Koordinaten im Gefängnis. Der Großteil ihrer Wahrnehmung konzentrierte sich auf das, was sie hören konnten.

Als Grundlage für Abu Hamdans Klanginstallation diente eine Untersuchung von Amnesty International zu den Bedingungen im Saydnaya-Gefängnis, die in Zusammenarbeit mit der Forschungsgruppe Forensic Architecture durchgeführt wurde, der auch der Künstler angehört. Physisch kamen die Menschenrechtsaktivist*innen Saydnaya nur durch Satellitenbilder nahe, da das Gefängnis noch in Betrieb ist und unabhängigen Beobachter*innen der Zutritt verwehrt wird. So erhielt der Künstler nur durch die Erinnerungen der Überlebenden einen Einblick in die Haftanstalt.

Für seine Klanginstallation nutzte Abu Hamdan neue Darstellungsformen, um auch die nicht greifbaren Aspekte des Gefängnisalltags zu dokumentieren und darzustellen. Nach der Fertigstellung einer umfassenden Studie und einer Website für Amnesty International ging der Künstler der Frage nach, wie Erinnerung mit Architektur und Gewalt zusammenhängt. Durch seine Soundarbeit mit „einer Reihe von Beweismitteln, die sich auf das Schweigen, das Flüstern, die Verzerrungen der Erinnerung und die seltsamen Verquickungen zwischen Raum, Körper und Wand konzentrieren“, schuf der Künstler ein Werk, von dem er meint, es berge „zerbrechliche Wahrheiten“.

Abu Hamdans stützt seine Arbeit auf gesetzlich anerkannte Beweismittel. Er will zeigen, wie vermeintlich ungeschützte Menschen ausgesondert oder, um Achille Mbembe zu zitieren, so manche Leben als „überflüssig" angesehen werden.

Lawrence Abu Hamdan, who goes by the moniker ‘private ear’ (independent audio investigator), engages with the politics of the silenced, and with the testimony of aural witnesses whose evidence is excised from history. Spanning video, performance and installation, his work analyses the political conditions that determine why some lives are rendered audible while others are made silent—or, as Abu Hamdan would assert, not yet intelligible—by state interest, colonial oppression, invasion or conflict.

These thresholds of audibility, ones that are equally the threshold of the political, become thresholds of reconstruction in *Saydnaya (The Missing 19db)* (2017). The installation comprises painful testimonials or ‘acoustic memories’ recounting the torture of surviving prisoners of the Saydnaya prison complex in Syria; these individuals were blindfolded and kept in enforced silence: a human rights black spot, where an estimated 5,000 to 13,000 executions took place between 2011 and 2015. Many of the executed were political prisoners held under Bashar al-Assad’s political regime. The prisoners were blindfolded when they arrived and forced to cover their eyes whenever guards were in the room; the four walls of their cells being the only visible co-ordinates. The majority of their perception centred on what they heard.

The basis of Abu Hamdan’s work was drawn from Amnesty International’s research with Forensic Architecture (of which the artist is a member) to help uncover the conditions of the Saydnaya prison. The closest they could get to the site was through satellite images taken miles away, as the prison remains in operation and no independent observers have been allowed to enter. The artist’s access to this location was solely through the memories of its survivors.

In this work, Abu Hamdan utilises new forms of representation to document and represent the intangible aspects of the prison. After producing a comprehensive study and website for Amnesty International, the artist paid attention to how memory conjoins with architecture and violence, proffering what he describes as ‘fragile truths’ through a sound work in which there is ‘a body of evidence that focuses on silences, on whispers, on the distortions of memory, on the weird conflations between space and the body and wall’. Abu Hamdan’s work reveals what is recognised by law as material evidence and elucidates how deemed outside its protection are excised or, to quote Achille Mbembe, how some lives are deemed ‘superfluous’.

Chris McCormack

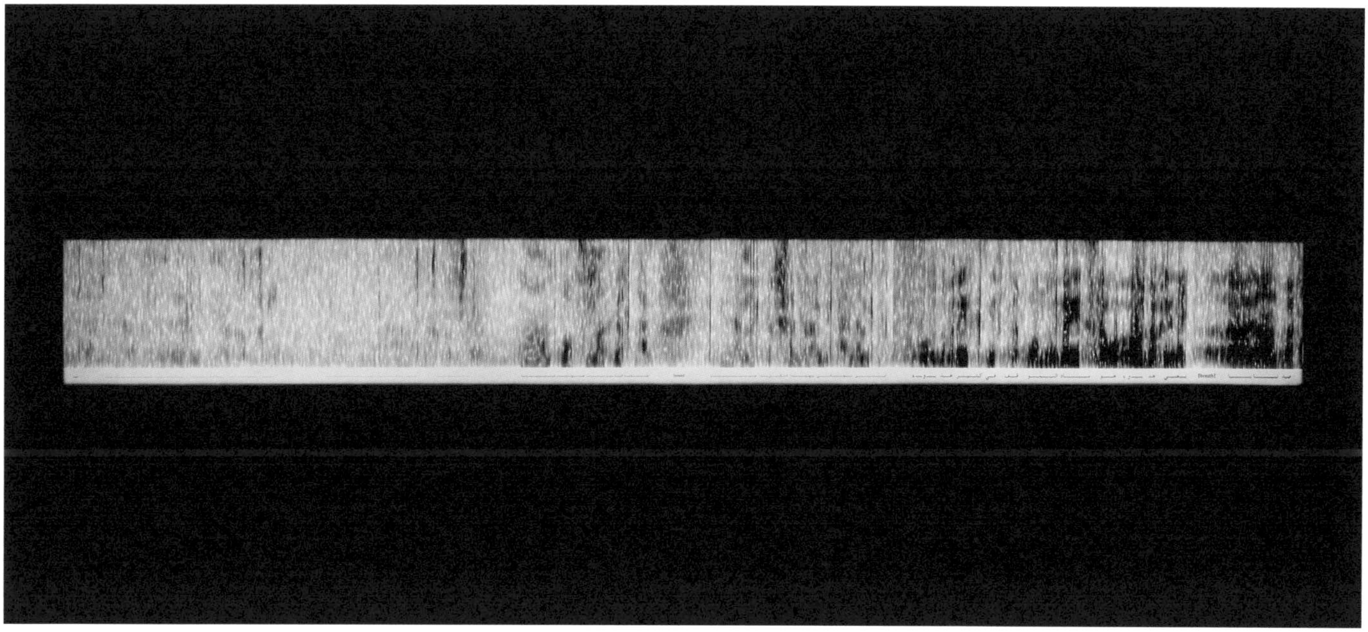

*Saydnaya (The Missing 19db) / Saydnaya (Die vermissten 19 db)*, 2017. Abzug; Sound, Mischpult mit Auto-Fader / Print; sound, mixing desk with automated faders, lightbox, electrical digital timer. 240 × 27,51 cm. Maße variabel / Dimensions variable. Im Auftrag der Sharjah Art Foundation / Commissioned by Sharjah Art Foundation. Installationsansicht / Installation view, Sharjah Biennial 13, Sharjah Art Foundation, 2017.

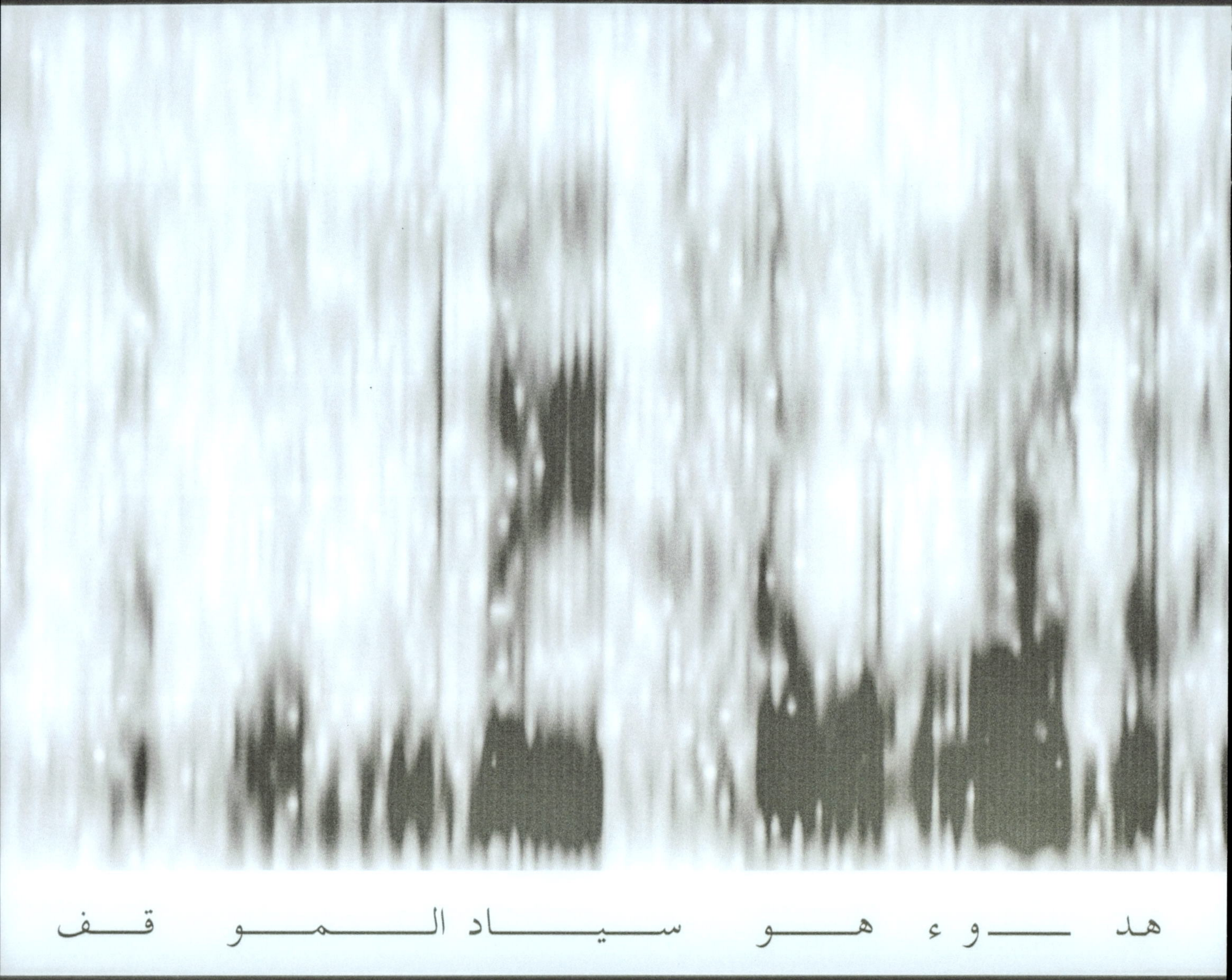
هد ــــــ و ء هـــو ســيــــاد الــــمـــو قـــف

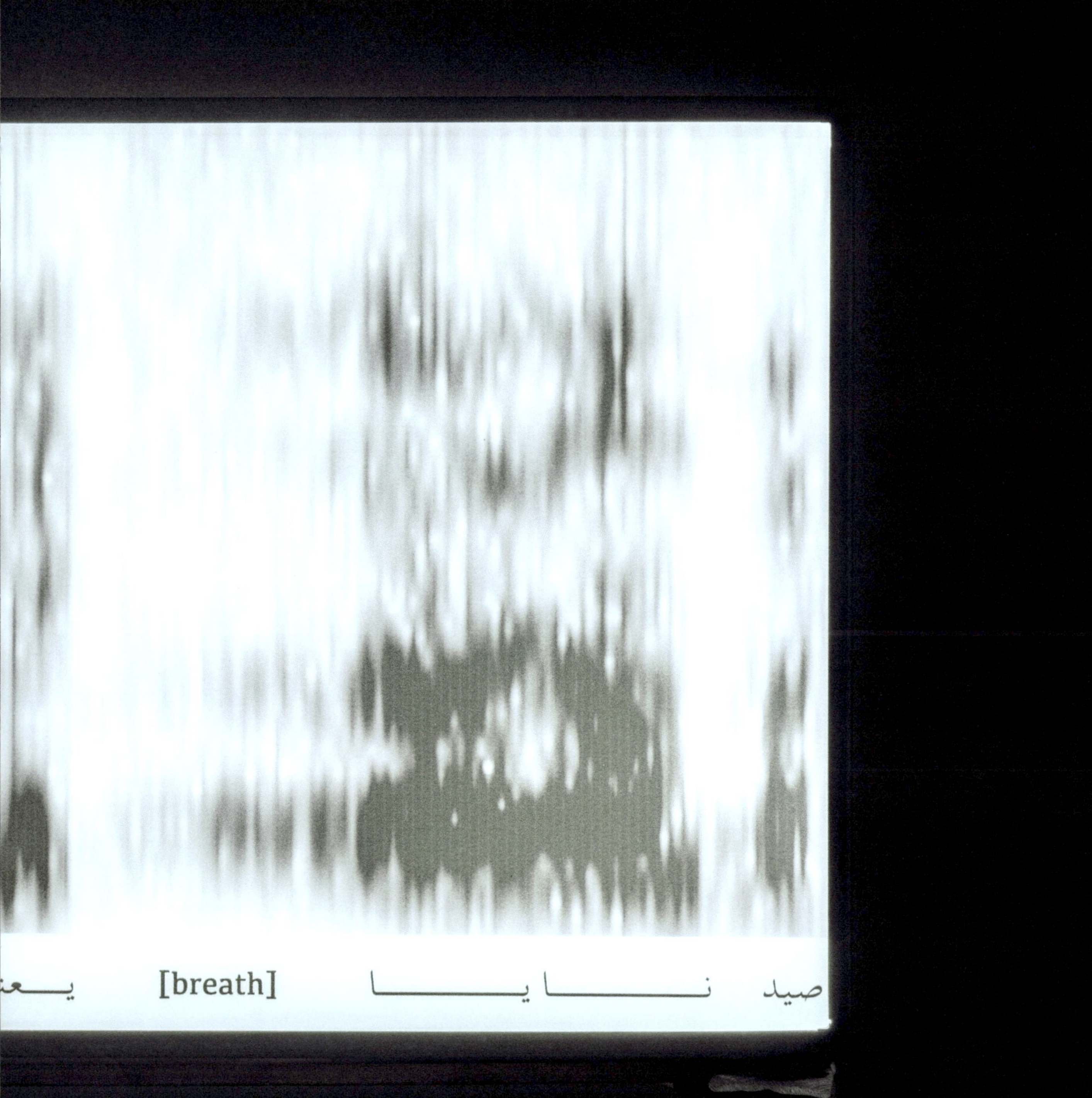
صيد نـــــــا يـــــــا
[breath]

# Khadim Ali

Der farbenfrohe, neun Meter lange Wandteppich *Invisible Border* („Unsichtbare Grenze", 2020) wurde von den Hazara handgewebt, einer ethnischen Gruppe in den afghanischen Bergen, der auch der Künstler angehört. Die kunstvollen Stickereien erzählen in Collagen von Tieren, Fabelwesen und Palästen anschauliche Geschichten über die Kultur und Vertreibung der Hazara. Sie erinnern an Illustrationen aus dem *Schahnameh (Buch der Könige)*, einem einflussreichen persischen Epos aus dem Jahr 1010 n. Chr., das der Künstler aus seiner Kindheit kennt. Die alten Geschichten von Gut und Böse aus der klassischen persischen Literatur werden hier mit Maschinengewehren, einer aufgebrachten Menschenmenge und anderen zeitgenössischen politischen Symbolen für Krieg, Auseinandersetzung und Gewalt konfrontiert.

Khadim Ali, der zunächst eine Ausbildung in Miniaturmalerei absolvierte, wandte sich der Stickerei und Tapisserie zu, nachdem zwei große Wandteppiche einen Selbstmordanschlag der Taliban mit einer Autobombe auf sein Elternhaus in Quetta, Pakistan, unbeschadet überstanden hatten. Die beiden Techniken stellen für ihn heute eine Form der künstlerischen Arbeit dar, die dem Terror gegen das Volk der Hazara standhält. Zudem betrachtet er sie als eine Möglichkeit der Zusammenarbeit mit anderen, um ihr Leben im Exil und ihre Erfahrungen als Geflüchtete zu erkunden.

Die Einnahmen aus dem Verkauf dieses Werks gingen an die Mitarbeiter*innen seines Ateliers in Kabul, das er selbst nicht besuchen konnte. Das Werk reflektiert die nach wie vor prekäre Situation der Hazara als Geflüchtete sowie der vielen anderen, die auf der ganzen Welt darauf warten, sich an einem Ort niederlassen zu können. Es entstand vor der Machtübernahme der Taliban im Jahr 2021 und ist auch eine Kritik an dem jüngsten militärischen Abzug des Westens – insbesondere der USA – aus Afghanistan.

A colourful nine-metre hanging tapestry, *Invisible Border* (2020) is hand-woven by the artist's native Hazara community, an ethnic group from a mountainous region of Afghanistan. The embroidery tells stories of their culture and displacement in vivid montages that include animals, mythical creatures and palaces, recalling illustrations from *The Shahnameh*, an epic and influential Persian poem written in 1010 CE, which the artist encountered as a child. The ancient stories of good and evil from classic Persian literature sit alongside machine guns, an angry mob of men and other contemporary political symbolisers of war, conflict and violence.

Khadim Ali's expansion into embroidery and tapestry from his early training as a miniature painter emerged when two large tapestries survived a Taliban suicide car-bombing at his parents' home in Quetta, Pakistan. For him, they now represent a form of art practice that can withstand the terror inflicted on the Hazara people and a methodology for collaboration with others to explore their life in exile and the experience of being a refugee.

The proceeds from the sale of this work were sent back to Ali's studio assistants in Kabul, where he was unable to visit. Its presence contemplates the Hazara, who remain refugees in a precarious situation, as well as the many others left waiting to find some form of settlement across the world. Whilst produced before the 2021 Taliban takeover, the work also represents a critique of the West's recent militaristic treatment of Afghanistan—particularly that of the United States.

Sarah Perks

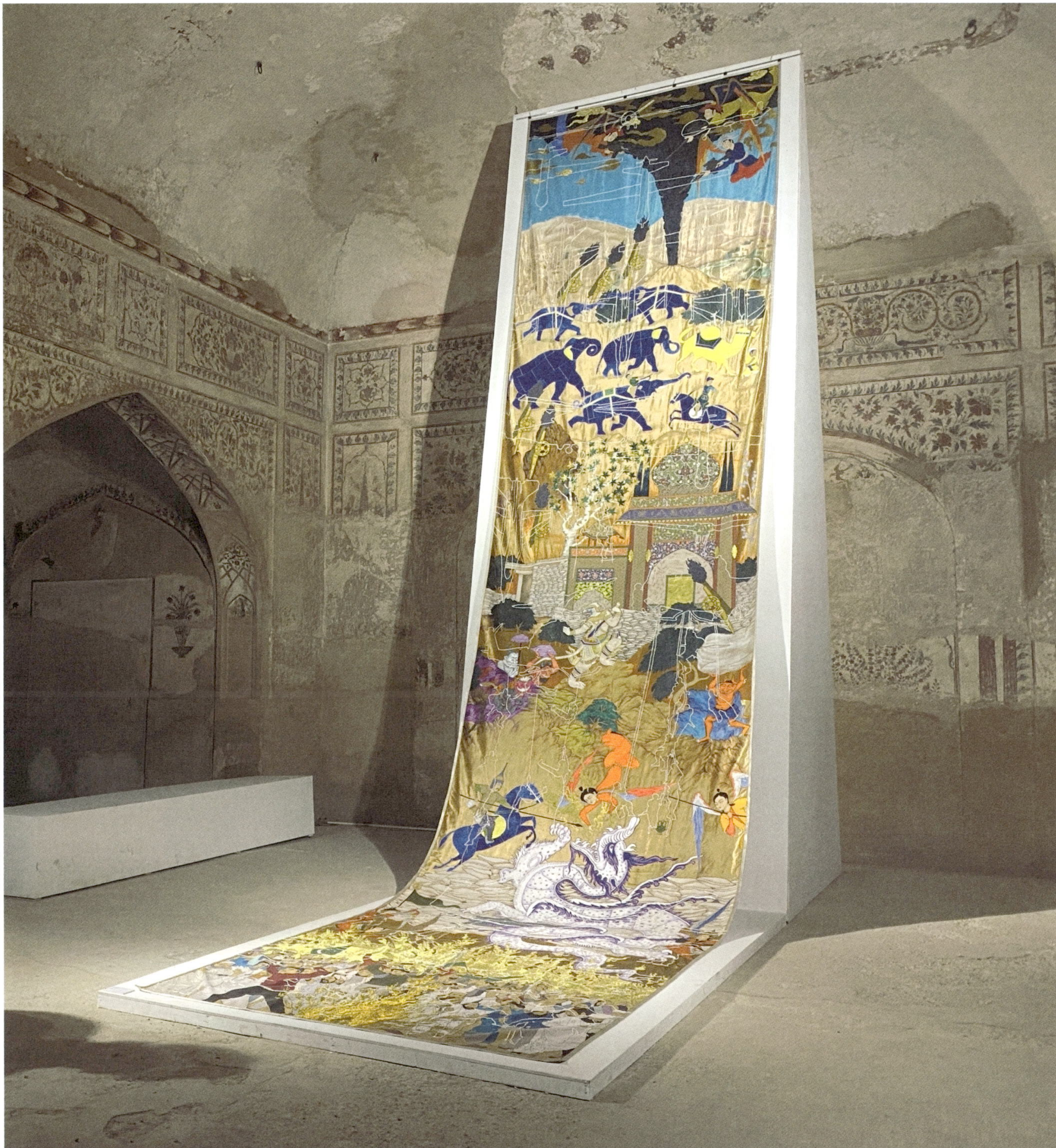

*Invisible Border / Unsichtbare Grenze*, 2020. Acrylfarbe und -lack, Hand- und Maschinenstickerei auf Stoff / Acrylic paint and dye, hand and machine embroidery on fabric. 210 × 900 cm

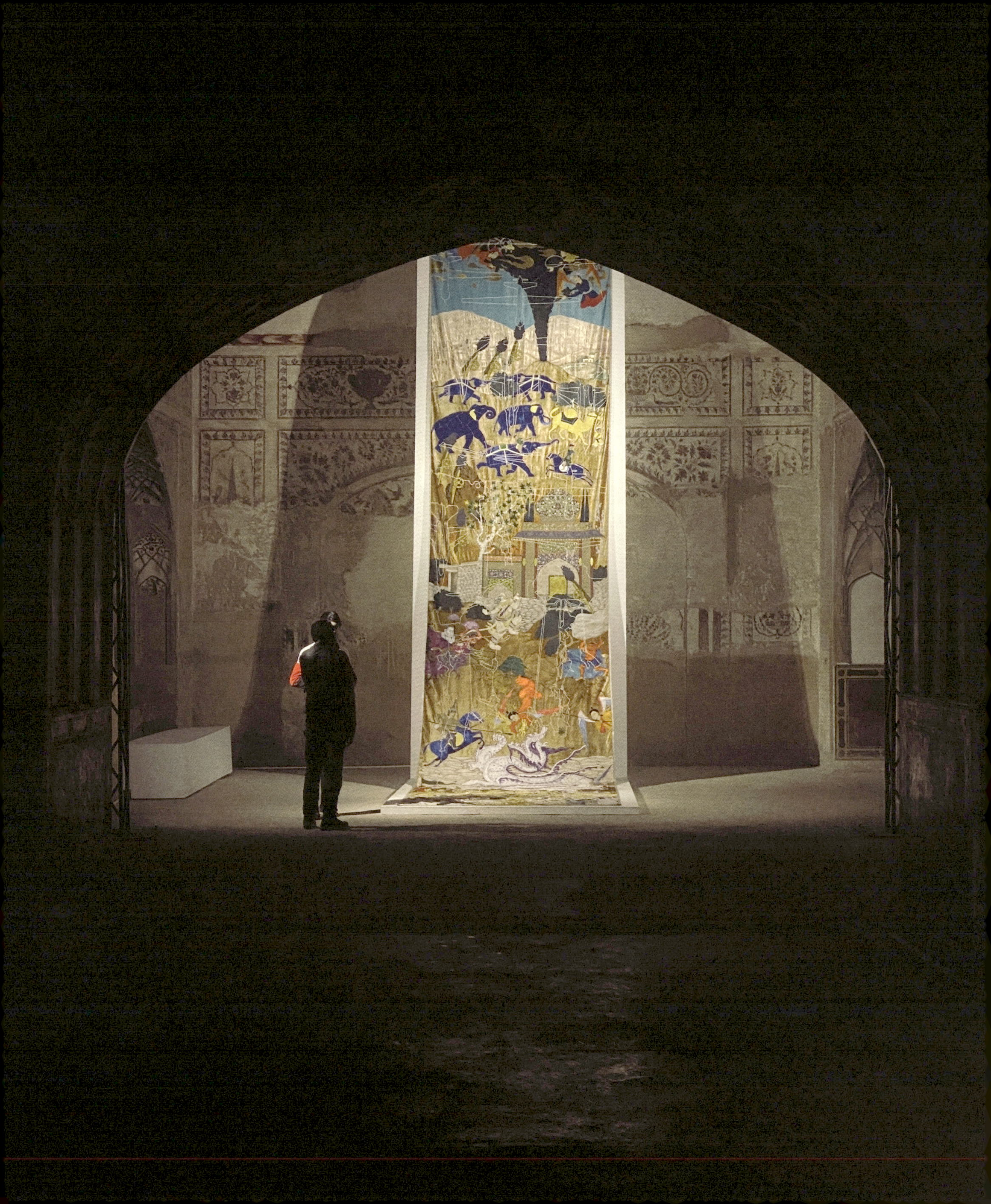

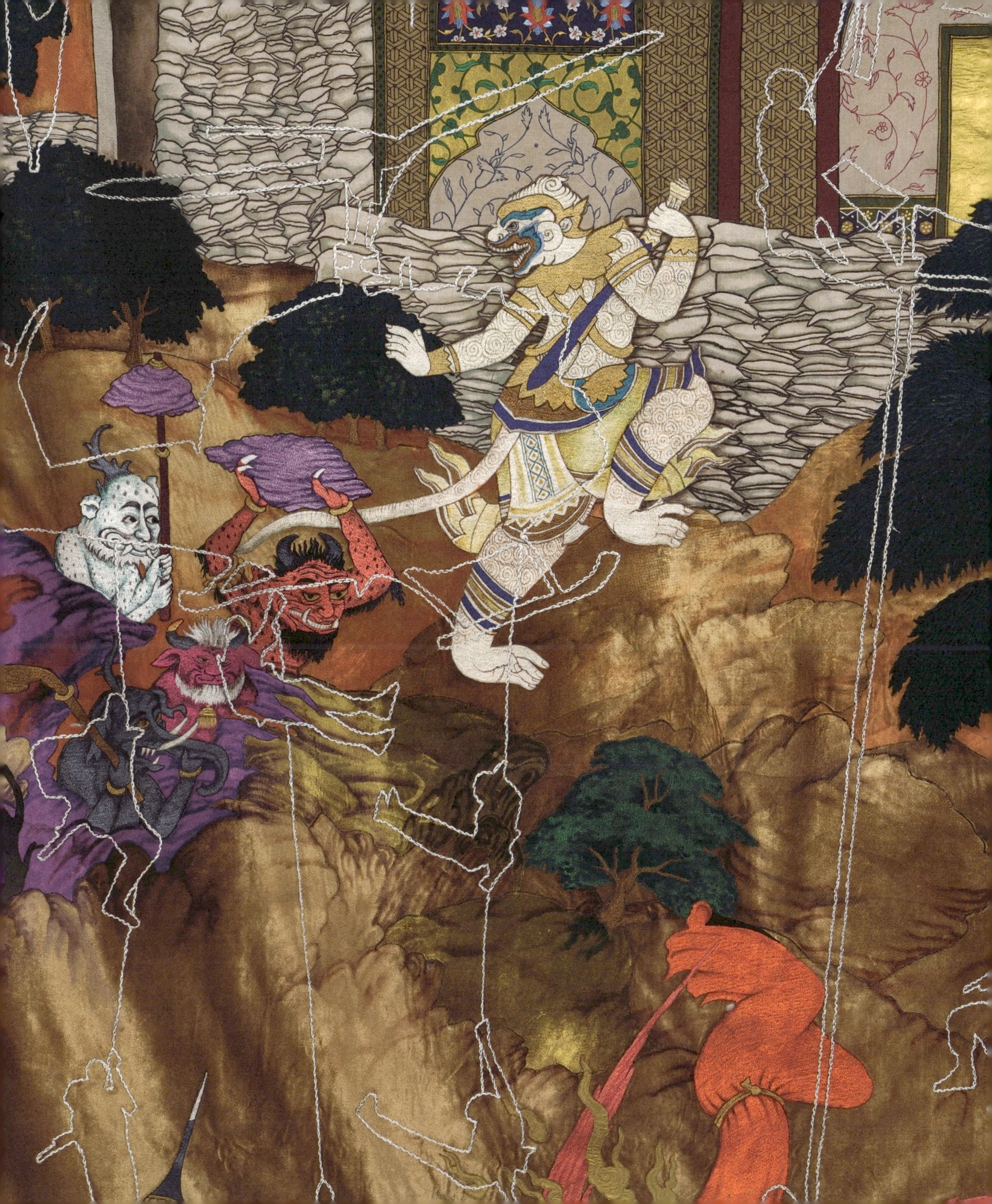

# Halil Altindere

Muhammed Ahmed Faris, der 2011 mit der demokratischen Oppositionsbewegung gegen das Regime von Bashar Al-Assad auf die Straße ging, flüchtete im Jahr 2012 in die Türkei, nachdem die syrische Revolution in einen Bürgerkrieg umgeschlagen war. Faris, Oberst, Militärberater und Leiter der syrischen Luftwaffenakademie, ist der erste und einzige Syrer, der je ins All reiste. Er wurde 1985 in das sowjetische Kosmonaut*innen-Programm aufgenommen und flog 1987 zusammen mit zwei russischen Kosmonauten zur Raumstation MIR. Halil Altindere porträtiert das Trio in seinem Öl- und Acryl-Porträt *Muhammed Ahmed Faris with Friends #2* („Muhammed Ahmed Faris mit Freunden #2", 2016) im Stil des sozialistischen Realismus. In *Stamp #2* („Briefmarke #2", 2016) tauchen die drei als gestandene Persönlichkeiten noch einmal auf. Der großformatige Siebdruck auf Leinwand zeigt eine vergrößerte russische Briefmarke, die an die Weltraumreise von 1987 erinnert – eine gemeinsame Mission und ein Spiegel der syrisch-sowjetischen Beziehungen zur Zeit des Kalten Krieges.

Altinderes Arbeiten zu Faris entstanden 2016 für eine Ausstellung im Neuen Berliner Kunstverein, bei der das Video *Space Refugee* („Weltraumflüchtling") im Mittelpunkt stand. Im Video schildert Faris seinen Weg vom außerordendlichen Astronauten zu einem von Millionen Flüchtlingen und entwirft eine Vision des Weltraums als zukünftiger Freistatt syrischer Geflüchteter. Das Video wurde von Modellen und Porträts umkreist, die Faris' Status als Nationalheld widerspiegeln, darunter das Gemälde *Mohammed Ahmed Faris, Portrait #1* im Stil des sozialistischen Realismus und eine in 3-D-Druck hergestellte Skulptur von Faris in Kosmonautenausrüstung, *Mini Faris* (2016).

Trotz der vom Propagandakitsch des Kalten Krieges durchdrungenen Ästhetik ist das Projekt von bemerkenswerter Aufrichtigkeit. Es reflektiert Faris' Erfahrungen im Weltraum und den Overview-Effekt, den Astronaut*innen nach ihrer Rückkehr zur Erde häufig beschreiben. So bemerkte Faris im Jahr 2016 in einem Interview mit dem *Guardian*: „Wenn Sie die ganze Welt durch Ihr Fenster gesehen haben, gibt es kein Wir und Sie, keine Politik."

Muhammed Ahmed Faris, who marched in democratic opposition to the Bashar Al-Assad regime in 2011, fled to Turkey in 2012 after the Syrian revolution erupted into civil war.

Faris, a colonel and military advisor who headed the Syrian Air Force Academy, is the first and only Syrian to date to have travelled into outer space. Joining the Soviet cosmonaut programme in 1985, he participated in a mission to the Mir space station in 1987 alongside two Russian cosmonauts. Halil Altindere portrays the trio in the Soviet Realist oil-and-acrylic portrait *Muhammed Ahmed Faris with Friends #2* (2016), and they show up again as standing figures in *Stamp #2* (2016). The large screen-print on canvas blows up a Russian stamp commemorating the 1987 journey into the cosmos—a joint mission reflecting Syrian-Soviet relations during the Cold War. Altindere's Faris-focused works were created for a 2016 exhibition at the Neuer Berliner Kunstverein in Berlin, which revolved around the video *Space Refugee*. In the video, Faris recounts his journey from singular astronaut to a refugee among millions, while projecting space as a future place for Syrian refugees to find a free home. Orbiting this video were models and portraits reflecting Faris's status as national hero, including the socialist realist painting *Muhammed Ahmed Faris, Portrait #1* (2016) and a 3D-printed sculpture of Faris in cosmonaut gear, *Mini Faris* (2016).

Despite an aesthetic steeped in the kitsch of Cold War propaganda, a striking sincerity pervades the artist's project: a reflection of Faris's experience in space as well as the Overview Effect astronauts often describe once returning to Earth. As Faris told *The Guardian* in 2016: 'When you have seen the whole world through your window, there is no us and them, no politics'.

Stephanie Bailey

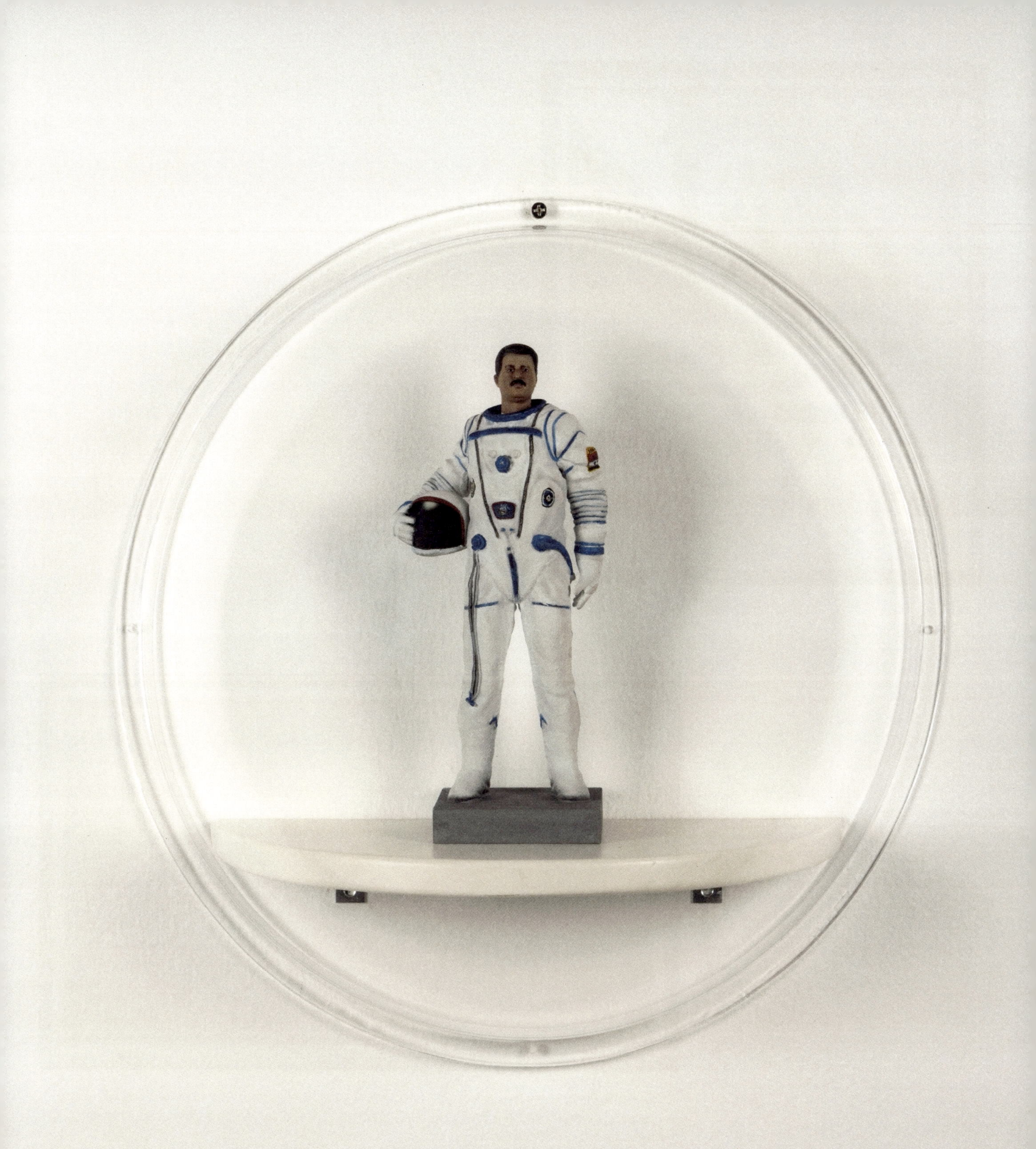

*Mini Faris*, 2016. Von Hand nachbearbeitete 3D-Druck-Skulptur aus Plexiglas / 3D printed sculpture processed by hand in plexiglass.
Höhe Skulptur 24 cm; Durchmesser Plexiglas 40 cm / Sculpture height 24 cm; plexiglass diameter 40 cm

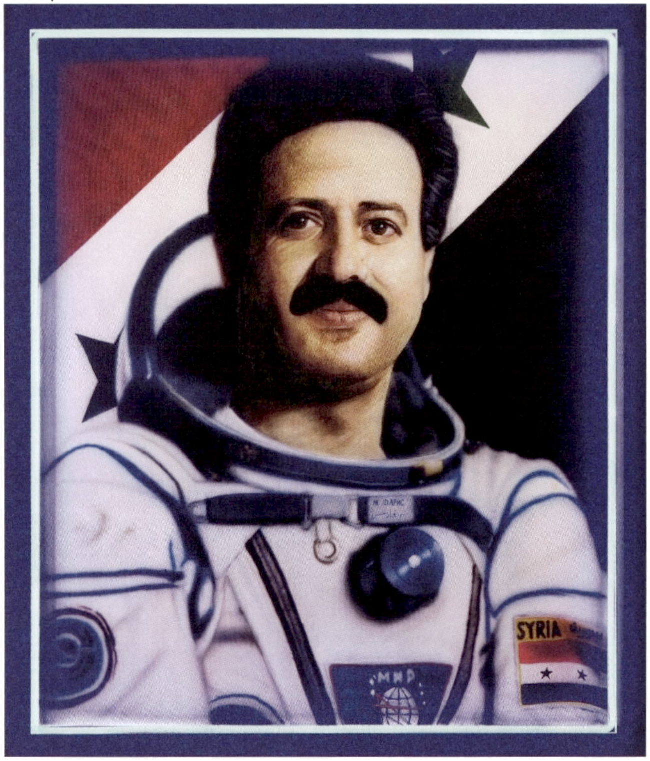

*Muhammed Ahmed Faris, Portrait #1*, 2016. Öl und Acryl auf Leinwand, Rahmen, flexible LED-Neonröhre / Oil and acrylic on canvas, frame, flexible LED neon tubing. 80 × 105 × 6 cm

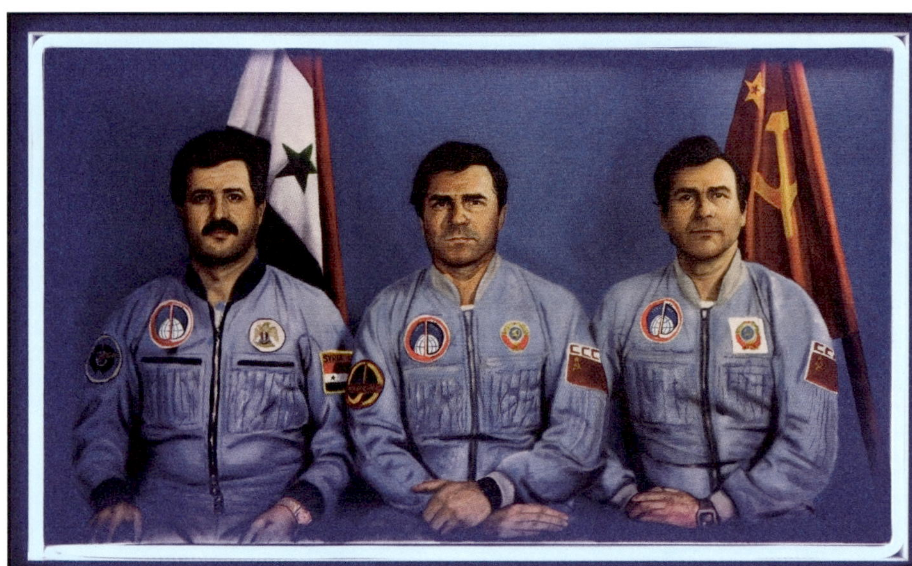

*Muhammed Ahmed Faris with Friends #2 / Muhammed Ahmed Faris mit Freunden #2*, 2016. Öl und Acryl auf Leinwand, Rahmen, flexible LED-Neonröhre / Oil and acrylic on canvas frame, flexible LED neon tubing. 65,5 × 39,5 × 6 cm

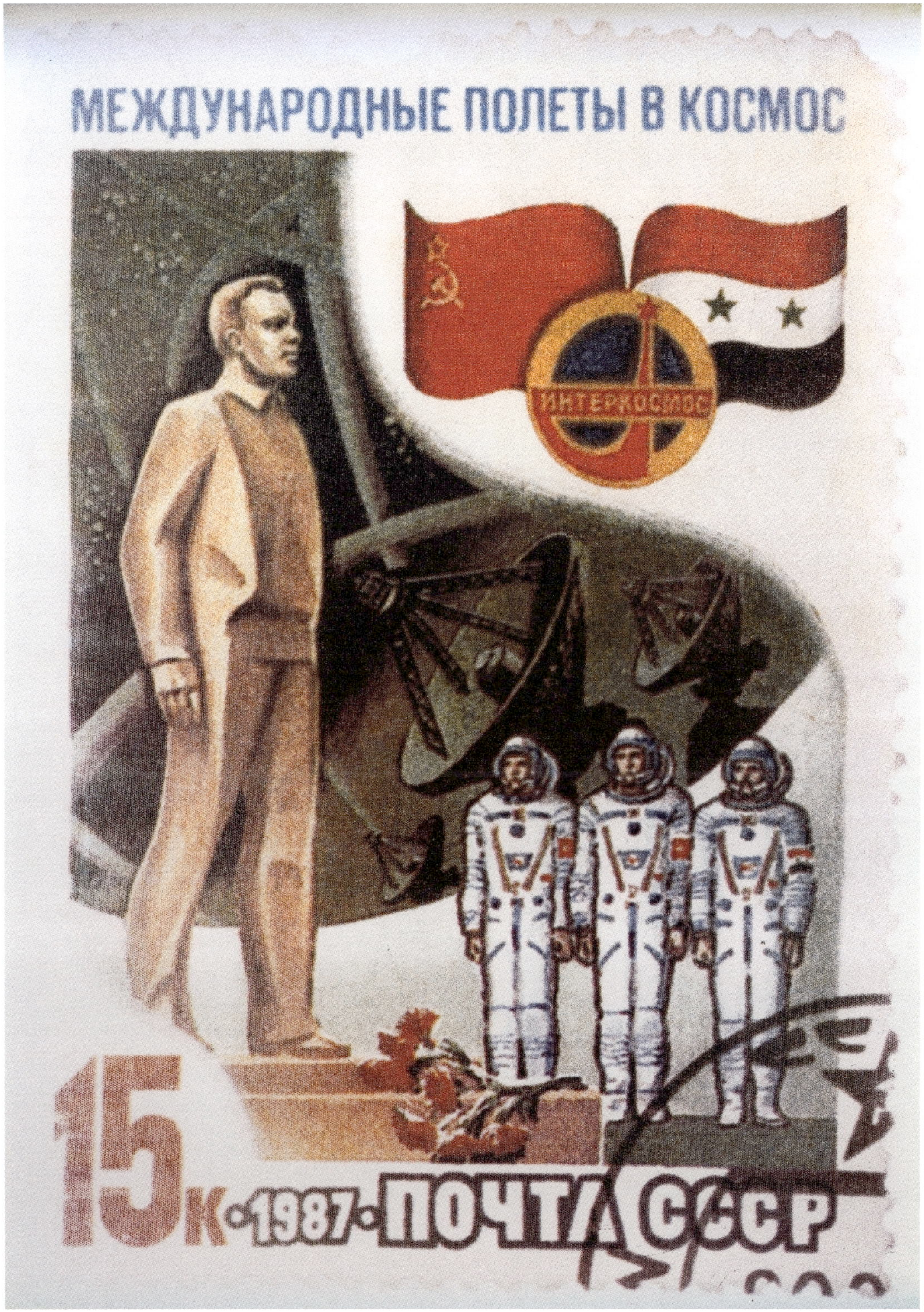


*Stamp #2 | Briefmarke #2*, 2016. Siebdruck auf Leinwand, gerahmt / Silkscreen on canvas, framed. 55 × 75 × 6 cm

# Minam Apang

Minam Apangs *Seas* („Meere", 2019) ist eine kaum sichtbare Kohlezeichnung auf Stoff, die ein bewegtes, fast glasartiges Meer zeigt. Das Werk der in Goa lebenden Künstlerin Apang ist flüchtig: Jede Zeichnung ist vage und kaum greifbar. Ihre Arbeiten fangen einen Augenblick in seiner schwungvollen Bewegung ein, bevor er wieder vergeht – so wie ein fliegender Fisch silbern im Licht aufglänzt, bevor er wieder ins Meer eintaucht. Die Materialwahl der Künstlerin spiegelt diese Tendenz zum Vergänglichen wider: Sie arbeitet vor allem mit Papier, Fäden und Kohle. Ihre Arbeiten erschließen „den fließenden, imaginären Raum des Mythos", indem sie sich bei ihrer Auseinandersetzung mit der Form in „eine expressive Traumlandschaft" begebe, erklärt Apang in einem Interview mit der *Arts Initiative Tokyo*. Einige dieser Mythen sind mündlich überlieferte Geschichten und Folklore aus ihrem Heimatstaat Arunachal Pradesh, andere beschäftigen sich mit der Reise zwischen Leben und Tod – der Zeit zwischen beidem und ihrer „engen, austauschbaren/zyklischen Beziehung im mythischen Raum". Für Adi, eine in Arunachal und Tibet gesprochene indigene Sprache, gibt es keine standardisierte Schrift. So sind Apangs Zeichnungen Positionsbestimmungen und Protokolle zugleich der Versuch, eine Entsprechung zur mündlichen Überlieferung und deren verbindendem Charakter zu finden. Apang zeichnet zunächst Markierungen auf ein Blatt Papier und baut dann nach und nach assoziativ auf diesen Markierungen auf. Die Bilder entwickeln sich – sie sind ebenso beabsichtigt wie vom Unterbewusstsein bestimmt. Sie wirken manchmal übertrieben, manchmal fantastisch und manchmal in eine bleierne Stille gehüllt. Apang behandelt Kohle als skulpturales Medium und stellt ihr Pulver selbst her, indem sie Pastellstifte zerreibt und die Grafitkerne aus Bleistiften schabt. Den Stoff, den sie häufig als Bildträger verwendet, befreit sie von sämtlicher Stärke und spielt mit dem Effekt, dass sich durch Falten im Stoff farbliche Abstufungen ergeben.

Minam Apang's *Seas* (2019) is a barely visible charcoal on cloth of a shifting, glassy seascape. Goa-based Apang's work is evanescent: each drawing is fleeting. Her works catch a moment in lively throw before it passes again—just as a flying fish flashes silver in the light before it dips back into the sea. The artist's use of material mirrors this elusive tendency; she works primarily with paper, thread and charcoal. The works extend 'the fluid, imaginative space of myth', as Apang explains in an interview with *Arts Initiative Tokyo*, where she accesses 'an expressive dream landscape' in her exploration of form. Some of these myths are passed-down oral histories and folklore from her home state of Arunachal Pradesh, others are preoccupied with journey: between life and death, between moments in time, and in the 'closely interchangeable/cyclical relationship [shared] in mythic space'. Adi, an indigenous language spoken in Arunachal and Tibet, does not have a formalised written script, and so Apang's drawings become both cursor and record. She overlaps history and fiction, moving between abstracted and figurative landscapes. Apang's process attempts to parallel the relational, generative quality so acquired from the ways in which oral histories are passed on: first, she will make markings on a page, and over time, through a kind of associative act, she will build on these markings. Images evolve through this—they are as much intentional as they are of the subconscious, they are sometimes hyperbolic, sometimes fantastical and sometimes cloaked in a leaden stillness. Apang finds that charcoal is a sculptural medium, and she often makes her own powders by crushing pastel and shaving the graphite cores of pencils. She strips the cloth, which forms her base, of any starch, welcoming the gradations that form as the fabric wrinkles.

Skye Arundhati Thomas

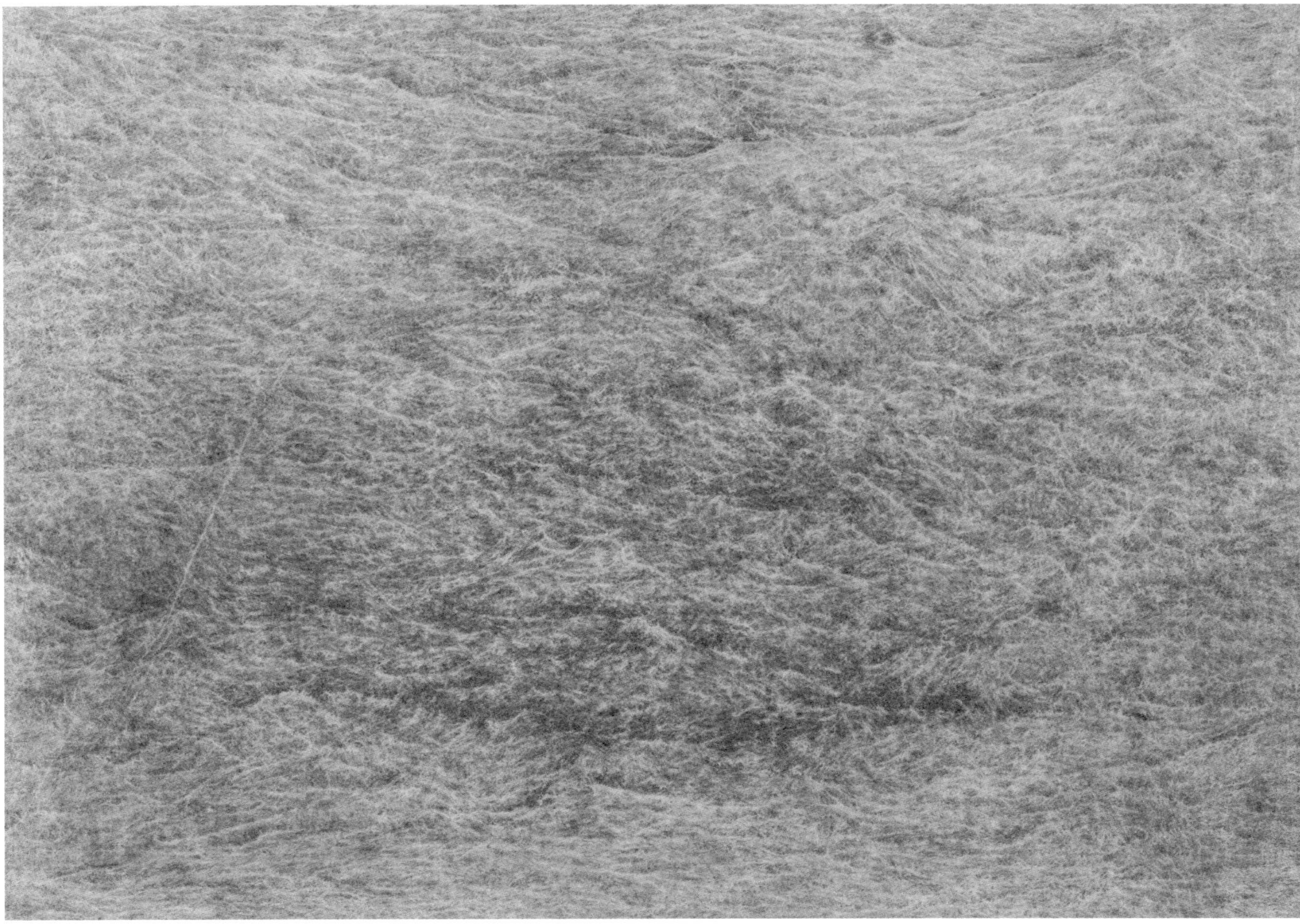

*Seas* / *Meere*, 2019. Kohle auf Stoff / Charcoal on cloth. 149,9 × 104,1 cm

# Shiraz Bayjoo

*Île de France* (2015) ist ein nicht-narrativer Film, dessen Titel einen der historischen Namen der Insel Mauritius zitiert, die von 1715 bis 1810 unter französischer Herrschaft stand. Der Film beruht auf dem fortwährenden Interesse des Regisseurs Shiraz Bayjoo an den Themen Identität und Nationalität – insbesondere was die Gesamtregion um den Indischen Ozean betrifft. *Île de France* macht sich auf eine Spurensuche quer über die Insel, die ursprünglich unbewohnt war, bevor sie ab dem 17. Jahrhundert erst durch die Niederlande, dann durch Frankreich und Großbritannien kolonialisiert wurde und 1968 ihre Unabhängigkeit erlangte. Entsprechend beschäftigt sich Bayjoo mit der Geschichte und dem Erbe von Kolonialismus, Sklaverei, Migration und Zwangsarbeit.

Der von Mauritius stammende Filmemacher, Fotograf und Bildhauer begann seine umfangreiche Arbeit an dem Projekt während eines Künstleraufenthalts in London. Er besuchte öffentliche und private Archive und interviewte Historiker*innen und Vertreter*innen lokaler Gruppen. Seine Recherchen vor Ort machte er zur Grundlage des malerischen Films, der Zuschauer*innen in bewegenden Bildern durch das Innere von Handelshäusern, das Haus seiner Großmutter in Port Louis, Ruinen von Industrieanlagen und Siedlungen sowie über Friedhöfe und durch Wälder führt.

*Île de France* ist mit einer emotionalen Tonspur unterlegt, in der volkstümliche Musik, Archivaufnahmen der Unabhängigkeitsfeierlichkeiten von 1968 und geflüsterte Worte aus dem Buch Genesis mit dem Code Noir verknüpft werden, der als theologische Rechtfertigung für die Sklaverei diente. Meeresklänge tauchen während des Films immer wieder auf. Für Bayjoo ist der Ozean eine Naturgewalt und ständiger Zeuge im Auf und Ab der Geschichte, die ihm wie „eine geliehene Zeit und ein geliehener Raum“ erscheint.

Der Film wurde im Rahmen einer größeren Installation zusammen mit Fotografien, Skulpturen, Acryl- und Kunstharzgemälden konzipiert, die dem Lebensgefühl auf Mauritius eine materielle Textur verleihen. Trotz der fehlenden menschlichen Präsenz zeigt *Île de France* die Auswirkungen der einzelnen Kolonialisierungsphasen auf die Sprachen, Kulturen und auf die gebaute und natürliche Umwelt der Insel und beleuchtet die Komplexität individueller und kollektiver Identitäten sowohl in der Vergangenheit wie auch im Heute.

*Île de France* (2015) is a non-narrative film titled after the name given to the island of Mauritius under French rule between 1715 and 1810. Reflecting Shiraz Bayjoo's ongoing interest in identity and nationhood, particularly in relation to the Indian Ocean region, *Île de France* traces the histories and legacies of colonialism, slavery, migration and indentured labour in Mauritius. The island country was uninhabited before successive colonisation from the 17th century, first by the Dutch, then the French and the British, until its independence in 1968.

During an artist's residency in Mauritius (which is also the artist's birthplace), Bayjoo carried out extensive research into public and private archives and met with historians and members of various local communities. His visits to locations across the island informed the development of a painterly film that evocatively shifts through domestic interiors of merchant houses, his grandmother's home in Port Louis, ruins of industrial sites and settlements, graveyards and forests.

The film is interspersed with an emotive use of sound, which includes vernacular music, archival footage of the 1968 Independence ceremonies and whispered words from the Book of Genesis, associated with the Code Noir, which provided a theological justification for the existence of slavery. Sounds of the ocean—a natural force that Bayjoo describes as a witness to histories that have come and gone—emerges throughout, like 'borrowed time and borrowed space'.

The film was conceived as part of a larger installation of photographs, sculptures and acrylic and resin paintings that gave material texture to this sense of place. Devoid of human presence, the film nonetheless communicates the impact of successive periods of colonisation of the island's languages, cultures, and built and natural environments, as well as the complexities of representing individual and collective identities both historically and today.

Anne Barlow

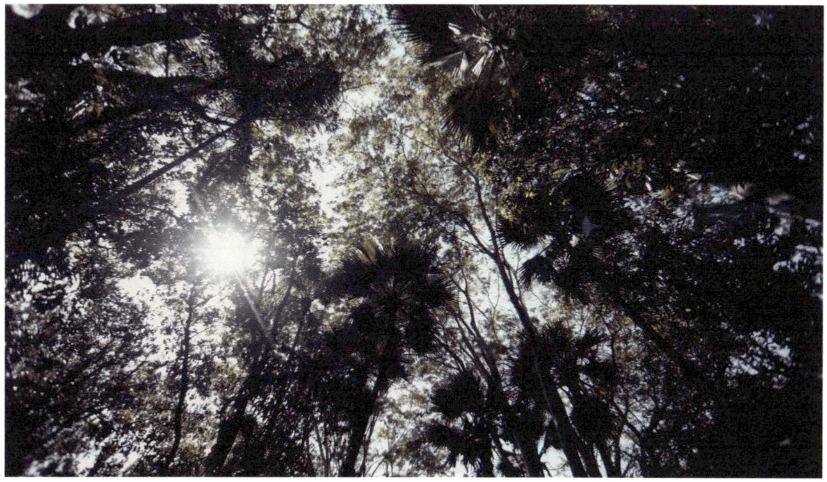

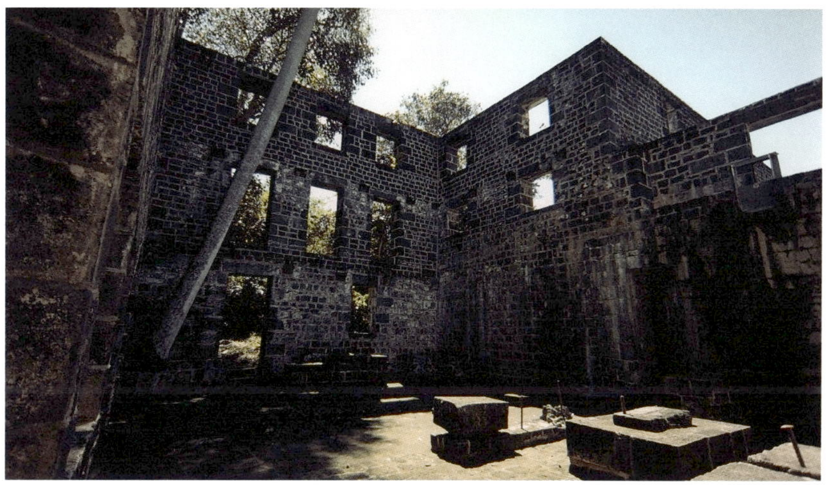

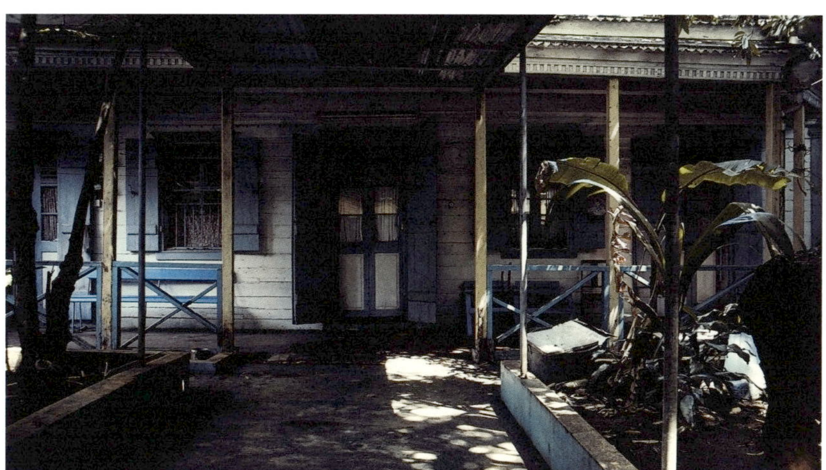

*Île de France*, 2015. 16mm-HD-Film / 16mm HD film. 31 Minuten, 18 Sekunden / 31 minutes 18 seconds

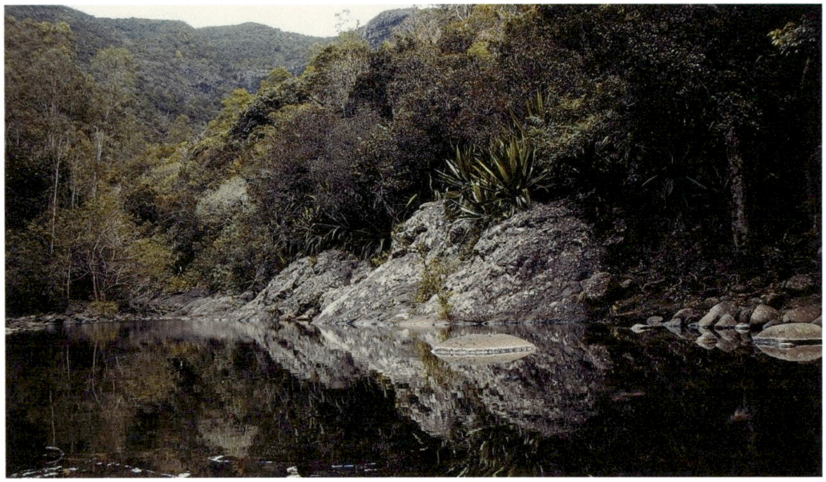

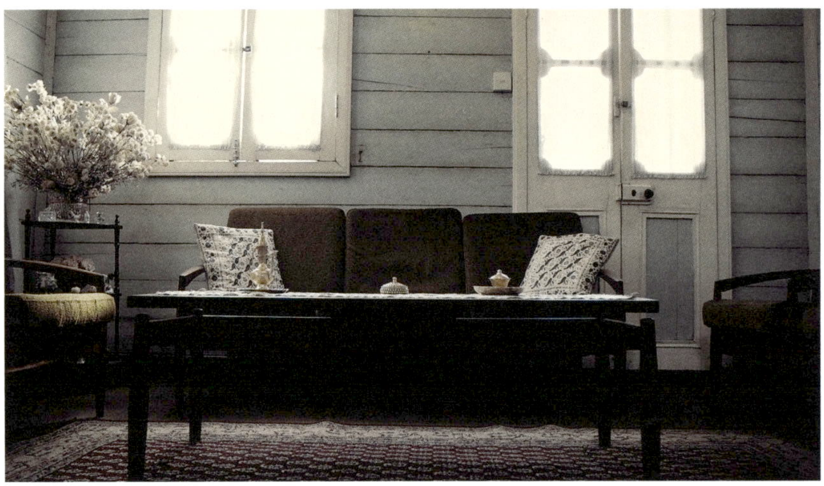

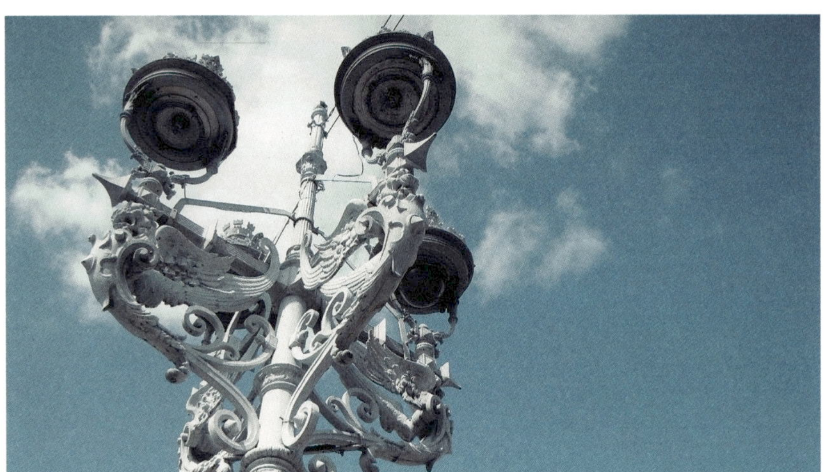

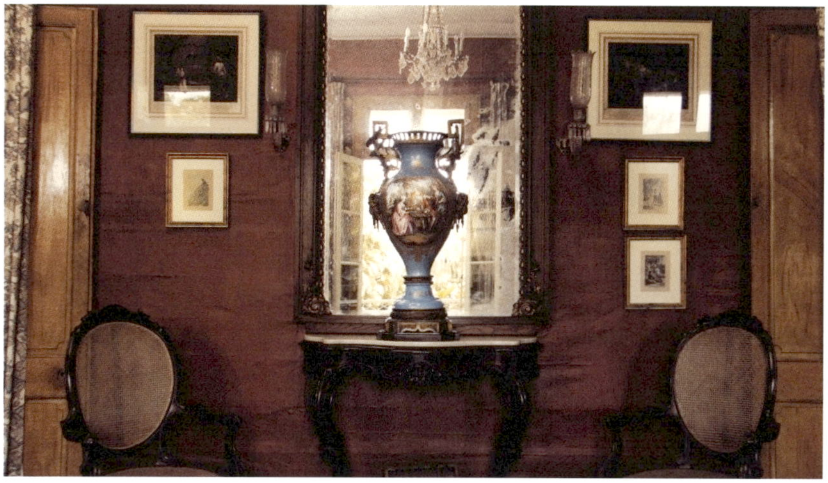

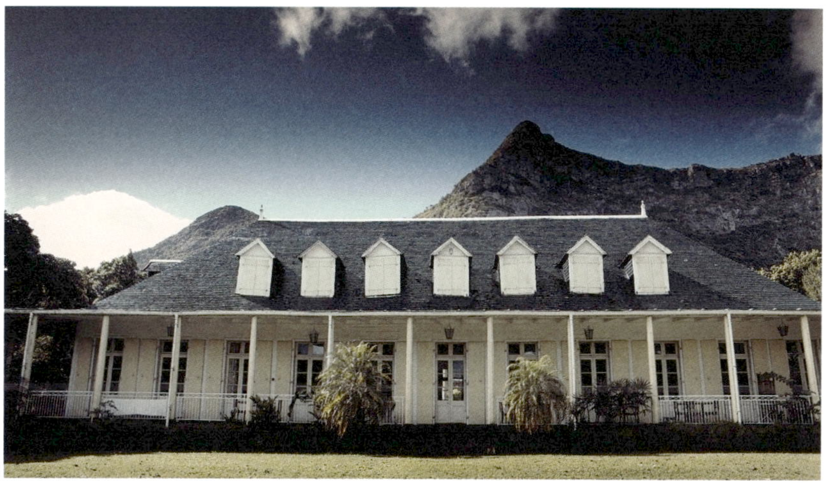

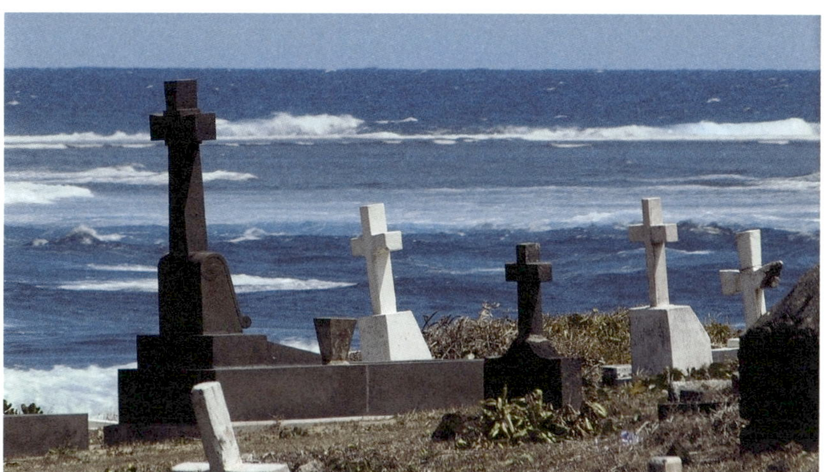

# CAMP

Die drei Golfe in CAMPs *From Gulf to Gulf to Gulf* („Von Golf zu Golf zu Golf", 2009–2013) sind der Golf von Kachchh (Gujarat, Indien), der Persische Golf und der Golf von Aden im Süden des Roten Meers. Zusammen zeichnen sie die einst bekannten Routen der Kauf- und Seeleute und einer transnationalen Gemeinschaft von Männern nach, die auf und an diesen Gewässern lebten und arbeiteten. Das Werk entstand innerhalb mehrerer Jahre und unter dem Einsatz unterschiedlicher Medien. Einen Hauptbestandteil bilden die Filmaufnahmen der Seeleute auf diesen Schiffen, die ihre tägliche Arbeit auf dem Indischen Ozean mit ihren Mobiltelefonen dokumentierten. In Kooperation mit dem Künstler*innenatelier CAMP wurde dieses Rohmaterial anschließend zusammen mit eigenem Material, das die Künstler*innen entlang dieser Routen aufgenommen hatten, auf Spielfilmlänge zusammengeschnitten.

Ausgangspunkt für das CAMP-Projekt war die Volksgruppe der Kuchi in Sharjah, die in der Vergangenheit ihre eigenen Boote bauten. Darauf verweist auch der hindisprachige Titel des Werks, *Kutchi Vahan Pani Wala*. Zu Beginn des Films intonieren zwei Männer auf einem Boot *Yaadon Ko Bas Wo Yaad*, ein beliebtes melancholisches Liebeslied auf Hindi. Das große Vergnügen und die gespielte Schüchternheit, mit der sie das Lied vortragen, geben den Takt für eine Geschichte über die sozio-ökonomischen Veränderungen vor, die diese Menschen an ihren jeweiligen Heimathäfen erleben.

„Die Videos zeigen, dass die Welt groß ist und der Bildschirm klein." Entsprechend dieser knapp formulierten Maßgabe verknüpften die Künstler*innen, deren Gemeinschaftsatelier CAMP 2007 in Mumbai von Ashok Sukumaran und Shaina Anand gegründet wurde, die verschiedenen Videos miteinander.

The three Gulfs alluded to in CAMP's *From Gulf to Gulf to Gulf* (2009–13) allude to the Gulf of Kutch (Gujarat, India), the Arabian Gulf and the Gulf of Aden at the tip of the Red Sea. Together, they map the once familiar routes taken by merchant sailors and a community of transnational men who lived and worked across these waters. The work was created over a number of years using a variety of media, of which one of the primary sources was footage of these individuals aboard these ships, documenting their daily activities on the Indian Ocean on their mobile phones. In collaboration with CAMP, an artist studio, over a period of four years, this raw material was subsequently edited into a feature-length film that incorporates some of the artists' own material, filmed across and throughout these routes.

The CAMP project began through the Kutchi community in Sharjah—individuals who historically built and owned their boats. This is reflected in the Hindi title of the work *Kutchi Vahan Pani Wala*. The film begins with two men on a boat performing a popular melancholic Hindi love song, *Yaadon Ko Bas Wo Yaad*. The sheer enjoyment and faux bashfulness surrounding their performance sets the pace for a story that maps the changing socioeconomics of these people and their respective shores.

CAMP is a collaborative studio that was founded in Mumbai in 2007 by Ashok Sukumaran and Shaina Anand. They explain the result of their experimental approach to stitching together the various videos with the following succinct phrase: 'These videos express that the world is big, and the screen is small'.

Sarah Perks

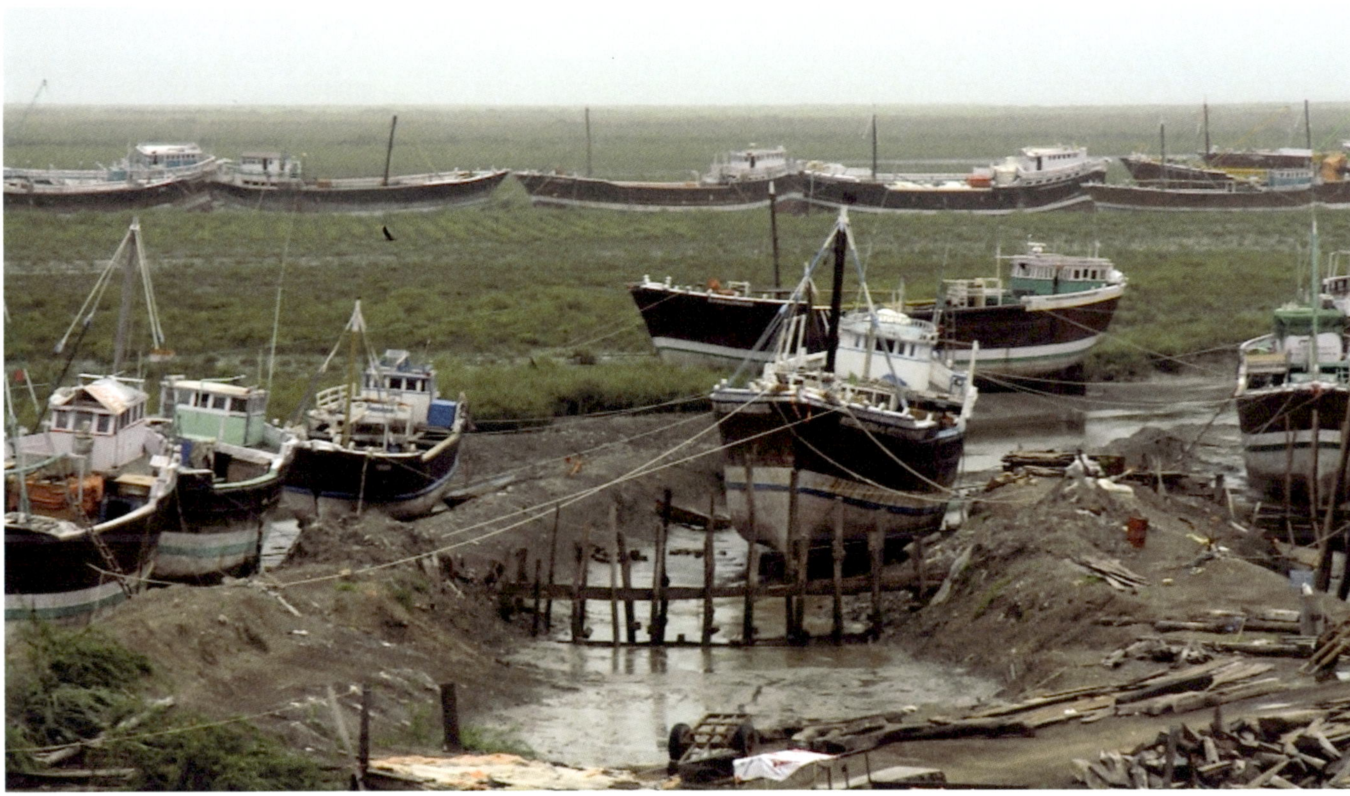

*From Gulf to Gulf to Gulf / Von Golf zu Golf zu Golf*, 2009–2013. Farbvideo-Projektion, Sound / Colour video projection, sound. 79 Minuten, 40 Sekunden / 79 minutes 40 seconds. Im Auftrag des Produktionsprogramms der Sharjah Art Foundation / Commissioned by Sharjah Art Foundation Production Programme

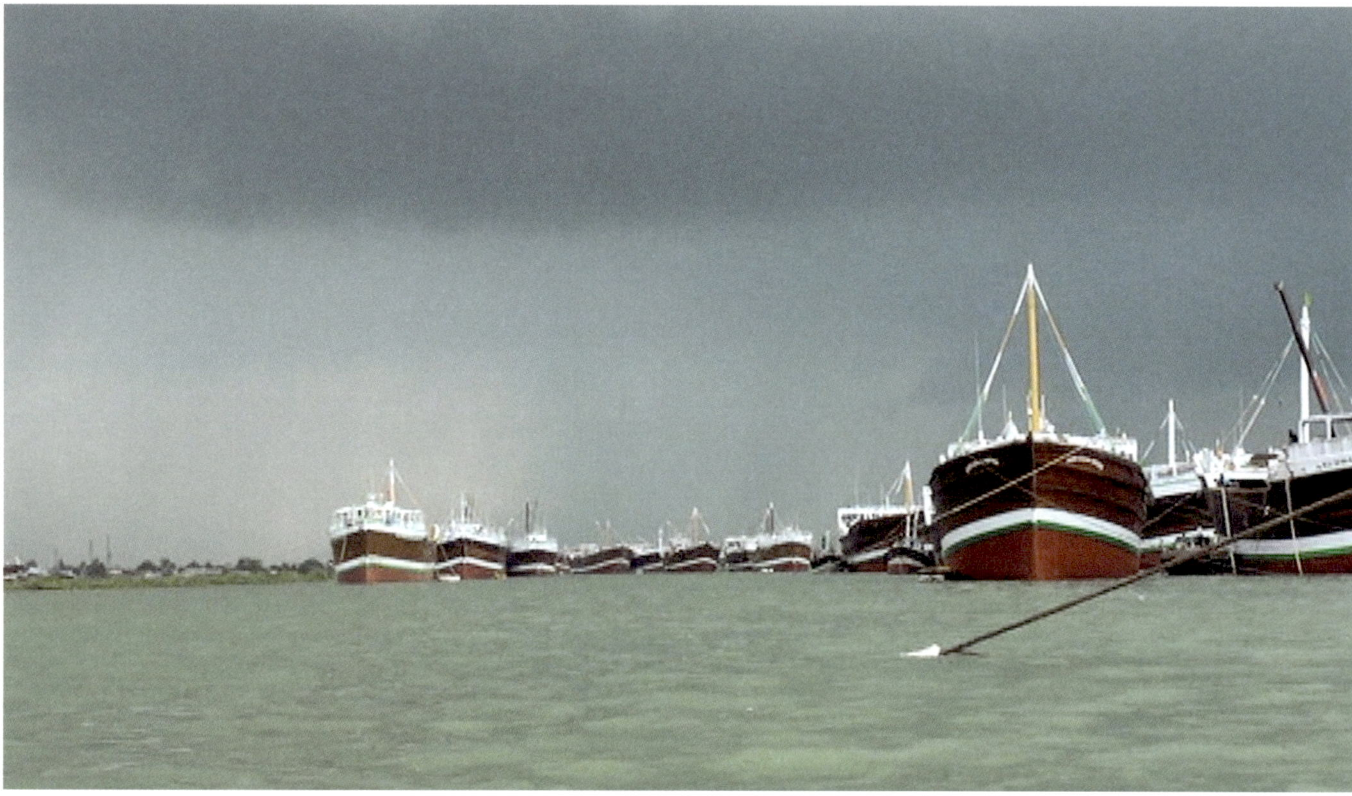

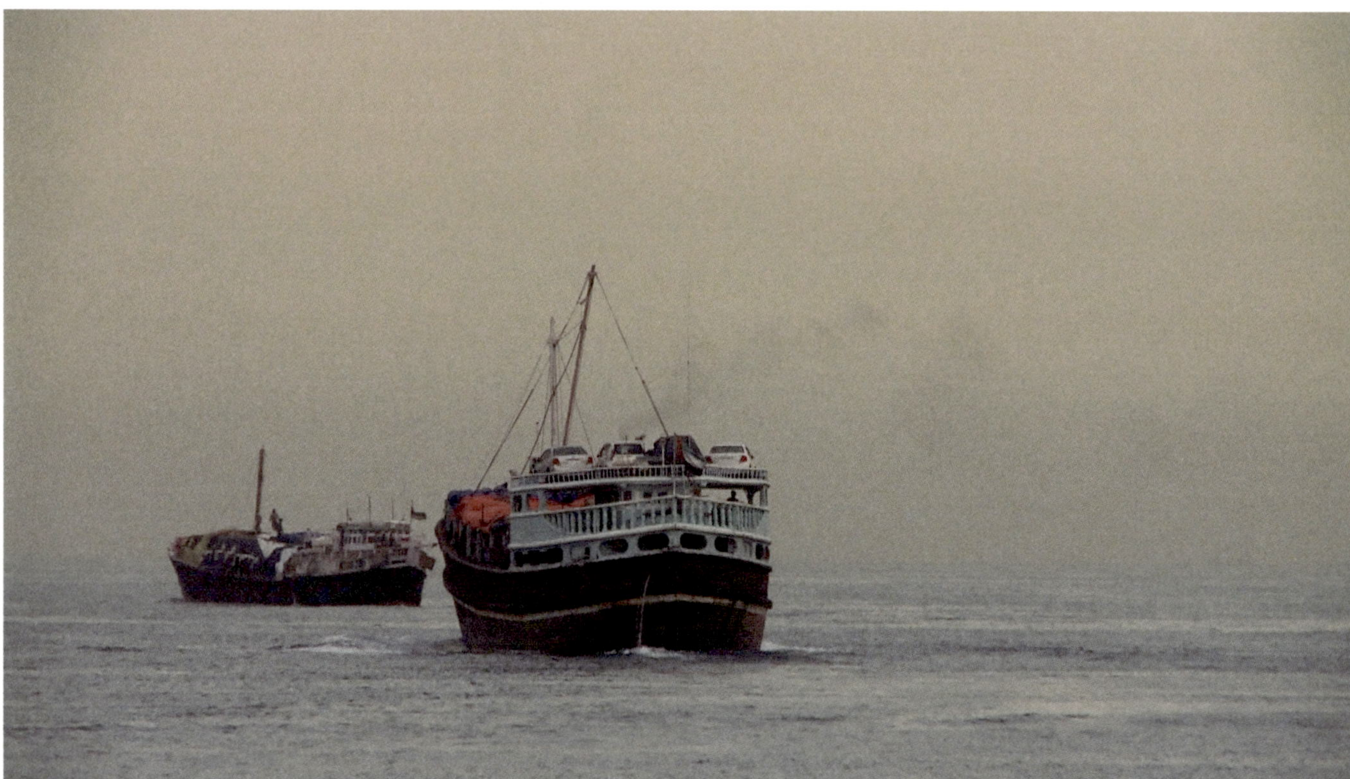

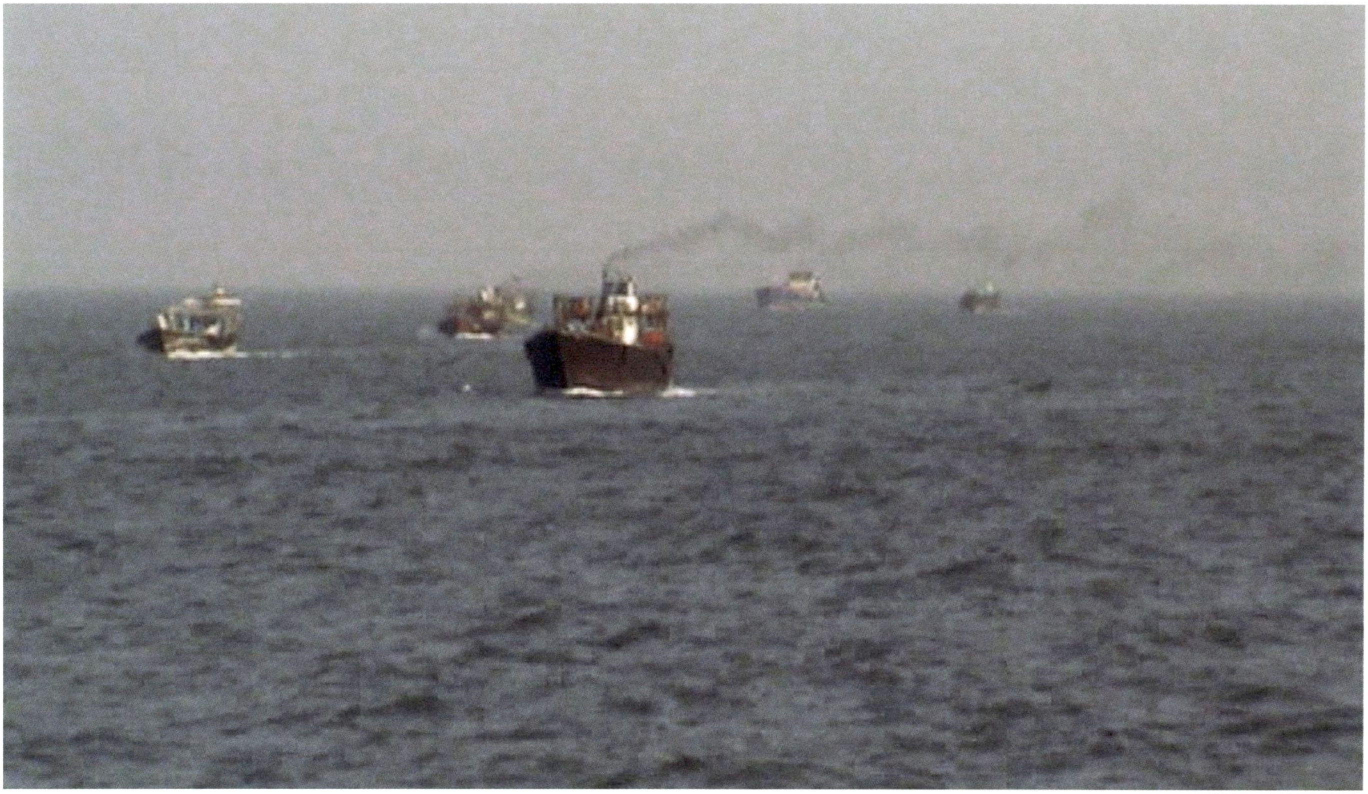

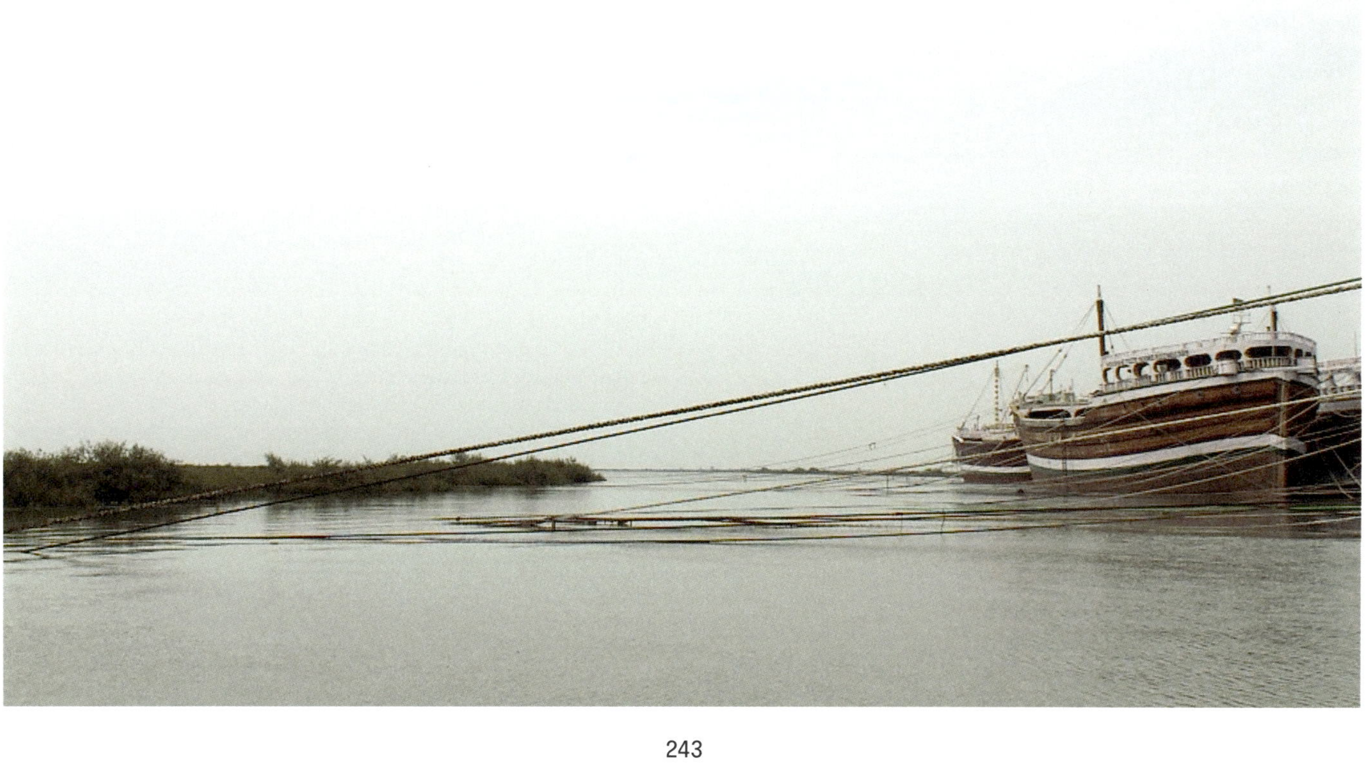

# Tony Chakar

*All that is Solid Melts into Air* („Alles was fest ist, löst sich in Luft auf", 2000), von Tony Chakar als „psycho-geografische Landkarte von Beirut" bezeichnet, existiert in verschiedenen Versionen. Für das *Hamra Street Project*, eine im Jahr 2000 vom Beiruter Kunstverein *Ashkal Alwan* organisierte Ausstellung von 13 Künstler*innen zur Geschichte dieser belebten Straße, reproduzierte Chakar den ersten modernen Stadtplan Beiruts. Die vom dänischen Konsul Julius Loytved gezeichnete Karte wurde 1876 mit einer Widmung an den osmanischen Sultan Abdul Hamid II. gedruckt. Chakar betont, dass sie nicht wie üblich genordet ist. Vielmehr liegt der Norden auf der Karte unten, wo sich die Küstenlinie Beiruts befindet – vielleicht eine Anspielung darauf, dass Loytved die Stadt vom Hafen aus betrat. Oder ein Verweis auf chinesische und arabische Konventionen, nach denen sich der Süden oben auf der Karte befindet.

Für das *Hamra Street Project* wurde Chakars Landkarte als Faltposter und als Druck in Schwarz-Weiß präsentiert, wobei der Künstler entlang der Straße runde Bilder platzierte – die meisten von modernen Gebäuden, mit Ausnahme der Kirche des heiligen Franz von Assisi. Am oberen Bildrand befinden sich kleine Texte, die Chakar aus einem Beutel mit Zitaten von Walter Benjamin, Karl Marx und Jean Baudrillard gezogen und in der entsprechenden Reihenfolge angeordnet hat. Im Rahmen von *On Becoming Two* („Über das Zweiwerden"), Chakars Ausstellung im Beirut Art Center von 2018, wurde die Karte zu einem Wandgemälde, dessen Text sich über den Bildrahmen hinaus auf die Wände der Galerie ausbreitete.

Bei dieser farbigen Reproduktion auf Leinwand mit denselben runden Schwarz-Weiß-Bildern entlang der Hamra Street ist der Text mit Bleistift geschrieben. Zu den Zitaten, die Landkarten generell als Konstrukt kritisieren, gehört eines von Roland Barthes, das Chakar durch die Wörter „Territorium" und „Karte" ergänzt hat. „Es schaudert mir vor einer Katastrophe, die bereits stattgefunden hat", heißt es in dem Satz. „Gleichviel, ob das Subjekt/Territorium, das sie erfährt, schon tot ist oder nicht, ist jegliche Fotografie/Karte diese Katastrophe."

*All that is Solid Melts into Air* (2000), which Tony Chakar has described as a 'psycho-geographic map of Beirut', has manifested in different forms. For *Hamra Street Project*, the 2000 exhibition organised by Beirut's Ashkal Alwan that invited 13 artists to respond to the history of one of Beirut's busiest streets, Chakar reproduced the first modern map of the city. Drawn by Danish Consul Julius Loytved, the map was printed in 1876 with a dedication to the Ottoman Sultan Abdul Hamid II. It does not follow the convention of placing north at the top, Chakar has pointed out. Rather, north is at the bottom, where Beirut's coastline is located—perhaps a reference to how Loytved entered the city from the port, or to Chinese and Arab map-making conventions where south points up.

For *Hamra Street Project*, Chakar's map was presented as a black-and-white fold-out poster and print, to which the artist added circular images along Hamra Street: mostly of modernist buildings, with the exception of the Church of St. Francis of Assisi. Written at the top of the image are lines of text Chakar created by pulling quotes from Walter Benjamin, Karl Marx and Jean Baudrillard, among others, out of a bag and ordering them in the sequence in which they were selected. As part of *On Becoming Two*, Chakar's 2018 exhibition at the Beirut Art Center, the map became a wall painting with text extending beyond the pictorial frame across the gallery's walls.

In this colour reproduction on canvas, with the same black-and-white circular images lining Hamra Street, text is written in pencil. Lines critiquing the map as a construct include a Roland Barthes quote, into which Chakar inserts the words 'territory' and 'map'. 'I shudder over a catastrophe which has already occurred', the sentence reads. 'Whether or not the subject/territory is already dead, every photograph/map is this catastrophe'.

Stephanie Bailey

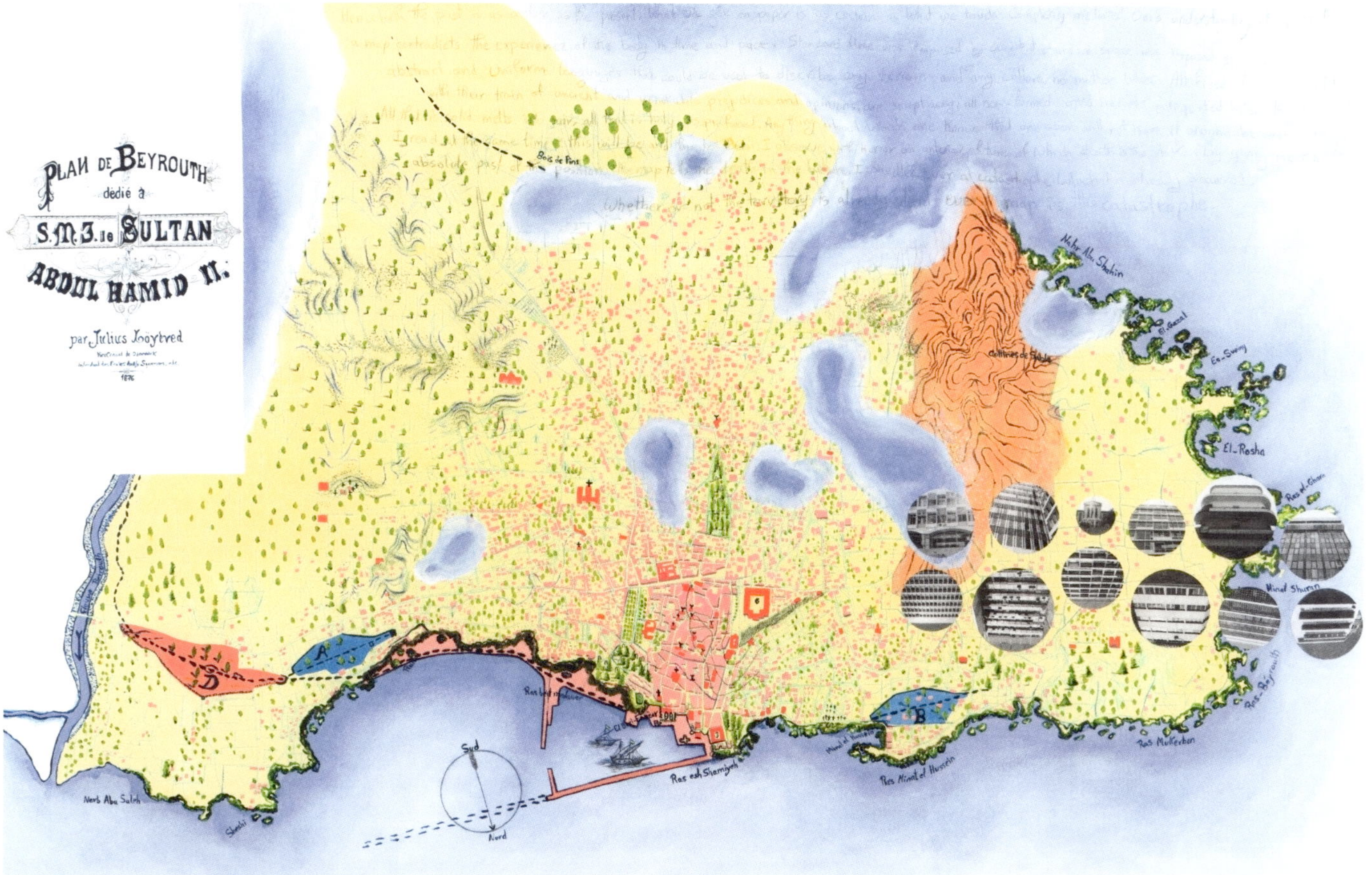


*All that is Solid Melts into Air | Alles, was fest ist, löst sich in Luft auf*, 2000. Acryl und andere Materialien auf Leinwand / Acrylic and other materials on canvas. 150 × 100 cm

# Rokni Haerizadeh

Im Rahmen der Ausstellung wird *Cursed into Slum2* („Verbannt in den Slum2“, 2011) präsentiert, ein multimediales Werk von Rokni Haerizadeh aus seiner charakteristischen *Fictionville*-Serie. Mit diesem Tableau, das aus neun in verschiedenen Techniken angefertigten Gemälden besteht, macht sich Haerizadeh Gedanken darüber, wie menschliches Leid in den Mainstreammedien ausgebeutet wird. Der Künstler verwendet Ausschnitte aus Fotografien, um Collagen aus sich überlagernden Formen zu schaffen und damit eine ganz eigene surrealistische Welt zu erfinden. Das Werk entstand im Jahr 2009 nach der Grünen Revolution im Iran und zur Zeit der arabischen Aufstände, die 2010 in Tunesien begannen und sich 2011 von Ägypten in weitere Länder ausbreiteten – also zu einem historischen Zeitpunkt, als Bilder im Zuge ihrer massenhaften Verbreitung eine neue Bedeutung erhielten.

Haerizadeh verwendet bei jedem Bild Schichten von Gesso und Kleber und arbeitet mit spontanen malerischen Gesten, die aus den Gewaltfantasien abgeleitet sind, welche hier als humorvolle, an die Seiten eines satirischen politischen Magazins erinnernde Szenen dargestellt werden. Man könnte annehmen, dass diese Bilder eine schonungslose Kritik an der politischen Instrumentalisierung und der Gewalt gegen die verschiedenen Bevölkerungsgruppen im Iran, im Kaukasus und generell in Westasien darstellen.

Haerizadeh ist allgemein für seine detaillierten, sorgfältig konzipierten und gestalteten Gemälde bekannt, in denen er antike Mythen und Sagengestalten mit Bezügen zum zeitgenössischen Film und zu epischen Erzählungen der modernen Geschichte verbindet. Seine Arbeiten sind eine kritische Auseinandersetzung mit seiner Heimat Iran – insbesondere mit Blick auf das Thema Geschlechterdiskriminierung. In *Cursed into Slum2* (2011) hat sich der Kopf eines Politikers in den eines Schweins verwandelt, eine beliebte Darstellung des „Bösen“ in der Kunst der Karikatur.

Haerizadeh erweitert seine künstlerische Arbeit in Kooperationen mit seinem Bruder Ramin Haerizadeh und dem gemeinsamen Freund Hesam Rahmanian. Das Trio lebt und arbeitet zusammen und erklärt: „In unserer Arbeit geht es darum, großzügig zu sein und das Leben zu zelebrieren. Es geht um die Hinwendung zu anderen Menschen als Antwort auf die Herausforderungen der Welt, in der wir alle leben. In gewisser Weise geht es auch darum, uns selbst aus dem Mittelpunkt des Denkens zu nehmen und eine Leere zu schaffen, in der wir andere schätzen können.“

Presented in the exhibition hall is *Cursed into Slum2* (2011), a multimedia work by Rokni Haerizadeh taken from his recognisable *Fictionville* series. Consisting of nine multimedia paintings, this constellation of images presents Haerizadeh's reflections on how human suffering is exploited in mainstream media. The artist uses photographic cut-outs to create collages of interpolating forms—inventing a distinctive surrealist realm all his own. Produced after the 2009 Green Revolution in Iran and at the same time as the Arab Uprisings, which began in 2010 in Tunisia and spread throughout Egypt and beyond in 2011, this work was created at a timely historical juncture, when images began to take on new meaning in an age of mass circulation.

Haerizadeh uses layers of gesso and bonding on each piece, as well as spontaneous painterly gestures conjured from violent imaginaries, reconceived here as humorous scenes that could resemble the pages of a satirical political magazine. One could infer that these images form a brutal critique of political exploitation and the violence presented against the multiple publics of Iran, the Caucuses and, more broadly, across western Asia.

The artist is popularly known for his detailed paintings, carefully structured and constituted, that layer ancient myths and legendary figures alongside references from contemporary cinema and epic tales of modern history. His works proffer critiques of his home of Iran—in particular, considerations of the issue of gender discrimination. In *Cursed into Slum2* (2011) a politician's head is transmuted into a pig's, a popular invocation of 'evil' in the art of caricature.

Haerizadeh's practice is expanded through collaborations with his brother, Ramin Haerizadeh, and their friend, Hesam Rahmanian. Living and working together, the trio have noted: 'Our work is about generosity and celebration, to embrace other people as an answer to the challenges of the world in which we all live. In a way, this is about decentring yourself, allowing a hollowness to make space to appreciate others'.

Omar Kholeif with Reem Sawan

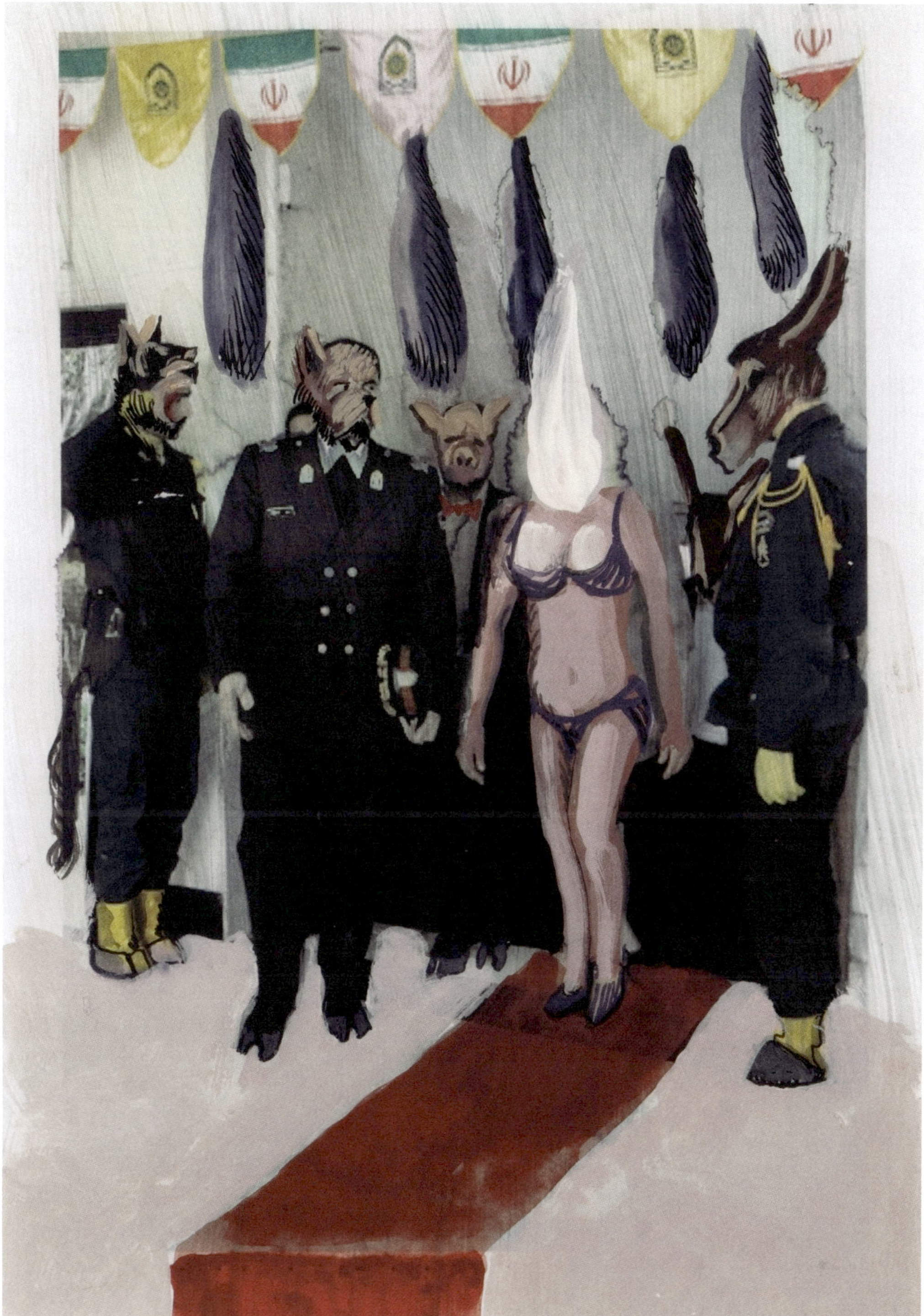

*Cursed into Slum* / *Verbannt in den Slum*, 2011. Aus / From *Fictionville*. 9 Abzüge, Gesso, Aquarellfarbe und Tinte auf Papier / 9 prints, gesso, watercolour and ink on paper. 8 Abzüge jeweils 30 × 21 cm; 1 Abzug 21 × 30 cm / 8 prints 30 × 21 cm each; 1 print 21 × 30 cm

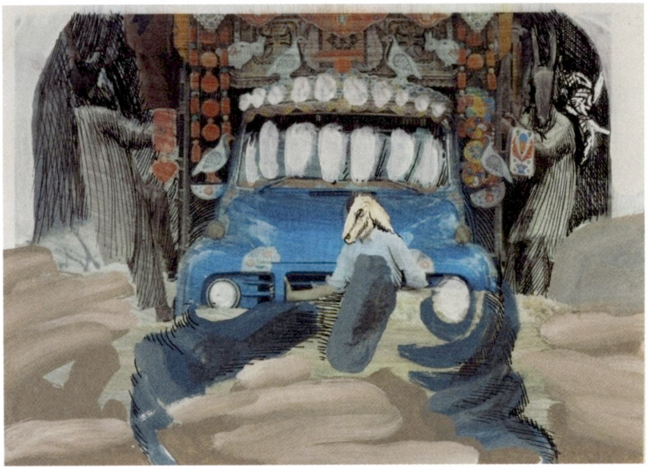

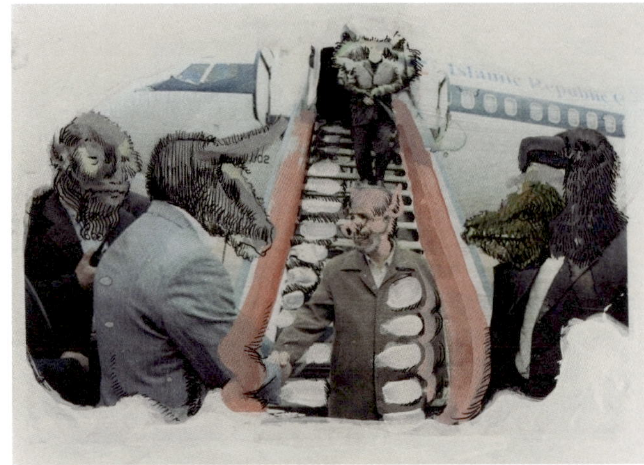

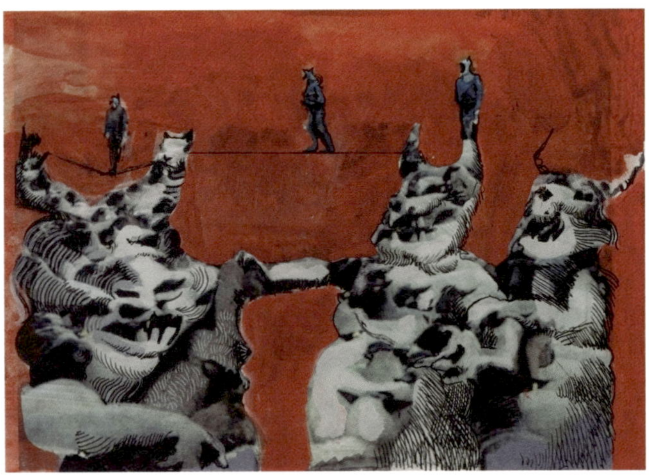

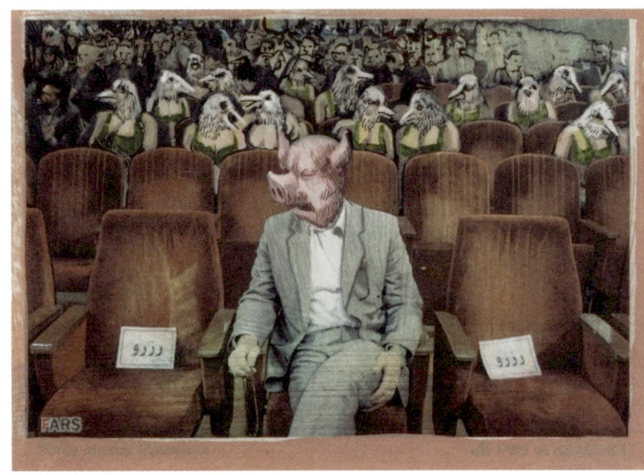
FARS

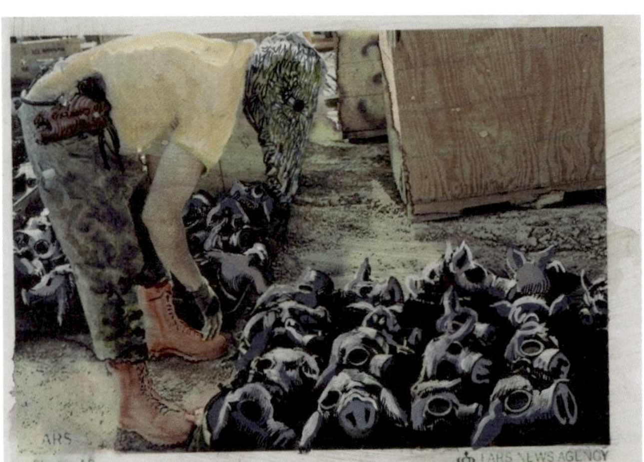
FARS
Photo : AP
FARS NEWS AGENCY

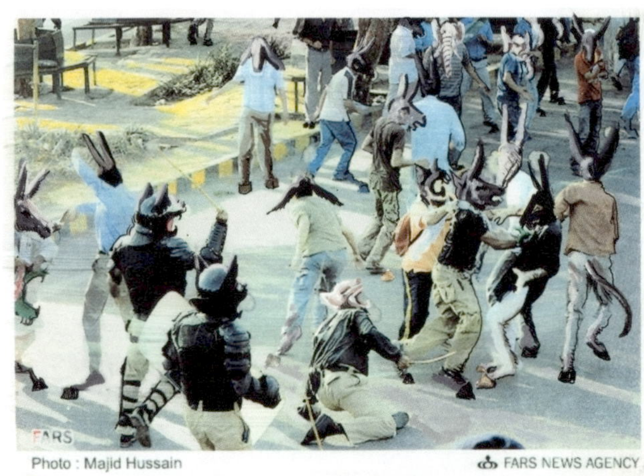
FARS
Photo : Majid Hussain
FARS NEWS AGENCY

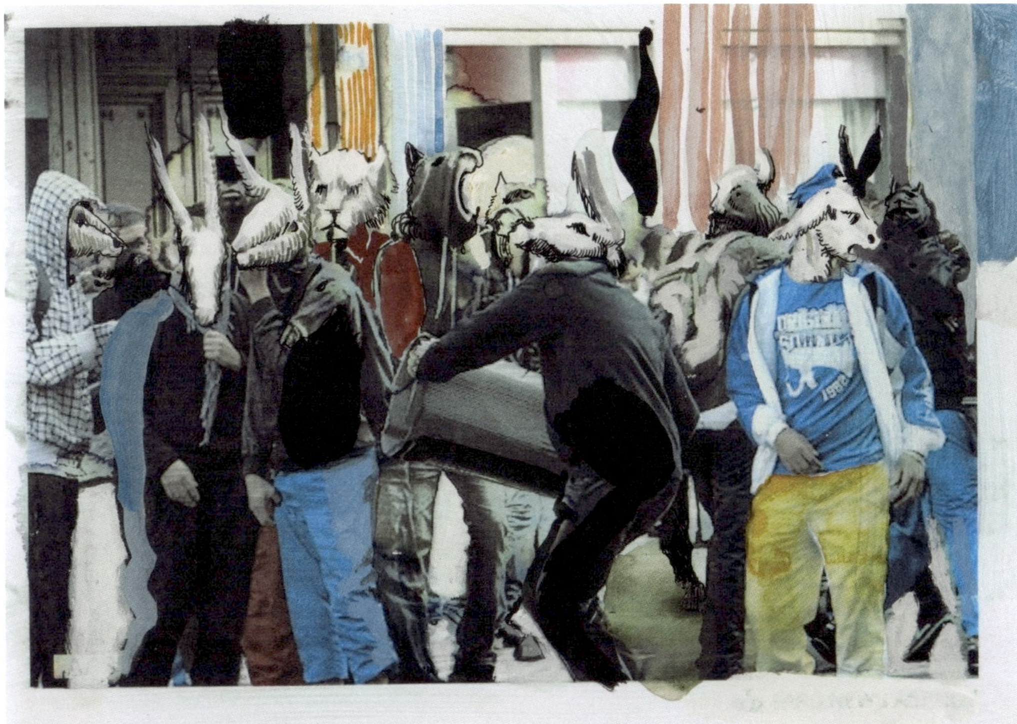

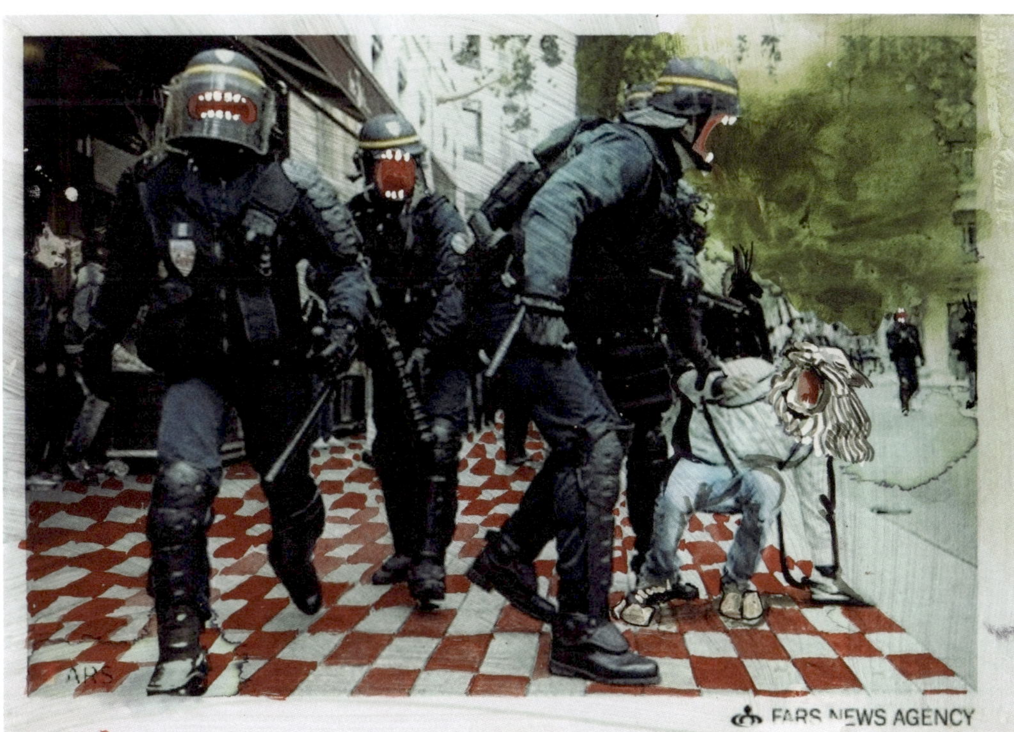
FARS NEWS AGENCY

Text siehe S. 168
see p. 168

# Joana Hadjithomas & Khalil Joreige

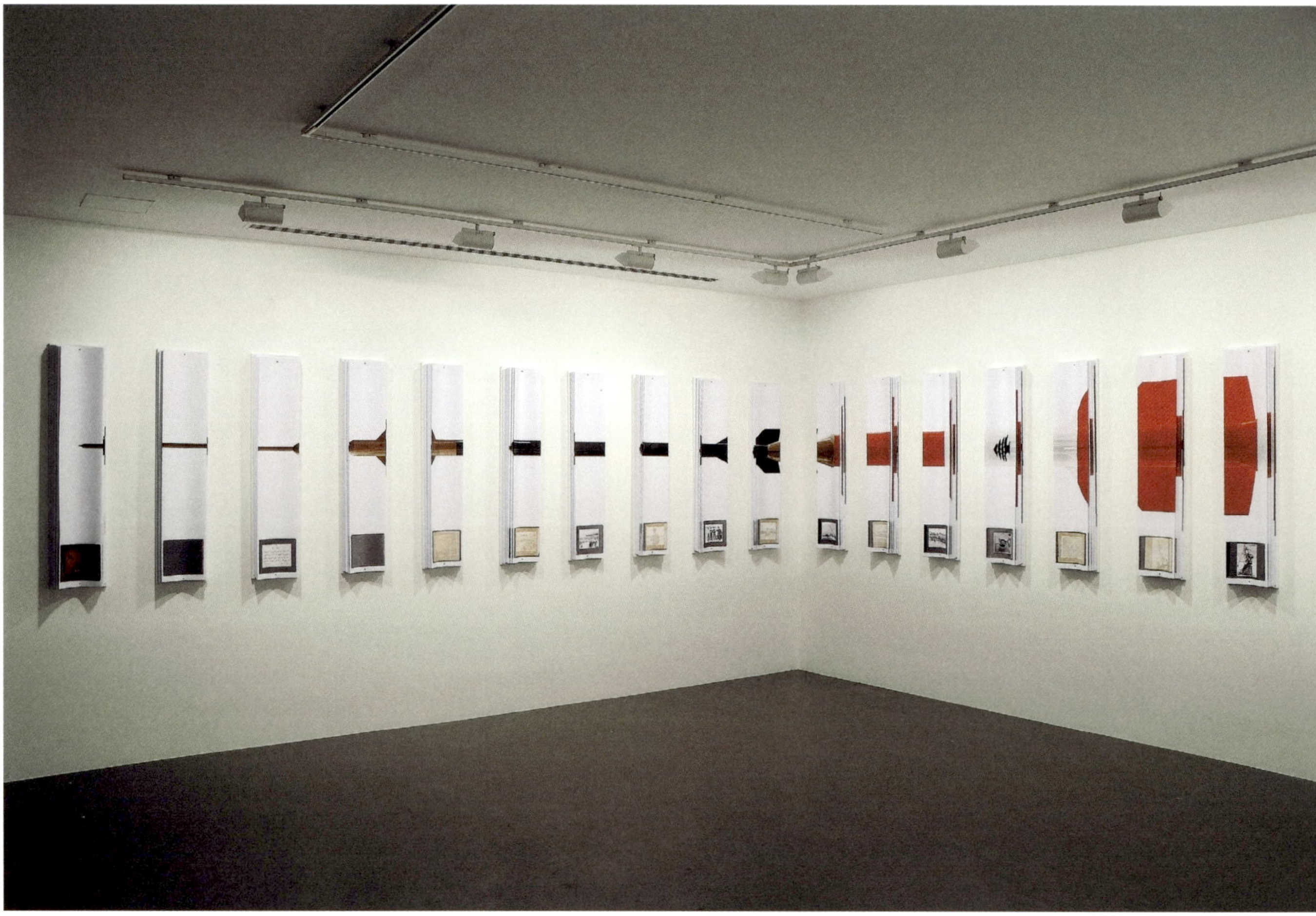

*Lebanese Rocket Society: The President's Album* / *Lebanese Rocket Society: Das Album des Präsidenten*, 2011. 32 Digitalabzüge, auf Holz gefaltet / 32 digital prints, folded on wood. Jeweils / each 141 x 41 x 12,7 cm / 141 x 41 x 12,7 cm. Produziert von der Sharjah Art Foundation / Produced by Sharjah Art Foundation. Installationsansicht / Installation view, *Two Suns in a Sunset*, Sharjah Art Foundation, 2016.

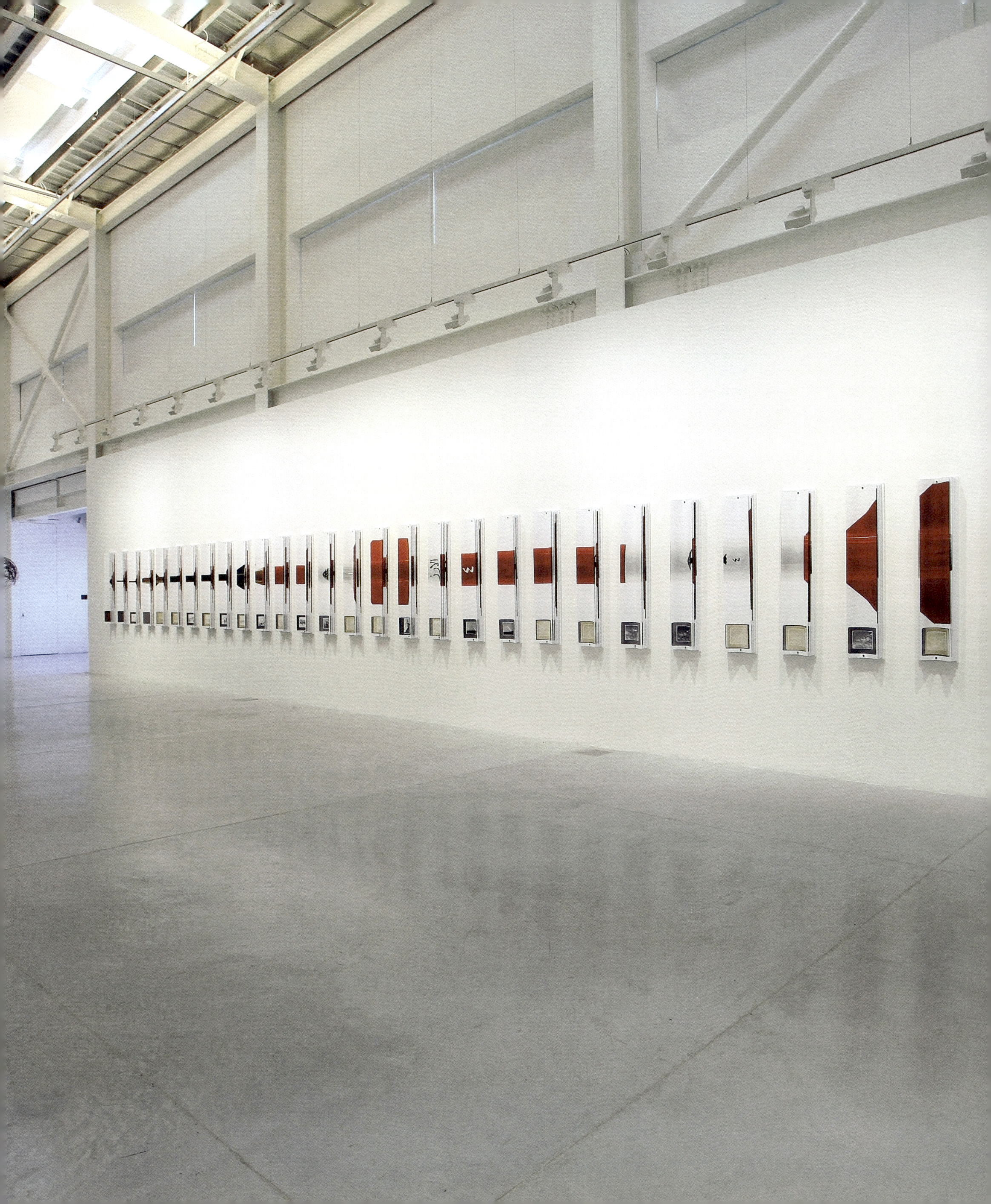

# Taloi Havini

Die Werke Taloi Havinis setzten sich mit den Wissens- und Produktionsökonomien des vor- und nachkolonialen Melanesiens auseinander, einer Unterregion Ozeaniens im südwestlichen Pazifik, zu der die heute gemeinhin als unabhängig bezeichneten Länder Fidschi, Vanuatu, die Salomonen und Papua-Neuguinea gehören. Havinis Praxis besteht bei jedem Projekt darin, dass zunächst umfangreiche Archiv- und Geschichtsrecherchen durchgeführt und dabei Fälle von Umweltzerstörung und Menschenrechtsverletzungen aufgedeckt werden, deren Nachwirkungen durch die Geschichte bis ins heutige Leben hineinreichen.

Die von der Sharjah Art Foundation für die 13. *Sharjah Biennial* nachgebildete und nun hier gezeigte Arbeit *Beroana (Shell Money) IV* („*Beroana [Muschelgeld] IV*", 2016) bezieht sich auf eine Muschelwährung, die auf der Insel Buka in der Autonomen Region Bougainville verwendet wurde, der Heimat der Künstlerin, von der sie während des Bürgerkriegs auf Bougainville (1988–1998) mit ihrer Familie nach Australien übersiedelte. Die an Stahldraht von der Decke hinabhängende Spirale mit Hunderten daran aufgereihten Perlen aus glasiertem Steingut, Ton und Porzellan beschwört eine andere Finanzordnung. Den Betrachter*innen wird hier eine verkörperte und mühsame Erfahrung präsentiert, die meist mit der Arbeit von Frauen in Verbindung gebracht wird, denen die Aufgabe zufällt, die Muscheln zu sammeln, von Hand zu schleifen und zu formen und Löcher in sie zu bohren – eine Arbeitsleistung, die den großen globalen Formen des heutigen Finanzwesens widerspricht. In der von Christine Tohmé, Kuratorin der Biennale, als „Wirbel" oder „Wirbelwind" von eleganter „Stille" bezeichneten Installation spiegelt sich sowohl die jüngere Tagebaugeschichte Bougainvilles (1969–1989) als auch die Geschichte dieser Muscheln als Artefakte. Heute werden sie häufig von Museen im südwestpazifischen Raum gesammelt.

Taloi Havini's artworks explore the economies of knowledge and production of pre- and post-colonial Melanesia, a subregion of Oceania in the southwestern Pacific Ocean, home to what today are commonly referred to as the independent countries of Fiji, Vanuatu, the Solomon Islands and Papua New Guinea. Undertaking extensive archival and historical research at the outset of each project, Havini's practice reveals instances of ecological destruction and human rights abuses, which continue to echo and resound throughout history into the life of the present.

Exhibited and reproduced by Sharjah Art Foundation for Sharjah Biennial 13, *Beroana (Shell Money) IV* (2016) refers to a shell-based currency that was used on the Buka Island in the Autonomous Region of Bougainville, where the artist was born before relocating with her family to Australia during the Bougainville civil war (1988–98). The rounded spire of stoneware, earthenware, porcelain and glaze hangs from steel wire, evoking a different financial order. Here, the spectator is presented with an embodied and laboured experience, most often associated with the work of women who are taxed with collecting, grinding, shaping and drilling these shells by hand, an act that contradicts major global examples of financial order in the contemporary sphere. Referred to by SB13 curator Christine Tohmé as a 'vortex' and a 'whirlwind' of elegant 'stillness', the installation reflects Bougainville's recent history of mining (1969–89) as much as it reflects these shells as artifact. Today, they are commonly collected by museums in the Southwest Pacific Basin.

Omar Kholeif

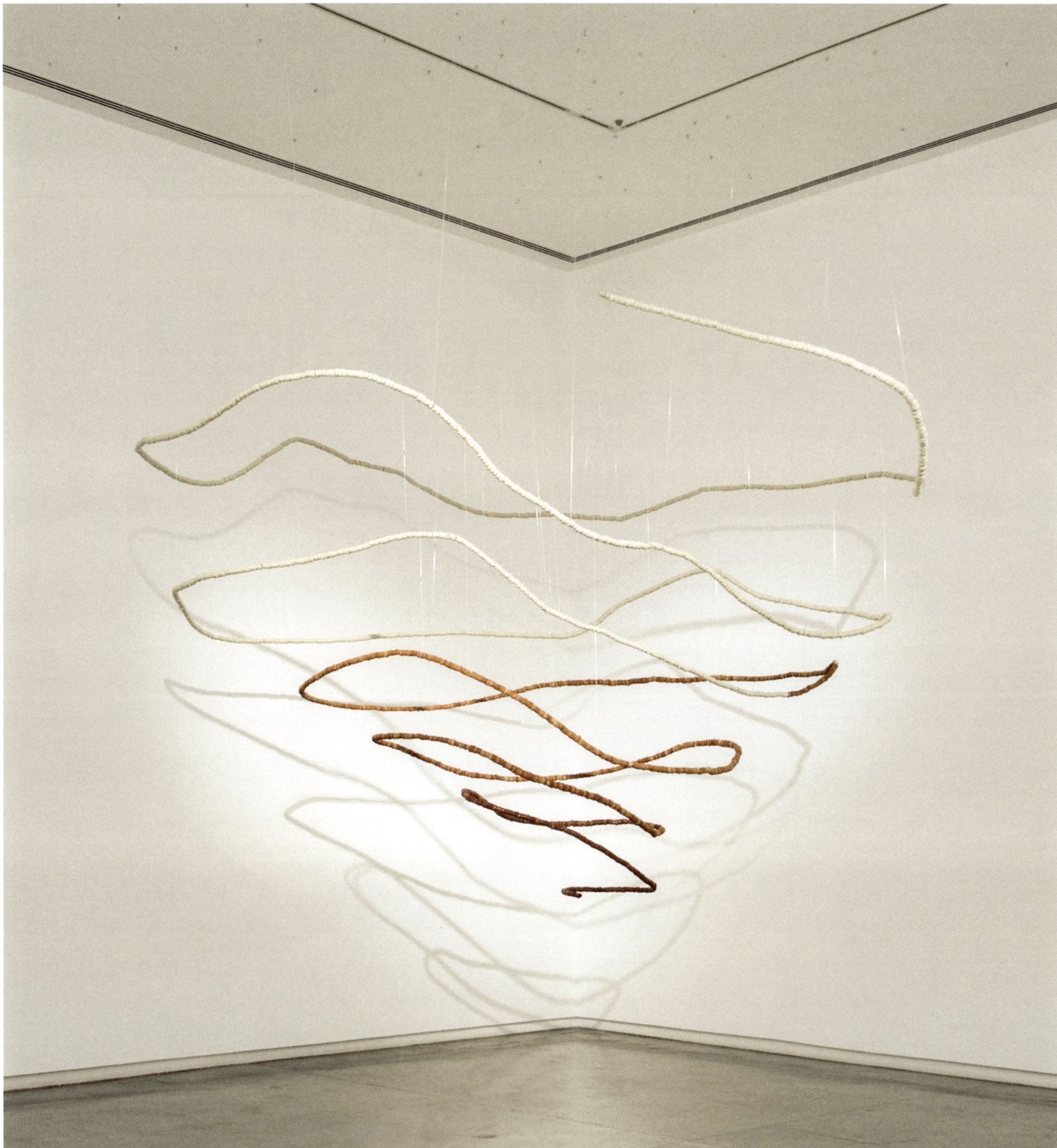

Taloi Havini, *Beroana (Shell money) IV / Beroana (Muscheldgeld) IV*, 2016. Steinzeug, Steingut, klare Glasur, Stahldraht / Stoneware, earthenware, cleare glaze, steel wire. Maße variabel / Dimensions variable. Reproduziert von / Reproduced by Sharjah Art Foundation

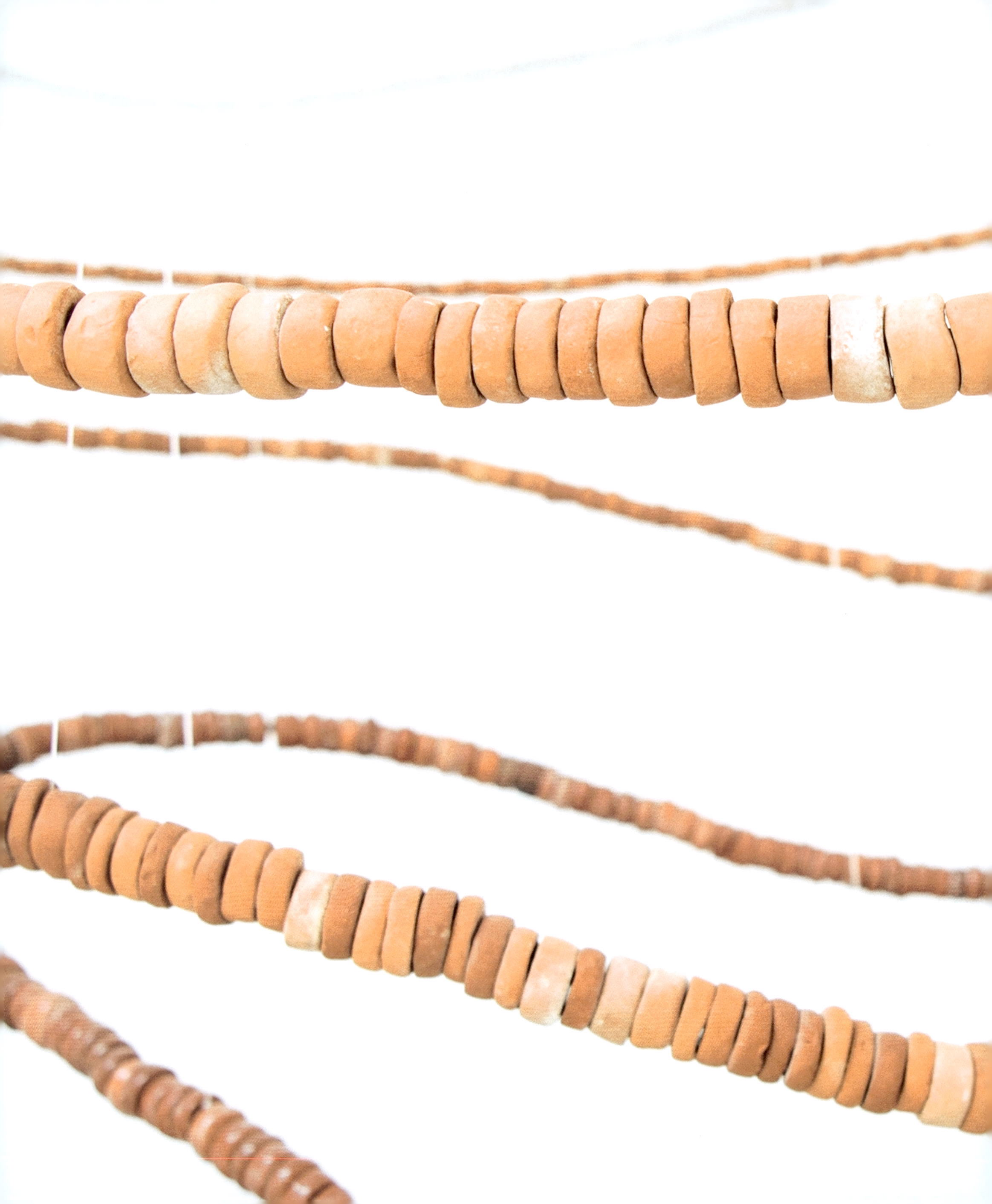

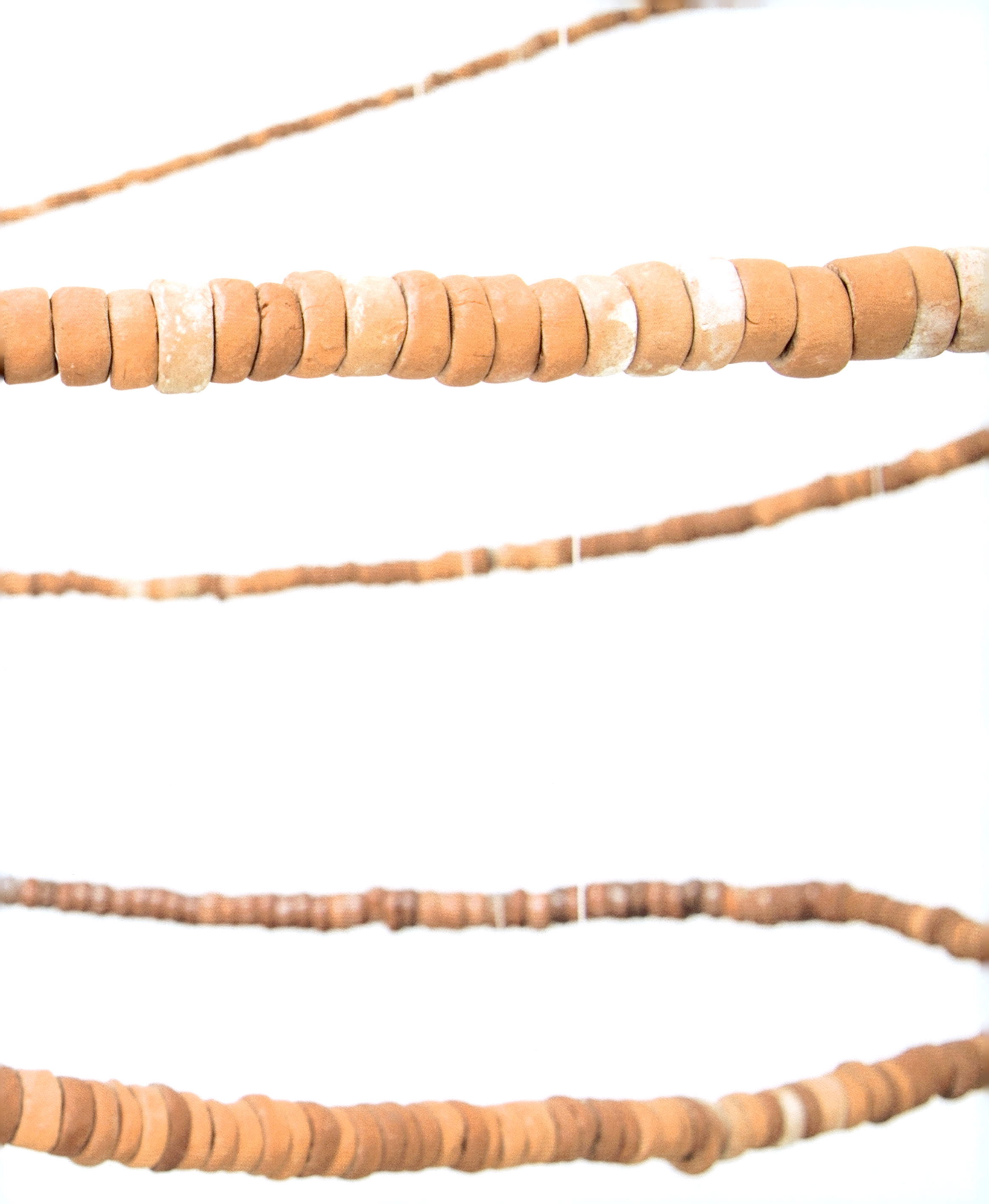

# Emily Jacir

*Lydda Airport* („Flughafen Lydda", 2009) ist eine zweiteilige Installation, die aus einem Kurzfilm und einem skulpturalen Modell des gleichnamigen Flughafens auf einem Tisch in einiger Entfernung hinter der Leinwand besteht. In dem schwarz-weißen Stummfilm hält eine von der Künstlerin Emily Jacir dargestellte Figur einen Blumenstrauß in der Hand, während auf dem Hintergrund, der wie die Archivaufnahme eines Passagierflugzeugs aussieht, die Worte „Palestine Airways Limited" auf Arabisch, Englisch und Hebräisch zu lesen sind. Doch es landen keine Flugzeuge. Der Flughafen Lydda, heute Flughafen Ben Gurion in Tel Aviv, wurde 1936 von den Briten als wichtige Station ihrer Imperial Airways Empire Route gebaut und war damals der größte Flugplatz der Welt.

Jacirs Arbeit wurde von zwei Geschichten über das Verschwinden inspiriert. Die erste erzählte der palästinensische Soziologe Salim Tamari der Künstlerin über seinen Vater Edmond, einen Flughafenangestellten aus Jaffa. Edmond sollte die berühmte US-amerikanische Fliegerin Amelia Earhart bei ihrer Landung auf dem Flughafen in Empfang nehmen. Diese verschwand jedoch während ihres Fluges im Juli 1937; sie kam nie an und wurde nie gefunden. Das Flugzeug im Film ist ein Short-Scion-Eindecker, wurde aber von der Geschichte der Hannibal inspiriert – dem Prototyp des damals größten Passagierflugzeugs der Welt, der Handley Page H.P.42 –, die während eines Linienflugs nach Sharjah über dem Golf von Oman verschwand und ebenfalls nie gefunden wurde.

*Lydda Airport* ruft Gefühle der Wiederkehr, Erwartung und Unruhe hervor. Die Betrachter*innen werden hier in eine kreisförmige Reisebewegung gezwungen, in der die Zeit stillzustehen scheint. Die detaillierten Recherchen auf verschiedenen Ebenen untermauern die Künstlichkeit des Werks, indem sie die Videoprojektion mit der monochromen geisterhaften Flughafenskulptur kombinieren, um bewusst die Grenzen zwischen Fakten und Fiktion, Vergangenheit und Gegenwart zu verwischen.

*Lydda Airport* (2009) is a two-part installation that begins with a short film and is followed, a short distance away and behind the screen, by a sculptural model of the titular airport on a table. In the silent, black-and-white film, a character played by the artist Emily Jacir herself holds a bouquet of flowers while on the backdrop, which resembles archival footage of a passenger airplane, read the words 'Palestine Airways Limited', written in Arabic, English and Hebrew. Yet no airplanes land. Lydda Airport, now named Ben Gurion, was built in 1936 by the British, a vital element of their Imperial Airways Empire Route and, at the time, the world's largest aerodrome.

Jacir's work is inspired by two stories of disappearance, the first told to the artist by Palestinian sociologist Salim Tamari about his father Edmond, an airport worker from Jaffa. Edmond was sent to greet the famous US aviator Amelia Earhart as she was due to land there; she disappeared, however, whilst flying in July 1937. She never arrived and has never been found. The aircraft in the film is a Short Scion monoplane, but is inspired by the story of the Hannibal, the prototype of the Handley Page H.P.42 passenger aircraft, at the time the largest in the world, which disappeared on a scheduled flight en route to Sharjah over the Gulf of Oman and was never found.

Repetition, expectation and restlessness are feelings evoked by *Lydda Airport*. Here, the viewer is forced into a circular motion of travel, suspended in time. The detailed layers of research rally the artifice of the work, demonstrating the collusion of the video projection and the monochrome, ghost-like airport sculpture, to intentionally blur fact and fiction, past and present.

Sarah Perks

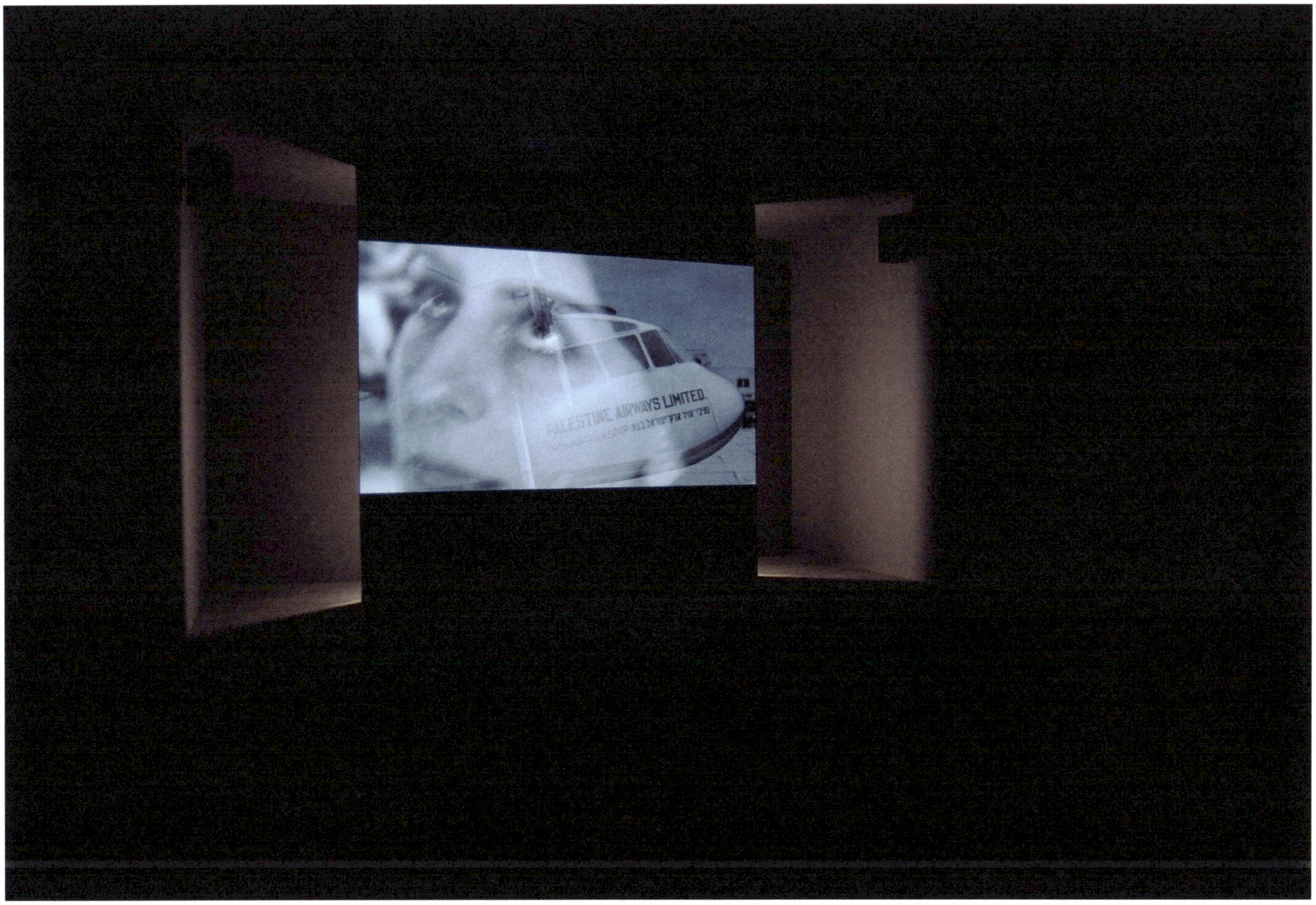


*Lydda Airport* / *Flughafen Lydda*, 2009. Skulptur, Harz, Glasfaser; Einkanal-Animation / Sculpture, resin, fiberglass; single-channel animation. 155,6 × 33 × 76,8 cm. 5 Minuten, 21 Sekunden / 5 minutes 21 seconds. Im Auftrag des Pick Laudati Fund for Arts Computing, Northwestern University / Commissioned by the Pick Laudati Fund for Arts Computing, Northwestern University. Installationsansicht / Installation view, Sharjah Biennial 10, Sharjah Art Foundation, 2011.

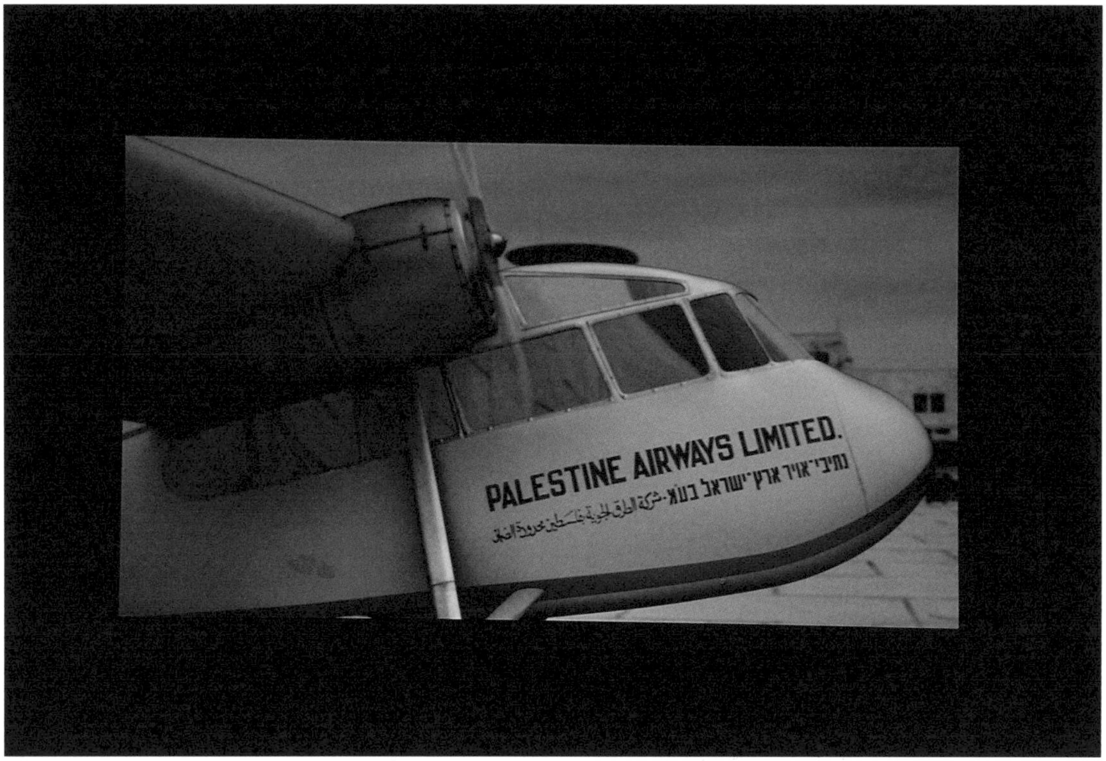
PALESTINE AIRWAYS LIMITED.

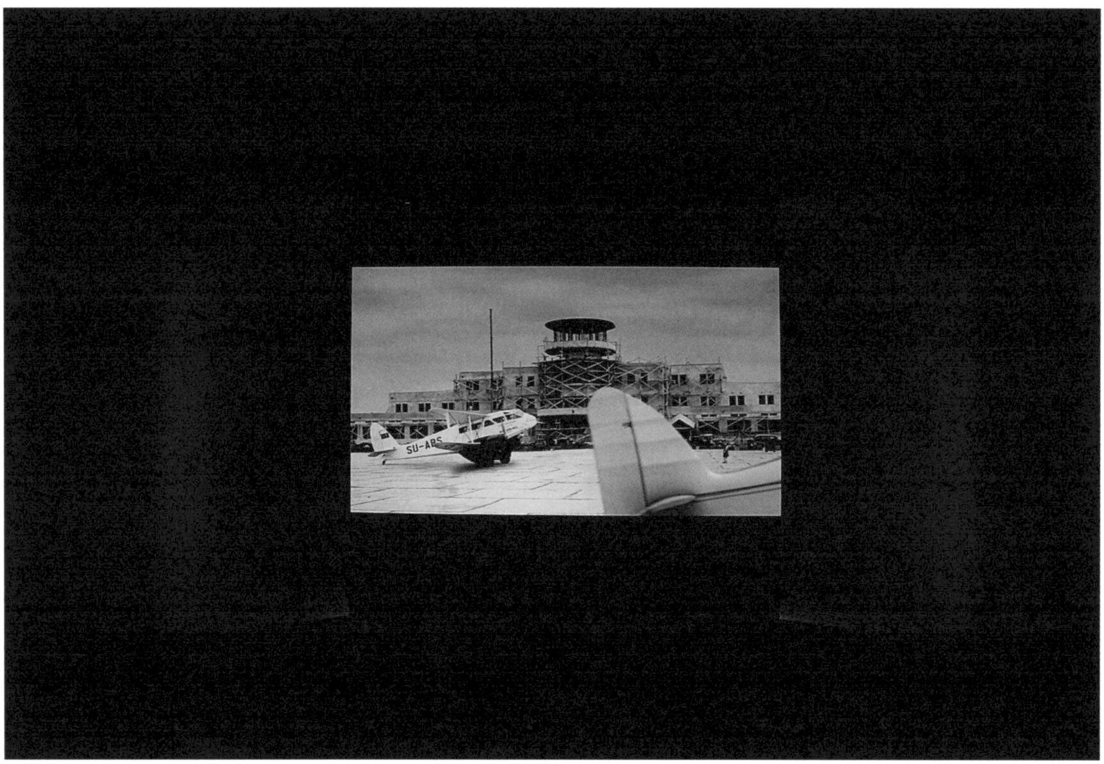

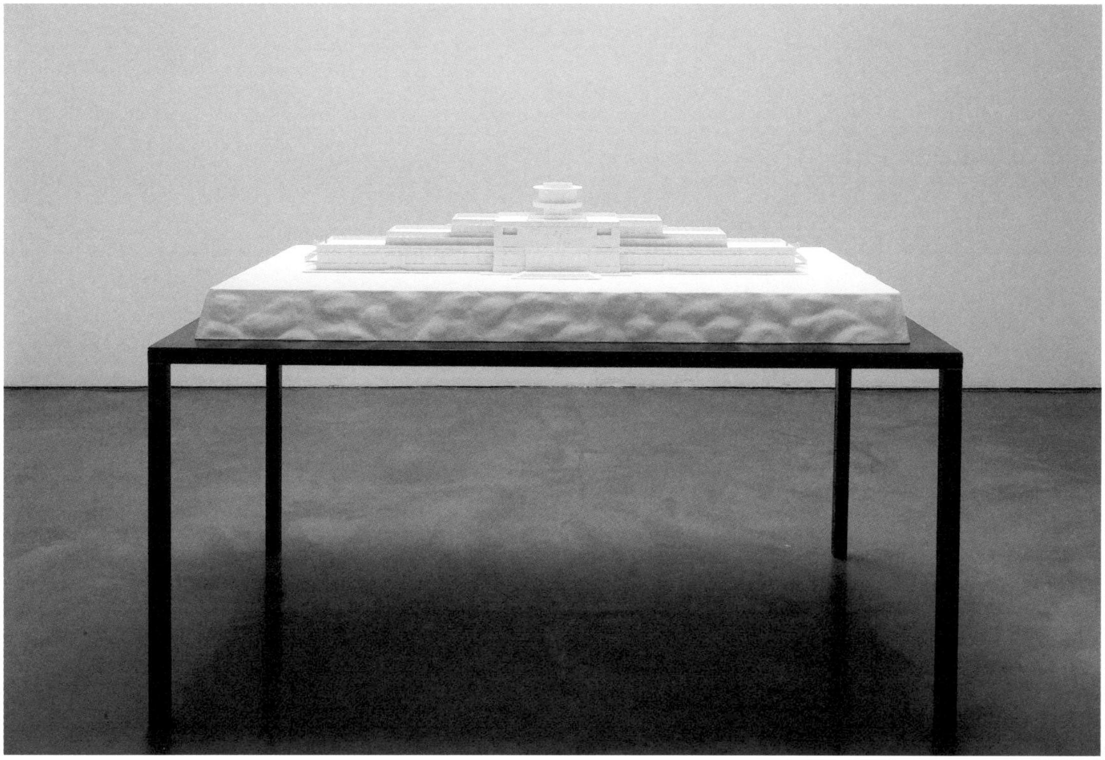

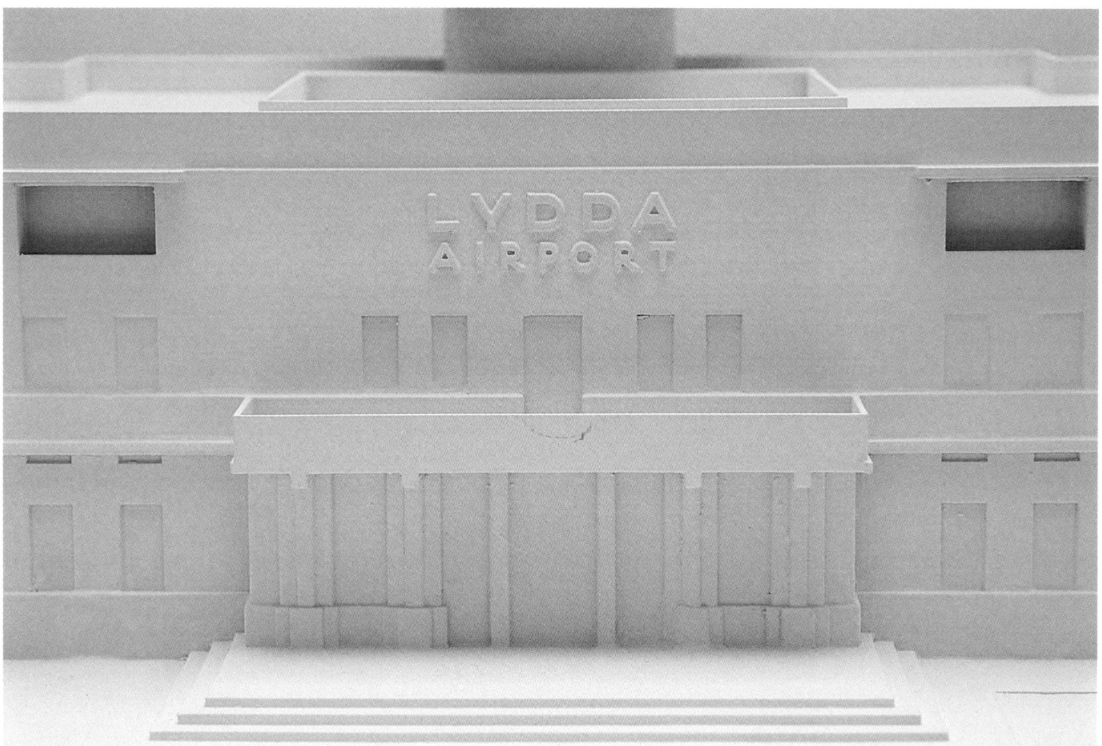
LYDDA
AIRPORT

# Amal Kenawy

Drei Werke der verstorbenen Multimediakünstlerin Amal Kenawy zeigen, wie sie die physischen und psychologischen Darstellungen ihrer selbst als Mittel zur Erforschung von Fragen der Macht, Gewalt und Unterdrückung einsetzt. Ihr Künstlerinnenbuch *Cairo Is Eating Me* („Kairo frisst mich auf", o.D.) entfaltet sich wie eine Ziehharmonika und offenbart ihre Notizen, Pläne und geheimsten Gedanken. *You Will Be Killed* („Du wirst getötet werden", 2006), eine animierte Videoarbeit, ist ein Zusammenschnitt ihrer Zeichnungen und Bilder, auf denen eine von der Künstlerin dargestellte gefangene weibliche Figur immer wiederkehrt. Ebenfalls zu sehen ist das großformatige Gemälde auf Leinwand *You Will Be Killed 2* (Mitte der 2000er Jahre), ein Selbstporträt der Künstlerin, die – offenbar flach am Boden liegend, möglicherweise bewusstlos –, zwischen Leben und Tod zu schweben scheint.

*You Will Be Killed* ist eine Werkgruppe, die Kenawy rund um ein Militärkrankenhaus schuf, das die Briten in den 1980er Jahren in Kairo errichteten. Während der Schauplatz die Aufmerksamkeit auf die Zerstörung und Heilung des physischen Körpers nach einem Kampf lenkt, drängt die Künstlerin zur Reflexion über die anhaltende Wirkung von psychischer Gewalt, indem sie zeigt, wie sie am Boden liegend in ihrem eigenen Bild gefangen ist und Zeichnungen der Träume und Sehnsüchte anderer entwirft. Trotz der temporeichen Verschmelzung der Formate in ihrem Video konzentriert sich Kenawy streng auf die Vermittlung von Ideen; die gewählte Technik war lediglich diejenige, die ihr Thema nach eigenen Angaben am besten zum Ausdruck bringen konnte.

Kenawy, die im Alter von nur 39 Jahren einer Krankheit erlag, entwickelte ein komplexes künstlerisches Verfahren an der Schnittstelle zwischen persönlicher Geschichte, Erinnerung und der performativen Kraft künstlerischer Darstellung. Sie war zu einer Zeit aktiv, als es noch möglich war, Kunst über Ägypten zu produzieren, ohne sich vor Zensur, Festnahme oder Inhaftierung fürchten zu müssen. Kenawys Arbeit war eng mit der in den späten 1990er und 2000er Jahren pulsierenden unabhängigen Kunstszene in Kairo verbunden, in der die Künstler*innen neue Medienformate erkundeten und neben der staatlich gelenkten Kunstszene auch alternative Räume etablierten.

Three works by the late multimedia artist Amal Kenawy display the use of her own physical and psychological portraits as a conduit through which to explore questions of power, violence and suppression. An artist book, *Cairo Is Eating Me* (n.d.), unfolds concertina style to display her notes, plans and innermost thoughts. *You Will Be Killed* (2006), an animated video work, edits together her drawings and imagery, including a recurring trapped female character performed by the artist. Also on view is *You Will Be Killed 2* (mid-2000s), a large-scale painting on canvas that incorporates a self-portrait of the artist, seemingly flat, potentially unconscious, suspended between life and death.

*You Will Be Killed* is a body of work Kenawy created around a military hospital built by the British in Cairo in the 1980s. Whilst the location draws attention to the breaking and healing of physical bodies from conflict, the artist forces a consideration of the sustained effect of violence on the mind, represented by being trapped, flat, in her own image, projecting drawings of others' dreams and desires. Despite the fast-paced convergence of formats in Kenawy's video, the artist remains rigorously focused on the communication of ideas; her choice of technique was only that which is 'best to articulate my subject'.

Kenawy, whose life was cut short from illness at a mere 39 years of age, evolved an expansive practice concerned with the intersection of personal history, memory and the performative power of artistic representation. She was working at a time in recent history while it was still possible to produce art about Egypt without explicit fear of censure, arrest or detention. Kenawy's work was closely associated with the once-growing independent art scene in Cairo in the late 1990s and 2000s, which saw artists embrace expanded media formats, alongside the rise of alternative spaces to the state-run art scene.

Sarah Perks

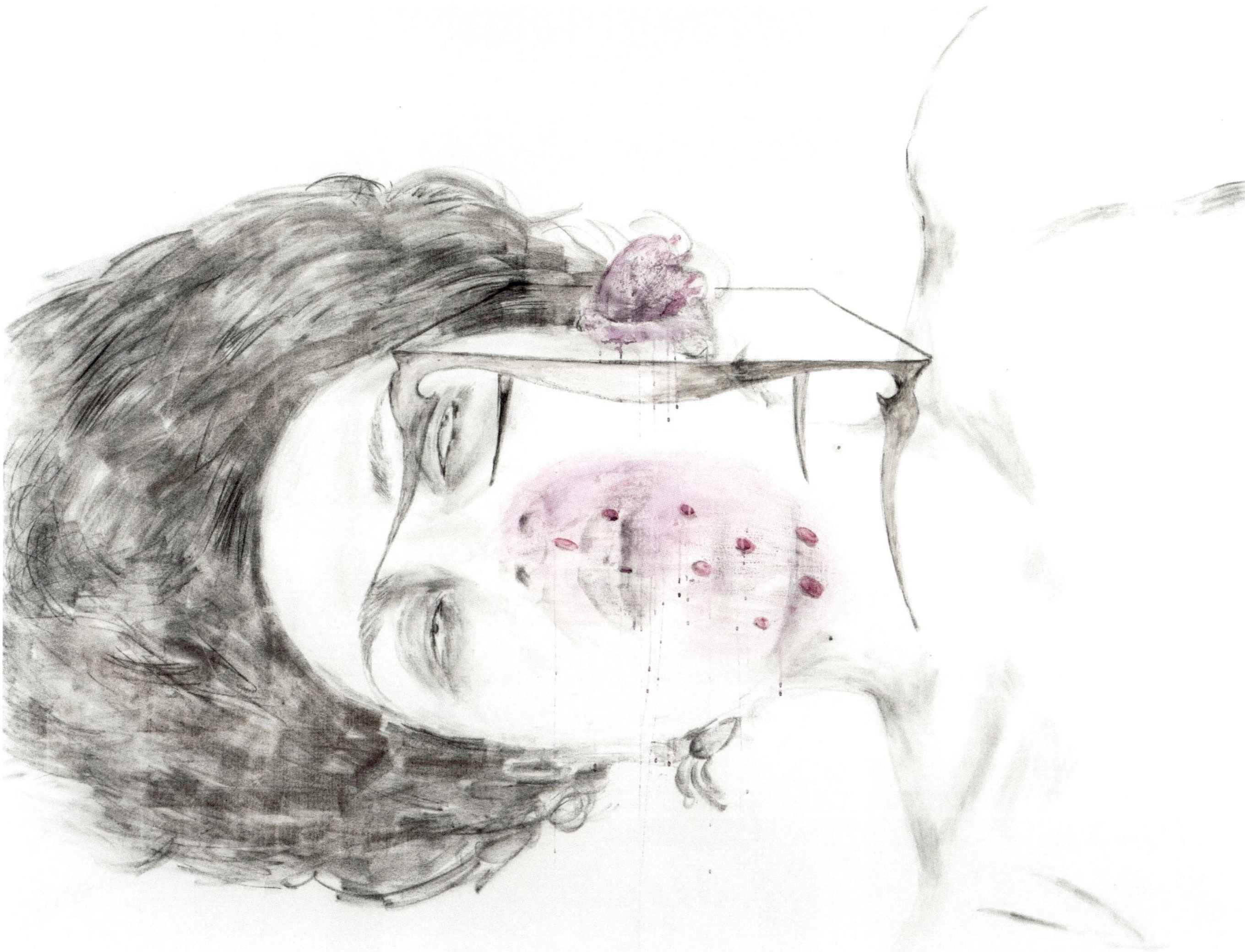

*You Will Be Killed 2 / Du wirst getötet werden 2*, Mitte der 2000er Jahre / mid-2000s. Mixed Media auf Leinwand / Mixed media on canvas. 200 × 150 cm

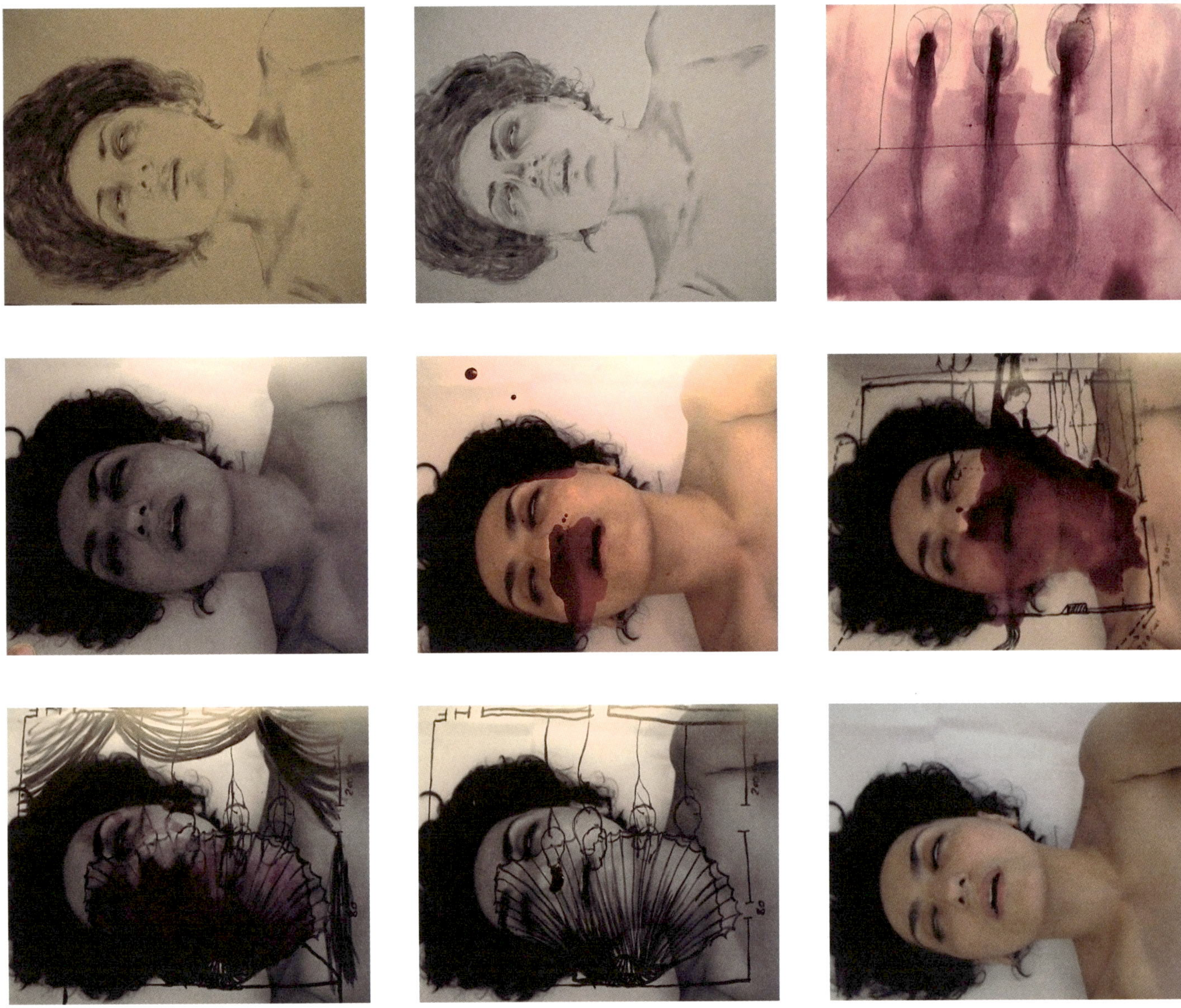

*You Will Be Killed / Du wirst getötet werden*, 2006. Video-Animation / Video animation. 5 Minuten, 56 Sekunden / 5 minutes 56 seconds

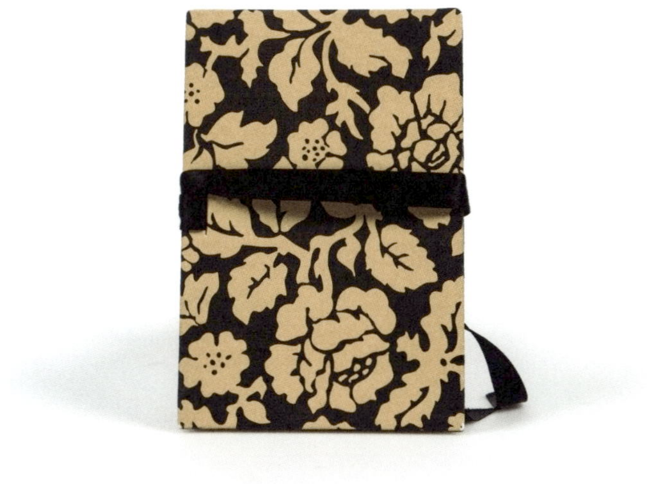

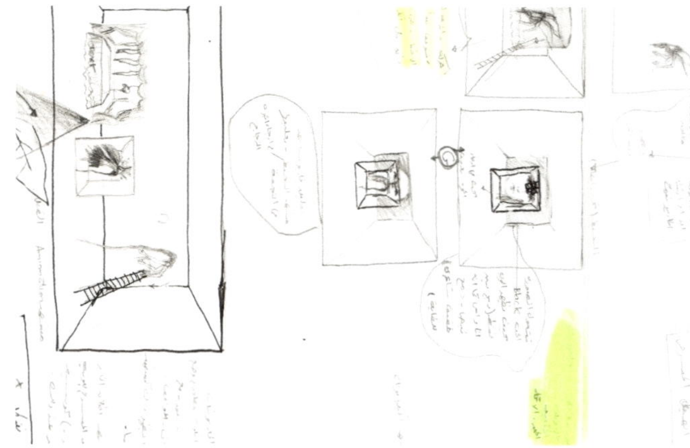

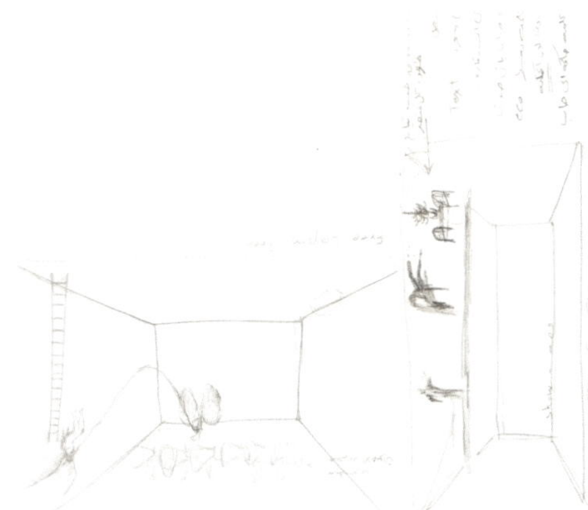

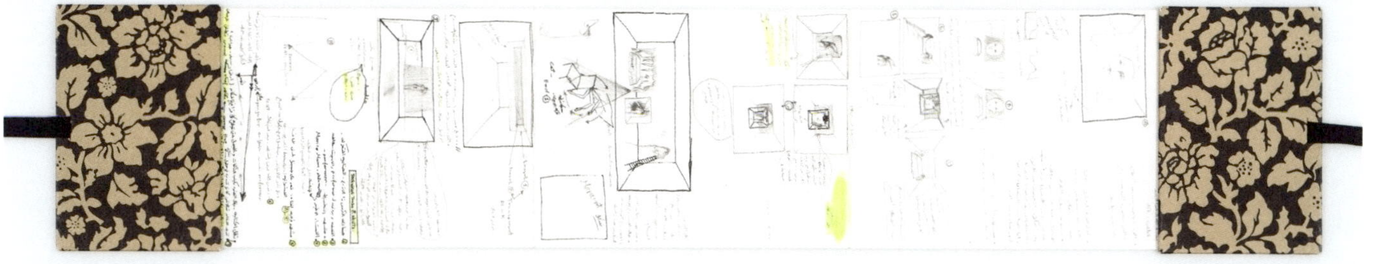

*Cairo is Eating Me* / *Kairo frisst mich auf*, o. D. / n. d. Künstlerinnenbuch / Artist book. Maße variabel / Dimensions variable.

# Tala Madani

Die Künstlerin Tala Madani untersucht in ihren Gemälden und Animationen auf sarkastische Weise die sinnlichen und geschlechterspezifischen Werte, die für das heutige politische Klima bestimmend sind. In Anlehnung an den Rabelais'schen bizarren und oft karikaturistischen Humor zerfallen schriftähnliche Umrisse von Einzelwesen, verbrennen in der Atmosphäre zu, bilden Pfützen aus goldener Flüssigkeit, lösen sich im kalten Licht einer Discokugel oder in den schmutzigen Flecken von Exkrementen auf. Tala Madani erklärte in einem Interview, dass Kunst für sie „in der Psyche gräbt, nicht im Frontallappen, nicht im Intellektuellen, nicht im Sagbaren, sondern im Unsagbaren". Das Rückgrat der eigenen Identität als totalisierendes Gebilde aus sprachlicher Gelassenheit und Selbstbeherrschung wird in Madanis Welt nicht nur entwertet, sondern oft schon im entstehenden Sumpf ausgelöscht.

Karikaturen zeichnen meist kein Bild komplexer Subjektivität. Nicht so Madanis Arbeiten. Ihre zunächst beliebig anonym anmutenden und replizierbaren Figuren – ein weißer oder iranischer „männlicher Körper", der durch Kindergekritzel dargestellt wird, oder eine „Mutter", von einem braunen Fleck symbolisiert, der von anhänglichen Kindern umgeben ist – gewinnen eine transgressive Perversität mit Blick auf erkennbar archetypische Rollen und Verhaltensweisen. *Corner Projection (Panic)* („Eckprojektion [Panik]", 2019) geht noch einen Schritt weiter, indem es zwischen Subjekt und Betrachter*in einen imaginären Ort einfügt, von dem aus das gemalte Bild erscheint. Es ist die fotorealistische Darstellung eines digitalen Videoprojektors und seines verträumt projizierten Bildes.

Dafür positioniert die Künstlerin zwei Leinwände in der Ecke eines Raumes so, dass sie sich berühren. Der Lichtkegel des projizierten Videolichts fällt darauf und enthüllt ein eingefrorenes Standbild oder vielleicht auch das mit Graffiti versehene Nachbild einer leeren Projektion. Durch die fast kosmisch anmutende Wolke aus gebrochenem Licht und einer dick aufgetragenen gemalten Verzerrungsschicht hindurch wird eine Gruppe von Figuren sichtbar, die offenbar in den schattigen Rand des projizierten Lichtrahmens flieht. Derart als Momentaufnahme gelesen, könnte man die unförmigen Figuren auch als Menetekel künftiger Konflikte in den USA verstehen, wo die Künstlerin lebt. Alternativ kann es sich auch um eine Gruppe von Menschen handeln, die aus Angst oder Scham um ihre Leben rennen.

The paintings and animations by Tala Madani caustically examine the libidinal and gendered currencies that thread today's political climate. Riffing on various Rabelaisian, scatological and often cartoonishly humorous forms, we see typefaces of identities dissolve and combust ambiently into ether or reduce into puddles of golden liquid, the cool glow of a disco light or the filthy stains of excrement. As Madani reveals in an interview: 'Art that excavates from the psyche, not the frontal lobe, not the intellectual, not the speakable, but the unspeakable'. The stability of one's identity as a totalising entity of linguistic composure and self-governance is not only made indeterminate in Madani's world, but is often extinguished in the resulting mire.

If cartoonish caricature typically eschews complex subjectivity, Madani reroutes what might be the groundless anonymity of replicable figures—for instance, the white or Iranian 'male body' reduced to that of an approximate scribble of a baby, or a 'mother' rendered as a brown stain surrounded by devoted children—into one that sticks transgressive perversity onto recognisably archetypal roles and behaviours. *Corner Projection (Panic)* (2019) develops these concerns further by inserting between subject and viewer the imagined construction of where the painted image is appearing from—a photorealist depiction of a digital video projector and its dreamily projected image. By abutting two canvases in the corner of a space, the cone of projected video light seemingly falls to reveal a frozen film still or, perhaps, the graffitied after-image of a blank projection. Through the somewhat cosmic cloud of refracted light and thickly applied painted distortion, we see a rabble of figures fleeing into the shadowed edge of the projected frame of light. In this snapshot, one might even read the plump figures as foreshadowing conflicts to emerge in the United States, where the artist lives, or perhaps a group fleeing for their lives out of fear or shame.

Chris McCormack

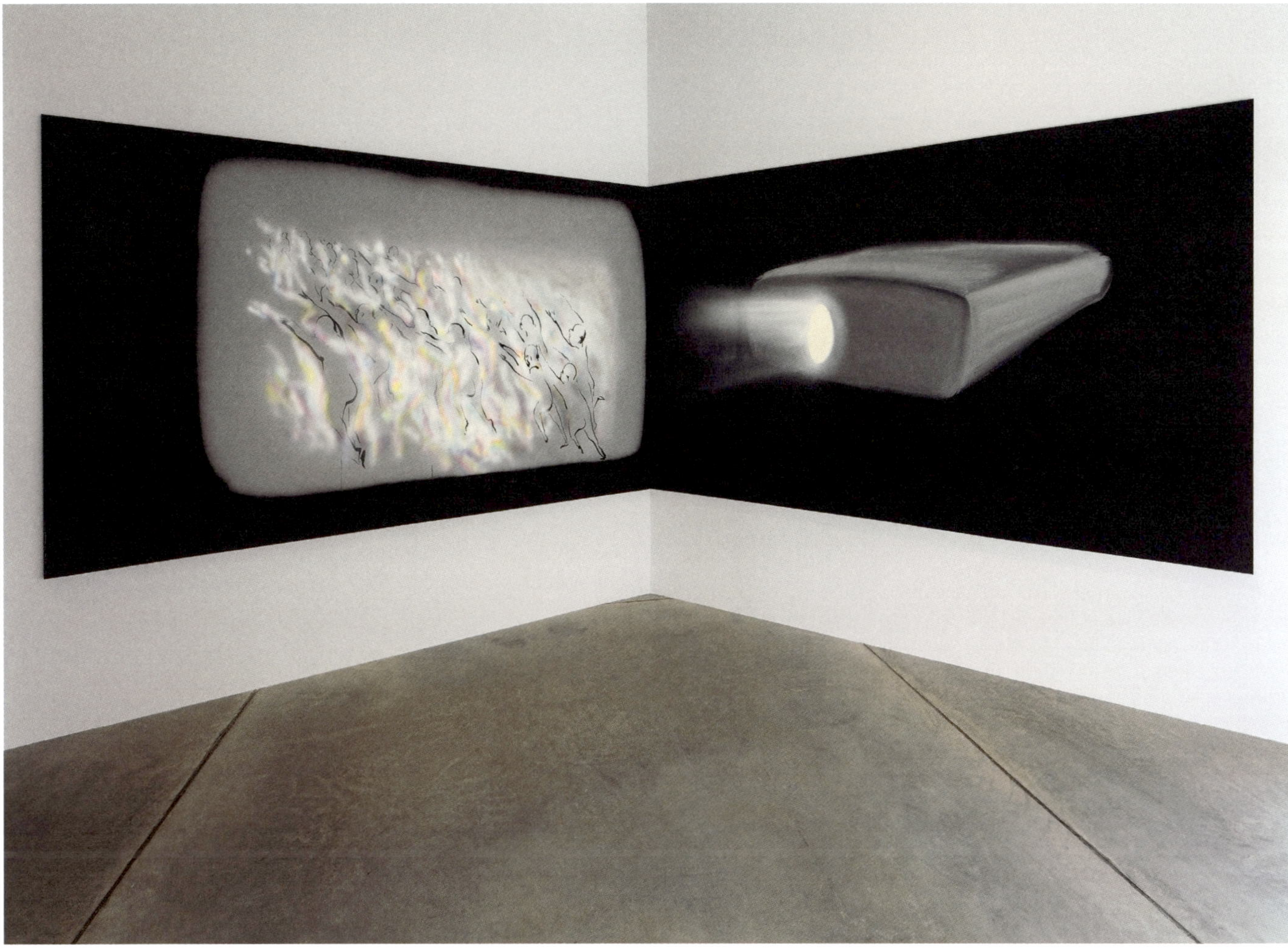

*Corner Projection (Panic) | Eckprojektion (Panik)*, 2019. 2 Gemälde, Öl auf Leinen / 2 paintings, oil on linen. Jeweils / Each 365,8 × 182,9 × 3,8 cm. Installationsansicht / Installation view, *Unsettled Objects*, Sharjah Art Foundation, 2021.

# Taus Makhacheva

Taus Makhacheva versetzt einen männlichen Darsteller in dem mittlerweile verlassenen avarischen Bergdorf Gamsutl in Dagestan. Der Film zeigt eine komplette Bewegungs- und Tanzperformance des Protagonisten und schafft so eine Erzählung mit Bezügen zu westlichen zeitgenössischen Performances, zu Kampfposen in den Panoramaschlachtengemälden des russischen Künstlers Franz Roubaud (1856–1928) und zu Schritten aus dem „Tanz des Kolchosbrigadeführers", einem nordossetischen Tanz aus den 1930er Jahren, der ethnische und sowjetsozialistische Erfahrungen gleichermaßen reflektiert. Die Performance versucht, die Geschichte der Konflikte um das Dorf (insbesondere den Kaukasuskrieg im 19. Jahrhundert) und den gesellschaftlich-politischen Wandel (sowjetische Revolution und Modernität, die postsowjetische Zeit) mitsamt den Mühen des Alltags zusammenzufügen, und verweist zugleich auf eine Rückkehr zum Felsen und natürlichen Lebensraum der vorzeitlichen Besiedlung.

Das Dorf Gamsutl (wörtlich: „am Fuß der Khan-Festung"), bei dem nicht bekannt ist, wann es zuerst besiedelt wurde, gilt als eines der ältesten in Dagestan und hatte zum Zeitpunkt der Entstehung dieser Arbeit nur noch einen einzigen Bewohner. Heute ist es vollkommen verlassen und nur noch eine bizarre Sehenswürdigkeit. Die Performance selbst ist brüchig, widersprüchlich und emotional mehrdeutig, womit sie auf die verlassene Trümmerlandschaft um sie herum reagiert und deren unbeabsichtigter Renaturalisierung Schönheit abgewinnt. Das Traditionelle und das Zeitgenössische stehen in der postkolonialen Erlebniswelt der Menschen im Nordkaukasus – einer historischen Konfliktregion mit bedeutenden Handelsrouten an der Schnittstelle zwischen Europa und Asien – in einem besonderen Spannungsverhältnis. In ihrer Rolle als wissbegierige Vermittlerin des kulturellen Erbes von Dagestan erkundet Makhacheva die Möglichkeiten der Zukunft, indem sie die Vergangenheit freilegt.

Taus Makhacheva positions a male performer into the now-deserted Avarian mountain village of Gamsutl in Dagestan. The duration of the film projection follows the protagonist's performance of movement and dance to create a narrative that includes references from Western contemporary performance, poses from battle scenes in the panoramic paintings of Russian artist Franz Roubaud (1856–1928) and steps from the Dance of the Collective Farm Brigade Leader, a 1930s North Ossetian dance reflecting both ethnic folk and Soviet socialist experiences. The performance attempts a summation of the history of conflicts on the village (in particular, the Caucasian War in the 19th century) and sociopolitical change (Soviet revolution and modernity, the post-Soviet condition), whilst also including labours of daily life and signifying a return to the rock and natural habitat of the pre-human settlement.

Its first date of settlement unknown but believed to be one of the oldest in Dagestan, the village Gamsutl (literally, 'at the foot of Khan's fortress') had only one resident left at the time of production of this work. Now, it is entirely uninhabited, left only as an obscure tourist attraction. The performance itself is fractured, contradictory and unfinished in feel, echoing its context in the debris of a forgotten place, yet finding a beauty in the unintended ecological revival. The traditional and the contemporary form a particular type of tension for the postcolonial experience of those in the North Caucasus, a significant trade route and historical site of struggle at the nexus of Europe and Asia. Makhacheva's role as a curious narrator of the cultural heritage of Dagestan interrogates the possibilities of the future by way of excavating the past.

Sarah Perks

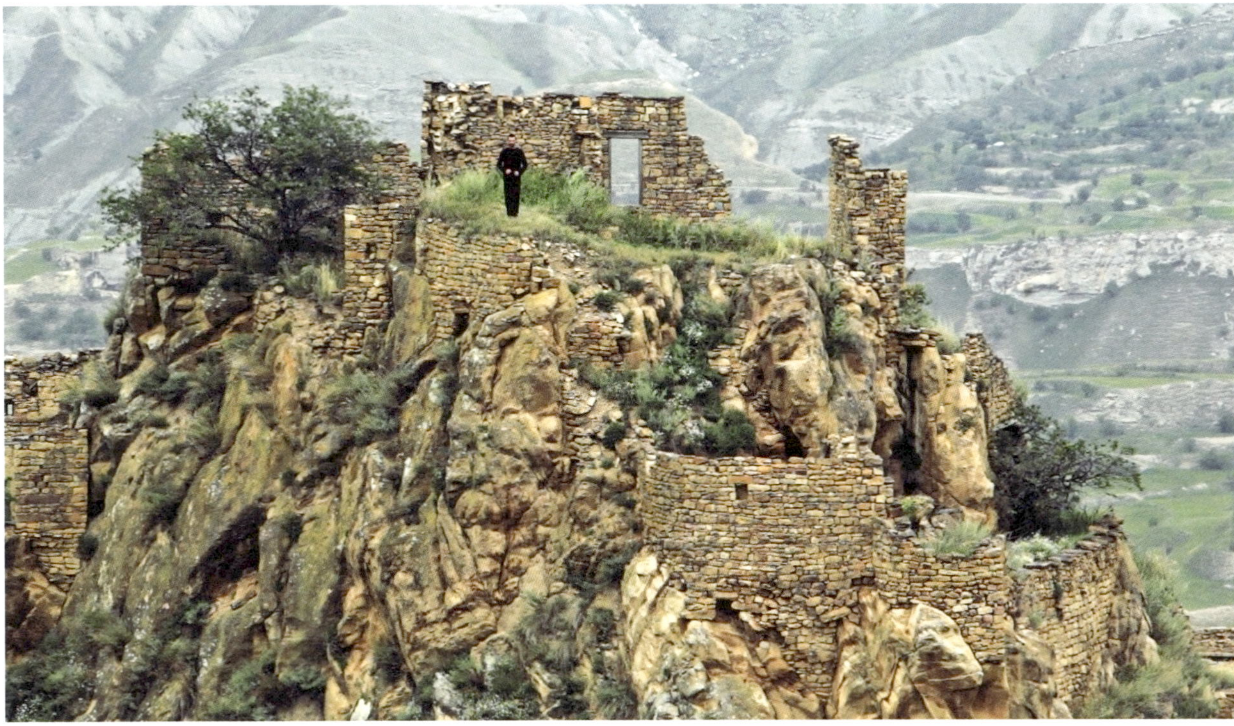

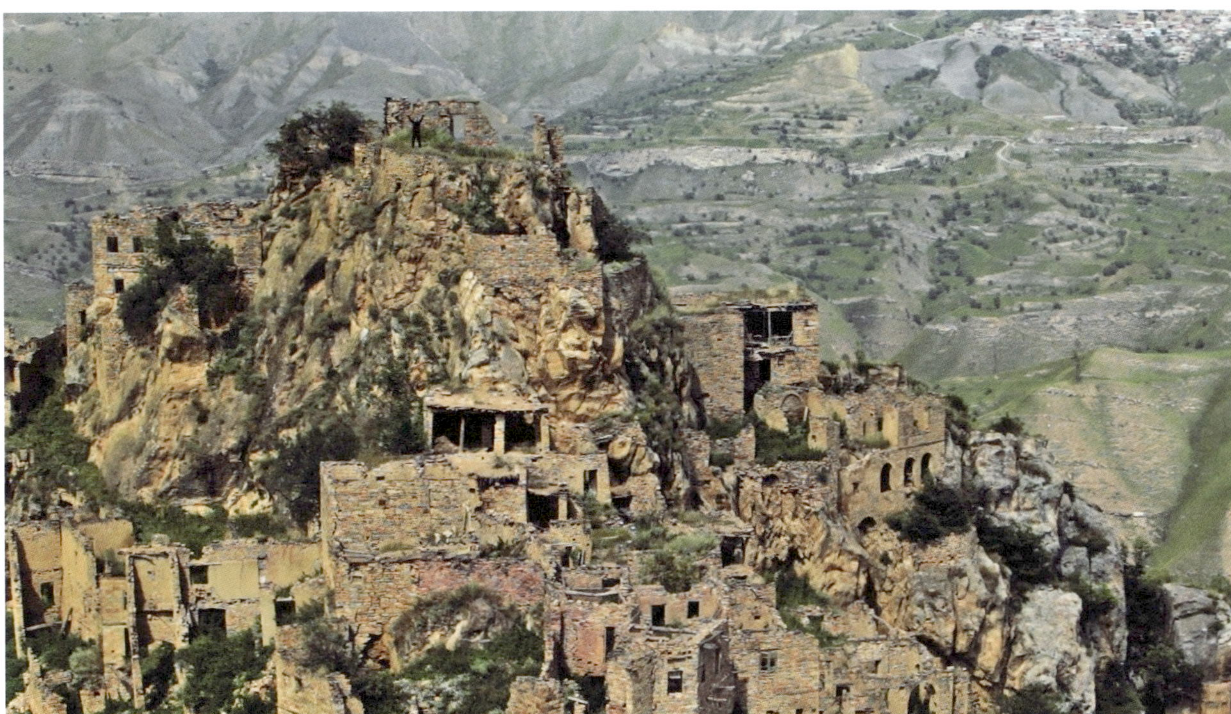

*Gamsutl*, 2012. HD-Farbvideo-Projektion / HD colour video projection. 16 Minuten, 1 Sekunde (Videoschleife) / 16 minutes 1 second (looped)

# Ahmed Mater

Im Jahr 2016 veröffentlichte Ahmed Mater den Fotobildband *Desert of Pharan* („Wüste von Pharan"), der die Entwicklung von Mekka, der heiligsten Stadt des Islam, dokumentiert. Der Titel des Buches verweist auf den alttestamentarischen Namen der Stadt und der sie umgebenden Landschaft. Er verleiht den Abbildungen die Bedeutung epischer Zeugnisse. Die Ansichten reichen von spektakulären Vogelperspektiven auf Bauprojekte, die prägend für das Mekka des 21. Jahrhunderts sind, in dem Einkaufszentren und Luxushotels den heiligen öffentlichen Raum einfassen, bis hin zu Fotos aus den beengten Wohnquartieren von Arbeitsmigranten.

„Die Geschichte von Mekka ist die Geschichte einer lebendigen Siedlung", sagte Mater der *New York Times* im Jahr 2016. Entsprechend repräsentieren die Menschen, die ihm beim Fotografieren behilflich waren, das gesamte gesellschaftliche Spektrum derer, die Mekkas Stadtentwicklung vorantreiben: vom Slumbewohner bis zum saudischen Prinzen. Die Sammlung *100 Found Objects* („100 Fundstücke", 2014) ergänzt diese Bestandsaufnahme von Menschen durch eine Vielzahl von Gegenständen wie Bustickets, den Schutzhelm eines Arbeiters und einen Mekka-Spielzeugbaukasten, den Mater als „Mecca Minecraft" bezeichnet.

Die Gegenstände dieses Archivs haben sich über Jahrzehnte angesammelt. Die Scheibe für einen View-Master, die in einem inzwischen abgerissenen Laden gefunden wurde, zeigt Schwarz-Weiß-Aufnahmen von Mekka. Die Fotos auf einer weiteren Scheibe, die der Vater dem Künstler nach dessen Hadsch im Jahr 1984 schenkte, wurden in Technicolor aufgenommen. Zwei Paar Colaflaschen stehen für die Vielschichtigkeit der Modernisierung, die Mater in seiner Arbeit thematisiert. Wie jedes der Archivobjekte sind auch sie datiert und wie Museumsstücke gekennzeichnet: Die Zam-Zam-Cola aus einem Trödelladen in Mekka stammt aus der Regierungszeit von König Saud (1953–1964). Die Ka'aki-Cola aus der Zeit um 1950 wurde der Mater-Sammlung im Jahr 2014 von der Familie Ka'aki gestiftet. Online werden diese Exponate von Ich-Erzählungen begleitet, die sich zwischen Tatsachen und Spekulation bewegen. Die Ka'aki-Cola-Flaschen erklären sich zu Kopien des echten Produkts – „eine Fälschung, eine Stellvertreterin, könnte man sagen (…), aber ich bin ebenso gut, und ich bin von hier."

In 2016, Ahmed Mater published *Desert of Pharan*, a book of photographs documenting the development taking place in Islam's holiest city, Mecca. The book's title, the Old Testament name that has been associated with the site and its surrounding landscape, lends the portrayals within a sense of epic testimony. Perspectives range from spectacular bird's-eye views of construction projects that define Mecca in the 21st century, where shopping malls and luxury hotels circle this sacred public space, to images inside cramped living quarters for migrant labourers.

'The story of Mecca is the story of a living settlement', Mater told *The New York Time*s in 2016. In keeping, the people who helped him photograph Mecca represent the societal spectrum who are driving the city's evolution, from slum dwellers to Saudi princes. *100 Found Objects* (2014) extends this human mapping with a multiplicity of items such as bus tickets, a worker's helmet and a toy Mecca construction kit, which Mater describes as 'Mecca Minecraft'.

The objects in this archive have evolved over decades. One reel for a View-Master, found in a since-demolished shop, depicts black-and-white captures of Mecca, while the images in another, a gift from the artist's father after the artist completed Hajj in 1984, are rendered in technicolour. Two pairs of cola bottles encapsulate the hybridity of modernisation Mater locates in his subject. As with every object in the archive, both pairs are dated and sourced akin to museum artefacts: Zam Zam Cola, found in a vintage shop in Mecca, belongs to the reign of King Saud (1953–1964); while Ka'aki Cola, from circa 1950, was donated to Mater's collection by the Ka'aki family in 2014. Online, these exhibits are accompanied by first-person narratives straddling fact and speculative fiction. The Ka'aki Cola bottles declare themselves copies of the real thing—'a sham, a proxy you could say… But I'm just as good, and home-grown'.

Stephanie Bailey

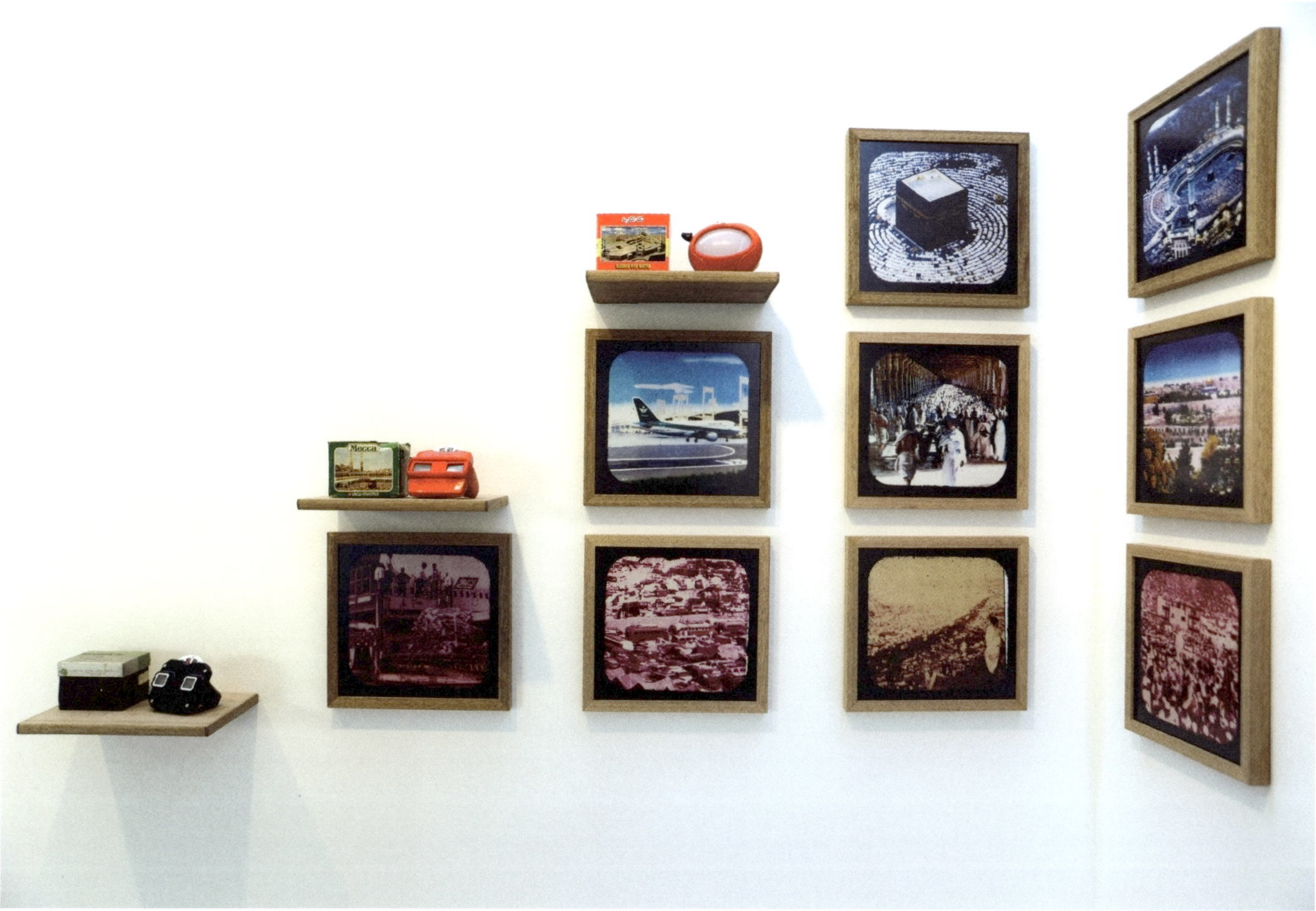

*100 Found Objects / 100 Fundstücke*, 2014. Mixed Media. Maße variabel / Dimensions variable. Installationsansicht / Installation view, Ahmed Mater: *100 Found Objects*, Sharjah Art Foundation, 2014.

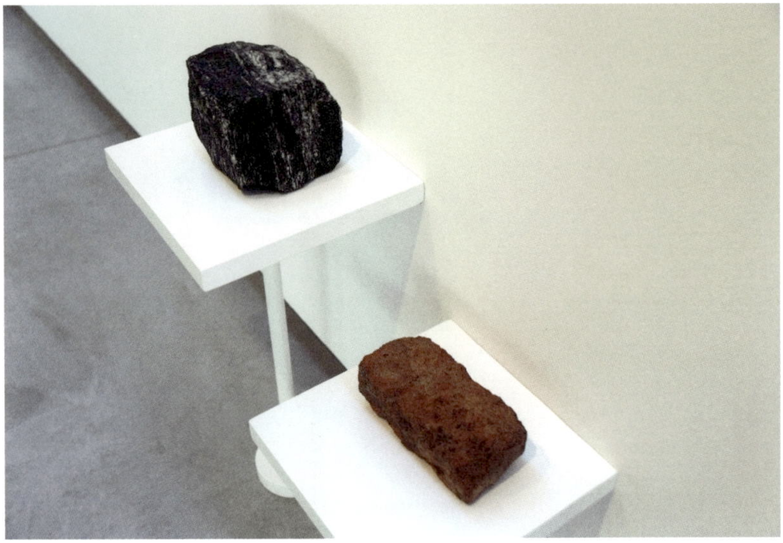

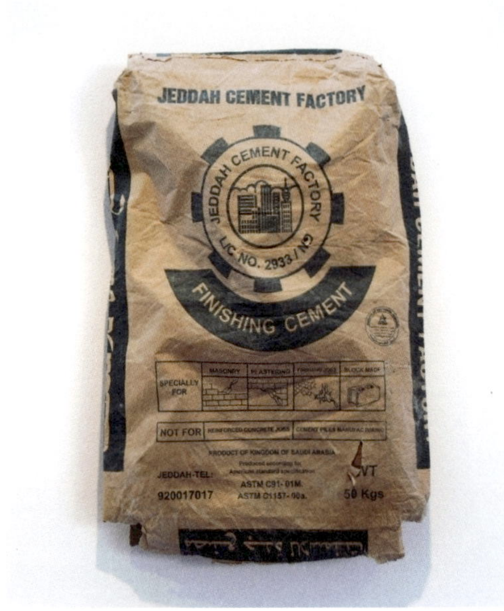
JEDDAH CEMENT FACTORY
JEDDAH CEMENT FACTORY
FINISHING CEMENT
SPECIALLY FOR
NOT FOR
JEDDAH-TEL:
920017017
50 Kgs

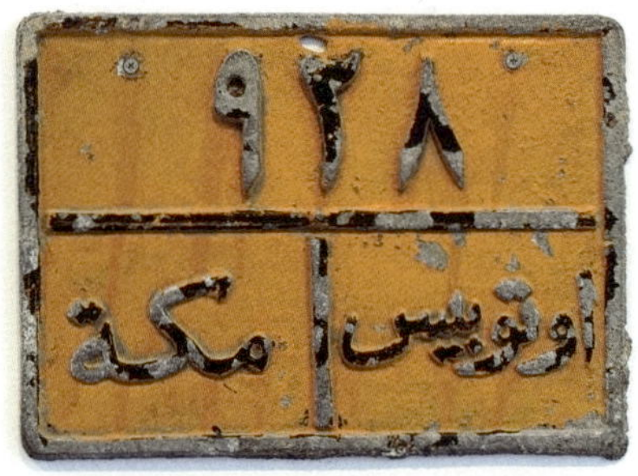
٩٢٨
اوتوبيس مكة

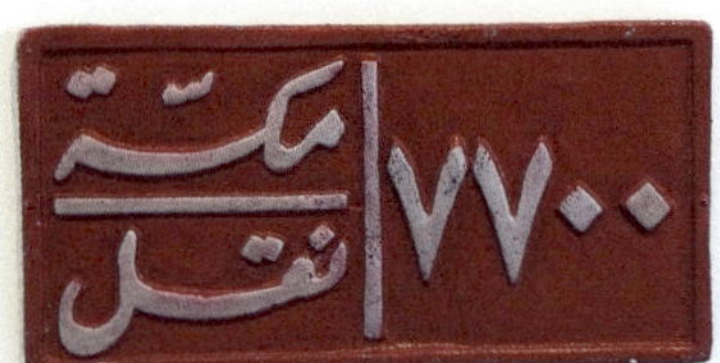
مكة
نقل
٧٧٠٠

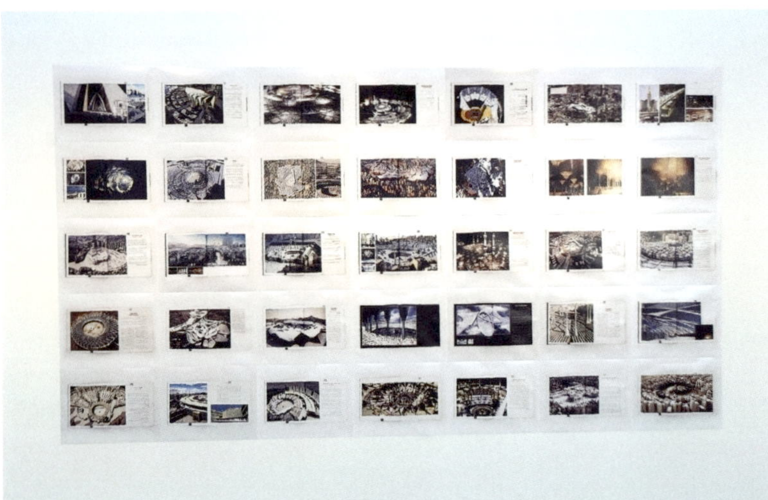

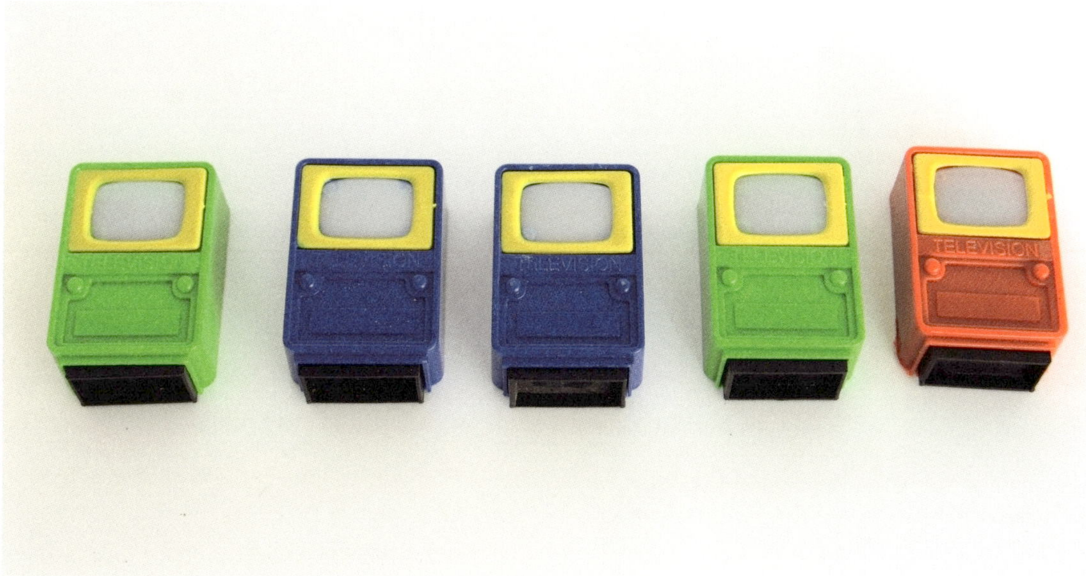
TELEVISION

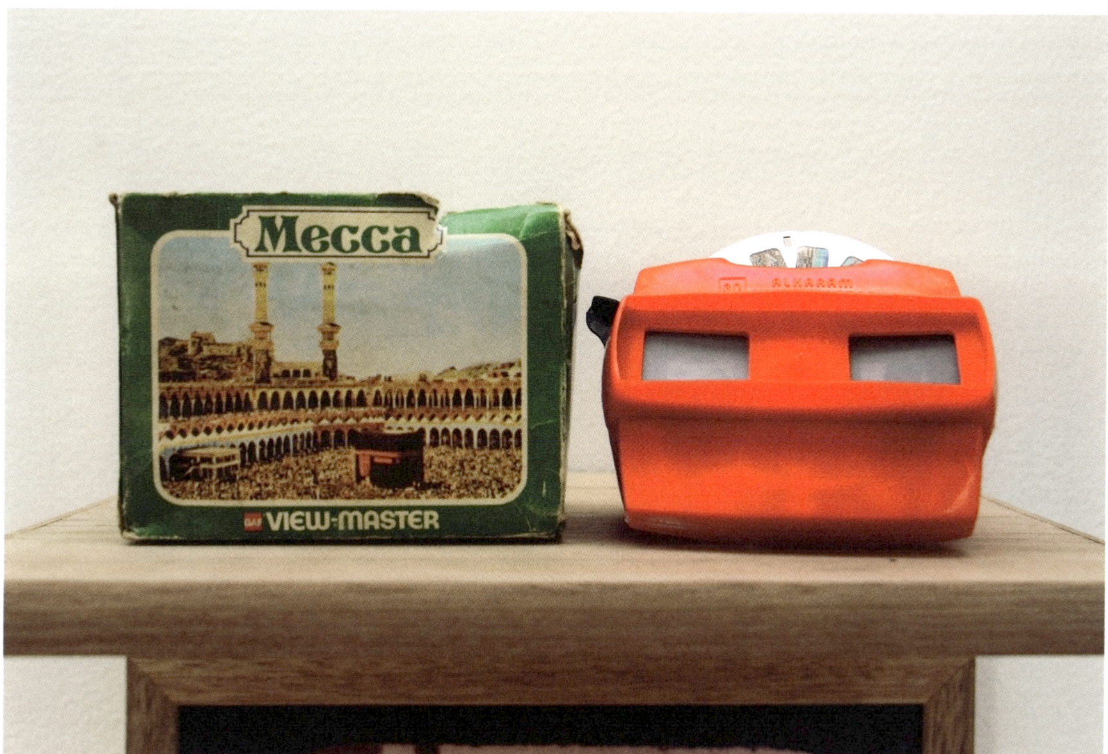
Mecca
VIEW-MASTER

# Khalil Rabah

Der Künstler Khalil Rabah vergleicht die Entwicklung und Fortführung institutioneller Machtstrukturen in Industrienationen mit der mangelhaften Administration in seiner palästinensischen Heimat. Indem der Künstler mit seinen Arbeiten die basalen kulturellen Institutionen, die einen Staat ausmachen – ein Museum, eine Biennale oder eine Fluggesellschaft etwa – nachbildet, übernimmt er die Funktion sogenannter Soft Power und spielt imaginär mit deren Potenzial.

Khalil Rabahs facettenreiches Werk *The Palestinian Museum of Natural History and Humankind* („Das palästinensische Museum für Naturkunde und Menschheit", 2003 bis heute) zeigt einfühlsam, wie Schlüsselmomente effektiv rekonstruiert und tradiert werden können, wenn ihre Präsenz nicht durch die israelischen Besatzungskräfte in Vergessenheit geraten. Rabah hat dafür monothematische Abteilungen entwickelt und sein „Museum" mit Kunstwerken ausgestattet, die exemplarisch dafür stehen, wie Bilder und Sprache das institutionelle Machtgefüge über das rein Physische hinaus ins Ideologische ausdehnen.

Die Arbeit *Area C Fields of Gold (Not Everything that Shines Is Gold)* („C-Zone Goldene Felder [Es ist nicht alles Gold, was glänzt]", 1994–2019) befasst sich mit einer ähnlich komplexen Konstellation von Territorium und Identität. Die ländliche C-Zone macht im Westjordanland rund 60 Prozent des Gebiets aus. Der nährstoffreiche Boden war einmal das Rückgrat der palästinensischen Landwirtschaft. In der heute von Israel verwalteten C-Zone wird es Palästinenser*innen praktisch unmöglich gemacht, eigene Gemeinden aufzubauen.

Der Künstler beschreibt dieses ländliche Bild mit Gold und lässt dabei das Material die Grenzen der herkömmlichen assoziativen Illusion sprengen, indem er es zur Darstellung der Gewalt der Grenzkontrollen verwendet. Denn bei genauerer Betrachtung entpuppt sich das Gold als aufgerollter Stacheldraht. Dessen Spulen sind in gitterartigen Formationen angeordnet, die als Barrikade von den Ausstellungsbesucher*innen wahrgenommen werden.

Eine völlig andere poetische Energie geht von den geflochtenen Spulen aus Goldfäden aus, die in Olivenöl getaucht wurden. Die materielle Sinnlichkeit, die an Kunstwerke von James Lee Byars oder sogar Joseph Beuys erinnert, wird von Rabah unmissverständlich zu einer Barriere umgedeutet, die den Zugang zu einem bestimmten Gebiet abschneidet und verwehrt. Die gitterartige Struktur, wie sie der Modernismus pflegte, erinnert somit nicht nur an die Unendlichkeit, sondern auch an die scharfen Grenzen, die von Besatzer*innen gesetzt werden.

Khalil Rabah mirrors the way in which the structures of institutional power are designed and replicated across industrialised nations in order to locate real politicised absences in his homeland of Palestine. By re-creating the cultural foundations of a nation-state—be it a museum, biennial or an airline—Rabah takes on the functions of so-called soft power and speculatively recasts it as one of imaginary potential.

This malleability is powerfully rendered in Rabah's multifaceted work *The Palestinian Museum of Natural History and Humankind* (2003–ongoing), which effectively constructs and preserves anchor points in history that are otherwise shaken from their connective moorings by Israeli occupying forces. The artist has extended specialised 'departments' and populated his 'museum' with artworks as if to further demonstrate the ways in which image and language comprise institutional power beyond the realm of the physical, moving into the ideological.

Rabah's *Area C Field of Gold (Not Everything that Shines Is Gold* (1994–2019) similarly distils a complex relationship to territory and identity. Area C is a rural area that covers more than 60 percent of the West Bank and that once formed a central plank of Palestine's agricultural wealth. It is now a contested colonised territory where Palestinian community development is rendered impossible. The artist weighs this rural image with that of gold, in a distillation where the material's appearance extends beyond the illusory to evoke the violence of border control. Indeed, the gold presented here is coiled barbed wire. The spools are arranged in grid-like formation as viewers enter the gallery, forming a barricade they must decide how to negotiate.

A different poetic is evoked by the installation's braided spools of golden thread submerged in olive oil. If the material sensuality here evokes that of James Lee Byars's or even Joseph Beuys's artworks, Rabah limpidly reframes it as one made of barriers; one in which entry to a given land is continually shorn and denied. The grid-like arrangement of Modernism is not one solely evoking infinity, but the sharply restrictive limits made by an oppressor.

Chris McCormack

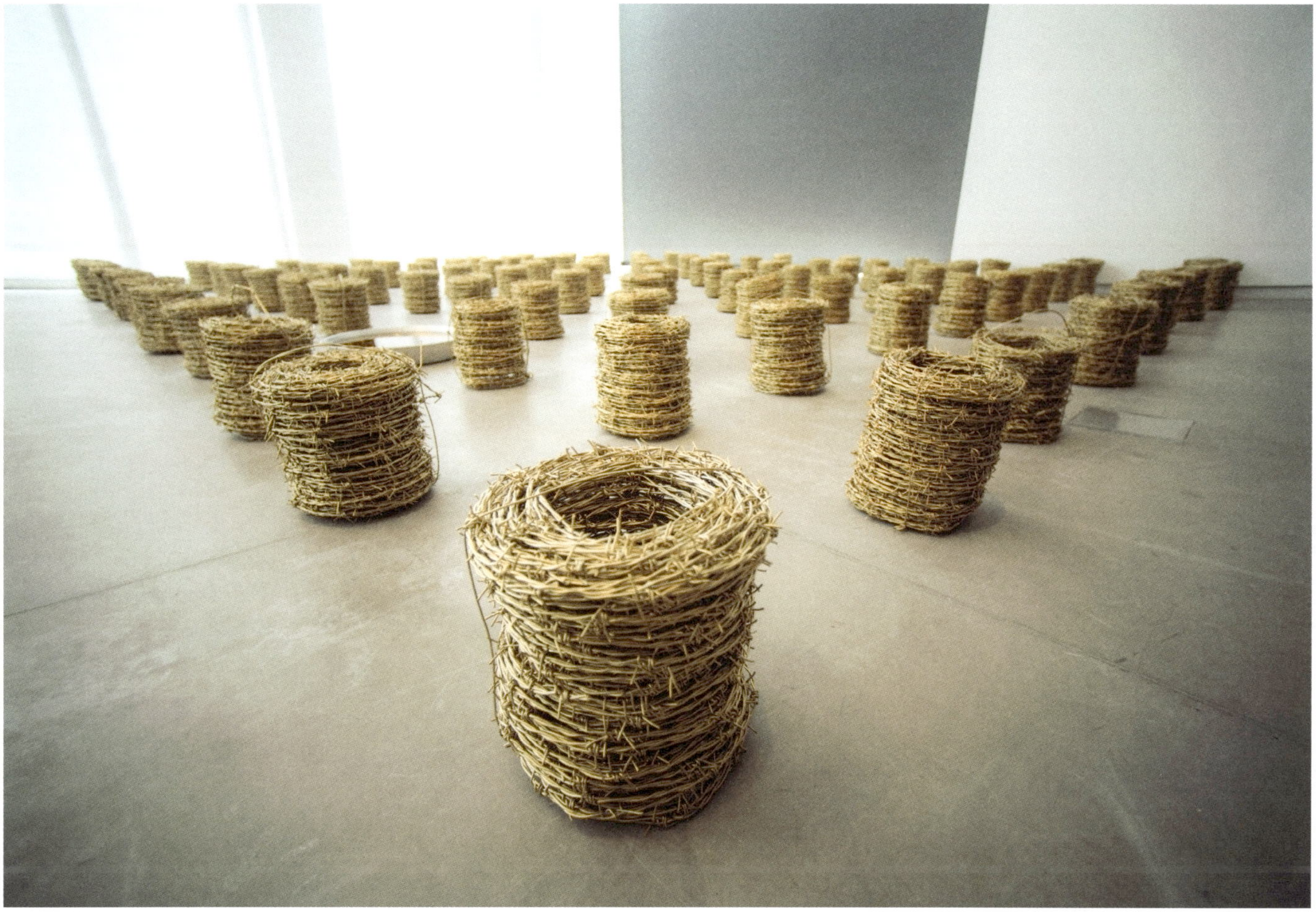

*Not Everything that Shines Is Gold* / *Es ist nicht alles Gold, was glänzt*, 2017. Aus *C-Zone Goldene Felder* / From *Area C Fields of Gold*, 1994–2019
90 Spulen mit Stacheldraht / 90 barbed wire coils. Höhe jeweils 40 cm, Durchmesser 40 cm / Height 40 cm; diameter 40 cm each. Reproduziert von der Sharjah Art Foundation / Reproduced by Sharjah Art Foundation. Installationsansicht / Installation view, Khalil Rabah: *What is not*, Sharjah Art Foundation, 2022.

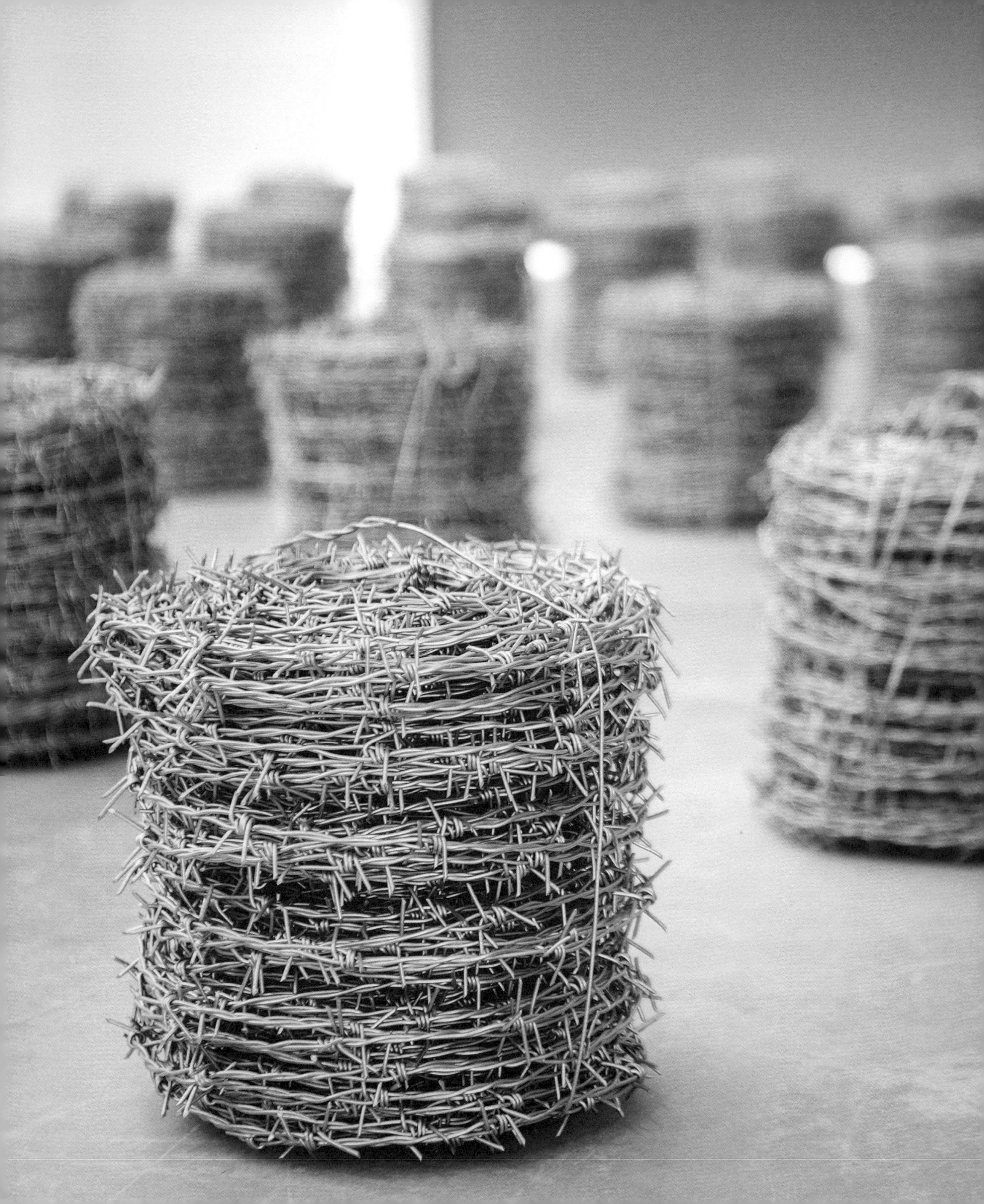

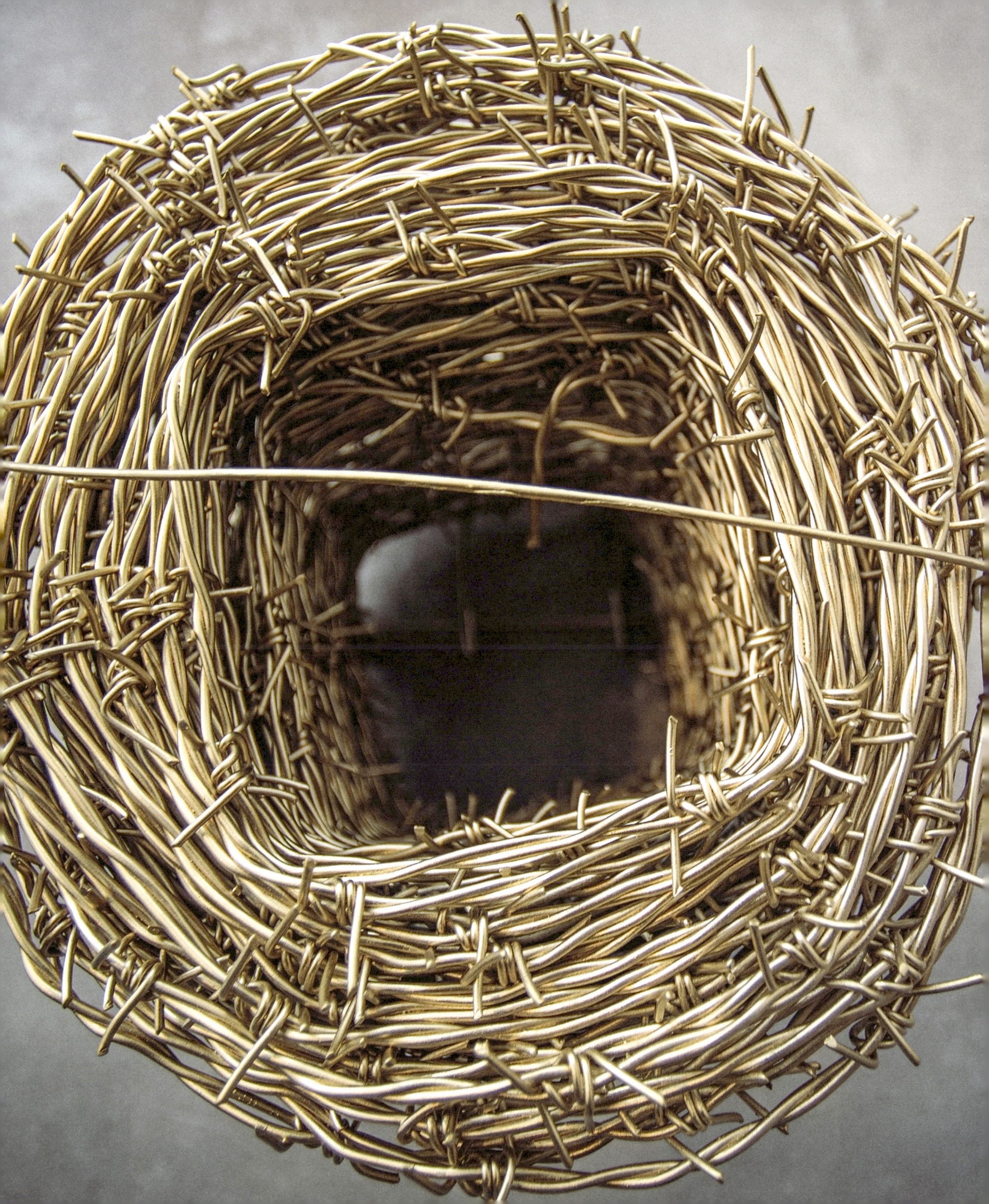

# Hrair Sarkissian

Hrair Sarkissian widmet sich der großformatigen Fotografie als konzeptuellem Medium. Daraus entstehen Projekte, die dokumentarische Fotografie und ihre Wirkung so harmonisch in Einklang bringen, dass der Blick des Fotografen zu einem Kaleidoskop der Bildsprache wird.

So inszenierte Sarkissian in seiner Installation *My Father and I* („Mein Vater und ich“, 2010) Selbstporträts seines Vaters aus dessen Jugendzeit, indem er sie jeweils neben einem großen Foto des väterlichen Fotolabors in Damaskus präsentierte, wo er seine eigene Ausbildung begann. Diese querformatige Ansicht, die von zwei sich über Jahrzehnte hinweg spiegelnden Gesichter dominiert wird, verwandelt eine intime Studie in ein erweitertes Porträt der Vergänglichkeit. Dabei enthält es Anklänge an Sarkissians Serie *Execution Squares* („Hinrichtungsplätze“) aus dem Jahr 2008: lebensgroße Farbfotografien, die Orte öffentlicher Hinrichtungen in ganz Syrien dokumentieren. Ebenso erinnert die Installation an *Last Seen* („Zuletzt gesehen“), ein 2018 begonnenes Projekt, das sich mit Orten im Libanon, in Argentinien, Brasilien, dem Kosovo und Bosnien befasst, die mit gewaltsamem Verschwindenlassen zu tun haben. In jedem Projekt verewigt Sarkissian die emotionalen Spuren, die trotz des unaufhaltsamen und oft zerstörerischen Fortschreitens der Zeit zurückbleiben.

Die gleiche Idee des Gedenkens liegt dem Projekt *Final Flight* („Letzter Flug“, 2018–2019) zugrunde, das dem Waldrapp gewidmet ist. Dieser majestätische Vogel, Nachfahre des schon vor Jahrtausenden in ägyptischen Hieroglyphen dargestellten Vogel, war in Syrien 1989 für ausgestorben erklärt worden. Bis im Jahr 2002 in der syrischen Wüste nahe Palmyra eine überlebende Kolonie von sieben Tieren gesichtet wurde. Trotz dieser erstaunlichen Entdeckung gerieten die Vögel in den Wirren des syrischen Bürgerkriegs in Vergessenheit und verschwanden etwa zu der Zeit, als der Islamische Staat Palmyra eroberte und den Ort verwüstete. Im Mittelpunkt von Sarkissians Installation stehen als stumme Zeugen sieben Knochenabgüsse eines 3-D-Schädelmodells von einem andalusischen Artgenossen, das sich in der Sammlung eines spanischen Zoos befindet. Diese auf eleganten Sockeln aufgereihten Schädel weisen auf ein Video mit Satellitenaufnahmen, die die vermutlichen Flugrouten der Zugvögel zu ihren Lebzeiten nachzeichnen.

Hrair Sarkissian's sustained exploration of large-format photography as a conceptual medium is defined by projects that mediate documentary image-making and its affects with such balance that the photographer's gaze transforms into a kaleidoscopic conduit of transmission.

For instance, in his installation *My Father and I* (2010), Sarkissian restaged self-portraits his father took in his youth, presenting each set in a line on either side of a large photograph of his father's photo lab in Damascus, where Sarkissian initially trained. This landscape view, marked by two faces mirroring one another across decades, turns an intimate study into an expanded portrait of time passing. There are resonances here with Sarkissian's *Execution Squares* series from 2008, life-sized colour photographs documenting sites of public executions across Syria, and *Last Seen*, a project initiated in 2018 centring on spaces connected to people who forcibly disappeared in Lebanon, Argentina, Brazil, Kosovo and Bosnia. In each project, Sarkissian monumentalises the affective traces that linger despite time's inevitable and often devastating passage.

That same commemoration infuses *Final Flight* (2018–19), which focuses on the northern bald ibis. This majestic bird, descended from those depicted in Egyptian hieroglyphs created millennia ago, was apparently declared extinct in 1989, until a surviving colony of seven was discovered in 2002 in the Syrian desert near Palmyra. Despite this remarkable discovery, the birds were lost amid the chaos of the Syrian civil war, and disappeared around the time ISIS seized Palmyra, devastating the site. Bearing witness, Sarkissian's installation centres on seven bone casts of a 3D model skull of an Andalusian specimen housed in the collection of a Spanish zoo. These skulls, poised on elegant plinths and positioned in a line, point to a video screening satellite footage that re-creates the migratory flight routes the ibis were believed to have taken in their lifetimes.

Stephanie Bailey

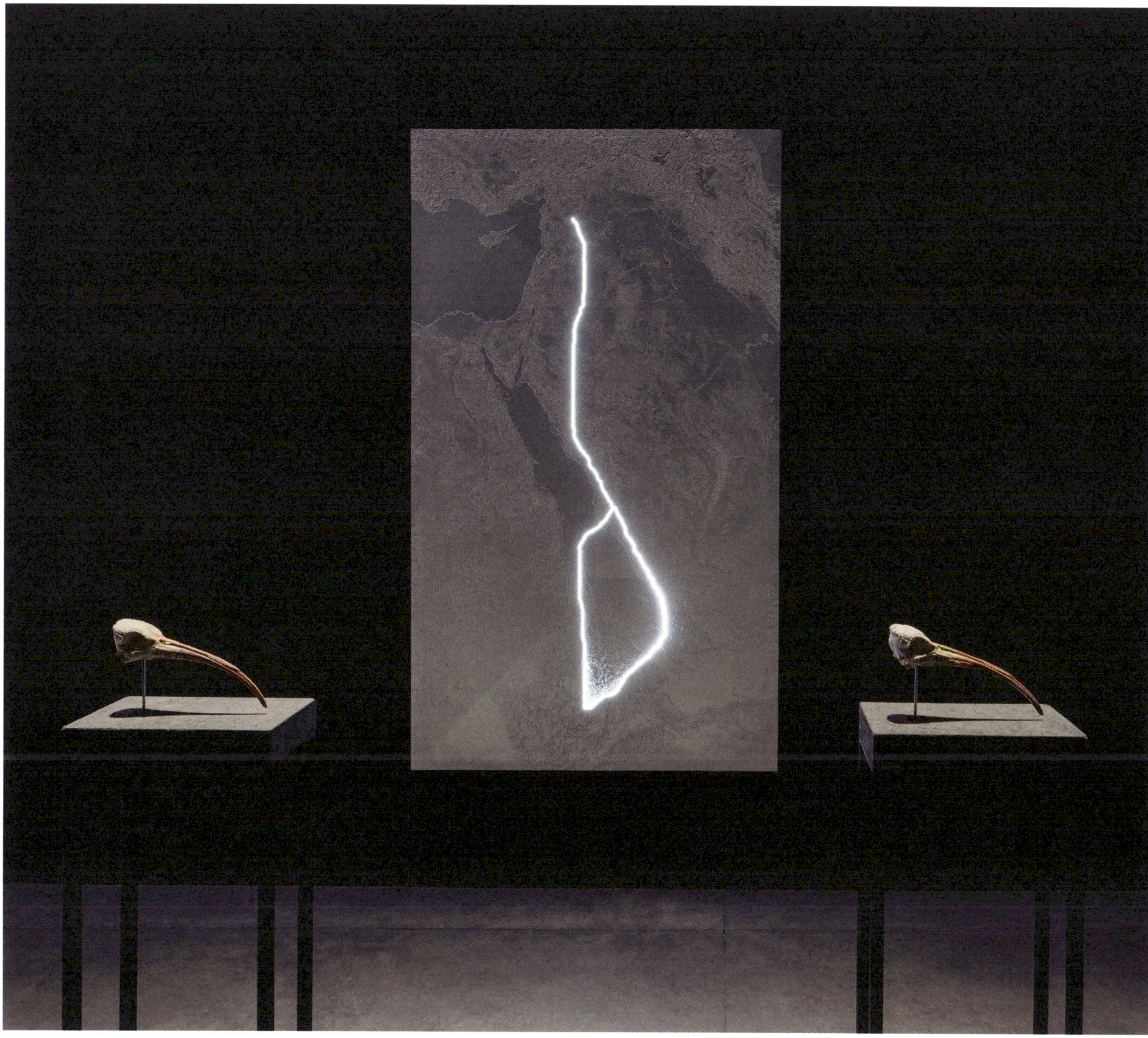

*Final Flight / Letzter Flug*, 2018–2019. Archiv-Inkjet-Druck; 7 handbemalte Knochenabgüsse aus Harz eines 3D-Schädelmodells; auf Aluminiumplatten; Einkanal-Video / Archival inkjet print; 7 hand-painted resin/bone casts of 3D-model skull; milled relief on aluminium plate; single-channel video. 185 × 85 cm; jeweils 26 × 6 × 5 cm; 125 × 230 × 0,6 cm; 9 Stunden / 185 × 85 cm; 26 × 6 × 5 cm each; 125 × 230 × 0,6 cm; 9 hours. Teilweise im Auftrag der Sharjah Art Foundation / Partially commissioned by Sharjah Art Foundation. Installationsansicht / Installation view, Hrair Sarkissian: *The Other Side of Silence*, Sharjah Art Foundation, 2021.

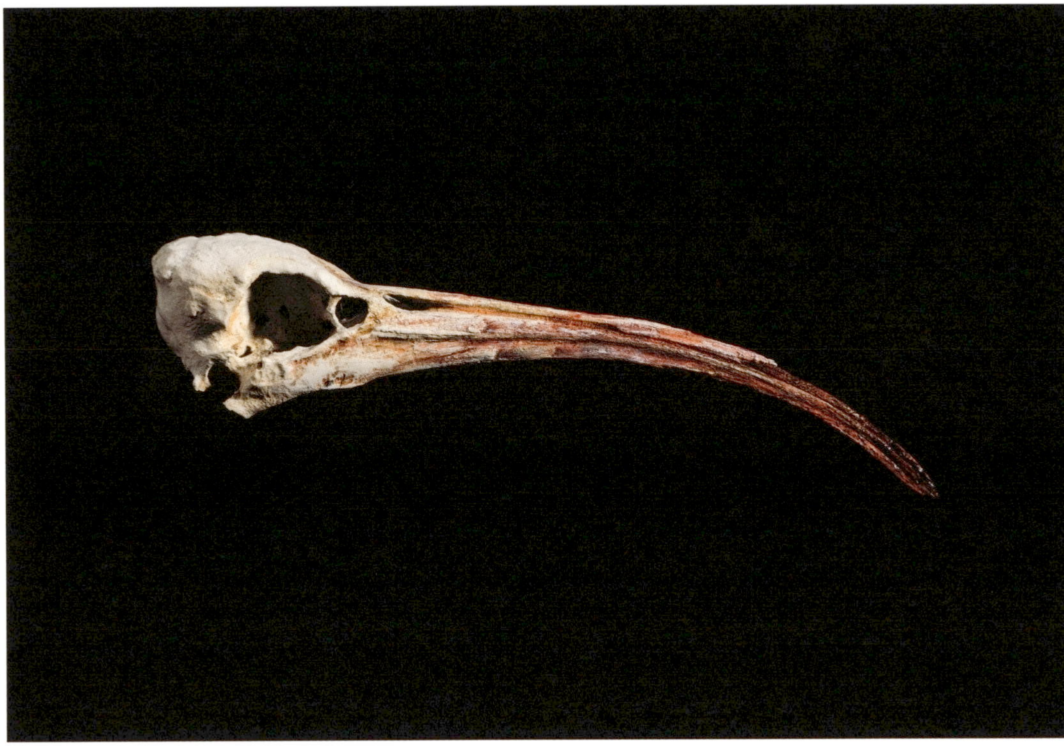

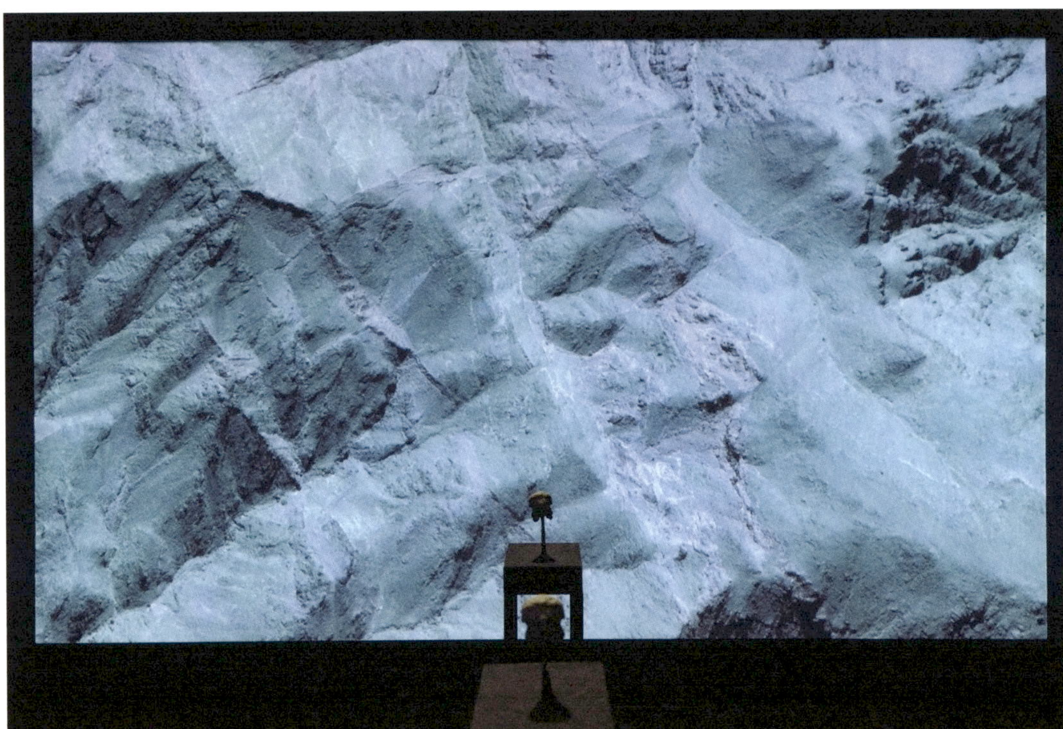

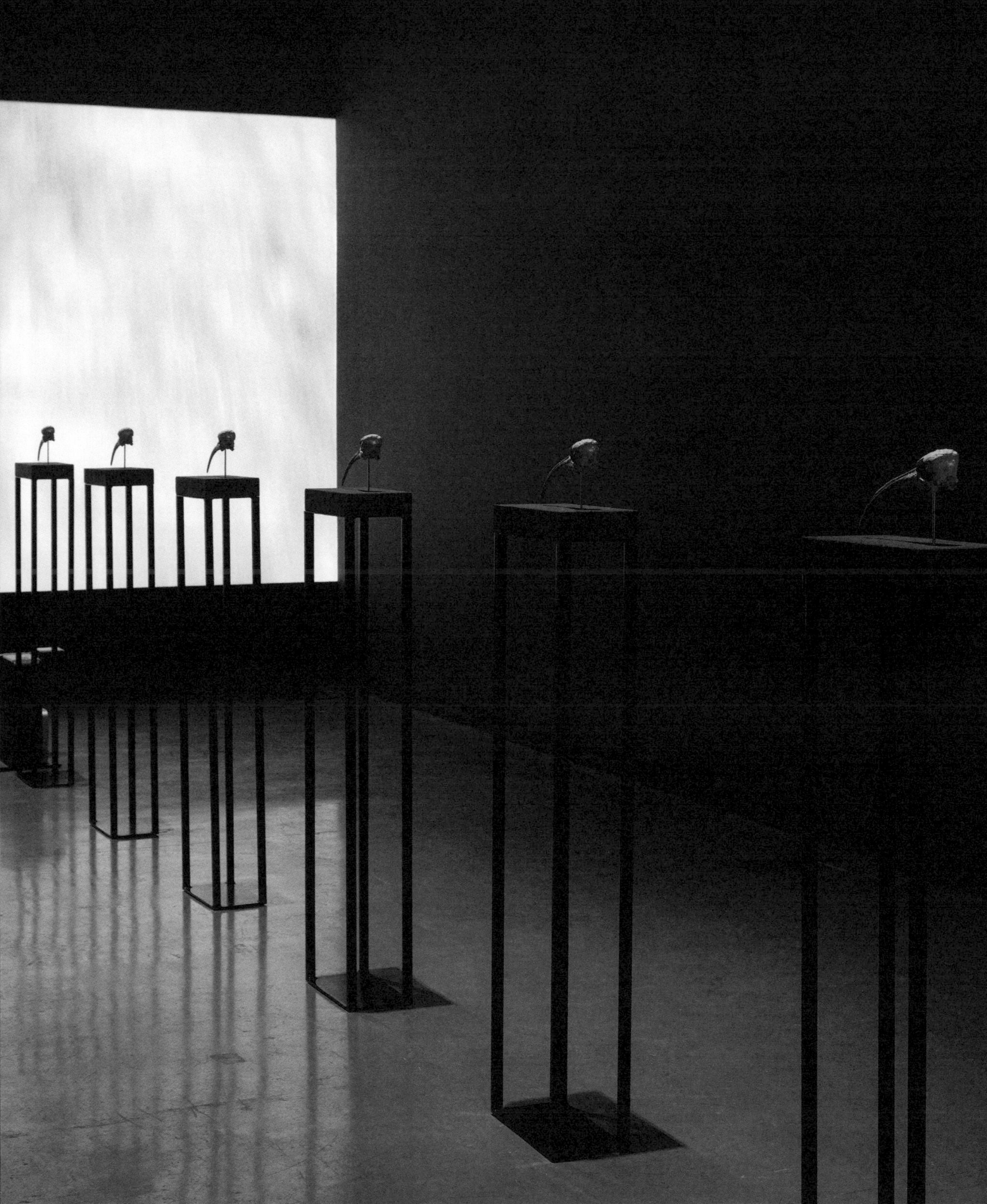

# Rayyane Tabet

Während eines Ausflugs an die Nordküste des Libanon im Jahr 2012 entdeckte die Familie von Rayyane Tabet nahe der Stadt Byblos ein Boot. Sie erkannte es wieder: Eben jenes Boot hatte Tabets Vater 29 Jahre zuvor angemietet, um während des libanesischen Bürgerkriegs (1975–1990) nach Zypern zu fliehen. Er hatte es nicht geschafft, das Boot war untauglich, nicht robust genug gewesen – die Fahrt hatte nur 30 Minuten gedauert. Und dennoch lag dieses Boot nun hier – ein Moment unwirklicher und unheimlicher Wiederkehr. Für seine Arbeit *Cyprus* („Zypern", 2015) hängte Tabet das Holzboot an die Decke. Mit seinem Gewicht von über 800 Kilogramm, das über Flaschenzüge von einem herabhängenden Stahlanker gehalten wird, hat es eine enorme Präsenz. Die Ankerflügel schweben über dem Boden, das daran befestigte Seil liegt zu einem flachen Bündel aufgerollt daneben. Der Anker ist mannshoch. *Cyprus* ist eines von fünf Objekten, die zusammen Tabets Serie *Five Distant Memories: The Suitcase, The Room, The Toys, The Boat and Maradona* („Fünf entfernte Erinnerungen: Der Koffer, Das Zimmer, Die Spielsachen, Das Boot und Maradona") bilden (2006 bis heute). In anderen Teilen dieser Serie wird ein Koffer für eine bevorstehende Reise gepackt; die Spielzeuge stammen aus dem von Bomben zerstörten Kinderzimmer des Künstlers in Beirut. Auf dem Fußboden der Galerie steht ein vergilbtes Sanyo-Radio, das fortlaufend eine Meldung von 1986 wiederholt – über den argentinischen Fußballspieler Diego Maradona und sein mit der Hand erzieltes Tor. Der Moderator Charif al-Akhawi unterbricht seine üblichen Ansagen über Sirenen und herannahende Bomben, um die Geschichte von der „Hand Gottes" zu erzählen – eine der frühesten Erinnerungen des Künstlers. Tabet, der ursprünglich Architekt war, bemerkte in einem Interview mit Chad Elias, er habe eine „komplizierte Beziehung zur Denkmalpflege". In der Tat verwandelt der Künstler gern einschneidende persönliche Augenblicke in historisch aufgeladene Sinnbilder, deren Einordnungsmöglichkeiten changieren. So verleiht Tabet den Gegenständen seiner Familiengeschichte ein für viele nachvollziehbares Pathos.

While on a trip to the northern coastline of Lebanon in 2012, by the city of Jbeil, Rayyane Tabet's family came across a boat. It was familiar: it was the very same boat chartered by Tabet's father, 29 years previous, in an attempt to flee to Cyprus during the Lebanese Civil War (1975–90). He hadn't made it, the boat was faulty, not strong enough, the trip had lasted a mere 30 minutes. And yet here it had returned, in a moment unreal and eerily circular. In Tabet's *Cyprus* (2015), the artist strings the wooden boat from the ceiling. It bears an enormous presence, weighing more than 800 kilograms, balanced by pulleys and a steel anchor, which hangs duly beside its hefty stature. Flukes float above the floor, attached rope curling into a low pile. The anchor is as tall as a human. *Cyprus* is one of five objects that form Tabet's series, *Five Distant Memories: The Suitcase, The Room, The Toys, The Boat and Maradona* (2006–ongoing). In other iterations of the sequence, the suitcase is packed in anticipation of a journey; the toys are collected from the artist's own bombed childhood bedroom in Beirut. A yellowing Sanyo radio sits on the gallery floor replaying the 1968 announcement of Argentinian footballer Diego Maradona's hand-touched goal. The presenter, Charif al-Akhawi, interrupts his regular announcements of sirens and incoming bombs to break the story of the 'Hand of God'—and listening to this is one of Tabet's earliest memories. Tabet, who initially trained as an architect, says in an interview with Chad Elias that he holds a 'complicated relationship to historical preservation'. Indeed, the artist takes penetratingly personal moments and turns them into charged emblems of history—slipping between methods of classification—infusing the objects of one family's story with a widely resonant pathos.

Skye Arundhati Thomas

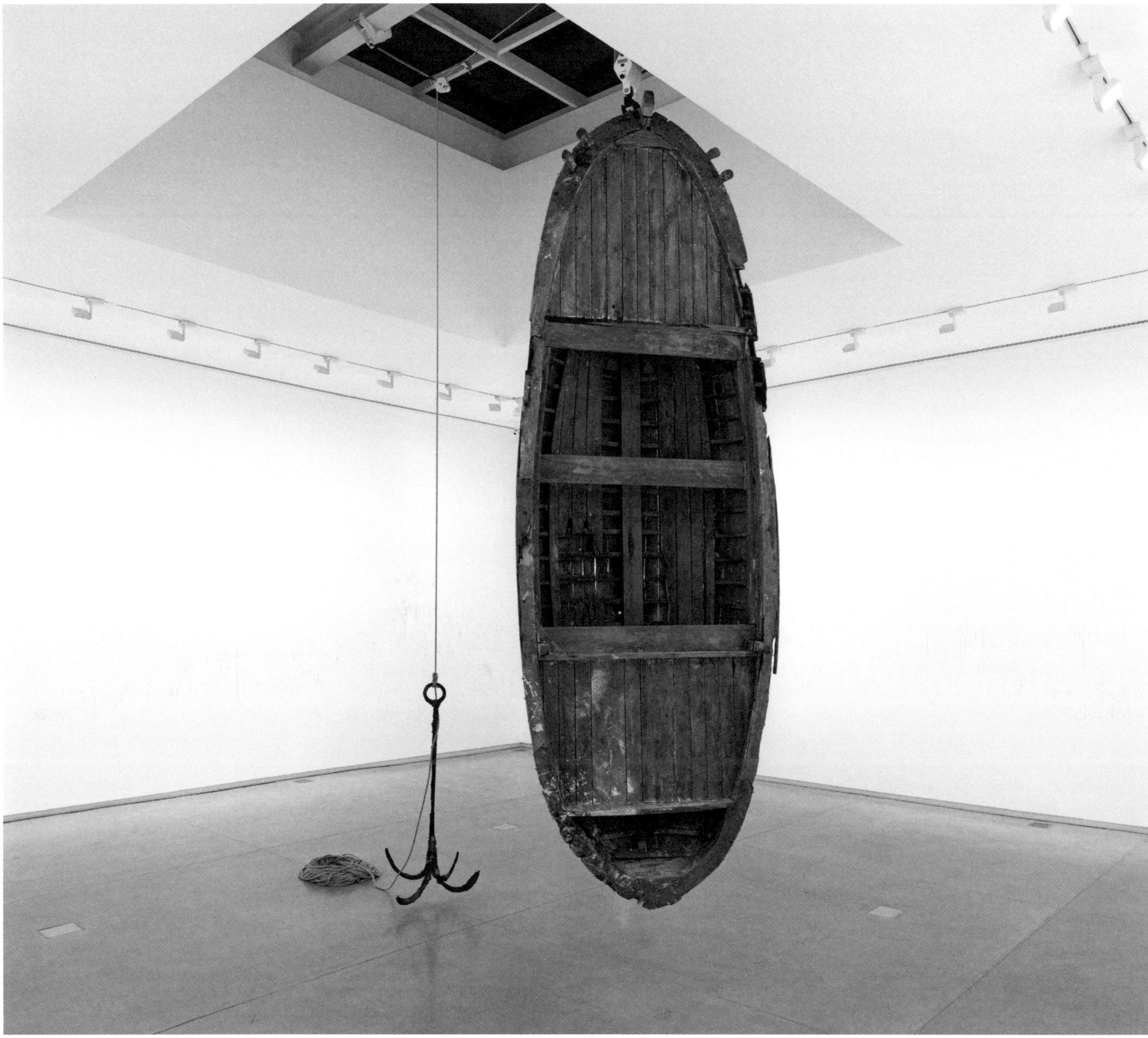

*Cyprus / Zypern*, 2015. Aus *Fünf entfernte Erinnerungen: Der Koffer, Das Zimmer, Die Spielsachen, Das Boot und Maradona* / From *Five Distant Memories: The Suitcase, The Room, The Toys, The Boat and Maradona*, 2006–. Holzboot, Stahlanker, Flaschenzug, Seil, Zubehör / Wooden boat, steel anchor, pulleys, rope, hardware. Maße variabel / Dimensions variable. Im Auftrag der Sharjah Art Foundation / Commissioned by Sharjah Art Foundation

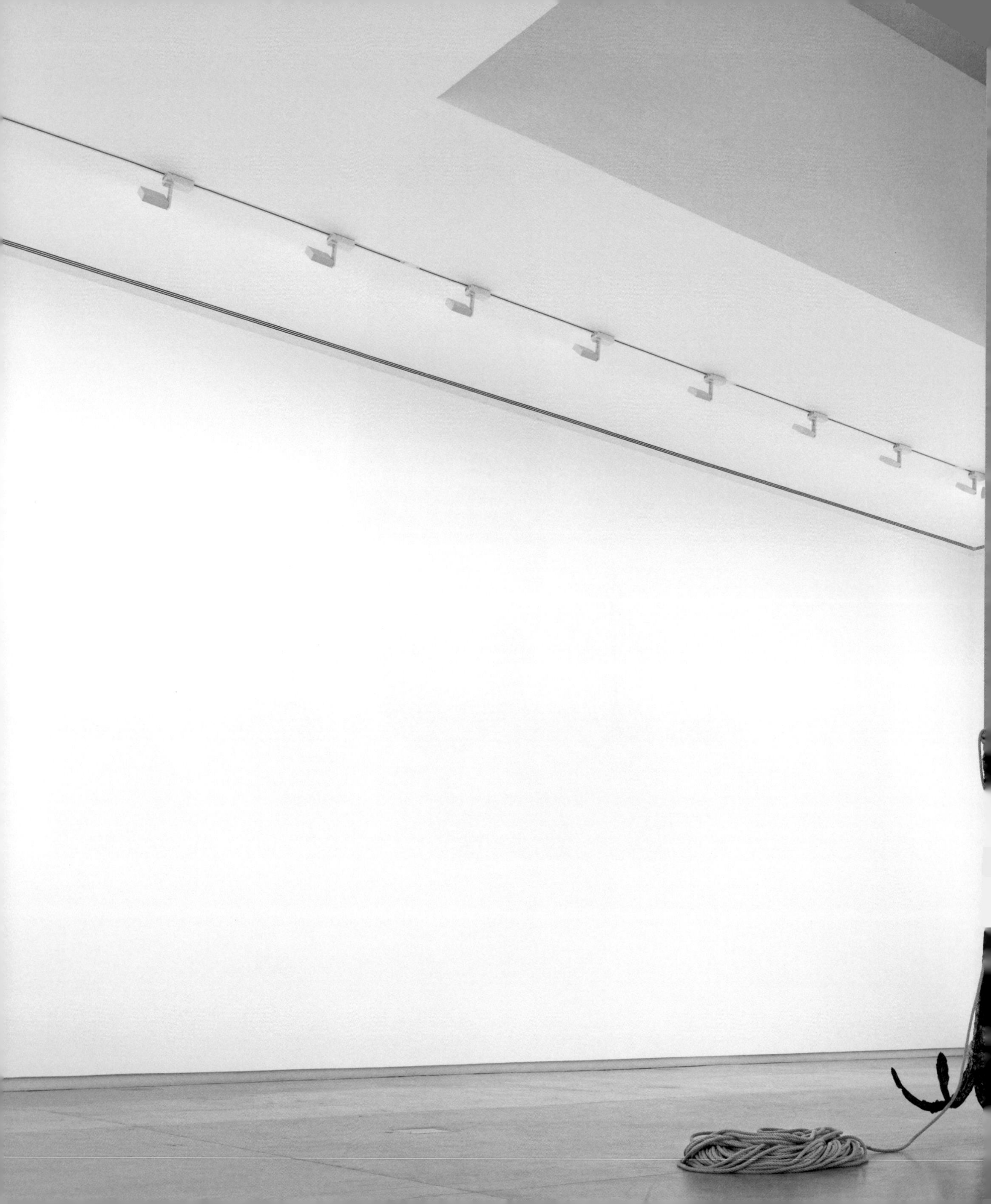

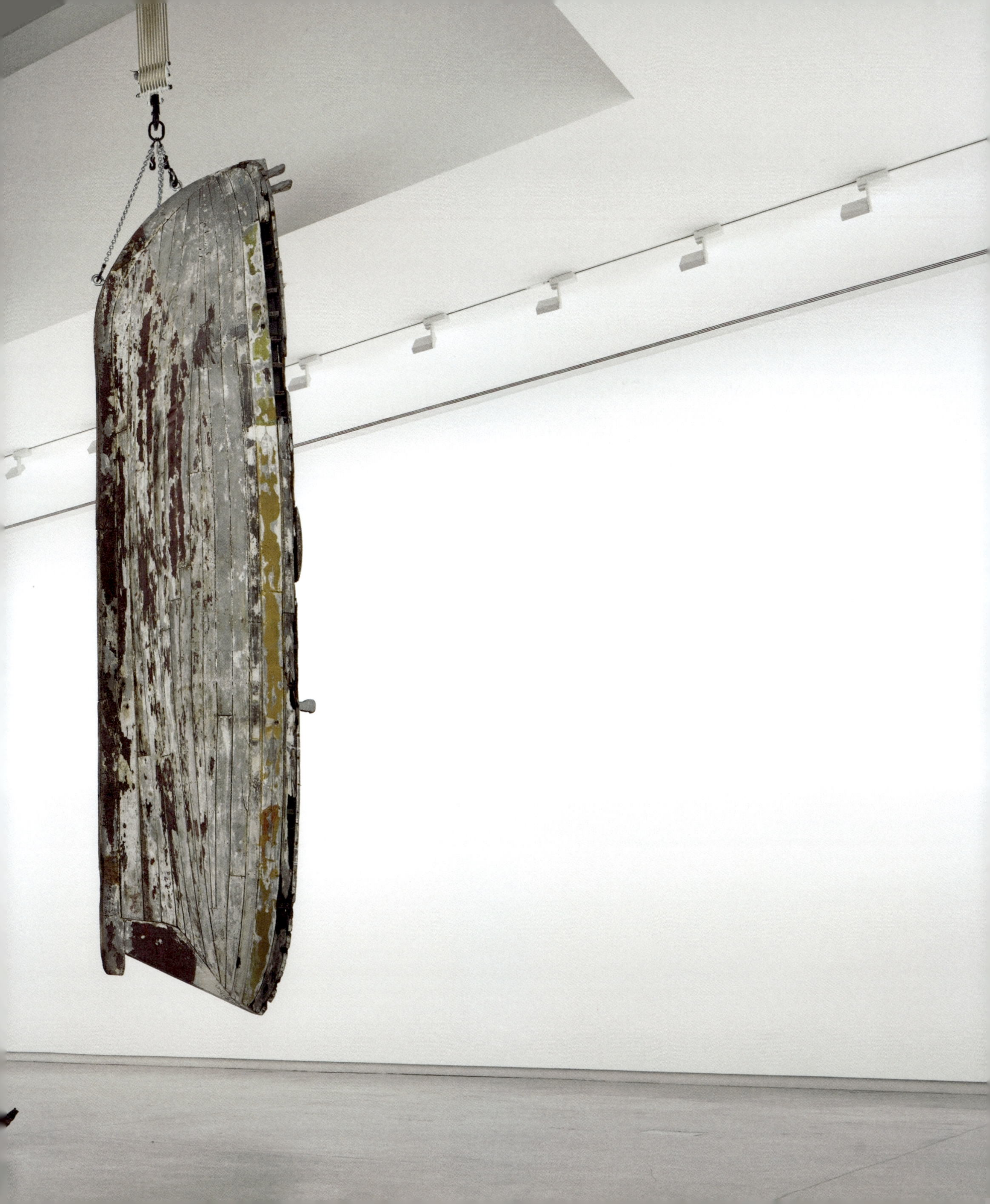

# Akram Zaatari

Der Künstler und Filmemacher Akram Zaatari lebt in Beirut. Er beschäftigt sich mitunter mit Ausgrabungen, um die oftmals fieberhaften politischen Ereignisse ans Licht zu bringen, die bestimmte historische Details verdrängt oder unter sich begraben haben. Zaatari macht auf die begrenzten Möglichkeiten der Verbreitung von Bildmaterial in Kriegszeiten aufmerksam und hebt so die Auslöschung oder Marginalisierung der Lebensgeschichten früherer libanesischer Oppositioneller hervor. Im Rahmen seiner Arbeit stößt er immer wieder auf Fotoarchive und Notizen, die Einblick in die Selbstorganisation radikaler oppositioneller Gruppierungen und in ihre Geschichten gewähren.

Ein wesentlicher Aspekt von Zaataris Arbeit ist seine Rolle als Mitgründer der Arab Image Foundation (AIF), die sich regelmäßig an den Diskursen über den Erhalt und die Archivpraxis von Orten beteiligt, wo keine offiziellen oder für die Öffentlichkeit zugänglichen Archive bestehen.

Sein Film *In This House* („In diesem Haus“, 2005) ist ein frühes Beispiel für Zaataris Interessengebiet und Arbeitsweisen. Es geht um die Suche nach einem Brief des früheren Widerstandskämpfer Ali Hashisho, den dieser Anfang der 1990er Jahre in einer Mörsergranate versteckt und in einem Garten in der südlibanesischen Stadt Saida vergraben hat. Zaatari, der ebenfalls aus Saida kommt, kontaktierte Hashisho, der inzwischen als Journalist tätig war, und stellte ihm sein Kunstprojekt über versteckte Archive vor. Zur Überraschung von Zaatari willigte Hashisho ein, an dem Filmprojekt teilzunehmen, und wurde zu dessen wichtigstem Protagonisten.

Die Stadt lag während der Besatzungszeit (1985–1991) – nach dem Einmarsch der israelischen Armee in den Libanon und dem anschließenden Rückzug aus Ain El Mir 1985 –innerhalb der Verteidigungslinie. Im Film wird diese Zeit mit Fotos und Notizen von Ali Hashisho nachgezeichnet – darunter auch die Geschichte der unerwartet einfühlsamen Entscheidung, den Olivenbaum der vertriebenen Hausbewohner*innen trotz der angespannten Lage nicht zu fällen, um Brennholz zu gewinnen.

Auch wenn der Gärtner letzten Endes die Mörsergranate nicht findet, macht der Film doch die damit zusammenhängenden Strukturen und politischen Ängste in Bezug auf das potenzielle Fundstück und seine mögliche Brisanz deutlich. Dass der Brief in einer Mörsergranate aufbewahrt wurde, ist dabei vermutlich kein zufälliges Detail: Es zeigt, wie explosiv Geschichte sein kann.

Akram Zaatari is an artist and filmmaker based in Beirut. His work uses the act of excavation as a means to uncover the often-febrile political circumstances that have rendered certain histories forgotten or buried. By calling attention to both the circulation and restriction of images in times of war, Zaatari centres the erasure and fragile histories of former militants' lives in Lebanon, often unearthing archives of photographs and notes that chronicle self-organised radical histories or groups. A central aspect of Zaatari's practice is his co-founding of the Arab Image Foundation (AIF), which has made numerous contributions to discourses on preservation and archival practices in sites where official archives do not formally exist, or are inaccessible to the public.

His film *In This House* (2005) is an early example of Zaatari's interests and methodology. It records the search for a letter buried inside a mortar shell written in the early 1990s by a former resistance fighter, Ali Hashisho, in the garden of a house in the city of Saida in southern Lebanon. Zaatari, who also hails from Saida, contacted Hashisho—now a journalist—as a potential conduit for an artwork he had in mind about hidden archives. To the artist's surprise, Hashisho became the central protagonist of this work. The village in question was a frontline defence against the occupation from 1985 to 1991 after Israel's invasion of Lebanon and its subsequent withdrawal from Ain el Mir in 1985. *In This House* recounts this period, showing numerous photographs and notes made by Hashisho, including unexpectedly tender decisions, such as the preservation of the displaced occupants' olive tree, which, during the warring tensions, was not cut down for firewood. If the work belies its central premise of the gardener attempting to locate the buried mortar shell, it does so to reveal attendant structures and political anxieties about what might be buried and the power it holds—that the letter has been preserved in a mortar shell is perhaps no coincidence: history is itself explosive.

Chris McCormack

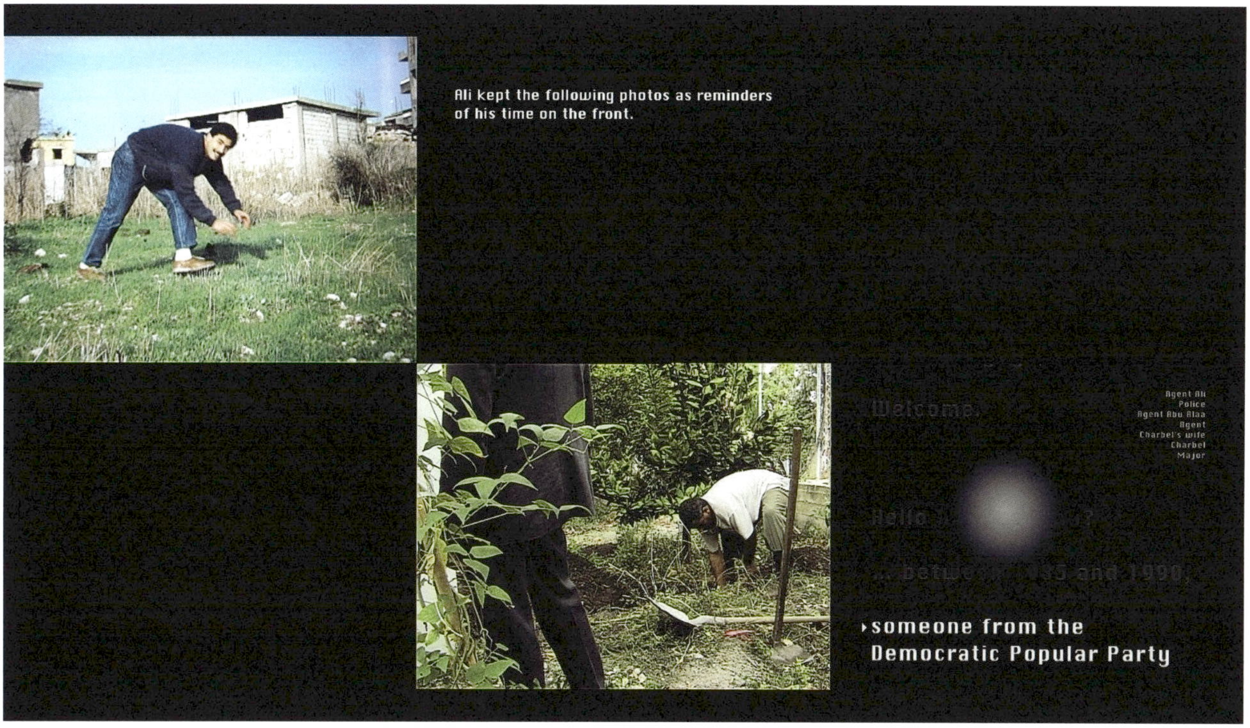


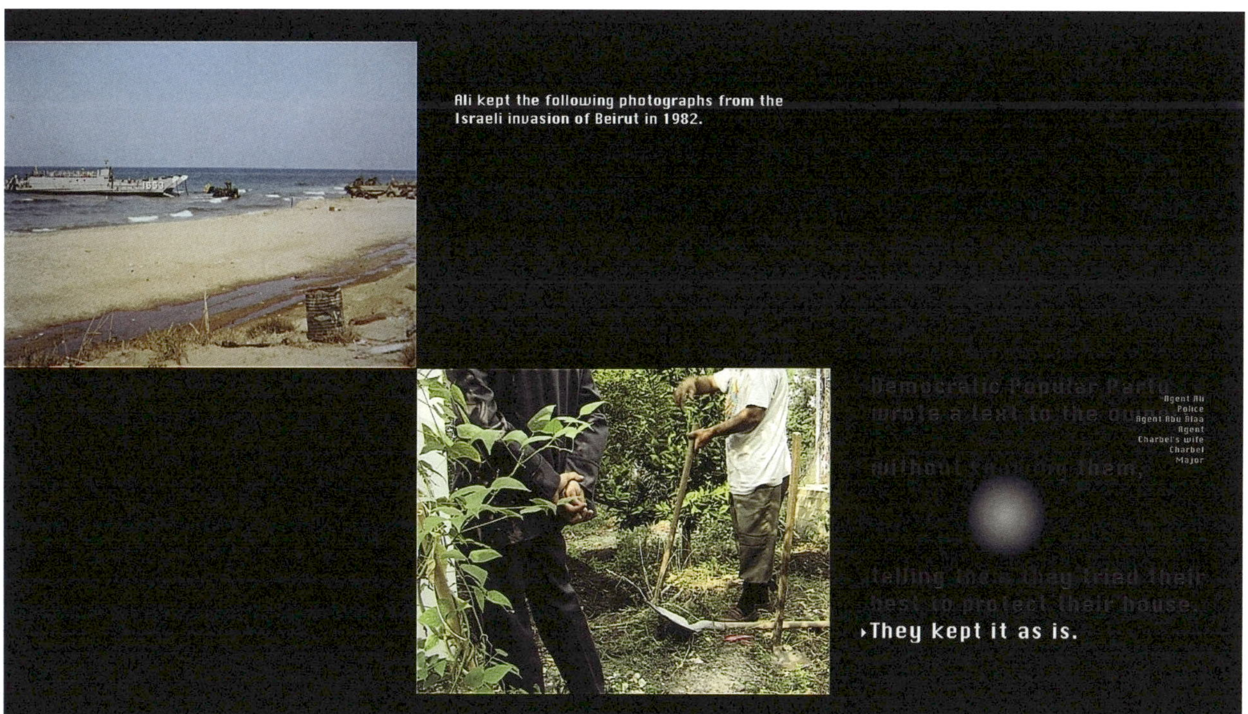


*In This House* / *In diesem Haus*, 2004–2012. Video, Farbe, Sound / Video, colour, sound. 30 Minuten / 30 minutes

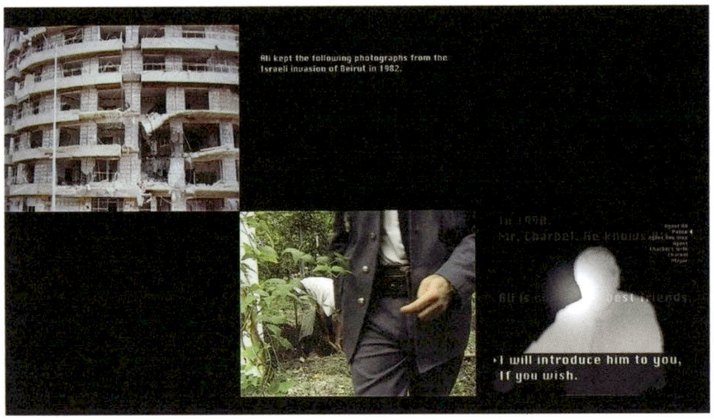
Ali kept the following photographs from the Israeli invasion of Beirut in 1982.
In 1990.
I will introduce him to you, If you wish.

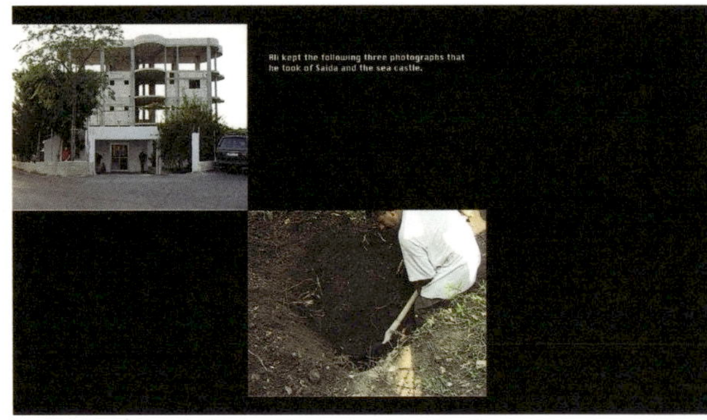
Ali kept the following three photographs that he took of Saida and the sea castle.

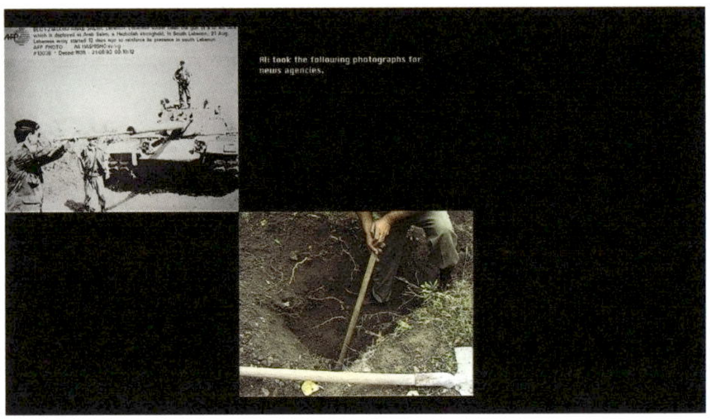
Ali took the following photographs for news agencies.

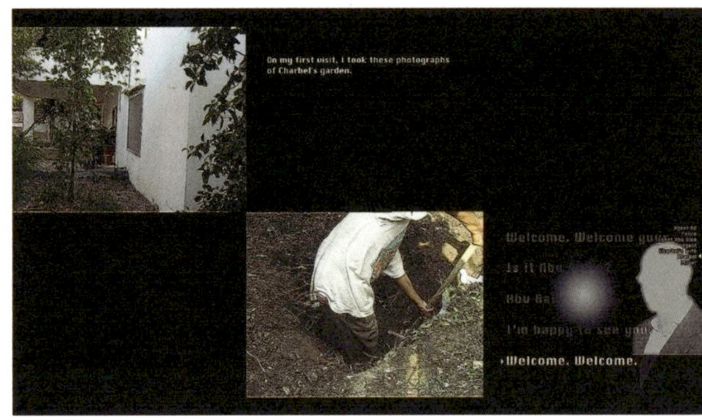
On my first visit, I took these photographs of Charbel's garden.
Welcome. Welcome.

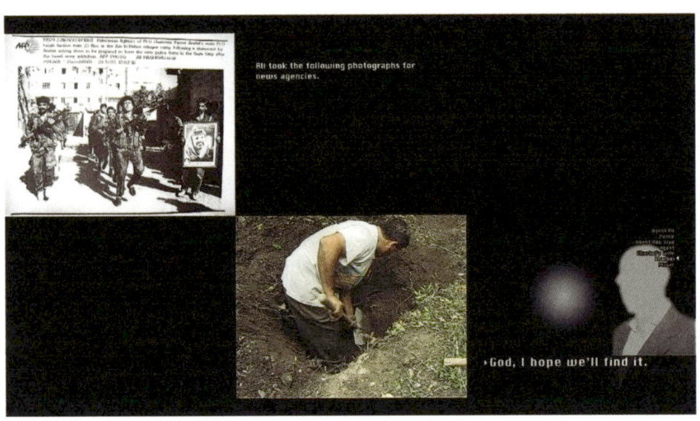
Ali took the following photographs for news agencies.
God, I hope we'll find it.

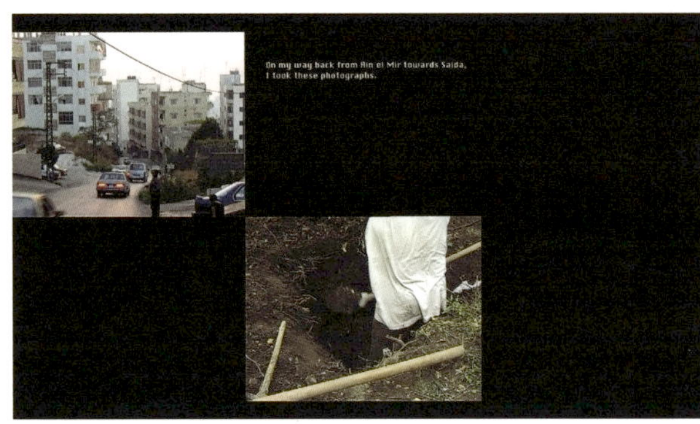
On my way back from Ain el Mir towards Saida, I took these photographs.

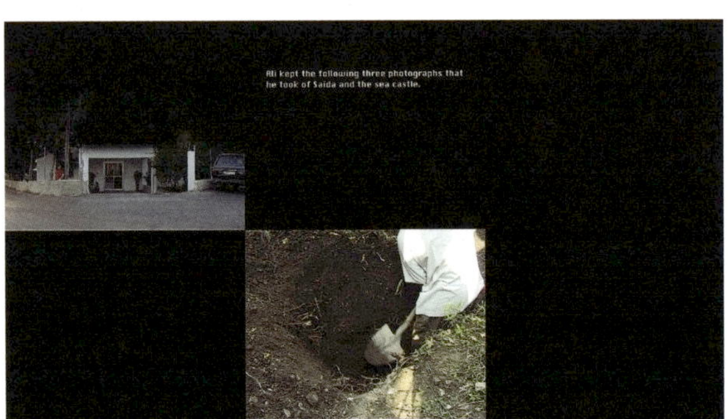
Ali kept the following three photographs that he took of Saida and the sea castle.

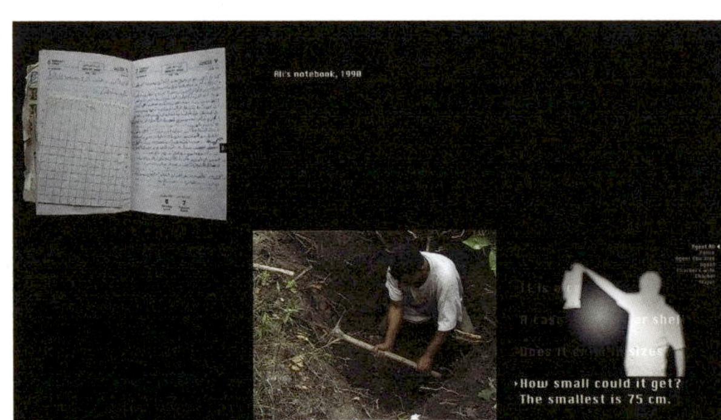
Ali's notebook, 1990
How small could it get? The smallest is 75 cm.

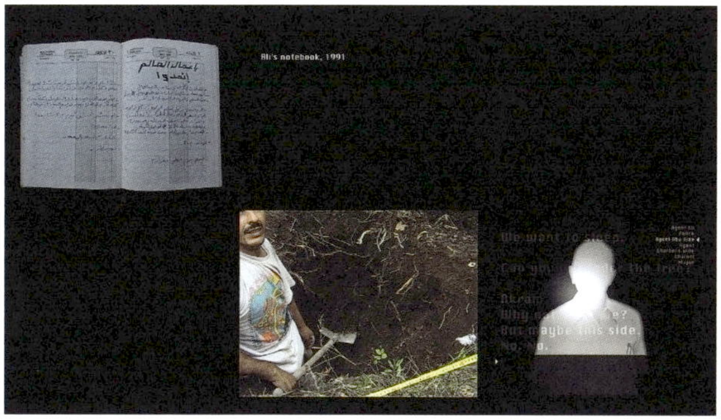
Ali's notebook, 1991

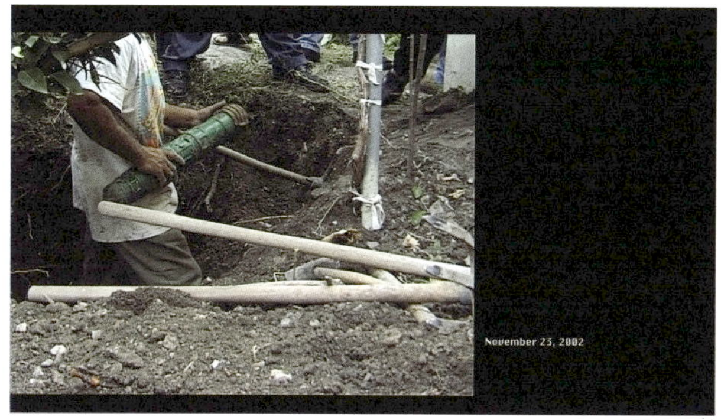
November 23, 2002

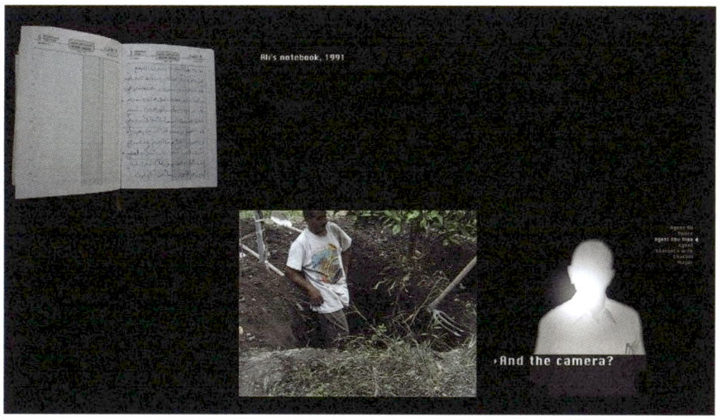
Ali's notebook, 1991
And the camera?

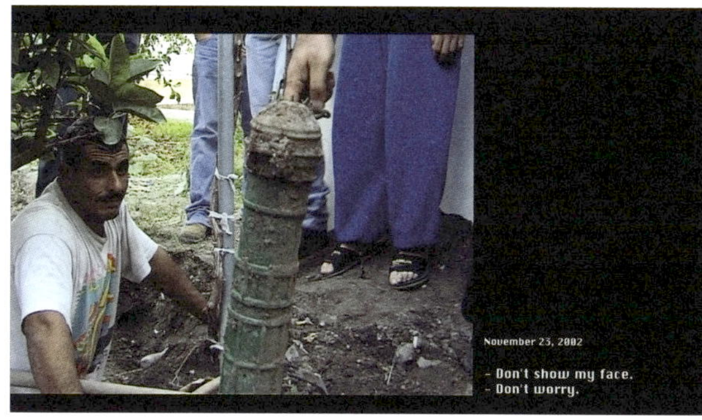
November 23, 2002
- Don't show my face.
- Don't worry.

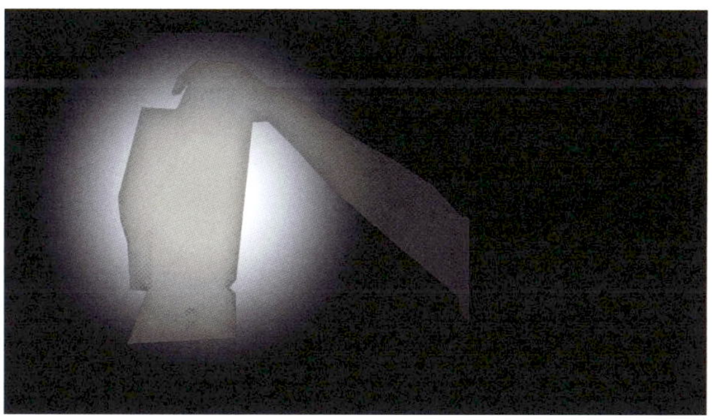

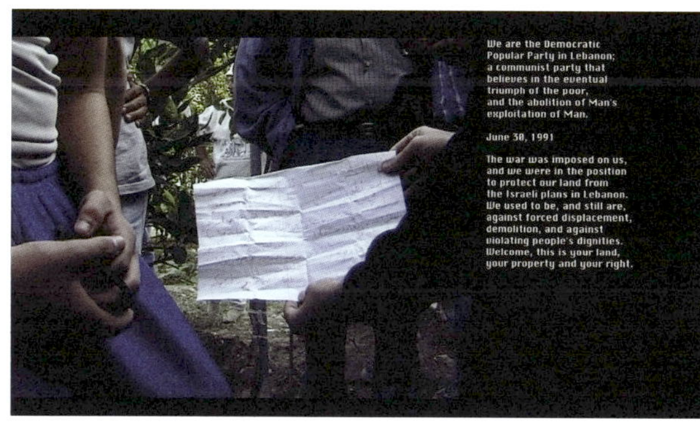
We are the Democratic
Popular Party in Lebanon;
a communist party that
believes in the eventual
triumph of the poor,
and the abolition of Man's
exploitation of Man.
June 30, 1991
The war was imposed on us,
and we were in the position
to protect our land from
the Israeli plans in Lebanon.
We used to be, and still are,
against forced displacement,
demolition, and against
violating people's dignities.
Welcome, this is your land,
your property and your right.

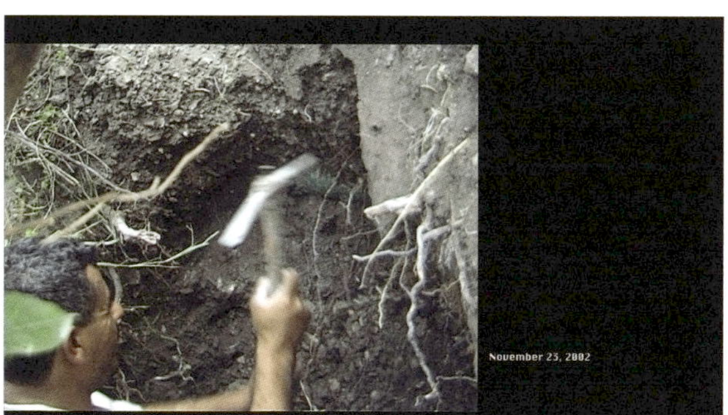
November 23, 2002

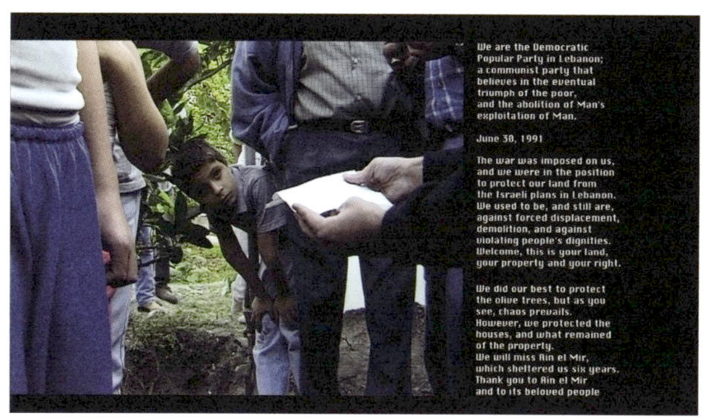
We are the Democratic
Popular Party in Lebanon;
a communist party that
believes in the eventual
triumph of the poor,
and the abolition of Man's
exploitation of Man.
June 30, 1991
The war was imposed on us,
and we were in the position
to protect our land from
the Israeli plans in Lebanon.
We used to be, and still are,
against forced displacement,
demolition, and against
violating people's dignities.
Welcome, this is your land,
your property and your right.
We did our best to protect
the olive trees, but as you
see, chaos prevails.
However, we protected the
houses, and what remained
of the property.
We will miss Ain el Mir,
which sheltered us six years.
Thank you to Ain el Mir
and to its beloved people

# "Wenn Du mir auf der Straße begegnest, sei Dir nicht sicher, dass ich es bin."

## Sofia Victorino im Gespräch mit: Bani Abidi, Lubaina Himid, Hrair Sarkissian

In diesem Podiumsgespräch geht es es um die Schnittstellen, die sich aus der künstlerischen Auseinandersetzung mit Geschichts- und Erinnerungspolitik, Unsichtbarkeit und Auslöschung, ethnischer Diskriminierung und sozialer und politischer Transformation, Archiven und Beweismitteln, Akten der Fürsorge sowie Lektionen in Resilienz ergeben.

Sofia Victorino Im Mittelpunkt der Ausstellung *In the Heart of Another Country* steht die Frage, auf welche Weise die Erfahrungen verschiedener Diasporagruppen miteinander verknüpft sind. Der Titel ist inspiriert von Etel Adnans bemerkenswerten Memoiren. Ich möchte daher gern mit einem Zitat von ihr beginnen:

„Stets bin ich entfernt von etwas, von einem Ort. Meine Sinne haben mich verlassen, einer nach dem anderen, um ihr eigenes Leben zu führen. Wenn du mir auf der Straße begegnest, sei dir nicht sicher, daß ich es bin. Mein Mittelpunkt liegt nicht im Sonnensystem."*

Erzählungen aus der Diaspora bilden den Kern des kuratorischen Konzepts dieser Ausstellung. Mit poetischen Worten vermittelt uns Etel Adnan hier einen Eindruck vom Leben in der Diaspora. Für mich persönlich ist die Diaspora ein Lebensentwurf, der auf einem Dasein zwischen den Dingen beruht und zugleich die Spuren der eigenen Geschichte nicht verwischt. Dabei geht es um das, was aus uns wird, und weniger um ein Beharren auf festen Vorstellungen von Identität oder Zugehörigkeit. Das Kunstschaffen verschiedener Diasporagruppen hat schon immer einen anderen als den imperialen und kolonialen Blick auf das Leben geworfen und Kunstwerke hervorgebracht, die sich der Auslöschung und dem Vergessen widersetzen.

Meine Verbindung zu eurer Arbeit ist unweigerlich mit London verbunden. Während meiner zehnjährigen Tätigkeit in der Whitechapel Gallery habe ich mich auch mit eurer künstlerischen Praxis auseinandergesetzt. Zu Beginn unseres Gesprächs möchte ich euch fragen, inwiefern ihr in eurer Arbeit durch die Wahl von Materialien und Formen eine Verbindung zwischen persönlichen Erfahrungen und größeren historischen Zusammenhängen herstellt.

Lubaina Himid In London habe ich eine Ausbildung zur Bühnenbildnerin gemacht. Meine künstlerische Praxis habe ich über Umwege oder auf eine für mich überraschende Weise entwickelt. Es war nie mein Plan, meine Kunst in Galerien auszustellen. Zumindest nicht zu Beginn. Damals in der Anfangszeit hat es mir Freude bereitet, mit allem zu arbeiten, was mir in die Hände fiel: mit Holzstücken aus dem Garten, Fundstücken von der Straße oder Dingen aus meinen Schrän-ken. Es fühlte sich natürlich an und wie eine Fortführung der falschen Realität des Theaters und der Illusion aus der Welt der Galeriekunst. Und das meine ich überhaupt nicht negativ. Allerdings fühlte ich mich zu keiner dieser beiden Welten richtig zugehörig. In keiner hatte ich bis dahin meinen Platz gefunden. Genauso wenig hatte ich eine Vorstellung davon, was meine Art von Kunst war oder sein könnte. An der Art des Arbeitens faszinierte mich aber, dass ich die Kontrolle hatte, und die Leichtigkeit des Umgangs mit Materialien wie Tellern oder Stühlen, Stoffstücken, Bettlaken oder Kissenbezügen. Außerdem fehlte mir das Geld für Leinwände und Ölgemälde. All das hat einen Einfluss auf mein aktuelles Kunstschaffen und darauf, dass ich sowohl mit Fundstücken arbeite als sie auch bemale. Beim Malen geht es um Momente, Momente des Wandels und der Bewegung.

# 'If you meet me on the street, don't be sure it's me'.

# Sofia Victorino in conversation with: Bani Abidi, Lubaina Himid, Hrair Sarkissian

This panel discussion seeks to unpick how distinct art practices overlap in their approaches to the politics of history and memory; invisibility and erasure; racial justice and social and political transformation; archives and material evidence; acts of care and lessons of resilience.

Sofia Victorino The exhibition *In the Heart of Another Country* addresses the question of how multiple diasporas and their histories intertwine. Its title is inspired by Etel Adnan's remarkable memoir, so I am keen to begin with one of her quotes:

'I'm always away from something and somewhere. My senses left me one by one to have a life of their own. If you meet me in the street, don't be sure it's me. My centre is not the solar system.'

The diasporic imagination is central to the curatorial framework of the exhibition. These words situate us poetically in relation to ideas of diaspora. Diaspora for me emerges as a concept that proposes an in-betweenness. It does not dissolve historical traces. It is about what we are becoming rather than the attachment to fixed notions of identity or belonging. Art practices from multiple diasporas have consistently proposed a way of looking that is against the imperial and colonial project—nurturing art that works against erasure and forgetting.

My relation to your work is inevitably connected to London. I've worked at Whitechapel Gallery for a decade, and I have followed and researched your practice over time. I would like to open the conversation with a question about the ways in which the material and formal elements in your work connect personal experience to larger historical narratives.

Lubaina Himid Well, I trained in London as a theatre designer, I was coming at my practice in an odd way or in a way that even surprised me. I never meant to be a gallery artist. It was not what I set out to do. That was my pleasure, once upon a time. In those very early days, I began to make work with whatever was to hand, from bits of wood that were in the garden or things that I found on the street or in the cupboard, that seemed very natural, and a sort of continuation of the false reality of theatre and the illusion of the world of gallery art. Not in a bad way, but I didn't particularly belong to either of those worlds. I hadn't made any kind of place in either of those worlds or hadn't really, in a way, understood what my practice even was or could be. And that understanding of the power and the ease of engagement one has with a plate or a chair or a piece of cloth, a sheet, or a pillowcase, drew me to working in that way. Also, I didn't have the funds to be stretching canvases and making oil paintings. A combination of those things is why the work really looks like it looks today and why I fluctuate between using found objects and painting on them. Painting is about moments, shifting, fluctuating moments.

Bani Abidi If I were to describe the personal and its effect on how I make work, I would say the transition from painting to a time-based practice. I trained in Lahore at the National College of Arts in painting and printmaking, and then I went to the School of the Art Institute of Chicago and kept on working with painting and installations. I never really studied video or film, but I had a lot of exposure to film just because it was cheaper to watch cinema and there was good programming. At some point, it was clear that there was a love for narrative, and that I was trying to squeeze a lot out of a painting and a still image. I grew up in a very oral narrative culture where there's a much deeper sensitivity to poetry. My parents were both literary people and

**Bani Abidi** Auf die Frage, welche persönlichen Erfahrungen meine Arbeit beeinflussen, würde ich meinen Wechsel von der Malerei zu einer zeitbasierten Praxis nennen. Meine Ausbildung in Malerei und Druckkunst habe ich am National College of Arts in Lahore absolviert. Anschließend besuchte ich das School of the Art Institute in Chicago, wo ich mich weiter der Malerei und Installationen widmete. Video- oder Filmkunst habe ich nie studiert. Doch ich habe viele Filme geschaut, weil Kinobesuche günstig waren und es ein gutes Programm gab. Irgendwann wurde mir klar, dass ich gern Geschichten erzähle und schon immer darauf ausgewesen bin, viele Themen in einem einzigen Gemälde oder einem unbewegten Bild zu verarbeiten. Ich bin in einer sehr mündlichen Erzählkultur mit einem besonders tiefen Verständnis für Poesie aufgewachsen. Meine Eltern waren Schriftsteller*innen, sie sprachen Urdu und konnten ein paar Brocken Persisch. Mit der Arbeit an meinem ersten Film betrat ich völliges Neuland. Gleichzeitig fühlte ich mich in diesem Medium zu Hause, weil ich mit Zeit, Sound und Bildern arbeiten konnte. Und auf diesen drei verschiedenen Ebenen kann ich Geschichten erzählen, die mir wirklich am Herzen liegen. Dies ist der biografische Aspekt meiner Arbeit.

**Hrair Sarkissian** Wie sagt man so schön: Ich bin nicht mit einem goldenen Löffel, sondern mit einer Kamera im Mund auf die Welt gekommen. Mein Vater ist Fotograf und hat mich an die Fotografie herangeführt. Als Kind habe ich meinem Vater während der Sommerferien in seinem Labor geholfen. Im Jahr 1976 hatte er sich einen großen Traum verwirklicht und das erste Farbfotolabor Syriens eröffnet. Und an diesem Ort bin ich im Grunde aufgewachsen. Das Labor war meine Schule. Ich habe dort viel über Fotografie und auch über das Leben gelernt. Ich wollte schon immer Fotograf werden. Doch nach meinem High-School-Abschluss lernte ich mit der zeitgenössischen französischen Fotografie eine ganz andere Form der Fotografie kennen, die mich dazu bewegte, als selbstständiger Fotograf zu arbeiten. Für mein erstes Projekt machte ich Aufnahmen von Körpern. In Syrien gibt es zahlreiche Einschränkungen, nicht in sexueller Hinsicht, sondern was unsere Freiheiten betrifft. Durch das Fotografieren von nackter Haut und Körpern als Landschaften konnte ich mehr oder weniger unabhängig meine eigenen Vorstellungswelten schaffen. Anschließend setzte ich mich in meiner Arbeit mit meinem familiären Hintergrund auseinander. Meine Familie stammt aus Armenien, und das Trauma des Völkermords an den Armeniern hat auch mein Leben geprägt. Dieser Aspekt soll immer den Kern meiner Arbeit bilden … dieses Gefühl soll stets im Mittelpunkt meiner Arbeit stehen.

**Sofia Victorino** Die Titel eurer Kunstwerke in der Ausstellung sprechen für sich. Bani, dein Werk heißt *Proposal for a Man in the Sea / Angebot für einen Mann im Meer* (2012), deines, Hrair, *Final Flight / Letzter Flug* (2018–2019), und deines, Lubaina, *Bone in the China: Success to the Africa Trade / Knochen im Porzellan: Erfolg dem afrikanischen Sklavenhandel* (1985). Könnt ihr etwas über die Entstehungsprozesse dieser Kunstwerke sagen?

**Lubaina Himid** Ja, bei meinem es handelt es sich um ein frühes Werk aus den 1980er Jahren. Damals folgte ich der Einladung eines Museums in den englischen Midlands an einen Ort namens Stoke, der das Zentrum der Keramikkunst in Großbritannien ist. Dort wird die jahrhundertealte Geschichte der englischen Keramik gewürdigt: berühmtes Steingut und Tafelgeschirr aus Manufakturen wie *Wedgwood*. Von mir wurde erwartet, dass ich mich durch die Exponate zu eigenen Werken inspirieren lasse. Ein zentrales Ausstellungsstück in einer hübschen Vitrine war eine wunderschön beleuchtete Schale in einem Glaskasten. Auf dem dazugehörigen Schild stand der Titel *Success to the Africa Trade / Erfolg dem afrikanischen Sklavenhandel.* Tatsächlich handelte es sich um eine Schale für Punsch, also für ein Festtagsgetränk. Mehr war auf dem Schild nicht zu lesen. Doch selbstverständlich hatte die Schale eine Geschichte: Sie war ein Geschenk der Stadt Liverpool an einen Kapitän für den erfolgreichen Transport von Erzeugnissen wie Nägeln und Eisenwaren und Baumaterialien aus Nordengland an die afrikanische Westküste. Im Anschluss beförderte das Schiff Gefangene von der Westküste Afrikas in die Karibik und brachte auf dem Rückweg Mahagoni und schwere Hölzer mit, auch um das Schiff zu stabilisieren. Die Schale würdigte also den Handel mit Afrikaner*innen, doch in der Ausstellung gab es darauf keinen Hinweis. Das Exponat wurde als exquisites Beispiel für englische Feinkeramik präsentiert. Mein Werk stammt aus den 1980er Jahren und damit aus einer Zeit, in der man über so etwas nicht sprach, ganz besonders nicht in englischen Museen und Galerien. Ich sagte, dass ich auf dieses Ausstellungsstück gern mit einem großen unförmigen Gemälde auf Holz reagieren würde, das nicht die elegante Form der Keramik nachahmen, sondern die unausgesprochenen Fragen aufwerfen sollte. Ich habe nichts dagegen, wenn schöne Objekte in einer Ausstellung nur für ihre Form und Funktion bewundert werden. Doch sie müssen unbedingt auch in ihren Kontext gesetzt werden. Ich halte nichts davon, Dinge zu zerstören oder verschwinden zu lassen. Viel mehr interessiert es mich, die Lücken zu füllen. In gewissem Sinne stelle ich mit meinem Kunstwerk all die Fragen, die im Zusammenhang mit der Schale

they read Urdu and understood a bit of Persian. To make my first film was really like discovering something new and feeling very much at home in that medium because I could use time, I could use sound and image. And there's three different layers over which I could reveal things that I'm really invested in. So that was my biographical kind of influence.

Hrair Sarkissian As they say, I was born with a camera in my mouth instead of a silver spoon. My father is a photographer, and that's how I came into photography. During my childhood, in summer holidays, I used to work with my dad in his lab. Then in 1976, he opened the first colour lab in Syria, which was like his big dream project. This is basically where I grew up, this was my academy, and I learnt a lot about photography and life at the same time. My focus in life was to be a photographer. But then, when I finished high school, I was introduced to contemporary French photographers, and that was a different kind of photography that pushed me to work as an independent photographer. In my first project, I photographed bodies. Coming from Syria, we have all these restrictions, not from a sexual side, but about having more freedom. Photographing the skin and the bodies as landscapes created a kind independence regarding my own ways of thinking. From there, I moved on to concentrate on my family background, having Armenian origins, and inheriting Armenian genocide traumas in my life. That has become the core that I always try to work from...

Sofia Victorino Your works in the exhibition have very evocative titles. Bani, yours is *Proposal for a Man in the Sea* (2012), Hrair, *Final Flight* (2018–19), and Lubaina, *Bone in the China: Success to the Africa Trade* (1985). Can you talk through the genesis of each of these artworks?

Lubaina Himid Yes, it's an early piece from the 1980s. I was invited to a museum in the Midlands in England, in a place called Stoke, which is the centre of the ceramics in Britain. Its history of making ceramics in that town goes back hundreds of years... all the famous plates, dinner services, and factories, like Wedgwood. The history of English ceramics is celebrated there. And this museum invited me to look at what they had and maybe make some work around that. A key piece that was on show in a very beautiful vitrine was a bowl, beautifully lit, covered in a glass case. The label said that it was called *Success to the Africa Trade* and, in fact, what it was, was a punch bowl, for serving punch... it's a celebratory drink, really. That was all the label said. But, of course, what it was, was a present from the City of Liverpool to a sea captain for having successfully taken goods from the North of England to the west coast of Africa. Materials like nails and iron and things for building, and then taken captured Africans from the West Coast to the Caribbean and come back with mahogany to balance the ship. It was a bowl that was celebrating the trade in buying and selling Africans, and yet there was no label that said this. It was admired as a piece of fine English ceramic. I made the work in the '80s, and those were the times when those sorts of acknowledgements or conversations were not had. They were certainly not had in museums and galleries in England. I said I would like to respond to that piece and make a big, clunky painting on wood that wasn't trying to match the ceramic elegance, but was asking all the questions that were not asked. I don't have an objection to beautiful objects being on show as something to be admired for their form and their function, but I absolutely insist that they're fully contextualised. I am not a believer in breaking things or smashing things or disappearing things, really. I'm much more interested in filling in the gaps. In a sense, that piece is very much about asking all the questions that were not asked of that piece, and eventually it did set up very intense conversations between audiences and the museum.

Sofia Victorino Do you recall any of those conversations?

Lubaina Himid The museum staff used it to think about their collection and about labels. Yes, they had a history of British ceramics. But what they had there was a history of colonialism, a history of industrialisation, a history of all sorts of other things. It helped them towards those sorts of rethinking.

Sofia Victorino Bani, the idea of the monument and how it appears in public space is something that *Proposal for a Man in the Sea* also touches upon. Can you tell us about that project?

Bani Abidi Listening to Lubaina, I think it's interesting that what happens today in terms of audiences is that people just get in touch and send you an Instagram message. There is a direct response, and it's moving. I really value that because there's no mediator.

I come from a place where there was a dictatorship for 11 years, and there's been a whole round of generals who ruled us, and the ruling class dictates the nature of how this country moves and exists. I think that negotiating or confronting that power has always been a running thread in my work. For me, the personal lens in *Proposal for a Man in the Sea* was that my parents were both teenagers at the time of independence and partition. They were patriotic in a way that we can never be because they

nicht gestellt wurden. Am Ende ergaben sich daraus auch intensive Gespräche zwischen dem Museum und seinem Publikum.

Sofia Victorino Kannst du dich noch erinnern, worum es damals ging?

Lubaina Himid Die Mitarbeiter*innen des Museums machten sich Gedanken über ihre Sammlung und die Beschilderung. Natürlich ging es um die Geschichte der britischen Keramik. Doch es ging auch um die Geschichte des Kolonialismus, die Geschichte der Industrialisierung, die Geschichte vieler anderer Dinge. Die Gespräche haben ein Umdenken bei ihnen ausgelöst.

Sofia Victorino Bani, in *Proposal for a Man in the Sea / Angebot für einen Mann im Meer* geht es auch um Denkmäler und ihre Wahrnehmung im öffentlichen Raum. Kannst du uns etwas über dieses Projekts erzählen?

Bani Abidi Im Zusammenhang mit Lubainas Geschichte finde ich es interessant, dass unser Publikum heute einfach Instagram benutzt, um seine Meinung mitzuteilen. Es reagiert direkt auf unsere Kunst, was ich sehr ergreifend finde. Solche Kommentare bedeuten mir wirklich sehr viel, weil sie mich direkt und unvermittelt erreichen.

In meiner Heimat herrschte 11 Jahre lang eine Militärdiktatur mit einer ganzen Reihe von Generälen an der Spitze, die über unser Leben bestimmten. Die herrschende Klasse diktierte die Abläufe und den Alltag der Menschen in meinem Land. Ich denke, ein roter Faden meiner Arbeit war immer die Auseinandersetzung oder Konfrontation mit dieser Macht. Der persönliche Blick in *Proposal for a Man in the Sea / Angebot für einen Mann im Meer* ist familiär bedingt: Zur Zeit der Unabhängigkeit und Teilung waren meine Eltern Teenager. Ihr damaliges Gefühl des Patriotismus kann es heute nicht mehr geben, denn sie hatten gegen die Kolonialherrschaft und für die Unabhängigkeit gekämpft. Diese junge Generation, die von einer neuen Nation träumte und dafür kämpfte, hat mich schon immer interessiert.

*Proposal for a Man in the Sea / Angebot für einen Mann im Meer* ist ein dokumentarisches Werk. Es enthält Fotoaufnahmen aus dem Atelier von Ram Sutar, der bei unserem ersten Treffen etwa 86 Jahre alt war. Als Bildhauer hat er Statuen von Politiker*innen in Indien angefertigt. Wir lernten uns im Jahre 2012 kennen, als ich an *Death at a 30 Degree Angle / Tod in einem 30-Grad-Winkel* arbeitete, einem Spielfilm über einen Mann, der eine Statue von sich selbst in Auftrag geben will und sich nicht für eine Pose entscheiden kann. Will er als Intellektueller, Kriegsherr oder Politiker dargestellt werden? Bei der Suche nach Drehorten stieß ich auf Ram Sutar. Zuerst dachte ich, oh mein Gott, die Lebensgeschichte dieses Mannes ist so unendlich viel interessanter als meine eigene Idee. Also machte ich ihn zu einem Teil meines Films. Sein Atelier war voller Statuen von Rabindranath Tagore, Gandhi, Nehru. Das gesamte Pantheon der politischen und intellektuellen Geschichte Indiens war dort vertreten. Die Zeit, die ich dort verbrachte, war eine bewegende und unvergessliche Erfahrung. Außerdem hatte Ram Sutar miterlebt, wie sich die Forderungen und die politische Landschaft über die Jahre veränderten. Er plante eine Statue von Gandhi, wie dieser zwei Dalit-Kinder an der Hand hält. Der Titel *Death at a 30 Degree Angle / Tod in einem 30-Grad-Winkel* geht darauf zurück, dass die Statue von Saddam Hussein bei ihrem Sturz zunächst in einem ungünstigen Winkel in der Luft hängen geblieben war. Es sollte eine Anspielung auf die Selbstverherrlichung der Politiker vergangener Zeiten sein. *Proposal for a Man in the Sea / Angebot für einen Mann im Meer* entstand im Anschluss an diesen Film. Sutar sagte,diese Statue von Ghandi solle im Arabischen Meer stehen und höher als die Freiheitsstatue sein.

Sofia Victorino Hrair, dein Werk *Final Flight / Letzter Flug* ist etwas jüngeren Datums. Trotzdem steht es im Bezug zu unserer Diskussion über Erinnerungskultur oder in diesem Fall das Verschwinden.

Hrair Sarkissian Ja, *Final Flight / Letzter Flug* ist meine erste Installation ohne Fotografien. Sie erzählt die Geschichte des Waldrapp, eines in Syrien heimischen Vogels. Diese Vogelart ist sehr alt, es gibt sie seit über 5.200 Jahren. Für die Ägypter war der Vogel Thot, der Gott des Schrifttums und der Weisheit. Im Alten Testament wird er auch als Botschafter der Fruchtbarkeit erwähnt. Im Islam glaubte man, dass der Vogel Pilgern den Weg nach Mekka weisen würde. In Palmyra in der syrischen Wüste war er bis in die 1930er Jahre heimisch und verschwand dort in den späten 1980er Jahren. Sein Aussterben wurde von der Regierung offiziell bestätigt. Doch 2003 fanden Beduinen eine Kolonie von sieben Vögeln, die nahe der Ruinen von Palmyra brüteten. Sie informierten die Regierung, dass die Vögel in die Region zurückgekehrt seien. Die Regierung nahm davon keinerlei Kenntnis, bis der italienische Ökologe und Naturschützer Gianluca Serra nach Palmyra reiste und dort neun Jahre verbrachte, um die Vögel zu beobachten und schließlich eine Auffangstation zu bauen.

Unter den Vögeln, die die Beduinen entdeckten, war ein Weibchen. Sie nannten es Zenobia, nach der Herrscherin des

had fought against colonialism and fought for independence. I have always had an interest in that young generation that had dreams of a new nation and had fought for that new nation.

*Proposal for a Man in the Sea* is a documentary work. It includes photographs taken in the studio of Mr Ram Sutar, who was 86 or something when I met him. He is a sculptor of political statues in India, and we met because in 2012, I was making *Death at a 30 Degree Angle*, a fictional film about a man who wants to have a statue commissioned of himself and can't decide on his posture. Does he want to be an intellectual, a warrior or a politician? In finding a location, I came across Ram Sutar. My first feeling was that, oh, my god, this man's life story is infinitely more interesting than my idea. So he became part of the film. His studio was full of statues of Rabindranath Tagore, Gandhi, Nehru, the entire pantheon of Indian political and intellectual history. It was a profound and incredible experience. He was also a witness to changing desires and politics, and he had collected different kinds of archives and sketches for this one statue that he wanted to make of Ghandi holding the hands of two Dalit children. The title *Death at a 30 Degree Angle* comes from the fact that Saddam Hussein's statue got stuck at a very awkward angle and just stayed there. It was a way of addressing the idea of self-aggrandisement that male politicians have had in the past. *Proposal for a Man in the Sea* came about as a result of that film. It relates to the fact that Ram Sutar had said 'I want to make this statue of Gandhi in the Arabian Sea, and it should be higher than the Statue of Liberty'.

Sofia Victorino Hrair, yours is a more recent work, *Final Flight*, but it connects to what we've been debating about memorialisation, or disappearance, in this case.

Hrair Sarkissian Yes, the project *Final Flight* is my first non-photographic installation. It tells the story of a bird that existed in Syria, the northern bald ibis. It's a very ancient bird, over 5,200 years old. For the Egyptians, the bird was Thoth, the god of writing and wisdom. The bird was also mentioned in the Old Testament as the fertility messenger, and in Islam they believed these birds were guides for pilgrims when travelling to Mecca. The bird existed in Syria until the '30s in the desert in Palmyra and disappeared in the late '80s, and the government officially confirmed their extinction. Yet, in 2003, the Bedouins found a colony of seven birds nesting near the ruins of Palmyra, and they informed the government that these birds were back again to the region. The government didn't pay attention until an Italian ecologist and conservationist Gianluca Serra travelled to Palmyra, where he lived for nine years, to study the birds and eventually to build a breeding centre.

Amongst the seven birds the Bedouins found, there was one female bird. They named her Zenobia, after the Queen of the Kingdom of Palmyra. She was the only one who knew the routes from Palmyra all the way to the highlands of Ethiopia, as they would travel across seven to eight countries during migratory seasons. Over the years, the numbers increased, and all the birds were tagged so they could be followed through satellites to study their speed, heights and where they stop. Later, in 2011, the numbers of the birds started to decrease. One day, they caught the signal of one of the birds and followed it all the way to Saudi Arabia. This is when they realised that the Saudis were hunting the birds. Until 2013, the numbers went down and there were only three birds left. When ISIS entered Palmyra, everyone fled, of course, including the birds. Zenobia, the female one, was seen for the last time in 2014. This type of bird exists in Morocco, Turkey, Spain, Italy and Ethiopia, but they are all in breeding centres, they do not migrate. The migrating ones are extinct, but there is a whole new conservation programme to introduce migratory birds. In this installation, I casted seven skulls of these birds, and it took me a while to find one. It was impossible to borrow a skull from the British Museum, and the Natural History Museum in London was another whole issue. But I found a small zoo in Granada, Spain, who very kindly sent me a table of 20 skulls, saying that I could borrow any of those and we 3D'd the skull and did the cast of seven. The installation includes a nine-hour-long video of the migratory route from Palmyra to Ethiopia, filmed on the same height and almost the same bird view angle. This project is about the bird, but it is also about the Syrians during war, and how politics and war interfere with people getting dispersed, and its aftereffects…

Sofia Victorino Let's return to Etel Adnan for a moment. 'My own writing was like my own breathing: something I was doing'. I'd like to use this quote to think about the 'decolonial'. Does the idea of decolonising art and knowledge carry for you, as artists, a meaning that emerges in the act of 'doing' rather than being a mere discursive construct?

Lubaina Himid Well, I think for me, when I started out, no one was admitting that colonising, or colonialism, was even a subject to be discussed in art making. That's why it took many of us so long to… well, we had to make our own forum for discussion, really. Because as Black British artists, we couldn't find a way into the debates that were happening. But for me, the very act of not

Königreichs von Palmyra. Sie war die Einzige, die die Zugrouten von Palmyra bis ins äthiopische Hochland durch sieben bis acht Länder kannte. Mit den Jahren wuchs die Population, und alle Vögel wurden mit einem Mikrochip ausgestattet, um über Satelliten ihre Fluggeschwindigkeit, Flughöhe und Reisestationen zu verfolgen. Später, im Jahr 2011, nahm ihre Zahl allerdings wieder ab. Eines Tages folgten die Forschenden dem Signal eines Vogels bis nach Saudi-Arabien und stellten fest, dass die Saudis Jagd auf die Vögel machten. Bis 2013 sank ihre Zahl dann auf nur noch drei Vögel. Als der Islamische Staat (IS) nach Palmyra kam, flohen natürlich alle, auch die Vögel. Das Vogelweibchen Zenobia wurde zuletzt 2014 gesehen. Es gibt die Vogelart in Marokko, der Türkei, Spanien, Italien und Äthiopien, allerdings ausschließlich in Auffangstationen und nicht als Zugvögel. Die Zugvögel sind ausgestorben, doch es wurde ein völlig neues Schutzprogramm zu ihrer Wiederansiedlung gestartet. In dieser Installation sind sieben Abgüsse von Schädeln dieser Vögel zu sehen, die nicht leicht zu bekommen waren. Eine Leihgabe des British Museum war nicht möglich, im Falle des Natural History Museum in London wäre es sogar noch komplizierter gewesen. Doch ich fand einen kleinen Zoo in Granada in Spanien, der mir freundlicherweise eine Tafel mit 20 Schädeln als Leihgabe zur Verfügung stellte. Wir fertigten 3D-Modelle der Schädel und anschließend sieben Abgüsse an. Die Installation zeigt ein neun Stunden langes Video von der Zugroute zwischen Palmyra und Äthiopien, das aus der Flughöhe und sogar fast aus der Perspektive der Zugvögel gefilmt wurde. In diesem Projekt geht es um den Waldrapp, aber auch um das Leben der syrischen Bevölkerung in Kriegszeiten und darum, wie Politik und Krieg die Menschen in alle Himmelsrichtungen treiben und welche Folgen damit verbunden sind …

Sofia Victorino Wenden wir uns für einen Moment wieder Etel Adnan zu: „Ich schrieb, wie ich atmete: Ich tat es einfach.“ Mit diesem Zitat möchte ich beginnen, über das „Dekoloniale“ nachzudenken. Hat die Idee einer Dekolonialisierung der Kunst und des Wissens für euch als Kunstschaffende eine Bedeutung, die eher im Schaffensakt selbst liegt, als dass sie den Diskurs betrifft?

Lubaina Himid In meiner Anfangszeit waren Kolonialisierung oder Kolonialzeit überhaupt kein Thema in der Kunstwelt. Deshalb haben viele von uns so lange gebraucht, um zu … Wir mussten uns tatsächlich ein eigenes Diskussionsforum schaffen. Denn als Schwarze Künstler*innen in Großbritannien konnten wir uns keinen Zugang zu den laufenden Debatten verschaffen. Ich setzte schon damit ein Zeichen, dass ich nicht den klassischen Weg einer bildenden Künstlerin in Europa beschritt. Ich habe zwar eine Kunstschule besucht, allerdings um eine künstlerische Ausbildung zur, wie es damals hieß, Theaterdesignerin zu machen, Bühnenbilder und Kostüme zu entwerfen und Teil der Theaterwelt zu werden. In der britischen Klassengesellschaft läuft alles nach festen Regeln ab … Komischerweise ist es noch immer üblich, dass es innerhalb der Kunstwelt beim Übergang von einer Klasse in eine andere einer Einführung bedarf. Ich würde wirklich behaupten, dass es in Großbritannien noch immer so ist, dass es bestimmte Verhaltensregeln gibt. Natürlich halten sich viele von uns nicht immer daran, doch das System ist immer noch sehr rigide.

In meiner Anfangszeit wurden solche Themen in der Akademie nicht besprochen. Wir konnten lediglich darauf eingehen, indem wir uns in unseren Kunstwerken direkt darauf bezogen und die Werke an anderen Orten als in Kunstgalerien ausstellten. Dies waren Kunst- oder Gemeindezentren, wo sich arbeitslose Menschen und Rentner*innen auf eine Tasse Tee treffen. Unser Geld verdienten wir beispielsweise mit dem Entwurf von Plakaten für lokale Veranstaltungen. Anfangs versuchten wir, diese Themen in die Alltagsdebatten, aber auch in den Alltagsdebatten der Kultureinrichtungen zu integrieren und so zu tun, als hätten wir unsere eigenen Netzwerke. Das war wohl auch so, aber oft waren wir auch einfach nur vollkommen pleite. Nicht arm, aber pleite. Das ist ein entscheidender Unterschied.

Heute denke ich, dass ich gemeinsam mit vielen der Künstler*innen aus meiner Anfangszeit in den 1980er Jahren sehr dankbar bin, lange genug überlebt zu haben, um hier einen Wandel und d. h. den Mut zur Zerstörung zu erleben. Auf gewisse Weise nehme ich mich als sehr vorsichtige Künstlerin wahr. Vermutlich ist dies einer der Vorwürfe, die ich mir machen könnte, dass ich zu lange versucht habe herauszufinden, worum es eigentlich geht, wo die Fehlstellen waren, wie die Lücken gefüllt werden konnten, wie ein solches Thema im Alltag angesprochen werden könnte. Zumindest ist es mir gelungen, Teil einer großen Bewegung von Kunstschaffenden zu sein, die mit dem Finger auf die Heucheleien und Lügen und auf die Verleugnung von Tatsachen gezeigt haben. Aber ich bin mir nicht mehr durchgehend sicher, wie ich dies effektiv mit meiner Arbeit erreichen kann – so wie es jüngere Künstler*innen tun können oder Menschen, die noch unvertrauter mit dem Prozess und darum weniger erschöpft von dieser Bewegung zum Positiven sind. In meinem späteren Werk habe ich mich mit dem anhaltend starken Einfluss der politischen Kräfte auf unser Leben auseinandergesetzt. Doch mich interessieren

conforming to the ways of working of a European fine artist... yes, I did go to art school, but I went in order to find my way into being an artist that was, as they were called then, a theatre designer, to design sets and costumes and be part of the performance world. Britain has that class system where everything does function in a rigid way... there's still that strange way of being where you have to be introduced from one class into another within the art world. And I would claim this still goes on today in Britain, that there are particular ways of doing things. Of course, many of us break these ways of doing things all the time, but it's still very rigid.

I started working when those issues were not discussed in the academy. And the only way we could talk about them was to make pieces of work that were addressing these issues head-on and showing the work in places that were not art galleries. These were art centres, or community centres where people met together because they didn't have jobs, or were elderly. Our jobs were jobs like making posters for community events. The very act of how we started was to try to bring up these subjects into the debates of the everyday, but also into the everyday debates in cultural institutions. We tried to behave as if we were running our own networks. I think we were, but lots of the time, we were very broke. Not poor, but broke. The difference between those things is important.

Today, I think that myself, and many of those artists that I started working with in the early 1980s, are grateful to have managed to stay alive long enough to see the development of that, having the courage to break something. In some ways, I still feel that I am really a rather cautious sort of artist. That's probably one of the criticisms I would have myself—that I spent such a long time trying to work out what the conversation was, what the absence was, how to fill the gaps, how to get a subject like that into an everyday conversation, that I can only feel that I've managed to at least be part of a huge movement of artists who exposed this hypocrisy and this set of lies and denials. But I'm not always that sure now how to effectively make work that does that in a way that, either younger artists or people newer to making and less exhausted by the upward trajectory can do. In later years, the work I'm making is dealing so much with how that political force still has a grip on our lives. But I've become more and more interested in tiny moments, in everyday lives, and I leave those bigger, mountain-climbing feats, to my colleagues who are coming at it from much better directions.

Sofia Victorino   Bani, how would you respond to the debates on decolonising art practices and institutions? How does that emerge in your doing and thinking process?

Bani Abidi   I'm working on a project right now looking at old art history books and Xeroxes that we had in the '90s in Pakistan. It's really fascinating because it got me thinking about the reception of art history and traditions. Being someone who was completely broken from precolonial traditions or even language, I'm more fluent in English than I'm in Urdu because my parents' generation believed that we must all be fluent in English, it's a whole world of knowledge that I've been cut off from. Even our own history in South Asia was written by the British. So how we understand ourselves is through British historiography. There's so much unpacking to be done. Okay, there's that first moment of, I'm a kind of a mongrel. I don't understand where I'm coming from. And then, our relationship with the Western art history canon, which was always through scratchy old slides and Xeroxes in college libraries. There would be one book that would appear because Thames & Hudson or Phaidon made things for circulation in a certain region. It's only recently that I realised that most of the things that I learnt were just in different shades of black and grey, and it was the materiality of Xerox copies that we saw. We kind of reinterpreted it, but we never fully understood it. When I was living and teaching in Chicago, I'd tell students to look at the original art piece in a museum. The whole museum-going experience that we were physically, culturally, politically away from.

I think that what you see in my work is multiple approaches; humour, narrative, storytelling, these are the words that I use to describe my practice, but I think people just can't place me. Yet, I feel so liberated as a result of being independent of any one space of any one canon, especially this question of the Western canon. That's just one canon. I'm coming from such a different world, where literally, the Muslim calendar and the Gregorian calendar live side by side. And this is a world that I cannot translate to anyone. I have lots of thoughts about the right to opacity. But that's my whole feeling about a decolonial practice: it is not about going back to pre-colonial ideas, but admitting the mishmash and the lack of purity.

Hrair Sarkissian   I didn't study abroad, and I didn't study in Syria, either. I see myself free from these references because the main thing that I relay in my work is pain. It's how to project the pain of others. And in that, I want to be free, and I don't want to rely on any sort of institution. For instance, I live in London. It's been almost 12 years, and I'm not into the London art scene. I do my things quietly and, yeah, I feel more liberated.

Sofia Victorino   Can you elaborate on some of your works that address key historical moments...

auch immer mehr die kleinen Alltagsmomente, und die bergsteigerischen Unternehmungen überlasse ich meinen Kolleg*innen, die sich ihnen aus einer viel besseren Perspektive nähern.

Sofia Victorino Bani, was sagst du zu den Debatten über eine Dekolonisierung des Kunstschaffens und der Einrichtungen? Wie schlägt sich dieser Aspekt in deinen Arbeits- und Denkweisen nieder?

Bani Abidi Aktuell beschäftige ich mich im Rahmen eines Projekts mit alten Büchern über Kunstgeschichte und mit Xerokopien, die wir in den 1990er Jahren in Pakistan verwendet haben. Diese Arbeit ist faszinierend, denn sie hat bei mir ein Nachdenken über die Rezeption von Kunstgeschichte und Traditionen angeregt. Ich persönlich habe keinerlei Bezug zu vorkolonialen Traditionen oder auch zur Sprache aus dieser Zeit. Mein Englisch ist besser als mein Urdu, weil die Generation meiner Eltern der Auffassung war, wir müssten alle fließend Englisch sprechen. Auf diese Weise wurde ich von einer ganzen Welt des Wissens abgeschnitten. Sogar unsere eigene Geschichte in Südasien wurde von den Briten geschrieben. Unser Selbstverständnis beruht damit auf der britischen Geschichtsschreibung. Es gibt noch so viel zu entdecken. Im ersten Moment dachte ich, okay, ich bin eine Art Mischling. Ich habe keine Vorstellung von meiner Herkunft. Und unser Verhältnis zum Kanon der Kunstgeschichte der westlichen Welt entwickelten wir ausschließlich über zerkratzte alte Dias und Xerokopien in den Universitätsbibliotheken. Vielleicht gab es auch ein Buch, weil *Thames & Hudson* oder *Phaidon* etwas zur Veröffentlichung in einer bestimmten Region herausgaben. Erst vor Kurzem ist mir klar geworden, dass ich die meisten Dinge nur in unterschiedlichen Schattierungen von Schwarz und Grau und auf dem Material der Xerokopien kennengelernt habe. Wir deuteten die Dinge gewissermaßen um, haben sie jedoch nie ganz verstanden. Während meiner Zeit in Chicago forderte ich meine Student*innen auf, sich die Originalkunstwerke in einem Museum anzuschauen. Eine Museumskultur, von der wir damals körperlich, kulturell, politisch weit entfernt waren.

Ich denke, ich nähere mich meinen Werken aus mehreren Richtungen. Meine Praxis würde ich als humorvoll, narrativ, erzählerisch beschreiben. Offenbar bin ich schwer einzuordnen. Trotzdem empfinde ich es als sehr befreiend, völlig unabhängig von einem Raum oder Kanon, insbesondere vom westlichen Kanon, zu arbeiten. Der ist nur einer von vielen. Ich komme aus einer völlig anderen Welt, in der der mulimische und der gregorianische Kalender buchstäblich Seite an Seite existieren. Und das Leben in dieser Welt kann ich niemandem vermitteln. Ich denke oft über das Recht darauf nach, undurchsichtig zu sein. Doch genau das empfinde ich im Zusammenhang mit einer dekolonialen Praxis. Es geht nicht darum, zu Ideen aus der vorkolonialen Zeit zurückzukehren, sondern darum, das Durcheinander und die fehlende Klarheit zuzugeben.

Hrair Sarkissian Ich habe weder im Ausland noch in Syrien studiert. Ich betrachte mich als unabhängig von diesen Bezügen, weil ich über meine Werke hauptsächlich das Gefühl des Schmerzes vermitteln will. Es geht darum, den Schmerz anderer Menschen zu projizieren. Und dabei möchte ich frei sein und mich nicht auf irgendeine Einrichtung verlassen. Beispielsweise lebe ich seit ungefähr 12 Jahren in London und bin dennoch nicht Teil der Londoner Kunstszene. Ich mache meine Kunst im Stillen und fühle mich dadurch tatsächlich freier.

Sofia Victorino Könnt ihr etwas zu euren Werken sagen, die sich mit wichtigen historischen Momenten beschäftigen?

Bani Abidi In diesem Zusammenhang kann ich etwas zu meinem Kunstwerk *Memorial to Lost Words / Denkmal für die verlorenen Wörter* sagen. Es entstand im Auftrag des *Edinburgh Arts Festival* 2016 im Anschluss an eine Ausschreibung für Künstler*innen zur Auseinandersetzung mit Denkmälern. In Edinburgh gibt es mehr als 200 Statuen. Interessanterweise werden zu bestimmten historischen Jubiläen auch die Archive geöffnet. Als zwischen 2014 und 2018 mit zahlreichen Jahrestagen an den Ersten Weltkrieg erinnert wurde, gab es plötzlich viel Material aus bisher nicht verfügbaren Archiven. Besonders interessant fand ich Berichte über Soldaten vom indischen Subkontinent, die für Großbritannien in den Ersten Weltkrieg gezogen waren. Vor der Einladung zur Teilnahme an dieser Ausstellung hatte ich mich bereits ausführlich mit diesem Thema beschäftigt, denn es war schon lange bekannt, dass es außerhalb von Berlin ein Kriegsgefangenenlager namens Halbmondlager gegeben hatte, wo die Deutschen Sikhs und Pathans und Menschen aus Südasien – die vielen indischen Soldaten – festhielten. Sie brachten in Berlin eine Zeitung namens *Al Dschihad* heraus. Die Idee war, die Muslime in dieser Gruppe zum Kampf aufseiten des Osmanischen Reichs zu bewegen. Es handelte sich um eine Politisierung des Konzepts des Dschihad, das viele mit dem 11. September und jüngeren politischen Ereignissen assoziieren, das aber über 100 Jahre alt ist.

Dieses Kriegsgefangenlanger wurde in den 1920er Jahren zu einer Art Menschenzoo. Ein renommierter Linguist machte

Bani Abidi *Memorial to Lost Words* is the title of the work that I can talk about in this context. It was commissioned by the Edinburgh Art Festival in 2016 as a call for artists to engage with the idea of monuments, Edinburgh being a city of more than 200 statues. It is interesting that when there's a particular anniversary in history, these are the moments when archives come alive. Between 2014 and 2018, the anniversary of the First World War, suddenly, there was a lot of material on previously unavailable archives. The one that drew my attention was the soldiers that came from the Indian subcontinent to fight for the British in the First World War. Before I got the invitation to participate in this exhibition, I was already immersed in it because we knew for a long time that outside Berlin, there had been a prisoner-of-war camp called the Halbmondlager, where Germans brought Sikhs and Pathans and people from South Asia, all these Indian soldiers. They then issued a newspaper called *El Dschihad*, from Berlin. The idea was to get the Muslims in this group to fight for the Ottomans. It was a politicisation of the concept of jihad, which people associate with 9/11 and more recent politics, but it's 100 years old.

That prisoner camp became a kind of a human zoo in the 1920s. But a prominent linguist at the time recorded samples of their voices and their dialects with a phonograph. These archives were lost, but closer to the 1990s, an academic in Germany uncovered them. These stories had never been heard, never been understood. They were translated and they were heard. Many were folk songs or stories or poems, others were SOS messages because people thought that somehow what is recorded will get heard somewhere. There were more than a million soldiers and there's no mention of that in the Imperial War Museum in London. I went searching for the Indian soldier, and there was maybe one photograph. It is just completely erased.

For the first time, I was looking into such a tough historical moment that I did not know what to do with it. When you get into archive research, it's endless. And you can lose interest in the world because you're immersing yourself in history. And history can really pull the carpet under your feet. It disables all concepts of what you think is true because you have these archival truths. I eventually decided to research letters written by Indian soldiers during the First World War from Brighton and from France, written from hospitals. Again, a lot of these letters were censored. And the reason why they came out in a book called *Indian Voices of the Great War*, by David Omissi, was because of the 100th anniversary.

I read these letters and then contacted an incredible man, Amarjit Chandan, who is a well-known Punjabi Naxalite poet living in England, and he cannot go back to India. He knew about the story of these soldiers. But he also had the verses of songs that were sung by women who stayed home. And what were the songs being sung at home when the men have all been taken away? They were revolutionary songs beseeching the British government not to take the men away, for Britain and Germany to stop the war, how it disrupted society. Then I had these texts composed as a song and presented as a sound installation in the old Scottish Parliament. The idea that a parliamentary space would be inhabited by Punjabi voices was important. I had never used music or songs in my work, and now, six years later, that sound work has had so many lives. In Lahore, I showed it around a statue of Queen Victoria, I surrounded her with eight speakers and these voices sang to her. The key thing for me is what form you give an archive and how to distil it down into an expansive experience for people. I think that's a struggle because you get sunk into these hard realities.

Sofia Victorino Would you like to comment on the connection to history, Lubaina?

Lubaina Himid Yes, the series that I made, *Le Rodeur* (2016), started when I was talking to an academic who had researched the archives of French newspapers and found the account of a French slave ship taking captured Africans from Mali across the Atlantic to the Caribbean. Halfway across, the Africans began to lose their sight, and because they were all packed together, it spread very quickly. Soon, they all had gone blind, hundreds and hundreds of people trapped on this wooden ship around 1819. Then the French crew caught this disease, an eye infection, and in the end, only one member of crew managed to see. Most of the captured Africans were thrown overboard, and the boat made its way to the Caribbean. They came across indigenous people who understood that it was an eye infection, quite a simple thing, and for some, they were able to make herbal remedies and their sight was restored.

My desire, once I'd heard this set of facts, these truths, was to make a work where one felt, as an artist, the fear of going blind; to share with an audience who are interested in visual art, the equal fear of going blind, the understanding of how it is to be in a place where you don't know where you are, and you don't know what's happening to you and why. I tried to express that double tragedy of having your sight restored, but facing a future as an enslaved person; fit to be in the slave market. What happened to me at the time that I was making these quite big paintings, was that my partner then was developing Alzheimer's without her or

damals dort Tonaufnahmen der Stimmen und Dialekte. Diese Phonogrammarchive galten als verloren, wurden jedoch in den 1990er Jahren von einem deutschen Wissenschaftler wiederentdeckt. Die Geschichten dieser Menschen waren nie gehört und nie verstanden worden. Nun wurden sie übersetzt und gehört. Viele Aufnahmen enthielten Volkslieder oder Geschichten oder Gedichte, andere Notrufe, weil die Menschen dachten, dass die Aufnahmen vielleicht von irgendwem gehört würden. Im Imperial War Museum in London gibt es keine Hinweise auf diese mehr als eine Million Soldaten. Ich habe dort nach einem indischen Soldaten gesucht und bin dabei vielleicht auf eine Aufnahme gestoßen. Ihre Geschichte(n) wurde(n) einfach ausgelöscht.

Zum ersten Mal habe ich mich mit einem historischen Ereignis beschäftigt, das derart kompliziert war, dass ich nicht wusste, was ich damit anfangen sollte. Archivrecherchen haben etwas Bodenloses. Man kann durch das Abtauchen in die Geschichte das Interesse an der Welt verlieren. Und die Geschichte kann dir wirklich den Boden unter den Füßen wegziehen. Sie bringt alles ins Wanken, was du bisher als Wahrheit betrachtet hast, weil du plötzlich mit Wahrheiten aus dem Archiv konfrontiert wirst. Schließlich beschloss ich, mich näher mit Briefen zu beschäftigen, die indische Soldaten im Ersten Weltkrieg aus Krankenhäusern in Brighton und Frankreich geschrieben hatten. Auch hier waren viele der Briefe zensiert. Und sie wurden im Rahmen des 100. Jahrestags in einem Buch mit dem Titel *Indian Voices of the Great War* von David Omissi veröffentlicht.

Nachdem ich diese Briefe gelesen hatte, kontaktierte ich den wunderbaren Amarjit Chandan, einen bekannten Punjabi-Dichter und Naxaliten, der in England lebt und nicht nach Indien zurückkehren kann. Er kannte die Geschichte dieser Soldaten. Aber er besaß auch die Strophen von Liedern, die Frauen sangen, die zu Hause geblieben waren. Waren dies die Lieder, die in der Heimat gesungen wurden, nachdem man die Männer fortgebracht hatte? Es waren revolutionäre Lieder, in denen die britische Regierung angefleht wurde, die Männer nicht mitzunehmen, Großbritannien und Deutschland aufgefordert wurden, den Krieg zu beenden, und Lieder darüber, wie der Krieg die Gesellschaft spaltete. Aus diesen Texten ließ ich ein neues Lied komponieren und präsentierte alles zusammen als Klanginstallation im alten schottischen Parlament. Wichtig war dabei die Tatsache, dass in einem Parlamentsgebäude Punjabi erklang. Bisher hatte ich nie mit Musik oder Songs gearbeitet. Und heute, sechs Jahre später, ist diese Sound-Arbeit schon an vielen verschiedenen Orten erklungen, unter anderem in Lahore neben einer Statue von Queen Victoria, um die ich acht Lautsprecher anordnete, aus denen die Stimmen ein Lied für sie sangen. Für mich geht es vor allem um die Form des Archivs und wie ich daraus ein vielseitiges Erlebnis für das Publikum machen kann. Das ist meines Erachtens keine leichte Aufgabe, weil man mit so vielen harten Realitäten konfrontiert wird.

Sofia Victorino Möchtest du etwas über deine Verbindung zur Geschichte sagen, Lubaina?

Lubaina Himid Ja, Startschuss für meine Reihe *Le Rodeur* (2016) war mein Gespräch mit einem Wissenschaftler, der in den Archiven französischer Zeitungen recherchiert und dabei einen Bericht über ein französisches Sklavenschiff namens *Le Rodeur* gefunden hatte, das Afrikaner*innen von Mali über den Atlantik in die Karibik transportierte. Auf halber Strecke verloren viele der Afrikaner*innen plötzlich ihr Augenlicht. Durch die beengten Verhältnisse griff die Erkrankung schnell um sich. Bald waren alle erblindet, Hunderte von Menschen waren auf diesem Sklavenschiff um das Jahr 1819 gefangen. Dann infizierte sich auch die französische Besatzung mit der Augenentzündung, sodass am Ende nur noch ein Crewmitglied sehen konnte. Die meisten der gefangenen Afrikaner*innen wurden über Bord geworfen, und das Schiff setzte seine Reise in die Karibik fort. Auf ihrem Weg begegneten die Seeleute Ureinwohner*innen, die erkannten, dass es sich um eine Augenentzündung handelte. Sie konnten einigen der Betroffenen mit pflanzlichen Heilmitteln helfen und ihr Sehvermögen wieder herstellen.

Nach der Lektüre dieser Geschichte verspürte ich den dringenden Wunsch, die Furcht vor dem Erblinden in einem Kunstwerk zu vermitteln. Und dieses Gefühl mit einem Publikum zu teilen, das sich für visuelle Kunst interessiert – das Gefühl, an einem Ort zu sein, den man nicht kennt, und nicht zu wissen, was geschieht und warum. Ich versuchte dieses doppelte Schicksal, dass es ein Unglück ist, wieder sehen zu können, weil dann eine Zukunft als Sklavin oder Sklave auf dich wartet, auszudrücken. Nun bist du wieder für den Verkauf geeignet. In der Zeit, als ich an diesen großen Gemälden arbeitete, erkrankte meine damalige Partnerin an Alzheimer, ohne dass wir beide etwas davon bemerkten. In meinen Gemälden ging es also nicht um erblindende Afrikaner*innen auf einem Schiff, sondern darum, dass niemand in den Gemälden verstand, was geschah. Viele Personen in den Gemälden wissen nicht einmal, ob die anderen Personen in den Gemälden dort sind oder nicht. Sie erforschen, was es bedeutet, dort zu sein –

me knowing that it was happening. So, I was making paintings that were not illustrating Africans on a boat going blind, but making paintings in which nobody in the painting understood what was happening. Many people in the paintings didn't even know if the other people in the paintings were there or not. They explore being there, not being there, seeing, not seeing. The sea is everywhere in the painting and outside. I was making them with a person in the room who had no idea whether she was in the room or not. I didn't know anymore whether she was in the room or not, even though she was in the room.

Over the years, I've worked with historians because I get very involved with making work about what they have discovered. Then, in turn, they use the work to make an expansive book or set of lectures where they're really exchanging instead of just telling the facts. So, it's very central to my life, those moments, that sort of turn on a sixpence, as we say.

Bani Abidi It's interesting, when you talk about the fact that historians use material produced by artists to take it back into the classroom. It's also just the history of history, right? It wasn't always books. It is also the fact that a lot of history is poetry and song. And it is subjective. It is authored by multiple people; it is authored by women. I think that artists today, when there's such a research-based practice, have become essential in some ways. We've brought back the possibility of a non-didactic relationship with knowledge and with history. And we're all very aware about the way history has been written up to this point.

Sofia Victorino Hrair, you've mentioned before 'doing things quietly', and for me, there is an idea that emerges quite poignantly in your work, which is about silence, also present in different ways in Bani and Lubaina's work, I believe.

Hrair Sarkissian I think it's more like screaming about the silence, especially with the project *Last Seen*, where I met 50 families from five different countries, Lebanon, Argentina, Brazil, Kosovo and Bosnia. Families that have lost loved ones during dictatorship or war. They are still waiting for answers. They still think this person is alive and they live with this person. For me, sitting with these families and listening to their stories, absorbing everything, in the end, I just don't know how I did it because there is so much pain. And the silence… I try to bring things in a very quiet and silent way, especially in the West, because if it makes noise, people will not listen or pay attention.

Lubaina Himid Apart from the fact that I live in a small town and next to a park, so it is very quiet, I'm quite a stranger to silence. Even when I'm making work, I'm listening to so much stuff that has nothing to do with what I'm making, because often I can't bear to hear what it is I'm making. When I'm making work, music is playing; I'm listening to operas or plays or listening to football matches, listening to politics, or there are children in the house. When I look at the work much later, sometimes I can see and hear the sound that was going on when I made it. Also, very often, there's text within the work, which describes a forest or describes going through rivers or hearing bombs or turning up at a place and not knowing whether the emptiness of it is before the disaster or after the disaster. I only really understood with this Tate Modern show, the sea is present in so many of the paintings, seen through a back window, always there because of the politics of maritime Britain, you know, the imagined glory of this country and its maritime past, its sense of itself despite all those murderous transatlantic crossings. I was born in Zanzibar, that understanding of what it is to live on an island, so the sea is there. I can hear the sea in all sorts of different ways, as well as seeing it in my work. I only speak one language, which is English, but my father spoke Swahili, however, because he died when I was four months old and my mother who is English came back from Zanzibar to here and brought me up without that language; I became afraid of that language and afraid that I couldn't speak the language and ashamed of that. Learning a language, understanding a language and speaking a language in order to belong in the place that you're in, I have never had to do, but I'm very aware of it.

Bani Abidi I've dealt with silence in different ways. The silence of censorship by the state, the silence that comes with self-censorship, with becoming irrelevant. What is the silencing of different voices? The silence of erasure. Most of my work deals with sound. These days, I'm making a film about acoustic displacement and acoustic loss. It is the first film that I'm making in Germany, because I've been living in Berlin for 10 years, but I have not got my teeth into understanding how to make art about… here. I have this whole diaspora thing… I live more in my head. This film is about an old man who has been displaced and who cannot deal with the silence of his apartment. He hears every sound and has acoustic memories, and then he goes around finding a way to solve that. For me, it's the opposite of growing up in Karachi. Every time I go back to my place in Berlin, it's so silent that I've had a ceiling fan installed in my room because the white noise of the ceiling fan is so South

nicht dort zu sein – nicht sehen zu können. Das Meer ist überall auf dem Gemälde und außer-halb davon. Während meiner Arbeit war eine Person bei mir, die nicht wusste, ob sie im selben Raum war oder nicht. Ich wusste auch nicht mehr, ob sie dort war oder nicht, obwohl sie im Raum war.

Ich arbeite schon länger gerne mit Historiker*innen, weil es mich sehr fasziniert, aus ihren Erkenntnissen etwas entstehen zu lassen. Im Gegenzug nutzen sie meine Kunstwerke in großen Buchprojekten oder Vortragsreihen, in denen sie mit dem Publikum ins Gespräch kommen und nicht nur von den Fakten berichten wollen. Diese Momente, dieser Blick über den Tellerrand, wie wir es nennen, ist ein wichtiger Teil meines Lebens.

Bani Abidi Es ist interessant, was du erzählst, dass Historiker*innen Material von Künstler*innen in der Lehre nutzen. Es ist außerdem einfach die Geschichte der Geschichte, oder? Es waren nicht immer Bücher. Geschichte wird auch oft in Gedichten und Liedern erzählt. Sie wird von vielen Menschen geschrieben. Sie wird von Frauen geschrieben. Ich denke, dass Künstler*innen heute wegen der umfangreichen Recherchen für ihre Kunstwerke eine wichtige Rolle übernehmen. Wir haben erneut die Möglichkeit einer nichtdidaktischen Herangehensweise an das Wissen und die Geschichte geschaffen. Und uns allen ist wohl bewusst, wie die Geschichtsschreibung bis heute funktioniert hat.

Sofia Victorino Hrair, du hast von deiner Arbeit „im Stillen" gesprochen. Für mich bringst du in deinen Werken auf sehr bewegende Weise das Schweigen zum Ausdruck, das auf andere Art auch in Banis und Lubanais Werken vorkommt, wie ich finde.

Hrair Sarkissian Meines Erachtens geht es vor allem darum, lautstark auf das Schweigen hinzuweisen, insbesondere in meinem Projekt *Last Seen*, für das ich 50 Familien aus fünf verschiedenen Ländern, aus dem Libanon, Argentinien, Brasilien, dem Kosovo und Bosnien, getroffen habe. Familien, die geliebte Menschen in einer Diktatur oder im Krieg verloren haben. Sie warten noch immer auf Antworten. Sie denken noch immer, dass diese Personen leben, und sie leben mit diesen Personen. Für mich war es sehr schwer, mir die Geschichten dieser Familien anzuhören und das alles zu verarbeiten. Im Grunde weiß ich nicht, wie ich es ausgehalten habe, denn es war sehr schmerzvoll. Und das Schweigen … Ich versuche, Dinge auf eine ruhige und stille Art zu vermitteln, vor allem im Westen, denn wenn ich zu viel Krach mache, hören die Menschen nicht zu oder werden unaufmerksam.

Lubaina Himid Ich lebe in einer Kleinstadt und an einem Park, also sehr ruhig, doch eigentlich ist mir die Stille fremd. Sogar während der Arbeit höre ich immer etwas, das nichts damit zu tun hat, weil ich es nicht ertragen kann, etwas zum selben Thema zu hören. Seit vielen Jahren läuft immer irgendetwas, während ich arbeite. Entweder eine bestimmte Musik, oder ich höre mir Theaterstücke oder Fußballspiele an, politische Reportagen, oder es laufen Kinder durch das Haus oder Ähnliches. Wenn ich dann später eines meiner Werke betrachte, kann ich mich manchmal an die Geräusche und Klänge erinnern, die ich während der Arbeit gehört habe. Häufig enthalten die Werke auch Texte, die einen Wald beschreiben oder das Laufen durch Flüsse oder das Geräusch von Bomben oder die Ankunft an einem Ort, von dem man nicht weiß, ob die Leere schon vor oder erst nach der Katastrophe da war. Ich habe tatsächlich erst durch die Ausstellung in der Tate Modern verstanden, dass in vielen meiner Gemälde das Meer zu sehen ist. Es kommt in großen Wellen durch ein Fenster im Hintergrund und steht für die glorreiche Geschichte und das Selbstbewusstsein unserer großen Seefahrernation. Aber auch für die vielen Atlantiküberquerungen. Ich wurde in Sansibar geboren und kenne das Leben in einem Inselstaat. Und ich kenne die unterschiedlichen Geräusche des Meeres, die ich auch in meinen Werken sehen kann. Und dann ist da natürlich die Sprache. Ich spreche nur eine Sprache, nämlich Englisch. Mein Vater hat zwar Swahili gesprochen, doch er ist gestorben, als ich vier Monate alt war. Und meine englische Mutter kehrte mit mir hierher zurück und hat mir diese Sprache nie beigebracht. Auf gewisse Weise hatte ich Angst vor der Sprache und Angst, sie nicht sprechen zu können, was mich beschämte. Ich musste nie eine Sprache verstehen und sprechen lernen, um mich an einem Ort zugehörig zu fühlen, doch ich kann mir gut vorstellen, was das heißt.

Merkwürdigerweise habe ich erst in letzter Zeit ein wirkliches Verhältnis zum Sound entwickelt. Meine Werke waren immer sehr klangvoll, auf geräuschlose Weise. Für meine letzte Ausstellung in London habe ich mit der Grafikerin und Klangkünstlerin Magda Stawarska-Beavan zusammengearbeitet, die ich schon lange kenne. Gemeinsam wollten wir den Klang meiner Werke in den Raum bringen, den Sound, den ich immer hören konnte.

Bani Abidi Ich habe mich mit verschiedenen Formen des Schweigens auseinandergesetzt. Es gibt das Schweigen durch staatliche Zensur, durch Selbstzensur oder das Verstummen in Bedeutungslosigkeit. Wie werden verschiedene Stimmen zum

Asian… we all need ceiling fans, but it's also the sound of the breeze moving. I just can't deal with the silence. It was very autobiographical in the sense that I think a lot about how sound can shake us out of one space and transport us into another, like the streets of Berlin. Then I've done work with the archives of soldiers from the First World War, bringing their letters into light through their songs. So, yeah, there's lots of interest in silence and giving space for reconstructing the sound.

Sofia Victorino Thinking about archives as repositories of history and memory, and how silenced histories are potentially narrated through them, can working with archives help repair erasures and absences? To what extent do archives enable us to question how oppressive memories are transmitted? Bani, you were just about to tell us of your work with Indian soldiers in the First World War. And I'm thinking also of Lubaina's archival project, *Making Histories Visible*, and Hrair's *Unexposed* (2015), a project which I saw years ago at the Armenian Pavilion in Venice, about the Armenians who converted to Islam.

Hrair Sarkissian I think, for me, it all depends on who owns the archive. The winner always controls the narrative. Once you own the narrative, you win. And in my case, when it comes to the Armenian genocide, all the archives that are within the hands of the Turkish authorities are not open to the public. In the '80s, they burned 60 percent of all the Ottoman archives that documented the Armenian genocide. I did a project called *Istory* (2010), where I photographed the books in the National Archive Centre, in Istanbul, all these books that contained the stories and documents within the period of the Armenian genocide until 1917 and '18. When I did this project, I was not allowed to touch or open any of these books. This was a right that I was not… It basically says that I don't exist, too, you know, and it was a big challenge to stand in front of these bookcases and meet the Turkish authorities. The moment they read Hrair Sarkissian, an Armenian name, the director of the National Archive Centre said, 'You can only photograph the reading room. We will not let you to go into the archives'. There is a message for me here, you know?

Sofia Victorino The idea of reparation is complex.

Hrair Sarkissian It's impossible. It's not even complex. It is completely impossible.

Lubaina Himid What I have to say is nothing in comparison to that. It's very, very painful. I gathered material from the early years of us, as young Black British artists, trying to be artists, trying to communicate with each other, trying to make a place in our surroundings. And I really was not very good at throwing things away, which is a different thing to collecting an archive, in a sense. I called it an archive because I thought that one day these things could be important. I collected books, visual materials, photographs, paintings, films, letters and catalogues or brochures. I had exhibition launch invitations, those old-fashioned things of the 1980s to encourage each other to keep making work or encourage our friends to come and see the work. I gathered this material in my house in boxes that I never threw away. Then I had a wonderful colleague at the university who said, 'Let's share it. We can find space at the university'. We spent a lot of time with students and artists cataloguing and organising it. I persuaded the university to give me a little terraced house on campus. Over the years, many curators and art historians, but mostly artists, would come and just 'be' in the space. It wasn't one of those archive projects where you had a very formal experience. It was more like going to visit somebody you knew, and they go and make dinner, and instead of helping them, you look through their letters and their bookcases… It was that sort of atmosphere that I wanted to have there. And you know, symposiums and conferences grew around it, and people began their PhDs or curated shows with it. If you wanted to know about all those Black women in Britain in the 1980s who had carried on working, but whose achievement was way below the surface, Claudette Johnson, Ingrid Pollard, Veronica Ryan, Sonia Boyce, Chila Burman, Maud Sulter and Marlene Smith… if you wanted to know how they began and why they appeared to disappear, the answer was in this small set of materials. Then I retired this February from the University of Central Lancashire. I had the intention to send some of the materials to Tate Britain and to take the books back to my house, but I couldn't really trust enough the funding streams there to leave it behind, so I took it to my studio in Preston. This was not what I had planned. However, in the moment at which I could implement that plan, I wanted it with me, readily available to view. If I'd donated it to a bigger institution, of course, there would be too many filters and barriers. I've made it very personal and informal again.

Sofia Victorino The final question is about collaborative practices, which is something to which I have dedicated my work as a curator at Whitechapel Gallery. But I would like to focus on your own works. Hrair meeting communities in extremely vulnerable situations; Lubaina's work with artists and engaging with a whole tradition of painting; and Bani dealing with

Schweigen gebracht? Das Schweigen der Auslöschung. In den meisten meiner Werke arbeite ich mit Sound. In meinem aktuellen Filmprojekt geht es um akustische Vertreibung und Klangverlust. Es ist der erste Film, den ich in Deutschland mache. Ich lebe zwar seit zehn Jahren in Berlin, doch bisher wusste ich nicht, wie ich hier Kunst machen könnte. Das hat bei mir auch viel mit dem Thema Diaspora zu tun … Ich lebe vor allem in meinen Gedanken. In dem Film geht es um einen Mann, der vertrieben wurde und mit der Stille in seiner Wohnung nicht klar kommt. Er hört jedes Geräusch und wird von akustischen Erinnerungen verfolgt, bis er eine Lösung für sein Problem findet. Für mich ist es das Gegenteil meiner Kindheit und Jugend in Karachi. In meiner Berliner Wohnung war es nach meiner Rückkehr immer so still, dass ich mir einen Deckenventilator angeschafft habe, weil mich das weiße Rauschen des Ventilators an Südasien erinnert. Dort sind Deckenventilatoren unerlässlich. Doch es ging mir auch um das Geräusch des Luftzugs. Mit der Stille komme ich nicht klar. Das hat etwas sehr Autobiografisches, denn ich denke sehr viel darüber nach, wie uns Klänge von einem Ort an einen anderen transportieren können, wie es oft in den Straßen von Berlin passiert. Und bei meiner Arbeit mit dem Feldpostarchiv aus dem Ersten Weltkrieg habe ich die Briefe der Soldaten mit ihren Liedern untermalt. Ich habe also ein großes Interesse am Schweigen und an der Rekonstruktion von Klängen.

Sofia Victorino Wenn wir Archive als Quellen der Geschichte und der Erinnerung und als Möglichkeit betrachten, verschwiegene Geschichten zu erzählen, kann die Arbeit mit Archiven dann dazu beitragen, ausgelöschte und abwesende Ereignisse und Personen erneut zum Leben zu erwecken? Inwiefern helfen uns Archive dabei zu verstehen, wie bedrückende Erinnerungen weitergegeben werden? Bani, du hast uns gerade von deiner Arbeit über indische Soldaten im Ersten Weltkrieg berichtet. Dazu fallen mir auch Lubainas Archivprojekt *Making Histories Visible / Geschichten sichtbar machen* und Hrairs Projekt über zum Islam konvertierte Armenier*innen, *Unexposed / Unbelichtet* (2015), ein, das ich vor Jahren im armenischen Pavillon in Venedig gesehen habe.

Hrair Sarkissian Aus meiner Sicht hängt alles davon ab, wem ein Archiv gehört. Der Gewinner hat immer die Kontrolle über das Narrativ. Wer das Narrativ besitzt, hat gewonnen. Und was meine Arbeit zum Völkermord an den Armenier*innen betrifft, sind alle Archive im Besitz der türkischen Behörden nicht öffentlich zugänglich. In den 1980er Jahren wurden 60% des Osmanischen Archivs mit Dokumenten zum Völkermord verbrannt. Für mein Projekt *Istory* (2010) fotografierte ich all die Bücher im Staatsarchiv in Istanbul, die Geschichten und Dokumente aus der Zeit des Völkermords bis 1917 bzw. 1918 enthalten. Bei meiner Arbeit war es mir nicht erlaubt, die Bücher zu berühren oder aufzuschlagen. Dieses Recht hatte ich nicht … Es war so, als ob auch ich nicht existierte. Und es war nicht leicht, vor diesen Bücherregalen zu stehen und mit den türkischen Behörden in Kontakt zu sein. Sobald der Leiter des Staatsarchivs meinen armenischen Namen, Hrair Sarkissian, sah, sagte er zu mir: „Sie dürfen nur im Lesesaal fotografieren, zu den Archiven erhalten Sie keinen Zugang."

Sofia Victorino Wiedergutmachung ist eine komplizierte Sache.

Hrair Sarkissian Wiedergutmachung ist nicht möglich. Sie ist nicht einmal kompliziert. Sie ist vollkommen unmöglich.

Lubaina Himid Was ich dazu beitragen kann, lässt sich nicht einmal annähernd mit diesen schmerzhaften Erfahrungen vergleichen. Ich habe eine Sammlung mit Materialien aus unseren Anfangsjahren als junge Schwarze britische Künstler*innen. Als wir versucht haben, in der Kunstwelt aktiv zu sein, miteinander zu kommunizieren und Fuß zu fassen. Und es fällt mir wirklich nicht leicht, Dinge wegzuschmeißen, was etwas ganz anderes als der Aufbau eines Archivs ist. Aber ich bezeichnete die Sammlung als Archiv, weil ich dachte, dass diese Dinge einmal wichtig sein könnten. Ich sammelte Bücher, Bildmaterial, Fotos, Gemälde, Filme, Briefe und Kataloge oder Broschüren, wirklich alles. Einladungen, diese altmodische Tradition aus den 1980er Jahren, mit denen wir uns gegenseitig in unserem Kunstschaffen motivierten oder unsere Freund*innen zu unseren Ausstellungen einluden. All dies hatte ich in meinem Haus in Kartons verstaut, die ich nie entsorgt habe. Dann gab es eine wunderbare Kollegin an der Universität, die zu mir sagte: „Wir können uns gemeinsam darum kümmern und die Sachen an der Universität lagern." Zusammen mit Student*innen und Künstler*innen verbrachten wir viel Zeit damit, alles zu katalogisieren und zu ordnen. Ich überzeugte die Universität davon, mir ein kleines Reihenhaus auf dem Campus zur Verfügung zu stellen. Im Verlauf der Jahre kamen viele Kurator*innen, aber vor allem Künstler*innen an diesen Ort, um einfach nur dort zu sein. Es war keines dieser eher förmlichen Archivprojekte. Sondern eher wie der Besuch bei Bekannten. Und dann half man nicht dabei, das Abendessen vorzubereiten,

multiple voices and ways of telling histories. Have different forms of collaboration impacted your work?

Hrair Sarkissian The only time I collaborated was in the project *Last Seen*. It was essential, because I needed to get in touch with NGOs in five countries who are in contact with the families of missing people, so they would allow me to enter their private space. It always takes a lot of time. The key thing is to be open about the aim of the entire project. The ones who accepted welcomed the idea of introducing their pain in a different way, different from the way it is usually dealt with in newspaper articles.

Bani Abidi I've actually collaborated in this sound piece with a poet, song composers and singers. But I generally feel that… it's more about the community and the way I operate as an artist, especially with a group of four girlfriends, one of whom is an art historian, and two are artists. We all share our ideas, and although we're living in different cities, we kind of move together, not just the four of us, but with others. What does community mean, intellectually, at any point in time? I've always been part of a group, and I like to address that at all times. Similarly, I had a show in Sharjah a couple of years ago… What was crucial for me to say was… hey, listen, Karachi in the '90s was a very important place for me, so I really would like to have a show about that time. That idea of collaboration is more like committing to, identifying and offering an intellectual universe that we belong to, at any given time, when we present ourselves. I love to quote what my friends have said about things that I'm interested in. Because it's that idea of how people exist in my work.

Sofia Victorino Thinking about friendship, so much of your practice has evolved in relation to close friends and to people who surround you.

Lubaina Himid Yes, in many ways, really. In the beginning, making those shows in the 1980s with those women I have mentioned earlier came from an MA I was doing at the Royal College of Art. I was trying to prove that Black people made art, you know? In 1984, you had to do an MA to prove that to the British art world, but in the process, I met all those women that I've known ever since 1982. We are part of each other's lives. In the early days, we were making those exhibitions together. However, in the making of my artwork, I wasn't always very collaborative. I was never a curator, but I would have an idea for an exhibition that, then, maybe five or six or eleven of us were working together to make it work, you know? Those were the collaborative things that I did. Even now, I'm curating a show in a year's time, September '23, with artists that I've been working alongside for many years.

One of the artists with whom I made the only practice-based collaboration I've participated in is Magda Stawarska-Beavan. We made this installation together, *Blue Grid Test*. In 2020, we spent a lot of time locked down in the same place. We talked about language and colour and sound. She thought about language and got me to speak languages that I don't speak, to talk about the colour blue, and I just took instruments, furniture, books from my house and my studio, my garage and cellar. I made a very thin blue line of patterns from everywhere. Japanese patterns, East African, West African patterns, Indian patterns, but all in blue. I painted patterns on the objects, so that around the room, you have this one thin blue line, but painted on a mandolin, tureens, maps, shopping baskets, a clock. A sound work composed by Magda emanating from six speakers, speaks about the colour blue. A friend of ours is playing the Joni Mitchell song *Blue* on the piano. In a sense, it's a like a kanga surrounding you. It's a place to hold yourself before you go to the next place, whichever that is. You go through this installation and into a much more dangerous set of artworks, and the caption that goes with it (I refused to have labels in my Tate show), the words on the wall ask, 'What does love sound like?' Even if we thought we were exploring codes and poetry, music and sound, while making patterns sound like something real, and music/voice look like something equally real, I think love is what we were really exploring.

Sofia Victorino It is extraordinary that we managed to be here together, across three time zones and four countries, Armenia, Pakistan, Portugal and the UK. Thank you for being so generous in sharing ideas and thoughts about your art practice.

16 August 2022
131 minutes

sondern stöberte in den Briefen und Bücherregalen … Genau diese Atmosphäre wollte ich dort vermitteln. Und so entwickelten sich daraus Symposien und Konferenzen, Doktorarbeiten oder kuratierte Ausstellungen. Hier konnte man etwas über die vielen Schwarzen Künstlerinnen erfahren, die im Großbritannien der 1980er Jahre aktiv, aber nicht allzu bekannt waren, Claudette Johnson, Ingrid Pollard, Veronica Ryan, Sonia Boyce, Chila Burman, Maud Sulter und Marlene Smith … Wenn man etwas über ihre Anfangsjahre und darüber erfahren wollte, warum sie da waren und dann wieder verschwanden, dann fand man die Antworten tatsächlich in dieser kleinen Materialsammlung. Als ich im Februar in den Ruhestand ging, wollte ich einen Teil des Materials an die Tate Britain übergeben und die Bücher mit nach Hause nehmen. Doch ich hatte kein Vertrauen in die Finanzierung, in neue Mitarbeiter. Also konnte ich mich nicht davon trennen und nahm alles mit in mein Studio in Preston. Das war wirklich nicht der Plan gewesen. Doch als ich die Möglichkeit hatte, wollte ich die Dinge bei mir haben. Ich wollte, dass sie weiter jederzeit zugänglich sind. Hätte ich sie einer größeren Einrichtung gegeben, wären viele Dinge sicherlich aussortiert und abgelehnt worden. Also habe ich daraus erneut ein sehr persönliches und informelles Archiv gemacht.

Sofia Victorino Meine letzte Frage bezieht sich auf kollaborative Prozesse, mit denen ich mich ausführlich während meiner Zeit als Kuratorin in der Whitechapel Gallery beschäftigt habe. Doch ich möchte mich gern auf eure eigenen Werke konzentrieren: Hrair, du hast Menschen aus verschiedenen Gemeinschaften in ausgesprochen verzweifelten Situationen getroffen; Lubaina, du hast mit anderen Künstler*innen zusammengearbeitet und dich der Tradition der Malerei gewidmet, und Bani, du hast dich mit unterschiedlichen Stimmen und Möglichkeiten des Geschichtenerzählens beschäftigt. Hatten verschiedene Formen der Zusammenarbeit einen Einfluss auf eure Arbeit?

Hrair Sarkissian Ich habe bisher nur für das Projekt *Last Seen* mit anderen zusammengearbeitet. In diesem Fall ging es nicht anders, weil ich über NGOs in fünf Ländern den Kontakt zu den Familien der Vermissten herstellen musste, um sie in ihrem privaten Umfeld besuchen zu können. So etwas ist immer sehr zeitaufwendig. Deshalb ist es auch immens wichtig, immer offen für Änderungen am Gesamtkonzept zu bleiben. Den Familien, die sich zu einer Teilnahme bereit erklärten, gefiel der Gedanke, ihren Schmerz anders darzustellen, als es normalerweise in Zeitungsartikeln üblich ist.

Bani Abidi Für die Klanginstallation habe ich mit einem Dichter, Komponist*innen und Sänger*innen zusammengearbeitet. Ganz grundsätzlich denke ich aber, dass es mehr um die Gemeinschaft und meine Arbeitsweise als Künstlerin geht. Insbesondere wenn ich mit einer Gruppe von vier Freundinnen, eine von ihnen ist Kunsthistorikerin, zwei sind Künstlerinnen, zusammenarbeite. Wir sprechen über unsere Ideen. Und obwohl wir in unterschiedlichen Städten leben, rücken wir auf gewisse Weise zusammen, nicht nur wir vier, auch andere. Wie genau lässt sich eine Gemeinschaft in einem bestimmten Moment definieren? Ich war immer Teil einer Gruppe, und das möchte ich auch immer zum Ausdruck bringen. Vor einigen Jahren hatte ich auch eine Ausstellung in Sharjah … Mir war wichtig zu sagen: In den 1990er Jahren war Karachi ein sehr wichtiger Ort für mich, ich möchte daher sehr gerne eine Ausstellung über diese Zeit machen. Der Gedanke der Zusammenarbeit hat für mich mehr mit Engagement, Identifikation und der Präsentation einer intellektuellen Welt zu tun, mit der unsere eigene Darstellung stets untrennbar verbunden ist. Ich zitiere gerne, was meine Freund*innen über meine Interessen gesagt haben. Denn auf diese Weise erwachen Personen in meinen Werken zum Leben.

Sofia Victorino Freundschaft ist ein gutes Stichwort für dich, Lubaina, weil ein großer Teil deiner künstlerischen Praxis über deine Beziehungen zu engen Freund*innen und zu den Menschen in deiner Umgebung entstanden ist.

Lubaina Himid Ja, das stimmt in vielerlei Hinsicht. Zu Beginn, in den 1980er Jahren, standen meine Ausstellungen mit diesen Frauen, die ich bereits erwähnte, in einem Zusammenhang mit meinem Magister am Royal College of Art. Ich wollte beweisen, dass auch Schwarze Menschen Kunst schaffen. Davon ließ sich die britische Kunstwelt des Jahres 1984 nur überzeugen, wenn man einen Masterabschluss vorzuweisen hatte. Allerdings lernte ich dadurch all die Frauen kennen, mit denen ich seit 1982 im Kontakt bin. In der Anfangszeit machten wir diese Ausstellungen gemeinsam. Doch meine künstlerische Praxis war nicht immer allzu kollaborativ ausgelegt. Ich war niemals als Kuratorin tätig, doch ich hatte die Idee, dass vielleicht fünf oder sechs oder elf von uns gemeinsam eine Ausstellung auf die Beine stellten könnten. Dies war meine Form der Zusammenarbeit. Das ist noch heute so. Nächstes Jahr, im September 2023, werde ich eine Ausstellung mit Künstler*innen kuratieren, mit denen ich seit langer Zeit zusammenarbeite.

Eine der Künstlerinnen, mit der ich die einzige praxisbezogene Zusammenarbeit gemacht habe, ist Magda Stawarska-

Beavan. Wir entwickelten gemeinsam die Installation *Blue Grid Test*. Im Jahr 2020 verbrachten wir während des Lockdowns viel Zeit gemeinsam an einem Ort. Wir unterhielten uns über Sprache und Farbe und Klang. Sie machte sich Gedanken zur Sprache und brachte mich dazu, Sprachen zu sprechen, die ich nicht beherrsche, auch über die Farbe Blau zu sprechen. Und ich schnappte mir Instrumente, Möbel, Bücher aus meinem Haus und meinem Atelier und meiner Garage und meinem Keller und malte eine dünne blaue Linie mit Mustern aus aller Welt. Muster aus Japan, Ostafrika, Westafrika, Indien, und zwar ausschließlich in blauer Farbe. Ich malte all diese Muster auf die Gegenstände, sodass sich eine dünne blaue Linie auf einer Mandoline, einer Uhr, Terrinen, Landkarten, Einkaufskörben durch den Raum zog. Eine von Magda komponierte Klangarbeit, die aus sechs Lautsprechern ertönte, handelte von der Farbe Blau. Eine gemeinsame Freundin spielte den Song *Blue* von Joni Mitchell auf dem Klavier. Es war, als wäre man von einem Kanga umgeben. Ein Ort, an dem man verweilt, bis man zum nächsten Ort weitergeht, was auch immer das sein mag. Man schreitet durch die Installation in eine weitaus gefährlichere Reihe von Kunstwerken mit den dazugehörigen Erläuterungen (in meiner Ausstellung im Tate wollte ich keine Erläuterungen haben). An der Wand steht die Frage „Wie hört sich Liebe an?". Wir haben zwar gedacht, dass wir Dinge wie Codes und Poesie und Musik und Sound erforscht und Muster zum Klingen gebracht und Musik und Stimmen ein Aussehen gegeben haben, doch eigentlich glaube ich, dass wir in Wirklichkeit die Liebe erforscht haben.

Sofia Victorino Es ist schon etwas Außergewöhnliches, dass wir es geschafft haben, miteinander zu sprechen, über drei Zeitzonen und vier Länder – Armenien, Pakistan, Portugal und Großbritannien – hinweg. Vielen Dank, dass ihr so bereitwillig eure Ideen und Gedanken zu eurem Kunstschaffen geteilt habt.

16. August 2022
131 Minuten

*
Aus: Etel Adnan, *Im Herzen des Herzens eines anderen Landes*, dt. Übersetzung aus dem Englischen von Christel Dormagen, Frankfurt a. M. 2004.

## Künstler*innen

BANI ABIDI
geb. 1971, Karachi, Pakistan
lebt und arbeitet in Berlin und Karachi
Bani Abidi versteht sich als Geschichtenerzählerin und urbane Archäologin. Ihre Videos, Fotos und Inszenierungen erkunden die emotionalen und psychologischen Aspekte, die mit Satire, surrealen Situationen und sozialen Kommentaren verbunden sind. Dabei entlarvt sie die Absurdität der Gesellschaft, indem ihre Protagonist*innen die Grenze zwischen Realität und Schauspielerei, zwischen geplanten und spontanen Momenten verschwimmen lassen.

SARAH ABU ABDALLAH
geb. 1990, Qatif, Saudi-Arabien
lebt und arbeitet in Qatif
Sarah Abu Abdallah befragt in ihren Werken Geschlechterrollen und erkundet weibliche Erfahrungen. Dabei fokussiert sie ebenso Obskures wie die den gängigen Normen entsprechende soziale und kulturelle Alltagspraxis im heutigen Saudi-Arabien.

LAWRENCE ABU HAMDAN
geb. 1985, Amman, Jordanien
lebt und arbeitet in Dubai
Lawrence Abu Hamdan versteht sich als „Lausch-Detektiv", der die Welt anhand von Klängen und Sprache erforscht. Seine Kunst und die Recherchen, die er zusammen mit seinen Kolleg*innen des Forensic-Architecture-Kollektivs durchführt, werden auch zur Beweisaufnahme beim britischen Asyl- und Einwanderungsgericht und von Menschenrechtsorganisationen wie Amnesty International oder Defence for Children International verwendet.

ETEL ADNAN
geb. 1925, Beirut, Libanon
gest. 2021, Paris
Die Dichterin, Dramatikerin, Essayistin und bildende Künstlerin Etel Adnan hat sich zeitlebens mit den emotionalen Aspekten von Heimat im Exil beschäftigt. Ihre Werke basieren auf den Erfahrungen der Diaspora, wofür insbesondere die Kluft zwischen Sprache und Identität zentral ist. Deshalb verwebt Adnan zunächst geschriebene und gehörte Wörter miteinander und verleiht ihnen dann in ihren abstrakten Gemälden durch Linien, Formen, Texturen und Farben poetischen Ausdruck.

LATIF AL ANI
geb. 1932, Karbala, Irak
gest. 2021, Bagdad
Latif Al Ani, der „Vater der irakischen Fotografie", dokumentierte das öffentliche Leben und die politischen Ereignisse wie auch die archäologischen Stätten des Landes. Seine Bilder bezeugen auf eindrucksvolle Art die damalige wirtschaftliche und kulturelle Blüte des Irak. Al Ani beendete seine Karriere 1979 noch vor dem Ausbruch des Iran-Irak-Krieges.

KHADIM ALI
geb. 1978, Quetta, Pakistan
lebt und arbeitet in Sydney
Khadim Ali erforscht die Veränderungen von Worten und Bildern, wie sie der Wechsel ideologischer Vorzeichen mit sich bringt. Seine Gemälde und Textilien sind beeinflusst von der traditionellen vorder- und mittelasiatischen Miniaturmalerei, Kalligrafie und Erzählkunst. Sie zeugen mitunter auch von der Zerstörung des kulturellen Erbes in Bamiyan, Afghanistan, und verleihen dem Gefühl von Verlust und Vertreibung Ausdruck, das ihn als in Pakistan geborener Sohn einer afghanischen Flüchtlingsfamilie zeitlebens begleitet.

HALIL ALTINDERE
geb. 1971, Mardin, Türkei
lebt und arbeitet in Istanbul
Der Künstler und Filmemacher Halil Altindere thematisiert in symbolischen Bildern den Widerstand gegen autokratische Systeme, wobei u. a. der urbane Wandel und das Geschlechterverhältnis in sein Blickfeld rückt. Altindere versteht sich dabei als Vermittler, der eng mit den jeweils Betroffenen zusammenarbeitet und auf deren Erfahrungen zurückgreift.

MINAM APANG
geb. 1979, Naharlagun, Indien
lebt und arbeitet in Goa
In ihren Zeichnungen verknüpft Minam Apang Erinnerungen und Fantasie, was ihr erlaubt, stets neue Beziehungen zu ihrer Umgebung zu knüpfen. Seit 15 Jahren greift sie hierbei verstärkt auf die tradierte Mythologie und Erzählkunst Nordostindiens zurück.

RASHEED ARAEEN
geb. 1935, Karachi, Pakistan
lebt und arbeitet in London
Der pakistanische Bauingenieur Rasheed Araeen ist fasziniert von architektonischen Strukturen, die auf geometrischer und abstrakter Formgebung beruhen. In den 1960er Jahren zog er nach London, wo er zum Vorreiter der minimalistischen Bildhauerei avancierte.

MARWAN KASSAB BACHI
geb. 1934, Damaskus, Syrien
gest. 2016, Berlin
Der als Marwan bekannte Künstler und Pädagoge Marwan Kassab Bachi verband in seiner Arbeit sein Interesse an der Dekonstruktion des Porträts mit soziopolitischer und -psychologischer Erinnerungsarbeit. In seiner postsurrealistischen Landschafts- und Porträtmalerei verhalf er dem ganzen Universum der Seele und den Qualen der menschlichen Existenz zum Ausdruck. Sein Werk ist häufig mit der deutschen Nachkriegsbewegung der Neuen Figuration in Verbindung gebracht worden.

THURAYA AL-BAQSAMI
geb. 1951, Kuwait
lebt und arbeitet in Kuwait
Die bildende Künstlerin, Schriftstellerin und Feministin Thuraya Al-Baqsami blickt über eine 50-jährige Karriere auf drei Kontinenten – Europa, Afrika und Asien – zurück. Ihre Werke befassen sich mit soziopolitischen Sachverhalten und Ereignissen, von der irakischen Invasion in Kuwait bis zur Unterdrückung der Frau. Die Erforschung des Weltraums und die Ideenwelt der Moderne sind weitere zentrale Themen ihrer Arbeit. Als Autorin hat sie sowohl Romane und Novellen wie auch Geschichten für Kinder veröffentlicht.

SHIRAZ BAYJOO
geb. 1979, Port Louis, Mauritius
lebt und arbeitet in London und Mauritius
Shiraz Bayjoo beschäftigt sich in seinen Videos, Gemälden, Fotos und Skulpturen mit Fragen der kulturellen Identität in seinem Heimatland Mauritius und der gesamten Region des Indischen Ozeans. Dabei widmet er sich Themen wie der kollektiven Identität, der Nationalität, Migration sowie dem Erbe der europäischen Kolonialisierung. Dazu nutzt er häufig historische Artefakte aus privaten und öffentlichen Sammlungen.

SEMIHA BERKSOY
geb. 1910, Istanbul, Türkei
gest. 2004, Istanbul
Die Malerin, Dichterin und Opernsängerin Semiha Berksoy ist dem Publikum aus vielen türkischen Filmen und Theaterproduktionen bekannt. In ihren autobiografischen Gemälden thematisiert die Künstlerin Stationen ihrer Karriere und lässt dabei spirituelle und fantastische Element mit einfließen.

HUMA BHABHA
geb. 1962, Karachi, Pakistan
lebt und arbeitet in New York
Die Künstlerin Huma Bhabha ist bekannt für ihre poetisch-figurativen postapokalytischen Skulpturen aus ungewöhnlichen Materialien. Auch für ihre abstrakten Figuren zieht sie die Inspiration u. a. aus der Filmwelt und der Science-Fiction und adressiert dabei Themen aus dem Kontext von Kolonialismus, Krieg und Vertreibung.

HUGUETTE CALAND
geb. 1931, Beirut, Libanon
gest. 2019, Beirut
Die interdisziplinäre Künstlerin Huguette Caland zeigt in ihren feinlinigen Zeichnungen menschliche gequetschte Körperteile, Liebkosungen und ineinander verschlungene Gliedmaßen. Ihre abstrakten Gemälde und Entwürfe überschritten oft die Grenzen dessen, wie Körper, Sexualität und Begehren bislang dargestellt worden waren.

CAMP
gegründet 2007, Mumbai, Indien
die Künstler*innen leben und arbeiten in Mumbai
Das Künstler*innenstudio CAMP wurde 2007 von Shaina Anand und Ashok Sukumaran gegründet. Es stellt mit seinen Arbeiten die Unterscheidungen zwischen Kunst und Nicht-Kunst, zwischen Kommerz und autonomer Kreativität, zwischen institutionellem Rahmen und künstlerischer Selbstbestimmung auf den Prüfstand. CAMPs Filme, Videos, Fotografien, Installationen und Aktionen spiegeln dabei häufig den Wertekosmos von Open-Source-Gemeinschaften wider.

TONY CHAKAR
geb. 1968, Beirut, Libanon
lebt und arbeitet in Beirut
Der Architekt, Künstler und Schriftsteller Tony Chakar beschäftigt sich insbesondere mit den Konflikten und ihren Auswirkungen in seiner Heimatstadt Beirut. Um deren Komplexität gerecht zu werden, setzt er in seinen Arbeiten Bilder, Architektur und philosophisch inspirierte Texte miteinander in Beziehung. Zudem lehrt und publiziert Chakar regelmäßig über Kunst und Architektur im Libanon.

SALOUA RAOUDA CHOUCAIR
geb. 1916, Beirut, Libanon
gest. 2017, Beirut
Saloua Raouda Choucair gilt als internationale Wegbereiterin der abstrakten Moderne. Sie wurde durch die Dekonstruktion und Neukodifizierung islamischer geometrischer Formen, Muster und Architekturen inspiriert, denen sie in Ägypten begegnete. Ebenso beeinflussten sie die klassischen und abstrakten Maltechniken, die sie in den 1940er Jahren während ihres Studiums in Paris kennenlernte. Ihre verschachtelten Formen in Malerei und Skulptur verweisen auf die unendliche Vielfalt möglicher Lebensentwürfe.

TIFFANY CHUNG
geb. 1969, Danang, Vietnam
lebt und arbeitet in Ho-Chi-Minh-Stadt
Tiffany Chung ist bekannt für ihre Arbeiten über politische Konflikte, erzwungene Migration und urbanen Wandel. Um den jeweiligen historischen und kulturellen Kontext auszuleuchten, bedient sich Chung so unterschiedlicher Medien wie Kartografie, Skulpturen, Film und Performance. Ihre Landkarten – real oder fiktiv – verweisen auf die positiven wie negativen Implikationen von Grenzziehungen und auf die in ihnen verborgenen „Wahrheiten".

MONIR SHAHROUDY FARMANFARMAIAN
geb. 1922, Qazvin, Iran
gest. 2019, Teheran
Für das enorme, sechs Jahrzehnte umspannende Werk von Monir Shahroudy Farmanfarmaian stehen vor allem ihre Spiegel-und Hinterglasmalereien mit wiederkehrenden Mustern und geometrischen Formen. Ihre filigranen Zeichnungen und Collagen, Spiegelmosaike und Skulpturen verweben die Tradition mit einem Bewusstsein für die Moderne, was die Iranerin zu einer der international anerkanntesten abstrakten Künstler*innen macht.

SIMONE FATTAL
geb. 1942, Damaskus, Syrien
lebt und arbeitet in Paris
Die Künstlerin und Verlegerin Simone Fattal lässt sich für ihre höchst poetisch wirkenden Gemälde, Collagen und Skulpturen – Letztere sind in Ton, Bronze, Stein oder Terrakotta gearbeitet – von der Geschichte und Mythologie der sogenannten Arabischen Welt inspirieren. In ihren politisch-sozial konnotierten Werken beschäftigt sie sich zum einen mit kultureller Identität und Nationalismus, zum anderen verleiht sie darin ihren Erinnerungen an syrische Landschaften Ausdruck.

MARCOS GRIGORIAN
geb. 1925, Kropotkin, Russland
gest. 2007, Jerewan
Marcos Grigorians Engagement reichte von Schauspiel, Lehre und bildender Kunst bis zu seiner Arbeit als Galerist, Kurator und Sammler. Zeitlebens pendelte er zwischen der Sowjetunion, dem Iran, Italien, den Vereinigten Staaten und Armenien und nahm Einfluss auf die dortigen Kunstszenen. Seine experimentellen Arbeiten umfassen performative Fotografie sowie figurative und expressionistische Malerei, bei der er häufig auch natürliche Materialien wie verderbliche Lebensmittel und Fundstücke einsetzte.

ABBAS HABIBALLA
geb. 1950, Sudan
gest. 2020, Ort unbekannt
Nach seiner Ausbildung und Beschäftigung als Fotograf durch das sudanesische Kulturministerium begann Abbas Habiballa, alltägliche, intime und feierliche Momente in seinem familiären Umfeld und in der sudanesischen Gesellschaft mit der Rolleiflex-Kamera festzuhalten. Insbesondere seine Gruppenporträts zeugen von dem großen Feingefühl, mit dem Habiballa seinen Protagonist*innen begegnete.

JOANA HADJITHOMAS & KHALIL JOREIGE
beide geb. 1969, Beirut, Libanon
leben und arbeiten in Beirut und Paris
Das Künstler*innenduo Joana Hadjithomas & Khalil Joreige hinterfragt in seinen Arbeiten die Entstehungskontexte von Bildern, Ideenwelten und Geschichtsschreibung, indem es formale und thematische Verbindungen zwischen Fotografie, Video, Performance, Installation, Skulptur und Spiel- oder Dokumentarfilm schafft und diese zugleich dekonstruiert.

ROKNI HAERIZADEH
geb. 1978, Teheran, Iran
lebt und arbeitet in Dubai
Rokni Haerizadeh fokussiert in seinen Arbeiten die Widersprüche und auch den Humor, die das gesellschaftliche Leben vorantreiben. Seine Skulpturen, Gemälde, Inszenierungen und Animationen nehmen meist Bezug auf bereits tote oder zurückgetretene Politiker*innen, auf Figuren der Literatur oder auf Protagonist*innen des Kinos und des Fernsehens.

TALOI HAVINI
geb. 1981, Arawa, Autonome Region Bougainville
Lebt und arbeitet in Brisbane, Australien
Taloi Havini (Nakas-Stamm, Volk der Hakö) wurde in Arawa in der Autonomen Region Bougainville geboren und lebt und arbeitet heute in Brisbane, Australien. Havinis Arbeit basiert auf umfangreichen Recherchen, die durch ihre matrilinearen Verbindungen zu ihrem Land und ihren Communities auf Bougainville geprägt sind.

SUSAN HEFUNA
geb. 1962, Berlin, Deutschland
lebt und arbeitet in Kairo, Düsseldorf und New York
Die deutsch-ägyptische Multimediakünstlerin Susan Hefuna setzt sich mit ihrer interkulturellen Sozialisation sowie den Korrespondenzen zwischen Ortsansässigkeit und Identität auseinander. Hefunas rasterartige, minimalistische Kompositionen untersuchen Bilder und Strukturen, die sie mithilfe von Zeichnungen, Videos, Fotografien, Skulpturen und Performances verschiedenartig kontextualisiert.

ADAM HENEIN
geb. 1929, Kairo, Ägypten
gest. 2020, Kairo
Der Bildhauer Adam Henein widmete sich in seiner 80-jährigen künstlerischen Schaffenszeit mit dem Gespür für die poetische Reduktion der visuellen Form. Seine Arbeit drehte sich um die Vorstellung von Ewigkeit, wofür er sich von pharaonischer Kunst wie auch der zeitgenössischen Ästhetik inspirieren ließ. Er hinterließ Skulpturen aus Bronze, Holz, Ton und Granit sowie abstrakte geometrische Gemälde, häufig auf Papyrus.

LUBAINA HIMID
geb. 1954, Sansibar, Tansania
lebt und arbeitet in Preston, Großbritannien
Lubaina Himids Werke gelten als Eckpfeiler der britischen Black-Art-Bewegung. Ihr Bühnenbildstudium und ihr ausgeprägtes Interesse an der Oper haben starken Einfluss auf ihre Malerei, figurativen Collagen und Installationen. Himid hinterfragt mit ihren Arbeiten die tradierten, auch in den akademischen Institutionen gepflegten Narrative, in denen das Vermächtnis der Sklaverei und die Rolle der afrikanischen Diaspora systematisch übergangen worden sind.

EMILY JACIR
geb. 1972, Bethlehem, Westjordanland
lebt und arbeitet in Bethlehem und Rom
Die Künstlerin und Filmemacherin Emily Jacir beschäftigt sich insbesondere mit den Themen Transformation, Übersetzung und unterdrückte Narrative. Ihre Arbeiten über Exil, Freiheit und Widerstand nutzen vielschichtige Medien wie etwa Performances, historische Aufzeichnungen und Analysen gesellschaftlicher, historischer und psychosozialer Zusammenhänge.

HAYV KAHRAMAN
geb. 1981, Bagdad, Irak
lebt und arbeitet in Los Angeles
Hayv Kahraman setzt ihre eigenen Vertreibungs- und Exilerfahrungen und ihr Leben in der Diaspora künstlerisch anhand von Frauenfiguren um, deren Charaktere semi-autobiografisch und gleichzeitig kulturell mehrdeutig sind. In ihren Gemälden, Zeichnungen, Objekten und Performances beschäftigt sie sich mit Begriffen wie Gewalt, Unterdrückung, Erinnerung und der Frage nach Zugehörigkeit.

ALI KAZIM
geb. 1979, Pattoki, Pakistan
lebt und arbeitet in Lahore
Inspiriert von Mogul-, Rajput- und Company-Malerei aus Südasien, erforscht Ali Kazim die Geschichte alter Zivilisationen, deren Hinterlassenschaft im Erdboden verborgen sind. Das Werk des zunächst in Pakistan und anschließend in London ausgebildeten Künstlers zeigt in ätherischer Manier häufig Figuren und archäologische Überreste, die fantastisch anmuten.

AMAL KENAWY
geb. 1974, Kairo, Ägypten
gest. 2012, Kairo
Amal Kenawy konzentrierte sich in ihrer Arbeit auf soziale und politische Themen. Sie erforschte den Körper, die Phänomene des Todes und des Begehrens ebenso wie die der Erinnerung und der Verletzlichkeit. Die hauptsächlich in Ägypten lebende Künstlerin verband in ihren Werken die Medien Performance, Installation, Video, Malerei und Zeichnung.

AISHA KHALID
geb. 1972, Faisalabad, Pakistan
lebt und arbeitet in Lahore
Politisch-soziales Denken, Spiritualität und eine an islamischen Mustern geschulte Präzision kennzeichnen die multimediale Praxis von Aisha Khalid. Ihre Stickereien, Gemälde, Videos und Installationen sind von ihrer Ausbildung in südasiatischer Miniaturkunst inspiriert und kombinieren dekorative Flächen häufig mit motivischen Darstellungen, die Sufi-Versen entlehnt sind.

ANUAR KHALIFI
geb. 1977, Lloret de Mar, Spanien
lebt und arbeitet in Barcelona und Tanger
Mit leuchtenden Farben schafft Anuar Khalifi, der Autodidakt mit spirituellen Interessen ist, transzendentale Porträts im neoimpressionistischen Stil. Seine Landschaftsgemälde kombinieren oftmals Figuren, die der Sufi-Tradition zu entstammen scheinen, mit autobiografisch konnotierten Motiven und Referenzen aus der Kunstgeschichte.

DAVID KOLOANE
geb. 1938, Johannesburg, Südafrika
gest. 2019, Johannesburg
David Koloane war multidisziplinär arbeitender Künstler, Aktivist, Schriftsteller und Kurator. Er war als Lehrer und Mentor tätig und gründete lokale Kunstinstitutionen, die wesentlich zur Entwicklung der Kunstszene im Südafrika der Apartheid beitrugen. Seine ins Abstrakte tendierenden Stadtlandschaften und fantasievoll bevölkerten Kompositionen thematisieren zumeist die conditio humana und die mit ihr verstrickten politisch-sozialen Verhältnisse.

FARIDEH LASHAI
geb. 1944, Rascht, Iran
gest. 2013, Teheran
Die bildende Künstlerin, Schriftstellerin und Übersetzerin Farideh Lashai hat über mehr als fünf Jahrzehnte ihre persönliche Geschichte mit ausdrucksstarker Lyrik und Erzähltechnik verwoben. Während ihre idyllischen Landschaften die Natur feiern und den Trost beschreiben, den sie spendet, ist Lashais Kunst dennoch zugleich tief im gesellschaftlichen und politischen Leben verwurzelt.

TALA MADANI
geb. 1981, Teheran, Iran
lebt und arbeitet in Kalifornien
Tala Madanis satirische Gemälde üben scharfe Kritik an der patriarchalen Gesellschaft. In ihren figurativen Werken dekonstruiert sie Geschlechterklischees und Männlichkeitsideale. Madanis Bilder entstehen aus Studien und Skizzenbüchern; ihre Gemälde entwickelt sie häufig in Stop-Motion-Animationen weiter.

TAUS MAKHACHEVA
geb. 1983, Dagestan, Russland
lebt und arbeitet in Moskau und Machatschkala
Taus Makhacheva erforscht in Videoarbeiten, Installationen, Fotografien und Performances den schmalen Grat, der Gleichheit und Differenz trennt. Dabei geht sie der Frage nach, was von der Vergangenheit ihres Landes noch überliefert ist und in welcher Form diese Traditionen wieder in den Alltag Einzug halten.

JUMANA MANNA
geb. 1987, Princeton, USA
lebt und arbeitet in Berlin and Jerusalem
Mit ihren Filmen, Installationen und Skulpturen erkundet Jumana Manna die Machtdynamiken, die den kolonisierten Körpern und dem Land innewohnen. Dabei untersucht sie die Vielschichtigkeiten und Widersprüche, in die sich Archäologie, Landwirtschaft und Rechtsprechung verwickeln – u. a. indem sie Begriffe wie Bewahrung, Zerstörung und Wiederbelebung in ihrem jeweiligen Anwendungskontext hinterfragt.

IBRAHIM MASSOUDA
geb. (vermutlich) 1925, Ägypten
gest. (vermutlich) 1965
Ibrahim Massouda wurde in Ägypten geboren, widersprüchlichen Quellen zufolge entweder 1925 oder 1938, wobei häufiger das frühere Datum angegeben wird. Verstorben ist er vermutlich in oder um das Jahr 1965. Nach dem Studium an der Akademie der Schönen Künste in Kairo entwickelte Massouda einen unverwechselbaren impressionistischen Stil, wobei er oft er politische Konflikte darstellte. Er trat der Gruppe für Kunst und Freiheit, der Keimzelle der surrealistischen Bewegung Ägyptens, spät bei und wurde um 1945 aktives Mitglied der gegründeten Gruppe für Zeitgenössische Kunst.

AHMED MATER
geb. 1979, Tabuk, Saudi-Arabien
lebt und arbeitet in Riad
Der ehemalige Arzt Ahmed Mater erforscht die Narrative und Ästhetik der islamischen Kultur unter den Vorzeichen des von Globalisierung und Massenkonsum geprägten gesellschaftlichen Wandels. Mater arbeitet mit Fotografie, Kalligrafie, Installation und Video, um die komplexen Realitäten des heutigen Saudi-Arabien zu dokumentieren und zu kritisieren.

AHMED MORSI
geb. 1930, Alexandria, Ägypten
lebt und arbeitet in New York City
Ahmed Morsi hat als Maler, Dichter, Grafiker und Kritiker seit den 1940er Jahren ein weitverzweigtes, von der Mythologie durchdrungenes Werk geschaffen. Seine figurativen wie fantastischen Gemälde zeigen seinem Interesse am Surrealismus entsprungene Welten, die von Pferden, Fischen, Vögeln und Menschen bevölkert sind.

FATEH MOUDARRES
geb. 1922, Aleppo, Syrien
gest. 1999, Aleppo
Der Maler, Schriftsteller und Dichter Fateh Moudarres gilt als Vorreiter der syrischen Moderne. Seine Werke wurden ebenso von den politischen Unruhen beeinflusst, die er in der Region miterlebte, wie von der alten syrischen Kunst und der christlichen Ikonografie. Moudarres ist für seinen unverwechselbaren abstrakten Stil bekannt, der sich durch multikulturelle Referenzen und erdige Farbtöne auszeichnet.

KHALIL RABAH
geb. 1961, Jerusalem, Israel / Palästina
lebt und arbeitet in Ramallah
Khalil Rabah beschäftigt sich eingehend mit Architektur und Städtebau, um alternative Visionen und halbfiktive Vorstellungen von Geschichte entwickeln zu können. Rabahs Arbeiten greifen Themen wie Vertreibung, Erinnerung und Identität auf, wobei im Vordergrund immer die Beziehung zwischen den Menschen und ihrer Umgebung steht.

MICHAEL RAKOWITZ
geb. 1973, New York City, USA
lebt und arbeitet in Chicago
Der Konzeptkünstler Michael Rakowitz schafft Projekte, Installationen und Aktionen im öffentlichen Raum – oft in Zusammenarbeit mit lokalen Akteuren. Sein einzigartiges, subversives Vorgehen kann als eine Form kontrakolonialer Geschichtsschreibung und als Intervention in aktuelle gesellschaftliche Prozesse gelesen werden. In seinen umfangreichen Recherchen spürt er den unterschiedlichsten Sachverhalten nach – vom persönlichen Lebensbereich bis hin zur Geopolitik.

MARWAN RECHMAOUI
geb. 1964, Beirut, Libanon
lebt und arbeitet in Beirut
Marwan Rechmaoui begann sein künstlerisches Schaffen mit Malerei, bevor er ein Interesse an architektonischen Formen, industriellen Materialien und kartografischer Arbeit entwickelte. Aus Teer, Gummi, Metall, Beton, Glas und Stoff entwickelt er Werke, die – inspiriert von der reichhaltigen Kultur und Geschichte Beiruts – die Vielschichtigkeit und soziopolitischen Unterströmungen dieser Stadt aufdecken.

IBRAHIM EL-SALAHI
geb. 1930, Omdurman, Sudan
lebt und arbeitet in Oxford
Ibrahim El-Salahi verbindet klassische westliche Kunsttechniken, die er in London studierte, mit afrikanischen und islamischen Mustern. In seinen Gemälden verschmelzen abstrakte Kalligrafien mit Naturmotiven – ein Spiegel seiner eigenen Lebenserfahrungen. El-Salahis multidisziplinäre Arbeiten rücken afrikanische Kunst in den Kontext eines neuen globalen Modernismus.

MOHAN B SAMANT
geb. 1924, Bombay (heute Mumbai), Indien
gest. 2004, New York City
Mohan Samant gilt als Pionier der modernen indischen Kunst. In den 1950er Jahren war er Mitglied der Progressive Artists' Group, einer Gruppe von Künstler*innen, die vor allem in Mumbai lebten. Seine Arbeiten speisten sich aus zahlreichen Quellen wie der Miniatur- und Basohli-Malerei sowie Hieroglyphen und Objekten aus dem alten Ägypten. Seinem Stil, seiner Technik, seiner Farbgebung und seinem Material sind historische, spirituelle und lebensweltliche Narrative eingeschrieben.

HRAIR SARKISSIAN
geb. 1973, Damaskus, Syrien
lebt und arbeitet in London
Hrair Sarkissian nutzt das Medium der Fotografie, um Geschichten zu erzählen, die in offiziellen Dokumenten oder Geschichtsbüchern nicht vorkommen. Mithilfe einer Großformatkamera schafft er konzeptionelle Arbeiten, die ihre Betrachter*innen einladen, sich mit dem auseinanderzusetzen, was unter der Oberfläche seiner großflächigen Aufnahmen liegt.

HASSAN SHARIF
geb. 1951, Iran
gest. 2016, Dubai
Hassan Sharif war ein Pionier der Konzeptkunst und experimenteller Methoden; außerdem ein engagierter Kritiker und Gründer mehrerer Kunsteinrichtungen in den Vereinigten Arabischen Emiraten. Zu seinen Ausdrucksmitteln gehörten Performances, Gemälde und Installationen, die er systematisch aus gefundenen Gegenständen zusammenwachsen ließ. Sharif beschäftigte sich in seiner Kunst auch mit gesellschaftlichen Themen wie der Massenproduktion von Gütern und der Konsumkultur.

WAEL SHAWKY
geb. 1971, Alexandria, Ägypten
lebt und arbeitet in Alexandria und Philadelphia
Wael Shawkys Filme, Installationen, Zeichnungen, Gemälde, Fotografien und Performances basieren auf ausgedehnten Recherchen, auf die der Künstler zurückgreift, um in seinen Arbeiten Fiktion und Fakten zu verschmelzen. Shawky betrachtet die zeitgenössische Gesellschaft aus der Perspektive subjektiver Geschichte(n), wobei insbesondere die Identitätspolitik sowie die Darstellung von Religion und Mythologie in den Fokus geraten.

ANWAR JALAL SHEMZA
geb. 1928, Shimla, Indien
gest. 1985, Stafford
Der Künstler, Schriftsteller und Kunstlehrer Anwar Jalal Shemza wurde für seine lyrisch-figurativen Arbeiten und als Gründer des pakistanischen Lahore Art Circle bekannt. Ab 1956 studierte er an der Londoner Slade School of Fine Art und begann, geometrische und kalligrafische Formen aus der islamischen Kunst mit Elementen und Denkweisen der abstrakten europäischen Kunst zu verknüpfen.

AHMED SHIBRAIN
geb. 1931, Berber, Sudan
gest. 2017, Khartum
Der Maler, Grafikdesigner und Pädagoge Ahmed Shibrain studierte an der Londoner Central School of Art, um anschließend in den Sudan zurückzukehren und dort in staatlichen Kulturinstitutionen und an der Hochschule leitende Funktionen zu übernehmen. Er wurde zu einem namhaften afrikanischen Vertreter der Moderne und in den 1960er Jahren zu einem der Gründungsmitglieder der Schule von Khartum. In seinem Werk vereinte er Aspekte der arabischen Kalligrafie mit ästhetischen und kulturellen Traditionen aus ganz Afrika.

SHAHZIA SIKANDER
geb. 1969, Lahore, Pakistan
lebt und arbeitet in New York
Shahzia Sikander Arbeiten initiieren kritische Dialoge zwischen indo-persischer Miniaturmalerei, Populärkultur, Mythologie und zeitgenössischer Theorie. Ihre detailreichen Zeichnungen, Gemälde, Videos, Installationen und Animationen widmen sich so aktuellen Themen wie Geschlecht, Sexualität, Religion und kulturelle Identität im Kontext der kolonialen und postkolonialen Geschichte.

RAYYANE TABET
geb. 1983, Achkout, Libanon
lebt und arbeitet in Beirut und San Francisco
Rayyane Tabet beschäftigt sich in seinen Installationen mit Narrativen, die ein alternatives Verständnis von soziopolitischen Ereignissen vermitteln. Vor dem Hintergrund seiner Architektur- und Bildhauerausbildung erkundet er die Paradoxien der urbanen Welt sowie die Umbrüche, die einst als treibende Kräfte der „objektiven" Geschichte gelten werden.

RICHARD LOKIDEN WANI
geb. 1974, Kajo Keji, Sudan
lebt und arbeitet in Juba
Richard Lokiden Wani erhielt seine informelle fotografische Ausbildung von amerikanischen und norwegischen Geistlichen, die sich während des zweiten sudanesischen Bürgerkriegs in Juba aufhielten. Seine Aufnahmen von Kirchgänger*innen, Prediger*innen und Nachbar*innen machen infolge des Einsatzes von Blitzlicht im Tageslicht einen erhabenen Eindruck: Die im Sitzen oder Stehen Porträtierten strahlen Entschlossenheit und Stolz aus.

NARI WARD
geb. 1963, St. Andrew, Jamaika
lebt und arbeitet in New York
Nari Ward ist für seine Installationen bekannt, die er mit weggeworfenen Materialien und Fundstücken aus seiner alltäglichen Umgebung gestaltet. Seine Arbeiten setzen sich mit dem historischen Gedächtnis, mit Race, Armut und Konsumkultur auseinander.

LIONEL WENDT
geb. 1900, Colombo, Sri Lanka
gest. 1944, Colombo
Lionel Wendt erhielt in England eine Ausbildung als Rechtsanwalt und Pianist, bevor er in den 1930er Jahren eine Karriere als professioneller Fotograf startete. Er experimentierte mit Fotogrammen, Fotomontagen, Doppelbelichtungen und Solarisationen und schuf Werke, die für die Fotografiegeschichte von grundlegender Bedeutung sind. Mit seinen Schriften und der Gründung der Künstler*innen vereinigung Gruppe '43 in Colombo war er außerdem aktiv an der Etablierung und Entwicklung der modernen Kunst in Sri Lanka beteiligt.

KAMAL YOUSSEF
geb. 1923, Kairo, Ägypten
lebt in Pennsylvania
In Kamal Youssefs Werk verschränken sich körperliche und geistige Welten. Seine Gemälde und Skulpturen sind im Laufe von sieben Jahrzehnten entstanden und von seinen Pendelreisen zwischen Ägypten, Frankreich und den USA geprägt. Zu seinen Inspirationsquellen gehören auch die Avantgardebewegungen in ihren jeweiligen kulturellen Kontexten, u. a. auch der ägyptische Surrealismus.

AKRAM ZAATARI
geb. 1966, Saida, Libanon
lebt und arbeitet in Beirut
Akram Zaatari gestaltet Videos und Installationen aus Fotomaterial sowie Bücher zu einer Vielzahl von Themen: Archäologische Ausgrabungen, politische Widerstandsbewegungen und die Bilderfluten während des Krieges sind wichtige Ankerpunkte seines kreativen Schaffens. Die zeitgenössische Kunstszene in Beirut ist stark von Zaatari geprägt worden, der bei der Gründung der Arab Image Foundation (AIF) eine Schlüsselfunktion ausübte.

## Autor*innen

*Direktor*innen*

HOOR AL QASIMI gründete 2009 die *Sharjah Art Foundation* (SAF), um die Kunst in Sharjah, in den Vereinigten Arabischen Emiraten und auf globaler Bühne zu fördern. Als Präsidentin und Direktorin der Stiftung hat sie bedeutende internationale Wanderausstellungen, Künstler*innen- und Kurator*innen-Residenzen, Auftragsarbeiten, Produktionsstipendien und Bildungsprogramme für junge Künstler*innen auf den Weg gebracht. Zudem ist sie seit 2003 die Direktorin der *Sharjah Biennale* sowie die Präsidentin der *International Biennial Association*, Präsidentin des *Africa Institute* und Vorsitzende des Vorstands der *Sharjah Architecture Triennial*. Weitere Positionen hat oder hatte sie im Aufsichtsrat von *MoMA PS1* (New York), des *KW Institute for Contemporary Art* (Kunst-Werke Berlin e.V.) und bei *Ashkal Alwan* (Beirut) inne.

Zudem ist Al Qasimi Vorsitzende des Hochschulbeirats für Bildende Künste und Design an der Universität von Sharjah, Mitglied der Beiräte der *Khoj International Artists' Association*, Neu-Delhi, und *Daratal Funun*, Amman, sowie Mitglied des *Prince Claus Award Committee*.

Sie hat des Weiteren bedeutende nationale und internationale Ausstellungen kuratiert, wie den Pavillon der Vereinigten Arabischen Emirate auf der *56. Biennale* von Venedig und der *2. Biennale* von Lahore und ist Kuratorin der *Sharjah Biennale 15*. Zu ihrer akademischen Laufbahn gehören drei Londoner Universitätsabschlüsse: ein MA in Kuratieren zeitgenössischer Kunst am *Royal College of Art*, ein Diplom in Malerei an der *Royal Academy of Arts* und ein BFA an der *Slade School of Fine Art*.

PROF. DR. DIRK LUCKOW ist seit 2009 Intendant der *Deichtorhallen Hamburg*. Seine Promotion über Joseph Beuys und die Antiform-Kunstbewegung schrieb er an der *Freien Universität Berlin*. Während seiner fast 30-jährigen Karriere absolvierte er Stationen an der *Kunstsammlung Nordrhein-Westfalen* (Düsseldorf), beim *Solomon R. Guggenheim Museum* (New York), beim *Württembergischen Kunstverein* (Stuttgart) und beim *Siemens Arts Program* (München). Von 2002 bis 2009 war Luckow als Direktor der *Kunsthalle zu Kiel* tätig. Des Weiteren hat Luckow zahlreiche Publikationen und Artikel verfasst, u. a. über Künstler*innen wie Richard Artschwager, Cecilia Edefalk, Charline von Heyl, William Kentridge, Hans-Peter Feldmann oder Marilyn Minter. Darüber hinaus war er Juror für den *Hauptstadtkulturfonds* (Berlin), bei *KÖR – Kunst im öffentlichen Raum* (Wien) und ist Mitglied des Kuratoriums der *Nordmetall-Stiftung* und der *Herbert-Gerisch-Stiftung/Skulpturenpark* (Neumünster).

Luckow ist zudem Honorarprofessor für Kunsttheorie an der *Hochschule für bildende Künste Hamburg*.

*Kurator*in, Redakteur*in und Autor*in der Ausstellung*

DR. OMAR KHOLEIF CF FRSA FKA Blake Karim Mitchell ist Autor*in von Poesie und Prosa, Historiker*in des akademischen Lebens und Kurator*in untergegangener und verborgener Archive. Im Laufe der Karriere von Dr. Kholeif hat diese*r als Rundfunksprecher*in, Filmemacher*in, Herausgeber*in, Verleger*in, Museumsdirektor*in und LGBTQ+-Aktivist*in in Südafrika, Großbritannien, den USA, den GKR-Staaten und Nordafrika gearbeitet. In den vergangenen 17 Jahren konzentrierte Dr. Kholeif sich vor allem auf die neu entstehende digitale Bildkultur an der Schnittstelle zu Ethnizität, Race, Geschlecht und Sexualität. Dr. Kholeifs Hauptaugenmerk liegt auf der Frage, wie diese Konzepte mit Begrifflichkeiten aus den Bereichen Gleichheit, Ableismus und öffentliche Gesundheit in der aktuellen Diskussion um soziale Gerechtigkeit zum Ausdruck gebracht werden.

Die hieraus entstandenen Fragen hat Dr. Kholeif in mehr als 60 Ausstellungen und als Autor*in, Ko-Autor*in und Herausgeber*in über 30 Büchern festgehalten, die in zwölf Sprachen übersetzt wurden. Dr. Kholeif war Ko-Kurator*in der *Sharjah Biennale 14: Leaving the Echo Chamber* und ist derzeit Sammlungsleiter*in und Senior Curator der *Sharjah Art Foundation* (Vereinigte Arabische Emirate). Dr. Kholeifs Monografie *Internet Art: From the Birth of the Web to the Rise of NFTs* wird im April 2023 bei *Phaidon* veröffentlicht.

*Autor*innen*

NAWAR AL QASSIMI ist Vizepräsidentin der *Sharjah Art Foundation* (SAF), wo sie seit 2010 zunächst die Entwicklung neuer Strategien für öffentliche Programmgestaltung und die Einbindung der Öffentlichkeit verantwortete. Anschließend leitete sie die Entwicklungsabteilung der Stiftung mit dem Schwerpunkt kulturelle Partnerschaften. In ihrer jetzigen Position ist Al Qassimi für die strategische Planung der SAF verantwortlich und stärkt die Rolle der Stiftung als Katalysator und Fürsprecher für Kunst in Sharjah, Vereinigte Arabische Emirate, sowie auf internationaler Ebene. Al Qassimi ist Mitglied des *Sharjah Tourism Advisory Committee*. Sie ist Absolventin der *American University of Sharjah*.

SKYE ARUNDHATI THOMAS ist Schriftstellerin im indischen Goa und Mitherausgeberin von *The White Review*. Ihr essayistisches Buch *Remember the Details* über viral gegangene Bilder, Gerichtssäle und die kurzlebige indische Protestbewegung von 2019 wurde 2021 bei Floating Opera Press veröffentlicht.

STEPHANIE BAILEY arbeitet als Chefredakteurin des *Ocula Magazine* und pendelt zwischen Hongkong und London. Sie ist zudem als Redakteurin bei *Artpapers* tätig, berät *das M+ Museum of Visual Culture* (Hongkong), ist Mitglied des Redaktionsausschusses von *Naked Punch*, Mitglied des Beirats von *D'ivan, A Journal of Accounts* sowie Gesprächskuratorin der *Art Basel Hongkong* und inhaltliche Beraterin für die *Art Basel, Asien*. Zuvor war Bailey geschäftsführende und leitende Redakteurin bei *Ibraaz Publishing*. Sie hat an zahlreichen Ausstellungskatalogen mitgewirkt und hält regelmäßig Vorträge über die Politik der Ästhetik in der zeitgenössischen Welt.

ANNE BARLOW ist Direktorin der *Tate St. Ives*. Zuvor war sie Direktorin von *Art in General* (New York) und Kuratorin für Bildungs- und Medienprogramme am New Yorker *New Museum*. Sie hat zahlreiche Publikationen veröffentlicht und Vorträge gehalten und war Mitglied einer Vielzahl von Auswahlgremien, beispielsweise für den *Kim? Residency Award* (Riga), *Exposure 8* (Beirut) und den britischen Pavillon der *58. Biennale* von Venedig. Barlow war zudem Kuratorin der *Bukarest Biennale 5* und Ko-Kuratorin des lettischen Pavillons auf der *55. Biennale* von Venedig. Zurzeit kuratiert sie den *Samdani Art Award 2023*.

CHRIS MCCORMACK ist Schriftsteller und Mitherausgeber von *Art Monthly*. Zu seinen jüngsten redaktionellen Projekten gehören Charlotte Prodgers Monografie *Selected Works* (Koenig Books, 2022), die Herausgabe von *ON&BY: Andy Warhol* (MIT Press/Whitechapel, 2016) sowie die Mitveröffentlichung von James Richards' *Requests and Antisongs* (Sternberg Press, 2016). McCormacks Forschung zur Stimmentwicklung, *Voce di testa*, wurde im walisischen Pavillon auf der *57. Biennale* von Venedig ausgestellt. Zu den von ihm kuratierten Ausstellungen und herausgegebenen Monografien gehört außerdem *Anarchic Sexual Desires of Plain Unmarried Schoolteachers* (2015).

PROF. SARAH PERKS ist eine interdisziplinäre Kuratorin und Autorin im nordenglischen Tees Valley. Die Professorin für Kuratieren an der *MIMA + School of Arts and Creative Industries* an der *Teesside University* erforscht vergleichende kuratorische Strategien und ihre wirtschaftlichen, ökologischen und soziopolitischen Aspekte. Zudem gestaltet sie Ausstellungen, Bücher und Projekte über zeitgenössische Kunst, Design, Wissenschaft und Film. Frühere Stationen waren u. a. die künstlerische Leitung von *HOME* und *Cornerhouse* in Manchester. Perks ist zudem Programmberaterin für das *BFI London Film Festival* und leitet *Natural Futures*, ein gemeinschaftliches Forschungsprojekt über kreative Naturerholung und Ökopsychologie.

SOFIA VICTORINO ist Kuratorin und Wissenschaftlerin. Aktuell untersucht sie, inwiefern künstlerische Ansätze als dekolonisierende Werkzeuge in Kunstinstitutionen dienen können. Von 2011 bis 2021 leitete Victorino als Direktorin die Bereiche Bildung und öffentliche Programme an der *Whitechapel Gallery* in London, wo sie ein integriertes Programm mit Residenzen und Auftragsarbeiten, Ausstellungen, Performances, Schul- und Gemeinschaftsprojekten sowie Experimenten mit diskursiven Programmen verantwortete. Von 2002 bis 2011 leitete sie die Ressorts Bildung und öffentliche Programme am *Museu de Arte Contemporânea de Serralves* (Porto). Victorino ist Mitglied des Beirats der Buchreihe *Documents of Contemporary Art*, die gemeinsam von der *Whitechapel Gallery* und *MIT Press* herausgegeben wird. Zudem hält sie Vorlesungen in *Curating Art and Public Programmes* an der London South Bank University.

## Artists

BANI ABIDI
b. 1971, Karachi
Lives and works between Berlin and Karachi
Playing the role of storyteller and urban archeologist, Bani Abidi explores an emotional and psychological space of satire, absurdity and social commentary through video, photography and performance. Her unexpected protagonists blur the lines between actors and non-actors, scripted and spontaneous moments, exposing the absurd theatre of society.

SARAH ABU ABDALLAH
b. 1990, Qatif, Saudi Arabia
Lives and works in Qatif
Through references to gender roles and the female experience, Sarah Abu Abdallah's work explores issues of obscurity and value alongside an investigation of the social and cultural in contemporary Saudi Arabia.

LAWRENCE ABU HAMDAN
b. 1985, Amman
Lives and works in Dubai
Lawrence Abu Hamdan, who refers to himself as a 'private ear', is an artist who investigates the world through the study of sound and linguistics. His artwork and research, along with fellow members of the collective Forensic Architecture, have been used as evidence at the UK Asylum and Immigration Tribunal and as advocacy for organisations such as Amnesty International and Defence for Children International.

ETEL ADNAN
b. 1925, Beirut
d. 2021, Paris
Etel Adnan was a formidable poet, playwright, essayist and visual artist. Diligently developing a sense of home in exile, she derived her creations from the diasporic experience and the gap between language and identity. Her work weaves together written and visual vocabularies, and uses abstract paintings as a form of poetic expression, replacing words with intersecting lines, shapes, textures and colours.

LATIF AL ANI
b. 1932, Karbala, Iraq
d. 2021, Baghdad
Latif Al Ani was known as the father of Iraqi photography and captured the nature of life in his country, including displays of public life, archeological sites and political events. His photographs bear witness to Iraq's golden age and economic rise. He stopped making images in 1979, before the outbreak of the Iran-Iraq War.

KHADIM ALI
b. 1978, Quetta
Lives and works in Sydney
Khadim Ali explores the way words and images change meaning when filtered through different ideological lenses. Drawing from traditions of miniature painting, calligraphy and epic storytelling, Ali's paintings and textiles tell stories of the destruction of his own cultural heritage in Bamiyan, Afghanistan, and the subsequent sense of loss and displacement.

HALIL ALTINDERE
b. 1971, Mardin, Turkey
Lives and works in Istanbul
Halil Altindere is an artist and filmmaker who uses irony and symbolic imagery to explore the resistance of oppressive systems. Acting as a mediator, Altindere chooses to engage with issues such as urban transformation and gender relations and collaborate with those who have direct experience of them.

MINAM APANG
b. 1979, Naharlagun, India
Lives and works in Goa
Minam Apang uses drawing as a way to mine her memories and creative imagination, and to rebuild interactions with her immediate environment. Over the past 15 years, Apang has focused on painting, where she increasingly uses, and often references, mythology and tales from Northeast India.

RASHEED ARAEEN
b. 1935, Karachi
Lives and works in London
Rasheed Araeen was trained as a civil engineer in Pakistan, where his fascination for architectural forms, inspired by his surroundings, fuelled his investigation of geometry and abstraction. In the 1960s, he moved to London, where he developed pioneering works in minimalist sculpture.

MARWAN KASSAB BACHI
b. 1934, Damascus
d. 2016, Berlin
Marwan Kassab Bachi, known as Marwan, was an artist and educator. His visual vocabulary is saturated with socio-political memory, an obsession with deconstructing portraiture and the inner human psyche. His Post-surrealist paintings, associated with the German New Figuration Movement, present landscapes and heads consolidated to form a universe of the soul, conveying his obsession with the anguish of the human condition.

THURAYA AL-BAQSAMI
b. 1951, Kuwait
Lives and works in Kuwait
Thuraya Al-Baqsami is a visual artist, feminist and writer whose career spans five decades and three continents: Europe, Africa and Asia. Her work engages with socio-political events, from the Iraqi invasion of Kuwait to the oppression of women. She is also deeply interested in space exploration and modernist ideas. She has published novels, children's books and short stories.

SHIRAZ BAYJOO
b. 1979, Port Louis, Mauritius
Lives and works between London and Mauritius
Shiraz Bayjoo addresses social, political and historical concerns essential to Mauritian cultural identity and the larger Indian Ocean region through his multidisciplinary work encompassing video, paintings, photography and sculpture. His practice examines collective identity, nationhood, migration and the legacy of European colonisation through historical artefacts taken from private and public collections.

SEMIHA BERKSOY
b. 1910, Istanbul
d. 2004, Istanbul
Semiha Berksoy was a painter, poet and opera singer from Turkey who performed in several major films and theatre productions. Her autobiographical paintings encompass an amalgam of fantasy, spirituality and imagination, and draw from her celebrated career.

HUMA BHABHA
b. 1962, Karachi
Lives and works in New York
Huma Bhabha is known for her post-apocalyptic and poetic figurative sculptures, created using unconventional materials. Her work is an intersection of figuration and abstraction, derived from cinema, science-fiction, cultural references, colonialism, war and displacement.

HUGUETTE CALAND
b. 1931, Beirut
d. 2019, Beirut
Huguette Caland was an interdisciplinary artist. Her delicate lines portrayed flattened flesh, caressing lovers and interwound body parts. Caland's abstract paintings and designs pushed the boundaries of representing the body, sexuality, desire and the politics surrounding it.

CAMP
Established 2007, Mumbai
Live and work in Mumbai
Artist studio CAMP was founded by Shaina Anand and Ashok Sukumaran. CAMP produces work that challenges the distinctions between art and non-art, commodity markets and free culture, the individual and the institutional. Their work encompasses films, video works, photography, installation and community programmes, which frequently reflect the values of open-source communities.

TONY CHAKAR
b. 1968, Beirut
Lives and works in Beirut
Tony Chakar is an architect, artist and writer whose practice frequently incorporates literature, philosophy and theory through an amalgam of text, images and architectural forms. His work often explores the complexities of conflict and its aftermath in his home city of Beirut. Chakar also teaches and writes widely on art and architecture in Lebanon.

SALOUA RAOUDA CHOUCAIR
b. 1916, Beirut
d. 2017, Beirut
Saloua Raouda Choucair is one of the pioneering figures in Abstract Modernism globally. Much of her work was inspired by a deconstruction and recodification of Islamic geometric forms, designs and architecture that she encountered in Egypt, as well as the abstract and classical painting techniques she observed during her studies in Paris in the 1940s. Her interlocking forms in painting and sculpture suggest infinite possible architectures of existence.

TIFFANY CHUNG
b. 1969, Danang, Vietnam
Lives and works in Ho Chi Minh City
Tiffany Chung is a multidisciplinary artist, renowned for her examination of political conflicts, forced migration and urban alteration in relation to history and cultural memory. Working across various mediums, including cartographic drawings, film, performance, sculpture and video, Chung's maps, whether fictional or real, demonstrate the strengths and limitations of cartography to convey hidden truths.

MONIR SHAHROUDY FARMANFARMAIAN
b. 1922, Qazvin, Iran
d. 2019, Tehran
Produced over the course of six decades, Monir Shahroudy Farmanfarmaian's prodigious output is epitomised by the repetitive patterns and structural geometric shapes seen in her mirrored and reverse glass paintings. Her delicate drawings and collages, alongside her mirrored mosaics and sculptures, weave together tradition with a modernist consciousness, which situated Farmanfarmaian amongst renowned abstract artists globally.

SIMONE FATTAL
b. 1942, Damascus
Lives and works in Paris
Artist and publisher Simone Fattal is inspired by the spirtuality, history and mythology of the so-called 'Arab World'. Her work contains socio-political undercurrents

where she explores notions of identity, nationalism and her memories of Syrian landscapes. Her poetic practice encompasses paintings, collages and sculptures made from clay, bronze, stone and terracotta, among other luminous forms.

MARCOS GRIGORIAN
b. 1925, Kropotkin, Russia
d. 2007, Yerevan, Armenia
Marcos Grigorian was an artist, actor, teacher, gallerist, curator and collector. He lived a nomadic life between the Soviet Union, Iran, Italy, the United States and Armenia, contributing to the art scene of each of these countries. His diverse experimentations defined his practice, which included performative photography as well as figurative and expressionist paintings that were often created using earth materials, found objects and perishable food.

ABBAS HABIBALLA
b. 1950, Sudan
d. 2020, location unknown
Initially trained as a photograper in Sudan's Ministry of Culture, Abbas Habiballa went on to record the commonplace, intimate and celebrative life moments of his family and neighbours in various facets of Sudanese culture. On his Rolleiflex camera, his group portraits were theatrically staged and his subjects were delicately captured.

JOANA HADJITHOMAS & KHALIL JOREIGE
b. 1969, Beirut (both)
Live and work between Beirut and Paris
Joana Hadjithomas & Khalil Joreige interrogate the creation of images, the development of imaginaries and the writing of history. Their work establishes formal and thematic connections between several mediums, including photography, video, performance, installation, sculpture and fiction or documentary film.

ROKNI HAERIZADEH
b. 1978, Tehran
Lives and works in Dubai
Rokni Haerizadeh examines the contradictions and unearths the humour within social behaviour. His work often references historical political leaders, literary figures and contemporary film. Haerizadeh's practice spans a variety of mediums, including sculpture, painting, performance, animation and assemblage.

TALOI HAVINI
b. 1981, Arawa, Autonomous Region of Bougainville
Lives and works in Brisbane, Australia
Taloi Havini (Nakas Tribe, Hakö people) was born in Arawa, Autonomous Region of Bougainville, and is currently based in Brisbane, Australia. Their work is developed through extensive research informed by their matrilineal ties to their land and communities in Bougainville.

SUSAN HEFUNA
b. 1962, Berlin
Lives and works between Cairo, Düsseldorf and New York
Of German-Egyptian heritage, Susan Hefuna's work is informed by her cross-cultural upbringing and the intersection of location and identity. The multimedia artist works with drawing, film, photography, sculpture and performance. Hefuna's grid-like minimalist compositions investigate images and structures, bridging the way they work in diverse contexts.

ADAM HENEIN
b. 1929, Cairo
d. 2020, Cairo
Over the course of eight decades, Adam Henein sought the poetic simplicity of visual form, drawing on a rich visual legacy in pharaonic art and contemporary aesthetics. His sculptures of bronze, wood, clay and granite, and his paintings of abstract geometric shapes, regularly rendered on papyrus, often embodied the notion of eternity.

LUBAINA HIMID
b. 1954, Zanzibar
Lives and works in Preston, UK
An educator, artist and curator, Lubaina Himid's work is widely considered is a cornerstone of the British Black Art Movement. Her degree in theatre design and her interest in opera have had a profound influence on her practice, which encompasses paintings, figurative cut-outs and installations. Himid's art challenges institutional narratives that have systematically overlooked the legacy of slavery and the foundational contributions to society made by the African diaspora.

EMILY JACIR
b. 1972, Bethlehem
Lives and works between Bethlehem and Rome
Artist and filmmaker Emily Jacir is particularly interested in transformation, translation and silenced narratives. She uses a variety of mediums and approaches, including historical research, performative gestures and in-depth study to investigate themes such as exile, freedom and resistance.

HAYV KAHRAMAN
b. 1981, Baghdad
Lives and works in Los Angeles
Artist Hayv Kahraman draws from her own experiences of exile, displacement and living in the diaspora. Her multifaceted practice, that encompasses painting, drawing, object-making and performance, often includes depictions of female figures which are at once semi-autobiographical and culturally ambiguous. Through these, she addresses notions of violence, oppression, memory and the crisis of belonging.

ALI KAZIM
b. 1979, Pattoki, Pakistan
Lives and works in Lahore
Inspired by Mughal, Rajput and Company paintings from South Asia, Ali Kazim's practice explores the hidden histories of ancient civilizations buried beneath the landscape. Primarily trained in Pakistan and subsequently in London, his work often encompasses figures and archeological remains, and has an ethereal, fantastical dimension to it.

AMAL KENAWY
b. 1974, Cairo
d. 2012, Cairo
Amal Kenawy's work focused on social and political themes, encompassing explorations of the body, death and desire, alongside memory and fragility. Primarily based in Egypt, her work often combined performance, installation, sound video, painting and drawing.

AISHA KHALID
b. 1972, Faisalabad, Pakistan
Lives and works in Lahore
Social and political ideologies, spirituality and the precision of Islamic geometric patterns are themes that inform Aisha Khalid's multimedia practice. Inspired by her training in South Asian miniature art, her embroidery works, paintings, videos and installations often juxtapose decorative surfaces with motifs from Sufi verses.

ANUAR KHALIFI
b. 1977, Lloret de Mar, Spain
Lives and works between Barcelona and Tangier
Anuar Khalifi uses vivid colours to create transcendental portraits inspired by his ongoing pursuit of creating a transcendental spiritual practice. Self-taught, Khalifi's paintings are presented in a Neo-Impressionist style. His landscapes often contain figures who invoke the Sufi tradition alongside autobiographical elements, as well as key references from the genre from art history.

DAVID KOLOANE
b. 1938, Johannesburg
d. 2019, Johannesburg
David Koloane was a multidisciplinary artist, activist, writer and curator who contributed immensely to the art scene in apartheid-era South Africa through his teaching, mentoring and establishment of local institutions. His abstract, textured cityscapes and imaginative, populated compositions often deal with the human condition and socio-political narratives.

FARIDEH LASHAI
b. 1944, Rasht, Iran
d. 2013, Tehran, Iran
Multidisciplinary visual artist, writer and translator Farideh Lashai's practice spanned more than five decades and weaved personal history with expressive abstraction, lyricism and narrative. Celebrating nature in her idyllic landscapes and depicting solace in it is scenery, Lashai's art was deeply rooted in the social and political realms.

TALA MADANI
b. 1981, Tehran
Lives and works in California
Tala Madani's satirical paintings offer a sharp critique of a patriarchal society. In her figurative works, which often proffer a critique of the male figure, she deconstructs notions of masculinity and gender stereotypes. Her images are derived from studies and sketchbooks, and her paintings are also often transformed into stop-motion animations.

TAUS MAKHACHEVA
b. 1983, Dagestan, Russia
Lives and works in Moscow and Makhachkala, Russia
Taus Makhacheva uses video, installation, photography and performance to explore the boundary between similarity and difference. She questions what remains of her country's past, asking in what form it has been reintroduced into daily life.

JUMANA MANNA
b. 1987, Princeton, US
Lives and works between Berlin and Jerusalem
Working in film, installation and sculpture, Jumana Manna explores the power dynamics inherent in colonised body and land. Her practice investigates the complexities and contradictions within the fields of archaeology, agriculture and the law, including notions of preservation, destruction and regeneration.

IBRAHIM MASSOUDA
b. (presumably) 1925, Egypt
d. (presumably) 1965
Ibrahim Massouda was born in Egypt. Conflicting accounts list his date of birth as 1925 and 1938, respectively, with most suggesting the former. His suspected date of death may be in or around 1965. Massouda studied at the School of Fine Arts in Cairo, after which point, he developed a distinctive impressionistic style—often painting scenes of political sacrifice. He was a later addition to the country's Art and Liberty Group, also recognised as the Egyptian Surrealists, before becoming an active member of Egypt's Group of Contemporary Art, formed circa 1945.

AHMED MATER
b. 1979, Tabuk, Saudi Arabia
Lives and works in Riyadh
Ahmed Mater is a physician-turned-artist who explores the narratives and aesthetics of Islamic culture in an era of globalisation, consumerism and flux. Mater uses photography,

calligraphy, installation and video to document and critique the complex realities of contemporary Saudi Arabia.

AHMED MORSI
b. 1930, Alexandria, Egypt
Lives and works in New York
A painter, poet, printmaker and critic, Morsi has created a diverse body of work abundant in its mythology from the 1940s until today. Both figurative and fantastical, Morsi's paintings contain worlds where horses, fish, birds and humans share space, reflecting his interest in Surrealism.

FATEH MOUDARRES
b. 1922, Aleppo, Syria
d. 1999, Aleppo, Syria
As a painter, writer and poet, and credited with spearheading modernism in Syria, Fateh Moudarres's paintings were influenced by the political turmoil he witnessed in the region as well as ancient Syrian art and Christian iconography. Moudarres is renowned for depicting various subjects in his distinctive abstract style drawn from multicultural references and earthen tones.

KHALIL RABAH
b. 1961, Jerusalem
Lives and works in Ramallah
Khalil Rabah draws upon his deep engagement with architecture, urbanism and performance to create alternative visions and semi-fictive imaginings of history. Rabah's practice engages with themes of displacement, memory and identity, examining the relationship between humans and their surroundings.

MICHAEL RAKOWITZ
b. 1973, New York
Lives and works in Chicago
Michael Rakowitz is a conceptual artist who creates public projects, installations and proactive events often devised in collaboration with local communities. His singular practice, subversive in style, can be read as a form of contra-colonial history and an intervention into current and public affairs. Employing extensive research methodologies, he engages in fact-finding, focusing on situations that range from the personal to the geopolitical.

MARWAN RECHMAOUI
b. 1964, Beirut
Lives and works in Beirut
Marwan Rechmaoui began his practice as a painter, before developing an interest in architectural forms, industrial materials and map-making. He uses tar, rubber, metal, concrete, glass and textile to create work that is inspired by the rich culture and history of Beirut, exposing the city's multiple complexities and socio-political undercurrents.

IBRAHIM EL-SALAHI
b. 1930, Omdurman, Sudan
Lives and works in Oxford
Ibrahim El-Salahi created his own artistic language by integrating the classical techniques he learned studying in London with African and Islamic pattern. His paintings blend abstract calligraphy with motifs from nature, reflecting his life experiences. El-Salahi's multidisciplinary practice has been noted for repositioning African artistic practices within the framework of a revived global modernism.

MOHAN B SAMANT
b. 1924, Bombay (now Mumbai)
d. 2004, New York
Mohan Samant is considered a pioneering Indian modernist artist. He was a member of the Progressive Artists' Group in the 1950s, a collective of creatives predominantly based in Mumbai. His work drew from multiple sources, such as miniature and Basohli painting, as well hieroglyphics and ancient objects from Egypt. His style, technique, colour and material consistently shifted, reflecting historical, spiritual and quotidian narratives.

HRAIR SARKISSIAN
b. 1973, Damascus
Lives and works in London
Hrair Sarkissian uses photography to narrate stories excluded from official records or histories. Employing a large-format camera to elucidate his conceptual work, his work often invites the viewer to contemplate what lies beneath the surface of his large-scale photographs.

HASSAN SHARIF
b. 1951, Iran
d. 2016, Dubai
Hassan Sharif was a pioneer of conceptual art and experimental practice, as well as a prolific writer on art and a founder of several art institutions within the UAE. His work included performance, paintings and repurposed found objects. These were often transformed into systematic, accumulating installations. He frequently dealt with pertinent themes, such as time, mass production and consumer culture in society.

WAEL SHAWKY
b. 1971, Alexandria, Egypt
Lives and works between Alexandria and Philadelphia, US
Wael Shawky's films, installations, drawings, paintings, photographs and performances often fuse fact with fiction, and are based upon periods of extensive research. His work explores contemporary society through the lens of subjective histories, identity politics, the representation of religion and its mythology.

ANWAR JALAL SHEMZA
b. 1928, Simla, India
d. 1985, Stafford, UK
Anwar Jalal Shemza was an artist, writer and teacher. He gained recognition in Pakistan for his lyrical figurative works and was a founding member of the Lahore Art Circle. In 1956, he moved to London, where he studied at the Slade School of Fine Art and began to place geometric and calligraphic forms from Islamic art in dialogue with elements and philosophies drawn from abstract art movements in Europe.

AHMED SHIBRAIN
b. 1931, Berber, Sudan
d. 2017, Khartoum
Painter, graphic designer and an educator, Ahmed Shibrain was a renowned African modernist and one of the founding members of the Khartoum School in the 1960s. His work integrated aspects of Arabic calligraphy and Pan-African aesthetic and cultural traditions. He studied at London's Central School of Art and Design before returning to found several institutions in Sudan.

SHAHZIA SIKANDER
b. 1969, Lahore
Lives and works in New York
Shahzia Sikander's practice creates critical dialogues between Indo-Persian miniature painting tradition, popular culture, mythology and contemporary theory. Her intricately detailed drawings, paintings, videos, installations and animations often deconstruct and resituate notions of gender, sexuality, religion, cultural identity, colonial and postcolonial histories.

RAYYANE TABET
b. 1983, Achkout, Lebanon
Lives and works between Beirut and San Francisco
Rayyane Tabet investigates narratives that provide an alternate understanding of sociopolitical events. Drawing on his training in architecture and sculpture, his installations explore paradoxes in the built environment and the ruptures often found in histories that were once perceived to be objective.

RICHARD LOKIDEN WANI
b. 1974, Kajo Keji, Sudan
Lives and works in Juba, South Sudan
Richard Lokiden Wani received informal training in photography from American and Norwegian evangelists present in Juba during Sudan's second civil war. His use of a flash during daytime adds a sublime touch to his photographs of churchgoers, preachers and neighbours. His subjects are captured either sitting or standing, while reflecting a sense of determination and pride.

NARI WARD
b. 1963, St Andrew, Jamaica
Lives and works in New York
Nari Ward is renowned for the installations he creates from discarded materials and found objects gleaned from his everyday environment. Ward creates art that addresses historical memory, race, poverty and consumer culture.

LIONEL WENDT
b. 1900, Colombo
d. 1944, Colombo
Trained as a lawyer and pianist in England, Lionel Wendt formally took up photography in the 1930s. He experimented with photograms, photomontage, double printing and solarisation to produce work that was foundational in the global history of photography. He also contributed to the development of modern art in Sri Lanka through his writing and founding of the '43 Group of artists in Colombo.

KAMAL YOUSSEF
b. 1923, Cairo
Lives in Pennsylvania, US
In Kamal Youssef's work, the tangible and the spiritual worlds intertwine. His paintings and sculptures, made over the span of seven decades, were often influenced by his travels between Egypt, France and the US, frequently inspired by the avant-garde movements of the time, including Egyptian Surrealism.

AKRAM ZAATARI
b. 1966, Saida, Lebanon
Lives and works in Beirut
Akram Zaatari creates videos, installations of photographic material and books on variety of intersecting themes. The experience of excavation, political resistance and the transmission of pictures during war time form a key anchor in his creative practice. The formal, intellectual and institutional architecture of Beirut's contemporary art scene has been greatly influenced by Zaatari, who was a pivotal figure in the founding of the Arab Image Foundation (AIF).

## Authors

*Directors*

HOOR AL QASIMI established Sharjah Art Foundation (SAF) in 2009 as a catalyst and advocate for the arts in Sharjah, UAE, as well as the greater region and abroad. As President and Director, she has expanded the Foundation's scope to include major international travelling exhibitions, artist and curator residencies, commissions and production grants for emerging artists, and a wide range of educational programming. She has also served as Sharjah Biennial Director since 2003. Beyond her role at SAF, Al Qasimi is currently President of the International Biennial Association, President of the Africa Institute and Chair of the Board of the Sharjah Architecture Triennial. She serves or has served on the Boards of Directors of MoMA PS1, New York; Kunst-Werke, Berlin e. V.; and Ashkal Alwan, Beirut.

Al Qasimi is Chair of the Advisory Board of the College of Fine Arts and Design at the University of Sharjah, is a member of the advisory boards of the Khoj International Artists' Association, New Delhi, and Darat al Funun, Amman, and is a member of the Prince Claus Awards Committee. Al Qasimi has curated major exhibitions and pivotal solo shows in Sharjah and abroad, including the UAE Pavilion at the 56th Venice Biennale and the 2nd Lahore Biennale, and is the curator of the Sharjah Biennial 15. She holds an MA in curating contemporary art from the Royal College of Art, London; a diploma in painting from the Royal Academy of Arts, London; and a BFA from the Slade School of Fine Art, London.

PROFESSOR DR DIRK LUCKOW has been Director of the Deichtorhallen Hamburg since 2009. He received his doctorate in art history from the Freie Universität Berlin, focusing on Joseph Beuys and the Anti-form art movement. Over the course of a career of nearly 30 years, he has held positions at institutions including the Kunstsammlung Nordrhein-Westfalen, Düsseldorf; the Solomon R. Guggenheim Museum, New York; the Württembergischer Kunstverein in Stuttgart; and the Siemens Arts Programme, Munich. From 2002 to 2009, Luckow served as director of the Kunsthalle zu Kiel.

Professor Luckow has authored numerous publications and essays on artists, including Richard Artschwager, Cecilia Edefalk, Charline von Heyl, William Kentridge, Hans-Peter Feldmann and Marilyn Minter, among others. He has served as a juror for the Capital Cultural Fund in Berlin, the KÖR – art in public space award, Vienna, and as a member of the board of trustees of the Nordmetall Foundation and the Herbert Gerisch Foundation/Sculpture Park Neumünster.

Luckow is an Honorary Professor of art theory at the Hochschule für bildende Künste Hamburg/the Hamburg University of Fine Arts.

*Exhibition Curator, Editor and Author*

DR OMAR KHOLEIF CF FRSA FKA Blake Karim Mitchell is an author of prose and poetry, a historian of the academy and its peripheries, and a curator of vanquished and/or suppressed archives. They have worked as a broadcaster, filmmaker, editor, publisher, museum director and LGBTQ+ campaigner in South Africa, the United Kingdom, the United States, the GCC and North Africa. Over the last 17 years, their work has concentrated on the evolving nature of networked image culture in relation to the intersectional questions emerging in the field and study of ethnicity, race, gender and sexuality. Specific attention is focused on how these concepts are reified through the language of equality, ableism and public health, as expressed through the critical fabulation around contemporary social justice movements.

The probing questions gleaned from these lines of inquiry have come to life in more than 60 exhibitions, and in over 30 authored, co-authored and edited books, which have been translated into 12 languages. Dr Kholeif was a co-curator of Sharjah Biennial 14: *Leaving the Echo Chamber* and currently serves as Director of Collections and Senior Curator, Sharjah Art Foundation, UAE. Their forthcoming monograph, *Internet_Art: From the Birth of the Web to the Rise of NFTs* is published by Phaidon in April 2023.

*Contributing Authors*

NAWAR AL QASSIMI is Vice-President of Sharjah Art Foundation (SAF), where she has worked since 2010. She began her tenure developing public programming and audience engagement strategy, later leading the Foundation's development department, with a focus on cultural partnerships. In her current capacity, Al Qassimi is responsible for SAF's strategic planning—strengthening the Foundation's role as a catalyst of and advocate for the arts in Sharjah, the UAE and internationally. Al Qassimi is a member of the Sharjah Tourism Advisory Committee. She is a graduate of the American University of Sharjah.

SKYE ARUNDHATI THOMAS is a writer based in Goa, India. She is co-editor of *The White Review*. Her essay-length book, *Remember the Details*, on viral images, courtrooms and a brief history of a protest movement, was published in 2021 by Floating Opera Press.

STEPHANIE BAILEY is *Ocula Magazine*'s editor-in-chief, and is based between Hong Kong and London. A contributing editor to *ARTPAPERS*, a consultant editor to the M+ Museum of Visual Culture, Hong Kong, a member of *Naked Punch*'s editorial committee and an advisory board member to *D'ivan, A Journal of Accounts*, Bailey is also Art Basel Hong Kong's Conversations Curator and a content advisor for Art Basel, Asia. Previously, Bailey served as managing and senior editor of Ibraaz Publishing. She has contributed to numerous exhibition catalogues and regularly lectures on the politics of aesthetics in the contemporary sphere.

ANNE BARLOW is Director of Tate St Ives. She was formerly Director of Art in General, New York, and Curator of Education and Media Programmes at the New Museum, New York. She has published and lectured widely and served on numerous selection panels, including the kim? Residency Award, Riga; Exposure 8, Beirut Art Center; and the British Pavilion, 58th Venice Biennale. Barlow was Curator of Bucharest Biennale 5 and Co-Curator of the Latvian Pavilion, 55th Venice Biennale, and is Curator of the Samdani Art Award 2023.

CHRIS MCCORMACK is a writer and a co-editor of *Art Monthly*. Recent editorial projects include Charlotte Prodger's monograph, *Selected Works* (Koenig Books, 2022); serving as commissioning editor of *ON&BY: Andy Warhol* (MIT Press/Whitechapel, 2016); and co-authoring James Richards's *Requests and Antisongs* (Sternberg Press, 2016). McCormack's research into vocal development, *Voce di testa*, was published as part of the Welsh Pavilion at the 57th Venice Biennale. Curated exhibitions and edited monographs include *Anarchic Sexual Desires of Plain Unmarried Schoolteachers* (2015).

PROFESSOR SARAH PERKS is an interdisciplinary curator and writer based in the Tees Valley, UK. She creates exhibitions, books and projects that work across contemporary art, design, science and film. She is Professor of Curating at MIMA × School of Arts and Creative Industries at Teesside University, where her research involves relational curatorial strategy and economic, environmental and socio-political issues. Previous roles include Artistic Director at HOME and Cornerhouse in Manchester. Perks is also Programme Advisor for the BFI London Film Festival and leads Natural Futures, a collaborative research project on creative nature recovery and ecopsychology.

SOFIA VICTORINO is a curator and researcher, currently considering how artistic practices can serve as decolonial tools within art institutions. From 2011 to 2021, Victorino served as Director of Education and Public Programmes at the Whitechapel Gallery, London, where she oversaw an integrated programme of artists' residencies and commissions, exhibitions, performance, schools and community projects, as well as experiments in discursive programming. From 2002 to 2011, she served as Head of Education and Public Programmes at the Museu de Arte Contemporânea de Serralves, Porto. Victorino sits on the advisory board of the Documents of Contemporary Art book series, co-published by Whitechapel Gallery and MIT Press, and lectures for the MA in Curating Art and Public Programmes at London South Bank University.

# Nachwort: Smile, You’re in Sharjah

## Nawar Al Qassimi

Sharjah bedeutet für mich Heimat. Als jemand, die dort geboren wurde und ihr ganzes Leben im Emirat gelebt hat, würde ich es am ehesten als einen Treffpunkt, einen dauerhaften Ort der Zusammenkunft beschreiben. Schon immer haben sich Menschen aus verschiedenen Teilen der Welt in Sharjah eingefunden: Einige machen nur kurz Halt, bevor sie ihre Reise anderswohin fortsetzen, andere bleiben ein Leben lang, ihrer eigenen und kommenden Generationen zuliebe. Es ist ein Zuhause, das sich ständig verändert.

Historisch gesehen war Sharjah eine wichtige Drehscheibe des Seehandels. Die Stadt entstand aus den Siedlungen entlang des geschützten Hafens, heute Sharjah Creek genannt. Hier gibt es noch immer die traditionellen hölzernen Dhaus zu sehen, voll beladen mit Gewürzen, gebrauchten Elektrogeräten und Gebrauchtwagen für die benachbarten Häfen der Region.

Entlang der nahe gelegenen Küstenstraße stößt man auf einen in den 1930er Jahren erbauten Suk oder Markt, wo sich Händler und Seeleute wie seit Jahrhunderten treffen. Die Sehenswürdigkeiten und Geräusche, denen man beim Spaziergang durch diesen Teil des historischen Zentrums von Sharjah begegnet, lassen die reiche Geschichte der Gegend lebendig werden.

Auf diesen Wegen hört man Arabisch, Urdu, Farsi und Englisch, ein Hinweis auf die verschiedenen Migrationshintergründe der Bevölkerung. Viele der Einwohner*innen in dieser Gegend führen noch immer Familienbetriebe, die von Generation zu Generation weitergegeben wurden. Dort gibt es Kleidung und auch Stoffe zu kaufen, die man zwecks Maßanfertigung zu einem benachbarten Schneider bringen kann. Man bekommt eine Tasse Karak angeboten, ein Milchtee, der traditionell aus Südasien stammt und heute überall in den VAE getrunken wird.

Kleine, gepflasterte Straßen und Gassen führen einen vom geschäftigen Souk in das heute „Heritage Area“ genannte ruhige Viertel, wo man auf die Reste ehemaliger Wohnhäuser und Villen aus dem 19. Jahrhundert stößt. Manche dieser Häuser wurden umfunktioniert, andere sind nur in Teilen erhalten, wobei ihre Grund- oder Hofmauern, aus in der Nähe vorkommenden Materialien wie Korallen und Meeressteine gebaut, uns an Sharjahs Lage am Meer erinnern.

Mit dem Wohlstand, den die Entdeckung von Erdölvorkommen im Land in den 1960er Jahren mit sich brachte, verließen die Bewohner*innen das Viertel und zogen ins Landesinnere in moderne klimatisierte Villen. Die denkmalgeschützten ehemaligen Wohnhäuser zeugen von dem, was einst das Zentrum von Sharjah war. Seit den 1980er Jahren ist dort ein Netz kleiner Museen und Zentren für Poesie, Kalligrafie und Theater entstanden, die dafür sorgten, dass das Gebiet nicht saniert wurde und sein historisches Aussehen bewahrte. In den letzten zwei Jahrzehnten hat die Sharjah Art Foundation nach und nach Räume in diesem Viertel instand gesetzt und für Ausstellungen und Veranstaltungen umfunktioniert, während die historische Bausubstanz vor Ort vielen Künstler*innen zur Inspiration dient.

# Afterword: Smile, You're in Sharjah

## Nawar Al Qassimi

For me, Sharjah means home. As someone who was born there and has lived in theEmirate my entire life, I can best describe it as a meeting point—a perpetual site of assembly. People from different parts of the world have always gathered in Sharjah; some may stop in briefly before continuing their journey elsewhere, others settle for a lifetime, for their own and for generations to come. It is a home that is forever changing.

Historically, Sharjah has been an important centre of maritime trade, the city growing from settlements along the protected harbor now known as Sharjah Creek. Here, you will still see the traditional wooden dhows piled high with their cargos of spices, sugar, used electronics, secondhand cars, destined for neighbouring ports in the region.

Along the corniche nearby, you will find a souk, or market, built in the 1930s, where tradesmen and sailors gather as they have for centuries. The sights and sounds you encounter while walking through this part of the Sharjah's historic centre bring the rich history of the area to life.

Along these paths, you will hear Arabic, Urdu, Farsi and English being spoken, hinting at the populace's various points of migration. Many of the inhabitants in this area still run family businesses—passed down across generations. The scent of spice and perfume consumes the spaces between the shops, where brightly colored fabrics and textiles from places like India and Japan are draped across windows. These colors entice you in to purchase a ready-made garment, or, for the more adventurous, metres of textiles that you can take to a neighboring tailor for a custom order. You will be offered a traditional cup of Karak, or milk tea, that is traditionally from South Asia and now a household staple in the UAE.

Small, paved streets and alleyways lead you from the bustling souk to the quiet serenity of what is now known as the heritage area, where you encounter the traces of former family homes and villas from the 1800s. Typically constructed of materials commonly found nearby, such as coral and sea stones, some of these homes have been repurposed, others remain as fragments, the footprints or courtyard walls reminding us of Sharjah's deep ties to the sea.

With the prosperity brought on by the discovery of oil in the country during the 1960s, residents abandoned the neighborhood and moved inland to modern, climate-controlled villas that offered a more comfortable life during the harsh UAE summers. The uninhabited dwellings and heritage homes remain as markers of what was once the centre of Sharjah. Since the 1980s, a network of small museums and centres for poetry, calligraphy and theatre has grown and ensured that the area avoided redevelopment and maintained its historic character. For the past two decades, Sharjah Art Foundation has slowly restored and repurposed spaces for exhibitions and events within this area, while the remaining fragments and courtyards often become sites of inspiration to artists for the creation of new work.

Sharjah wird oft als die Kulturhauptstadt der Vereinigten Arabischen Emirate bezeichnet. Seit über 70 Jahren werden im Emirat Bildung und Kultur gefördert, was darauf zurückzuführen sein mag, dass die älteste Schule der VAE in Sharjah gegründet wurde. Dank dieses Erbes ist das Emirat heute fruchtbares Terrain für die Art von Engagement und Experimentierfreude, die für die Arbeit von Künstler*innen wie auch für die Tätigkeit der Sharjah Art Foundation grundlegend ist.

Während das Emirat über das historische Zentrum hinaus zur heute drittgrößten Stadt der VAE gewachsen ist, verdankt Sharjah seinen besonderen Charakter einer Geschichte, die durch den verschmelzenden Einfluss des Seehandels, eine hohe Wertschätzung von Bildung sowie durch wechselseitige kulturelle Akzeptanz und Unterstützung geprägt ist. Das Emirat bekennt sich zu dieser Vielfalt, die Teil seiner humanistischen Kulturgeschichte ist. Seine Atmosphäre erinnert denn auch an viele Hafenstädte, wo vertraute Lebensweisen Assoziationen an Heimat wecken.

Für viele Menschen, Künstler*innen eingeschlossen, die sich oftmals in ihrer Bewegungsfreiheit eingeschränkt sahen, erwies und erweist sich Sharjah als ein gastfreundlicher Ort, der Begegnungen und Interaktionen zwischen Menschen fördert und denjenigen Zuflucht bietet, die aus ihrer Heimat vertrieben worden sind. Wie der florale Willkommensgruß des Emirats auf dem zentralen Verkehrsrondell der Stadt besagt: „Smile, You're in Sharjah".

Sharjah is often described as the capital of culture in the UAE. Perhaps a legacy of being home to the first school in the country, the Emirate has invested in access to education and culture for over 70 years. This legacy has made the Emirate a fertile ground for the type of engagement and experimentation that is so fundamental to the work of artists and of Sharjah Art Foundation.

While the Emirate has grown beyond the historic centre to become the third-largest contemporary city in the UAE, the character of Sharjah has been built on a history coloured by the amalgamating influence of maritime trade, by the prioritization of learning and education, alongside cultural acceptance and support. The Emirate bristles with the warmth of a collective humanity—a place that embraces difference as part of its cultural history. Its slow-paced, humble atmosphere is reminiscent of many coastal port cities whose shared sense of intimacy evokes home.

For many people, including artists, for whom mobility has often been limited, Sharjah has been a welcoming site, one that has nourished and nurtured encounters and interactions between and amongst people, offering a form of refuge for those often displaced from home. As the Emirate's welcome sign reads, in flora, on the city's central roundabout, 'Smile, You're in Sharjah'.

Dieser Katalog erscheint anlässlich der Ausstellung *In the Heart of Another Country – Erzählungen aus der Diaspora. Werke der Sharjah Art Foundation Collection* in der Halle für aktuelle Kunst, Deichtorhallen Hamburg vom 28. Oktober 2022 bis zum 12. März 2023.

This catalogue is published on the occasion of the exhibition *In the Heart of Another Country – The Diasporic Imagination in the Sharjah Art Foundation Collection* at the Hall for Contemporary Art, Deichtorhallen Hamburg from October 28, 2022 until March 12, 2023.

KATALOG / CATALOGUE

*Herausgeber*in / Editor*
Omar Kholeif

*Redaktion / Catalogue Editorial Management*
Omar Kholeif, Zeina Al-Kattan, Cosima Grosser, Reem Sawan, Annette Sievert

*Redaktionsassistenz / Editorial assistance*
Frances Fürst

*Grafische Gestaltung / Graphic design*
Daly & Lyon, London

*Mitwirkende Autor*innen / Contributing authors*
Hoor Al Qasimi, Nawar Al Qassimi, Skye Arundhati Thomas, Anne Barlow, Stephanie Bailey, Omar Kholeif, Dirk Luckow, Chris McCormack, Sarah Perks, Reem Sawan *und / and* Sofia Victorino

*Lektorat / Copyediting and proofreading*
Eti Bonn-Muller, Nicholas Davies

*Übersetzungen / Translations*
Nadja Bossmann, Kathrin Hadeler, Jennifer Holleis, Bram Opstelten, Sylvia Zirden

*Erschienen im / Published by*
Snoeck Verlagsgesellschaft mbH

Gedruckt in / Printed in Germany
ISBN: 978-3-86442-399-4



Bildnachweise / Credits

Trotz intensiver Recherche war es nicht in allen Fällen möglich, die Rechteinhaber*innen der Abbildungen ausfindig zu machen. Ansprüche von Berechtigten werden daher im Rahmen der üblichen Vereinbarungen abgegolten. / Should despite intensive research any person entitled to rights have been overlooked, legitimate claims will be met within the usual provision.

Wenn nicht anders angegeben, für die abgebildeten Werke / Unless otherwise stated, for the works illustrated:

Photo: CHROMA, André Carvalho & Tugba Carvalho, S. / p. 232/233
Photo: Plamen Galabov, S. / p. 254/255, 257
Photo: Genevieve Hanson, S. / p. 281
Photo: Shanavas Jamaluddin, S. / p. 113, 124/125, 131, 133, 145, 147, 167–169, 187, 189, 198/199, 223, 225, 265, 277, 320
Photo: Motaz Mawid. S. / p. 273–275
Photo: Shafeek Nalakath, S. / p. 69, 73, 78, 85/86, 99, 107, 137–139, 162–165, 191, 215, 217–219, 227–229, 231, 247–249
Photo: Alfredo Rubio, S. / p. 143, 258/259, 269–271
Photo: Danko Stjepanovic, S. / p. 65–67, 70/71, 75, 77, 79, 81–83, 87, 89, 91–93, 95–97, 103–105, 133, 115–117, 119–123, 127–129, 153, 155–157, 183–185, 192/193, 195, 201–203, 205–207, 209–211, 235, 245, 261–263, 278/279
Photos: We Document Art, S. / p. 109–111

*Cover*
Etel Adnan, *Mount Tamalpaïs*, 2015
Im Auftrag der Sharjah Art Foundation / Commissioned by Sharjah Art Foundation
Wolle / Wool
170 × 212 cm

Die Ausstellung wurde kuratiert von Dr. Omar Kholeif, Direktor*in der Sammlungen und Chefkurator*in, Sharjah Art Foundation. / The exhibition is curated by Dr. Omar Kholeif, Director of Collections and Senior Curator, Sharjah Art Foundation.

*Ausstellungsdesign / Exhibition design*
Todd Reisz

Kommunikation / Communications

*Leitung Kommunikation / Head of communications*
Angelika Leu-Barthel

*Volontariat / Assistant*
Caroline Huzel

Digitale Projekte

Julia Schulze Darup, Matthias Schönebäumer

Kulturelle Bildung / Education

*Leitung Kulturelle Bildung / Head of education*
Birgit Hübner

*Mitarbeit Kulturelle Bildung / Collaboration education*
Rebecca Janko

*Bundesfreiwilligendienst / Federal Volunteer Service*
Pia Harz

Sponsoring, Marketing und Vermietung / Sponsoring, marketing and event spaces

*Leitung Sponsoring, Marketing und Vermietung / Head of sponsoring, marketing and event spaces*
Daniela Guhl

*Vermietung Parkplatz / Letting of parking spaces*
Mareile Hanke

Verwaltung / Administration

*Leitung Finanzen und Controlling / Head of finances and controlling*
Ole Stark

*Buchhaltung / Accounting*
Hendrik Günther

*Personalreferentin / Human resources*
Claudia Herzer-Hendrischke

*Personal Kassen- und Aufsichtsdienste / Museum desk and custodial staff*
Mareile Hanke

*Aufsichtsdienste / Custodial staff*
René-Martin Kellmann

Technik / Technical staff

*Technische Leitung / Head of technical staff*
Henning Best

*Architektur und Grafik / Architecture and graphics*
Jutta Wasser

*Haus- und Medientechnik / Building services and media technology*
Nils Handschuh

*Haus- und Betriebstechnik / Building services and operations maintenance*
Karsten Chmielewski

SHARJAH ART FOUNDATION

*Präsidentin und Direktorin / President and Director*
Hoor Al Qasimi

*Vizepräsidentin / Vice President*
Nawar Al Qassimi

*Direktor*in der Sammlungen und Chefkurator*in / Director of Collections and Senior Curator*
Omar Kholeif

Entwicklung, Partnerschaften und Kommunikation / Development, Partnership and Communications

Judith Greer, *Direktorin für internationale Programme / Director of International Programmes*
Tuba Tortop, *Marketing und Kommunikation / Marketing and Communications Manager*
Alyazeyah Al Reyaysa, *Marketing- und Kommunikationskoordinatorin / Senior Marketing and Communications Coordinator*
Nawale Lacroix, *Kommunikationsberaterin / Communications Consultant*
Resnicow and Associates (R&A), *Agentur für strategische Kommunikation / Strategic Communications Agency*

Ausstellungsplanung und -management / Exhibition Planning and Management

John Labib, *Sammlungs- und Restaurierungsmanager / Collections and Conservation Manager*

Ausstellungsrecherche und -management / Exhibition Research and Management

Zeina Al Kattan, *Kuratorische Assistentin / Curatorial Assistant*
Reem Sawan, *Koordinatorin der Sammlungen / Collections Coordinator*

Ausstellungsdesign, -entwicklung und -modelle / Exhibition Design, Development and Modelling

Souraya Kreidieh, *Stellvertretende Registrarin der Sammlungen / Associate Registrar for Collections*

Ausstellungsproduktion / Exhibition Production

Hassan Ali Mahmoud Al Jaddah, *Abteilungsleitung / Director of Operations*
Younus Suliman, *Technischer Leiter / Audio-visual and Technical Manager*
Mahmoud Habib, *Lagerhausleitung / Warehouse Manager*

Design und Archiv / Design and Archives

Dima Bittard, *Leiter Design und Multimedia / Design and Multimedia Manager*
Unnikrishnan. SB, *Leitender Multimedia-Koordinator / Senior Multimedia Coordinator*
Louie De La Torre, *Video und Redaktion / Videographer and Editor*

Publikationen / Publications

Ahmad Makia, *Leitung Publikation / Head of Publications*

Sharjah Art Foundation Förder*innen / Sharjah Art Foundation Patrons

Mohammed Afkhami
Maysoune Ghobash
Badr Jafar
Olivier Georges Mestelan
HH Sheikh Zayed bin Sultan Al Nahyan
Haleema Al Owais
Catherine Petitgas
HE Sheikha Bodour bint Sultan Al Qasimi
Sultan Sooud Al Qassemi
Abdelmonem bin Eisa Al Serkal

Hauptsponsor / Gold Sponsor

بنك الإستثمار Invest bank

Unterstützt von / Supported by

FÖRDERKREIS DEICHTORHALLEN HAMBURG

Hamburg | Behörde für Kultur und Medien

Partner der Deichtorhallen Hamburg / Partners of Deichtorhallen Hamburg

Hapag-Lloyd

WHITE WALL

Kölln

KULTURPARTNER

NDR kultur

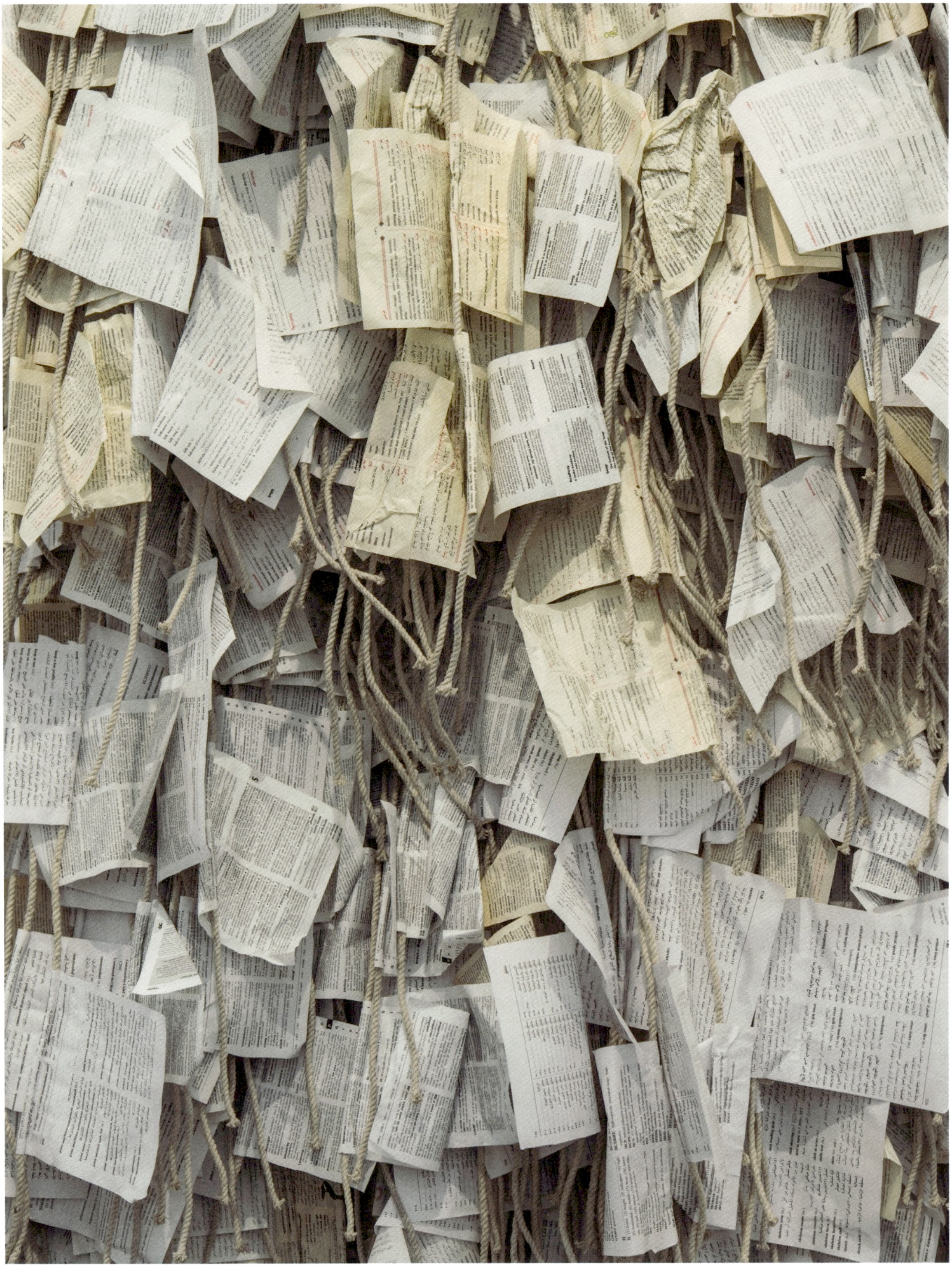

Hassan Sharif, *Dictionary*, 2015, Kleber, Wörterbuchseiten und Baumwollseil / Glue, dictionary pages and cotton rope, 385 × 170 × 65 cm